Thalia Dorwick

Ana M.
Pérez-Gironés
WESLEYAN UNIVERSITY

Anne Becher
UNIVERSITY OF
COLORADO, BOULDER

Puntos de partida

SPAN 1442
Beginning Spanish II
Department of Modern Languages
University of Texas at Arlington

6 7 8 9 0 SCI SCI 19

ISBN-13: 978-1-259-95732-1
ISBN-10: 1-259-95732-2

Solutions Program Manager: Joyce Berendes
Project Manager: Gina Schilling

It's more than a text. It's a program.

Success in the language classroom requires so much more than just a text. In any language-learning setting, students require numerous and various opportunities to read, write, hear, and speak. *Puntos de partida* sets the standard for Spanish-language teaching. An innovative program that has been continuously refined for today's classroom, *Puntos* delivers proven pedagogy with clear and effective presentations, comprehensive teaching resources, and powerfully adaptive digital tools.

Now in its anniversary Tenth Edition, *Puntos* builds on the holistic, five-skills approach it pioneered. It's the *Puntos* you know. It's the *Puntos* of today.

Proven Approach

Puntos has been the starting point for over a million students beginning to learn Spanish. The best-selling program combines digital innovations with the program's solid foundation and proven approach.

This is what *Puntos* offers that continues to set the standard for Introductory Spanish programs:

• Comprehensive scope and sequence

Puntos' hallmark approach to vocabulary and grammar focuses on the acquisition of vocabulary during the early stages of language learning (**Capítulo 1: Ante todo**) and then at the start of each chapter throughout the text. Grammar is introduced in thorough explanations, with careful attention given to skill development rather than grammatical knowledge alone.

To this end, the overall organization carefully progresses from formulaic expressions to vocabulary and grammar relevant to daily life and personal interests (studies, family, home, leisure activities), then goes on to prepare students for survival situations (ordering a meal, traveling), and finally branches out to broader themes (current events, social and environment issues). This forward progress is reinforced by a cyclical structure where vocabulary, grammar, and language functions are continuously reviewed and recycled.

• Clear and effective vocabulary and grammar presentations

The thorough, effective grammar explanations in *Puntos* are in keeping with the extensive changes made in the ninth edition. These explanations are now even more accessible to students, featuring conversational language, increased clarity, additional examples, and organization of complex, dense explanations into manageable chunks of concise grammar summary. Students will find the grammar explanations to be clear and comprehensible, and particular care has been taken to bolster those grammar points that traditionally prove difficult.

- Integrated four-skills approach with scaffolded activities that move students from input to open-ended communication

One of the hallmark features of *Puntos* is its careful sequencing of activities, moving students from controlled to free-form tasks. In the tenth edition, this scaffolding is improved and introduced at the individual activity level. Starting with the very first activity following the grammar explanation, additional *Pasos* have been added to give students the opportunity to use the new grammar in a controlled but more personalized way, facilitating practice and communication with their peers as soon as new concepts are introduced. The activities following each vocabulary topic and grammar point also build up to one or more free- expression activities in which students communicate more independently and creatively.

- Inclusion of all Spanish-speaking countries

The tenth edition of *Puntos* highlights the proven concept that introducing students to the Spanish-speaking world goes beyond asking them to simply absorb information about each country. Instead, a few key cultural insights, appearing at various moments throughout each chapter, serve to spark students' interest and, by closing with a question that asks students to reflect on cultural comparisons, encourage them to create personal connections with the cultures of the Spanish-speaking world.

Práctica y comunicación

A. Los gustos y preferencias para las vacaciones

Paso 1. Autoprueba. Complete las siguientes oraciones con -a or -an.

1. Me gust_____ nadar.
2. Por eso me gust_____ las playas caribeñas.
3. A mi familia y a mí nos gust_____ esquiar.
4. Por eso nos gust_____ las vacaciones de invierno.
5. A mi mejor amigo le gust_____ el sol.
6. Por eso siempre le gust_____ la República Dominicana para las vacaciones.
7. ¿A ti te gust_____ las vacaciones activas o relajantes (*relaxing*)?

Paso 2. Use las siguientes frases en oraciones completas para expresar sus gustos.

MODELOS: ¿viajar? → (No) Me gusta viajar.
　　　　　 ¿los aviones? → (No) Me gustan los aviones.

1. ¿viajar?
2. ¿los viajes con mi familia?
3. ¿los vuelos?
4. ¿el calor?
5. ¿el invierno?
6. ¿las playas caribeñas?
7. ¿los aeropuertos?
8. ¿viajar en coche?

Paso 3. Ahora, en parejas, túrnense para entrevistarse sobre las ideas del Paso 2. Luego díganle al resto de la clase algo que Uds. tienen en común.

MODELO: E1: A mí me gusta viajar. ¿Y a ti?
　　　　　 E2: A mí también. →
　　　　　 A nosotros nos gusta viajar.

EL MUNDO HISPANOHABLANTE*

- El español es la lengua que más se habla* en el mundo* después del* mandarín. Más de* 500 (quinientos) millones de personas hablan español.

- Es la lengua oficial de 20 (veinte) naciones y de Puerto Rico.

*El...The Spanish-speaking world *Is...the language spoken most *world *después... *Más...More than

Comprehensive *Teaching Resources* to **Create a Successful Face-to-Face, Hybrid, or Online Class**

Puntos de partida was designed to provide novice and experienced instructors alike with the tools needed to walk into the classroom—be it face-to-face or online—well-prepared to teach an engaging class. As a comprehensive program, *Puntos* offers a wide array of resources and supporting materials, so it functions as a flexible framework that can be tailored to individual teaching situations and goals. Whether you're using the program for your face-to-face, hybrid, or online class, the wealth of resources sets up both instructors and students for success.

• New and enhanced instructor's annotations

The program's user-friendliness and solid teaching support are strengthened in this edition with extensively rewritten annotations in the Instructor's Edition. With improved and added notes, instructors will now find teaching suggestions for each and every grammar presentation and practice activity in the text, with point-by-point suggestions for presenting the material in class, in addition to a wealth of helpful facts and resources, variations on and supplements to the existing material, and suggestions for follow-up and extension. Taking into account that Introductory Spanish classrooms typically contain a mix of true beginners, false beginners, and even heritage speakers, a new streamlined organization and a designated space for expanded suggestions for heritage speakers makes it even easier to meet the needs of students with varying levels of language proficiency.

---

234 ■ doscientos treinta y cuatro   Capítulo 8 De viaje

HERITAGE SPEAKERS

• Hay muchas maneras de decir *autobús* dependiendo del país en que uno se encuentre. Por ejemplo, en México se dice *el camión* o *la ruta* para referirse a un autobús de transporte público. En la Argentina se dice *el colectivo*, mientras que en las Islas Canarias, las Antillas, Cuba y la República Dominicana, se dice *la guagua*. Sin embargo, la palabra *guagua* significa *bebé, niño* o *infante* en el Perú y en otros países andinos. Pregúnteles a los hispanohablantes qué palabra usan ellos para referirse a un autobús.

(Cont.)

- Brand-new digital and print testing program

A key part of the instructor resources available with *Puntos* is the comprehensive testing program, now completely rewritten and available in both print and digital formats. Whether you use the testing program as a model to customize your own tests, or you want to quickly and easily assign existing exams or poolable questions to your students, the new testing program offers multiple versions for each chapter from which instructors can draw.

- Updated supplemental activities manual

The tenth edition can be accompanied by the updated *Supplementary Materials to Accompany* Puntos de partida, by Sharon Foerster. The supplementary materials are an updated teacher's guide to *Puntos* and consist of worksheets, short pronunciation practice, listening exercises, grammar worksheets, integrative communication-building activities, comprehensive chapter reviews, and language games.

- In-class grammar and culture presentations on Connect under the Library tab

Connect houses other important resources to support instruction. In addition to the Instructor's Manual and an Instructor's Guide for Connect, you will find a digital Image Bank to support your classroom presentations and activities, as well as updated cultural and grammar content for in-class use. With engaging images and cultural facts about the countries of focus, the updated Cultural PowerPoint Presentations offer students additional contact with culture, and offer the instructor detailed notes and suggestions for how to present these in class. To build on the grammar presentations in the text, Grammar PowerPoint Presentations provide an additional way for students to absorb grammatical knowledge, which is especially useful for hard-to-grasp concepts where students often benefit from multiple and varied modes of presentation.

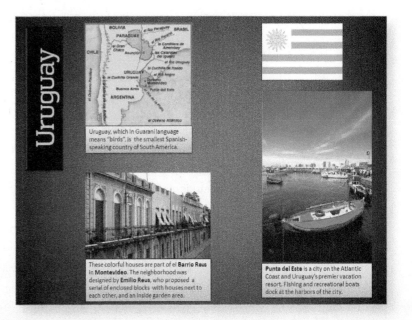

Uruguay, which in Guaraní language means "birds", is the smallest Spanish-speaking country of South America.

These colorful houses are part of el **Barrio Reus** in **Montevideo**. The neighborhood was designed by **Emilio Reus**, who proposed a serial of enclosed blocks with houses next to each other, and an inside garden area.

Punta del Este is a city on the Atlantic Coast and Uruguay's premier vacation resort. Fishing and recreational boats dock at the harbors of the city.

Engaging and Immersive
Digital Tools

Connect is the most powerful and flexible course management system available. Rooted in research on effective student learning practices, the platform integrates adaptive learning tools with dynamic, engaging language practice activities. The result is better student learning of the Spanish language.

• A personalized and adaptive learning and teaching experience

No two students learn a language the same way or at the same rate. Students enter the Introductory Spanish course with a wide range of knowledge and experience, from true beginners to heritage speakers. So how do you know what to teach and to whom?

McGraw-Hill's LearnSmart provides each student with a personalized and adaptive learning experience based on individual needs. As the student works through a series of probes around the vocabulary and grammar presented in each chapter, LearnSmart identifies what the student knows and doesn't know, and continuously adapts the subsequent probes to focus on those areas where the student needs the most help. Each student learns and masters core vocabulary and grammar at his or her own pace and comes to class better prepared to communicate in the target language.

And just as no two students learn a language the same way, no two Spanish courses are taught the same way. Connect provides the instructor with both the ability and flexibility to pull from the robust set of content available in the platform and craft a unique learning path based on the goals of the course. Be it in a face-to-face, hybrid, or fully online course, Connect can adapt to you and to your students to create the ideal learning environment.

• Student-centered

Students learn best when they are involved and interested in the material being taught. *Practice Spanish: Study Abroad*, the market's first 3-D immersive language game designed exclusively by McGraw-Hill Education, brings the language to the students in a fun, engaging, and immersive gaming experience. Students "study abroad" virtually in Colombia where they will create their very own avatar, live with a host family, make new friends, and navigate a variety of real-world scenarios using their quickly developing Spanish language skills. Students earn points and rewards for successfully accomplishing these tasks via their smartphones, tablets, and computers, and instructors have the ability to assign specific tasks, monitor student achievement, and incorporate the game into the classroom experience. *Practice Spanish: Study Abroad* is available upon request. Your Learning Technology Representative can provide more information.

• Robust data

Instructors and students alike want to know how students are performing in the course and where they can improve. The powerful reporting tools in Connect surface actionable data to both instructors and students so steps can be taken by both groups to ensure student success.

The first and only analytics tool of its kind, Connect Insight is a series of visual data displays—each framed by an intuitive question—to provide instructors at-a-glance information regarding how your class is doing. Connect Insight provides analysis on five key insights, available at a moment's notice from your Connect course.

LearnSmart provides powerful reports to view student progress by module and detail with completion breakdown, along with class performance data, frequency of missed questions, and a view into the most challenging learning objectives. Metacognitive reports allow instructors to view statistics on how knowledgeable their students are about their own comprehension and learning. What's more, LearnSmart provides students their own progress reports so they can take full responsibility for their own learning.

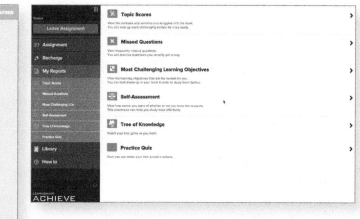

WHAT'S NEW

Functional design and easy reference

- **Identifiable goals:** Each chapter opener details what students can hope to accomplish.

- **Significance of color:** Updated color patterns allow for easy navigation and concept identification.

- **Visually fresh:** Many new photos, realia, and updated drawings.

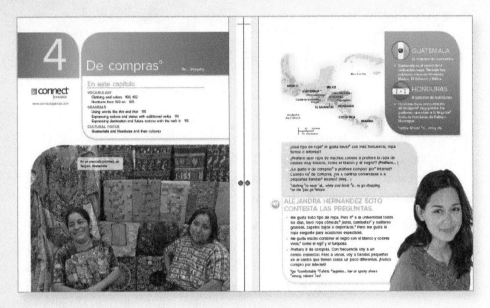

Solidifying grammar and vocabulary

- **Clarity:** Grammar explanations are simpler and more straightforward, with particular care given to points that are often challenging for students.

- **Grammar summaries:** Short summaries now appear at the end of all grammar explanations.

- **More input:** More models in the target language to guide students through activities.

- **Seamless progression:** *Práctica* and *Conversación* are now a single section, *Práctica y comunicación*, for seamless transition from controlled to free-form activities, while maintaining careful sequencing. Each initial activity in *Práctica y comunicación* incorporates an *Autoprueba* for students to check their comprehension and builds up to personalized and communicative grammar practice.

- **Self-checks:** *En resumen* now includes a chapter-ending checklist for students to assess their progress toward attaining the goals stated at the beginning of the chapter.

New opportunities for communicative practice

- **Chapter opener:** New personal chapter opener questions and answers from native speakers from various parts of the Spanish-speaking world get students listening and talking in the target language from the very first page of each chapter.

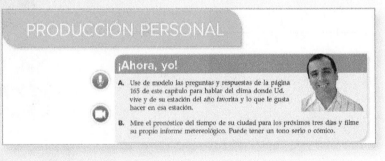

- **Communicative grammar practice:** Grammar activity sections are scaffolded to carefully move students into free-form practice activities after each grammar point.

- *Producción personal*: This new chapter-ending section guides students to create a capstone portfolio of writing, speaking, and filming activities.

- **Information gap activities:** New activities designed for every chapter.

Integrated culture

- Culturally based activities: More grammar and vocabulary exercises center on cultural context.
- *Algo sobre...* : Appearing three to four times per chapter, these new windows into the countries of focus weave culture into the linguistic workflow.
- *A leer*: Readings are simplified and include more interactive activities (*Y ahora, Uds.*).
- *Un poco de todo*: Each section starts with a *Lengua y cultura* activity to practice newly acquired and recycled grammar and vocabulary.

Video integration:

- In each chapter, the *Salu2* (formerly *Telepuntos*) video is divided into two shorter segments, one that is integrated into the vocabulary presentation, providing the opportunity for additional practice, and one that remains at the end of the chapter to reinforce a variety of skills.

SALU2

Salu2 desde° Los Ángeles

Antes de mirar°

What is a morning news
all of the phrases that a

- ☐ un poco (*a little*
- ☐ un poco serio
- ☐ informativo
- ☐ muy dramático
- ☐ para (*for*) una a
- ☐ solo para las pe

Digital tools

- Embedded audio: Audio recordings throughout the ebook; students hear new vocabulary as it is introduced.
- LearnSmart: Grammar modules for every grammar topic and updated vocabulary modules.
- *Practice Spanish: Study Abroad*: This interactive 3D game, accessible on computers and mobile devices, immerses students in a virtual study abroad experience in Colombia. *Practice Spanish* facilitates real-world application that integrates culture, grammar, and vocabulary.
- English grammar guides: Assignable explanations and practice with basic grammar concepts in English.

Instructor resources

- Even more comprehensive instructor annotations: Strengthened and reorganized annotations have consistent suggestions for expansion, oral practice, and grammar explanations.
- Well-organized: Easy-to-navigate Annotated Instructor's Edition with a dedicated area for heritage speakers.
- Testing program: Completely revised in both digital and print forms.

ABOUT THE AUTHORS

Thalia Dorwick retired as McGraw-Hill's Editor-in-Chief for Humanities, Social Sciences, and Languages. For many years she was also in charge of McGraw-Hill's World Languages college list in Spanish, French, Italian, German, Japanese, and Russian. She has taught at Allegheny College, California State University (Sacramento), and Case Western Reserve University, where she received her Ph.D. in Spanish in 1973. She was recognized as an Outstanding Foreign Language Teacher by the California Foreign Language Teachers Association in 1978. Dr. Dorwick is the coauthor of several textbooks and the author of several articles on language teaching issues. She is a frequent guest speaker on topics related to language learning, and she was also an invited speaker at the II Congreso Internacional de la Lengua Española, in Valladolid, Spain, in October 2001. In retirement, she consults for McGraw-Hill, especially in the area of world languages, which is of personal interest to her. She is a Vice President of the Board of Trustees of Case Western Reserve University and a past President of the Board of Directors of Berkeley Repertory Theatre.

Ana María Pérez-Gironés is an Adjunct Associate Professor of Spanish at Wesleyan University, Middletown, Connecticut, where she teaches and coordinates Spanish language courses. She received a Licenciatura en Filología Anglogermánica from the Universidad de Sevilla in 1985, and her M.A. in General Linguistics from Cornell University in 1988. Professor Pérez-Gironés' professional interests include second language acquisition and the use of technology in language learning. She is a coauthor of *A otro nivel, Puntos en breve,* Second Edition, and *¿Qué tal?,* Seventh Edition. She is also a coauthor of the Student Manuals for Intermediate Grammar Review and Intensive and High Beginner Courses that accompany *Nuevos Destinos.*

Anne Becher received her M.A. in Hispanic Linguistics in 1992 from the University of Colorado—Boulder, and now coordinates the Beginning Spanish One course and teaches pedagogy and methods courses for the Department of Spanish and Portuguese there. She has taught beginning through advanced levels of Spanish since 1996, including several years teaching Modified Spanish classes for students with difficulty learning languages. She has published several reviews in *Hispania,* presents frequently at the Colorado Congress of Foreign Language Teachers (CCFLT) conferences, and has served on the boards of CCFLT and the Colorado chapter of American Association of Teachers of Spanish and Portuguese. She co-edited the bilingual literary journal *La selva subterranea* from 1987–1996.

ACKNOWLEDGMENTS

We would like to thank the overwhelming number of friends and colleagues who served on boards of advisors or as consultants, completed reviews or surveys, and attended symposia or focus groups. Their feedback was indispensible in creating the *Puntos* program. The appearance of their names in the following lists does not necessarily constitute their endorsement of the program or its methodology.

Practice Spanish: Study Abroad Board of Advisors

James Abraham
Glendale Community College

Kalynn Aguirre
Florida Atlantic University

Adam Ballart
Ball State University

Kelly Conroy
Western Kentucky University

Ari Gutman
Auburn University

Patricia Harrigan
Community College of Baltimore County

Felix Kronenberg
Rhodes College

Melissa Logue
Columbus State Community College

Leticia McGrath
Georgia Southern University

David Neville
Elon University

Michelle Ocasio
Valdosta State University

Aaron Salinger
Mount San Antonio College

Jacquelyn Sandone
University of Missouri

Practice Spanish: Study Abroad Colombia Consultants

Lourdes Arevalo
University of California, Los Angeles

Jorge Cubillos
University of Delaware

Fabio Espitia
Grand Valley State University

Martiza Nemoga
University of Pittsburgh

Beatriz Potter
Valdosta State University

Chayree Santiago Thomas
Rowan-Cabarrus Community College

Amy Uribe
Lone Star College

Juan Villa
University of Rhode Island

Practice Spanish: Study Abroad Student Board of Advisors

Kaitlin Anderson
Illinois State University

Jasmine Arias
University of Illinois, Urbana-Champaign

Joyce Bolivar
University of Rhode Island

Mike Churvis
Georgia Perimeter College, Dunwoody

Julian Colonia
University of Rhode Island

Brian de la Cruz
University of Rhode Island

Katherine Foss
University of Rhode Island

Brandi Glenn
Georgia Southern University

Michael R. Herrera
University of Cincinnati

Tricia Hogan
University of Rhode Island

Abigael Mandenberg
University of Illinois, Urbana-Champaign

Jen McGunigal
University of Rhode Island

Johan Molina
University of Rhode Island

Deandra Moorman
University of Cincinnati

Isaac Reeves
Ben Davis University

Gulya Tlegenova
San Diego Mesa College

Kari Uhle
Indiana University

Victoria Vanderaa
Illinois State University

Juan Villa
University of Rhode Island

Kayla Warren
Georgia Southern University

Practice Spanish: Study Abroad Student Ambassadors

Daniel Carroll
Northern Virginia Community College

Marie-Claire Levy
Florida State University

Tuyen Lieu
Central Piedmont Community College

Matt Lozano
Clarke University

Colin McCullough
Ohio University

Emily Ousterhout
Mississippi State University

Paige Tabler
California State University, Chico

Maggie Wilson
George Mason University

Vanessa Wismeier
Loras College

Matt Wolf
Kansas State University

Practice Spanish: Study Abroad Pilots and Beta Testers

James Abraham
Glendale Community College

Julie Alwehieby
Coastline Community College

Melba Amador
Western Kentucky University

Jeanette Banashak
Grand Valley State University

Tulio Cedillo
Lynchburg College

Daren Crasto
Houston Community College

Paul Cristofaro
Minot State University

Luis Delgado
Olive Harvey College

Mark A. Dowell
Randolph Community College

Muriel Gallego
Ohio University

Audrey R. Gertz
Indiana University-Purdue University Indianapolis

Scott Gibby
Austin Community College

Adrienne Gonzalez
University of Denver

Michael Harrison
San Diego Mesa College

Claudia Jaramillo
Purdue University Calumet

Ryan LaBrozzi
Bridgewater State University

Jude Thomas Manzo
Saint Phillip's College

Leticia McGrath
Georgia Southern University

Peggy McNeil
Louisiana State University

Marco Mena
Mass Bay Community College

Wendy Mendez-Hasselman
Palm Beach State College

Jerome Mwinyelle
East Tennessee State University

Danae Orlins
University of Cincinnati

Hector Iglesias Pascual
Ohio University

Erika M Southerland
Muhlenberg College

Amber Workman
California Lutheran University

ACTFL 2014 Workshop Participants

Susana Solera Adoboe
Southern Methodist University

Berta Chópite
Earlham College

Abby Dings
Southwestern University

Jude Thomas Manzo
Saint Phillip's College

Leticia McDoniel
Southern Methodist University

Javier Morin
Del Mar College

Samuel Sommerville
Johnson County Community College

Gloria Yampey-Jorge
Houston Community College

Symposia

Atlanta, GA

Juan Alcarría
Georgia College & State University

Barbara A. Bateman
Georgia Perimeter College

María Elena Bermudez
Georgia State University

María Guadalupe Calatayud
University of North Georgia

Aurora Castillo-Scott
Georgia College & State University

Jose A. Cortés
Georgia Perimeter College

Lisa Davie
Georgia Perimeter College

Janan Fallon
Georgia Perimeter College

Carolina Ganem-Cameron
Georgia Perimeter College

Gael Guzmán Medrano
University of West Georgia

Kristi Hislope
University of North Georgia

Nicolas Hu
University of North Georgia

Melissa Logue
Columbus State Community College

Leda Lozier
The University of Georgia

Raúl Llorente
Georgia State University

Rosaria Meek
University of North Georgia

Oscar H. Morena
Georgia State University

Sharon Nuruddin
Clark Atlanta University

Teresa Pérez-Gamboa
The University of Georgia

Rick Robinson
Georgia Perimeter College

Daniel Sanchez
The University of Georgia

Pamela Simpson
Georgia Perimeter College

Elizabeth Z. Solis
University of West Georgia

Mariana Stone
University of North Georgia

Sherry von Klitzing
Kennesaw State University

Alvaro Torres Calderón
University of North Georgia

Ami L. Travillian-Vonesh
University of North Georgia

Napa, CA

Tanya Chroman
California Polytechnic State University

Laurie de González
University of Oregon

Mari Carmen García
Sacramento City College

Ana Hartig-Ferrer
California Polytechnic State University

Deborah Holmberg
Azusa Pacific University

Keith Johnson
California State University, Fresno

Anne Kelly-Glasoe
South Puget Sound Community College

Milagros Ojermark
Diablo Valley College

Marcelo Paz
California State University, East Bay

Beatriz Robinson
University of Nevada, Reno

Judy Rodríguez
California State University, Sacramento

Julio Torres
University of California, Irvine

Chicago, IL

Maxi Armas
Triton College

An Chung Cheng
University of Toledo

Chyi Chung
Northwestern University

Luis Delgado
Olive-Harvey College

Ronald Gest
Milwaukee Area Technical College

Ileana Hester
Governors State University

Alfonso Illingworth-Rico
Eastern Michigan University

Franklin Inojosa
City Colleges of Chicago

David Migaj
Wilbur Wright College

Octavian Stinga
City Colleges of Chicago

Lucero Tonkinson
City Colleges of Chicago

Los Angeles, CA

Ashlee Balena
University of North Carolina at Wilmington

Tracy Bishop
University of Arkansas

Aymara Boggiano
Rice University

Oscar Cabrera
Community College of Philadelphia

Sara Casler
Sierra College

Christine Cotton
University of Arkansas at Little Rock

Christopher DiCapua
Community College of Philadelphia

Concepción Domenech
University of Wyoming

Mandy Faretta-Stutenberg
Northern Illinois University

Erin Finzer
University of Arkansas at Little Rock

Anna Kalminskaia
University of Nevada, Reno

David Leavell
College of S. Nevada

Maria Manni
University of Maryland, Baltimore County

Anne-Marie Martin
Portland Community College

Juan Carlos Moraga
Folsom Lake College

Christine Núñez
Kutztown University of Pennsylvania

Eva Núñez
Portland State University

Norma Rivera-Hernández
Millersville University of Pennsylvania

Baton Rouge, LA

Gina Breen
Louisiana State University

Brigitte Delzell
Louisiana State University

Dorian Dorado
Louisiana State University

Ann Francois
Louisiana State University

Stephanie Gaillard
Louisiana State University

Amy George-Hirons
Tulane University

Melissa Guerry
Louisiana State University

Sheldon Lotten
Louisiana State University

Cathy Luquette
Louisiana State University

Peggy McNeil
Louisiana State University

Sulagna Mishra
Louisiana State University

John Patin
Louisiana State University

Alfonso Quinones
Louisiana State University

Mariela Sanchez
Southeastern Louisiana University

Jack Yeager
Louisiana State University

Miami, FL

Emmanuel Alvarado
Palm Beach State College

Elisabeth D'Antoni
Broward College Central

Domenica Diraviam
Broward College Central

Mónica Durán
University of Miami, Coral Gables

Trenton Hoy
Broward College Central

Wendy Mendez-Hasselman
Palm Beach State College, Lake Worth

Sandy Oakley
Palm Beach State College, Eissey

Celia Roberts
Broward College Central

Alyse Schoenfeldt
Palm Beach State College, Eissey

Alina Vega-Franco
Broward College Central

Justin White
Florida Atlantic University, Boca Raton

Amelia Island, FL

Flavia Belpoliti
University of Houston

Sarah Bentley
Portland Community College

Sara Casler
Sierra College

Jorge Cubillos
University of Delaware

Paul Larson
Baylor University

María Elizabeth Mahaffey
University of North Carolina, Charlotte

Leticia McGrath
Georgia Southern University

Catherine Ortiz
University of Texas at Arlington

Yanira Paz
University of Kentucky

Carlos Ramírez
University of Pittsburgh

Carmen Sotolongo
El Camino College

Edda Temoche-Weldele
Grossmont College

Amy Uribe
Lone Star College

Karen Zetrouer
Santa Fe Community College

Key West, FL

Michelle Cipriano
Wright State University

Edward Erazo
Broward College–Central

Cindy Espinosa
Central Michigan University

Vanessa Lazo-Wilson
Austin Community College–Round Rock

Kathy Leonard
University of Nevada, Reno

Melissa Logue
Columbus State Community College

Germán Negrón
University of Nevada, Las Vegas

Sylvia Nikopoulos
Central Piedmont Community College

Isabel Parra
University of Cincinnati, Batavia

Carlos Pedroza
Palomar College

Beatriz Potter
Valdosta State University

Latasha Russell
Florida State College, South Campus

Nancy Stucker
Cabrillo College

Lucero Tenorio
Oklahoma State University, Stillwater

Lilia Vidal
Miracosta College

Practice Spanish: Study Abroad - Hollywood, FL

Kelly Conroy
Western Kentucky University

Darren Crasto
Houston Community College, Northwest College

Richard Curry
Texas A & M University

Dorian Dorado
Louisiana State University, Baton Rouge

Leah Fonder-Solano
University of Southern Mississippi

Luz Font
Florida State College, South Campus

Muriel Gallego
Ohio University, Athens

Scott Gibby
Austin Community College, Northridge

Ryan LaBrozzi
Bridgewater State University

Melissa Logue
Columbus State Community College

Alejandro Muñoz
Garces Coastal Carolina University

Aaron Roggia
Oklahoma State University

Aaron Salinger
Mt. San Antonio College

Jacquelyn Sandone
University of Missouri, Columbia

Michael Vrooman
Grand Valley State University

Reviewers

Dean Allbritton
Colby College

Tim Altanero
Austin Community College

Virginia Arreola
Hiram College

Silvia Arroyo
Mississippi State University

Barbara Avila-Shah
University at Buffalo, State University of New York

Wanda Baumgartel
Snead State Community College

Anne Becher
University of Colorado at Boulder

Brian Beeles
Arizona Western College

Clare Bennett
University of Alaska Southeast, Ketchikan

Donna Binkowski
Southern Methodist University

Diane Birginal
Gonzaga University

Joseph Brockway
Mountain View College

Francis Canedo
Northeast State Community College

Beth Cardon
Georgia Perimeter College

Gabriela Carrion
Regis University

Mayra Cortes-Torres
Pima Community College

Laurence Covington
University of the District of Columbia Community College

Darren Crasto
Houston Community College

Betsy Dahms
University of West Georgia

Kit Decker
Piedmont Virginia Community College

Heriberto Del Porto
Westminster College, MO

David Detwiler
MiraCosta College

John Deveny
Oklahoma State University, Stillwater

Dorian Dorado
Louisiana State University

Indira Dortolina
Lone Star College, Univeristy Park

Denise Egidio
Guilford Technical Community College

Hector Fabio Espitia
Grand Valley State University

Abra Figueroa
Oklahoma City Community College

Sarah Finley
University of Kentucky

Timothy Foxsmith
Univeristy of Texas, Arlington

Ellen Lorraine Friedrich
Valdosta State University

Daniel Fulmer
Snead State Community College

Javier A. Galvan
Santa Ana College

Luis Garcia-Torvisco
Gonzaga University

Alejandro Garza
Tarrant County College, Northwest Campus

Scott Gibby
Austin Community College

Debbie Gill
Penn State University, DuBois

Elena Grajeda
Pima Community College

Ileana Gross
University of Colorado Denver

Sergio A. Guzmán
College of Southern Nevada

Karen Hall Zetrouer
Santa Fe College

Patricia Harrigan
Community College of Baltimore County

Haydn
Campbell University

Lynn Healy
Grand Valley State University

Laurie Huffman
Los Medanos College

Elena Iglesias-Villamel
Hiram College

Kelsey Ihinger
University of Wisconsin, Madison

Casilde Isabelli
University of Nevada, Reno

Roberto Jimenez-Arroyo
University of South Florida Sarasota-Manatee

Julie Kleinhans-Urrutia
Austin Community College

Chris Kneifl
University of Oklahoma

Dr Jeremy Larochelle
University of Mary Washington

Luis E Latoja
Columbus State Community College

Rachele Lawton
The Community College of Baltimore County

Vanessa Lazo-Wilson
Austin Community College

Peter Lebron
Moberly Area Community College

Kathleen Leonard
University of Nevada, Reno

Talia Loaiza
Austin Community College

Rosemary LoDato
Houston Community College Southwest

Kathy Lopez
Saginaw Valley State University

Kimberly Louie
Southeast Missouri State University

Monica Malamud
Canada College

Jude Thomas Manzo
Saint Philip's College

Sandra M. Manzon - Omundson
Anoka Ramsey Community College

Ornella Mazzuca
Dutchess Community College

Peggy McNeil
Louisiana State University

Marco Mena
Massbay Community College

Wendy Mendez-Hasselman
Palm Beach State College

Jise L. Mendoza
The University of San Diego

Joseph Menig
Valencia College

Lizette Moon
Houston Community College Northwest

Patricia Moore-Martinez
Temple University

Sandra J. Mulryan
Community College of Baltimore County

Heather Nylen
University of Hawaii at Manoa

Dale Omundson
Anoka-Ramsey Community College

Ann Ortiz
Campbell University

Catherine Ortiz
University of Texas at Arlington

Patricia Orozco Watrel
University of Mary Washington

Philip Pack
Connors State College

Elizabeth Petree
Joliet Junior College

Maria Portal
Hamilton College

Tim Robbins
Drury University

Silvia Roca-Martinez
The Citadel

Angelo J. Rodriguez
Kutztown University of Pennsylvania

Margarita Rodriguez
Lone Star College System

Ulises Rodriguez
Mountain View College

Francisco Salgado
The College of Staten Island

Francisco Salgado-Robles
University of Kentucky

Bethany Sanio
University of Nebraska at Lincoln

Roman Santos
Mohawk Valley Community College

David Schultz
College of Southern Nevada

Dr. Dennis Seager
Oklahoma State University

Georgia Seminet
St. Edward's University

Louis Silvers
Monroe Community College

Natalie Sobalvarro
Merced College

Samuel Sommerville
Johnson County Community College

Stacy Southerland
University of Central Oklahoma

Clay Tanner
The University of Memphis

Joe Terantino
Kennesaw State University

Rosa Tezanos-Pinto
Indiana University-Purdue University Indianapolis

Giovanna Urdangarain
Pacific Lutheran University

Amy Uribe
LoneStar College CyFair

Vangie Vélez-Cobb
Palo Alto College

Hilde Votaw
University of Oklahoma

Michael Vrooman
Grand Valley State University

Natalie S. Wagener
University of Texas, Arlington

Sara Walker
Holy Family University

Tina Ware-Walters
Oklahoma Christian University

Sandra Watts
University of North Carolina, Charlotte

Susan Wehling
Valdosta State University

Christopher Weimer
Oklahoma State University

Joseph Wieczorek
College of Baltimore

Karen Zetrouer
Santa Fe College

The authors wish to thank the following friends and professional colleagues. Their feedback, support, and contributions are greatly appreciated.

- Arni C. Álvarez , Rodrigo Figueroa, Nathan Gordon, Melissa Logue, Christina D. Miller, and Mark Pleiss for their work as user diarists, and Anne Becher and Jeanette Sánchez Naranjo for helping us identify many members of this fine team
- The Teaching Assistants and colleagues of Anne Becher at the University of Colorado, Boulder, whose thought-provoking conversations and annotations truly shaped the revision of the grammar, vocabulary, and activities. "Their work was perhaps the single most important kind of input that I received for this edition."—Thalia Dorwick
- The colleagues of Ana Pérez-Gironés at Wesleyan University
- Dora Y. Marrón Romero and Claudia Sahagún (Broward Community College), for their helpful comments about culture
- Alejandro Lee (Central Washington University), for the many comments and suggestions on the eighth edition
- Laura Chastain, for her meticulous work on the language and linguistic accuracy of the manuscript, over many editions but especially this one

Finally, the authors would like to thank their families and close personal friends for all of their love, support, and patience throughout the creation of this edition. **¡Los queremos mucho!**

Contributors

Kalynn Aguirre, Sarah Alem, Allen Bernier, Denise Nicole Casnettie, Eileen Fancher, Lorena Gómez Mostajo, Danielle Havens, Shelly Hubman, Emilia Illana Mahiques, Constance Kihyet, Christopher LaFond, Lily Martínez, Leticia McGrath, Wendy Mendez-Hasselman, Louise Neary, Ron Nelms, Pennie Nichols, Jodi Parrett, Maritza Salgueiro-Carlisle, John Underwood, Annie Rutter Wendel, Sam Sommerville, Nina Tunac-Basey, Amy Uribe, Alina Vega Franco

Product Team

Editorial and Marketing: Mike Ambrosino, Jorge Arbujas, Allen J. Bernier, Susan Blatty, Chris Brown, Laura Ciporen, Craig Gill, Helen Greenlea, Misha Maclaird, Pennie Nichols, Sadie Ray, Kimberley Sallee, Katie Stevens, Alina Vega Franco

Art, Design, and Production: Matt Backhaus, Amber Bettcher, Francine Cronshaw, Kelly Heinrichs, Patti Isaacs, Lynne Lemley, Erin Melloy DeHeck, Sylvie Pittet, Margaret Potter, Terri Schiesl, Emily Tietz, Beth Thole, Shawntel Schmitt

Media Partners: Aptara, BBC Motion Gallery, Eastern Sky Studios, Hurix, Klic Video Productions, Inc., Laserwords, Latinallure Voiceover, LearningMate

CONTENTS

GET THE MOST FROM YOUR SPANISH STUDIES!

In the 21st century global society we live in now, there is an ever-growing demand for those who have proficiency in more than one language. The Spanish language is at the top of the list in the United States. Regardless of your career path, there is not a single profession that would not benefit from proficiency in Spanish!

In addition to **majoring** or **minoring in Spanish**, the Department of Modern Languages also offers a **B.A. in Translation and Interpreting**. You may also wish to consider other options such as completing one of the **Certificate Programs**. And if you are looking for a way to build your proficiency in the language while expanding your cultural horizons, be sure to check out details of our **Study Abroad Program**. **Accelerated courses for Lower Level Spanish** (1441-1442 and 2313-2314) can help you begin these programs more quickly by taking two levels in one semester. See details for these options below and on the following page.

Full course descriptions for **all undergraduate Spanish courses** are listed at the end of this section of your textbook. For more information, please consult with our **Undergraduate Advisor** in the Department of Modern Languages by sending an email to **modladvisor@uta.edu** or by phoning **817.272.3161**. More information is also available on the Department of Modern Languages website: **http://www.uta.edu/modl**

CERTIFICATE IN SPANISH FOR THE PROFESSIONS

Students interested in receiving theoretical and practical training in **Spanish for the Professions** are eligible to apply to the Department of Modern Languages for this **15-hour certificate program** which will prepare them to work with Spanish-speaking individuals and in Spanish-language contexts. Topics to be covered by coursework in this program include Spanish for law enforcement, social services, education, medical professions, business, communications, Hispanic culture and intercultural competence. Prerequisites: To take SPAN 3314 or SPAN 3305, students need credit for SPAN 2314 or SPAN 2315 with a grade of C or better. Other prerequisites are listed below and also require a grade of C or better.

REQUIRED COURSES:

❖ **SPAN 3314** - Advanced Spanish Grammar OR:
  SPAN 3305 - Advanced Spanish for Heritage Speakers
❖ **SPAN 3315** - Composition through Literature (Prerequisite: SPAN 3314 or SPAN 3305)
❖ **SPAN 3309** - Spanish for the Professions (Prerequisite: SPAN 3315)

❖ **Two (2) 4000-level courses** from the following. (Prerequisites: All <u>required</u> courses above.)
  SPAN 4312 - Intercultural Competence for Global Communication
  SPAN 4334 - Contemporary Hispanic Culture
  SPAN 4335 - Business Spanish
  SPAN 4336 - Topics in Spanish for the Professions

CERTIFICATE IN TRANSLATION

PREREQUISITES:
- ❖ SPAN 3305 - Advanced Spanish for Heritage Speakers OR:
  SPAN 3314 - Advanced Spanish Grammar
- ❖ SPAN 3315 - Composition through Literature

REQUIRED COURSES:
- ❖ SPAN 3340 - Introduction to Translation
- ❖ SPAN 4341 - Business and Legal Translation
- ❖ SPAN 4342 - Medical, Scientific and Technical Translation

translation	traducción
english	inglés
spanish	español

CERTIFICATE IN INTERPRETING

PREREQUISITES:
- ❖ SPAN 2314 - Intermediate Spanish II OR:
  SPAN 2315 - Intermediate Spanish for Heritage Speakers
- ❖ SPAN 3305 - Advanced Spanish for Heritage Speakers OR:
  SPAN 3314 - Advanced Spanish Grammar

REQUIRED COURSES:
- ❖ SPAN 3341 - Introduction to Interpreting
- ❖ SPAN 4343 - Interpreting in Medical Settings
- ❖ SPAN 4344 - Interpreting in Legal Settings

ACCELERATED LOWER LEVEL SPANISH COURSES

ACCELERATED BEGINNING SPANISH: SPAN 1441-032 + SPAN 1442-032. Take Beginning Spanish I and Beginning Spanish II in one semester. This class meets MWF from 10-11:50.

ACCELERATED INTERMEDIATE SPANISH: SPAN 2313-132 + SPAN 2314-132. Take Intermediate Spanish I and Intermediate Spanish II in one semester. This class meets MWF from 10-11:50. Prerequisite: Grade of C or better in SPAN 1442.

SPANISH DEGREE PROGRAMS

B.A. in SPANISH FOR GLOBAL COMPETENCE
B.A. in TRANSLATION AND INTERPRETING
MINOR in SPANISH

Detailed information on the MODL website: **http://www.uta.edu/modl/spanish/Spanish_Programs.php**

SUMMER STUDY ABROAD PROGRAM IN MEXICO

- Study Spanish in Cuernavaca, Mexico – a colonial city in the heart of Mexico known for its eternal spring weather.
- Live with a Mexican family.
- Interact with native speakers.
- Experience Mexican culture first hand: in the classroom, on the cobblestone streets or in the market.
- Attend classes on the beautiful campus of the Spanish Language Institute.
- Students pay in-state tuition to UTA in addition to program fees, room, board, and excursions. Student Financial Aid applies! Scholarships are available at the Department of Modern Languages for eligible students, in addition to UTA.

WEBSITE: **http://utaencuernavaca.wordpress.com**
PROGRAM DIRECTOR: **Dr. Ray Elliott – elliott@uta.edu**

SPANISH COURSE DESCRIPTIONS

SPAN 1441. BEGINNING SPANISH I. 4 Hours. (TCCN = SPAN 1411). Beginning study of Spanish language with emphasis on speaking, listening, reading, and writing. No prerequisites. Native or heritage speakers of Spanish may not take this course.

SPAN 1442. BEGINNING SPANISH II. 4 Hours. (TCCN = SPAN 1412). Continuation of beginning Spanish. Prerequisite: SPAN 1441 with a grade of C or better. Native or heritage speakers of Spanish may not take this course.

SPAN 2301. TOPICS IN SPANISH LITERATURE IN TRANSLATION. 3 Hours. Study of the works of major authors and intellectual trends of a given period or periods. May be repeated for credit as topics or periods vary. SPAN 2301 may be taken to fulfill the foreign language literature requirement. Prerequisite: ENGL 1301 and ENGL 1302.

SPAN 2313. INTERMEDIATE SPANISH I. 3 Hours. (TCCN = SPAN 2311). Intermediate study of Spanish language with emphasis on speaking, listening, reading, and writing. Prerequisite: SPAN 1442 with a grade of C or better. Native or heritage speakers of Spanish may not take this course.

SPAN 2314. INTERMEDIATE SPANISH II. 3 Hours. (TCCN = SPAN 2312). Continuation of intermediate Spanish. Prerequisite: SPAN 2313 with a grade of C or better. Native or heritage speakers of Spanish may not take this course.

SPAN 2315. INTERM SPAN HERITAGE SPEAKERS. 3 Hours. This course focuses on the development of reading, writing, speaking and listening skills in Spanish, as well as an understanding of Hispanic cultures and issues of identity of heritage speakers in the United States. This course is intended for heritage speakers of Spanish and is the equivalent of SPAN 2314. Prerequisite: SPAN 2313 with a Grade of C or better or the equivalent, or consent of the department.

SPAN 2391. CONFERENCE COURSE. 3 Hours. Independent study; consultation with instructor on a regular basis. Prerequisite: Permission of the instructor.

SPAN 3302. HISPANIC LITERATURE IN TRANSLATION. 3 Hours. The works of major authors and intellectual trends of a given period. May be repeated for credit as topics or periods vary. SPAN 3302 cannot be applied toward the B.A. in Spanish or toward a Spanish minor, but may be taken to fulfill the foreign language literature requirement. Prerequisite: 2314 of a Modern or Classical language and 6 hours of English.

SPAN 3303. ADVANCED SPANISH CONVERSATION. 3 Hours. Practice in oral expression with an emphasis on vocabulary building and grammar review. Of special interest to students who wish to improve their skills in pronunciation, comprehension, and oral expression. Credit will not be granted to native or heritage speakers of Spanish. Prerequisite: SPAN 2314 with a grade of C or better.

SPAN 3305. ADVANCED SPANISH FOR HERITAGE SPEAKERS. 3 Hours. A detailed study of Spanish grammar for heritage speakers. Capitalizes upon students' existing language skills, expands their knowledge base, and develops their ability to read, write, and communicate more effectively. Special attention is given to regional and dialectal differences. Prerequisite: SPAN 2315, or the equivalent, with a grade of C or better.

SPAN 3309. SPANISH FOR THE PROFESSIONS. 3 Hours. Practice in Spanish-language skills needed in the professional fields in order to communicate with Spanish-speaking individuals. Emphasis on specialized vocabulary building, role play, and an understanding of Hispanic culture. Topics may include Spanish for law enforcement, social services, education, medicine, business, and communications. Prerequisite: SPAN 3315 with a grade of C or better.

SPAN 3311. SPANISH CULTURE AND CIVILIZATION. 3 Hours. Spanish history with emphasis on cultural, intellectual, and artistic trends and existing social institutions. Prerequisite: SPAN 2314 or SPAN 2315 with a grade of C or better.

SPAN 3312. LATIN AMERICAN CULTURE AND CIVILIZATION. 3 Hours. An interdisciplinary introduction to Latin American society, history and culture. Offered as MAS 3312 and SPAN 3312; credit will be granted for either MAS or SPAN. Prerequisite: SPAN 2314 or SPAN 2315 with a grade of C or better.

SPANISH COURSE DESCRIPTIONS

SPAN 3313. TOPICS IN HISPANIC LANGUAGE, LITERATURE & CULTURE. 3 Hours. Topics may include Peninsular or Latin American film, music, radio, politics, human rights movements, literature, language or Hispanic linguistics. May be repeated as the topic changes. Prerequisite: SPAN 2314 or SPAN 2315 with a grade of C or better.

SPAN 3314. ADVANCED SPANISH GRAMMAR. 3 Hours. A detailed study of Spanish grammar for non-native speakers. Credit will not be granted to native or heritage speakers of Spanish. Prerequisite: SPAN 2314 with a grade of C or better.

SPAN 3315. COMPOSITION THROUGH LITERATURE. 3 Hours. Practice in original composition and critical thinking through the study of selected literary and cultural texts. Of special interest to students who wish to improve their reading comprehension and their writing skills. Prerequisite: SPAN 3305 or SPAN 3314, with grade C or better.

SPAN 3319. INTRODUCTION TO SPANISH LINGUISTICS. 3 Hours. Introductory study of the structure of the Spanish language including phonology, morphology, and syntax, as well as historical, regional, and social variation. Prerequisite: SPAN 3314 or SPAN 3305 with a grade of C or better.

SPAN 3320. INTRODUCTION TO HISPANIC LITERATURE AND CULTURE. 3 Hours. An introduction to the tools of literary and cultural criticism as well as Spanish and Latin American literary history. Study of representative literary texts with the object of developing students' understanding of historical change and cultural crosscurrents. Prerequisite: SPAN 3315 with a grade of C or better.

SPAN 3340. INTRODUCTION TO TRANSLATION. 3 Hours. This course is an introduction to the theory, methods and practice of English to Spanish translation and Spanish to English translation. The student will learn how to address translation problems related to culture and language as well as the fundamentals of translating general material from different fields such as journalism, advertisement, tourism, gastronomy, health, business, etc. The student will also acquire basic knowledge of translation theory. SPAN 3340 cannot be applied toward the B.A. in Spanish. Prerequisite: SPAN 3315 with grade of C or better.

SPAN 3341. INTRODUCTION TO INTERPRETING. 3 Hours. Introduction to the theory, methods and practice of interpreting. The student will become familiar with community interpreting (interpreting in school, medical and legal settings) and interpreting theory. The student will begin to interpret in the simultaneous and consecutive (bilateral) modes. The student will also learn about sight translation. Non-native/heritage speakers are also encouraged to take SPAN 3303 prior to enrolling in SPAN 3341. SPAN 3341 cannot be applied toward the B.A. in Spanish. Prerequisite: SPAN 3305 or SPAN 3314 with a grade of B or better.

SPAN 3345. INTRODUCTION TO COMPUTER-ASSISTED TRANSLATION. 3 Hours. Introduction to computer-assisted translation (CAT), machine translation (MT), translation memory (TM) and terminology management tools in modern translation and localization workflows. Prepares students for real-world careers in the language services industry. For students enrolled in Localization and Translation/Interpreting programs only. SPAN 3345 cannot be applied toward the B.A. in Spanish.

SPAN 3391. CONFERENCE COURSE. 3 Hours. Independent study; consultation with instructor on a regular basis. Offered primarily in summer study abroad programs. May be repeated for credit. Prerequisite: Permission of the instructor.

SPAN 4310. TOPICS IN PENINSULAR SPANISH LITERATURE AND CULTURE TO THE EIGHTEENTH CENTURY. 3 Hours. Topics may include: Medieval Spanish literature and culture, Golden Age Spanish literature and culture, or any particular movement, genre, work or author prior to the eighteenth century. May be repeated for credit when content changes. Prerequisite: SPAN 3315 with a grade of C or better.

SPAN 4311. TOPICS IN PENINSULAR SPANISH LITERATURE AND CULTURE, EIGHTEENTH CENTURY TO THE PRESENT. 3 Hours. Topics may include: Neoclassical peninsular Spanish literature and culture, peninsular Spanish literature and culture of the Romantic period, Realist or Naturalist Spanish literature and culture, peninsular Spanish literature and culture since 1900, as well as any particular movement, genre, work or author from the eighteenth century to the present. May be repeated for credit when content changes. Prerequisite: SPAN 3315 with a grade of C or better.

SPANISH COURSE DESCRIPTIONS

SPAN 4312. INTERCULTURAL COMPETENCE FOR GLOBAL COMMUNICATION. 3 Hours. A study of the cultural differences between the U.S. and the Hispanic world with a focus on the development of intercultural competence: verbal and non-verbal communication, interpersonal skills, effective management strategies, and professional etiquette in multicultural settings. Prerequisite: SPAN 3315 with a grade of C or better.

SPAN 4313. TOPICS IN HISPANIC CULTURE. 3 Hours. Among the topics are Spanish or Latin American music, television, radio, film, and literature as culture. May be repeated for credit as topic changes. Prerequisite: SPAN 3315 with a grade of C or better. Offered as MAS 4313 and SPAN 4313; credit will be given for MAS 4313 or SPAN 4313 but not both in a given semester.

SPAN 4314. TOPICS IN LATIN-AMERICAN LITERATURE AND CULTURE TO MODERNISM. 3 Hours. Topics may include: Colonial Latin-American literature and culture, pre-modern Latin-American literature and culture, Latin-American literature and culture of the Enlightenment, or any particular movement, genre, work or author prior to Modernism. May be repeated for credit when content changes. Prerequisite: SPAN 3315 with a grade of C or better.

SPAN 4315. TOPICS IN CONTEMPORARY LATIN-AMERICAN LITERATURE AND CULTURE, MODERNISM TO THE PRESENT. 3 Hours. Topics may include: Latin-American literature and culture of Modernism, modern Latin-American literature and culture, or any particular movement, genre, work or author from Modernism to the present. May be repeated for credit when content changes. Offered as MAS 4315 and SPAN 4315; credit will be given for MAS 4315 or SPAN 4315 but not both in a given semester. Prerequisite: SPAN 3315 with a grade of C or better.

SPAN 4317. CHICANO LITERATURE. 3 Hours. Mexican-American literature, with special attention to its social, cultural, and linguistic background. Offered as MAS 4317 and SPAN 4317; credit will be given for MAS 4317 or SPAN 4317 but not both in a given semester. Prerequisite: SPAN 3315 with a grade of C or better.

SPAN 4318. MEXICAN LITERATURE. 3 Hours. Studies in Mexican fiction, poetry, drama, and literary essay. Offered as MAS 4318 and SPAN 4318; credit will be given for MAS 4318 or SPAN 4318 but not both in a given semester. Prerequisite: SPAN 3315 with a grade of C or better.

SPAN 4320. TOPICS IN SPANISH LANGUAGE, WRITING AND THEORY. 3 Hours. Review of advanced research methods and topics in Spanish, Latino and Latin American literature, culture and linguistics. Topics may include: literary and cultural theory in relation to Hispanic literature and culture, research trends, and methods in Spanish linguistics. Students conduct original research or writing projects in relation to the course topic. May be repeated for credit as topic changes. Prerequisite: SPAN 3315 with a grade of C or better.

SPAN 4327. WOMEN IN HISPANIC LITERATURE. 3 Hours. Considers women as characters in and writers of Hispanic literature. Includes the analysis of themes, language, and how the writings of women often give voice to lesser known aspects of culture. Offered as SPAN 4327, MAS 4327, and WOMS 4327; credit will be granted only once. Prerequisite: SPAN 3315 with a grade of C or better.

SPAN 4330. TOPICS IN SPANISH LINGUISTICS. 3 Hours. Topics may include: Spanish phonetics and phonology, morphology, syntax, semantics, lexicography, history of the Spanish language, Old Spanish, Spanish sociolinguistics, as well as the application of any theoretical approach to the study of the Spanish language, excluding the study of either peninsular or American Spanish dialectology. May be repeated for credit when content changes. Prerequisite: SPAN 3319 with a grade of C or better.

SPAN 4332. TOPICS IN SPANISH DIALECTOLOGY. 3 Hours. Topics may include: Modern peninsular Spanish dialectology, modern Spanish-American dialectology, Old Spanish dialectology, early American Spanish dialectology, as well as a detailed study of any one dialect or regional dialect of Spanish from either a synchronic or a diachronic perspective. Emphasis may be given to phonetics, phonology, morphology, syntax, semantics, or lexicon, as applied to the study of peninsular or American Spanish dialectology. May be repeated for credit when content changes. Prerequisite: SPAN 3319 with a grade of C or better.

SPANISH COURSE DESCRIPTIONS

SPAN 4334. CULTURE AND ECONOMIC GLOBALIZATION IN THE HISPANIC WORLD. 3 Hours. An introduction to social, political and economic structures in Spain and Latin America, with special emphasis on current events affecting the business world. Prerequisite: SPAN 3315 with a grade of C or better. Exclusively for International Business Spanish students. SPAN 4334 cannot be applied toward the B.A. in Spanish.

SPAN 4335. BUSINESS SPANISH. 3 Hours. An introduction to business terminology, skills needed for writing business letters, conducting telephone conversations, commercial transactions, and international procedures. Operational and strategic issues involved in interaction with Hispanic firms and markets; international trade; competitive, vendor-customer, and collaborative relations. Prerequisite: SPAN 3315 with a grade of C or better. Exclusively for International Business Spanish students. SPAN 4335 cannot be applied toward the B.A. in Spanish.

SPAN 4336. TOPICS IN SPANISH FOR THE PROFESSIONS. 3 HOURS. Development of Spanish-language skills needed to work in a specific profession. Emphasis on reading and formal communication, including technical papers, letters, reports, proposals, and presentations. Topics may include Spanish for legal, medical, educational, or communications fields. May be repeated for credit when content changes. Prerequisite: SPAN 3315 with a grade of C or better.

SPAN 4339. THE ACQUISITION OF SPANISH. 3 Hours. Topics, methods, and techniques specific to the teaching of the Spanish language. Prerequisite: SPAN 3319 with a grade of C or better.

SPAN 4341. BUSINESS AND LEGAL TRANSLATION. 3 Hours. An advanced course in translation with a focus on business and legal texts. Students deepen their knowledge of translation theory and are trained to build and consolidate their skills in specialized translation. May be taken concurrently with SPAN 4342. SPAN 4341 cannot be applied toward the B.A. in Spanish. Prerequisite: SPAN 3340 with a grade of C or better.

SPAN 4342. MEDICAL, SCIENTIFIC & TECH TRANSLATION. 3 Hours. An advanced course in translation with a focus on medical, scientific and technical translation. Students deepen their knowledge of translation theory and are trained to build and consolidate their skills in specialized translation. May be taken concurrently with SPAN 4341. SPAN 4342 cannot be applied toward the B.A. in Spanish. Prerequisite: SPAN 3340 with a grade of C or better.

SPAN 4343. INTERPRETING IN MEDICAL SETTINGS. 3 Hours. A study of different types of interpretation. Medical terminology in English and Spanish will be addressed with a special emphasis on the diverse roles of medical interpreters as well as various locations where they are needed, such as hospital clinics, doctor's offices, and hearings that deal with medical issues. Ethical standards of practice in medical interpreting will be examined. SPAN 4343 cannot be applied toward the B.A. in Spanish. Prerequisite: SPAN 3341 with a grade of B or better.

SPAN 4344. INTERPRETING IN LEGAL SETTINGS. 3 Hours. A study of different types of interpretation. Legal terminology in English and Spanish will be addressed with special emphasis on the diverse roles of legal interpreters as well as various locations where they are needed, such as courtrooms, lawyer's offices, and state, federal, or local law-enforcement facilities. Ethical standards of practice in legal interpreting will be examined. SPAN 4344 cannot be applied toward the B.A. in Spanish. Prerequisite: SPAN 3341 with a grade of B or better.

SPAN 4391. CONFERENCE COURSE. 3 Hours. Independent study in the preparation of a paper on a research topic; consultation with instructor on a regular basis. May be repeated for credit. Prerequisite: two 3000 level courses and permission of the instructor.

SPAN 4393. SPANISH INTERNSHIP. 3 Hours. A combination of field-related experience in the business or service sector with an academic component. Coursework may include journal writing in Spanish, outside readings, and formal presentations. Prerequisite: two 3000 level courses and permission of the instructor.

SPAN 4394. HONORS THESIS / SENIOR PROJECT. 3 Hours. Required of all students in the University Honors College. During the senior year, the student must complete a thesis or a project under the direction of a faculty member in the major department. May not be repeated for credit. Prerequisite: two 3000 level courses and permission of the instructor.

7

¡A comer!°

¡A... *Let's eat!*

En este capítulo

www.connectspanish.com

Una frutería, en la Ciudad de Panamá, Panamá

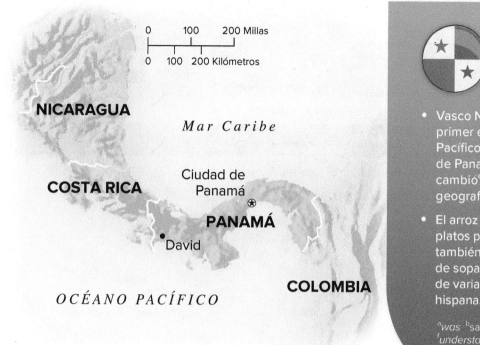

PANAMÁ

3.8 (punto ocho) millones habitantes

- Vasco Núñez de Balboa fue[a] el primer europeo que vio[b] el océano Pacífico en 1514, desde una colina[c] de Panamá. Este descubrimiento[d] cambió[e] la comprensión[f] de la geografía de nuestro planeta.

- El arroz con pollo[g] es uno de los platos panameños más típicos. Es también típico el sancocho, un tipo de sopa que muestra[h] la influencia de varias culturas: la indígena, la hispana, la africana y la afroantillana.[i]

[a]*was* [b]*saw* [c]*hill* [d]*discovery* [e]*changed* [f]*understanding* [g]*arroz... chicken with rice* [h]*shows* [i]*Afro-Caribbean*

- ¿Cuál es su comida[a] favorita?
- ¿Cuáles son algunos[b] de los platos[c] típicos de su país?
- ¿Dónde y a qué hora almuerza y cena[d] Ud., por lo general?

[a]*food* [b]*some* [c]*dishes* [d]*have dinner*

MANUEL GIL DEL VALLE CONTESTA LAS PREGUNTAS.

- Eso es difícil de contestar porque me gusta comer bien y me gusta casi todo. Pero si tengo que elegir un plato, elijo la paella de mariscos.[a]

- Los «nacatamales» son muy populares. Son tamales muy grandes, rellenos de carne, verduras, arroz, ciruelas[b] y otros ingredientes más. Una bebida típicamente nicaragüense es el pinolillo, una especie de horchata hecha de harina de maíz.[c] Pero en Nicaragua también son populares las comidas originarias de otros países, como la española, italiana, mexicana, china, etcétera.

- Trabajo en el centro de Managua. Así que,[d] por lo general, almuerzo en uno de los muchos restaurantes pequeños que hay en el centro. La hora siempre depende del trabajo, pero con frecuencia almuerzo al mediodía. ¿Y la cena? Casi siempre cenamos en casa con toda la familia, a eso de[e] las ocho. Mi esposa es una cocinera[f] estupenda.

[a]paella... *seafood paella* [b]rellenos... *stuffed with meat, vegetables, rice, cherries* [c]hecha... *made with corn flour* [d]Así... *So* [e]a... *around* [f]*cook*

La comida y las comidas°

La... *Food and meals*

el desayuno

07:00

desayunar

el cereal

el jugo (de fruta)

el café

la leche

el pan tostado

la mantequilla

el té

el huevo

el almuerzo

12:00

almorzar (almuerzo)

el queso

la ensalada

la pimienta

la sal

la hamburguesa

la sopa

el refresco

el sándwich

la manzana

el agua* mineral

la cena

06:00

cenar

el bistec

la patata/papa

el vino blanco

el vino tinto

el pan

el pastel

los espárragos

el pollo (asado)

el pescado

el arroz

la cerveza

You can hear the pronunciation of theme vocabulary words and phrases in the Connect eBook.

*The noun **agua** (water) is feminine, but the masculine articles are used with it in the singular: el **agua**. Adjectives that modify it are feminine: el **agua frí**a. This occurs with all feminine nouns that begin with a stressed **a** sound, for example, el/un **ama de casa** (homemaker).

Otras frutas

la banana	banana
la naranja	orange

Otras verduras

el aguacate	avocado
las arvejas	green peas
la cebolla	onion
los champiñones	mushrooms
los frijoles	beans
los garbanzos	chickpeas
la lechuga	lettuce
el pepino	cucumber
el tomate	tomato
la zanahoria	carrot

Otras carnes

la barbacoa	barbeque
la chuleta (de cerdo)	(pork) chop
el jamón	ham
el pavo	turkey
la salchicha	sausage; hot dog

Otros pescados y mariscos

el atún	tuna
los camarones	shrimp
la langosta	lobster
el salmón	salmon

Otros postres

los dulces	sweets; candy
el flan	(baked) custard
la galleta	cookie
el helado	ice cream

Otras comidas

el aceite (de oliva)	(olive) oil
el azúcar	sugar
la salsa	salsa
el yogur	yogurt

Los verbos

desayunar	to have (eat) breakfast
almorzar (almuerzo)	to have (eat) lunch
cenar	to have (eat) dinner, supper
cocinar	to cook

Así se dice

There is great variety in the words used to refer to foods in the Spanish-speaking world. The following are only a few of the most common ones.

las arvejas = los guisantes (*Sp.*)	la papa = la patata (*Sp.*)
los camarones = las gambas (*Sp.*)	el refresco = la gaseosa, la soda (¡**OJO!** = *soda water* in some areas)
el jugo = el zumo (*Sp.*)	

There are many ways to express **la tienda de comestibles** (*grocery store*): **la abacería, el almacén** (which you have learned means *department store* in most areas), **la bodega** (popular in the Caribbean), **la pulpería** (*C.A., S.A.*), **la trucha** (*C.A.*).

Nota **comunicativa**

Más vocabulario para hablar de la comida

tener (mucha) hambre	to be (very) hungry
tener (mucha) sed	to be (very) thirsty
merendar (meriendo)	to snack
la merienda	snack
la cocina	cuisine
los comestibles	groceries, foodstuff
el plato	dish (*food prepared in a particular way*); course
el plato principal	main course
caliente	hot (*in temperature, not taste*)
frito/a	fried
picante	hot, spicy
rico/a	tasty, savory; rich (*in calories*)

La merienda (typically a late afternoon snack) is a traditional custom in those countries where the dinner hour is quite late, such as Spain, for example, where people may have dinner at 10:00 or 11:00 P.M. or even later. **La merienda** tides people over until the late evening meal.

You will use these words and phrases in **Comunicación A** and **B**.

Comunicación

A. **¿Qué quiere tomar?** Empareje las descripciones con las comidas.

DESCRIPCIONES

1. __C__ una sopa fría, langosta, espárragos, ensalada de lechuga y tomate, vino blanco y, para terminar, un pastel
2. __d__ jugo de fruta, huevos con jamón, pan tostado y café
3. __e__ un vaso (*glass*) de leche y unas galletas
4. __a__ pollo asado, arroz, arvejas, agua mineral y, para terminar, una manzana
5. __b__ una hamburguesa con patatas fritas, un refresco y un helado

COMIDAS

a. un menú ligero (*light*) para una dieta
b. una comida rápida
c. una cena elegante
d. un desayuno estilo estadounidense
e. una merienda

B. **Definiciones**

Paso 1. Dé las palabras definidas.

1. un plato de lechuga y tomate
2. una bebida alcohólica blanca o roja
3. una verdura anaranjada
4. una carne típica para una barbacoa en este país
5. la comida favorita de los ratones (*mice*)
6. una verdura que se come frita con las hamburguesas
7. una fruta roja o verde

Paso 2. Ahora, en parejas, túrnense para crear (*create*) definiciones de comidas y bebidas, según el modelo del **Paso 1.** Una persona da (*gives*) la definición y la otra da la palabra correspondiente.

Nota **cultural**

La comida del mundo hispano

No se puede hablar de una sola comida hispana, porque en el mundo hispanohablante hay una gran variedad culinaria.

- La comida cambia de país a país, dependiendo de los productos locales y de influencias nativas y externas. Sin embargo, sí hay productos de origen americano que se utilizan[a] en prácticamente todas las cocinas latinoamericanas: el maíz, las papas, los frijoles, los tomates, los aguacates.
- El arroz es también fundamental, pero es de origen asiático. Fue introducido en América por[b] los españoles.

Una de las influencias básicas en la cocina de todos los países latinoamericanos es la cocina española. Se combina con la tradición culinaria indígena de cada región y, en algunos[c] países, también con la tradición culinaria africana, gracias a la influencia de los esclavos[d] que fueron traídos[e] a América.

El maíz, uno de los ingredientes básicos de casi todos los países latinoamericanos

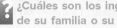 ¿Cuáles son los ingredientes básicos de la cocina de su familia o su país?

[a]se... *are used* [b]by [c]some [d]slaves [e]fueron... *were brought*

C. Consejos (Advice) a la hora de comer. ¿Qué puede comer o beber su compañero/a en las siguientes situaciones? Déle consejos, según el modelo.

[handwritten: what can your partner eat or drink in the following situations?]

MODELO: Tengo mucha/poca hambre (sed). →
E1: Tengo mucha hambre.
E2: Puedes comer un bistec con papas fritas.

1. Tengo mucha/poca hambre (sed). *[handwritten: mucha, little]*
2. Tengo hambre a las cuatro de la mañana, después de una fiesta. *[handwritten: desayuno (breakfast)]* *[handwritten: 2) to have an afternoon snack]*
3. Estoy a dieta. *[handwritten: ensaladas, frutas, agua]*
4. Estoy de vacaciones en Maine (Texas, California, la Florida,...).
5. Es hora de merendar. Estoy en casa (la universidad).
6. Soy vegano/a. *[handwritten: vegan]*

D. Las preferencias gastronómicas

Paso 1. Complete las siguientes oraciones para describir lo que Ud. come y no come. *[handwritten: following sentences / what you eat]*

1. Por la mañana siempre como desayuno *[handwritten: (juevos, pan tostado, etc.)]* (No como langosta o hamburguesa) *[handwritten]*
2. En el desayuno me gusta comer _____.
3. Para cenar, prefiero comer _____. *[handwritten: for dinner]*
4. Nunca como naranjas y nunca bebo vino. *[handwritten: never, naranjas, vino]*
5. No me gusta comer _____, pero lo/la como (*I eat it*) en casa de mis padres/hijos/abuelos. *[handwritten: 3) dislike]*

Paso 2. Haga una lista de los tres tipos de cocinas que Ud. prefiere.

Paso 3. Entre todos, comparen las listas. ¿Cuáles son los platos, lugares para comer y cocinas favoritos de la clase? ¿Cuáles son los ingredientes más necesarios para cocinar sus platos favoritos?

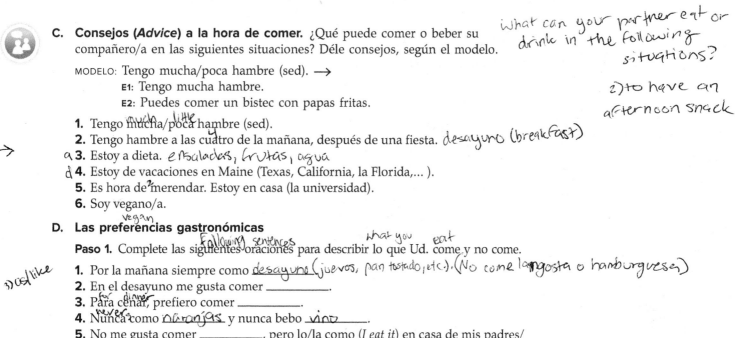

¿Qué sabe Ud. y a quién conoce?

As you know, two Spanish verbs express *to be:* **ser** and **estar.** They are not interchangeable, and their use depends on the meaning the speaker wishes to express. Similarly, two Spanish verbs express *to know:* **saber** and **conocer.** Note their uses in the drawings and text below. Also note that **conocer** is frequently used with the word **a** when referring to a person (as in the phrase **¿a quién conoce?** from the title of this section).

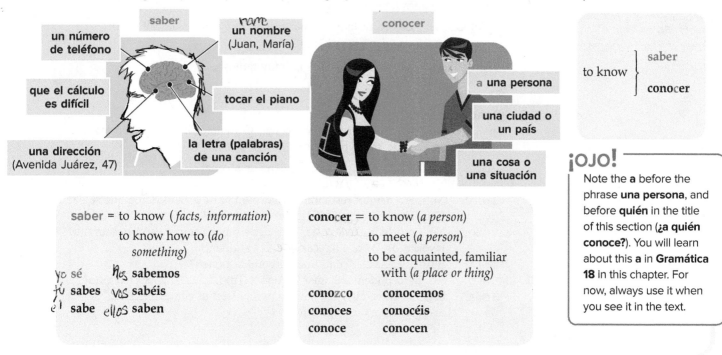

saber
un número de teléfono
un nombre (Juan, María) *[handwritten: name]*
que el cálculo es difícil
tocar el piano
una dirección (Avenida Juárez, 47)
la letra (palabras) de una canción

conocer
a una persona
una ciudad o un país
una cosa o una situación

to know { saber / conocer }

saber = to know (*facts, information*)
to know how to (*do something*)

yo sé	*[handwritten: nos]* sabemos
[handwritten: tú] sabes	*[handwritten: vos]* sabéis
[handwritten: él] sabe	*[handwritten: ellos]* saben

conocer = to know (*a person*)
to meet (*a person*)
to be acquainted, familiar with (*a place or thing*)

conozco	conocemos
conoces	conocéis
conoce	conocen

¡OJO!
Note the **a** before the phrase **una persona,** and before **quién** in the title of this section (**¿a quién conoce?**). You will learn about this **a** in **Gramática 18** in this chapter. For now, always use it when you see it in the text.

Comunicación

A. **¿Cuánto sabe Ud. de Panamá?**

Paso 1. ¿Cierto o falso? Complete las oraciones con la forma **yo** del verbo **saber** o **conocer**. Luego diga si las oraciones son ciertas o falsas para Ud.

		CIERTO	FALSO
1. _conozco_	Panamá.	☐	☐
2. _sé_	dónde está Panamá.	☐	☐
3. _s_	el nombre de la capital de Panamá.	☑	☐
4. _c_	a una persona panameña famosa.	☐	☑
5. _c_	quién es Rubén Blades.	☐	☑
6. _c_	la música de Blades.	☐	☑
7. _s_	la letra de una canción de Blades.	☐	☑
8. _s_	bailar salsa.	☐	☑
9. _c_	un restaurante panameño.	☐	☐

Paso 2. Ahora, en parejas, túrnense para hacer y contestar preguntas basadas en las oraciones del **Paso 1**.

MODELO: E1: ¿Conoces Panamá?
E2: No, no conozco Panamá. ¿Y tú?
E1: Yo sí. / Yo tampoco. (*Me neither.*)

B. **Los usos de *saber* y *conocer***

Paso 1. Llene (*Fill in*) los espacios en blanco con la forma apropiada de **saber**. Luego dé su equivalente en inglés.

—¿(Tú) _sabes_ [1] la dirección de un restaurante panameño?

—¡Cómo no![a] Hay uno en la calle[b] Park. El chef, Felipe, _sabe_ [2] hacer unos platos muy originales.

—¿(Tú) _sabes_ [3] a qué hora abren los sábados?

—No (yo) _sé_ [4] exactamente. ¡Pero _sé_ [5] la dirección electrónica!

[a]¡Cómo… *Of course!* [b]*street*

Paso 2. Ahora llene los espacios en blanco con la forma apropiada de **conocer**. Luego dé su equivalente en inglés.

—¿(Tú) _conoces_ [1] ese restaurante panameño que está en la calle Park?

—Sí, y también (yo) _conozco_[2] al chef, Felipe.

—¿Ah sí? Yo lo[a] quiero _conozco_ [3]. Es muy famoso.

[a]*him*

C. **¿Dónde cenamos?**

Paso 1. Lola y Manolo quieren salir a cenar. Complete su diálogo con las formas apropiadas de **saber** o **conocer**.

LOLA: ¿(Tú) ~~conoces~~ _sabes_ [1] adónde quieres ir a cenar?

MANOLO: No ~~conozco~~ _sé_ .[2] ¿Y tú?

LOLA: No, pero hay un restaurante nuevo en la calle Betis. Creo que se llama Guadalquivir. ¿_conoces_ [3] el restaurante?

MANOLO: No, pero (yo) _conozco_ [4] que tiene mucha fama. Es el restaurante favorito de Pepa. Ella _conoce_ [5] al dueño.[a]

LOLA: ¿(Tú) _____[6] qué tipo de comida tienen?

MANOLO: No, pero podemos llamar a Pepa. ¿(Tú) _____[7] su teléfono?

LOLA: Está en mi celular. Llámala[b] y pregúntale[c] si ella _____[8] si aceptan reservaciones o no.

MANOLO: De acuerdo.

[a]*owner* [b]*Call her* [c]*ask her*

Paso 2. Comprensión. Conteste las siguientes preguntas.

1. ¿Saben Lola y Manolo dónde quieren cenar?
2. ¿Conocen el nuevo restaurante?
3. ¿Saben qué tipo de comida se sirve allí?
4. ¿Saben el número de teléfono de Pepa?
5. ¿Conocen al dueño del restaurante?

D. ¿Sabe Ud. mentir (*to lie*) bien?

Paso 1. Escriba dos oraciones con **saber** sobre algunas (*some*) cosas que sabe hacer y dos oraciones con **conocer** sobre personas interesantes que conoce. Algunas oraciones deben ser falsas. **¡OJO!** No olvide (*Don't forget*) usar la **a** con **conocer.**

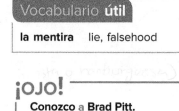

Vocabulario **útil**

la mentira   lie, falsehood

Paso 2. En grupos de tres, túrnense para presentar sus oraciones. Los compañeros que escuchan deben adivinar (*guess*) cuáles son las oraciones falsas.

E. Encuesta (*Poll*) sobre los talentos especiales de la clase

Paso 1. Haga una lista de tres cosas interesantes que Ud. sabe hacer bien. Use infinitivos, según el modelo.

MODELO: tocar el acordeón, hacer paella, esquiar

¡OJO!
Conozco a Brad Pitt.

Paso 2. Ahora haga una encuesta entre los compañeros de clase para ver si los talentos de Ud. son únicos o comunes en su clase. Si sus compañeros tienen un talento que Ud. también tiene, deben firmar (*sign*) en el espacio indicado.

MODELO: tocar el acordeón → ¿**Sabes** tocar el acordeón? Si **sabes, firma** aquí.

Talento 1: _____	Talento 2: _____	Talento 3: _____

F. Intercambios

1. ¿Qué restaurantes conoces en esta ciudad? ¿Cuál es tu restaurante favorito? ¿Por qué es tu favorito? ¿Es buena la comida allí? ¿Qué tipo de comida sirven? ¿Te gusta el ambiente (*atmosphere*)? ¿Comes allí con frecuencia? ¿Llamas para hacer reservaciones?

2. ¿Qué platos sabes hacer? ¿Tacos? ¿enchiladas? ¿pollo frito? ¿hamburguesas? ¿Te gusta cocinar? ¿Cocinas con frecuencia? ¿Qué ingredientes usas con más frecuencia? ¿Tienes una receta (*recipe*) favorita?

«¡Qué rico!°» Segmento 1

¡Qué... *How delicious!*

Antes de mirar

Indique con qué comida del día se relacionan las siguientes comidas y bebidas. Y si le gusta mucho una comida o bebida, ¡indíquela (*mark it*) con una estrella (*star*) también! Si no conoce una comida o bebida, escriba **no sé.**

D = el desayuno **A** = el almuerzo **C** = la cena **M** = la merienda

1. ___D___ el café
2. ___D___ la leche
3. ___M___ el chocolate
4. ___C___ el arroz
5. _____ el jamón *ham*
6. _____ el queso
7. _____ las tapas
8. _____ los mariscos *seafood*

Ana saluda, tomando café: «Me entusiasmé (*I became a fan*) con el café cubano durante los meses que viví (*I lived*) en Miami. Y va muy bien con el primer segmento de hoy... »

Este segmento

En este segmento Laura va a Miami y después a Barcelona para hablar de comidas... ¡y de bebidas!

Estrategia

To maximize your comprehension of *Salu2*, go beyond actively looking at the texts and photo on this page. Try to imagine what you will see in the segment. What do you expect to see and hear in a show devoted to food?

Vocabulario **del segmento**

fuerte	strong	**la sartén**	frying pan
¡a mí me encanta!	I love it!	**se cocina**	it is cooked
la calle	street	**vine**	I came
cortado/a con	diluted, cut with	**para que la vean**	for you to see
un poquito de	a little bit of	**no es nada barato**	not at all cheap
yo no sabía nada	I didn't know anything	**una auténtica delicia**	a true delicacy
Se ve bien rico.	It looks great (very delicious).	**algo dulce**	something sweet
		espeso/a	thick, dense
estuvo	was	**¡Riquísimo!**	Very delicious!
dicen	(they) say		

Después de mirar

A. ¿Está claro? Empareje las palabras de las dos columnas para describir las comidas que se mencionan en el segmento.

1. _____ la «medianoche»
2. _____ los churros
3. _____ la paella
4. _____ el jamón serrano

a. una tapa
b. el chocolate
c. los mariscos
d. un sándwich cubano

B. Un poco más. Conteste las siguientes preguntas.

1. ¿Qué adjetivos usan los presentadores para hablar del café cubano?
2. ¿Qué ingredientes varían en la paella? ¿Cuál es la paella favorita de Laura?
3. ¿Cómo es el chocolate español? Según Laura, ¿cuándo se toma un chocolate con churros?

Vocabulario **útil**

¿Has probado... ? Have you tried ... ?
Ya he probado... I have already tried ...
Me/Te gustaría probar... I'd/You'd like to try ...

C. Y ahora, Uds. En parejas, hablen de las comidas y bebidas que se presentan en el segmento. ¿Son Uds. gourmets o se resisten a probar (*trying*) cosas nuevas?

MODELO: E1: Ya he probado el café cortado.
E2: ¿Te gusta?
E1: ¡Me encanta! Es intenso.

Grammar Tutorial 18
connect
SPANISH
www.connectspanish.com

18 Expressing *what* or *who(m)*

Direct Objects; The Personal **a**; Direct Object Pronouns

Gramática en acción: La pirámide alimenticia

ᵃAlgunas... *Sometimes* ᵇVegetales *Vegetables*

¿Y Ud.?

Indique cuáles de estas declaraciones expresan lo que Ud. hace.

1. el pollo
- Lo como todos los días. Por eso tengo que comprarlo con frecuencia.
- Lo como de vez en cuando (*once in a while*). Por eso no lo compro a menudo (*often*).
- Nunca lo como. No necesito comprarlo.

2. la fruta
- La como todos los días. Por eso tengo que comprarla con frecuencia.
- La como de vez en cuando. Por eso no la compro a menudo.
- Nunca la como. No necesito comprarla.

3. los refrescos
- Los bebo todos los días. Por eso tengo que comprarlos con frecuencia.
- Los bebo de vez en cuando. Por eso no los compro a menudo.
- Nunca los bebo. No necesito comprarlos.

4. las bananas
- Las como todos los días. Por eso tengo que comprarlas con frecuencia.
- Las como de vez en cuando. Por eso no las compro a menudo.
- Nunca las como. No necesito comprarlas.

Direct Objects / Los complementos directos

In English and in Spanish, the *direct object* (**el complemento directo**) of a sentence answers the question *what?* or *who(m)?* in relation to the subject and verb.

> the direct object / **el complemento directo** = the noun or pronoun that receives the action of the verb

SUBJECT (S)	VERB (V)	DIRECT OBJECT (DO)
Ana	is preparing	**dinner.**
They	can't hear	**the waiter.**

What is Ana preparing? ⟶ **dinner**
Who(m) can't they hear? ⟶ **the waiter**

Indicate the subjects, verbs, and direct objects in the following sentences.

1. *I don't see Betty and Mary here.*
2. *We don't have any money.*
3. No veo a Betty y María aquí.
4. No tenemos dinero.
5. Julio va a poner la sopa en la mesa.
6. ¿Necesitas el libro y un bolígrafo?

The Personal a / La a personal

In Spanish, the word **a** immediately precedes the direct object of a sentence when the direct object refers to a specific person or persons. This **a**, called the *personal a* (**la a personal**), has no equivalent in English.*

Vamos a visitar **a nuestros abuelos.**
We're going to visit our grandparents.
but
Vamos a visitar **la casa de nuestros abuelos.**
We're going to visit our grandparents' house.

Necesitan **a sus padres.**
They need their parents.
but
Necesitan **el coche de sus padres.**
They need their parents' car.

The personal **a** is not used when the direct object is a nonspecific person or an unknown person.

Conozco **a un buen chef.**
I know a great chef.
but
Necesito **un buen chef para una fiesta.**
I need a great chef for a party.

Pets (but not all animals) are treated like people and take the personal **a.**

¿Ves **a Bear**, mi perro?
Do you see Bear, my dog?
but
¿Ves **el perro** allí?
Do you see the dog over there?

¡OJO!
The personal **a** is used before the interrogative words **¿quién?** and **¿quiénes?** when they function as direct objects.

¿**A quién** llamas? ¿**al** camarero?
Who(m) are you calling? The waiter?

¡OJO!
The English verbs *to listen to / look at / look for / wait for* are all followed by prepositional phrases (a *preposition* + *noun* or *pronoun*). However, the Spanish equivalents of those verbs (**escuchar, mirar, buscar,** and **esperar**) are not followed by prepositions. They *are* followed by the personal **a** before a specific person or pet. Compare these pairs of sentences.

Miro el menú. *I'm looking at the menu.*
Miro **al** niño. *I'm looking at the boy.*

Espero el autobús. *I'm waiting for the bus.*
Espero **al** niño. *I'm waiting for the boy.*

¡OJO!
Don't confuse the personal **a** with other uses of the word **a** that you have learned so far.
- **a** = the preposition *to*
- **a** = used after some verbs before an infinitive

Voy **a** la universidad.
En esta clase **aprendemos a** hablar español.
Vamos a salir mañana.

*The personal **a** is not generally used with **tener** or **hay**: Tenemos cuatro hijos. Hay tres niños en la sala.

me	me	nos	us
te	you (*fam. sing.*)	os	you (*fam. pl.*)
lo	you (*form. sing.*), him, it (*m.*)	los	you (*form. pl.*), them (*m., m. + f.*)
la	you (*form. sing.*), her, it (*f.*)	las	you (*form. pl.*), them (*f.*)

1. Direct Object Pronouns

Like direct object nouns, *direct object pronouns*
(**los pronombres del complemento directo**) are
the first recipient of the action of the verb.

    If the direct object noun were repeated in the
English answer to the right, it would sound very repetitive:
"Where are the carrots?" "Do you need the carrots right now?"
Direct object pronouns avoid that kind of unnecessary
repetition: *"Do you need **them** right now?"*

—¿Dónde están **las zanahorias**?
—¿**Las** necesitas ahora mismo?
*"Where are **the carrots**?"*
*"Do you need **them** right now?"*

2. Placement of Direct Object Pronouns

Direct object pronouns are placed:
- before a conjugated verb
- after the word **no** when it appears

—¿Conoces a **Diego**?
—No, no **lo** conozco.
"Do you know Diego?"
"No, I don't know him."
—¿Quién **te** llama más por teléfono?
—Mi madre **me** llama más.
"Who calls you the most?
"My mother calls me the most."

3. With Infinitives or Present Participles

When the conjugated verb is followed by an
infinitive or a present participle, the pronouns
either precede the conjugated verb *or* follow
(and are attached to):

- the infinitive
- the present participle

Las tengo que leer. }
Tengo que **leerlas**. } *I have to read them.*

Lo estoy comiendo. }
Estoy **comiéndolo**. } *I am eating it.*

¡OJO!
When the pronoun is added to the end of a present
participle, an accent mark is added to retain the
original stress: **mirando** ⟶ **mirándolo**.

4. Multiple Meanings of *lo/la/los/las*

Note that the direct object pronouns **lo/la/los/las** have
different meanings depending on the context. In the first
sentence to the right, it is impossible to know what
lo means.

    Notice how the meaning of **lo** is clear in the three
sentences that follow.

No lo veo por la niebla.

I don't see { *it* / *him* / *you (form.)* } *because of the fog.*

¿El coche? No lo veo por la niebla. (**lo** = *it*)
¿El niño? No lo veo por la niebla. (**lo** = *him*)
¿Ud.? No lo veo por la niebla. (**lo** = *you* [*form.*])

5. The Pronoun *lo*

Note that the direct object pronoun **lo** can refer to
actions, situations, or ideas in general. When used in
this way, **lo** expresses English *it* or *that*.

Lo comprende muy bien.
He understands it (that) very well.

No lo creo.
I don't believe it (that).

Lo sé.
I know (it).

Summary of Direct Object Pronouns

yo	→	me
tú	→	te
Ud., él	→	lo
Ud., ella	→	la
nosotros/as	→	nos
vosotros/as	→	vos
Uds., ellos	→	los
Uds., ellas	→	las

Práctica y comunicación

A. Correspondencias

Paso 1. Autoprueba. Complete las siguientes oraciones. **¡OJO!** Use la **a** personal cuando sea (*whenever it is*) necesaria.

Conozco...

1. una persona famosa
2. la ciudad de Nueva York
3. el estado de Montana
4. el profesor / la profesora de _____
5. los padres de mi compañero/a de cuarto

Necesito...

6. el libro de texto en esta clase
7. más clases para graduarme
8. mi familia
9. mis buenos amigos
10. mi perro/gato

Paso 2. Ahora complete las oraciones del **Paso 1** con el pronombre del complemento directo apropiado.

MODELO: Conozco... al profesor de historia latinoamericana. → **Lo** conozco.

Paso 3. Ahora, en parejas, túrnense para hacer y contestar preguntas usando las oraciones del **Paso 2.**

MODELO: Conozco... al profesor de historia latinoamericana. →
    E1: ¿Conoces al profesor de historia latinoamericana?
    E2: Sí, **lo** conozco. (No, no **lo** conozco.) ¿Y tú?
    E1: Yo sí/también. / Yo tampoco. (*Me neither.*)

B. Más correspondencias.
Empareje los pronombres del complemento directo con las personas. A veces hay más de una correspondencia posible.

PRONOMBRES

1. _c_ los
2. _a_ la
3. _b_ te
4. _e_ lo
5. _f_ las
6. _d_ nos

PERSONAS

a. Ana
b. tú
c. Pedro y Carolina
d. María y yo
e. Jorge
f. Elena y Rosa
g. Uds.
h. Ud.

C. ¿Qué comen los vegetarianos?
Aquí hay una lista de diferentes comidas. ¿Cree Ud. que las come un vegetariano? Conteste según los modelos.

MODELOS: el bistec → No **lo** come.
          la banana → **La** come.

1. las patatas
2. el arroz
3. las chuletas de cerdo
4. las zanahorias
5. las manzanas
6. los camarones
7. los champiñones
8. los frijoles
9. la ensalada

D. La cena de Lola y Manolo

Paso 1. La siguiente descripción de la cena de Lola y Manolo es muy repetitiva. Combine las oraciones, según el modelo.

MODELO: El camarero (*waiter*) trae un menú. Lola lee el menú. →
    El camarero trae un menú y Lola **lo** lee.

1. El camarero trae una botella de vino tinto. Pone la botella en la mesa.
2. Lola quiere la especialidad de la casa. Va a pedir la especialidad de la casa.
3. Manolo prefiere el pescado fresco (*fresh*). Pide el pescado fresco.
4. Lola quiere una ensalada también. Por eso pide una ensalada.
5. El camarero trae la comida. Sirve la comida.
6. «¿La cuenta (*bill*)? El dueño está preparando la cuenta para Uds.»
7. Manolo quiere pagar con tarjeta (*card*) de crédito. Pero no trae su tarjeta.
8. Por fin, Lola toma la cuenta. Paga la cuenta.

Paso 2. Las siguientes oraciones describen la cena de Lola y Manolo. Diga en español a qué se refieren los pronombres indicados. Luego diga quién hace cada acción.

1. **Lo** pide.
2. **La** sirve.
3. No **la** trae.
4. **La** paga.

E. Minidiálogos

Paso 1. Complete los siguientes minidiálogos con los pronombres del complemento directo que faltan (*are missing*).

1. —¿Me quieres (*do you love*)?

   —¡_____ quiero muchísimo!

2. —Voy a Panamá y tengo un boleto (*ticket*) de avión gratis. ¿Me acompañas?

   —¡Claro que _____ acompaño! ¿Cuándo nos vamos?

3. —Buenas noches, señor. ¿_____ atienden ya (*Is someone already helping you*)?

   —No, todavía no, gracias.

   — Perdón. Entonces (*Then*) voy a atender_____ yo.

4. —¡Mi hija nunca me llama por teléfono!

   — ¡Tu hija solo tiene 19 años! Seguro que _____ llama si necesita dinero.

5. —¿Cuándo van a visitar a Uds. sus primos panameños?

   —_____ van a visitar este verano.

6. —Buenos días, señora. ¿En qué puedo ayudar_____ (*to help*)?

   —Buenos días. Busco una blusa negra de mi talla (*size*).

7. —¡Qué perro tan bonito (*What a beautiful dog*) tienes!

   —Si quieres, puedes tocar_____ (*to touch*).

Paso 2. Las siguientes oraciones añaden (*add*) un intercambio más a cada minidiálogo del **Paso 1.** Emparéjelos e identifique en cada caso a quién se refiere el pronombre del complemento directo.

a. ¿Desde cuándo lo tienes?
b. ¿Qué desea tomar?
c. ¡Y yo te adoro!
d. ¿La quiere de algodón o de seda?
e. Pues yo quiero conocerlos también.
f. La primera semana de julio.
g. Sí, eso es lo que hace.

Nota **comunicativa**

Cómo expresar una acción muy reciente: *acabar* + de + *infinitivo*

To talk about what you have *just* done, use the phrase **acabar** + **de** + *infinitive*.

Acabo de almorzar con Beto.	*I just had lunch with Beto.*
Acabas de celebrar tu cumpleaños, ¿verdad?	*You just celebrated your birthday, didn't you?*

Note that the infinitive follows the preposition **de**.

You will practice talking about what you have *just* done in **Práctica F.**

F. ¡Acabo de hacerlo! Imagine that a friend is pressuring you to do the following things. With a classmate, tell him or her that you just did each one, using either of the structures in the model.

MODELO: E1: ¿Por qué no haces la ensalada? →
E2: Acabo de hacer**la**. (**La** acabo de hacer.)

1. ¿Por qué no preparas las chuletas para la fiesta?
2. ¿Vas a comprar la fruta hoy?
3. ¿Por qué no pagas los cafés?
4. ¿Vas a cocinar la comida para la cena?
5. ¿Quieres ayudarme?
6. ¿Por qué no me invitas a cenar?

G. ¡Ayuda! (Help!)

Paso 1. Todos necesitamos ayuda alguna vez (*at some point*), ¿no? ¿Quién ayuda a Ud. en los siguientes casos?

MODELO: con el coche → **Mi padre me** ayuda con el coche.

1. con las cuentas (*bills*)
2. con la tarea
3. con la matrícula
4. con el horario de clases
5. con el español
6. pagar las deudas (*debts*)
7. estudiar para los exámenes
8. resolver los problemas personales

Paso 2. Ahora, en parejas, túrnense para hacer y contestar preguntas basadas en el **Paso 1.**

MODELO: con el coche →
E1: ¿Quién **te** ayuda con el coche?
E2: Generalmente, **mis padres me** ayudan un poco. A veces también **me** ayudan **mis abuelos.**

H. Intercambios. En parejas, túrnense para hacer y contestar preguntas sobre los alimentos (*foods*) que consumen y con qué frecuencia. Expliquen por qué tienen esos hábitos. Luego digan a la clase algo (*something*) que tienen en común.

MODELO: E1: ¿Comes pan sin gluten?
E2: No, no **lo** como porque no soy celiaco.

Vocabulario **útil**

la cafeína	ser **bueno/a para la salud** (health)
las calorías	ser **celiaco/a**
el colesterol	
la grasa fat	**me pone(n) nervioso/a** it/they make me nervous
estar **a dieta**	**me sienta(n) mal** it/they don't
ser **alérgico/a a**	agree with me
	lo/la/los/las detesto

1. pan sin gluten
2. refrescos sin azúcar
3. productos bajos en sodio
4. frutas y verduras orgánicas
5. pescados y mariscos
6. hamburguesas
7. bebidas alcohólicas
8. café
9. productos lácteos (*milk*)
10. comidas congeladas (*frozen*)

You have been using a few words that express indefinite and negative qualities since the first chapter of this text. Review what you already know about the content of **Gramática 19** by giving the English equivalent of the following words.

1. siempre *always* 2. nunca *never* 3. también *also/too*

19 Expressing Negation
Indefinite and Negative Words

Grammar Tutorial 19
connect
|SPANISH
www.connectspanish.com

Gramática en acción: ¿Un refrigerador típico?

Empareje las siguientes respuestas con el refrigerador A o el B.

1. ¿Hay algo bueno de comer en este refrigerador?
   _____ Sí, hay algo.
   _____ No, no hay nada.
2. ¿Hay fruta y pan?
   _____ Sí, hay fruta y pan.
   _____ No, no hay fruta. Tampoco hay pan.
3. ¿Hay chuletas de cerdo?
   _____ No, no hay ninguna chuleta.
   _____ Sí, hay algunas chuletas.
4. En esta casa, ¿alguien compra comida con frecuencia?
   _____ No, nadie la compra.
   _____ Sí, alguien la compra.

¿Y Ud.?

¿Cuál de los dos refrigeradores se parece (*resembles*) más al refrigerador de su casa o apartamento? ¿Cuál se parece más al típico refrigerador de los estudiantes? ¿de una familia con hijos? ¿de jóvenes profesionales?

Indefinite and Negative Words / Las palabras indefinidas y negativas

Los adverbios indefinidos y negativos		
siempre	always	Siempre estudio en casa. Estudio en casa siempre.
nunca, jamás	never	Nunca estudio en la biblioteca. No estudio nunca en la biblioteca.
también	also	Yo también sé preparar una paella. Yo sé preparar una paella también.
tampoco	neither, not either	Tampoco sé preparar una paella. Yo no sé preparar una paella tampoco.

A typical refrigerator? **1.** *Is there something good to eat in this refrigerator? Yes, there is something. No, there is nothing.* **2.** *Is there (some) fruit and bread? Yes, there is (some) fruit and bread. No, there is no fruit. There isn't any bread either.* **3.** *Are there pork chops? No, there aren't any chops. (Lit., No, there is no chop.) Yes, there are some chops.* **4.** *In this house, does anyone buy food frequently? No, no one buys it. Yes, someone buys it.*

Los sustantivos indefinidos y negativos

alguien	someone, anyone	En esta clase **alguien** habla chino.
nadie	no one, nobody, not anybody	En esta clase **nadie** habla chino.
		En esta clase **no** habla chino **nadie**.
		Conozco **a alguien** en esa fiesta.
		No conozco **a nadie** en esa fiesta.
algo	something, anything	Sé **algo** de la cocina panameña.
nada	nothing, not anything	No sé **nada** de la cocina panameña.

¡OJO!

The personal **a** is used with **alguien** and **nadie** when they function as direct objects, as in the examples.

Pronunciation Hint: Pronounce the **d** in **nada** and **nadie** as a fricative, that is, like the *th* sound in *the*: [**na-d̯a**], [**na-d̯ie**].

Los adjetivos indefinidos y negativos

algún, alguna, algunos/as	some, any	**algún** tomate, **algunas** chuletas
ningún, ninguna	no, not any	**ningún** tomate, **ninguna** chuleta

¡OJO!

Note how **alguno** and **ninguno** shorten (**algún, ningún**) before masculine singular nouns. You've seen something similar with **uno** (⟶ **un**), **bueno** (⟶ **buen**), and **grande** (⟶ **gran**).

algún / ningún problema
alguna / ninguna cosa
algunos problemas
algunas cosas

The Double Negative / La negativa doble

A double negative is avoided in English but is often necessary in Spanish.
- When the negative word comes *before* the conjugated verb, that is all that is needed.
- When the negative word comes *after* the conjugated verb, another negative word—usually **no**—must be placed before the verb.

negative word + verb

no + *verb + negative word*

¿**Nadie estudia**?
¿**No estudia** nadie? } *Isn't anyone studying?*

Nunca estás en clase.
No estás en clase **nunca**. } *You're never in class.*

Tampoco quieren cenar aquí.
No quieren cenar aquí **tampoco**. } *They don't want to have dinner here either.*

The Adjectives algún and ningún / Los adjetivos *algún* y *ningún*

Algún (**Alguna/os/as**) and **ningún** (**ninguna**) are adjectives. Unlike the other indefinite and negative words you have learned (which are nouns or adverbs), **algún** and **ningún** must agree with the noun they modify. **Ningún** (**Ninguna**) is rarely used in the plural.

—¿Hay **algunos recados** para mí hoy?
—Lo siento, pero hoy no hay **ningún recado** para Ud.
"Are there any messages for me today?"
"I'm sorry, but there are no messages for you today."
(*"There is not a single message for you today."*)

Summary of Indefinite and Negative Words

algo	nada
alguien	nadie
algún/alguna/os/as	ningún, ninguna
siempre	nunca, jamás
también	tampoco

Práctica y comunicación

A. Cosas esenciales

Paso 1. Autoprueba. Dé la palabra negativa correspondiente.

always *also* *something* *someone* *someone*
1. siempre   **2.** también   **3.** algo   **4.** alguien   **5.** alguna

Paso 2. Complete las siguientes oraciones.

1. Siempre tengo _____ (algo) en mi cuarto y también tengo _____ (otra cosa).

2. Nunca _____ (una acción) temprano por la mañana. Tampoco _____ (otra acción que no me gusta hacer).

3. Algo que siempre hay en mi refrigerador es _____. Algo que nunca hay es _____.

4. Para mí, no hay nada tan importante como mi(s) _____ (alguien).

5. En este momento, nadie es tan importante en mi vida (*life*) como mi(s) _____.

Paso 3. Ahora, en parejas, comparen sus oraciones del **Paso 2** y digan a la clase algo que tienen en común.

MODELO: Para nosotros/as dos, no hay nada tan importante como nuestras familias.

B. ¿Qué pasa esta noche en esta casa?

Paso 1. Complete las siguientes oraciones con la palabra indefinida o negativa apropiada según el dibujo.

1. Hay _____ cantando en el baño.

2. Hay _____ niños jugando en su alcoba.

3. Hay _____ en la mesa del comedor.

4. Hay _____ comida en la barbacoa.

5. Hay _____ personas en la sala.

6. No hay _____ en la cocina.

7. No hay _____ plato en la mesa del comedor.

Estrategia

Remember that **ninguno** is always used in the singular and that it shortens to **ningún** before a masculine, singular noun.

Paso 2. Ahora haga otras oraciones ciertas, pero contrarias a las (*those*) del **Paso 1**.

MODELO: **1. No** hay **nadie** cantando en **el jardín**.

C. ¡Nadie come allí! Exprese negativamente, usando la negativa doble.

MODELO: Hay alguien en el restaurante. → **No** hay **nadie** en el restaurante.

1. Hay algo interesante en el menú.
2. Tienen algunos platos típicos.
3. El profesor cena allí también.
4. Mis amigos siempre almuerzan allí.
5. Preparan algo especial para grupos.
6. Siempre hacen platos nuevos.
7. Y también sirven paella, mi plato favorito.

Prác. A, Paso 1. Answers: 1. nunca 2. tampoco 3. nada 4. nadie 5. ninguna

D. **Extremos**

Paso 1. Modifique las siguientes declaraciones para hacerlas negativas.

MODELO: Hay muchas personas antipáticas en mi familia. →
No hay **ninguna persona** antipática (**No** hay **nadie** antipático) en mi familia.

1. Tengo muchos planes interesantes para este fin de semana.
2. Todas mis clases este semestre/trimestre son maravillosas (*wonderful*).
3. Me gusta toda la comida de la cafetería.
4. Hay muchos programas interesantes en la tele últimamente (*lately*).
5. Siempre estudio en la biblioteca.
6. Todos los estudiantes de esta universidad son internacionales.

Paso 2. Ahora modifique las oraciones del **Paso 1** para que expresen (*so that they express*) su opinión.

MODELOS: Hay muchas personas antipáticas en mi familia. →
No hay ninguna persona antipática en mi familia.
En mi familia hay algunas personas antipáticas, pero muy pocas.

Paso 3. Ahora, en parejas, túrnense para hacer y contestar preguntas basadas en las oraciones del **Paso 2**.

MODELO: En mi familia hay algunas personas antipáticas, pero muy pocas. →
E1: En tu familia ¿hay alguna persona antipática (alguien antipático)?
E2: Sí, mi tío Gerry es muy antipático. (No, no hay nadie antipático.)

E. **Intercambios**

Paso 1. En parejas, túrnense para entrevistarse sobre los siguientes temas. Deben obtener detalles interesantes y personales de su compañero/a.

MODELO: E1: ¿Tienes alguna buena excusa para no ir al gimnasio esta semana?
E2: No, no tengo ninguna buena excusa esta semana. (Sí, tengo una buena excusa. ¡No tengo tiempo!)

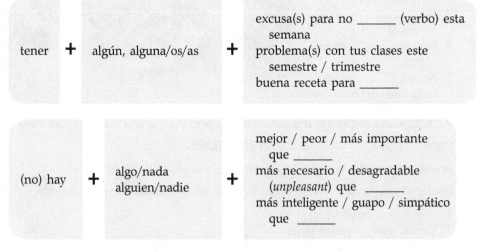

tener	+	algún, alguna/os/as	+	excusa(s) para no _____ (verbo) esta semana problema(s) con tus clases este semestre / trimestre buena receta para _____
(no) hay	+	algo/nada alguien/nadie	+	mejor / peor / más importante que _____ más necesario / desagradable (*unpleasant*) que _____ más inteligente / guapo / simpático que _____

Paso 2. Ahora digan a la clase una respuesta interesante o peculiar.

MODELOS: Algo interesante de Jim es que tiene una excusa muy buena para no hacer la tarea esta noche. Va a...
Algo interesante de Aurora es que, en su opinión, no hay nada más desagradable que la arrogancia.

Algo sobre...

los emberás

Unas casas típicas de los emberás

Los emberás son un pueblo amerindio del este de Panamá y también de la región noroeste de Colombia y del Ecuador. Tradicionalmente viven en la selva,[a] junto a ríos,[b] en zonas donde llueve todo el año. Por eso sus casas están en alto.[c] Están cubiertas[d] de hojas[e] de palma.

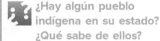
¿Hay algún pueblo indígena en su estado? ¿Qué sabe de ellos?

[a]*jungle* [b]*rivers* [c]*en... raised up* [d]*covered* [e]*leaves*

¿Recuerda Ud.?

Review what you already know about irregular first person present tense forms by giving the **yo** form of the following infinitives. You will need to know this information in **Gramática 20**.

1. salir _____   **3.** conocer _____   **5.** hacer _____   **7.** perder _____
2. tener _____   **4.** pedir _____   **6.** dormir _____   **8.** traer _____

20 Influencing Others

Commands (Part 1): Formal Commands

Grammar Tutorial 20
connect
|SPANISH
www.connectspanish.com

Gramática en acción: Receta para guacamole

El guacamole

1 aguacate
1 diente de ajo,[a] prensado[b]
1 tomate
jugo de un limón[c]
sal
un poco de cilantro fresco[d]

Cómo se prepara

Corte el aguacate y el tomate en trozos[e] pequeños. Añada el jugo del limón, el ajo, el cilantro y la sal a su gusto. Mezcle bien todos los ingredientes y sírvalo con tortillas de maíz[f] fritas.

[a]diente... *clove of garlic* [b]*crushed* [c]*lime* [d]*fresh* [e]*pieces* [f]*corn*

En español, los mandatos se usan con frecuencia en las recetas. Los siguientes verbos se usan en forma de mandato en esta receta. ¿Puede encontrarlos?

añadir	to add
cortar	to cut
mezclar	to mix
servir (sirvo) (i)	

¿Y Ud.?

¿Le gusta el guacamole? ¿Lo hace con frecuencia? ¿Con qué lo sirve?

Formal Command Forms / Los mandatos formales (Ud., Uds.)

In *Puntos de partida* you have seen formal commands in the direction lines of activities since the beginning of the text: **haga, complete, conteste,** and so on.

Commands (imperatives) are verb forms used to tell someone to do something. In Spanish, *formal commands* (**los mandatos formales**) are used with people whom you address as **Ud.** or **Uds.*** Here are some of the basic forms.

> *a command* or *imperative* / **un mandato** = a verb form used to tell someone to do something

	hablar	**comer**	**escribir**	volver	poner
Ud.	hable	coma	escriba	vuelva	ponga
Uds.	hablen	coman	escriban	vuelvan	pongan
English	*speak*	*eat*	*write*	*come back*	*put, place*

1. Regular Verbs

Most formal command forms can be derived from the **yo** form of the present tense.

Note that the "opposite" vowel is used:

-ar   → e
-er/-ir → a

-ar: -o → -e, -en	-er/-ir: -o → -a, -an
hablo → hable	como → coma
hablen	coman
	escribo → escriba
	escriban

2. Stem-changing Verbs

Formal commands for stem-changing verbs show the stem change, since the stem vowel is stressed. Base the command on the **yo** form to get the stem change right.

pensar (**pienso**) → **piense** Ud., **piensen** Uds.
volver (**vuelvo**) → **vuelva** Ud., **vuelvan** Uds.
pedir (**pido**) → **pida** Ud., **pidan** Uds.

---

*You will learn how to form informal (**tú**) commands in **Gramática 36** (Cap. 13).

3. Verbs Ending in -car, -gar, -zar

These verbs have a spelling change to preserve the -c-, -g-, and -z- sounds of the infinitives.

c → qu	buscar: busque Ud., busquen Uds.
g → gu	pagar: pague Ud., paguen Uds.
z → c	empezar: empiece Ud., empiecen Uds.

¡OJO!

From this chapter on, these three spelling changes for verbs in formal commands will be indicated in parentheses in vocabulary lists. If these three verbs were active in this chapter, they would be listed in the end-of-chapter vocabulary list as follows: buscar (qu), pagar (gu), empezar (empiezo) (c).

4. Verbs with Irregular Present Tense yo Forms

Verbs that have an irregular **yo** form in the present tense will keep the irregularity in the **Ud./Uds.** commands.

conocer: **conozco**	→ **conozca** Ud., **conozcan** Uds.
decir* (to say, tell): **digo**	→ **diga** Ud., **digan** Uds.
hacer: **hago**	→ **haga** Ud., **hagan** Uds.
oír: **oigo**	→ **oiga** Ud., **oigan** Uds.
salir: **salgo**	→ **salga** Ud., **salgan** Uds.
tener: **tengo**	→ **tenga** Ud., **tengan** Uds.
traer: **traigo**	→ **traiga** Ud., **traigan** Uds.
venir: **vengo**	→ **venga** Ud., **vengan** Uds.
ver: **veo**	→ **vea** Ud., **vean** Uds.

5. Irregular Formal Commands

A few verbs have irregular **Ud./Uds.** command forms.

dar* (to give)	→ dé Ud., but den Uds.
estar	→ esté Ud., estén Uds.
ir	→ vaya Ud., vayan Uds.
saber	→ sepa Ud., sepan Uds.
ser	→ sea Ud., sean Uds.

Position of Pronouns / El lugar de los pronombres

1. Pronouns with Affirmative Commands

Direct object pronouns and reflexive pronouns must *follow* affirmative commands and are attached to them. In order to maintain the original stress of the verb form, an accent mark is added to the stressed vowel if the original command has two or more syllables.

una palabra:	mandato + pronombre
Pídalo Ud.	*Order it.*
Siéntese, por favor.	*Sit down, please.*

2. Pronouns with Negative Commands

Direct object and reflexive pronouns must *precede* the verb form in negative commands.

tres palabras:	**no** + pronombre + mandato
No lo pida Ud.	*Don't order it.*
No se siente.	*Don't sit down.*

¡OJO!

Now that you know how to form formal commands, be sure to use them carefully when speaking to native speakers of Spanish. Commands are strong forms in any language. It is wise to soften formal commands with **por favor** and by using a polite tone, just as you would in English. Example: **Abra la puerta, por favor.**

---

*Decir and dar are used primarily with indirect objects. Both of these verbs and indirect object pronouns will be formally introduced in **Gramática 21 (Cap. 8)**.

Práctica y comunicación

A. Mandatos de esta clase

Paso 1. Autoprueba. Complete los siguientes mandatos formales de **Ud.** con las terminaciones apropiadas. **¡OJO!** Es necesario escribir más de una letra en algunos casos.

1. habl_____
2. escrib_____
3. lleg_____
4. aprend_____
5. cierr_____
6. duerm_____
7. le_____
8. ha_____
9. empie_____
10. bus_____

Summary of Formal Commands

$-ar \longrightarrow$ -e(n)
$-er/-ir \longrightarrow$ -a(n)

Affirmative: command + pronoun (1 word)

Negative: no + pronoun + command (3 words)

Paso 2. Cambie las siguientes frases en mandatos lógicos y típicos de una clase de español. **¡OJO!** Pueden ser afirmativos o negativos.

MODELO: abrir los libros en la página x →
    Abr**an** los libros en la página x.

1. cerrar los libros
2. traer la tarea mañana
3. sentarse en círculo
4. dormirse
5. leer el texto
6. hacer preguntas
7. hablar en inglés
8. repetir (*like* pedir) más alto (*louder*)

Paso 3. En parejas, indiquen cuáles de los mandatos del **Paso 2** se oyen en su clase de español. Luego añadan (*add*) otros tres mandatos típicos de su clase.

B. El mundo al revés (*The world upside down*)

Paso 1. Hoy, los estudiantes son los «jefes» (*bosses*)... pero ¡solo por un día! Cambie las siguientes acciones en mandatos «lógicos» para todos sus profesores, no solo para su profesor(a) de español. Haga mandatos afirmativos y negativos.

1. llegar a tiempo
2. venir a la universidad
3. pedir la tarea
4. volver a casa
5. poner música de _____
6. pensar en _____
7. traer _____ (¿comida?) a clase
8. sentarse en _____
9. hacer _____
10. dar _____ a los estudiantes

Vocabulario útil

el examen	
la nota	grade (*academic*)
la prueba	quiz

Paso 2. ¿Qué otros mandatos pueden dar a sus profesores hoy? En parejas, inventen tres mandatos para ellos.

C. ¡Pobre Sr. Casiano!

Paso 1. El Sr. Casiano no se siente (*feel*) bien. Lea la descripción que él da de las cosas que hace.

Trabajo[1] muchísimo[a] —¡me gusta trabajar! En la oficina, soy[2] impaciente y critico[3b] bastante[c] a los otros. En mi vida personal, a veces soy[4] un poco impulsivo. Fumo[5d] bastante y también bebo[6] cerveza y otras bebidas alcohólicas, a veces sin moderación... Almuerzo[7] y ceno[8] fuerte,[e] y desayuno[9] poco. Por la noche, con frecuencia salgo[10] con los amigos —me gusta ir a las discotecas— y vuelvo[11] tarde a casa.

[a]*a great deal* [b]critico → criticar [c]*a good deal* [d]Fumo → fumar (*to smoke*) [e]*a lot*

Prác. A, Paso 1: Answers: 1. hable 2. escriba 3. llegue 4. aprenda 5. cierre 6. duerma 7. lea 8. haga 9. empiece 10. busque

(*Continúa.*)

Paso 2. Comprensión. ¿Cierto o falso?

	CIERTO	FALSO
1. El Sr. Casiano es una persona muy simpática.	☐	☐
2. Tiene algunos hábitos malos.	☐	☐
3. Por la noche, siempre está en casa.	☐	☐

Paso 3. ¿Qué *no* debe hacer el Sr. Casiano? Aconséjelo (*Advise him*) y dígale (*tell him*) lo que no debe hacer. Use los verbos en rosado o cualquier (*any*) otro.

MODELOS: **1.** Trabajo ⟶ Sr. Casiano, **no trabaje** tanto.
 2. soy ⟶ **No sea** tan impaciente.

D. Estrategias para adelgazar (*lose weight*). ¿Qué debe o no debe comer y beber una persona que quiere adelgazar? En parejas, imaginen una conversación entre esa persona y su médico.

MODELOS: ensalada ⟶ **E1:** ¿Ensalada?   postres ⟶ **E1:** ¿Postres?
 E2: Cóma**la**.   **E2:** No **los** coma.

1. bebidas alcohólicas
2. verduras
3. pan
4. dulces

5. leche entera (*whole*)
6. hamburguesas con queso
7. frutas frescas
8. refrescos dietéticos

E. ¡Qué desastre! Imagine los mandatos que esta madre va a darles a sus hijos adolescentes. ¿Le resultan (*Do they sound*) familiares a Ud. estos mandatos?

MODELO: no acostarse muy tarde ⟶
 ¡No se acuesten muy tarde!

1. levantarse más temprano
2. bañarse todos los días
3. quitarse esa ropa sucia
4. ponerse ropa limpia
5. no divertirse todas las noches con los amigos
6. ir más a la biblioteca y estudiar más
7. ¿ ?

F. Consejos sobre los buenos modales (*good manners*) en la mesa

Paso 1. Use las siguientes ideas para dar consejos en forma de mandatos formales sobre cómo se debe comer en una ocasión formal. **¡OJO!** Algunos consejos son normas de los buenos modales en los países hispanos y *no* coinciden con los modales que se practican en este país. ¿Puede decir cuáles son los modales hispanos?

1. poner las dos manos en la mesa
2. no poner los codos (*elbows*) en la mesa
3. para cortar, agarrar (*to hold*) el tenedor con la mano izquierda y el cuchillo con la derecha
4. cortar solo el pedazo (*piece*) de comida que puede poner en la boca
5. no cambiar (*to change*) de mano el tenedor para llevar la comida a la boca
6. no eructar (*to burp*) en público

Paso 2. Ahora, en grupos, inventen por lo menos (*at least*) cuatro consejos más.

Un poco de todo

A. Lengua y cultura: La cocina panameña

Paso 1. Complete the following paragraphs with the correct form of the words in parentheses, as suggested by context. When two possibilities are given in parentheses, select the correct word. ¡OJO! As you conjugate the verbs in this activity, note that you will make formal commands with some infinitives.

El arroz con pollo, un típico plato panameño

¿Creen Uds. que la comida panameña es similar a la[a] de México y que los tacos y las tortillas (ser / estar[1]) parte de la comida típica de los panameños? Si creen eso, entonces[b] no (*Uds.:* saber / conocer[2]) (algo / nada[3]) de la comida de (este[4]) nación. (*Uds.:* Seguir[5]) (leer[6]), porque van a aprender mucho.

La influencia (extranjero[7]) en la comida de la cosmopolita Ciudad de Panamá es muy visible. Hay (mucho[8]) restaurantes que (servir[9]) comida italiana, china, (francés[10]), etcétera.

Sin embargo, los panameños no (perder[11]) su identidad nacional, y frecuentemente (preferir[12]) la comida tradicional. En la cocina panameña hay muchos platos de mariscos y pescados, entre ellos **el ceviche.** Las personas vegetarianas no (tener[13]) problema (también / tampoco[14]) porque hay una variedad de platos (preparado[15]) con arroz y verduras. El arroz es un ingrediente importante en la comida de Panamá. Si Ud. desea (saber / conocer[16]) cuál es el plato nacional de Panamá, los panameños (contestar[17]): «el arroz con pollo.» (*Ud.:* Pedirlo[18]). Le va a gustar.

[a]*a... to that* [b]*then*

Paso 2. Comprensión. Conteste las siguientes preguntas.

1. ¿Cómo se sabe que la Ciudad de Panamá es cosmopolita?
2. ¿Cuál es el plato que representa mejor la cocina panameña?
3. ¿Qué ingredientes son comunes en la comida de Panamá?

Paso 3. En parejas, imaginen que un extranjero busca donde comer. Quiere saber dónde preparan de manera excelente las siguientes comidas, que son típicas de algunas partes de los Estados Unidos. Denle recomendaciones en forma de consejos o mandatos. Luego comparen sus recomendaciones con las (*those*) del resto de la clase para ver si todos están de acuerdo.

1. la mejor barbacoa
2. los mejores mariscos
3. la mejor comida china

4. la mejor comida hispana
5. el mejor queso
6. la mejor langosta

B. Publicidad. Como se ve en este anuncio de un periódico argentino, en español (como en inglés) los mandatos se usan con frecuencia en los anuncios y en la publicidad en general. En parejas, creen (*create*) un anuncio publicitario para un lugar de su universidad o de su ciudad, como un restaurante, un estadio, un cine, etcétera. El humor es siempre apreciado por sus compañeros.

[a]*grows* [b]*acercarse = to approach, draw near*

En **su** comunidad

Entreviste a una persona hispana de su universidad o ciudad sobre la cocina y la comida de su país.

PREGUNTAS POSIBLES

- ¿Cuáles son los ingredientes más importantes?
- ¿Puede encontrar estos ingredientes en los supermercados de aquí?
- ¿Cuál es la comida principal del día? ¿Comen un desayuno fuerte (*heavy*)?
- ¿Cuáles son algunos de los platos típicos?
- ¿Hay muchos restaurantes especializados en la comida de su país en este estado? ¿Cuál es su favorito?

Antes de mirar

Conteste las siguientes preguntas.

1. ¿Hay restaurantes de comida hispana donde Ud. vive? ¿En qué tipo de cocina se especializan?
2. ¿Se puede comprar comida en la calle (*street*) donde Ud. vive? ¿Hay muchos *food trucks*?

Este segmento

Los presentadores introducen un reportaje sobre la comida que se puede comprar en la calle (*street*). Luego cierran el programa haciendo planes para almorzar.

«Sin duda (*Undoubtedly*), los tacos son la comida callejera (*street*) por excelencia. Los hay de muchos tipos: al pastor, de carne, de pescado, etcétera. En efecto, cualquier alimento sabroso envuelto (*any tasty food wrapped*) en tortillas de esta manera puede llamarse taco.»

Fragmento del guion

¡Esa paella! Este reportaje de Laura me ha abierto el apetito.[a] El castellano[b] y la comida son la herencia[c] más positiva que nos dejó[d] la colonización española. Y lo mejor es que la comida española se adaptó fácilmente[e] a los ingredientes locales de cada país. Y se mezcló[f] con las tradiciones indígenas y también con las africanas que llegaron con los esclavos.[g] Y para qué hablar[h] del efecto de los productos americanos en la cocina de España y de toda Europa.

[a]*me... has whet my appetite* [b]*Spanish language* [c]*heritage, inheritance* [d]*nos... gave (lit. left) to us* [e]*se... easily adapted itself* [f]*se... it mixed* [g]*llegaron... arrived with the slaves* [h]*para... what can we say*

Vocabulario del segmento

neoyorquino/a	de Nueva York
el chorizo	type of sausage
la empanada	turnover
relleno/a	stuffed
el horneado de puerco	pork roast
me dijo	told me
el vendedor ambulante	street vendor
ya se imaginarán	you can imagine
cuidado con	(be) careful with
me muero de hambre	I'm starving
te apetece	do you feel like
la pupusa	filled corn tortilla
nos despedimos	that's all
¡No se lo pierdan!	Don't miss it!
¿Nos acompañan?	Won't you come with us?

Después de mirar

A. ¿Está claro? Empareje las siguientes comidas con su lugar de origen.

COMIDAS	LUGARES DE ORIGEN
1. _____ el horneado de puerco	a. la Argentina
2. _____ el choripán	b. América
3. _____ el chocolate y el tomate	c. el Ecuador
4. _____ el taco	d. El Salvador
5. _____ la pupusa	e. México

B. Un poco más. Conteste las siguientes preguntas.

1. ¿Qué es el choripán? ¿Cuál es el origen de su nombre?
2. ¿Cuál es la comida callejera por excelencia en México?
3. ¿Cómo se siente (*feels*) Víctor al final del programa? ¿Por qué?

C. Y ahora, Uds. En parejas, preparen un cierre del programa similar al (*to that*) de este segmento, usando algunas de las expresiones que usan los presentadores e información sobre la comida hispana de su ciudad.

Antes de leer

¿Cuáles son algunos de los platos típicos de su país? ¿Hay alguna comida típica de su ciudad o estado?

Lectura cultural: Panamá
La comida panameña

El arroz con pollo al estilo panameño es uno de los platos más típicos de Panamá. Otro plato típico es el sancocho, una sopa que también es parte de la cocina de otros países caribeños y que lleva algún tipo de carne, verduras y legumbres.[a] Y es necesario mencionar también las frituras, es decir,[b] la comida frita. Hay gran variedad de frituras: la yuca frita, las carimañolas (unas bolas de masa[c] de yuca con carne dentro[d]), los patacones (rebanadas[e] de plátano frito), las empanadas[f] al estilo panameño, etcétera.

De beber, se debe probar[g] las chichas, que son refrescos naturales de frutas panameñas, como el coco, la guanábana y el maracuyá.[h]

[a]*beans* [b]*es... that is* [c]*bolas... balls of dough* [d]*inside* [e]*slices* [f]*see* **En otros países** [g]*try* [h]*coco... coconut, soursop, and passion fruit*

En otros países hispanos

- **En todo el mundo hispanohablante** Las empanadas son probablemente la constante culinaria más notable de todos los países hispanohablantes. Consisten en una masa de pan[a] rellena[b] de algo dulce o salado.[c] Pueden ser pequeñas e individuales o grandes para ser compartidas.[d] Las empanadas son de procedencia española... y los españoles las heredaron[e] de los árabes. ¡Una larga y deliciosa tradición!

- **En los Estados Unidos** La comida latina es omnipresente en los Estados Unidos hoy día. La cocina mexicana es muy popular, como también lo es su variante Tex-Mex, genuinamente estadounidense. Pero también se puede encontrar la comida de casi todas las otras cocinas hispanas: las pupusas[f] salvadoreñas, la tortilla[g] española (con papas y cebollas), el arroz con gandules[h] puertorriqueño, el dulce de leche[i] (una comida panhispana), etcétera.

[a]*masa... bread dough* [b]*filled* [c]*salty* [d]*shared* [e]*inherited* [f]*corn masa stuffed with cheese, refried beans, or meat, then fried like a tortilla* [g]*omelet* [h]*pigeon peas* [i]*dulce... caramel*

El Canal de Panamá: 48 millas de canales y esclusas (*locks*)

Un símbolo panameño: El canal de Panamá

Es una de las obras[a] de ingeniería más importantes del mundo por su impacto en el transporte mundial. Une el mar Caribe con el océano Pacífico. Fue inaugurado[b] en 1914. Antes de su existencia, los barcos tenían que dar la vuelta por el Estrecho de Magallanes.[c] La ruta del canal fue descubierta[d] en 1514 por el explorador español Vasco Núñez de Balboa. Desde entonces[e] los españoles tuvieron[f] la idea de construir un canal. Pero su construcción no se hizo[g] realidad hasta principios del siglo XX.[h] En la actualidad,[i] el canal se está ampliando.[j]

[a]*works* [b]*opened* [c]*tenían... had to go around the Straight of Magellan* [d]*discovered* [e]*Desde... Since then* [f]*had* [g]*no... didn't become* [h]*principios... the beginning of the 20th century* [i]*En... Currently* [j]*se... is being enlarged*

COMPRENSIÓN

1. ¿Qué son las frituras panameñas?
2. ¿Qué es la chicha?
3. ¿Qué comida es muy típica de todo el mundo hispano?
4. ¿Qué cocina genuinamente estadounidense es de origen hispano?
5. ¿Cuándo empezó (*began*) a funcionar el Canal de Panamá? ¿Cuándo empezaron los españoles a pensar en hacer un canal?

Y ahora, Uds.

- ¿Cuáles son los platos más tradicionales de la cocina de los Estados Unidos? Escojan entre los/las dos el plato más representativo de este país y luego comparen su respuesta con las (*those*) de otros grupos o parejas.

- ¿Hay alguna obra de ingeniería muy importante en su país? ¿Por qué es importante?

Del mundo hispano

Antes de leer

Piense en la lasaña, un plato italiano tradicional. ¿Qué ingredientes contiene una lasaña típica? ¿pollo, aceite de oliva, papas, pimienta, pasta, tomates, sal, champiñones, tortillas, frijoles, agua, salchicha, lechuga, queso?

Lectura: Una receta

Lasaña de tortillas Para 6 porciones

INGREDIENTES

18 tortillas de maíz[a] en cuadrados[b]
480 gramos de queso ricotta
60 gramos de espinacas[c]
60 gramos de cebolla picada[d]
60 gramos de tomates en cuadrados
2 cucharadas[e] de mantequilla
Sal y pimienta

Salsa de tomate

4 tomates
1/2 cebolla
1 diente de ajo[f]
2 cucharadas de mantequilla
100 gramos de puré de tomate
100 mililitros de agua
Sal, pimienta y orégano al gusto[g]

Variación

PREPARACIÓN

Salsa de tomate

1. Corte los tomates y la cebolla en cuadrados y póngalos a hervir en una cacerola[h] con el agua, el puré de tomate, el ajo y el orégano. Licúelo[i] todo.
2. Vuelva a calentarlo[j] con la mantequilla y sazone con sal y pimienta.

Lasaña

1. Lave las espinacas y póngalas a hervir en un poco de agua; después, séquelas y saltéelas en una sartén[k] con la mantequilla, sal y pimienta.
2. En una fuente,[l] ponga la mitad de la salsa de tomate en el fondo[m] y encima[n] coloque las tortillas, el queso, las espinacas, el tomate y la cebolla en capas[ñ] hasta formar dos capas de todo. Después, cúbralo[o] con el resto de la salsa de tomate.
3. Meta la lasaña al horno[p] 30 o 40 minutos a 180° centígrados.

[a]*corn* [b]*squares* [c]*spinach* [d]*minced* [e]*tablespoons* [f]*diente... clove of garlic* [g]*al... to taste* [h]*póngalos... boil them in a pot* [i]*Blend it* [j]*Vuelva... Reheat it* [k]*séquelas... dry them (the spinach leaves) and sauté them in a frying pan* [l]*serving dish* [m]*bottom* [n]*on top* [ñ]*layers* [o]*cover it* [p]*oven*

Comprensión

A. Los mandatos de la receta. Todos los verbos para preparar esta receta son mandatos formales. Empareje los siguientes mandatos con su traducción en inglés, según el contexto de la receta.

MANDATOS

1. _____ corte
2. _____ sazone
3. _____ lave
4. _____ coloque
5. _____ meta

TRADUCCIONES

a. *put (into)*
b. *wash*
c. *place, arrange*
d. *cut*
e. *season*

B. Paso por *(by)* paso. Ponga en orden cronológico (de 1 a 4) los siguientes pasos para la lasaña, según la receta.

_____ Cocinar la lasaña en el horno.
_____ Hervir las espinacas y luego cocinarlas en una sartén.
_____ Preparar la salsa de tomate.
_____ Poner en una fuente, en capas, todos los ingredientes preparados para formar la lasaña.

Antes de escuchar

¿Sale con frecuencia a comer en restaurantes? ¿Tiene algún restaurante favorito? ¿En qué se especializa?

Vocabulario para escuchar

la carta	menu	**mixto/a**	mixed (with **paella** = having
los entrantes	starters, first courses		both meat and seafood)
el segundo plato	main course	**cómo no**	of course

Después de escuchar

A. ¿Qué desean? Los señores Robles cenan esta noche en un restaurante elegante. ¿Qué piden?

1. El Sr. Robles:

Entrante _____   Segundo plato _____

2. La Sra. Robles:

Entrante _____

Segundo plato _____

3. De beber:

_____

B. Más detalles. Conteste las siguientes preguntas.

1. ¿Qué platos tienen fama en este restaurante?
2. ¿Cuándo van a pedir el postre los Sres. Robles?

PRODUCCIÓN PERSONAL

¡Ahora, yo!

A. Use de modelo las preguntas y respuestas de la página 201 de este capítulo para hablar de la comida de su país y de sus preferencias culinarias.

B. Filme un programa culinario en el que (*which*) presente al menos dos platos o ingredientes tradicionales de una cocina nacional o regional.

A ESCRIBIR
La comida de las cafeterías de esta universidad

Preparar

Paso 1. ¿Qué piensan Uds. de la comida que sirven en las cafeterías de su universidad?

En parejas, compartan (*share*) sus ideas sobre este tema. Usen las siguientes preguntas de guía (*as a guide*). La conversación los/las ayudará (*will help you*) a clarificar sus propias (*own*) ideas y determinar un enfoque para su ensayo.

- ¿Ofrecen las cafeterías una buena variedad de comidas? Ejemplos: platos vegetarianos, comida baja en calorías
- ¿Cuáles son los platos que más piden los estudiantes?
- En general, ¿es rica la comida? ¿Es cara o barata?
- ¿Hay alguna cafetería mejor que otra?

Paso 2. Ahora use sus opiniones y las (*those*) de su compañero/a (no olvide citarlo/la [*quote him or her*] para escribir su ensayo). Escoja (*Choose*) un enfoque desde el principio (*from the beginning*) para organizar bien su texto. Hay más ayuda en Connect.

Más ideas para su portafolio

- Incluya una lista de sus comidas y bebidas favoritas. Incluya los lugares (restaurantes, la casa de alguien) donde las come o las bebe porque son mejores.
- Incluya una receta familiar favorita.
- Entreviste a un(a) hispanohablante sobre los platos más tradicionales de su cultura y pídale (*ask him/her for*) una receta fácil.
- Si ha estado jugando (*have been playing*) Practice Spanish: Study Abroad, en Quest 4 Ud. participó (*participated*) en una telenovela (*soap opera*) sobre una compañía que se especializa en (*specializes in*) la moda. En grupo, escriban una escena (*scene*) de una telenovela que tenga lugar (*that takes place*) en un restaurante. Usen vocabulario de este capítulo ¡y sean creativos (*be creative*)! Después, ustedes pueden interpretar (*act out*) su escena para la clase.

Sugerencia: You are now ready to play Quest 4 in **Practice Spanish: Study Abroad** (www.mhpractice.com).

EN RESUMEN En este capítulo

 ■LEARNSMART

Visit **www.connectspanish.com** to practice the vocabulary and grammar points covered in this chapter.

AFTER STUDYING THIS CHAPTER I CAN...

- ☐ talk about food and the meals of the day (202–203)
- ☐ use the verbs **saber** and **conocer** to express *to know* (205)
- ☐ use direct object pronouns to avoid repetition in conversation (209–211)
- ☐ use negative and indefinite words (215–216)
- ☐ give and understand formal commands (219–220)
- ☐ recognize/describe at least 2–3 aspects of Panamanian cultures

Gramática en breve

18. Direct Object Pronouns

  me, te, lo/la, nos, os, los/las

19. Indefinite and Negative Words

algo	nada
alguien	nadie
algún (alguna/os/as)	ningún (ninguna)
siempre	nunca, jamás
también	tampoco

  no + verb + negative word
  negative word + verb

20. Formal Commands

  -ar $\longrightarrow$ -e(n)
  -er/-ir $\longrightarrow$ -a(n)

  Affirmative: *command + pronoun* (1 word)
  Negative: *no + pronoun + command* (3 words)

Vocabulario

Los verbos

acabar de + *inf.*	to have just (*done something*)
ayudar	to help
ayudar a + *inf.*	to help to (*do something*)
conocer (conozco)	to know, to be acquainted, familiar with; to meet
contestar	to answer
esperar	to wait (for); to expect
invitar	to invite
llamar	to call
saber (sé)	to know
saber + *inf.*	to know how to (*do something*)

La comida

cenar	to have/eat dinner, supper
cocinar	to cook
desayunar	to have/eat breakfast
merendar (meriendo)	to have a snack
preparar	to prepare

Repaso: almorzar (almuerzo) (c)

> Remember that this letter indicates the spelling change that happens in the formal commands of verbs that end in **-car**, **-gar**, or **-zar**.

el aceite (de oliva)	(olive) oil
el aguacate	avocado
el arroz	rice
las arvejas	green peas
el atún	tuna
el azúcar	sugar
el bistec	steak
los camarones	shrimp
la carne	meat
la cebolla	onion
los champiñones	mushrooms
la chuleta (de cerdo)	(pork) chop
la comida	food
los dulces	sweets; candy
los espárragos	asparagus
el flan	(baked) custard
los frijoles	beans
la galleta	cookie
los garbanzos	chickpeas
el helado	ice cream
el huevo	egg
el jamón	ham
la langosta	lobster
la lechuga	lettuce
la mantequilla	butter
la manzana	apple
los mariscos	shellfish
la naranja	orange
el pan	bread
el pan tostado	toast
la papa (frita)	(French fried) potato
el pastel	cake; pie
el pavo	turkey
el pepino	cucumber
el pescado	fish
la pimienta	pepper
el pollo (asado)	(roast) chicken
el postre	dessert
el queso	cheese
la sal	salt
la salsa	salsa; sauce
la salchicha	sausage; hot dog
la sopa	soup
las verduras	vegetables
la zanahoria	carrot

Cognados: la banana, la barbacoa, el cereal, la ensalada, la fruta, la hamburguesa, el salmón, el sándwich, el tomate, el yogur

Las bebidas

el agua (but *f.*) (mineral)	(mineral) water
la cerveza	beer
el jugo (de fruta)	(fruit) juice
la leche	milk
el refresco	soft drink
el vino (blanco, tinto)	(white, red) wine

Cognado: el té

Repaso: la bebida, el café

Las comidas

el almuerzo	lunch
la cena	dinner, supper
la comida	meal
el desayuno	breakfast
la merienda	snack

En un restaurante

el/la camarero/a	waiter/waitress
la cuenta	check, bill
el plato	dish; course
el plato principal	main course

Cognado: el menú

Otros sustantivos

la ayuda	help
la canción	song
la cocina	cuisine
los comestibles	groceries, foodstuff
el consejo	(piece of) advice

la dirección	address
el/la dueño/a	owner
la letra	(*song*) lyrics
el mandato	command
el nombre	name
la receta	recipe
la tarjeta de crédito	credit card

Los adjetivos

asado/a	roast(ed)
caliente	hot (*in temperature, not taste*)
fresco/a	fresh
frito/a	fried
ligero/a	light, not heavy
picante	hot, spicy
rico/a	tasty, savory; rich (*in calories*)
tostado/a	toasted

Las palabras indefinidas y negativas

algo	something, anything
alguien	someone, anyone
algún (alguna/os/as)	some, any
jamás	never
nada	nothing, not anything
nadie	no one, nobody, not anybody
ningún (ninguna)	no, not any
tampoco	neither, not either

Repaso: nunca, siempre, también

Palabras adicionales

estar a dieta	to be on a diet
tener (mucha) hambre	to be (very) hungry
tener (mucha) sed	to be (very) thirsty

Vocabulario personal

8

De viaje°

De... *On a trip, Traveling*

www.connectspanish.com

En este capítulo

En la zona colonial de Santo Domingo, República Dominicana

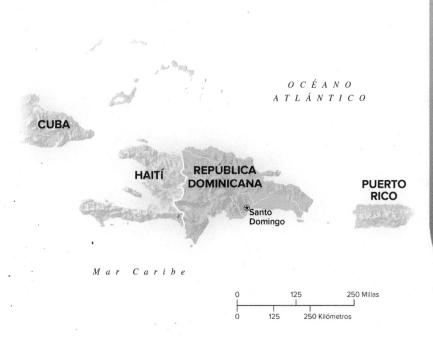

LA REPÚBLICA DOMINICANA

10.4 (punto cuatro) millones de habitantes

- La República Dominicana comparte[a] la isla de La Española (*Hispaniola,* en inglés) con el país de Haití.

- La ciudad de Santo Domingo, capital del país, fue fundada[b] por el hermano de Cristóbal Colón en 1496. Es la más antigua de todas las ciudades fundadas por los europeos en América.

[a]*shares* [b]*founded*

- ¿Dónde le gusta pasar las vacaciones? ¿En la playa? ¿en las montañas? ¿visitando una ciudad o un país que Ud. no conoce? (¿una nueva ciudad o un nuevo país?)

- ¿Qué le gusta hacer cuando está en la playa? ¿nadar[a]? ¿tomar el sol[b]? ¿hacer *surfing* u otros deportes[c]?

- ¿Qué es lo peor[d] de hacer un viaje? ¿hacer la maleta,[e] el viaje mismo[f] o volver a casa?

[a]*swim* [b]*tomar... sunbathe* [c]*sports* [d]*lo... the worst part* [e]*hacer... packing* [f]*el... the trip itself*

CECILIA FIGUEROA MARTÍN CONTESTA LAS PREGUNTAS.

- Prefiero ir de viaje a otros países y también visitar a mis parientes en los Estados Unidos. Como[a] soy de Puerto Rico y tengo el mar[b] y el calor todo el tiempo, me gusta ir de vacaciones a lugares con un clima diferente. ¡Me encanta[c] ver la nieve!

- Cuando voy a la playa, me gusta nadar y estar en la arena[d] leyendo.

- Para mí, lo peor de un viaje es tener que trasladarse.[e] Odio[f] especialmente los viajes en avión.[g] Pero si el viaje es muy divertido,[h] ¡odio volver!

[a]*Since* [b]*ocean* [c]*¡Me... I love* [d]*sand* [e]*change locations* [f]*I hate* [g]*en... by plane* [h]*muy... a lot of fun*

De viaje°   **De...** *On a trip, Traveling*

el maletero

la piloto

el piloto

en el aeropuerto

el asistente de vuelo

la asistente de vuelo

Vuelo 33
Salida 10:35

el equipaje

la maleta

Jorge

Anita

el pasajero

Alejandro

Javier

Josefina

Juana

la agente (el agente)

la pasajera

facturar el equipaje

el mostrador

You can hear the pronunciation of theme vocabulary words and phrases in the Connect eBook.

Los medios de transporte

la cabina	cabin (*on a ship*)
el crucero	cruise (ship)
la estación	station
de autobuses	bus station
de trenes	train station
el puerto	port
la sala de espera	waiting room
la sala de fumar / de fumadores	smoking area
el vuelo	flight
ir en...	to go/travel by . . .
autobús	bus
avión	plane
barco	boat, ship
tren	train

El viaje

el asiento	seat
el billete (*Sp.*) / el boleto (*L.A.*)	ticket
de ida	one-way ticket
de ida y vuelta	round-trip ticket
el billete/boleto electrónico	e-ticket
la demora	delay
la llegada	arrival
el pasaje	fare, price (*of a transportation ticket*)
el pasaporte	passport
la puerta de embarque	boarding gate
la salida	departure
la tarjeta de embarque	boarding pass

anunciar	to announce	**ir al extranjero**	to go abroad
bajarse (de)	to get down (from); to get off (of) (*a vehicle*)	**pasar por la aduana**	to go/pass through customs
estar atrasado/a	to be late	**el control de seguridad**	security (check)
facturar el equipaje	to check baggage		
guardar (un puesto)	to save (a place [*in line*])	**quejarse (de)**	to complain (about) ·
		salir/llegar (gu) a tiempo	to depart/arrive on time
hacer cola	to stand in line	**subir (a)**	to go up; to get on (*a vehicle*)
hacer escala/parada	to make a stop		
hacer la(s) maleta(s)	to pack one's suitcase(s)	**viajar**	to travel
hacer un viaje	to take a trip ·	**volar (vuelo) en avión**	to fly; to go by plane

Comunicación

A. Hablando de medios de transporte. ¿Con qué medio de transporte relaciona Ud. las siguientes personas y cosas? Hay más de una respuesta posible en algunos casos.

1. un crucero *cruise*
2. un(a) asistente de vuelo *flight attendant*
3. un puerto *a port*
4. una estación *station*
5. una cabina *cabin*
6. una agencia de viajes *travel agency*
7. un asiento *seat*
8. un(a) piloto *pilot*
9. un capitán / una capitana *captain*
10. la llegada *arrival*

Así se dice

El autobús is expressed in a variety of ways in different parts of the Spanish-speaking world. Here are a few of the most common ones.

el camión (*Mex.*)
el bus (*C.A.*)
la guagua (*Cuba, P.R.*)
el colectivo (*Arg.*)

Here are some other common travel-related variations.

la maleta = la valija (*Arg.*), la petaca (*Mex.*)

El boleto is generally understood to express ticket* throughout the Spanish-speaking world. The word **el tiquete** is heard in Mexico and Central America, as well as in this country, and **el billete** is used in Spain.

B. Un viaje al extranjero

Paso 1. Use los números del 1 al 9 para organizar un viaje de manera lógica.

a. _____ subir al avión cuando se anuncia el vuelo *get on the plane when the flight is announced*
b. _____ pasar por el control de seguridad *to go through the security check*
c. _____ hacer cola para obtener la tarjeta de embarque y facturar el equipaje *to get the boarding pass & check the baggage*
d. _____ pedir un taxi y llegar al aeropuerto *ask for a taxi to get to the airport*
e. _____ oír el anuncio de la salida del vuelo *hear the announcement of the flight exit*
f. _____ hacer la maleta y poner el pasaporte en el bolso *pack up the suitcase, put the sport in the bag*
g. _____ esperar en la puerta de embarque mandando mensajes *wait at the boarding gate by sending messages*
h. _____ sentarse en el asiento junto a la ventanilla (*window*) *sit in the seat by the window*
i. _____ llegar al aeropuerto de destino (*destination*) y pasar por el control de inmigración y la aduana *get to the destination airport & go through the immigration control & customs*

Paso 2. Ahora narre la secuencia en primera persona (**yo**).

C. Definiciones

Paso 1. Dé las palabras definidas.

1. Es necesario pasar por este control al llegar a otro país.
2. Es la cosa que se compra antes de hacer un viaje.
3. Es el antónimo de **subir a.**
4. Se va allí cuando se hace un viaje en avión.
5. Se va allí cuando se hace un viaje en tren.
6. Es la persona que nos ayuda durante un vuelo.

Paso 2. Ahora prepare dos definiciones para leer a toda la clase. Sus compañeros van a dar (*give*) la palabra que Ud. define.

Frases útiles del Paso 1: Es necesario para... Es la cosa que... Se va allí... Es la persona que... Es el antónimo de...

Otras frases útiles: Es el sinónimo de... Es el lugar donde... Es cuando... Es lo que...

---

*The words **la entrada** and **la localidad** are used to refer to tickets for movies, plays, or other events.

D. **En el aeropuerto.** En parejas, nombren o describan las cosas y acciones representadas en este dibujo.

VUELO 430

SALA DE ESPERA

ALMACÉN Rodríguez

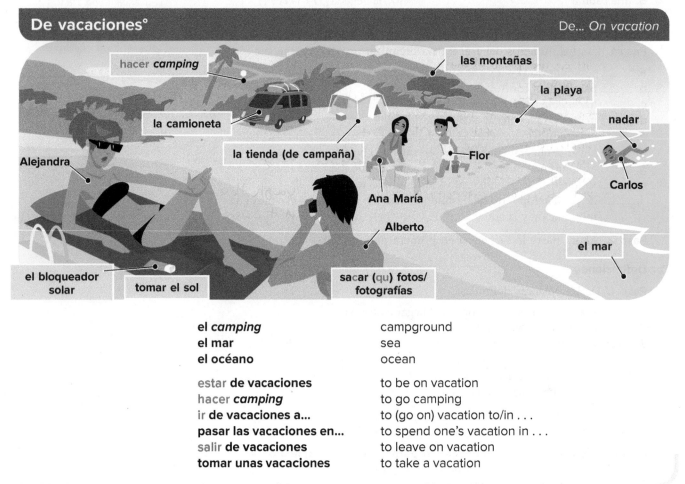

De vacaciones°

De... *On vacation*

hacer *camping*

las montañas

la playa

la camioneta

nadar

la tienda (de campaña)

Flor

Alejandra

Carlos

Ana María

el bloqueador solar

tomar el sol

Alberto

sacar (qu) fotos/ fotografías

el mar

el *camping*	campground
el mar	sea
el océano	ocean
estar de vacaciones	to be on vacation
hacer *camping*	to go camping
ir de vacaciones a...	to (go on) vacation to/in . . .
pasar las vacaciones en...	to spend one's vacation in . . .
salir de vacaciones	to leave on vacation
tomar unas vacaciones	to take a vacation

Comunicación

A. ¿Qué hace Ud.?

Paso 1. Diga si las siguientes declaraciones son ciertas o falsas para Ud. Corrija las declaraciones falsas.

	CIERTO	FALSO
1. Cuando estoy de vacaciones, tomo el sol.	☐	☐
2. Prefiero ir de vacaciones a las montañas.	☐	☐
3. Duermo muy bien en una tienda de campaña.	☐	☐
4. Saco muchas fotos cuando estoy de vacaciones.	☐	☐
5. Es fácil ir a playas bonitas desde (*from*) aquí.	☐	☐
6. Escribo muchas tarjetas postales.	☐	☐

Paso 2. En parejas, túrnense para hacer y contestar preguntas basadas en las oraciones del **Paso 1**.

Nota **cultural**

Tipos de turismo en el mundo hispano

En el mundo hispano hay ciudades y lugares impresionantes que visitar y playas maravillosas donde pasar las vacaciones. Pero hay también una gran variedad de lugares de destino para las personas que desean disfrutar de[a] unas vacaciones excepcionales.

- **El ecoturismo**
  Consiste en visitar lugares poco explotados por los seres[b] humanos. La selva costarricense y la selva amazónica (en el Ecuador y el Perú) son destinos populares, así como[c] la Patagonia (en la Argentina y Chile) y las Islas Galápagos. En el norte de España, muchos caminantes[d] de todas partes del mundo hacen el Camino de Santiago.[e] Su origen fue como un camino de peregrinación,[f] pero ahora muchas personas lo hacen sin motivo religioso. Es una actividad física no extrema que le permite a uno[g] hacer compañeros de viaje interesantes y variados.

- **El agroturismo**
  Este tipo de vacaciones implica pasar las vacaciones en un lugar rural. Los turistas pueden quedarse[h] en casas renovadas que ofrecen la experiencia de hacer trabajo agrícola y excursiones educativas. En la isla chilena de Chiloé, por ejemplo, hay ofertas agroturísticas interesantes.

- **El aventurismo**
  Es para aquellos[i] que buscan aventuras emocionantes y físicas. Se puede esquiar en los Andes o en las montañas españolas, hacer ciclismo de montaña, navegar en rápidos, etcétera.

Un grupo de estudiantes en una excursión ecoturística en la selva (*jungle*) amazónica, Perú

¿Practica Ud. alguno de estos tipos de turismo? ¿Dónde lo hace?

[a]disfrutar... *to enjoy* [b]*beings* [c]así... *as are* [d]*hikers* [e]Camino... *St James's Trail, Way* [f]un... *a (religious) pilgrimage* [g]le... *allows one* [h]*stay, be lodged* [i]*those (people)*

B. Intercambios

Paso 1. Complete el siguiente párrafo sobre sus vacaciones típicas y sus vacaciones más memorables.

En mis vacaciones típicas, voy a _____[1] en _____[2] (medio de transporte) en el mes de _____.[3] Voy con _____[4] (personas) y esto es lo que hago: _____.[5]

En mis vacaciones más memorables, fui[a] a _____[6] en _____[7] en el mes de _____.[8] Fui con _____.[9] Hice[b] las siguientes actividades: _____[10] (infinitivos).

[a]*I went* [b]*I did*

Paso 2. Ahora, en parejas, túrnense para hacer y contestar preguntas basadas en las ideas del **Paso 1.** Obtengan (*Get*) mucha información de su compañero/a.

MODELOS: ¿Adónde vas para tus vacaciones, generalmente? ¿Hay un lugar que siempre visitas para las vacaciones? ¿Vas allí todos los años? ¿Por qué vas allí? Y para tus vacaciones más memorables, ¿a qué lugar fuiste (*did you go*)?

Nota **comunicativa**

Otro uso de la palabra *se:* para expresar acciones impersonales

If there are native Spanish speakers living in your area, you probably have seen signs like the one in the photo: **Se habla español.** The word **se** in front of the verb (rather than a specific subject, like **Juan** or **ellos**) changes the English equivalent of the verb. In English, **se habla español** can mean: *Spanish is spoken here. They speak Spanish here. People speak Spanish here.* You have already seen this use of **se** in direction lines and readings in *Puntos de partida.*

Here are some additional examples of this use of **se** to talk about things that "people," rather than specific individuals, do.

Se va al aeropuerto para tomar un vuelo.	*One goes / People go / You go to the airport to catch a flight.*
Se aprende mucho viajando.	*One learns / People learn / You learn a lot by traveling.*

Be alert to this use of **se** in *Puntos de partida* as well as in real-life Spanish; it is very frequent and you need to understand it. You will practice it in **Comunicación C.** You will also see (and hear) plural verbs, but you will not practice using them in this text.

C. ¿Dónde se hace esto?

Indique el lugar (o los lugares) donde se hacen las siguientes actividades.

MODELO: Se come. $\longrightarrow$ Se come en un restaurante, en casa, en la cafetería...

1. Se factura el equipaje y se anuncia el vuelo.
2. Se hace la maleta.
3. Se compra un boleto.
4. Se espera el avión.
5. Se pide una bebida.
6. Se mira una película.
7. Se nada y se toma el sol.
8. Se habla francés.
9. Se habla portugués.
10. Se viaja en barco.

D. La publicidad. En parejas, lean este anuncio de una aerolínea latinoamericana y contesten las preguntas. ¡Piensen como expertos en *marketing*!

1. ¿Cómo se llama la aerolínea?
2. ¿A qué tipo de persona va dirigido (*directed*) el anuncio?
3. ¿Por qué se usa un plato con comida en el anuncio?
4. ¿Qué se ve en el plato? ¿Qué representa?
5. ¿En qué tipo de publicación creen Uds. que se encuentra (*is found*) este anuncio?

En LAN convertimos Latinoamérica en una gran red para tus negocios.
Vuela directo con el mejor servicio, a todas las capitales de América del Sur.

EEUU / Caribe / México

Caracas
Bogotá
Quito
Guayaquil
Lima
La Paz

España / Alemania / Resto de Europa

Rio de Janeiro
Sao Paulo

Isla de Pascua / Tahiti / Australia / Nueva Zelanda

Santiago
Buenos Aires
Montevideo

¿Recuerda Ud.?

In **Gramática 18 (Cap. 7),** you learned how to use direct object pronouns to avoid repetition. Can you identify the direct object pronouns in the following exchange? To what or to who(m) do these pronouns refer?

ROBERTO: ¿Tienes los boletos?

ANA: No, no los tengo, pero mi agente de viajes ya los tiene listos (*ready*).

ROBERTO: Si quieres, te acompaño a la agencia.

ANA: Encantada. Casi nunca te veo.

«¡De viaje!» Segmento 1

Un arcoíris (*rainbow*) en las Cataratas (*Falls*) del Iguazú: «La caída (*plunging*) de agua desde una altura de ochenta metros es simplemente indescriptible... Hay que estar allí para oír el rugido (*roar*) de las cataratas, sentir (*to feel*) el vapor del agua... »

Antes de mirar

¿Qué espera Ud. ver en un programa de viajes?

☐ la gente (*people*) del lugar que se visita
☐ el ambiente en las calles (*the atmosphere in the streets*)
☐ la naturaleza (selvas [*jungles*], animales autóctonos [*native*])
☐ la comida
☐ otras cosas: _____

So far you have talked almost exclusively about the present time. What verb tense do you think a traveler would use to talk about a trip?

Este segmento

Este segmento introduce un programa que muestra (*shows*) videos filmados por telespectadores sobre sus viajes favoritos a lugares de Latinoamérica. El primer video es sobre la Argentina.

Vocabulario **del segmento**

la elección	choice	**visité**	I visited	**me pareció**	it seemed
estar listo/a	to be ready	**enterrado/a**	buried	**impresionante**	impressive
la voz	voice	**me encantó**	I loved	**me gustó**	I liked
hice	I took, made	**fui/encontré**	I went / I found	**estuve**	I was
el año pasado	last year	**el puesto**	stall, stand		
llegué	I arrived	**vi**	I saw		

Después de mirar

A. ¿Está claro? Empareje los lugares con las descripciones de Jaime.

LUGARES

1.

2.

3.

4.

DESCRIPCIONES DE JAIME

a. _____ la tumba de Eva Perón en el Cementerio de la Recoleta

b. _____ un espectáculo (*show*) de gauchos en la Feria de Mataderos

c. _____ las increíbles Cataratas del Iguazú

d. _____ la famosa Plaza de Mayo

B. Un poco más. Las siguientes oraciones son falsas. Corríjalas, según el video.

1. Ana y Víctor recibieron (*received*) más de mil videos para este programa.
2. El video que se ve en este segmento es sobre Chile.
3. El turista solo fue (*went*) a las Cataratas del Iguazú.
4. Los gauchos son similares a los tucanes.

C. Y ahora, Uds. En parejas, escojan un lugar que a los dos les gustaría (*you would both like*) visitar. Luego completen la siguiente descripción del viaje.

En el futuro, nos gustaría[a] ir a _____ en el/la _____ (estación del año) porque nos gusta _____ (infinitivos). Nos gustaría ir con _____ y pasar _____ (período de tiempo) allí.

[a]nos... *we would like*

GRAMÁTICA

Grammar Tutorial 21
connect SPANISH
www.connectspanish.com

21 Expressing *to who(m)* or *for who(m)*
Indirect Object Pronouns; **Dar** and **decir**

Gramática en acción: En el aeropuerto

En el mostrador
—¿**Me** puede dar un asiento de ventanilla, por favor?
—Lo siento, pero ya no hay. Pero sí puedo asignar**le** un asiento de pasillo.

En el control de seguridad
—¿**Le** enseño la tarjeta de embarque?
—No es necesario, señorita.
—¿**Le** enseño el pasaporte?
—Tampoco es necesario.

Comprensión

¿Dónde se oye, en el mostrador o en el control de seguridad?

1. «¿Puede enseñar**me** (*show me*) lo que hay en su bolso?»
2. «No **me** gusta sentarme en el asiento de en medio (*middle*).»
3. «En un momento **le** doy la nueva tarjeta de embarque.»
4. «¿**Me** enseña el pasaporte, por favor?»

> *the indirect object* / **el complemento indirecto** = the noun or pronoun that indicates *to who(m)* or *for who(m)* an action is performed

Indirect Object Pronouns / Los pronombres del complemento indirecto

me	to/for me	nos	to/for us
te	to/for you (*fam. sing.*)	os	to/for you (*fam. pl.*)
le	to/for you (*form. sing.*), him, her, it	les	to/for you (*form. pl.*), them

> **¡OJO!**
> Note that indirect object pronouns have the same form as direct object pronouns, except in the third person: **le, les.**

At the airport *At the counter:* "Could you please give me a window seat?" "I'm sorry, but there aren't any more (*available*). But I **can** give you an aisle seat." *At the security check:* "Do I show you my boarding pass?" "That's not necessary, miss." "Do I show you my passport?" "That isn't necessary either."

1. Indirect Objects

Indirect object nouns and pronouns are the second recipient of the action of the verb. They usually answer the question *to who(m)?* or *for who(m)?* in relation to the verb. The word *to* is frequently omitted in English.

	INDIRECT	DIRECT	
Ana is preparing	**them**	dinner.	
I'll give	**her**	the gift	tomorrow.

For who(m) is Ana preparing dinner? → **(for) them**
To who(m) am I giving the gift? → **(to) her**

Indicate the direct and indirect objects in the following sentences.

1. *He'll give me the car tomorrow.*
2. *Please tell me the answer now.*
3. *Me va a dar el coche mañana.*
4. Dígame la respuesta ahora, por favor.
5. El profesor nos va a hacer algunas preguntas.
6. ¿No me compras una revista ahora?

2. Placement of Indirect Object Pronouns

Like direct object pronouns, *indirect object pronouns* (**los pronombres del complemento indirecto**) can precede the conjugated verb.

When the conjugated verb is followed by an infinitive or a present participle, the pronouns either precede the conjugated verb *or* follow (and are attached to):

- the infinitive
- the present participle

Remember to add an accent mark to the present participle when you attach a pronoun to it.

No, no **te** **presto** el coche.
No, I won't lend you the car.

Voy a **guardarte** el asiento.
Te **voy** a guardar el asiento.
I'll save your seat for you.

Le **estoy** escribiendo una carta a Marisol.
Estoy **escribiéndole** una carta a Marisol.
I'm writing Marisol a letter.

3. With Commands

As with direct object pronouns, indirect object pronouns:

- are attached to the affirmative command form
- precede the negative command form.

Remember to add an accent to most affirmative commands when you attach a pronoun.

Sírvanos un café, por favor.
Serve us some coffee, please.

No me **dé** su número de teléfono ahora.
Don't give me your phone number now.

4. Redundancy of the Indirect Object

Even when a sentence has a third person indirect object *noun*, it must also have a third person indirect object *pronoun*. The noun object is preceded by **a,** which expresses *to* or *for*. This redundancy may sound repetitive to you, but it is what happens in Spanish most of the time.

Vamos a **mandarle** un mensaje a Juan.
Let's send Juan a message.
(Lit., *Let's send **to him** a message **to Juan**.*)

¿**Les** guardo los asientos a los niños?
Shall I save the seats for the kids?
(Lit., *Shall I **for them** save the seats **for the kids**?*)

5. Multiple Meanings of *le(s)*

Le and **les** can have several different meanings. When context does not make the meaning clear, the meaning is clarified with a prepositional phrase: **a** + *pronoun object of a preposition.* This redundancy is appropriate in Spanish.

Voy a **mandarle** un telegrama. = meaning of **le** unclear unless specified
Voy a mandarle un telegrama a Ud. / ...a él. / ...a ella.
I'm going to send you/him/her a telegram.

¡OJO!

Object of prepositions = subject pronouns, except for **mí** and **ti**.

6. Clarification or Emphasis of Indirect Object Pronouns

To clarify or emphasize the indirect object pronouns **me, te, nos,** and **os,** a phrase with **a** + *object pronoun* is also used. English accomplishes this by tone of voice, but Spanish does it with redundancy.

¿Ud. **me** habla a mí?
*Are you talking to **me**?*

Pedro **te** dio el pasaporte a ti, no a mí.
*Pedro gave **you** the passport, not (to) **me**.*

7. Verbs Often Used with Indirect Objects

Here are some verbs frequently used with indirect objects. You already know the meaning of the ones marked with*.

contar (cuento)	to tell; to narrate	*pedir (pido) (i)	to ask for
entregar (gu)	to hand in	preguntar	to ask (*a question*)
*escribir	to write	prestar	to lend
explicar (qu)	to explain	prometer	to promise
*hablar	to speak	recomendar (recomiendo)	to recommend
*mandar	to send	regalar	to give (*as a gift*)
mostrar (muestro)	to show	*servir (sirvo) (i)	to serve
ofrecer (ofrezco)	to offer		

Dar and decir

dar (*to give*)		decir (*to say; to tell*)	
doy	damos	digo	decimos
das	dais	dices	decís
da	dan	dice	dicen

Juan **dice** que tiene muchos gastos (*expenses*) en la universidad. Por eso Juan les **dice** a sus padres que necesita dinero.

Sus padres le **dan** un cheque.

1. *dar*

Dar means *to give*. It is almost always used with indirect object pronouns.

¡OJO!
Another Spanish verb expresses *to give* as a gift: **regalar**.

Mis profesores **nos dan** mucha tarea en todas las clases.
My professors give us a lot of homework in all my classes.

Mis abuelos **me regalan** dinero para mi cumpleaños.
My grandparents give me money for my birthday.

2. *decir*

Decir means *to say* or *to tell*. When **decir** means *to tell*, it is almost always used with indirect object pronouns, like **dar**.

¡OJO!
Other verbs related to speaking are used to express different meanings.

hablar	to speak
contar (cuento)	to tell; to narrate

Mi profesor **dice** que la historia es fascinante.
My professor says that history is fascinating.

Y **nos dice** que tenemos mucho que aprender de la historia.
And he tells us that we have a lot to learn from history.

El profesor **habla** varias lenguas.
The professor speaks several languages.

A veces **nos cuenta** algunas de sus experiencias en Latinoamérica.
At times he tells us some of his experiences in Latin America.

3. Formal Commands of *dar* and *decir*

As you know, **dar** and **decir** also have irregular formal command forms. There is a written accent on **dé** to distinguish it from the preposition **de**.

Mandatos formales

dar → dé, den
decir → diga, digan

Práctica y comunicación

A. Asociaciones. ¿Qué verbos asocia Ud. con los siguientes objetos y situaciones?

1. un coche, el dinero
2. la comida en un restaurante
3. las fotos
4. hacer algo por (*for*) alguien
5. la gramática, un profesor

6. la tarea, un informe (*report, paper*)
7. algo para un cumpleaños
8. un restaurante, una película, un libro
9. flores (*flowers*), un e-mail
10. un secreto, un chiste (*joke*)

B. Dar y recibir

Paso 1. Autoprueba. Complete las siguientes oraciones con el pronombre del objeto indirecto apropiado.

1. _____ presto el coche a ti, Carolina, no a tu hermano.
2. Los señores Gómez _____ mandan saludos a su amigo dominicano.
3. No _____ dé más galletas a los niños, por favor.
4. ¿_____ pasas el pan, por favor? Está muy lejos de mí.
5. Profesora, no podemos terminar el examen si no _____ da más tiempo.
6. El tío Juan siempre _____ dice a mis hermanos y a mí que la ciudad de Santa Domingo es muy bonita.

Paso 2. Complete las siguientes declaraciones sobre su vida (*life*) con el pronombre del objeto indirecto apropiado. Si la oración no es cierta para Ud., hágala negativa usando **no** u otras palabras negativas.

1. Todos los años _____ doy una tarjeta de cumpleaños a mi mejor amigo/a.
2. Todos los años mi mejor amigo/a _____ da una tarjeta de cumpleaños.
3. Todos los días _____ escribo un mensaje a mis padres o a mis abuelos.
4. Todos los días mis padres o mis abuelos (mis hijos) _____ mandan un mensaje.
5. Todos mis profesores _____ cuentan chistes en clase con frecuencia.
6. Con frecuencia, _____ cuento historias a mis profesores y compañeros de clase.
7. Mis abuelos _____ regalan dinero con frecuencia.
8. _____ regalo dinero a mis abuelos con frecuencia.

Paso 3. Ahora, en parejas, túrnense para hacer y contestar preguntas, usando las oraciones del **Paso 2**. Luego díganle al resto de la clase algo que Uds. tienen en común. **¡OJO!** Hagan los cambios necesarios, según el modelo.

MODELO: Todos los años _____ doy una tarjeta de cumpleaños a mi mejor amigo/a. →

> E1: ¿Todos los años **le das** una tarjeta de cumpleaños a **tu** mejor amiga?
> E2: No, nunca **le doy** una tarjeta de cumpleaños a **mi** mejor amiga. ¿Y tú?
> E1: Yo tampoco. →
>
> Nosotros nunca **les damos** una tarjeta de cumpleaños a **nuestras** mejores amigas.

C. De vuelta (*Returning*) a la República Dominicana

Paso 1. Unos amigos dominicanos necesitan ayuda para arreglar (*arrange*) su vuelta (*return*) a casa. Explíqueles cómo Ud. los puede ayudar.

MODELO: imprimir (*to print*) el boleto electrónico → **Les** imprimo el boleto electrónico.

1. llamar un taxi
2. bajar (*to carry down*) las maletas de su habitación
3. guardar (*to keep an eye on*) el equipaje
4. guardar un puesto en la cola
5. comprar una revista
6. por fin dar un abrazo (*hug*)

Summary of Indirect Object Pronouns

a mí → **me**
a nosotros/as → **nos**

a ti → **te**
a vosotros/as → **vos**

a Ud., él, ella → **le**
a Uds., ellos, ellas → **les**

Paso 2. Ahora describa las acciones, pero desde el punto de vista (*point of view*) de sus amigos.

MODELO: imprimir el boleto electrónico → **Nos** imprimes el boleto electrónico.

D. **¿Qué hacen estas personas?** Complete las siguientes oraciones lógicamente con un verbo y un pronombre del complemento indirecto.

MODELO: El vicepresidente _____ consejos al presidente.

→ El vicepresidente **le ofrece** consejos al presidente.

1. Romeo _____ flores a Julieta.
2. Snoopy _____ besos (*kisses*) a Lucy... ¡Y a ella no le gusta!
3. Eva _____ una manzana a Adán.
4. Los psicólogos _____ consejos a la gente (*people*) que los necesita.
5. Los bancos _____ dinero a las personas que quieren comprar una casa.
6. Los asistentes de vuelo _____ bebidas a los pasajeros.
7. Yo siempre _____ la verdad a todos.

Vocabulario útil

dar
decir
ofrecer (ofrezco)
prestar
regalar
servir (sirvo) (i)

E. **En un restaurante.** Explíquele al pequeño Benjamín, que solo tiene 4 años, lo que se hace en un restaurante. Llene los espacios en blanco con pronombres del complemento indirecto.

Primero el camarero _____¹ ofrece una mesa desocupada.ª Luego tú _____² pides el menú al camarero. También _____³ haces preguntas sobre los platos y las especialidades de la casa y _____⁴ dices lo que quieres comer. El camarero _____⁵ trae la comida. Por fin tu papá _____⁶ pide la cuenta al camarero. Si tú quieres pagar, _____⁷ pides dinero a tu papá y _____⁸ das el dinero al camarero.

ª*vacant*

F. **Intercambios.** En parejas, túrnense para entrevistarse sobre los siguientes temas. Traten de (*Try to*) continuar la conversación.

hacer buenos regalos →

MODELO: E1: **¿Quién te** hace buenos regalos?
E2: Mis padres siempre me hacen buenos regalos.
E1: **¿Qué te** regalan, por ejemplo?
E2: Bueno, me regalan dinero, CDs, cosas para mi apartamento...

1. hacer buenos / interesantes regalos / regalar cosas feas
2. decir la verdad / mentiras (*lies*)
3. contar secretos / los secretos de otras personas
4. hacer favores / recomendaciones / la cena
5. escribir e-mails / poemas de amor / tarjetas postales cuando están de vacaciones
6. mostrar las fotos de sus vacaciones / las notas (*grades*) de sus exámenes
7. servir la comida / bebidas
8. pedir / dar ayuda / consejos
9. prestar dinero / ropa / su coche
10. prometer cosas que luego no hace
11. recomendar películas / restaurantes / clases en la universidad
12. ¿?

Algo sobre...

el casabe

El casabe, un producto que representa la cultura de la República Dominicana

El casabe es una especie de tortilla que se hace con la yuca.ª Es un producto básico de alimentaciónᵇ de los dominicanos. Como comida, el casabe es una tradición que viene de los taínos, los indígenas de la isla de La Española (hoy día, Haití y la República Dominicana).

En su cultura, ¿qué alimento se puede comparar con el casabe?

ª*manioc, cassava root* ᵇ*diet, what people eat*

¿Recuerda Ud.?

In **Capítulo 1** you started to use forms of **gustar** to express your likes and dislikes. Review what you know by answering the following questions. Then, changing their form as needed, interview your instructor.

1. ¿Te gusta el café (el vino, el té...)?
2. ¿Te gusta jugar al béisbol (al golf, al voleibol, al...)?
3. ¿Te gusta viajar en avión (fumar, viajar en tren...)?
4. ¿Qué te gusta más, estudiar o ir a fiestas (trabajar o descansar, cocinar o comer)?

Grammar Tutorial 22
connect |SPANISH
www.connectspanish.com

22 Expressing Likes and Dislikes
Gustar (Part 2)

Gramática en acción: Vacaciones en la República Dominicana

En la República Dominicana se puede hacer de todo en las vacaciones.

- A algunas personas les gusta relajarse en la playa.
- A otras personas les gustan las vacaciones que les permiten hacer actividades deportivas (*sporting*).
- A algunos turistas les gustan los museos y los monumentos históricos.
- A mucha gente le gusta hacer de todo un poco.

¿Y a Ud.?

¿Qué le gusta hacer en sus vacaciones? ¿Le gusta ir a un sitio donde hace buen tiempo? ¿Le gustan las actividades deportivas o las culturales (*cultural ones*)?

Using gustar / Los usos de *gustar*

Spanish	English Phrasing	Literal Equivalent
Me gusta la playa.	*I like the beach.*	The beach is pleasing to me.
No le gustan sus cursos.	*He doesn't like his courses.*	His courses are not pleasing to him.
Nos gusta esquiar.	*We like to ski.*	Skiing is pleasing to us.

You have been using the verb **gustar** since the beginning of *Puntos de partida* to express likes and dislikes. However, **gustar** does not literally mean *to like*, but rather *to be pleasing*.

Me gusta viajar.
Traveling is pleasing to me. (I like to travel.)

Me gustan los viajes de aventura.
Adventure trips are pleasing to me. (I like adventure trips.)

1. *Gustar* + Indirect Object Pronouns

Gustar is always used with an indirect object pronoun: Something is pleasing to someone. The verb agrees with the subject of the sentence = the thing that is pleasing. In the first two examples, **gusta** is used with the singular noun **asiento, gustan** with the plural **asientos**.

¡OJO!

An infinitive is a singular subject in Spanish. **Gusta** is used even if there are two or more infinitive subjects.

(no) *indirect object pronoun* + **gusta(n)** + *subject*

Me gusta **este asiento** de pasillo.
This aisle seat is pleasing to me. (I like this aisle seat.)

No **me** gustan **los asientos** de ventanilla.
Window seats are not pleasing to me. (I don't like window seats.)

Me gusta mucho **volar** en avión.
Flying is really pleasing to me. (I really like to fly.)

Me gusta nadar y **tomar** el sol.
I like to swim and sunbathe.

---

2. Redundancy of Indirect Object

When the person pleased is a noun or a proper name, the indirect object pronoun is still used. This redundancy (repetition) is the same concept you learned with *le* and *les* in **Gramática 21**.

¡OJO!

Remember: The indirect object pronoun *must* be used with **gustar** even when the prepositional phrase *a* + *noun* or *pronoun* is used.

---

a + *noun* + **(no) le / les gusta(n)** + *subject*
(no) le / les gusta(n) + *subject* + **a** + *noun*

Al niño no **le** gustan los aviones.
No **le** gustan los aviones **al niño**.
The child doesn't like airplanes.

A Raquel y a Arturo les gusta viajar juntos.
Les gusta viajar juntos **a Raquel y Arturo**.
Raquel and Arturo like to travel together.

---

3. Clarification or Emphasis

A phrase with **a** + *pronoun* is often used for clarification or emphasis. The prepositional phrase can appear before the indirect object pronoun or after the verb.

¡OJO!

Remember that subject pronouns (**Ud., él, ella**...) are used as the object of prepositions, except for **mí** (accent) and **ti** (no accent). (Exceptions: **conmigo, contigo.**)

CLARIFICATION
¿**Le** gusta **a Ud.** viajar? ¿**A Ud. le** gusta viajar?
Do you like to travel?

¿**Le** gusta **a él** viajar? ¿**A él le** gusta viajar?
Does he like to travel?

EMPHASIS
A mí me gusta viajar en avión, pero **a mi esposo le** gusta viajar en coche. Y **a ti**, ¿en qué **te** gusta viajar?
I like to travel by plane, but my husband likes to travel by car. How do you like to travel?

---

4. *Gustar* + determiner + noun

When the thing liked is a noun, it is always preceded by a determiner of some kind: an article, an adjective of quantity (like **muchos**), a possessive, or a demonstrative.

¡OJO!

In English, the definite article is omitted with the verb *like*. The definite article is *never* omitted with **gustar** unless another determiner is used.

Me gusta **el** chocolate. Me gustan **los** dulces.
I like chocolate. I like sweets.

Me gustan **muchas** canciones de Shakira.
I like many of Shakira's songs.

Me gustan **tus** sugerencias, pero no me gusta **ese** tipo de vacaciones.
I like your suggestions, but I don't like that type of vacation.

Would Like / Wouldn't Like = Gustaría

To express what you *would* or *would not* like to do, use **gustaría** + *infinitive* with the appropriate indirect objects.

A mí me gustaría viajar a Colombia.
I would like to travel to Colombia.

No nos gustaría hacer camping este verano.
We would not like to go camping this summer.

Práctica y comunicación

A. Los gustos y preferencias para las vacaciones

Summary of the Uses of *gustar*

me (te...) gusta + singular noun or infinitive(s)

me (te...) gustan + plural noun

Vocabulario útil

A mí también.	So do I.
A mí tampoco.	I don't either. / Neither do I.
Pues a mí, sí.	Well, I do.
Pues a mí, no.	Well, I don't.

Paso 1. Autoprueba. Complete las siguientes oraciones con **-a** or **-an.**

1. Me gust_____ nadar.
2. Por eso me gust_____ las playas caribeñas.
3. A mi familia y a mí nos gust_____ esquiar.
4. Por eso nos gust_____ las vacaciones de invierno.
5. A mi mejor amigo le gust_____ el sol.
6. Por eso siempre le gust_____ la República Dominicana para las vacaciones.
7. ¿A ti te gust_____ las vacaciones activas o relajantes (*relaxing*)?

Paso 2. Use las siguientes frases en oraciones completas para expresar sus gustos.

MODELOS: ¿viajar? → (No) Me **gusta** viajar.
¿los aviones? → (No) Me **gustan** los aviones.

1. ¿viajar?
2. ¿los viajes con mi familia?
3. ¿los vuelos?
4. ¿el calor?
5. ¿el invierno?
6. ¿las playas caribeñas?
7. ¿los aeropuertos?
8. ¿viajar en coche?

Paso 3. Ahora, en parejas, túrnense para entrevistarse sobre las ideas del **Paso 2.** Luego díganle al resto de la clase algo que Uds. tienen en común.

MODELO: E1: A mí me gusta viajar. ¿Y a ti?
E2: A mí también. →
A nosotros nos gusta viajar.

B. ¿Cómo van a organizar las vacaciones los Soto?

Vocabulario útil

hacer surfing
la discoteca
el hotel
el museo
el parque nacional

Paso 1. Los Soto tienen gustos muy diversos: ¡a cada uno le gusta solo una cosa! Explique el gusto de cada persona con oraciones completas. Luego nombre una actividad que probablemente le gusta hacer en las vacaciones.

MODELO: 1. la madre: las novelas de Julia Álvarez →
A la madre le gustan las novelas de Julia Álvarez. **Seguro que le gusta** leer en la playa.

1. la madre: las novelas de Julia Álvarez
2. el padre: los deportes (*sports*) acuáticos
3. los abuelos: el arte
4. Lucas: la naturaleza (*nature*)
5. Elena, la hija adolescente: la música pop
6. los mellizos (*twins*) de 11 años: jugar en la piscina

Paso 2. Ahora, en parejas, nombren un lugar al que a cada una de esas personas les gustaría ir para las vacaciones.

MODELO: A la madre le **gustaría** ir a una playa tranquila.

Paso 3. Finalmente, escojan un destino en el que (*which*) todos los miembros de la familia puedan (*can*) hacer algo que les gusta.

C. ¿Conoce bien a... ?

Paso 1. ¿Cree Ud. que conoce bien a su profesor(a) de español? Haga oraciones completas para decir si a él/ella le gustan o no las siguientes cosas.

MODELO: **1.** la música clásica →
    (No) Le gusta la música clásica.

1. la música clásica
2. bailar salsa
3. los niños pequeños
4. las canciones de los años 80
5. viajar
6. los destinos exóticos
7. el arte surrealista
8. ¿ ?

Paso 2. Ahora entreviste a su profesor(a) para saber si le gustan las cosas del **Paso 1** o no.

MODELOS: ¿A Ud. le gusta la música clásica?
    A Ud. le gusta la música clásica, ¿verdad?

Paso 3. Ahora entreviste a un compañero o una compañera sobre las mismas cosas.

MODELO: **E1:** ¿Te gusta la música clásica?
    E2: Sí. ¿Y a ti?

D. Perfiles personales. En parejas, inventen con detalles las preferencias de las siguientes personas.

> **Vocabulario útil**
>
> **la música** *rap*, *hip hop*
> **jugar (juego) (gu) a los videojuegos**
> **patinar en monopatín** to skateboard

1. Toño

2. los Sres. Sánchez

3. Memo

Nota comunicativa

Otras maneras de expresar los gustos y preferencias

Here are some ways to express intense likes and dislikes.

INTENSE LIKES

- **mucho/muchísimo** (with **gustar**)

  Me gusta **mucho/muchísimo.** *I like it a lot / a whole lot.*

- **encantar** (*like* **gustar**), **interesar** (*like* **gustar**)

  Me encantan las películas extranjeras. *I love foreign films.*

  Me interesa aprender otras lenguas. *I'm interested in learning other languages.*

Verbs that are used like **gustar** will be noted in vocabulary lists with the parenthetical note (like **gustar**).

INTENSE DISLIKES

- **no... (para) nada** (with **gustar**)

  No me gusta **(para) nada** la comida japonesa. *I don't like Japanese food at all.*

- **odiar**

  Unlike **encantar** and **interesar,** which are used like **gustar, odiar** is conjugated like regular **-ar** verbs. It is a transitive verb, that is, a verb that can take a direct object.

  Odio los champiñones. *I hate mushrooms.*

  Mi madre **odia** viajar sola. *My mother hates traveling alone.*

Use as many of these verbs and expressions as you can in **Práctica E**.

E. Intercambios. En parejas, túrnense para describir lo que les gusta y lo que odian cuando están en las siguientes situaciones. Inventen los detalles necesarios.

MODELO: en la playa ⟶ Cuando estoy en la playa, me encanta nadar en el mar, pero no me gusta el sol ni me gusta la arena (*sand*). Por eso odio pasar todo el día en la playa. Prefiero nadar en una piscina.

Situaciones

en un autobús	en el salón de clase
en un avión	en el coche
en la biblioteca	en una discoteca
en una cafetería	en una fiesta
en casa con mis amigos	en un parque
en casa con mis padres/hijos	en la playa
en un centro comercial	en un tren

¿Recuerda Ud.?

You have already learned one of the irregular past tense verb forms that is presented in **Gramática 23**. Review it now by telling what day yesterday was: **Ayer...**

23 Talking About the Past (Part 1)

Preterite of Regular Verbs and of **dar, hacer, ir,** and **ser**

Gramática en acción: Un viaje a la República Dominicana

Elisa es reportera. Hace poco, fue a la República Dominicana para escribir un artículo sobre la isla de La Española. Habla Elisa.

- Hice el viaje en avión.
- El vuelo fue largo porque el avión hizo escala en Miami.
- Pasé una semana entera en la Isla.
- Visité muchos sitios de interés turístico e histórico.
- Comí mucha comida típica del Caribe.
- Tomé el sol, nadé en el mar y escribí muchas tarjetas postales.
- ¡Lo pasé muy bien!

Comprensión

¿Cierto o falso? Corrija las oraciones falsas.

	CIERTO	FALSO
1. Elisa fue a la República Dominicana para pasar sus vacaciones.	☐	☐
2. El avión hizo escala en los Estados Unidos.	☐	☐
3. Elisa no visitó ningún lugar importante de la Isla.	☐	☐
4. No lo pasó bien en la playa.	☐	☐

So far, you have almost always talked in the present tense. In this section, you will use forms of the preterite, one of the past tenses in Spanish.

To talk about the past in Spanish, there are two simple tenses:* the preterite and the imperfect. In this chapter, you will learn the regular forms of the preterite and those of four irregular verbs: **dar, hacer, ir,** and **ser.** Then in **Capítulos 9, 10,** and **11,** you will learn more about both tenses.

Preterite: Regular Verbs / El pretérito: Los verbos regulares

-*ar* Verbs		-*er/-ir* Verbs		
hablar		**com**er		**viv**ir
hablé	I spoke (did speak)	**com**í	I ate (did eat)	**viv**í	I lived (did live)
hablaste	you spoke	**com**iste	you ate	**viv**iste	you lived
habló	you/he/she spoke	**com**ió	you/he/she ate	**viv**ió	you/he/she lived
hablamos	we spoke	**com**imos	we ate	**viv**imos	we lived
hablasteis	you spoke	**com**isteis	you ate	**viv**isteis	you lived
hablaron	you/they spoke	**com**ieron	you/they ate	**viv**ieron	you/they lived

---

A trip to the Dominican Republic Elisa is a reporter. A little while ago, she went to the Dominican Republic to write an article about the island of Hispaniola. Here's Elisa. ■ I made the trip by plane. ■ The flight was long because the plane made a stop in Miami. ■ I spent a whole week on the Island. ■ I visited a lot of interesting tourist and historical sites. ■ I ate a lot of typical Caribbean food. ■ I sunbathed, swam in the ocean, and wrote a lot of postcards. ■ I had a really good time!

*Simple tenses are those formed without an auxiliary or "helping" verb. Examples of simple tenses in English: I ate, I saw.
Examples of tenses with an auxiliary: I have eaten, I have seen.

1. Uses of the Preterite

As you saw in the chart on p. 251, the *preterite* (**el pretérito**) has several English equivalents.

The preterite is used to report finished, completed actions or states of being in the past. If the action or state of being is viewed as completed—no matter how long it lasted or took to complete—it will be expressed with the preterite. A two-month period is specified in the first example sentence; that period is over. No time span is specified in the second sentence, but the action is clearly over since it took place *last summer*.

hablé = I spoke, I did speak

Pasé dos meses en el Caribe.
I spent two months in the Caribbean.

El verano pasado **hicimos** *camping* en Puerto Rico.
Last summer we went camping in Puerto Rico.

2. *Nosotros* forms

Note that the **nosotros** forms of regular preterites for **-ar** and **-ir** verbs are the same as the present tense forms. Context usually helps determine meaning. If the translation were not available, what words would tell you that the first **hablamos** means *we spoke* and the second one *we're speaking*?

Ayer **hablamos** del viaje con nuestros amigos. Hoy, más tarde, **hablamos** con el agente de viajes a las dos de la tarde.
Yesterday we spoke about the trip with our friends. Today, later on, we'll speak with the travel agent at 2:00 P.M.

3. Accent Marks

Note the accent marks on the first and third person singular of the preterite tense. These accent marks are not used in the conjugation of **ver: vi, vio.**

bailé, bailó

bebí, bebió

asistí, asistió

but

vi, vio

4. Verbs ending in *-car*, *-gar*, and *-zar*

These verbs show a spelling change in the first person singular (**yo**) of the preterite. This is the same change you have already learned to make in formal commands, **Gramática 20 (Cap. 7).**

-car → qu buscar		
busqué	buscamos	
buscaste	buscasteis	
buscó	buscaron	

-gar → gu pagar		
pagué	pagamos	
pagaste	pagasteis	
pagó	pagaron	

-zar → c empezar		
empecé	empezamos	
empezaste	empezasteis	
empezó	empezaron	

5. Unstressed *-i-*

An unstressed **-i-** between two vowels becomes **-y-**. Also, note the accent on the **í** in the **tú, nosotros,** and **vosotros** forms.

creer		leer	
creí	creímos	leí	leímos
creíste	creísteis	leíste	leísteis
creyó	creyeron	leyó	leyeron

6. *-ar* and *-er* Stem-changing Verbs

Stem-changing verbs that end in **-ar** and **-er** are completely regular in the preterite. However, the preterite of **-ir** stem-changing verbs is not regular. You will learn the preterite of those verbs in **Gramática 25 (Cap. 9).**

despertar (despierto): desperté, despertaste,...
volver (vuelvo): volví, volviste,...

Irregular Forms / Las formas irregulares

1. Dar

The preterite endings for **dar** are the same as those used for regular **-er/-ir** verbs, except that the accent marks are dropped.

dar	
di	dimos
diste	disteis
dio	dieron

2. Hacer

All forms of **hacer** are irregular in the preterite, especially the third person singular, **hizo,** which is spelled with a **z** rather than a **c** to keep the [s] sound of the infinitive.

hacer	
hice	hicimos
hiciste	hicisteis
hizo	hicieron

3. Ir and ser

These verbs have identical forms in the preterite. Context will make the meaning clear. For example, in the first sentence to the right, the word **a** is a clue that **Fui** means I went, since forms of the verb **ir** are often followed by **a.** In the second sentence, **Fui** is followed directly by a noun; forms of **ir**/to go are never directly followed by a noun, so **fui** must mean I was.

ir/ser	
fui	fuimos
fuiste	fuisteis
fue	fueron

Fui a la playa el verano pasado.
I went to the beach last summer.

Fui agente de viajes.
I was a travel agent.

Práctica y comunicación

A. El verano pasado

Paso 1. Autoprueba. Dé la forma apropiada del pretérito para cada sujeto.

1. **tú:** comprar, ir, acostarse, beber, hacer
2. **Ud.:** comprender, empezar, creer, afeitarse, dar
3. **nosotros:** hacer, ser, ir, pagar, leer
4. **ellas:** asistir, volver, terminar, despertarse, salir

Summary of Preterite Endings
-ar: **-é, -aste, -ó, -amos, -asteis –aron**
-er/-ir: **-í, -iste, -ió, -imos, -isteis, -ieron**
dar: **di...**   hacer: **hice...** ir/ser: **fui...**

Paso 2. Complete las siguientes oraciones sobre el verano pasado con las terminaciones apropiadas de la primera persona singular (**yo**). Si es necesario, use **no** para hacer oraciones que son ciertas para Ud.

El verano pasado...

1. tom_____ clases en la universidad.
2. asist_____ a un concierto en otra ciudad.
3. trabaj_____ mucho y gan_____ mucho dinero. (**ganar** = to earn)
4. hi_____ *camping* con unos amigos.
5. viv_____ todo el tiempo con mi familia.
6. me qued_____ trabajando y estudiando en la universidad.
7. fu_____ a la playa.
8. me levant_____ tarde casi todos los días.

Paso 3. Ahora, en parejas, túrnense para entrevistarse sobre las ideas del **Paso 2.** Luego díganle a la clase dos cosas que Uds. tienen en común.

MODELO: tomé clases en la universidad. →
   E1: El verano pasado, ¿**tomaste** alguna clase en la universidad?
   E2: No, ¿y tú?
   E1: Yo tampoco. →

   Nosotros no **tomamos** ninguna clase el verano pasado.

Prác. A, Paso 1: Answers: 1. compraste, fuiste, te acostaste, bebiste, hiciste 2. comprendió, empezó, creyó, se afeitó, dio 3. hicimos, fuimos, fuimos, pagamos, leímos 4. asistieron, volvieron, terminaron, se despertaron, salieron

B. El viernes pasado por la tarde

Paso 1. Narre la secuencia de las acciones que hizo Julio el viernes pasado por la tarde. ¡OJO! **Julio** es el sujeto de muchas oraciones, pero no de todas. A veces el sujeto es **ellos** (Julio y su amigo Roberto).

El viernes por la tarde, Julio...

1. volver a casa después de trabajar todo el día

2. llamar a su amigo Roberto y los dos: decidir ir al cine juntos

3. ducharse y afeitarse

4. salir de casa rápidamente e ir al cine en autobús

5. los dos: hacer cola para comprar las entradas y comprar palomitas (*popcorn*)

6. entrar en la sala y sentarse

7. ver la película pero no gustarles nada

8. ir a un restaurante a cenar y quedarse conversando hasta muy tarde

Paso 2. Comprensión. ¿Cierto, falso o no lo dice?

	CIERTO	FALSO	NO LO DICE
1. El amigo de Julio se llama Roberto.	☐	☐	☐
2. Son compañeros de clase.	☐	☐	☐
3. A los dos amigos les interesa el cine.	☐	☐	☐
4. Vieron una película extranjera.	☐	☐	☐
5. Odiaron la película.	☐	☐	☐
6. Comieron después de la película.	☐	☐	☐
7. Julio regresó a casa en autobús.	☐	☐	☐

Paso 3. Ahora, en parejas, vuelvan a contar la historia, usando las siguientes palabras en su narrativa: **primero, segundo** (*second*), **después, luego, finalmente.**

las hermanas Mirabal

Un billete^a de 200 pesos dominicanos con fotos de las hermanas Mirabal

Patria (1924–1960), Minerva (1926–1960) y María Teresa (1935–1960) Mirabal son heroínas dominicanas que

lucharon contra la terrible dictadura^b de Rafael Trujillo. (Se conocen también como las Mariposas.^c) Las tres fueron brutalmente asesinadas por orden del dictador. La hermana sobreviviente,^d Dedé, dedicó el resto de su vida a preservar la memoria de sus hermanas. Ahora hay una provincia dominicana con el nombre de Hermanas Mirabal. Las Mariposas también aparecen^e en los billetes de 200 pesos dominicanos.

La Asamblea General de las Naciones Unidas designó el día de la muerte^f de las Mirabal como el Día Internacional de la No Violencia Contra la Mujer.

 ¿Cuáles son algunos de los héroes y heroínas nacionales más importantes de su país? ¿Por qué son importantes?

^abill ^bdictatorship ^cButterflies ^dsurviving ^eappear ^fdeath

---

C. El día de ayer de dos compañeras

Paso 1. Teresa y Liliana son compañeras de apartamento en la universidad. Haga oraciones completas según el modelo para describir su día.

MODELO: 7:30 **levantarse** → **Se levantó a** las siete y media.

TERESA
1. 8:00   ducharse y desayunar
2. 9:00   salir de casa / ir a la universidad
3. 10:00   estudiar toda la mañana
4. 12:00   almorzar con unos compañeros de la universidad
5. 1:00   hacer experimentos en el laboratorio de química
6. 3:15   volver a casa

LILIANA
7. 9:45   despertarse, pero no levantarse pronto
8. 10:30   desayunar y empezar a hacer la tarea de matemáticas
9. 12:30   terminarla y ver la tele
10. 2:00   empezar a hacer un pastel para el cumpleaños de Miriam
11. 2:30   mandar unos e-mails.
12. 4:30   terminar el pastel / decorarlo

TERESA Y LILIANA
13. 5:00   ir al gimnasio cerca de su apartamento / allí hacer ejercicio por una hora
14. 6:30   volver a casa / ducharse y hablar de la fiesta de Miriam
15. 9:30   ir a casa de Miriam / cantarle «Cumpleaños feliz» / darle su regalo y comer el pastel

¿Quién es, Teresa o Liliana? ¿Cómo lo sabe?

Paso 2. En parejas, túrnense para hacer y contestar preguntas basadas en las oraciones del **Paso 1**.

MODELO: E1: ¿**Te duchaste** a las ocho, como Teresa?
E2: No, **me duché** por la noche. ¿Y tú?
E1: No **me duché**. Me bañé.

D. **Un semestre en la República Dominicana.** Cuente la siguiente historia desde el punto de vista de la persona indicada, usando el pretérito de los verbos.

MODELO: *yo:* viajar a la República Dominicana el año pasado →
Viajé a la República Dominicana el año pasado.

1. *yo:* pasar todo el semestre en Santo Domingo
2. mis padres: pagarme el vuelo
3. *yo:* trabajar para ganar el dinero para los otros gastos (*expenses*)
4. vivir con una familia dominicana
5. aprender mucho sobre la la cultura dominicana
6. visitar muchos sitios de interés turístico e histórico
7. mis amigos: escribirme con frecuencia
8. *yo:* mandarles muchas tarjetas postales
9. comprarles recuerdos (*souvenirs*) a todos
10. volver a Denver a fines de agosto

E. **La última (*last*) vez**

Paso 1. Conteste las siguientes preguntas. Añada más detalles si puede.

MODELO: La última vez que Ud. fue a una fiesta, ¿le llevó un regalo al anfitrión / a la anfitriona (*host/hostess*)? →
Sí, **le** llevé flores / una botella de vino. (No, no **le** llevé nada.)

La última vez que Ud....

1. hizo un viaje, ¿le mandó una tarjeta postal a algún amigo o amiga?
2. tomó el autobús/metro, ¿le ofreció su asiento a una persona mayor?
3. vio a su profesor(a) de español en público, ¿le habló en español?
4. comió en un restaurante, ¿le recomendó algún plato a su compañero/a?

5. entró en un edificio, ¿le abrió la puerta a otra persona?
6. voló en avión, ¿le pidió algo a uno de los asistentes de vuelo?
7. le regaló algo a alguien, ¿le gustó el regalo a la persona?
8. le prometió a alguien hacer algo, ¿lo hizo?
9. se quejó de algo, ¿a quién habló?

Paso 2. Ahora, en parejas, túrnense para hacer y contestar preguntas basadas en las oraciones del **Paso 1.**

Paso 3. Ahora díganle a la clase dos cosas interesantes sobre su compañero/a.

F. **Intercambios**

Paso 1. Escriba una lista de diez de las acciones que Ud. hizo ayer. Use los siguientes verbos y añada cuatro más de su preferencia. Haga oraciones completas.

MODELO: levantarse → Ayer **me levanté** a las seis de la mañana.

1. levantarse	4. dar	7. ¿ ?	9. ¿ ?
2. empezar	5. hacer	8. ¿ ?	10. ¿ ?
3. leer	6. ir		

Paso 2. En parejas, túrnense para entrevistarse sobre las acciones de su lista del **Paso 1.**

MODELO: E1: Ayer **me levanté** a las seis de la mañana. ¿A qué hora **te levantaste tú**?
E2: **Me levanté** a las diez.

Paso 3. Ahora díganle a la clase en qué acciones los dos coincidieron ayer.

G. **Más intercambios**

Paso 1. En parejas, túrnense para entrevistarse sobre su último viaje. Deben obtener información relacionada con las siguientes preguntas.

1. ¿cuándo?
2. ¿adónde?
3. ¿en qué medio de transporte?
4. ¿cuántos días?
5. ¿con quién?

Paso 2. Ahora díganle a la clase los detalles esenciales del viaje de su compañero/a.

MODELO: Susie fue a Puerto Rico el verano pasado. Hizo el viaje en avión. Se quedó en Puerto Rico una semana. Viajó con su novio y su familia.

Un poco de todo

A. Lengua y cultura: Mi abuela dominicana

Paso 1. Complete the following paragraphs with the correct form of the words in parentheses, as suggested by context. When two possibilities are given in parentheses, select the correct word. **¡OJO!** The verbs in the paragraphs will be present tense or preterite; the context will indicate which tense to use.

Ayer llegó de visita mi abuela Manuela. Ella vive en Santo Domingo, con mi tía Zaira, la (hermana / sobrina[1]) de mi mamá. (*Nosotros*: Ir[2]) a recibir(la / le[3]) al aeropuerto y nos (*ella*: dar[4]) un abrazo[a] muy fuerte. (Mi / Mí[5]) abuela va (a / de[6]) pasar dos meses con nosotros en Connecticut, y luego (ir[7]) a quedarse un mes con el tío Julián en Nueva York. Así es la vida[b] de muchas abuelas con hijos en otro país.

A mi abuela le (gusta / gustaría[8]) tener a todos sus hijos y (nietos / sobrinos[9]) en Santo Domingo y siempre (ser / estar[10]) muy triste cuando (volver[11]) a la República Dominicana (antes de / después de[12]) visitarnos. Pero también (le / la[13]) gusta mucho la vida en los Estados Unidos. (*Ella*: Decir[14]) que aquí se vive muy bien y que las casas (ser / estar[15]) muy buenas. (El / La[16]) problema es que no le (gustan / gustarían[17]) los inviernos de (este / esto[18]) país. ¡Es lógico! A ella le (gusta / gustan[19]) las playas y las palmeras, porque es lo que (conoce / sabe[20]) bien.

Cuando mi abuela regresa a Santo Domingo, (les / los[21]) mandamos con ella muchos regalos a nuestros (padres / parientes[22]). Casi todos los años mi familia (viaje / viaja[23]) a la República Dominicana, porque mis padres (vivir[24]) allá hasta que (ir[25]) a estudiar a la Universidad de Massachusetts. ¡(A / —[26]) mí me encanta ir de vacaciones a la República Dominicana!

[a]*hug* [b]**Así...** *Such is the life*

Una abuela con su hija y su nieta

Paso 2. Comprensión. Conteste las siguientes preguntas.

1. ¿Quién habla en la narración? ¿Se sabe si es hombre o mujer?
2. ¿Dónde vive la tía Zaira?
3. ¿Qué le gusta de la vida en los Estados Unidos a la abuela?
4. ¿Qué no le gusta?
5. ¿Cuándo emigraron a los Estados Unidos los padres del narrador / de la narradora?

Paso 3. La gran mayoría de estadounidenses es descendiente de inmigrantes; muchos son inmigrantes recientes. En parejas, túrnense para saber algo de la historia de la familia de su compañero/a, haciéndole las siguientes preguntas.

1. ¿Tienes un pariente que nació (*was born*) en otro país? ¿Quién(es)?
2. ¿Cuándo llegó a los Estados Unidos?
3. ¿Vino solo/a? ¿A quién(es) dejó (*did he/she leave behind*) en su país de origen?
4. Si ese pariente vive todavía, ¿visita a veces su país de origen? Si ya murió (*he/she is already deceased*), ¿volvió a visitar su país de origen antes de morir (*die*)? ¿Cuántas veces fue?

B. Humor viajero. En parejas, lean el dibujo y contesten las preguntas.

HUMOR VIAJERO

-¿Y cómo pasó...?
-No sé... Te juro que no lo vi venir.

David Sebastián Ojeda, Pasaje Blanco 1662, Morón, prov. de Buenos Aires, tel. 4697-6858; artepiero@hotmail.com

¿El piloto o Superhombre? ¿Quién...

1. no vio el avión?
2. no vio a Superhombre?
3. sufrió un accidente?
4. juró (*swore*) algo?
5. no llegó a su destino?
6. va a ir al hospital?
7. hizo un informe (*report*) sobre el accidente?

En **su** comunidad

Entreviste a una persona hispana de su universidad o ciudad sobre sus últimas (*last*) vacaciones y los lugares más populares de su país para ir de vacaciones.

PREGUNTAS POSIBLES

- ¿Cuándo fue de vacaciones a su país la última vez? ¿Con quién fue? ¿Cuánto tiempo pasó allá? ¿Se quedó en casa de su familia o en un hotel? ¿Con cuánta frecuencia va de vacaciones a su país?

- ¿Cuáles son los lugares de vacaciones más famosos de su país? ¿Los visitan solo los turistas extranjeros o los nacionales también? ¿Cuál es su lugar favorito? ¿Por qué?

«¡De viaje!» Segmento 2

Antes de mirar

¿Le gustaría visitar el Perú? ¿Por qué? ¿Qué sabe del país?

Este segmento

Este segmento muestra otro video filmado por un telespectador de *Salu2*. Este turista hizo un viaje inolvidable (*unforgettable*) al Perú.

«Primero estuvimos (*we were*) varios días en Cusco, la antigua capital del Imperio inca. Está a más de 3.000 metros de altitud, y esta altitud puede provocar malestar (*discomfort*) físico. ¡Pero el malestar no es nada comparado a la belleza (*beauty*) de la ciudad!»

Vocabulario del segmento

con razón	rightly so	el fuerte	fort
la piedra	stone	al final	at the end
rodeado/a de	surrounded by	la fuente	fountain
permanecer	to remain	el espectáculo	show
oculto/a	hidden	no dejen de	don't miss out
descubrir	to discover	visitar	on visiting

Fragmento del guion

De Cusco nos fuimos al Valle Sagrado[a] de los Incas para visitar un santuario de llamas. Estuvimos[b] con personas de esta comunidad mientras hacían tejidos tradicionales.[c] Es un arte que ha pasado[d] de generación en generación y un gran ejemplo de la hermosa[e] artesanía peruana. Pero lo mejor[f] del viaje fue Machu Picchu, considerada una de las siete maravillas del mundo actual.[g]

[a]Valle... *Sacred Valley* [b]*We were* [c]mientras... *while they made traditional weavings* [d]ha... *has been passed down* [e]*beautiful* [f]lo... *the best part* [g]*modern*

Después de mirar

A. ¿Está claro? Ponga los lugares que visitó el turista en el orden de su visita. Luego empareje cada lugar con las frases del video.

LUGARES

1. _____ Machu Picchu
2. _____ Cusco
3. _____ Lima
4. _____ el Valle Sagrado de los Incas

FRASES DEL VIDEO

a. «la ciudad más visitada de todo Perú»
b. «el nuevo Parque de las Fuentes»
c. «un santuario de llamas»
d. «una de las siete maravillas del mundo actual»

B. Un poco más. Conteste las siguientes preguntas.

1. ¿Por qué se puede sentir (*feel*) malestar físico en Cusco?
2. ¿Qué tipo de artesanía hacen en el Valle Sagrado de los Incas?
3. ¿Por qué es misterioso Machu Picchu?

C. Y ahora, Uds. En parejas, preparen un resumen de este segmento de *Salu2*, contando lo que hizo este turista e incluyendo algo interesante que vio o aprendió en cada sitio. También deben decir lo que más le gustó a él.

MODELO: Primero fue a la ciudad de Cusco. Allí...

Antes de leer

¿Es el turismo un sector económico muy importante en su ciudad o estado?

Lectura cultural: La República Dominicana

El turismo en la República Dominicana

El turismo es el sector económico más importante de la República Dominicana. Es un país que ofrece lugares de interés para cualquier[a] visitante: bosques,[b] parques nacionales, ríos, lagos, playas, ciudades y zonas rurales. Uno de los destinos turísticos más populares es Punta Cana, al este del país. Allí se puede disfrutar de[c] un clima tropical y de bellas[d] playas de arena[e] blanca y fina. Santo Domingo, la capital del país, tiene una hermosa[f] zona colonial con museos, casas antiguas y otros monumentos históricos. En 1990, fue reconocida[g] como Patrimonio Cultural de la Humanidad[h] por la UNESCO.

[a]*any* [b]*forests* [c]*disfrutar... enjoy* [d]*beautiful* [e]*sand* [f]*beautiful* [g]*recognized* [h]*Patrimonio... World Cultural Heritage site*

Un grupo de merengueros dominicanos

En **otros** países hispanos

- **En todo el mundo hispanohablante** En muchos países hispanos, y no solo en los países tropicales, hay playas maravillosas.[a] El Uruguay, la Argentina y Chile tienen costas fabulosas sin estar en el trópico.

- **En España** La industria del turismo es un importante motor[b] de la economía española. España es el cuarto[c] país del mundo receptor de turistas extranjeros, después de China, Francia y los Estados Unidos.

- **En los Estados Unidos** Gran parte del actual[d] territorio estadounidense fue antes territorio español. Así que podría[e] visitar lugares históricos en Florida, Texas, California, etcétera, para saber de la historia del mundo hispano... ¡sin salir de este país!

[a]*wonderful* [b]*engine* [c]*fourth* [d]*present-day* [e]*Así... So you could*

COMPRENSIÓN

1. ¿Cuáles son dos de los lugares turísticos importantes en la República Dominicana?
2. ¿Qué país hispanohablante está muy alto en la lista de países receptores de turistas?
3. ¿Por qué se puede decir que en los Estados Unidos es muy importante la presencia histórica de los países hispanos?
4. ¿En qué países hispanos no tropicales hay playas fabulosas?
5. ¿Qué es el merengue?

Un símbolo dominicano: El merengue

El merengue es un tipo de música de origen dominicano. Sin embargo, se conoce y se baila en todo el mundo hispano. Empezó a tocarse[a] con instrumentos de cuerda,[b] pero se incorporó el acordeón (de influencia europea), el güiro[c] (de origen taíno) y la tambora[d] (de origen africano). Hoy se incluyen el piano y los instrumentos de viento.

[a]*Empezó... It was first played* [b]*string* [c]*percussion instrument made of the gourd of the calabash tree* [d]*bass drum*

Y ahora, Uds.

Escojan un destino turístico en los Estados Unidos o en su país de origen e indiquen todas las razones para visitarlo, incluyendo el clima y un poco de su historia.

Del mundo hispano

Antes de leer

En la **Nota cultural** (pág. 237) de este capítulo se describen varios tipos de turismo, incluyendo el aventurismo. ¿A Ud. le interesa esta forma de turismo? ¿Por qué? En su opinión, ¿cómo son las personas que practican este estilo de viajar? ¿Conoce a algunos «aventuristas»?

Vocabulario para leer

aventurarse	to venture out
la belleza	beauty
descubrir	to discover
desconocido/a	unknown
disfrutar de	to enjoy
encontrar (encuentro)	to find
salvaje	wild, untamed

Lectura: I love viajes

Norte de África en 4x4[a]
Explora el Marruecos[b] más desconocido[c] y aventúrate[d] en 4x4 entre las dunas del Sahara. Descubre oasis perdidos[e] en lo más profundo[f] del desierto y disfruta de una flora que no esperarías[g] encontrar en estas latitudes. ¡Pon rumbo a[h] la aventura!

Tierra del Fuego
Lugar de belleza única con sus nevados picos[i], montañas, bosques[j] y maravillosos lagos. Ushuaia es la ciudad más al sur del mundo. Tierra del Fuego es una isla de belleza extrema que une[k] el Pacífico y el Atlántico. Parajes vírgenes[l] por explorar.

Safari por África
El espectacular parque natural del delta del Okavango (Botsuana) es una gran concentración de animales salvajes. Visita las Cataratas[m] Victoria (en Zimbabue) donde observarás[n] la cortina[o] de agua más caudalosa[p] del mundo. ¡Refréscate![q]

[a]*four-wheel drive* [b]*Morocco* [c]*unknown* [d]*venture out, go exploring* [e]*lost* [f]lo... *the deepest part* [g]no... *you wouldn't expect* [h]¡Pon... *Get ready for* [i]nevados... *snowy peaks* [j]*forests* [k]conecta [l]Parajes... *Virgin expanses, territories* [m]*Falls* [n]vas a observar [o]*curtain* [p]más... *fastest flowing* [q]*Cool off!*

Comprensión

A. ¡Sea agente de viajes! ¿Adónde deben ir de viaje las siguientes personas? Dé una recomendación lógica para cada caso, explicando por qué hace esa sugerencia. Use **Le recomiendo...** o **Les recomiendo...** , según el caso.

MODELO: **El profesor Legrán:** «Tengo todo el verano para viajar. Quiero escaparme del calor de Nuevo México en el verano y visitar lugares remotos.» ⟶ Le recomiendo la Tierra del Fuego, porque allí no hace calor y está en el extremo sur de Sudamérica. Hay montañas, lagos y bosques allí. También hay una ciudad interesante.

1. **Los Sres. Ávila:** «Queremos viajar a un lugar cálido (*warm*) y seco (*dry*) durante el invierno.»
2. **El Sr. Sorkin:** «A mí me gusta observar los animales, pero solo los he visto (*I've seen*) en mi estado. Este año quiero ver animales exóticos en un lugar diferente.»
3. **Alejandra:** «Conozco Norteamérica, Europa y África. Para mis próximas vacaciones, quiero visitar un continente totalmente nuevo para mí.»
4. **Jorge y Jimena:** «Somos ecologistas, especialistas en la flora tropical. Pero para estas vacaciones queremos algo diferente.»

B. Preferencias personales. En parejas, hagan y contesten las siguientes preguntas sobre los destinos turísticos que Uds. prefieren y conocen.

1. De los tres destinos que sugiere (*suggests*) la lectura, ¿cuál es el más atractivo para ti? ¿Por qué? ¿Cuál es la mejor estación del año para visitar ese lugar? ¿Por qué?
2. ¿Hay algún lugar de los tres destinos que no te gustaría visitar? ¿Por qué?
3. ¿Qué otros lugares conoces o puedes nombrar donde se pueda (*one can*) hacer el mismo tipo de turismo de los destinos mencionados en los anuncios?

Las actividades de Arturo y David, de ayer y hoy

Antes de escuchar

Por lo general, ¿qué hace Ud. en su tiempo libre (*free time*)? ¿Qué actividades le gusta hacer cuando va a la playa? ¿y cuando va al centro de su ciudad?

Vocabulario para escuchar

¡No me digas que... !	Don't tell me that . . . !
apagado/a	turned off
¿De veras?	Really?
corriendo	running (in a hurry)

Después de escuchar

A. **¿Qué pasó ayer?** Conteste las siguientes preguntas según la conversación telefónica para decir lo que hicieron ayer unos amigos dominicanos.

1. ¿Qué hicieron David y Paula?
2. ¿Qué hicieron Arturo y Cristina?
3. ¿Cuál de los cuatros amigos hizo la actividad más relajada (*relaxing*)?

B. **¿Qué va a pasar hoy?** ¿Cierto o falso? Corrija las oraciones falsas.

	CIERTO	FALSO
1. Arturo y Cristina no quieren salir con David y Paula.	☐	☐
2. Hace viento hoy.	☐	☐
3. Van a la playa en coche.	☐	☐
4. No van a llevar nada de comer.	☐	☐

PRODUCCIÓN PERSONAL

¡Ahora, yo!

A. Use de modelo las preguntas y respuestas de la página 233 de este capítulo para hablar de sus vacaciones favoritas.

B. Haga un fotomontaje con voz en off (*voiceover*) sobre un destino turístico. Puede ser un destino que Ud. ya conoce o uno que le gustaría visitar.

A ESCRIBIR
Un ensayo sobre el verano pasado

¿Qué hizo Ud. el verano pasado? ¿Tomó vacaciones o solo trabajó?

Preparar

Paso 1. En parejas, hagan una lista de las preguntas básicas que se pueden hacer para hablar de lo que hicieron el verano pasado.

Paso 2. Ahora usen esas preguntas para entrevistarse mutuamente, buscando detalles interesantes, como por ejemplo, lo que más les gustó del verano y lo que menos les gustó.

Paso 3. Con esa información, escriba un ensayo individual sobre cómo pasaron el verano. Hay más ayuda en Connect.

Más ideas para su portafolio

- Haga una lista de seis palabras que Ud. asocia con la palabra **vacaciones**.
- Incluya una imagen de unas vacaciones memorables, explicando qué hizo durante ese tiempo.
- Ponga la foto de un lugar que le gustaría conocer y diga qué cosas se ven y se hacen allí típicamente.
- Si ha estado jugando (*have been playing*) Practice Spanish: Study Abroad, en Quest 5 Ud. fue a un mercado al aire libre en Colombia y tuvo que regatear (*had to haggle*). En parejas, conversen sobre la costumbre de regatear. ¿Dónde se hace típicamente? ¿Es aceptable regatear en el país donde viven Uds.? ¿En qué situaciones es regatear aceptable (o incluso esperado)? Luego, hagan una lista de instrucciones para una persona que quiera aprender a regatear.

Sugerencia: You are now ready to play Quest 5 in **Practice Spanish: Study Abroad (www.mhpractice.com).**

EN RESUMEN En este capítulo

LEARNSMART

Visit **www.connectspanish.com** to practice the vocabulary and grammar points covered in this chapter.

AFTER STUDYING THIS CHAPTER I CAN. . .

☐ talk about travel, transportation, and vacations (234–236)

☐ understand and use pronouns to explain *to* or *for who(m)* an action is done (241–243)

☐ use **gustar** and other verbs to talk about likes and dislikes in more detail (246–247)

☐ talk about actions in the past with many types of verbs (251–253)

☐ recognize/describe at least 2–3 aspects of Dominican culture

Gramática en breve

21. Indirect Object Pronouns; *Dar* and *decir*

me, te, le, nos, os, les

dar: **doy, das, da, damos, dais, dan**
decir: **digo, dices, dice, decimos, decís, dicen**

22. *Gustar*

(no) *indirect object pronoun* + **gusta** + *singular subject*

(no) *indirect object pronoun* + **gustan** + *plural subject*

Would like: **gustaría**

23. Preterite of Regular Verbs and of *dar, hacer, ir, and ser*

-ar Verbs: **-é, -aste, -ó, -amos, -asteis, -aron**
-er/-ir Verbs: **-í, -iste, -ió, -imos, -steis, -ieron**

dar: **di diste, dio, dimos, disteis, dieron**
hacer: **hice, hiciste, hizo, hicimos, hicisteis, hicieron**
ir/ser: **fui, fuiste, fue, fuimos, fuisteis, fueron**

Vocabulario

Los verbos

contar (**cuento**)	to tell; to narrate
dar (**doy**)	to give
decir (**digo**) (**i**)	to say; to tell
encantar (*like* **gustar**)	to like very much; to love
entregar (**gu**)	to hand in

explicar (**qu**)	to explain
gustar	to be pleasing
interesar (*like* **gustar**)	to interest (*someone*)
mostrar (**muestro**)	to show
odiar	to hate
ofrecer (**ofrezco**)	to offer
preguntar	to ask (*a question*)
prestar	to lend
prometer	to promise
recomendar (**recomiendo**)	to recommend
regalar	to give (*as a gift*)

Repaso: escribir, hablar, mandar, pedir (pido) (i), servir (sirvo) (i)

De viaje

de viaje	on a trip, traveling
la aduana	customs (*at a border*)
el aeropuerto	airport
el/la agente	agent
el asiento	seat
el/la asistente de vuelo	flight attendant
el autobús	bus
el avión	airplane
el barco	boat, ship
el billete (*Sp.*) / el boleto (*L.A.*)	ticket
de ida	one-way ticket
de ida y vuelta	round-trip ticket
electrónico	e-ticket
la cola	line (*of people*)
el control de seguridad	security (check)
el crucero	cruise (ship)
la demora	delay
el destino	destination
el equipaje	baggage, luggage
la escala	stop
la estación	station
de autobuses	bus station
de trenes	train station
la llegada	arrival
la maleta	suitcase
el maletero	porter
el medio de transporte	means of transportation
el mostrador	counter
la parada	stop
el pasaje	fare, price (*of a transportation ticket*)
el/la pasajero/a	passenger
el pasillo	aisle
la puerta de embarque	boarding gate
el puerto	port

el puesto	place (*in line*)
la sala de espera	waiting room
la sala de fumar / de fumadores	smoking area
la salida	departure
la tarjeta (postal)	(post)card
la tarjeta de embarque	boarding pass
la ventanilla	small window (*on a plane*)
el vuelo	flight

Cognados: el/la agente, la cabina, el pasaporte, el/la piloto, el tren

Repaso: el viaje

anunciar	to announce
bajarse (de)	to get down (from); to get off (of) (*a vehicle*)
facturar el equipaje	to check baggage
fumar	to smoke
guardar (un puesto)	to save (a place [*in line*])
hacer cola	to stand in line
hacer escala/parada	to make a stop
hacer la(s) maleta(s)	to pack one's suitcase(s)
ir al extranjero	to go abroad
ir en...	to go/travel by . . .
autobús	bus
avión	plane
barco	boat, ship
tren	train
pasar por	to go/pass through
el control de seguridad	security (check)
la aduana	customs
quejarse (de)	to complain (about)
subir (a)	to go up; to get on (*a vehicle*)
viajar	to travel
volar (vuelo) en avión	to fly, go by plane

Repaso: hacer un viaje, llegar (gu), salir

De vacaciones

de vacaciones	on vacation
el bloqueador solar	sunscreen
la camioneta	station wagon; van
el *camping*	campground
la foto(grafía)	photo(graph)
el mar	sea
la montaña	mountain
el océano	ocean
la tienda (de campaña)	tent

Repaso: la playa, el sol

estar de vacaciones	to be on vacation
hacer *camping*	to go camping
ir de vacaciones a...	to go on vacation to/in . . .
nadar	to swim
pasar las vacaciones en...	to spend one's vacation in . . .
sacar (qu) fotos	to take photos
salir de vacaciones	to leave on vacation
tomar el sol	to sunbathe
tomar unas vacaciones	to take a vacation

Otros sustantivos

el chiste	joke
la flor	flower
la gente	people
la historia	story

Los adjetivos

atrasado/a (*with* estar)	late
juntos/as	together

Palabras adicionales

a tiempo	on time
me gustaría (mucho)...	I would (really) like . . .
muchísimo	an awful lot
(para) nada	at all
por	through; for

Vocabulario personal

9

Los días festivos° Los... *Holidays*

www.connectspanish.com

En este capítulo

El Carnaval de Santiago de Cuba, que se celebra en julio, con música, bailes y desfiles (*parades*)

CUBA

11.5 (y medio) millones de habitantes

- La isla de Cuba está a solo 150 kilómetros (90 millas) de la costa sur de Florida.

- Cuba es un destino turístico importante para europeos y canadienses.

- Es un país con una tradición musical impresionante y que también se destaca[a] en el béisbol y en la danza.

[a]se... *excels*

ESTADOS UNIDOS (Florida)

Golfo de México

Estrecho de Florida

OCÉANO ATLÁNTICO

ISLAS BAHAMAS

La Habana

CUBA

•Camagüey

| 0 | 100 | 200 Millas |
| 0 | 100 | 200 Kilómetros |

Mar Caribe

Santiago de Cuba

HAITÍ

JAMAICA

- ¿Cuáles son las celebraciones más importantes de su país?

- ¿Qué días celebran más Ud. y su familia? ¿Cómo los celebran Uds.?

- ¿Tuvo Ud.[a] una fiesta en su último cumpleaños? ¿Quién se la dio[b]?

[a]¿Tuvo... *Did you have* [b]se... *gave it for you*

CECILIA FIGUEROA MARTÍN CONTESTA LAS PREGUNTAS.

- En Puerto Rico celebramos las fiestas de los Estados Unidos: el Día de los Presidentes, el Cuatro de Julio, el Día de Gracias, la Navidad. Y luego hay las fiestas patronales[a] de cada ciudad.

- Para nosotros la Navidad es un día muy importante de reunión familiar. Aunque,[b] en realidad,[c] nosotros festejamos[d] en Nochebuena.[e] La familia se reúne,[f] vienen amigos, comemos, bebemos, cantamos, bailamos...

- ¡Sí! Mi marido me hizo una fiesta muy grande para mi cumpleaños. Invitó a toda la familia y a nuestros amigos. ¡Estuvimos[g] de fiesta hasta las 4 cuatro de la mañana!

[a]fiestas... *holidays of the patron saints* [b]*Although* [c]en... *actually* [d]nosotros... *we celebrate* [e]*Christmas Eve* [f]se... *gets together* [g]*We were*

Una fiesta de cumpleaños para Javier

¡FELICITACIONES!

el anfitrión

la anfitriona

Sí, la fiesta es en casa de Javier.

Jorge

Melisa

bailar

Carmen

Pedro

los regalos

Javier

las tarjetas

los refrescos

Javier

el champán

las botanas / las tapas

el pastel de cumpleaños

las velas

20 años

You can hear the pronunciation of theme vocabulary words and phrases in the Connect eBook.

Para comer y beber

las botanas (*Mex.*) / las tapas	appetizers

Otros sustantivos

el anfitrión / la anfitriona	host (*of an event*)
el cumpleaños	birthday
el día festivo	holiday
el invitado / la invitada	guest

Los verbos

celebrar	to celebrate
comer/beber (demasiado)	to eat/drink (too much)
cumplir años	to have a birthday
darle una fiesta (a alguien)	to give (someone) a party
divertirse (me divierto) (i)	to have a good time, enjoy oneself
faltar (a)	to be absent (from), not attend

gastar	to spend (*money*)
hacerle una fiesta (a alguien)	to give (someone) a party; to have a party (for someone)
invitar	to invite
pasarlo bien/mal	to have a good/bad time
regalar	to give (*as a gift*)
reunirse (me reúno) con*	to get together (with)
ser + en + *place*	to take place in/at (*a place*)
¿Dónde es la fiesta?	Where is the party (at)?

Palabras adicionales

¡Felicitaciones!	Congratulations!
gracias por + *noun*	thanks for + *noun*
Gracias por el regalo.	Thanks for the present.
gracias por + *inf.*	thanks for + *verb* (-ing)
Gracias por invitarme.	Thanks for inviting me.

*Note the accent that occurs on -u- in forms of **reunirse** when the weak vowel -u- is stressed: **me reúno, te reúnes, se reúne, nos reunimos, os reunís, se reúnen.** This pattern is like that of stem-changing verbs (that is, the stem vowel changes when it is stressed.)

¡OJO!

Only the highlighted items are active vocabulary. Learn the Spanish names of the holidays that you need to talk about your activities and those of your family and write them in **Vocabulario personal** at the end of the chapter.

Los días festivos hispanos

el Día de los Reyes Magos	Day of the Magi (Three Kings) (Jan. 6)
la Pascua	Easter
la Pascua judía	Passover
el Día de la Raza	Columbus Day (Oct. 12)
el Día de los Muertos	Day of the Dead (Nov. 2)
el Janucá	Hanukkah
la Nochebuena	Christmas Eve
la Navidad	Christmas
la Nochevieja	New Year's Eve
la quinceañera	young woman's fifteenth birthday party

Los días festivos estadounidenses

el Día de San Patricio, el Cinco de Mayo, el Cuatro de Julio, el Día de (Acción de) Gracias

Note that **el Día de la Raza** corresponds to *Columbus Day* in the U.S. In some areas it is called *Hispanic Awareness Day.*

Algo sobre...

las parrandas cubanas

Una parranda en Remedios, Cuba

Las parrandas son grandes fiestas navideñas[a] típicas de los pueblos y ciudades de una región de la Cuba central. Las más famosas son las[b] de Remedios. La costumbre de las parrandas data del siglo XVIII.[c] Cada barrio[d] de una ciudad monta[e] una parranda y hay una competición entre los barrios para ver cuál es la mejor.[f] Estas fiestas incluyen fuegos artificiales y disfraces,[g] como las fiestas de carnaval.

¿En qué fiestas de su país hay fuegos artificiales? ¿y disfraces?

[a]*Christmas* [b]*those* [c]*data... dates back to the 18th century* [d]*neighborhood* [e]*throws, organizes* [f]*la... the best one (parranda)* [g]*fuegos... fireworks and costumes*

Así se dice

hacer una fiesta = hacer un juerga (*Sp.*), armar (un) bochinche (*Cuba*)
la quinceañera = la fiesta de quince años
el pastel = la torta, la tarta, el queque (*L.A.*)

la Pascua = la Pascua Florida
el Día de los Muertos = el Día de los Difuntos
la Navidad = las Pascuas

The figure of **Santa Claus** is a familiar one in Hispanic countries. That is what he is called in Mexico and Puerto Rico. In other parts of the Spanish-speaking world, he is more often called **Papá Noel.**

Comunicación

A. Una fiesta de cumpleaños para Javier. Conteste las siguientes preguntas sobre el dibujo de la página 268.

1. ¿Qué tipo de fiesta es? ¿Dónde es la fiesta?
2. ¿Quiénes son los anfitriones de la fiesta? ¿Quién es el invitado de honor?
3. ¿Qué hay de comer y de beber? ¿Qué hacen los invitados?
4. ¿Qué le dan los invitados a Javier, además de (*besides*) regalos?
5. ¿Quién falta a la fiesta? ¿Quién lo invita por teléfono?
6. ¿Qué le van a decir todos a Javier cuando corte (*cuts*) el pastel?
7. ¿Qué cree Ud. que Javier les va a decir a Carmen y Pedro después de la fiesta?

B. Asociaciones. ¿Qué palabras asocia Ud. con las siguientes ideas? Dé por lo menos (*at least*) dos palabras asociadas con cada idea.

1. un cumpleaños
2. una fiesta
3. los fuegos artificiales (*fireworks*)
4. un árbol (*tree*)
5. los regalos
6. una comida grande

C. Definiciones

Paso 1. Dé las palabras definidas.

1. Algo de comer o beber que se sirve en las fiestas.
2. El día en que, por tradición, algunas personas visitan los cementerios.
3. La fiesta de una muchacha que cumple 15 años.
4. Lo que uno le dice a un amigo que celebra algo.
5. Una fiesta de los judíos (*Jewish people*) que dura 8 días.

Paso 2. Ahora, en parejas, creen (*create*) por lo menos dos definiciones como las del **Paso 1.** La clase va a adivinar (*guess*) la palabra definida.

Vocabulario útil	
el fin	end
el nacimiento	birth

Nota **cultural**

Los días festivos importantes del mundo hispano

Algunas fiestas se celebran en casi todos los países hispanos.

- **La Nochebuena**
  Esta fiesta se celebra con una gran cena en casa. Luego los hispanos cristianos van a la Misa del Gallo,[a] un servicio religioso que se celebra a medianoche. En algunos países, los niños reciben la visita de Papá Noel, quien les deja[b] regalos.
- **La Nochevieja**
  Es una ocasión para grandes celebraciones, tanto entre familia como en lugares públicos. En España y otros países algunos siguen la tradición de comer una uva[c] por cada una de las doce campanadas[d] de medianoche.
- **El Día de los Reyes Magos**
  Esta fiesta se celebra en muchos países el 6 de enero. Los Reyes Magos son los encargados[e] de traer regalos. Muchos niños ponen sus zapatos en la ventana o balcón antes de acostarse la noche del 5 de enero. Los Reyes llegan en camellos durante la noche y llenan los zapatos con regalos y dulces.
- **El Día de la Independencia**
  Todos los países latino americanos celebran el día de la declaración de su independencia de España. Por ejemplo, Cuba celebra su independencia el 10 de octubre; México, el 16 de septiembre; Bolivia, el 6 de agosto; el Paraguay, el 15 de mayo y El Salvador, el 15 de septiembre.

[a]Misa... *Midnight Mass* [b]les... *leaves ... for them* [c]*grape* [d]*bell strokes* [e]los... *in charge*

Unos bailarines (*dancers*) durante las celebraciones del Día de los Reyes Magos, en La Habana, Cuba

- **La quinceañera**
  Esta fiesta, celebrada en muchos países latinoamericanos y en este país, celebra la llegada de las niñas a los 15 años, es decir, su transición de niña a mujer. La familia y los amigos de la joven le dan una gran fiesta, en la que[f] ella se viste de largo.[g] A veces se celebra una misa especial, pero siempre hay una cena y una fiesta con música para bailar.

¿Cuáles de estas fiestas se celebran en su familia? Si no se celebra ninguna de ellas, ¿cuáles son las fiestas familiares de más importancia para Ud.?

[f]la... *which* [g]se... *dresses up (in a gown)*

Vocabulario útil	
el árbol	tree
el barrio	neighborhood
la corona	wreath
el desfile	parade
el globo	balloon

D. Hablando de fiestas

Paso 1. ¿Cuáles de estas fiestas le gustan a Ud.? ¿Cuáles no le gustan? Explique por qué. Compare sus respuestas con las (*those*) de sus compañeros de clase.

MODELO: el Cuatro de Julio → Me gusta mucho el Cuatro de Julio porque vemos fuegos artificiales (*fireworks*) en el parque y...

1. el Cuatro de Julio
2. el Día de (Acción de) Gracias
3. la Nochevieja
4. la Navidad

Paso 2. Ahora piense en su fiesta favorita. Puede ser una de la lista del **Paso 1** o una del **Vocabulario útil** de la página 269. Piense en cómo celebra Ud. esa fiesta, para explicárselo (*explain it*) luego a la clase. Debe pensar en lo siguiente.

- los preparativos que Ud. hace de antemano (*beforehand*)
- la ropa especial que lleva
- las comidas o bebidas especiales que compra o hace
- el lugar donde se celebra
- la decoración especial que hay o que Ud. pone

Paso 3. ¿Hay algún día festivo que debe existir, según Uds., pero que no existe? En grupos, inventen por lo menos dos días festivos: **el Día de...** Presenten sus días festivos originales a la clase y expliquen cómo se deben celebrar.

Las emociones y los estados afectivos° estados... *emotional states*

llorar

discutir con (alguien) por/sobre (algo)

enojarse con (alguien) por (algo)

ponerse rojo/a

Otros verbos

olvidar	to forget
portarse bien/mal	to (mis)behave
quejarse de	to complain about
recordar (recuerdo)	to remember
reírse* (me río) (i) (de)	to laugh (about)
sonreír* (sonrío) (i)	to smile

Para expresar *to become/get* y *to feel*

ponerse + *adj.*	to become/get + *adj.*
sentirse (me siento) (i) + *adj.*	to feel + *adj.*

Adjetivos: alegre, contento/a, enojado/a (*angry, upset*), **feliz** (*pl.* **felices**) (*happy*), **furioso/a, nervioso/a, tranquilo/a** (*calm*), **triste**

Comunicación

A. Asociaciones

Paso 1. ¿Con qué verbos asocia Ud. las siguientes cosas y situaciones? Use verbos de **Las emociones...** o cualquier (*any*) otro.

1. ver un bebé
2. una situación injusta
3. un número de teléfono nuevo
4. algo memorable que pasó
5. tener un examen importante
6. un chiste muy bueno
7. un perro muy joven
8. un desacuerdo (*disagreement*) con un amigo
9. conocer a una persona muy interesante
10. estar equivocado (*wrong*) en público / enfrente de una clase

---

*The verbs **reír** and **sonreír** are e → i stem-changing verbs. An accent is required on all present tense forms of these verbs (as well as on the infinitives) to show the breaking of dipthongs io, ie, ei by stressing the weak vowel i: (**son**)**río**, (**son**)**ríes**, (**son**)**ríe**, (**son**)**reímos**, (**son**)**reís**, (**son**)**ríen**. No accent mark is needed on the present participle, in which the i is not stressed: (**son**)**riendo**.*

Paso 2. Ahora, en parejas, digan las palabras o frases que Uds. asocian con los siguientes verbos o frases.

1. recordar
2. sonreír

3. ponerse nervioso/a
4. discutir con alguien

Nota **comunicativa**

Cómo enfatizar: *-ísimo*

To emphasize the quality described by an adjective or an adverb in English, you can put *very very* or *really really* before the word: *I tried very very hard. I really really like it.* This is expressed in Spanish by adding **-ísimo** to an adverb and **-ísimo/a(os/as)** to an adjective. You already know one adverb formed like this: **muchísimo.**

- If the word ends in a consonant, **-ísimo** is added to the singular form and any accents on the original word are dropped: **difícil → dificilísimo.**

  Estas tapas son **dificilísimas** de preparar.
  These appetizers are very, very hard to prepare.

- If the word ends in a vowel, that vowel is dropped before adding **-ísimo** and any accents on the original word are also dropped.

  tarde → tardísimo   rápida → rapidísima

- There are spelling changes when the final consonant is a **c, g,** or **z.** This is the same spelling change you have learned to make in the formal command and preterite forms of verbs that end in **-car, -gar,** and **-zar.**

  rico → riquísimo   largas → larguísimas
  feliz → felicísimo

You can use adjectives and adverbs formed in this way in **Comunicación B** and **C.**

Vocabulario útil

avergonzado/a
  embarrassed
de buen/mal humor
contento/a
feliz/triste
furioso/a
impaciente
nervioso/a
preocupado/a

B. Reacciones. ¿Cómo se pone o se siente Ud. en estas situaciones? Use los adjetivos y verbos que Ud. sabe y también algunas formas enfáticas (**-ísimo**). ¿Cuántas emociones puede Ud. describir?

MODELO: Llueve todo el día. → Me pongo / Me siento **triste/tristísima.**

1. Llueve el día de su cumpleaños.
2. Es Navidad. Alguien le hace un regalo carísimo.
3. Ud. quiere bañarse. No hay agua caliente.
4. Ud. está solo/a en casa una noche y oye un ruido.
5. Ud. da una fiesta en su apartamento. Los invitados están aburridísimos.
6. Ud. tiene un examen importantísimo pero no estudió nada la noche anterior (*before*).
7. Ud. cuenta un chiste pero nadie se ríe.
8. Ud. acaba de terminar un examen difícil. Cree que lo hizo muy mal.

C. ¿Cuándo... ?

Paso 1. En parejas, completen las siguientes oraciones con un lugar y una acción o situación, según su experiencia. Sigan el modelo.

MODELO: Me quejo en... (lugar) cuando... (acción o situación) →
  E1: Me quejo en **el aeropuerto** cuando **tengo que hacer cola... ¡y la cola es larguísima!**
  E2: Yo también, y también me quejo en **una tienda cuando tengo que esperar demasiado tiempo.**

1. Me quejo en... cuando...
2. Me río muchísimo en... cuando...
3. Sonrío en... cuando...
4. Lloro en... cuando...
5. Mis padres se enojan en... cuando... (Mis hijos... Mi esposo/a... Mi novio/a...)

6. Los niños se portan bien/malísimo en... cuando...
7. Las mascotas se portan bien/mal en... cuando...
8. Me pongo rojo/a en... cuando...

Paso 2. Ahora comparen sus respuestas con las (*those*) del resto de la clase. ¿En qué son similares o diferentes las respuestas de todos?

«De fiesta en fiesta» Segmento 1

Antes de mirar

Indique las religiones más representadas en su comunidad.

- ☐ el budismo
- ☐ el cristianismo
  - **a.** ☐ católicos
  - **b.** ☐ evangélicos
  - **c.** ☐ protestantes
  - **d.** ☐ otros
- ☐ el Islam
- ☐ el judaísmo

Este segmento

En este segmento Víctor y Ana presentan datos estadísticos sobre la afiliación religiosa de los hispanos estadounidenses y hablan de las fiestas que celebran. Luego Laura presenta un reportaje desde el Perú.

Mucha gente limeña (*from Lima*) participa en la procesión del Señor de los Milagros (*Our Lord of the Miracles*). Es una imagen de un Cristo crucificado (*Christ on the cross*) muy venerada (*worshipped*) por más de cinco siglos (*centuries*).

Vocabulario del segmento

de nuevo nos encontramos	here we are again	**el/la muchacho/a**	boy/girl
aunque	although	**el/la esclavo/a**	slave
el/la seguidor(a)	follower	**el muro**	wall
atraer	to attract	**el terremoto**	earthquake
la escuela	school	**asolar**	to devastate
conocido/a	known	**rendir (rindo) (i) culto**	to worship
la fe	faith	**caminar despacio**	to walk slowly
alrededor de	circa, about	**la mantilla**	lace veil

Estrategia

The following Christian holidays are mentioned in **Segmento 1.** You do not need to know any details about them, but this list will help you recognize their names when you hear them.

- **la Navidad** (the celebration of the birth of Christ)
- **la Semana Santa** (*Holy Week* = the week leading up to Easter Sunday)
- **el Viernes Santo** (*Good Friday* = the day Christ was crucified on the cross)
- **el Domingo de Pascua de Resurrección** (*Easter Sunday* = the celebration of Christ's resurrection)

Después de mirar

A. ¿Está claro? Empareje los siguientes porcentajes con la explicación apropiada.

PORCENTAJES Y FECHAS

1. 60% (por ciento)
2. 22%
3. 12%
4. 1%

FRASES

a. población hispana cristiana pero no católica
b. población hispana religiosa pero no cristiana
c. población hispana católica
d. población hispana sin afiliación religiosa

B. Un poco más. Conteste las siguientes preguntas.

1. ¿En qué mes se celebra el Mes Morado? ¿Cuál es el origen del nombre de la celebración?
2. ¿Quién pintó la imagen del Señor de los Milagros? ¿En qué año?
3. En Panamá, ¿qué representan las fechas 3/11 y 28/11?

C. Y ahora, Uds. En grupos, hablen de las fiestas más importantes que se celebran en su ciudad o estado. Por ejemplo, ¿hay grandes celebraciones para el Día de la Independencia (el Cuatro de Julio)? ¿Cómo lo celebra su familia? ¿Qué otros días de fiesta se celebran en su ciudad o estado?

GRAMÁTICA

¿Recuerda Ud.?

You already know the irregular preterite stem and endings for **hacer**. All verbs presented in **Gramática 24** have irregular stems used with the same preterite endings as **hacer**. Review those endings by completing these forms.

1. yo: hic_____   **2.** nosotros: hic_____   **3.** Ud.: hiz_____   **4.** ellos: hic_____

Grammar Tutorial 24
connect
|SPANISH
www.connectspanish.com

24 Talking About the Past (Part 2)
Irregular Preterites

Gramática en acción: ¿Qué pasó en la fiesta de fin de año en casa de Sofía y Paco?

Mire con atención los verbos en rojo. Son formas del pretérito. ¿Puede Ud. dar el infinitivo?

1. ¿Quién estuvo hablando por teléfono?
2. ¿Quién dio la fiesta?
3. ¿Quién no pudo ir a la fiesta?
4. ¿Quién puso su copa sobre la televisión?
5. ¿Quién hizo mucho ruido?
6. ¿Quién no quiso beber más?
7. ¿Quién probablemente tuvo que irse temprano?

¿Y Ud.?

1. ¿Estuvo Ud. alguna vez en una fiesta de fin de año como esta? (**Estuve...**)
2. ¿Tuvo que irse temprano de la fiesta? (**Tuve...**) ¿O se quedó hasta medianoche? (**Me quedé...**)
3. ¿Recuerda qué ropa se puso para la fiesta? (**Me puse...**)

Irregular Forms / Las formas irregulares

1. Additional Irregular Forms

You have already learned the irregular preterite forms of **hacer**. The verbs to the right are also irregular in the preterite, like **hacer**.

• Their stem (shown in red) is irregular.
• They use the same preterite endings as **hacer**.

Only the first and third person singular endings are irregular (they have no accent marks). The verb **estar** is conjugated for you. The other verbs listed are conjugated like **estar**.

estar	
estuve	estuvimos
estuviste	estuvisteis
estuvo	estuvieron

¡OJO!
There are no accents on -e and -o.

estar:	estuv-
poder:	pud-
poner:	pus-
querer:	quis-
saber:	sup-
tener:	tuv-
venir:	vin-

Las terminaciones irregulares	
-e	-imos
-iste	-isteis
-o	-ieron

2. Preterite of *decir* and *traer*

The irregular preterite stems of these two verbs end in **-j-**. They use the same endings as the verbs on page 274, except that the **-i-** of the third person plural is omitted: **dijeron, trajeron**.

decir: dij- ⎫
traer: traj- ⎬ **-e, -iste, -o, -imos, -isteis, -eron**
　　　　　 ⎭

---

3. Preterite of *hay*: *Hubo*

Hay (*There is/are*) comes from the infinitive **haber**. Its preterite form is **hubo** = *there was/were*.

Hubo un accidente ayer en el centro.
There was an accident yesterday downtown.

Hubo muchas fiestas de Navidad el año pasado.
There were a lot of Christmas parties last year.

Changes in Meaning / Cambios de significado

The following Spanish verbs have an English equivalent in the preterite tense that is different from that of the infinitive.

Infinitive	Present Tense	Preterite Meaning
saber =	to know (*facts, information*)	to find out, learn
	Ya lo **sé**. *I already know it.*	Lo **supe** ayer. *I found it out (learned it) yesterday.*
conocer =	to know, be familiar with (*people, places*)	to meet (*for the first time*)
	Ya la **conozco**. *I already know her.*	La **conocí** ayer. *I met her yesterday.*
querer =	to want	to try
	Quiero hacerlo hoy. *I want to do it today.*	**Quise** hacerlo ayer. *I tried to do it yesterday.*
no querer =	not to want	to refuse
	No quiero hacerlo hoy. *I don't want to do it today.*	**No quise** hacerlo anteayer. *I refused to do it the day before yesterday.*

Práctica y comunicación

A. La última Nochevieja.

Paso 1. Autoprueba. Dé la forma indicada del pretérito.

1. yo: saber
2. ellos: tener
3. tú: venir
4. él: poner
5. nosotros: querer
6. Ud.: poder
7. ellos: decir
8. haber

> **Summary of Irregular Preterites**
>
> Endings: **-e, -iste, -o, -imos, -isteis, -ieron**
> Irregular stems: **dij-, estuv-, hic-, pud-, pus-, quis-, sup-, traj-, tuv-, vin-**

Paso 2. Ahora diga lo que Ud. hizo o no hizo el último día del año pasado. Haga oraciones completas con la forma apropiada del pretérito.

MODELO: 1. (no) querer hacer algo / nada especial ese día →
　　　　　Quise hacer **algo** especial ese día. **No quise** hacer **nada** especial ese día.

El último día del año pasado, (yo)...

1. (no) querer hacer algo / nada especial ese día
2. (no) dar una fiesta en mi casa / apartamento
3. (no) estar con unos buenos amigos
4. (no) tener que hacer algo / nada de comida

(Continúa.)

5. (no) conocer a alguien / nadie interesante

6. (no) decirle ¡Feliz Año Nuevo! a alguien / nadie

7. (no) poder quedarme despierto/a (*awake*) hasta la medianoche

8. (no) ponerse ropa elegante esa noche

Paso 3. Ahora, en parejas, túrnense para hacer y contestar preguntas basadas en las oraciones del **Paso 2**. Luego díganle a la clase lo que tienen en común.

MODELO: E1: ¿**Quisiste** hacer algo especial ese día?

E2: No, no **quise** hacer nada especial. ¿Y tú?

E1: Yo tampoco. ⟶

Ninguno de nosotros **quiso** hacer nada especial ese día.

B. En una fiesta. ¿Cómo se dice en inglés?

1. Conocí al primo cubano de una amiga.

2. Quise abrir una botella de champán.

3. Supe algo interesante sobre los anfitriones.

4. No quise bailar. ¡Bailo malísimo!

C. Una Nochebuena en Santiago de Cuba

Paso 1. Complete la siguiente narración sobre la celebración de la Nochebuena de una familia cubana de la ciudad de Santiago, al sur de la isla de Cuba. Habla Manuel, el padre de la familia. Use el pretérito de los verbos.

Estrategia

Not all of the verbs in this story are irregular in the preterite. As you conjugate each infinitive, first ask yourself if its preterite is regular or irregular.

El lechón (*suckling pig*) con moros (= frijoles) y cristianos (= arroz)

El año pasado mi esposa y yo celebramos la Nochebuena en casa con toda la familia. (Estar[1]) con nosotros mi primo Andrés, de la Florida, quien (quedarse[2]) con nosotros toda la semana. (Venir[3]) mis padres, mis suegros,[a] hermanos y cuñados[b] con sus hijos. También (*nosotros*: invitar[4]) a nuestros vecinos[c] de toda la vida,[d] los Benjumea. Pero ellos no (poder[5]) asistir porque (irse[6]) a La Habana para estar con su hija, que (tener[7]) un niño en noviembre.

Mi esposa (preparar[8]) lechón asado, moros y cristianos, yuca y tostones.[e] ¡Qué sabroso todo! Mi cuñado (traer[9]) turrón[f] español y cava.[g] A las 10:30, mi hermana (decir[10]) que era[h] hora de ir a la Misa del Gallo[i] y (llevar[11]) a los abuelos a la iglesia.[j] Los demás[k] no (querer[12]) ir y seguimos armando bochinche hasta que (volver[13]) los otros. Todo (ir[14]) bien chévere.[l] Como regalo de Navidad, mi primo Andrés me (dar[15]) un álbum con fotos y cartas de mis parientes en la Florida y Nueva Jersey. Yo (ponerse[16]) tan emocionado[m] que (llorar[18]).

[a]*in-laws* [b]*brothers- and sisters-in-law* [c]*neighbors* [d]*de... long-time (lit., of one's whole life)* [e]*fried plantains* [f]*sweet Christmas candy* [g]*Spanish champagne* [h]*it was* [i]*Misa... Midnight Mass* [j]*church* [k]*Los... The others* [l]*great* [m]*touched, emotional*

Paso 2. Comprensión

1. ¿Qué tuvo de especial la Nochebuena del año pasado para Manuel?

2. ¿Por qué no pudieron asistir los Benjumea?

3. ¿Quiénes fueron a la Misa del Gallo?

4. ¿Qué comieron y bebieron todos?

Prdc. A, Paso 1: Answers: 1. supe 2. tuvieron 3. viniste 4. puso 5. quisimos 6. pudo 7. dijeron 8. hubo

Paso 3. Ahora complete las siguientes oraciones basadas en lo que pasó en la celebración de la pasada Navidad, Pascua judía u otra fiesta de importancia para su familia. Conjugue los verbos en el pretérito, añadiendo el sujeto y otra información apropiada.

MODELO: celebrar _____ (fiesta) en _____ (lugar) →
        Mi familia **celebró** la Nochebuena en casa de mis abuelos.

1. celebrar _____ (fiesta) en _____ (lugar)
2. querer asistir / (no) poder
3. ir _____ (servicio religioso) antes / después de cenar
4. comer _____ (platos) y beber _____ (bebidas)
5. ponerse muy emocionado/a porque _____
6. darle un regalo a _____ (persona)

D. **Hechos (Events) históricos.** Describan Uds. algunos hechos históricos, usando una palabra o frase de cada columna. Usen el pretérito de los verbos. Su profesor(a) los puede ayudar con los datos (information) que no saben.

en 1957 los rusos en 1969 los estadounidenses Adán y Eva George Washington los europeos los aztecas Stanley	**+** conocer estar poner saber traer	**+**	en Valley Forge con sus soldados a un hombre en la luna (moon) un satélite en el espacio por primera vez el significado (meaning) de un árbol especial a Livingston en África el caballo (horse) al Nuevo Mundo a Hernán Cortés en Tenochtitlán

E. **Intercambios**

Paso 1. Haga preguntas en el pretérito con los siguientes verbos. En el **Paso 2,** Ud. va a usar las preguntas para entrevistar a un compañero o una compañera de clase.

MODELO: conocer → ¿Cuándo **conociste** a tu mejor amigo/a?

1. conocer   3. estar   5. hacer
2. saber   4. tener   6. dar

Paso 2. En parejas, túrnense para hacer y contestar sus preguntas. Luego díganle a la clase algo que los/las dos tienen en común.

MODELO: conocer → Los dos **conocimos** a nuestros mejores amigos en la
        escuela secundaria.

F. **La última fiesta que Ud. dio**

Paso 1. Haga una lista de todos los detalles (details) que Ud. recuerda de la última fiesta a la que (which) fue. Puede ser una fiesta que Ud. organizó o que otra persona dio. Use los siguientes verbos: **conocer, dar, estar, invitar, organizar, poder, saber, ser, venir.**

MODELO: Di una fiesta para el cumpleaños de mi mejor amigo.
        Mi amigo Clark y yo organizamos la fiesta...

Paso 2. Ahora entreviste a un compañero o una compañera sobre la última fiesta que organizó él o ella. Haga preguntas con las palabras interrogativas y el pretérito.

Palabras interrogativas: ¿cuándo?, ¿dónde?, ¿quién?, ¿con quién?, ¿qué?, ¿por qué?

MODELOS: **¿Cuándo dieron** la fiesta?
        ¿Qué sirvieron de comer y beber?

Paso 3. Luego díganle a la clase dos detalles interesantes sobre las fiestas que Uds. organizaron.

¿Recuerda Ud.?

You learned in **Gramática 15 (Cap. 6)** to make a change in the **-ndo** form of **-ir** stem-changing verbs. That same change occurs in some forms of the preterite of that type of verb. Review the change in the present participle by completing the following forms.

1. pedir: p___diendo

2. dormir: d___rmiendo

You will learn about this change in the preterite in **Grámatica 25.**

Grammar Tutorial 25

connect |SPANISH
www.connectspanish.com

25 Talking About the Past (Part 3)
Preterite of Stem-changing Verbs

Gramática en acción: Una fiesta de quinceañera

Escoja las respuestas más lógicas para describir la fiesta de quinceañera de Lupe Carrasco. Al leer (*As you read*), mire con atención los verbos en rojo. Son formas del pretérito. ¿Puede Ud. dar el infinitivo de esos verbos?

1. Para su fiesta, Lupe se vistió con...
  ☐ un vestido blanco muy elegante.
  ☐ una camiseta y *bluejeans.*

2. Mientras Lupe cortaba[a] el pastel de cumpleaños, la madre de ella...
  ☐ empezó a llorar.
  ☐ se rio mucho.

3. Lupe pidió un deseo[b] al cortar[c] el pastel. Ella...
  ☐ les dijo a todos qué fue lo que pidió.
  ☐ prefirió guardarlo en secreto.

4. En la fiesta sirvieron...
  ☐ champán y refrescos.
  ☐ solo té y café.

5. Todos los invitados...
  ☐ se divirtieron mucho.
  ☐ se quejaron.

6. A las tres de la mañana, el último invitado
  ☐ se despidió.[d]
  ☐ se sonrió.

[a]Mientras... *While she was cutting* [b]*wish* [c]al... *as she cut*
[d]se... *said good-bye*

Otra costumbre de quinceañera común en Cuba: ir por la ciudad en coche, como los recién casados (*newlyweds*) en este país

¿Y Ud.?

1. ¿Recuerda Ud. qué hizo cuando cumplió 15 años?
2. ¿Qué regalos pidió? (**Pedí...**)
3. ¿Qué sirvieron en la fiesta? (**Sirvieron...**)
4. ¿Se divirtió? (**Me divertí...**)
5. ¿Cómo se sintió ese día? (**Me sentí...**)

1. Preterite of -ar and -er Stem-changing Verbs

In **Gramática 23** (**Cap. 8**) you learned that **-ar** and **-er** stem-changing verbs have no stem change in the preterite (or in the present participle).

El pretérito de los verbos en -ar/-er			
recordar (recuerdo)		**perder (pierdo)**	
recordé	recordamos	perdí	perdimos
recordaste	recordasteis	perdiste	perdisteis
recordó	recordaron	perdió	perdieron
recordando		perdiendo	

2. Preterite of -ir Stem-changing Verbs

-Ir stem-changing verbs *do* have a stem change in the preterite.

- The change occurs only in the third person singular and plural forms.
- The stem vowels **e** and **o** change to **i** and **u**, respectively. This is the same change that occurs in the present participle of **-ir** stem-changing verbs.

El pretérito de los verbos en -ir			
e → i		o → u	
pedir (pido) (i)		**dormir (duermo) (u)**	
pedí	pedimos	dormí	dormimos
pediste	pedisteis	dormiste	dormisteis
pidió	pidieron	durmió	durmieron
pidiendo		durmiendo	

¡OJO!

Remember that this change is indicated in parentheses after the infinitive in vocabulary lists: **pedir (pido) (i)**, **dormir (duermo) (u)**. Now you know that it indicates two different changes: (1) in the present participle, and (2) in the third person singular and plural of the preterite.

3. Important -ir Stem-changing Verbs

You already know or have seen many of these verbs. New ones are indicated with*.

*conseguir (consigo) (i)	to get; to obtain	servir (sirvo) (i)	to serve
conseguir + *inf.*	to succeed in (*doing something*)	sonreír (sonrío) (i)	to smile
		sugerir (sugiero) (i)	to suggest
*despedirse (me despido) (i) (de)	to say good-bye (to)	vestirse (me visto) (i)	to get dressed
divertirse (me divierto) (i)	to have a good time		
dormir (duermo) (u)	to sleep		
dormirse	to fall asleep		
morir(se) ([me] muero) (u)	to die		
pedir (pido) (i)	to ask for; to order		
preferir (prefiero) (i)	to prefer		
reírse (me río) (i) (de)	to laugh (at)		
seguir (sigo) (i)	to continue; to follow		
sentirse (me siento) (i)	to feel		

¡OJO!

The verbs **reírse** and **sonreír** are e → i stem-changing verbs, but they drop the **e** completely in the third persons of the preterite and in the present participle.

(me reí, te reíste)	(nos reímos, os reísteis)
se rio	se rieron → riendo
(sonreí, sonreíste)	(sonreímos, sonreísteis)
sonrió	sonrieron → sonriendo

Práctica y comunicación

A. ¿Quién lo hizo?

Paso 1. Autoprueba. Complete las siguientes formas del pretérito.

1. nos divert____mos
2. se d____rmieron
3. tú s____rviste
4. se v____stió
5. yo sug____rí
6. Uds. p____dieron

Summary of the Preterite of Stem-changing Verbs

-ar / -er = no change
-ir = change in the third persons singular and plural

e → i

o → u

Prác. A, Paso 1: Answers: 1. nos divertimos 2. se durmieron 3. tú serviste 4. se vistió 5. yo sugerí 6. Uds. pidieron

Gramática

doscientos setenta y nueve ■ **279**

Paso 2. Ahora indique quiénes de sus compañeros de clase hicieron las siguientes acciones la semana pasada (*last week*). Use verbos en el pretérito. Si nadie lo hizo, simplemente diga **Nadie...** Si más de una persona lo hizo, use el verbo en plural.

MODELO: 1. _____ vestirse con ropa elegante / extravagante para venir a clase →
Tom **se vistió** con ropa **elegante** para venir a clase.

1. _____ vestirse con ropa elegante / extravagante para venir a clase
2. _____ dormirse en clase
3. _____ pedirle al profesor / a la profesora más tarea
4. _____ sentirse bien / mal con el resultado de un examen
5. _____ divertirse muchísimo en un concierto
6. _____ reírse a carcajadas (*out loud*)
7. _____ sugerir tener la clase afuera (*outside*)
8. _____ no recordar traer la tarea a clase
9. _____ despedirse en español de sus amigos de la clase
10. _____ morirse de vergüenza (*embarrassment*) por algo

Paso 3. Ahora, en parejas, comparen sus respuestas del **Paso 2**. Luego díganle a la clase una o dos de las respuestas que tienen en común. Mencionen el día, si lo recuerdan.

MODELO: Pensamos que Tom **se vistió** con ropa **elegante** para venir a clase **el miércoles de la semana pasada.**

B. José Martí

Paso 1. Complete la siguiente narración con formas del pretérito para saber más sobre José Martí.

José Martí (servir[1]) la causa de la independencia cubana toda su vida.[a] Siempre (pedir[2]) la libertad de Cuba, de España, y se opuso a la esclavitud.[b] Nació[c] en 1853 en Cuba, hijo de españoles. (Estudiar[3]) en España, donde (recibir[4]) el título de abogado[d] en 1874. Pero no (poder[5]) ejercer[e] esta profesión en Cuba. Luego (vivir[6]) en México, Guatemala y los Estados Unidos.

En 1876 (conocer[7]) a la mujer que luego (ser[8]) su esposa, María, y se casaron.[f] (*Ellos*: Tener[9]) un hijo, pero el matrimonio se separó y Martí (perder[10]) contacto con su hijo.

En 1895 (decidir[11]) empezar una guerra de independencia en Cuba. (Morir[12]) en acción en su querida[g] Isla.

Algunos de sus versos son especialmente famosos en todo el mundo gracias a la canción «Guantanamera».

[a]*life* [b]*slavery* [c]*He was born* [d]*título... law degree* [e]*practice* [f]*se... they got married* [g]*beloved*

Paso 2. Ahora, haga cinco preguntas usando verbos en el pretérito que se puedan contestar (*can be answered*) con información del texto.

MODELO: ¿Cuántos años vivió Martí?

C. Las historias que todos conocemos

Paso 1. Empareje los personajes (*characters*) de la columna de la izquierda con las acciones de la columna de la derecha para crear oraciones en el pretérito basadas en unos cuentos o historias muy famosos. ¿Puede adivinar (*guess*) quiénes son Caperucita Roja, la Cenicienta y Blancanieves?

(Continúa.)

José Martí, llamado el Apóstol (*founding voice*) de la independencia cubana

José Martí fue un escritor[a] y periodista[b] cubano que se considera un héroe nacional por su lucha[c] por la independencia y por la libertad de su país. Fue uno de los grandes intelectuales hispanohablantes del siglo XIX.[d]

¿Hay algún héroe político o social que Ud. admira mucho? ¿Por qué lo/la admira?

[a]*writer* [b]*journalist* [c]*fight* [d]*siglo... 19th century*

PERSONAJES	ACCIONES
1. Caperucita Roja el lobo (*wolf*)	**a.** conocer a una mujer misteriosa en un baile
	b. divertirse bailando con un joven muy guapo
2. la Cenicienta el Príncipe las hermanastras de la Cenicienta	**c.** dormirse después de comer una manzana
	d. morirse por el amor de su novia
	e. perderse en el bosque (*forest*)
	f. perder un zapato muy bonito
3. Blancanieves los siete enanos (*dwarves*)	**g.** encontrar (*to find*) un zapato de cristal (*glass*)
	h. sentirse preocupados por su amiga
4. Romeo Julieta	**i.** vestirse de (*as a*) abuela
	j. no conseguir ponerse el zapato de cristal
	k. hablar con un joven guapo desde su balcón

Paso 2. Ahora, en parejas, inventen dos acciones más en el pretérito para cada historia, pero sin incluir el nombre del personaje. La clase va a adivinar a qué personaje, cuento o historia se refieren sus oraciones.

MODELO: Una mujer **quiso** ponerse el zapato de cristal, pero no **pudo** ponérselo. ⟶ la hermanastra de la Cenicienta

D. Una entrevista indiscreta

Paso 1. Lea las siguientes preguntas y escriba una respuesta para cada una. ¡OJO! Tres de sus respuestas deben ser falsas.

1. ¿A qué hora te dormiste anoche?
2. ¿Perdiste mucho dinero alguna vez?
3. ¿Con qué programa de televisión te divertiste mucho en los días o meses pasados... pero te avergüenzas de (*you're ashamed to*) admitirlo?
4. ¿Seguiste haciendo algo después de que tu padre/madre (compañero/a, esposo/a) te dijo que no lo hicieras (*not to do it*)?
5. ¿Pediste una bebida alcohólica antes de tener 21 años?
6. ¿Qué cosa o tarea no conseguiste terminar el mes pasado?

Paso 2. En parejas, usen las preguntas del **Paso 1** para entrevistarse. Traten de (*Try to*) adivinar las respuestas falsas de su compañero/a.

Paso 3. Ahora presenten a la clase una de las respuestas interesantes de su compañero/a. La clase va a adivinar si la respuesta es cierta o falsa.

MODELO: E1: Julie, ¿a qué hora te dormiste anoche?
    E2: Me dormí a las tres de la mañana.
    E1: (*a la clase*): Julie se durmió a las tres de la mañana anoche.
    CLASE: No es cierto.
    E1: Tienen razón. No es cierto. Me dormí a las once.

E. Una fiesta de Halloween

Paso 1. En grupos, usen las siguientes ideas como guía para entrevistarse sobre la última fiesta de Halloween a la que (*which*) asistieron.

MODELO: vestirse de ⟶ E1: ¿De qué **te vestiste**?
    E2: **Me vestí** de vampiro. ¿Y tú?
    E3: Yo **me vestí** de bruja.

1. la fiesta: ser en _____ (lugar)
2. llegar _____ (modo de transporte)
3. vestirse de (*as*) _____ (disfraz)
4. ir con _____ (persona[s])
5. pedir / conseguir / dar _____ (comida)
6. bailar / hablar / beber / ¿ ?
7. divertirse mucho/poco
8. despedirse a la(s) _____ (hora)
9. ¿ ?

> **Vocabulario útil**
>
> **la bruja** witch
> **el disfraz** costume
> **el esqueleto**
> **el fantasma** ghost
> **la máscara**
> **la momia**
> **el monstruo**
> **el vampiro / la vampira**

Paso 2. Escojan a la persona que asistió a la mejor fiesta y díganle a la clase dos cosas interesantes que esa persona hizo en la fiesta.

In **Gramática 18 (Cap. 7)** you learned about direct object nouns and pronouns. In **Gramática 21 (Cap. 8),** you learned about indirect object nouns and pronouns. Review both types of object pronouns by identifying the indicated pronouns in the following sentences.

	DIRECT OBJECT	INDIRECT OBJECT
1. El profesor **les** dio la tarea.	☐	☐
2. El profesor **la** asignó para hacer en casa.	☐	☐
3. La profesora **me** vio.	☐	☐
4. La profesora **me** dio la tarea.	☐	☐

Grammar Tutorial 26
connect
|SPANISH
www.connectspanish.com

26 Avoiding Repetition
Expressing Direct and Indirect Object Pronouns Together

Gramática en acción: La fiesta de Anita

Berta   Anita

① Berta le hizo un pastel a Anita y **se lo** dio en la fiesta.

Anita   Berta

② Anita le prestó unos aretes a Berta.

Anita   Berta

③ Berta le sacó una foto a Anita y **se la** mostró.

Comprensión

¿Quién lo dijo? ¿De qué habla?

1. «Me lo hizo para mi cumpleaños.»
2. «Me los prestó para la fiesta.»
3. «Se la mostré en el celular.»

¿Y Ud.?

Describa los siguientes detalles de su último cumpleaños.

1. ¿Un pastel? ¿Alguien se lo hizo? **(Alguien / Nadie me...)**
2. ¿Unas fotos? ¿Alguien se las sacó?
3. ¿Algo de vestir? ¿Alguien se lo prestó?

complemento indirecto		complemento directo	complemento indirecto		complemento directo
me	+	lo / la / los / las	nos	+	lo / la / los / las
te	+	lo / la / los / las	os	+	lo / la / los / las
(le →) se	+	lo / la / los / las	(les) → se	+	lo / la / los / las

1. Both Object Pronouns in the Same Sentence

When both an indirect and a direct object pronoun appear in the same sentence, the indirect object pronoun comes first, followed by the direct object pronoun. You can remember the order of the pronoun by thinking of **ID**.

This is the *opposite* of the order in English. In addition, while a word (like *ready*, first example) can come in between the two pronouns in English, that is not possible in Spanish.

¿El almuerzo? **Te lo** hago ahora mismo.
Lunch? I'll get it ready for you right now.

¿El trofeo? No **nos lo** dieron.
The trophy? They didn't give it to us.

---

2. Position of Double Object Pronouns

The placement of double object pronouns in relation to the verb is the same as for single object pronouns. The pronouns come:
- before a conjugated verb
- after an infinitive or present participle *or*

- before the conjugated verb that precedes them

- before a negative command
- after an affirmative command

¿El libro? **Me lo dio.**

¿El equipaje? Acaban de **dármelo.** Están **dándomelo** ahora mismo.

¿Los pronombres? **Te los acabo** de explicar. **Te los estoy** explicando ahora.

¿La comida? **No me la traiga** ahora.

¿Las bebidas? **Tráigamelas**, por favor.

Le(s) → se

1. Use of *se*

When both the indirect and the direct object pronouns begin with the letter **l,** the indirect object pronoun *always* changes to **se.**

This **le(s)** → **se** change only happens in third person expressions, the equivalents of English (*Give*) *it to him/her/them;* (*Give*) *them to him/her/them.*

Only four third-person pronoun combinations are possible in Spanish: **se lo, se la, se los, se las.** In these combinations:
- se = indirect object pronoun (**le** or **les**)
- **lo/la/los/las** = direct object pronouns (no change)

So, in third-person combinations, all you need to focus on is the gender of the direct object pronoun (**lo, la, los, las**), since **se** will always be the same.

Indirect direct

Les dimos el coche.
↓ (les lo)
Se lo dimos.
We gave them the car.
We gave it to them.

Le escribí la carta ayer.
↓ (le la)
Se la escribí ayer.
I wrote her the letter yesterday.
I wrote it to her yesterday.

Le regaló esos zapatos.
↓ (le los)
Se los regaló.
He gave him those shoes.
He gave them to him.

Les mandamos las invitaciones. (les las)
Se las mandamos.
We sent them the invitations.
We sent them to them.

---

2. Clarifying *se*

Since **se** can stand for **le** (*to/for you* [sing.], *him, her*) or **les** (*to/for you* [pl.], *them*), it is often necessary to clarify its meaning by using **a** plus the prepositional pronoun.

You learned to clarify the indirect object pronouns **le** and **les** in this way in **Capítulo 8.** This is exactly the same thing, since **se** represents **le** and **les.**

¿La carta de recomendación? Voy a escribír**sela**.
(meaning of **se** unclear unless specified)

¿La carta de recomendación? Voy a escribír**sela** a Ud. / a Uds.
a él / a ellos.
a ella / a ellas.

The letter of recommendation? I'm going to write it
for you (sing.) / you (pl.).
for him / for them (m. or m. and f.).
for her / for them (f.).

Summary of Indirect and Direct Object Pronouns

INDIRECT	DIRECT
me/te/nos/os	
	+ lo/la/los/las
le(s) → se	

A. Oraciones «familiares»

Paso 1. Autoprueba. Complete las siguientes oraciones con los pronombres apropiados del complemento directo e indirecto: **se lo, se la, se los, se las.**

1. Le dieron el libro. → _____ _____ dieron.
2. Les sirvieron la paella. → _____ _____ sirvieron.
3. Le di las direcciones. → _____ _____ di.
4. Les trajo los boletos. → _____ _____ trajo.

Paso 2. Indique cuáles pueden ser los complementos posibles en las siguientes oraciones. Para cada oración, escoja un complemento indirecto y otro directo. **¡OJO!** A veces hay solo una posibilidad. A veces hay varias.

	COMPLEMENTOS INDIRECTOS	COMPLEMENTOS DIRECTOS
1. Se lo digo.	a mí	un consejo sobre algo
2. Me la hacen.	a ti	el dinero
3. Se los hago.	a mis parientes	los favores
4. Me lo dan.	a mis amigos	la fiesta de cumpleaños
5. «¡Te lo dije!»		«Te quiero».

Paso 3. Ahora, en parejas, digan si alguno de Uds. (u otras personas) hace las siguientes acciones con frecuencia.

MODELO: decirle «te quiero» a algún miembro de la familia →
E1: ¿Le **dices** «te quiero» a algún miembro de tu familia?
E2: Sí, **se lo digo a mi madre** con frecuencia. ¿Y tú?
E1: Yo **se lo digo a mi madre** también.

1. decirle «te quiero» a un miembro de la familia
2. hacerle una fiesta de cumpleaños a alguien
3. decirle «¡te lo dije!» a alguien
4. darle dinero a alguien
5. hacerle favores a alguien

B. En la mesa. Ud. todavía tiene hambre. Pida más comida, según el modelo. Preste atención al uso del tiempo presente para pedir algo de manera informal.

MODELO: ensalada → ¿Hay más **ensalada**? ¿Me **la** pasas, por favor?

1. pan
2. tortillas
3. tomates
4. fruta
5. vino
6. jamón

C. En el aeropuerto. Cambie los sustantivos por pronombres para evitar (*avoid*) la repetición.

MODELO: ¿La maleta? Van a prestarme la maleta mañana. →
Van a prestár**mela** (**Me la** van a prestar) mañana.

1. ¿La hora de la salida? Acaban de decirnos la hora de la salida.
2. ¿El horario (*schedule*)? Sí, léame el horario, por favor.
3. ¿Los boletos? No, no tiene que darle los boletos aquí.
4. ¿El equipaje? ¡Claro que le guardo el equipaje!
5. ¿Los boletos? Ya te compré los boletos.
6. ¿El puesto? No te preocupes. Te puedo guardar el puesto.

D. ¿Una madre típica? La madre de Aurora le recuerda (*reminds*) a su hija todo lo que debe hacer. Conteste las preguntas afirmativamente por Aurora, usando pronombres del complemento directo e indirecto.

MODELO: ¿Le diste un beso a papá antes de salir? →Sí, **se lo** di.

(Continúa.)

1. ¿Les diste las gracias a los abuelos por el regalo de cumpleaños?
2. ¿Le llevaste el ensayo al profesor de historia?
3. ¿Le mandaste las fotos a tu amiga?
4. ¿Me mandaste la cuenta de la matrícula?
5. ¿Te dio tu amiga el dinero para la blusa que le compraste?
6. ¿Les dijiste a tus amigos que están invitados para el Día de Gracias?

Algo sobre...

el son cubano

El son es un género musical cubano que dio lugar^a al mambo, a la rumba y a la salsa, entre otros bailes. También está presente en el *latin jazz*.

El son se originó en el este de Cuba a finales del siglo XIX^b con elementos musicales africanos y españoles. A principios^c del siglo XX llegó a La Habana y de allí salió al mundo. Los grupos soneros originales tocaban^d con un tres cubano (una guitarra con tres pares de cuerdas^e), bongós y maracas. Después empezaron a usar la guitarra, el contrabajo^f y la trompeta.

En su opinión ¿cuál es el género musical de su país que más influencia tiene en el mundo? ¿Qué sabe de esa música?

^adio... *gave rise, created* ^bsiglo... *19th century* ^cA... *At the beginning* ^d*played* ^e*strings* ^f*string bass*

Celia Cruz (1925–2003), la gran cantante cubana que llevó el son por todo el mundo

---

E. ¿Quién le regaló eso?

Paso 1. Haga una lista de los cinco mejores regalos que Ud. ha recibido (*have received*) en su vida (*life*).

Paso 2. Ahora dele a un compañero o una compañera su lista. Él/Ella le va a preguntar: **¿Quién te regaló ?** Use pronombres en su respuesta. **¡OJO!** Preste atención a estas formas en plural **(ellos): regalaron, dieron, mandaron.**

MODELO: E1: ¿Quién te regaló **los aretes de oro**?
        E2: Mis padres **me los** regalaron.

Paso 3. Ahora descríbale a la clase por lo menos uno de los regalos interesantes que recibió su compañero/a.

MODELO: Cintia recibió **unos aretes de oro** como regalo. **Se los** regalaron sus padres.

Un poco de todo

A. Lengua y cultura: La Virgen de Guadalupe, quince siglos (*centuries*) de historia

Paso 1. Complete the following paragraphs with the correct form of the words in parentheses, as suggested by context. When two possibilities are given in parentheses, select the correct word. Use the present tense or the preterite of the infinitives, according to context.

En todos los países hispanohablantes, hay festividades religiosas que son días de fiesta nacionales. Por ejemplo, el día de Navidad se (celebrar¹) en todo el mundo hispano. Otra celebración religiosa que también (es / está²) una fiesta nacional en (mucho³) países es el 12 de diciembre. Es el día de la fiesta de la

(Continúa.)

La tilma (*shawl*) de Juan Diego en la Basílica de Nuestra Señora (*Lady*) de Guadalupe, en la Ciudad de México

Virgen de Guadalupe, una imagen venerada[a] por todo el mundo católico, especialmente en México.

La historia de la Virgen de Guadalupe (venir[4]) a México desde[b] España. En el siglo VI,[c] el Papa[d] Gregorio tenía[e] una estatua de la Virgen y (se lo / se la[5]) regaló al Obispo[f] de Sevilla. Pero luego la estatua (desaparecer[6]) durante los siglos en que los árabes ocuparon la Península. Después de la expulsión de los árabes, un pastor[g] cristiano (le / la[7]) (encontrar[8]) cerca de la ciudad de Guadalupe. Por eso la estatua (tomar[9]) el nombre de la Virgen de Guadalupe.

En lo que hoy es México, en el siglo XVI, un campesino[h] indígena, Juan Diego, se convirtió[i] al cristianismo. Un día (*él*: ver[10]) a la Virgen en un lugar llamado Tepeyac. Por un milagro,[j] la Virgen (dejar[k11]) su imagen impresa[l] en la tilma[m] de Juan Diego. Esta imagen (recibir[12]) el nombre de Virgen de Guadalupe porque Tepeyac (es / está[13]) cerca del pueblo mexicano de Guadalupe.

La tilma de Juan Diego, con la imagen de la Virgen, todavía se puede (ver[14]) en la Basílica[n] de Nuestra Señora de Guadalupe, en la Ciudad de México.

[a]imagen... *image venerated, adored* [b]*from* [c]*el... the sixth century* [d]*Pope* [e]*had* [f]*Bishop* [g]*shepherd* [h]*peasant* [i]se... *converted* [j]*miracle* [k]*to leave* [l]*imprinted* [m]*shawl* [n]*large church*

Paso 2. Comprensión. ¿Cierto o falso? Corrija las oraciones falsas.

	CIERTO	FALSO
1. La Virgen de Guadalupe española es una estatua.	☐	☐
2. El Papa Gregorio vio a la Virgen en Tepeyac.	☐	☐
3. El campesino Juan Diego era (*was*) de origen español.	☐	☐
4. La tilma de Juan Diego ya no (*no longer*) existe.	☐	☐

Paso 3. En parejas, vuelvan a contar la historia de la Virgen de Guadalupe. Primero, hagan una lista de los hechos importantes en la historia, usando infinitivos. Ejemplo: **venir de España.** Luego, cuenten la historia.

B. ¿Qué pasó cuando... ? ¿Les pasó a Uds. alguna de estas cosas este año? En parejas, túrnense para hacer y contestar preguntas. Digan cuándo ocurrió y cómo reaccionaron. Luego díganle a la clase algo interesante.

MODELO: **1.** Su compañero/a de cuarto (esposo/a...) volvió anoche a casa muy tarde haciendo mucho ruido. →
    E1: ¿Tu compañero de cuarto volvió tarde alguna vez?
    E2: Sí, el domingo pasado volvió a las 4 de la mañana haciendo ruido. Me puse furioso. ¿Y tu compañero?
    E1: No, él nunca vuelve tarde. ¡Yo sí!

1. Su compañero/a de cuarto (esposo/a...) volvió anoche a casa muy tarde haciendo mucho ruido.
2. Un profesor le dio un examen «sorpresa».
3. Ud. perdió algo importante o de otra persona.
4. Un amigo/pariente de Ud. le dijo algo ofensivo / muy triste.
5. Ud. sacó una nota sorprendentemente (*surprisingly*) buena.
6. Ud. fue a una celebración familiar muy entrañable (*touching*).

En su comunidad

Entreviste a una persona hispana de su universidad o ciudad sobre las celebraciones tradicionales de su país y de su familia.

PREGUNTAS POSIBLES

- ¿Cuáles son los días festivos más importantes de su país? ¿Son celebraciones de origen civil o religioso? ¿Se celebran en familia? ¿También hay eventos en la ciudad?
- ¿Cuáles son las celebraciones más importantes en su familia? ¿Y sus favoritas?
- ¿Cuál fue la última fiesta que Ud. celebró en su país? ¿Cómo y con quién la celebró?

Antes de mirar

¿Qué asocia Ud. con una gran fiesta nacional?

_____ música
_____ comida
_____ mucha gente
_____ banderas (*flags*)
_____ colores patrióticos
_____ celebraciones en la calle (*street*)
_____ ¿ ?

La Fiesta Broadway, una celebración que conmemora una victoria mexicana

Este segmento

Laura presenta un reportaje sobre el Cinco de Mayo, y los presentadores, Ana y Víctor, cierran el programa.

Vocabulario del segmento

sino	but rather	**la manzana**	(city) block
la fuerza invasora	invading force	**el escenario**	stage
ha llegado a ser	has become	**órale**	right on
en grande	in a big way		

Fragmento del guion

ANA: Bueno, con sabor a^a fiesta mexicana, despedimos^b el programa de hoy. No se olviden que nos volvemos a ver aquí muy, muy pronto.

VÍCTOR: Hasta entonces,^c cuídense mucho.^d Nos vemos pronto.

^acon... *with the taste of... in mind* ^b*we close* ^c*then* ^dcuídense... *take good care of yourselves*

Después de mirar

A. **¿Está claro?** Complete las siguientes oraciones con las cifras (números) que se oyen en el segmento.

1. _____ fue el año de una victoria mexicana.
2. En la Fiesta Broadway hay _____ escenarios musicales diferentes.
3. Se calcula que _____ de personas asisten a la Fiesta Broadway.
4. La Fiesta Broadway ocupa _____ manzanas.

B. **Un poco más.** Conteste las siguientes preguntas.

1. ¿Dónde tiene lugar (*take place*) la Fiesta Broadway?
2. ¿Qué tiene de raro (*What's odd about*) la celebración del Cinco de Mayo?
3. ¿Qué otra fiesta muy conocida (*well known*) en los Estados Unidos está asociada con otro grupo nacional?

 C. **Y ahora, Uds.** En parejas, preparen un segmento informativo sobre una fiesta que se celebra en su ciudad o estado. El segmento debe comenzar con un saludo a los telespectadores y la introducción de Uds., los presentadores del programa. El segmento debe cerrarse formalmente. Usen el **Fragmento del guion** como modelo para el cierre.

A LEER

¿Hubo en este país alguna época de intolerancia política o religiosa?

Lectura cultural: Cuba
Dos días festivos cubanos

En Cuba se conmemoran dos días muy importantes. El primero es el 10 de octubre, que se conoce como el Día de la Independencia Nacional. En este día el patriota cubano Carlos Manuel de Céspedes declaró libres a todos los esclavos.[a] También llamó a todos los cubanos a liberarse del dominio[b] colonial de España. Esto marca el inicio[c] de la primera guerra[d] de independencia de Cuba.

El otro día festivo de mucha importancia para los cubanos es la Navidad. Como resultado del cambio[e] político de 1959 y durante muchos de los años bajo el régimen de Fidel Castro, no se les permitió a los cubanos celebrar la Navidad de manera oficial. Todo cambió[f] con la visita a Cuba del Papa[g] Juan Pablo II (Segundo) en el año 1998. Desde entonces[h] los cubanos pueden asistir a la iglesia y celebrar este día tan importante con su familia y amigos.

[a]slaves [b]control [c]beginning [d]war [e]change (that is, the regime of Fidel Castro) [f]changed [g]Pope (Head of the Catholic Church) [h]Desde... Since then

Unas palmas reales en La Habana, Cuba

Un símbolo cubano: La palma

La palma real[a] (también llamada palmera en otros países) es un ícono nacional que se encuentra por toda la Isla. Forma parte del escudo[b] nacional como símbolo del espíritu cubano: siempre alto y orgulloso.[c] José Martí la menciona en sus famosos versos[d]:

> Yo soy un hombre sincero
> De donde crece[e] la palma,
> Y antes de morirme quiero
> Echar[f] mis versos del alma.[g]

[a]royal [b]coat of arms [c]proud [d]lines (of a poem) [e]grows [f]Release [g]soul

En otros países hispanos

En todo el mundo hispanohablante Estas festividades se celebran en todas partes.

- **La Semana Santa** Así[a] se llama a la semana que va desde el Domingo de Ramos[b] hasta el Domingo de Pascua. En muchas ciudades hay procesiones[c] para conmemorar la pasión, muerte[d] y resurrección de Jesús. Coincide con el principio[e] de la primavera o el otoño, según el hemisferio.

- **El Carnaval** Esta fiesta precede al comienzo de la Cuaresma.[f] El Carnaval más famoso del mundo es el[g] de Río de Janeiro (Brasil), pero hay Carnavales hispanos que también son famosos por la exuberancia de su música, bailes y colorido, como los Carnavales de Cádiz (España), Barranquilla (Colombia) y Santiago de Cuba (Cuba).

[a]That's how [b]el... Palm Sunday [c]street processions [d]la... passion (that is, suffering), death [e]beginning [f]Lent (period from Ash Wednesday to Good Friday) [g]that

COMPRENSIÓN

1. ¿Cuáles son los días festivos más importantes de Cuba?
2. ¿Desde cuándo se permite celebrar la Navidad sin restricciones otra vez en Cuba?
3. ¿Cuáles son otros de los días festivos importantes del mundo hispano?
4. ¿Cuándo se celebra la Semana Santa?
5. ¿Por qué es la palma un símbolo apropiado del espíritu cubano?

Y ahora, Uds.

Piensen en los símbolos nacionales de los Estados Unidos. ¿Cuáles son? ¿Se usan en los días festivos? ¿en otros eventos? ¿Se usan símbolos nacionales similares en otras partes del mundo?

Del mundo hispano

Antes de leer

Es muy común hacer algunos propósitos (*resolutions*) cuando un año empieza. ¿Los hace Ud., generalmente? Haga una lista de cuatro propósitos que Ud. hizo en años pasados o tuvo la intención de hacer. Use infinitivos en su lista. ¿Los cumplió todos? (*Did you achieve all of them?*)

Lectura: Una declaración de propósitos

12 propósitos para el Año Nuevo

Complete la siguiente declaración:

Yo, _____ (nombre), me comprometo[a] a cumplir _____ (número) propósitos de esta lista en los próximos 365 días.

- Leer un libro cada dos meses.
- No excederte en tus horas de trabajo.
- Comer más sano.[b]
- Asistir a una muestra[c] de cine o de arte.
- Comprar la membresía[d] de un gimnasio.
- Tomar dos litros de agua diariamente.
- Ir a una ceremonia religiosa ajena a la tuya.[e]
- Regalar sin razón.[f]
- Desayunar bien.
- Ir a votar.
- Ir de excursión a un lugar remoto.
- Separar la basura en orgánica e inorgánica.

[a]me... *I promise* [b]más... *in a more healthy manner* [c]*exhibition* [d]*membership* [e]ajena... *different from yours* [f]sin... *for no reason*

Comprensión

Una vida mejor. La gente generalmente hace propósitos para el año nuevo con la intención de mejorar (*improving*) su vida (*life*) de alguna manera. Clasifique los (*those*) de esta lectura según las tres categorías a continuación y explique por qué puso cada propósito en la categoría que Ud. escogió (*chose*). (Algunos se pueden poner en más de un grupo.)

1. Los que pueden mejorar la salud (*health*) física
2. Los que pueden mejorar la salud mental o espiritual
3. Los que pueden mejorar las relaciones con los otros y con el medio ambiente (*environment*)

El mensaje telefónico de Pilar

Antes de escuchar

¿Qué actividades generalmente se hacen en una boda (*wedding*)? Haga una lista de todas las actividades que pueda imaginar. Consulte el **Vocabulario para escuchar** al hacer (*while making*) su lista.

Vocabulario para escuchar

¡qué lástima!	what a shame!	**tirar**	to throw, toss
los novios	bride and groom	**lo sintió mucho**	was very sorry
cortar	to cut	**el recuerdo**	souvenir, party
ensuciarse la cara	to dirty each other's faces		favor

Después de escuchar

A. ¿Quién hizo qué? Indique quién hizo qué, emparejando las acciones con las personas que las hicieron. Hay más de una opción en algunos casos.

ACCIONES

_____ **1.** bailar
_____ **2.** cortar el pastel y tirarlo
_____ **3.** llorar
_____ **4.** mandar un recuerdo
_____ **5.** tocar salsa
_____ **6.** no ir a la boda

PERSONAS

a. Estela
b. un conjunto (*group*) musical
c. Pilar
d. la mamá de Estela
e. los novios
f. la amiga de Pilar y de Estela

B. Más información. ¿Qué más se sabe o deduce Ud. del mensaje?

1. La amiga de Pilar, ¿es amiga de Estela también?
2. ¿Cómo se llama el novio?
3. ¿Por qué no fue la amiga de Pilar a la boda?
4. ¿Por qué cree Pilar que su amiga no contesta su llamada (*call*)?
5. ¿Cuál es la profesión de la amiga de Pilar?

PRODUCCIÓN PERSONAL

¡Ahora, yo!

A. Use de modelo las preguntas y respuestas de la página 267 de este capítulo para hablar de los días festivos que Ud. celebra.

B. Filme una entrevista con una persona hispana no estadounidense en su universidad o su comunidad. Hágale preguntas sobre un día festivo muy especial que se celebra en su ciudad o país, pero que no se celebra en los Estados Unidos.

A ESCRIBIR

Un ensayo sobre una celebración memorable

¿Cuál es la celebración más memorable de su vida (*life*)? ¿un baile de fin de curso (*prom night*)? ¿una boda (*wedding*)? ¿un cumpleaños? ¿una fiesta de Nochevieja? ¿el bautizo (*baptism*) de una hija o un hijo? ¿Qué es memorable de esa celebración?

Preparar

Paso 1. En parejas, hagan una lista de los aspectos que su ensayo debe incluir, sin olvidar lo que más le gustó.

Paso 2. Use las ideas del **Paso 1** para escribir su ensayo. Debe expresar sus sentimientos o los (*those*) de otras personas que estuvieron o no estuvieron en la celebración. Hay más ayuda en Connect.

Más ideas para su portafolio

- Escriba una o dos oraciones sobre unos momentos emocionantes de su vida: cuándo se puso más feliz (rojo/a, triste...), cuándo lloró más desconsoladamente (*nonstop*) o se rio con más ganas (*most uproariously*), etcétera.

- Escriba unas oraciones sobre una fiesta de un país hispanohablante a la que (*which*) Ud. quiere asistir algún día.

- Si ha estado jugando (*have been playing*) Practice Spanish: Study Abroad, en Quest 6 Ud. pasó tiempo en el museo del pueblo. Si hay una galería de arte en el campus de la universidad a la que asiste Ud. (o en su ciudad), haga un afiche (*poster*) o un folleto (*brochure*) con información sobre la galería para la comunidad hispanohablante.

Sugerencia: You are now ready to play Quest 6 in **Practice Spanish: Study Abroad** (www.mhpractice.com).

LEARNSMART

Visit **www.connectspanish.com** to practice the vocabulary and grammar points covered in this chapter.

AFTER STUDYING THIS CHAPTER I CAN . . .

☐ talk about holidays (268)

☐ express more feelings and emotions (271)

☐ use more types of verbs in the preterite (274–275, 278–279)

☐ understand double object pronouns and use them to avoid repetition (282–283)

☐ recognize/describe at least 2–3 aspects of Cuban cultures

Gramática en breve

24. Irregular Preterites

Irregular Preterite Endings

estuv- pud- pus- quis- sup- tuv- vin-		-e -imos = -iste -isteis -o -ieron	dij- traj-	-e -imos = -iste -isteis -o -eron

hay: haber → **hubo** (*there was/were*)

25. Preterite of Stem-changing Verbs

Preterite Stem-changing Patterns

-ar/-er = no change

-ir = change in the third person singular and plural

e → i

o → u

26. Direct and Indirect Object Pronouns Together

Indirect
me/te/nos/os

le(s) → se

Direct
☒ lo/la/los/las

Vocabulario

Los verbos

adivinar	to guess
conseguir (*like* seguir)	to get; to obtain
conseguir +inf.	to succeed in (*doing something*)
despedirse (*like* pedir) (de)	to say good-bye (to)

encontrar (encuentro)	to find
morir(se) ([me] muero) (u)	to die
sugerir (sugiero) (i)	to suggest

Repaso: dormir(se) ([me] duermo) (u), pedir (pido) (i), preferir (prefiero) (i), servir (sirvo) (i), vestirse (me visto) (i)

Los días festivos y las fiestas

el anfitrión, la anfitriona	host (*of an event*)
las botanas (*Mex.*)	appetizers
el champán	champagne
el día festivo	holiday
el/la invitado/a	guest
el pastel de cumpleaños	birthday cake
las tapas	appetizers
la vela	candle

Repaso: el cumpleaños, la fiesta, el pastel, el refresco, el regalo, la tarjeta

cumplir años	to have a birthday
darle una fiesta (a alguien)	to give someone a party
faltar (a)	to be absent (from); to not attend
gastar	to spend (*money*)
hacerle una fiesta (a alguien)	to give someone a party, have a party (for someone)
pasarlo bien/mal	to have a good/bad time
reunirse (me reúno) (con)	to get together (with)
ser en + *place*	to take place in/at (*a place*)

Repaso: bailar, beber, celebrar, comer, divertirse (me divierto) (i), invitar, regalar

Las emociones y los estados afectivos

el estado afectivo	emotional state
discutir con (alguien) por/sobre (algo)	to argue with (someone) about (something)
enojarse con (alguien) por (algo)	to get angry with (someone) about (something)
llorar	to cry
olvidar	to forget (about)
ponerse + *adj.*	to become, get + *adj.*
ponerse rojo/a	to blush
portarse bien/mal	to (mis)behave
recordar (recuerdo)	to remember
reírse (me río) (i) (de)	to laugh (about)
sentirse (me siento) (i) + *adj.*	to feel (*an emotion*) + *adj.*
sonreír (*like* reír)	to smile

Repaso: quejarse (de)

Otros sustantivos

el árbol	tree
el detalle	detail
el fin de año	end of the year
el hecho	fact; event

Los adjetivos

avergonzado/a	embarrassed
enojado/a	angry; upset
feliz (*pl.* **felices**)	happy
festivo/a	festive, celebratory
tranquilo/a	calm
-ísimo/a	very very

Repaso: alegre, contento/a, furioso/a, nervioso/a, triste

Vocabulario personal

El tiempo libre

En este capítulo

|SPANISH

onnectspanish.com

Un grupo de bomba en San Juan, Puerto Rico

OCÉANO
ATLÁNTICO

REPÚBLICA
DOMINICANA

PUERTO
RICO

San Juan ⊛

Ponce •

Mar Caribe

0		100		200 Millas
0	100		200 Kilómetros	

PUERTO RICO

3.6 (punto seis) millones de habitantes

- Puerto Rico es un Estado Libre Asociado a los Estados Unidos. Esto significa que Puerto Rico no es independiente, pero sí tiene autonomía interna. Los puertorriqueños son ciudadanos[a] estadounidenses.

- Los puertorriqueños tienen una gran conciencia[b] de su historia y de la importancia de su cultura. Se sienten muy orgullosos[c] de su herencia indígena, africana e hispana.

[a]*citizens* [b]*awareness* [c]*proud*

- ¿Qué le gusta a Ud. hacer en su tiempo libre? ¿Prefiere las actividades al aire libre[a]? ¿O prefiere las actividades sedentarias?

- ¿Es el baile una de sus diversiones preferidas? ¿Qué tipo de música le gusta más para bailar?

- ¿Tiene que pasar a veces parte de su tiempo libre haciendo quehaceres domésticos[b]?

[a]al... *outdoor* [b]quehaceres... *household tasks*

CECILIA FIGUEROA MARTÍN CONTESTA LAS PREGUNTAS.

- En mi tiempo libre, además de[a] descansar, me gusta hacer cosas con mi familia y con mis amigos. Algunas de las actividades que me gustan son sedentarias, como leer, ver películas, jugar al dominó y a las cartas. Pero también juego al tenis y me encanta nadar en el mar.

- ¡Claro que sí![b] Ahora no bailo tanto como cuando era[c] joven, pero me encanta bailar siempre que[d] puedo. Cualquier[e] tipo de música: pop, rock, salsa, merengue... lo que sea.[f]

- ¡Quién no! Tengo dos niños chicos.[g] Pero, en mi opinión, hacer los quehaceres domésticos no es parte del tiempo libre. ¡Es otro trabajo[h]!

[a]además... *besides* [b]¡Claro... *Of course!* [c]*I was* [d]siempre... *whenever* [e]*Any* [f]lo... *whatever* [g]niños... *small, young kids* [h]*job*

Los pasatiempos, diversiones y aficiones°

Los... *Pastimes, fun activities, and hobbies*

montar a caballo

caminar

hacer (el) yoga

esquiar (esquío), el esquí

jugar (juego) (gu) a los videojuegos

correr

dar una caminata

ir a una fiesta

You can hear the pronunciation of theme vocabulary words and phrases in the Connect eBook.

Los pasatiempos

los ratos libres	spare (free) time
dar/hacer una fiesta	to give a party
dar un paseo	to take a walk
hacer *camping*	to go camping
hacer planes para + *inf.*	to make plans to (*do something*)
hacer un *picnic*	to have a picnic
ir...	to go . . .
a un bar	to a bar
al cine	to the movies
a una discoteca	to a disco
a un museo	to a museum
al teatro / a un concierto	to the theater / to a concert
a ver una película	to see a movie
jugar (juego) (gu) a las cartas / al ajedrez	to play cards/chess
sacar (qu) fotos	to take pictures
tomar el sol	to sunbathe
aburrirse	to get bored
ser...	to be . . .
aburrido/a	boring
divertido/a	fun

Los deportes

el ciclismo	bicycling
el fútbol	soccer
el fútbol americano	football
hacer *surfing*	to surf
montar/pasear en bicicleta	to ride a bicycle
nadar	to swim
la natación	swimming
patinar	to skate

Cognados: el basquetbol, el béisbol, el golf, el hockey, el tenis, el voleibol

el equipo	team
el jugador / la jugadora	player
el partido	game, match
la pelota	ball
entrenar	to practice; to train
ganar	to win
jugar (juego) (gu) al + *sport*	to play (*a sport*)
perder (pierdo)	to lose
practicar (qu)	to participate (*in a sport*)
ser aficionado/a (a)	to be a fan (of)

Comunicación

A. El tiempo libre

Paso 1. ¿Cierto o falso? Corrija las oraciones falsas, según su opinión.

	CIERTO	FALSO
1. Es más aburrido ver un partido en la tele que en el estadio.	☐	☐
2. Lo paso mejor con mi familia que con mis amigos.	☐	☐
3. Las actividades creativas y artísticas me gustan más que las deportivas (*sport-related ones*).	☐	☐
4. Odio el béisbol tanto como el fútbol.	☐	☐
5. Los estudiantes universitarios tienen tanto tiempo libre como los (*those*) de la escuela secundaria.	☐	☐
6. La mejor actividad para un viernes por la noche es estudiar.	☐	☐
7. Jugar al ajedrez es más aburrido que jugar a las cartas.	☐	☐
8. No me gustan las actividades al aire libre (*outdoor*).	☐	☐

Paso 2. Ahora haga una lista de sus pasatiempos favoritos y de los que Ud. odia o no le interesan.

Paso 3. Compare su lista con la (*that*) de un compañero o una compañera de clase con quien Ud. no habla con frecuencia. ¿Les gustan los mismos pasatiempos?

B. Definiciones

Paso 1. Dé las palabras definidas.

MODELO: entrar en un lugar para ver una película → ir al cine

1. un grupo de jugadores
2. salir bien en una competencia; salir mal
3. practicar un deporte intensamente
4. asistir a todos los partidos de un equipo en particular
5. un deporte que se practica en una piscina

Paso 2. Ahora defina las siguientes palabras, según el modelo del **Paso 1.**

1. un jugador	**4.** hacer un *picnic*
2. un partido	**5.** dar un paseo
3. aburrirse	

Nota **cultural**

Los deportes más populares del mundo hispano

Dos deportes predominan en el panorama deportivo del mundo hispano: el fútbol y el béisbol.

- **El fútbol** Sin duda este es el rey[a] de los deportes en el mundo hispano, como en el resto del mundo. Ningún evento deportivo se compara en seguimiento[b] a la Copa Mundial de Fútbol. Se estima que mil millones de telespectadores miraron el partido final de la Copa 2014, entre Alemania y la Argentina. En todos los países hispanos, el fútbol se juega en cualquier calle,[c] plaza o espacio abierto y hay innumerables ligas[d] de todo tipo.

- **El béisbol** Un deporte inmensamente popular en los países de la costa caribeña es el béisbol. En las grandes ligas estadounidenses hay muchos jugadores de primer orden con apellidos hispanos. Muchos de estos «peloteros[e]», como se les llama[f] en muchos países, vienen de las ligas de sus respectivos países de origen, como la República Dominicana, Venezuela y México.

[a]*king* [b]*following* [c]*cualquier... any street* [d]*leagues* [e]*ball-players* [f]*se... they are called*

El equipo nacional de béisbol puertorriqueño, que celebra una victoria

- **El basquetbol, el tenis y el ciclismo** Estos deportes también tienen gran seguimiento en el mundo hispano. El basquetbol está creciendo[g] en cuanto al[h] número de espectadores y tiene dos grandes potencias[i] hispanas: España y la Argentina. Estos países tienen varios jugadores en la NBA estadounidense.

 ¿Qué otros deportistas hispanos puede Ud. nombrar?

[g]*growing* [h]*en... as far as the* [i]*superpowers*

Así se dice

el basquetbol = el baloncesto (*Sp.*)
dar una caminata = hacer senderismo (*Sp.*)
hacer *camping* = hacer acampada, acampar
hacer *surfing* = hacer *surf* (*P.R.*), surfear
pasear en bicicleta = andar en bicicleta, montar en bicicleta
la película = el filme, el film
el voleibol = el vólibol, el volibol

Actividad	Mediaª de tiempo diario (aproximada)
Estudios	
Vidaᵇ social con los amigos (en persona o a distancia)	
Vida familiar	
Tareas domésticas	
Deportes	
Ver medios de comunicaciónᶜ	
Leer por placer	
Otras actividades	

ªAverage ᵇLife ᶜmedios... media

C. ¿Cómo pasa Ud. su tiempo?

Paso 1. Complete la siguiente tabla con el tiempo medio (*average*) que Ud. pasa diariamente haciendo las actividades indicadas.

Paso 2. Ahora, en parejas, hagan comparaciones sobre el tiempo que Uds. pasan haciendo las actividades de cada categoría. Díganle a la clase algo que tienen en común.

MODELO: E1: ¿Cuánto tiempo pasas en los estudios?

E2: Paso cinco horas aproximadamente. ¿Y tú?

E1: Yo paso seis horas. Yo paso más horas estudiando que tú.

Los quehaceres domésticos°

Los... *Household chores*

limpiar (la casa)°　　　　　**limpiar...** *to clean (house)*

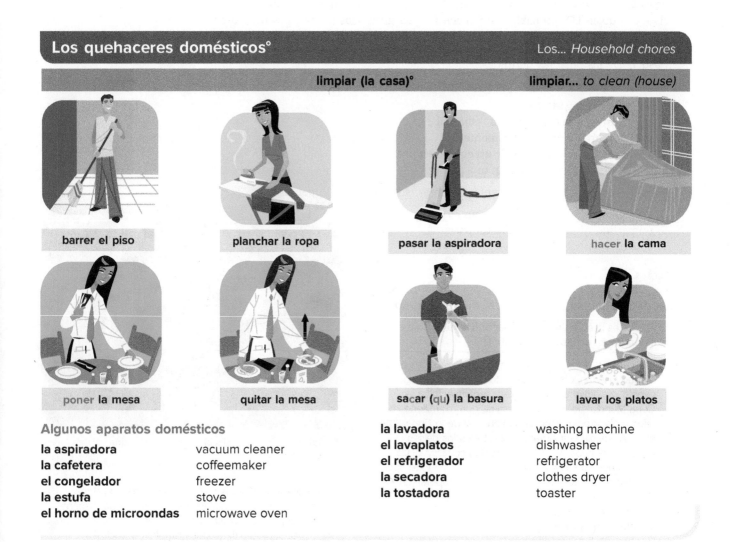

barrer el piso　　planchar la ropa　　pasar la aspiradora　　hacer la cama

poner la mesa　　quitar la mesa　　sacar (qu) la basura　　lavar los platos

Algunos aparatos domésticos

la aspiradora	vacuum cleaner
la cafetera	coffeemaker
el congelador	freezer
la estufa	stove
el horno de microondas	microwave oven

la lavadora	washing machine
el lavaplatos	dishwasher
el refrigerador	refrigerator
la secadora	clothes dryer
la tostadora	toaster

Comunicación

Así se dice

A. Los quehaceres domésticos. ¿En qué cuarto o parte de la casa se hacen las siguientes actividades? Hay más de una respuesta en muchos casos.

1. Se hace la cama en _____.
2. Se saca la basura de _____ y se pone en _____.
3. Uno se baña en _____ pero baña al perro en _____.
4. Se barre el piso del / de la _____.
5. Se pasa la aspiradora en _____.
6. Se lava y se seca la ropa en _____.
7. La ropa se plancha en _____.
8. Se usa la cafetera en _____.

Así se dice

el congelador = la nevera
la estufa = la cocina
hacer la cama = tender la
 cama
lavar los platos = fregar
 los platos
el refrigerador = el frigorífico,
 la heladera, la
 refrigeradora,
 la nevera

B. Las marcas (*Brand names*). ¿Para qué se usan o para qué sirven los siguientes productos?

MODELO: Mr. Coffee ⟶ Mr. Coffee sirve para hacer el café.

1. Windex
2. Glad bags
3. Lysol
4. Tide
5. Cascade
6. Palmolive

Vocabulario útil

el fregadero   sink
se usa para...
sirve para

C. Intercambios

Paso 1. En parejas, túrnense para hacer y contestar preguntas sobre cómo pasan Uds. el fin de semana. Basen sus preguntas en las siguientes ideas. Deben obtener detalles interesantes y personales de su compañero/a.

1. cuándo empieza el fin de semana (¿día? ¿hora?)
2. cómo se divierten
3. cuánta tarea hacen
4. cuánto duermen (¿por la noche? ¿la siesta?)
5. los quehaceres domésticos que tienen que hacer
6. cómo se sienten el domingo por la noche

Paso 2. Díganle a la clase dos detalles interesantes sobre lo que hace su compañero/a.

Algo sobre...

el coquí

Los coquíes son ranas[a] de varias especies de un género[b] nativo de Puerto Rico. Son muy pequeños (alrededor de una pulgada[c]) y viven en los árboles.[d] Su nombre es una versión onomatopéyica del sonido[e] que algunas especies de coquíes machos[f] hacen cuando cantan desde la caída del sol[g] hasta el amanecer.[h] La canción del coquí se puede oír por toda la isla y por eso esta ranita es uno de los grandes símbolos puertorriqueños. Desgraciadamente, los coquíes están en peligro[i] de extinción.

¿Qué animales son considerados símbolos de su estado o país? ¿Por qué lo representan?

[a]*frogs* [b]*genus* [c]alrededor... *about an inch* [d]*trees* [e]*sound* [f]*male* [g]caída... *sunset* [h]*dawn* [i]*danger*

Un coquí puertorriqueño

Nota **comunicativa**

Cómo expresar la obligación

You already know several ways to express the obligation to do something.

Tengo que		I have to	
Necesito	barrer el piso.	*I need to*	*sweep the floor.*
Debo		*I should, must*	

Of the three, **deber** + *infinitive* expresses the strongest sense of obligation, and **tener que** expresses the greatest sense of urgency or immediacy.

The concept *to be someone's turn or responsibility* (to do something) is expressed in Spanish with the verb **tocar (qu)** plus an indirect object.

—¿**A quién le toca** lavar los platos esta noche?   *"Whose turn is it to wash the dishes tonight?"*

—**A mí me toca** solamente sacar la basura. Creo que **a papá le toca** lavar los platos.   *"I only have to take out the garbage. I think it's Dad's turn to wash the dishes."*

You will use these expressions in **Comunicación D** and **E.**

D. Las tareas domésticas de esta semana

Paso 1. ¿Tiene Ud. que hacer los quehaceres de la siguiente lista esta semana? Conteste usando los verbos de la **Nota comunicativa.** Si tiene que hacerlos, diga cuándo. Si no tiene que hacerlos, puede decir: **No me toca _____ (quehacer) esta semana.**

MODELO: 1. hacer la cama →
         Debo / Tengo que hacer la cama todos los días.

1. hacer la cama   **6.** sacar la basura
2. poner la mesa   **7.** pasar la aspiradora
3. lavar los platos   **8.** barrer el piso
4. lavar la ropa   **9.** limpiar el piso
5. planchar la ropa   **10.** ¿ ?

Paso 2. Ahora, en parejas, túrnense para entrevistarse sobre sus hábitos omésticos, basándose en el **Paso 1.** De los dos, ¿quién se preocupa más por su hogar (*home*)? ¿por la limpieza (*cleanliness*)? ¿Quién mantiene (*keeps*) más limpia la casa?

MODELO: hacer la cama →
     E1: ¿Con qué frecuencia haces la cama? (¿A quién **le toca** hacer las camas en tu casa?)
     E2: la hago. (Las hago a veces. En mi casa, **le toca** a mi madre hacer las camas.)

E. Las obligaciones. Piense en las cosas que todos tenemos que hacer, no solo las tareas domésticas. ¿Cuáles son las obligaciones que no le gustan a Ud. para nada? ¿Cuáles son las (*those*) que hace de buena gana (*willingly*)? Dígale a la clase una de las obligaciones en cada categoría.

Antes de mirar

¿Qué deportes le gustan a Ud.? ¿Es Ud. aficionado/a o lo(s) practica?

☐ el basquetbol
☐ el béisbol
☐ el fútbol
☐ el fútbol americano
☐ la lucha libre (*wrestling*)
☐ otros: _____

Este segmento

Ana y Víctor introducen un programa sobre los deportes, que incluye un reportaje sobre el Museo del Deporte en Puerto Rico.

El Museo del Deporte de Puerto Rico es un lugar maravilloso (*wonderful*) para las personas de todas las edades (*ages*) y especialmente para los aficionados al béisbol, el deporte rey (*number one*) de los puertorriqueños.

Vocabulario del segmento

veamos	let's see	**de primer orden**	first rate	**el campeonato**	championship
de hecho	in fact	**el pelotero**	**el beisbolista**	**las destrezas**	skills
yo jugaba	I played	**el lanzador**	pitcher	**recaen en**	fall on, are the
la magnitud	size	**el compromiso**	commitment		responsibility of
los comienzos	beginnings	**el fuerte de**	teaching strength	**han practicado**	have played
el lugar de nacimiento	birthplace	**enseñanza**			

Después de mirar

A. ¿Está claro? Empareje los años con los acontecimientos importantes del béisbol.

LOS AÑOS

_____ **1.** 1942
_____ **2.** 1898
_____ **3.** 1973
_____ **4.** a fines del siglo XIX (*at the end of the 19th century*)
_____ **5.** la década de 1940

LOS ACONTECIMIENTOS

a. Los norteamericanos empezaron a llegar a Puerto Rico.
b. Los Estados Unidos tomó posesión de Puerto Rico después de ganar una guerra (*war*) contra España.
c. El primer pelotero puertorriqueño jugó para los Chicago Cubs en las Grandes Ligas (*Leagues*).
d. Terminó la segregación entre blancos y negros en los equipos estadounidenses de béisbol.
e. El primer beisbolista hispano entró en el Salón de la Fama.

B. Un poco más. Conteste las siguientes preguntas.

1. ¿Qué deportes le gustan a Víctor? ¿Y qué equipos?
2. ¿A qué pelotero se le otorga (*is awarded*) anualmente el Premio (*Prize*) Roberto Clemente?
3. Según el Director del Museo, ¿quiénes son las personas más importantes en la enseñanza de los jóvenes beisbolistas puertorriqueños?
4. ¿Qué tipo de visitantes recibe el museo?

C. Y ahora, Uds. En parejas, hablen sobre los deportes más populares en su universidad. ¿Cuáles son? ¿De qué manera son populares, por el número de aficionados o por el número de jugadores? ¿Eran (*Were*) esos mismos deportes los más populares en su escuela secundaria?

GRAMÁTICA

♻ **¿Recuerda Ud.?**

In **Capítulos 8** and **9,** you learned the forms and some uses of the preterite. Before you learn the other simple past tense (in **Gramática 27**), you might want to review the forms of the preterite in those chapters. The verbs in the following sentences are in the preterite. Can you identify any words in the sentences that emphasize the completed nature of the actions expressed by the verbs?

1. Esta mañana me levanté a las seis.
2. Ayer fui al cine con un amigo.

3. La semana pasada pinté las paredes de la cocina.

Grammar Tutorial 27
connect
|SPANISH
www.connectspanish.com

27 Talking About the Past (Part 4)

Descriptions and Habitual Actions in the Past: Imperfect of Regular and Irregular Verbs

Gramática en acción: Los indígenas taínos

Antillas Mayores

Los indígenas taínos eran los habitantes originales de las Antillas Mayores, que son las islas de Puerto Rico, Cuba, Haití y la República Dominicana (que comparten la que antes fue la isla de La Española) y Jamaica. Allí vivían cuando los españoles llegaron al Caribe a finales del siglo XV. El pueblo taíno era pacífico y generoso y tenía una sociedad matrilineal. Llamaban a su jefe «cacique» y hablaban una lengua que nos ha dejado en el español palabras como *barbacoa, hamaca, canoa, tabaco* y *huracán.*

Comprensión

1. ¿De cuántas islas están formadas las Antillas Mayores? ¿De cuántos países?
2. ¿Cómo era el pueblo taíno?

¿Y Ud.?

1. ¿Qué significan en inglés las últimas palabras del párrafo?
2. ¿Conoce algunos de los pueblos que vivían en lo que hoy son los Estados Unidos, cuando llegaron los europeos?

The Taíno Indians *The Taíno Indians were the original inhabitants of the Greater Antilles, which are the islands of Puerto Rico, Cuba, Haiti, and the Dominican Republic (which share what was formerly the island of Hispaniola), and Jamaica. They were living there when the Spaniards arrived in the Caribbean at the end of the fifteenth century. The Taíno people were peaceful and generous, and they had a matrilineal society. They called their chief* cacique, *and they spoke a language that has left us words such as* barbacoa, hamaca, canoa, tabaco, *and* huracán *in Spanish.*

You have already used the *preterite* (**el pretérito**) to express events in the past. The *imperfect* (**el imperfecto**) is the second simple past tense in Spanish. The preterite is used when you view actions or states of being as begun or completed in the past. The imperfect is used when you view past actions or states of being as habitual or as "in progress." It is also used for describing the past, especially for giving background details.

Forms of the Imperfect / Las formas del imperfecto

hablar		comer		vivir	
hablaba	hablábamos	comía	comíamos	vivía	vivíamos
hablabas	hablabais	comías	comíais	vivías	vivíais
hablaba	hablaban	comía	comían	vivía	vivían

Pronunciation Hints
- The **b** between vowels, such as in the imperfect ending **-aba,** is pronounced as a fricative [b] sound.
- In **-er/-ir** imperfect forms, it is important not to pronounce the ending **-ía** as a diphthong, but to pronounce the **i** and the **a** in separate syllables. The accent mark over the **í** helps remind you of this.

Los verbos en *-ar*		Los verbos en *-er/-ir*	
-aba	-ábamos	-ía	-íamos
-abas	-abais	-ías	-íais
-aba	-aban	-ía	-ían

1. **English Equivalents**
   As you can see at the right, the imperfect has several English equivalents. Most of them indicate that the action was still in progress (*was/were -ing*) or that it was habitual (*used to, would*).

   yo hablaba = *I spoke, I was speaking, I used to speak, I would speak*

   comíamos = *we ate, we were eating, we used to eat, we would eat*

   él vivía = *he lived, he was living, he used to live, he would live*

   ¡OJO!
   The simple English equivalent (*I spoke, we ate, he lived*) can correspond to either the preterite or the imperfect, but it usually corresponds to the preterite. You'll learn more about this in **Capítulo 11.**

   ¡OJO!
   would = repeated action ⟶ imperfect

   Comíamos allí todos los domingos.
   We would eat there every Sunday.

2. **Stem-changing Verbs and *hay***
   Stem-changing verbs do not show a change in the imperfect.

   The imperfect of **hay** is **había**. It means *there was, there were, there used to be,* and its form never changes.

   almorzar (almuerzo) ⟶ almorzaba, almorzabas,...
   perder (pierdo) ⟶ perdía, perdías,...
   pedir (pido) (i) ⟶ pedía, pedías,...

   Había **muchos estudiantes** en el salón de clase.
   There were a lot of students in the class.

3. **Irregular Imperfect Forms**
   Only three verbs are irregular in the imperfect: **ir, ser,** and **ver.**

ir		ser		ver	
iba	íbamos	era	éramos	veía	veíamos
ibas	ibais	eras	erais	veías	veíais
iba	iban	era	eran	veía	veían

4. **First and Third Person Singular Forms**
   Note that the first and third person singular forms are identical for **-ar, -er,** and **-ir** verbs. When context does not make meaning clear, subject pronouns are used.

   Los sábados **yo** jugaba al tenis y **él** paseaba en bicicleta.
   On Saturdays I used to play tennis and he used to ride his bike.

Uses of the Imperfect / Los usos del imperfecto

If you know when to use the imperfect, it will be easy to understand when the preterite is used. When talking about the past, the preterite *is* used when the imperfect *isn't*. That's an oversimplification, but at the same time it's a general rule of thumb that will help you out at first.

The imperfect has the following uses. Notice that the first three are very clearly indicated by the English equivalents of the imperfect.

1. To describe *repeated habitual actions* in the past

$$\left.\begin{array}{l}\text{used to}\\\text{would}\end{array}\right\} + verb$$

De niños, **siempre** jugábamos en el parque todas las tardes.
As children, we always played (used to play, would play) in the park in the afternoon.

Todos los agostos iban a la costa.
Every August they went (used to go, would go) to the coast.

2. To describe an *action that was in progress* (when something else happened)

was/were + -ing

Ramón pedía la cena (cuando Cristina **llamó**).
Ramón was ordering dinner (when Cristina called).

Los taínos vivían en Puerto Rico (cuando **llegó** Colón).
The Taíno Indians were living in Puerto Rico (when Colombus arrived).

3. To describe two *simultaneous past actions in progress*, with **mientras**

was/were + -ing

Tú leías **mientras** Juan escribía la carta.
You were reading while Juan was writing the letter.

Mientras yo veía la tele, los niños jugaban a las cartas.
While I was watching TV, the kids were playing cards.

4. To describe ongoing *physical, mental,* or *emotional states* in the past

Estaban muy **distraídos.**
They were very distracted.

La quería muchísimo.
He loved her a lot.

Hacía calor, pero Luis tenía frío.
It was hot (out) but Luis was cold.

5. To tell *time* in the past and to express *age* with **tener**

Era **la una.** / Eran **las dos.**
It was one o'clock. / It was two o'clock.

Tenía **18 años.**
She was 18 years old.

¡OJO!
Just as in the present, the singular form of the verb **ser** is used with one o'clock, the plural form from two o'clock on.

Summary of the Uses of the Imperfect

used to, would
was/were + -ing
simultaneous actions (**mientras**)
physical, mental, and emotional states
time
age

Práctica y comunicación

A. Cuando yo tenía 16 años...

Paso 1. Autoprueba. Dé la terminación apropiada del imperfecto para cada verbo.

1. yo habl_____   **3.** nosotros com_____   **5.** tú ten_____
2. Uds. er_____   **4.** Pedro ib_____

Paso 2. Haga oraciones basadas en las siguientes frases, usando el imperfecto para hablar de su vida a los 16 años. Si alguna oración no es cierta para Ud., use **No...** .

1. ser muy estudioso/a
2. saber conducir (*to drive*)
3. tener la licencia de conducir
4. ir a la escuela secundaria en autobús
5. levantarse muchos domingos antes de las 10
6. tocar un instrumento en la banda de la escuela
7. ver mis programas favoritos en internet
8. querer un celular mejor que el que (*the one*) tenía

Paso 3. Ahora, en parejas, túrnense para entrevistarse usando como base las oraciones del **Paso 2**. Luego díganle a la clase algo que Uds. tenían en común.

MODELO: E1: Cuando tenías 16 años, ¿eras muy estudioso?
       E2: No, no era nada estudioso. ¿Y tú?
       E1: Yo sí.

B. La vida a los 7 años

Paso 1. Haga oraciones sobre la vida de Tina Acevedo, que vivía en Puerto Rico cuando tenía 7 años. Use el imperfecto de los verbos.

1. Tina: vivir en Bayamón, Puerto Rico
2. asistir a una escuela católica
3. hablar español todo el tiempo
4. aprender inglés en la escuela
5. dibujar (*to draw*) mucho en clase
6. jugar con sus compañeros en el parque
7. ir a casa de sus abuelos después de la escuela
8. ver sus programas favoritos en la tele
9. sus padres: llegar por ella a las 7:30
10. sus padres: llevarla a casa

Paso 2. Ahora haga oraciones similares a las oraciones del **Paso 1** pero con información de su propia (*own*) vida a los 7 años.

MODELO: Tina: vivir en Bayamón, Puerto Rico. →
       Yo **vivía** en St. Louis, Missouri.

Nota **comunicativa**

El progresivo en el pasado

Just like the present progressive, the *past progressive* (**el imperfecto progresivo**) emphasizes that an action was happening at that very moment. The past progressive is formed with the imperfect of estar plus the present participle (**-ndo**) of another verb.

Cuando mi tío llamó, **estábamos cenando.**
When my uncle called, we were having dinner.

El sábado a las 10 de la noche, ¿**estabas estudiando**?
Saturday night at 10, were you studying?

You will use the past progressive in **Práctica C.**

Prác. A, Paso 1: Answers: 1. hablaba 2. eran 3. comíamos 4. iba 5. tenías

C. El trabajo de niñera (*baby-sitter*)

Paso 1. El trabajo de niñera puede ser muy pesado (*difficult*). ¿Qué estaba pasando cuando la niñera perdió por fin la paciencia? Describa todas las acciones que pueda, usando **estaba(n)** + *present participle* (**-ndo**).

MODELO: El bebé **estaba llorando.**

Paso 2. De adolescentes, ¿trabajaban Uds. de niñeros/as? ¿Tenían que cuidar a sus hermanos menores? ¿a los niños de sus parientes? En parejas, túrnense para hablar de sus experiencias trabajando como niñero/a. Háganse preguntas para obtener mucha información. Si no trabajaron de niñeros/as, cuenten sus experiencias en otros trabajos o sus experiencias *con* un niñero o niñera.

MODELO: E1: Cuando yo tenía 15 años, cuidaba a mi hermano menor.
E2: ¿Lo cuidabas todos los días? ¿Cuánto te pagaban tus padres? ¿Se portaba bien tu hermano menor? ¿Te daba mucho trabajo? ¿Qué cosas malas hacía siempre?

D. Los tiempos cambian (*change*).
Las siguientes oraciones describen aspectos de la vida de hoy. En parejas, comparen estos aspectos con el estilo de vida alrededor del (*around the*) año 1900. Luego, describan dos cambios más.

MODELO: E1: Ahora la gente se comunica electrónicamente. →
E2: Alrededor del año 1900, la gente **se comunicaba por carta.**

1900   **HOY**

1. Ahora muchísimas mujeres trabajan fuera de (*outside of the*) casa.
2. Hoy día la gente lee libros en formato electrónico.
3. Ahora la gente puede escuchar música en casa todo el tiempo.
4. Hoy día las mujeres se ponen pantalones.

(Continúa.)

***Sonar** *is a stem-changing verb. Remember that the stem of present participles does not change with* **-ar** *verbs* (**sonando**).

†*The present participle of* **caer** *is like that of* **leer**: **cayendo**.

5. Ahora hay hombres enfermeros (*nurses*) y maestros (*teachers*).

6. Hoy, tenemos más máquinas y por eso hacemos menos trabajo físicamente.

7. Las familias son más pequeñas.

8. Muchas parejas viven juntas sin estar casadas (*married*).

E. Intercambios

Paso 1. En parejas, túrnense para entrevistarse sobre su adolescencia y los años de la escuela secundaria. Usen las siguientes categorías para organizar su conversación. Deben obtener detalles interesantes y personales de su compañero/a.

MODELO: gustar: molestar (*to annoy*) a alguien →
> **E1:** Cuando tenías 15 años, ¿a quién te gustaba molestar?
> **E2:** Me gustaba molestar a mi hermano menor. Él a veces tomaba mis cosas sin mi permiso.
> **E1:** ¿Y ahora todavía te gusta molestarlo?
> **E2:** La verdad es que sí. (*Actually, yes.*)

1. gustar: molestar a alguien, oír un tipo de música, vestirse con un estilo de ropa

2. preferir: programas de tele, películas, materias, comidas y bebidas

3. comer: a qué hora, dónde, con quién

4. leer: revistas, novelas

5. hacer: los fines de semana, después de las clases

6. discutir: con quién, sobre qué

Paso 2. Ahora díganle a la clase dos cosas que Uds. tenían en común.

MODELO: A Frank y a mí nos gustaba oír música rock. Preferíamos ver películas de acción.

Algo sobre...

Borinquen

Borinquen es el nombre que los taínos, los habitantes originales de Puerto Rico, le daban a su isla. El pueblo taíno se extinguió[a] en el siglo XVI, como consecuencia de la colonización. Pero los puertorriqueños están muy orgullosos[b] de su origen taíno. Los términos[c] **boricua** y **borinqueño/a** se usan con frecuencia para referirse a las personas, instituciones y tradiciones de la Isla. De hecho,[d] el himno oficial[e] puertorriqueño se llama «La borinqueña».

¿Sabe Ud. quiénes eran los habitantes originales de su estado? ¿Está presente su herencia en el folclore de su estado?

[a]se... *died out* [b]*proud* [c]*terms* [d]De... *In fact* [e]himno... *national anthem*

El emblema del *Coast Guard* de Puerto Rico, que lleva dos símbolos puertorriqueños: el coquí y el nombre Borinquen

¿Recuerda Ud.?

You have been using interrogative words since the beginning of *Puntos de partida*, so not much will be new for you in **Gramática 28.** Review what you already know by telling which interrogative word or phrase you associate with the following phrases.

1. un lugar

2. la hora

3. una persona

4. la manera de hacer algo

5. una selección

6. la razón (*reason*) por algo

7. el lugar de origen de una persona

8. un destino

9. una cantidad

10. ser el dueño de algo

 28 Getting Information (Part 2)
Summary of Interrogative Words

Gramática en acción: Un restaurante de Connecticut

1. ¿Cómo se llama el restaurante?
2. ¿En qué ciudad de Connecticut está?
3. ¿En qué tipo de cocina se especializa el restaurante?
4. ¿Qué grupo toca el viernes, 6 de octubre?

¿Y Ud.?

¿Cuántas preguntas más puede Ud. hacer sobre este restaurante, por (*based on*) lo que dice el anuncio?

Here are all of the interrogatives that you have learned so far. Only more information about using **¿qué?** and **¿cuál(es)?**, both of which express *what?* or *which?* in Spanish, is new.

¡OJO!

Remember that interrogative words always have an accent mark in Spanish, and that questions have two question marks: **¿ ?**

¿Cómo?	How?	**¿Dónde?**	Where?
		¿De dónde?	From where?
¿Cuándo?	When?	**¿Adónde?**	Where (to)?
¿A qué hora?	At what time?		
		¿Cuánto/a?	How much?
¿Qué?	What? Which?	**¿Cuántos/as?**	How many?
¿Cuál(es)?	What? Which one(s)?		
		¿Quién(es)?	Who?
¿Por qué?	Why?	**¿De quién(es)?**	Whose?

Uses of *¿qué?* and *¿cuál?* / Los usos de *¿qué?* y *¿cuál?*

1. **¿Qué? + es/son = Definition**
   Use **¿Qué es/son... ?** to ask for a definition.

   ¿Qué es esto?
   What is this?

   ¿Qué son las Antillas?
   What are the West Indies?

2. **¿Qué? + *verb* = Explanation/Identification**
   Use **¿Qué... ?** with any verb other than **ser** to ask for an identification or an elaboration.

   ¿Qué quieres?
   What do you want?

   ¿Qué tocas?
   What (instrument) do you play?

3. **¿Qué? + *noun* = Identification**
   The interrogative **¿qué?** can be directly followed by a noun. The question asks the listener to identify or specify information, often making a choice.

   ¿Qué deporte prefieres?
   What (Which) sport do you prefer?

   ¿Qué playa te gusta más?
   What (Which) beach do you like most?

   ¿Qué instrumento musical tocas?
   What (Which) musical instrument do you play?

4. ¿Cuál(es)? + *verb* **= Choice**

Use **¿cuál(es)?** to express *what* when it means *which one*, that is, when it calls for a choice.

¡OJO!

¿Qué?, not **¿cuál?**, is followed by a noun. Compare these sentences:

¿Qué libro quieres? = *which book?*

¿Cuál quieres? = *which one?*

¿Cuál de los dos quieres? = *which one of the two?*

Sometimes a phrase like **de los dos (tres...)** makes the choice more obvious.

¿Cuál es la clase más grande?
What (Which [one]) is the biggest class?

¿Cuáles son tus jugadores favoritos?
What (Which [ones]) are your favorite players?

¿Cuál es tu (número de) teléfono?
What is your phone number?

¿Cuál prefieres?
Which one do you prefer?

¿Cuál de los dos coches vas a comprar?
Which of the two cars are you going to buy?

Práctica y comunicación

A. Preguntas personales

Paso 1. Autoprueba. Empareje las palabras interrogativas con la información que piden.

1. ¿Cuándo?
2. ¿Dónde?
3. ¿Qué?
4. ¿Cuánto?
5. ¿Cuál?

a. un lugar
b. una selección
c. un número o una cantidad

d. una definición
e. la hora
f. una explicación

> **Summary of ¿qué? Versus ¿cuál?**
>
> **¿qué?** + **es/son** = definition
>   + *verb* = explanation
>   + *noun*
> **¿cuál(es)?** + *verb* = choice

Paso 2. Complete las siguientes preguntas con **qué** o **cuál(es)** y contéstelas.

1. ¿Tiene Ud. un segundo nombre (*middle name*)? ¿_____ es? ¿_____ son sus dos apellidos, según el sistema hispano de apellidos?
2. ¿_____ es su número de teléfono?
3. ¿_____ es su dirección (*address*) postal? ¿_____ es su e-mail?
4. ¿_____ estado es su lugar de origen?
5. ¿_____ son las materias que Ud. toma este semestre/trimestre? ¿_____ es su favorita?
6. ¿_____ es más divertido para Ud., practicar un deporte o ir al cine?
7. ¿_____ tarea doméstica odia más?
8. ¿_____ es un equipo? ¿_____ es su equipo de fútbol americano favorito?

Paso 3. Ahora, en parejas, túrnense para hacer y contestar las preguntas del **Paso 2.** Luego díganle a la clase algo que Uds. tienen en común.

B. Intercambios

Paso 1. En parejas, túrnense para entrevistarse sobre los siguientes temas. Empiecen las preguntas con **¿Qué... ?** or **¿Cuál(es)...?** Hablen de sus preferencias actuales (*current*) o de sus preferencias de niño/a (usando el imperfecto).

MODELOS: estaciones del año →

    ¿Qué estación del año **prefieres?** (**¿Qué** estación **preferías** de niño/a?)
    ¿Cuál es / Cuál era tu estación del año favorita?

1. estilo de música
2. pasatiempos o deportes
3. programas de televisión

4. materias este semestre/trimestre
5. colores
6. tipos de comida

Paso 2. Ahora, díganle a la clase una cosa que tienen en común y otra en la que (*which*) no están de acuerdo.

Prác. A, Paso 1: Answers: 1. e 2. a 3. d, f 4. c 5. b

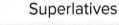

¿Recuerda Ud.?

You learned how to make comparisons in **Gramática 17 (Cap. 6)**. Before you start **Gramática 29,** review what you remember about comparisons by completing the following comparative phrases with the appropriate word.

1. más dinero _____ tú
2. tan simpáticos _____ ellos
3. _____ hermanas como...

4. menos libros _____ Cecilia
5. correr _____ como Ud.
6. viejo, _____

Grammar Tutorial 29
connect SPANISH
www.connectspanish.com

29 Expressing Extremes
Superlatives

Gramática en acción: Los puertorriqueños más famosos

¿Está Ud. de acuerdo? Corrija las declaraciones falsas, según su opinión.

	CIERTO	FALSO

1. Jennifer López es la cantante puertorriqueña más conocida del mundo. ☐ ☐
2. Benicio del Toro es el actor puertorriqueño más famoso del mundo. ☐ ☐
3. Roberto Clemente, de origen puertorriqueño, es el mejor beisbolista hispano de todos los tiempos. ☐ ☐

¿Y Ud.?

Complete las siguientes declaraciones para expresar su opinión.

1. El cantante hispano o hispana más popular del momento es _____.
2. La mejor actriz (*actress*) del momento es _____.
3. En la actualidad (*Currently*), la música más popular es _____ (la música de _____, la música de estilo _____).

Comparatives / Los comparativos	Superlatives / Los superlativos
Julio es **más** alto **que** Juanito.	Julio es el niño más alto de la clase. (Julio es el más alto de la clase.*)
El fútbol es **más** popular **que** el golf.	El fútbol es el deporte más popular del mundo. (El fútbol es el más popular del mundo.*)
La comida italiana es **buena,** pero la comida mexicana es **mejor**.	La comida mexicana es la mejor comida de todas las comidas del mundo. (La comida mexicana es la mejor de todas las comidas del mundo.*)

the superlative / **el superlativo** = an adjective or adverb that expresses an extreme

The most famous Puerto Ricans *Do you agree?* **1.** *Jennifer Lopez is the best known Puerto Rican singer in the world.* **2.** *Benicio del Toro is the most famous Puerto Rican actor in the world.* **3.** *Roberto Clemente, of Puerto Rican descent, is the best Hispanic baseball player of all time.*

*Notice how adjectives can be used as nouns: **el niño más alto** (the tallest child) → **el más alto** (the tallest), and so on. You can learn more about using adjectives in this way in Appendix 2, Using Adjectives as Nouns.*

Superlatives / Los superlativos

1. Forming the Superlative

To express the *most/best/least/worst,* and so on, the comparative forms are used with the definite article.

¡OJO!
in/of = **de**

el / la / los / las + *noun* + **más / menos** + *adjective* + **de**

El basquetbol es **el deporte** más **competitivo** del mundo.
Basketball is the most competitive sport in the world.

El golf es **el deporte** menos **peligroso** de todos.
Golf is the least dangerous sport of all.

2. Irregular Superlatives

Mejor and **peor** generally precede the noun.

el / la / los / las + **mejor(es) / peor(es)** + *noun* + **de**

Son **los mejores refrigeradores** de la tienda.
They're the best refrigerators in the store.

La verdad es que es **el peor jugador** del equipo.
The truth is that he's the worst player on the team.

Note that **mejor** and **peor** are often used alone (without the article or **de**).

Ana es **mi mejor** amiga.
Ana is my best friend.

¡Esa fue **tu peor** idea!
That was your worst idea!

Mayor and **menor** are often used without the noun.

Lorenzo es **el mayor de** los hermanos y Leticia es **la menor**.
Lorenzo is the oldest of the siblings and Leticia is the youngest.

Práctica y comunicación

A. Opiniones personales

Paso 1. Autoprueba. Ordene las palabras para hacer oraciones con sentido (*meaningful*) que expresan ideas superlativas.

1. **Es...** ciudad / más / el / grande / la / parque / de
2. **Son...** clase / los / difíciles / de / niños / la / más
3. **Visité...** del / los / mundo / museos / mejores
4. **Vi...** peor / año / película / la / del

Summary of Superlatives

el / la / los / las + *noun* + **más / menos** + *adjective* + **de**

el / la / los / las + { **mejor(es) / peor(es)** / **mayor(es) / menor(es)** } + *noun* + **de**

Paso 2. Use las siguientes ideas para dar su opinión sobre lo que es «más» en cada categoría.

MODELO: una estación del año (frío) ⟶ El invierno es **la** estación **más fría del** año.

1. un día festivo del año (divertido)
2. una materia de este semestre/trimestre (difícil)
3. una persona de la familia (vieja)
4. una persona de la familia (joven)
5. un mes del año (bueno)
6. un día de la semana (malo)
7. un amigo / una amiga (bueno/a)

Paso 3. Ahora, en parejas, usen las ideas del **Paso 2** para entrevistarse. Luego, díganle a la clase algo que tienen en común.

MODELO:: **E1:** ¿Cómo se llama tu mejor amigo o amiga?
  E2: Mi mejor amigo es Jacobo. ¿Y tu mejor amigo?
  E1: (Es) Luis.

B. Superlativos

Paso 1. Modifique las siguientes oraciones para hacer una forma superlativa.

MODELO: Es una estudiante muy alta. (la clase) ⟶
Es **la** estudiante **más alta de la clase.**

1. Son unos días festivos muy divertidos. (el año)
2. Es una clase muy interesante. (todas mis clases)
3. Es una persona muy inteligente. (todos mis amigos)
4. Son ciudades muy grandes. (los Estados Unidos)
5. Es un estado muy pequeño. (el país)
6. Es un perro muy pequeño. (el mundo)
7. Es una residencia muy ruidosa (*noisy*). (la universidad)
8. Es una montaña muy alta. (el mundo)

Paso 2. Ahora repita cada oración con información verdadera.

MODELO: **Carla** es la estudiante más alta de la clase.

C. Intercambios. En parejas, túrnense para expresar sus opiniones sobre las siguientes ideas. Luego compartan (*share*) sus opiniones con la clase.

MODELO: el peor / mejor restaurante de la ciudad ⟶
E1: Yo creo que _____ es **el peor** restaurante **de** la ciudad.
E2: En mi opinión, **el peor** restaurante **de** la ciudad es _____.
⟶ No estamos de acuerdo. Yo creo que _____ es **el peor** restaurante **de** la ciudad. Mi compañero/a cree que **el peor** es _____.

1. el peor / mejor **restaurante de la ciudad**
2. un libro interesantísimo / aburridísimo
3. un plato riquísimo / malísimo
4. un programa de televisión interesantísimo / pesadísimo
5. un lugar tranquilísimo / animadísimo / peligrosísimo (*very dangerous*)
6. la canción más bonita / fea del año
7. la mejor / peor película del año

Nota **comunicativa**

Los diminutivos

In Spanish, it is very common to add a suffix to nouns and adjectives to express littleness or affection. The most common diminutive ending is **-ito/a.**

- If the word ends in a consonant, **-ito/a** is added to the singular form (and any accent on the word is dropped): **papel** ⟶ **papelito, fácil** ⟶ **facilito.**
- If the word ends in a vowel, the final vowel is dropped before adding **-ito/a** (and any accent on the

word is dropped): **guap**o ⟶ **guapito, libr**o ⟶ **librito (libr**os ⟶**libritos), rápido** ⟶ **r**apido.
- Spelling changes occur when the final consonant is **c, g,** or **z: poc**o ⟶ **poquito, amig**a ⟶ **amiguita, peda**zos **(chunks)** ⟶ **pedacitos.**

You will use diminutives in **Práctica D.**

D. ¿Diminutivos para Ud.? Los diminutivos se usan para hablar de algo con afecto y ternura (*tenderness*). ¿Usarían Uds. (*Would you use*) un diminutivo para hablar de las siguientes personas y cosas? Expliquen sus respuestas.

MODELO: 1. ¿su cuarto? ⟶
E1: Sí, mi **cuartito,** porque es muy pequeño / es un lugar especial.
E2: No, no quiero llamarlo **cuartito,** porque no es pequeño / no me gusta.

1. ¿su cuarto?
2. ¿su libro de español?
3. ¿su hermano/a (sobrino/a) menor?

4. ¿su gorra favorita?
5. ¿su libro favorito cuando Ud. era pequeño/a?

Un poco de todo

A. Lengua y cultura: Un poco de la historia de Puerto Rico

Paso 1. Complete the following passage with the correct form of the words in parentheses, as suggested by context. When two possibilities are given in parentheses, select the correct word. **¡OJO!** Give the preterite form of the verbs marked *P:* and the imperfect of those marked *I:*.

En la isla de Puerto Rico, como en todas las Antillas Mayores, (*I: vivir*[1]) los indígenas taínos. Cristóbal Colón (*P: llegar*[2]) a la Isla en 1493, en su segunda[a] expedición al Nuevo Mundo. (*Se / Le*[3]) dice que el jefe[b] de los taínos, que (*I: tener*[4]) el título de cacique, (*P: recibir*[5]) a Colón con un collar[c] de oro. (*Por / Para*[6]) eso Colón pensó que (*I: haber*[7]) mucho oro en la Isla, pero no tenía (*razón / prisa*[8]). De todas formas,[d] los españoles explotaron la Isla intensamente. En poco tiempo, la población taína prácticamente (*P: desaparecer*[e9]) debido a[f] tres factores: (*el / la*[10]) explotación física causada por labores intensas,[g] las rebeliones de los nativos y las enfermedades[h] que los españoles (*P: llevar*[11]) consigo,[i] que (*I: ser*[12]) nuevas para los taínos. La población africana, que los españoles llevaron a la Isla como esclavos,[j] (*P: empezar*[13]) a llegar en el siglo[k] XVI.

En el siglo XIX, por toda Latinoamérica, (*I: haber*[14]) guerras[l] contra España para obtener la independencia. Pero las Antillas no (*P: independizarse*[15]). En 1898 Puerto Rico se convirtió en[m] territorio de los Estados Unidos, después de que España (*P: perder*[16]) la guerra que en los Estados Unidos (*P: recibir*[17]) el nombre de «*the Spanish American War*» (la Guerra Hispanoamericana).

En 1917 los puertorriqueños (*P: ser*[18]) declarados ciudadanos[n] (*estadounidense*[19]) y, desde 1953, su país es un Estado Libre Asociado a los Estados Unidos de América. Esto significa que aunque[ñ] no es independiente, tiene plena[o] autonomía interna.

Estatua y fuente (*fountain*) de La India Taína, en Caguas, Puerto Rico

[a]second [b]chief [c]necklace [d]De... In any case [e]to disappear [f]debido... due to [g]labores... hard labor [h]illnesses [i]with them [j]slaves [k]century [l]wars [m]se... became a [n]citizens [ñ]although [o]full

Paso 2. Comprensión. Conteste las siguientes preguntas.

1. ¿De qué grupo de islas forma parte Puerto Rico?
2. ¿Quiénes eran los habitantes originales de Puerto Rico?
3. ¿Cuándo llegaron los españoles a Puerto Rico por primera vez?
4. ¿Después del siglo XVI, qué otros grupos raciales había en la Isla?
5. ¿Desde cuándo es Puerto Rico territorio de los Estados Unidos?
6. ¿Cuál es la situación política actual de Puerto Rico?

Paso 3. Ahora, en parejas, den información histórica sobre su estado (o país) comparable a la información sobre Puerto Rico. Aquí hay unas sugerencias.

1. qué pueblo(s) vivía(n) en su estado (país) originalmente
2. qué otros pueblos llegaron más tarde y cuándo
3. si hubo guerra(s) con otro país y cuándo
4. si ganó su independencia de otro país y cuándo
5. cuándo se convirtió en estado de la Unión estadounidense

B. ¿Qué hizo Ricardo ayer?

Paso 1. Narre lo que Ricardo hizo ayer, usando como base los dibujos y las ideas debajo de ellos.

MODELO: despertarse **temprano** / ser 6:30 →
Ricardo **se despertó** temprano. **Eran** las seis y media de la mañana.

Vocabulario útil

primero...
luego... y...
después... y...
finalmente (por fin)...

Estrategia

- La primera frase debajo del dibujo indica una acción. Por eso el verbo se conjuga en el **pretérito**.
- La segunda frase describe un aspecto de la situación en ese momento. Por eso el verbo se conjuga en el **imperfecto**.

1. quedarse **en cama durmiendo** / tener **sueño**
2. ducharse **y vestirse rápidamente** / tener **prisa**
3. llegar **tarde a clase** / la profesora: explicar **el nuevo capítulo**
4. almorzar **con unos amigos** / tener **muchísima hambre**

5. jugar **un partido de basquetbol** / haber **mucha gente en el gimnasio**
6. regresar **a casa y** preparar **la cena** / ser **temprano todavía** (*still*)
7. alguien: llamarlo **por teléfono** / ser **su mamá**
8. acostarse **y dormirse inmediatamente** / estar **cansadísimo**

Paso 2. Ahora, en parejas, hablen de su día de ayer, siguiendo las ideas del **Paso 1.** Luego díganle al resto de la clase algo que tuvieron en común.

En **su** comunidad

Entreviste a una persona hispana de su universidad o ciudad sobre lo que hace en su tiempo libre.

PREGUNTAS POSIBLES

- ¿Practica algún deporte? ¿Es su deporte favorito uno de los deportes más populares de su cultura?
- ¿Cuáles son sus pasatiempos favoritos? ¿Cuáles eran sus pasatiempos favoritos cuando era niño/a?
- ¿Hace muchos quehaceres domésticos? ¿Cuáles son? ¿Cuáles son los quehaceres que más odia? ¿Qué tareas domésticas tenía que hacer cuando tenía 12 o 13 años?

«Deportes que mueven masas» Segmento 2

Antes de mirar

Conteste las siguientes preguntas.

¿Vio Ud. recientemente la final de algún campeonato (*championship*) importante? ¿Qué equipos se disputaron (*fought for*) el campeonato? ¿Cuál ganó?

Este segmento

Laura presenta un reportaje sobre el deporte rey (*number one*) en México.

«Y muchos [mexicanos] se unen a una porra (*fan club*) para acompañar a su equipo hasta el campo de fútbol y defenderlo a gritos (*with shouts* [*of support*]).»

Vocabulario del segmento

hasta	even	**el/la**	commentator
chévere	great	**comentarista**	
gritar	to yell; to scream	**angloparlante**	English-speaking
cualquier sitio	any place	**sabio/a**	wise
el asiento	seat	**la cita**	date; appointment
disfrutar	to enjoy	**que la pasen**	have a good
el grito	yell; scream	**bien**	time
¿han	have you	**que gane su**	may your
escuchado?	heard?	**equipo**	team win

Fragmento del guion

Pero el auténtico deporte rey del planeta es el fútbol. Les voy a dar un dato[a] fascinante: se calcula que más de mil millones de personas en todo el mundo vieron la final de la Copa Mundial[b] de Fútbol del año 2010, que se disputaron[c] España y Holanda. ¡Más de mil millones!

[a]*fact* [b]*Copa... World Cup* [c]*se... was fought out by*

Después de mirar

A. ¿Está claro? Complete las oraciones con información del video.

   1. El _____ por ciento de los beisbolistas de las grandes ligas es de origen hispano.

   2. El deporte rey del planeta es el _____.

   3. El deporte rey en México es el _____.

   4. _____ ganó la Copa Mundial en 2010.

   5. Los comentaristas _____ no saben gritar bien «¡gol!».

B. Un poco más. Conteste las siguientes preguntas.

   1. ¿Dónde vio Ana la final de la Copa del Mundo?

   2. ¿Qué hizo Ana durante el partido?

   3. ¿Quién prefería ver los partidos de fútbol en español? ¿Por qué?

C. Y ahora, Uds. En parejas, escojan uno de los dos deportes de este programa (el béisbol, **Segmento 1**, o el fútbol, este **Segmento**) y hablen de la situación de este deporte en su país. ¿Es este deporte uno de los más populares? ¿Es popular por el número de espectadores o por el número de personas que lo practican? ¿Dónde se practica?

A LEER

¿Hay playas muy frecuentadas por la gente cerca de su ciudad o estado? En la zona donde Ud. vive, ¿cuáles son los lugares que más visita la gente en el tiempo libre?

Lectura cultural: Puerto Rico
El tiempo libre en Puerto Rico

A muchos puertorriqueños les gusta pasar el tiempo junto al[a] mar. Es lógico: Puerto Rico y sus islas más pequeñas, como Vieques y Culebra, están rodeadas de[b] deliciosas aguas cálidas[c] y hermosas[d] playas. Muchas son de arena[e] fina y mar tranquilo, ideales para relajarse y nadar. Otras, especialmente en el norte, son excelentes para hacer *surfing*. Y otras (al este y al sur) ofrecen el espectáculo natural de la bioluminiscencia: unos microorganismos llamados dinoflagelados iluminan el agua del mar en la noche.

Aunque[f] en Puerto Rico hace buen tiempo todo el año, es en los meses de verano (de mayo a septiembre) cuando los puertorriqueños van más a la playa. Amigos y familia, música, comida, una hamaca entre palmeras... ¿Qué más se puede pedir?

[a]junto... *next to* [b]rodeadas... *surrounded by* [c]*warm* [d]*beautiful* [e]*sand* [f]*Although*

El Fuerte de San Felipe del Morro, que guardaba el puerto (*port*) de la bahía de San Juan, Puerto Rico

En **otros** países hispanos

- **En todo el mundo hispanohablante** Jugar al dominó y hacer la sobremesa son pasatiempos muy populares en muchos países hispanos. El dominó es un juego muy fácil de aprender, pero el juego se complica muchísimo —y también se hace más interesante— jugando en parejas. La sobremesa es el tiempo que se pasa charlando[a] en la mesa después de la comida. No es nada extraño[b] que un grupo de parientes o amigos hispanos pase dos o tres horas sentados[c] a la mesa, primero comiendo, luego tomando café y charlando, hasta unir el almuerzo con la merienda.

- **En la Argentina** En este país sudamericano hay gran afición por el deporte del polo. La Argentina domina ese deporte en el panorama mundial.

[a]*chatting* [b]*strange* [c]*seated*

Un símbolo puertorriqueño: El Viejo San Juan

Los puertorriqueños se sienten muy orgullosos[a] de su herencia cultural y de sus tradiciones, heredadas de los taínos, africanos y españoles. El Viejo San Juan representa la cultura y tradición españolas. Sus edificios coloniales, sus calles adoquinadas,[b] el Fuerte[c] San Felipe del Morro, la Catedral y otros edificios históricos representan la historia de la Isla.

[a]*proud* [b]*cobblestone* [c]*Fort*

COMPRENSIÓN

1. ¿Cuáles son los meses en que los puertorriqueño van más a la playa?
2. ¿Qué es la bioluminiscencia?
3. ¿Dónde están las mejores playas puertorriqueñas para hacer *surfing*?
4. ¿Cuáles son dos de los pasatiempos populares en algunos países hispanohablantes?
5. ¿Qué deporte es muy popular en la Argentina?
6. ¿Con qué herencia cultural se identifica el Viejo San Juan?

Y ahora, Uds.

¿Cuáles son los pasatiempos que Uds. asocian más con la vida familiar estadounidense? ¿Son típicos en su familia también? Si no, ¿cuáles son los pasatiempos de su familia?

Del mundo hispano

Antes de leer

Piense Ud. en cómo usa Ud. su teléfono celular. ¿Cuáles son los aspectos positivos y negativos de su uso?

Lectura: Los teléfonos celulares

Volver a conectar

Aunque[a] tabletas, *smartphones* y otros dispositivos están pensados y diseñados[b] para servirnos, los estudios realizados[c] hasta ahora... constatan[d] nuestra «dependencia electrónica». Sin embargo, desconectar es posible. El psicólogo Fernando Azor nos aporta[e] algunas sugerencias:

PRIORIZAR Hay que atender[f] primero a aquellos que se dirigen a[g] nosotros en persona; después las llamadas; después mensajes instantáneos y, por último, los correos electrónicos.

RESPONDER MÁS TARDE No responder de inmediato es un buen entrenamiento[h] para combatir la ansiedad. Ni nosotros estamos obligados a contestar al instante,[i] ni ellos pueden sentirse cuestionados[j] porque no se les escriba en el acto.[k]

ABSTENERSE[l] Ser capaz[m] de pasar un fin de semana o un día entero con el teléfono apagado es una señal[n] de sana independencia. Si este período es demasiado largo, hay que tratar de desconectar todas las redes[ñ] (si no, al menos[o] el wifi) en determinados momentos del día, por ejemplo durante la noche.

CONFIGURAR Configure su dispositivo para que los nuevos correos o mensajes instantáneos solo lleguen cuando usted actualice[p] manualmente. Evitará así[q] las constantes miradas a la pantalla en busca de notificaciones.

HUMANIZAR La tecnología crea una ilusoria sensación de intimidad y contacto. Por ello[r] es aconsejable,[s] al menos una vez a la semana, «desvirtualizar» nuestras relaciones y quedar con ese interlocutor[t] para tomar un café o dar un paseo real.

SELECCIONAR A menudo[u] mantenemos relaciones virtuales que, en realidad, no aportan[v] nada a nuestra vida,[w] o que incluso nos restan[x] energía y tiempo. Por ello, es muy saludable ser un poco más darwinistas[*] con nuestra agenda de contactos, y no dudar a la hora de dejar de[y] ser «amigo» de aquellas personas a las que, en el fondo, no nos une nada.[z]

[a]*Although* [b]pensados... *imagined and designed* [c]*completed* [d]*show* [e]*offrece* [f]*pay attention* [g]se... *address* [h]*training* [i]al... *immediately* [j]*let down* [k]en... *immediately* [l]*Abstain* [m]*capable* [n]*sign* [ñ]hay... *it's necessary to try to disconnect the networks* [o]al... *at least* [p]*refresh, update* [q]Evitará... *That way you will avoid* [r]Por... Por eso [s]*advisable* [t]*conversation partner* [u]A... Con frecuencia [v]*contribuyen* [w]*life* [x]incluso... *even take away from us* [y]no... *not hesitate when it comes to stop* [z]a... *whom, in the final analysis, we have no ties with*

Vocabulario para leer

apagado/a	turned off
el dispositivo	device
la llamada	(phone) call
la pantalla	screen
quedar con	to meet, make a date with
saludable	healthy
sano/a	healthy

Comprensión

A. Ideas principales. ¿Cuál de las siguientes oraciones resume mejor la lectura? Señale (*Point out*) evidencia en el texto para la respuesta que seleccione.

1. Los teléfonos celulares son dispositivos esenciales para la vida moderna y no se puede vivir sin ellos.
2. La dependencia de los teléfonos celulares y otros dispositivos es un problema, pero es posible controlarla.
3. Es mejor vivir sin teléfonos celulares y otros dispositivos.

B. Aplicación personal. De las seis sugerencias que ofrece la lectura, ¿cuáles implementa Ud. ahora? ¿Cuáles quiere implementar? ¿Cuáles no son ni (*neither*) apropiadas ni (*nor*) aceptables para Ud.? Explique sus respuestas.

---

*Darwinistas *refers to Charles Darwin, the nineteenth-century theorist of biological evolution. In this context, the term refers to an action that will lead to self-preservation.*

Antes de escuchar

¿Qué quehaceres hace Ud. para mantener limpio su apartamento o alcoba? ¿Cuál de los quehaceres hace con más frecuencia? ¿Cuál le molesta más hacer?

Vocabulario **para escuchar**

verdadero/a	real	**no discutamos**	let's not argue
no te preocupes	don't worry	**yo me encargo de**	I'll take care of
arreglar	to tidy up	**¡muévete!**	move it!, get a move on!

Después de escuchar

A. **¿Quién lo va a hacer?** Empareje cada tarea con la persona que la va a hacer.

TAREAS

1. _____ limpiar la cocina
2. _____ limpiar el baño
3. _____ pasar la aspiradora
4. _____ sacar la basura

PERSONAS

a. Jorge
b. Hilda
c. Ana

B. **Otros detalles.** Conteste las siguientes preguntas según el diálogo.

1. ¿Por qué es urgente limpiar el apartamento?
2. ¿Quién está dispuesto (*willing*) a ayudar?
3. ¿Quién no tiene muchas ganas de ayudar?

PRODUCCIÓN PERSONAL

¡Ahora, yo!

A. Use de modelo las preguntas y respuestas de la página 295 de este capítulo para hablar de su tiempo libre y de sus pasatiempos favoritos.

B. Filme una entrevista con un(a) atleta hispanohablante de su universidad. Si no encuentra ninguno/a, entreviste a un(a) atleta anglohablante (*English-speaking*) y use su voz en off (*voiceover*) para traducir al español las ideas principales de lo que dice el/la atleta.

A ESCRIBIR
Un ensayo sobre los pasatiempos y diversiones

En el Bosque Nacional el Yunque, en Puerto Rico

¿Cuáles son las actividades típicas de los estudiantes de su universidad? ¿Y qué hacía Ud. cuando era más joven? ¿Era similar a lo que hace ahora? Ud. va a escribir un ensayo sobre estas ideas.

Preparar

Paso 1. En parejas, piensen en las actividades típicas de la gente de su edad (*age group*) y en concreto de los estudiantes de su universidad. La tabla sugiere (*suggests*) algunas categorías, pero Uds. las pueden ampliar o modificar.

Actividades durante el tiempo libre	La gente de nuestra edad, en general	Los estudiantes de esta universidad
Físicas		
Intelectuales		
Vida (*Life*) social		
Otras		

Paso 2. Ahora use la información del **Paso 1** para escribir un ensayo comparativo. ¿Es Ud. una persona representativa de su generación y de su universidad? Cuando Ud. era más joven, ¿hacía las mismas cosas? Hay más ayuda (*help*) en Connect.

Más ideas para su portafolio

- Si Ud. juega en un equipo o hace un deporte a nivel competitivo, incluya una foto de Ud. haciendo ese deporte. Describa su posición en el equipo y otros detalles importantes (ranking, nombre del entrenador / de la entrenadora, etcétera). Si no practica ningún deporte, describa el tipo de ejercicio físico que hace, incluyendo una foto si es posible. Y si no hace ningún tipo de ejercicio físico, explique cómo pasa su tiempo libre.

- Incluya dos imágenes de lugares favoritos o especiales que Ud. relaciona con el tiempo libre y los pasatiempos de su infancia o adolescencia. Explique por qué iba allí, y qué hacía, con quiénes, etcétera.

- Si ha estado jugando (*have been playing*) Practice Spanish: Study Abroad, en Quest 7 Ud. supo que su amigo David está leyendo *El ingenioso hidalgo don Quijote de la Mancha*, de Miguel de Cervantes Saavedra, en su tiempo libre. Busque información sobre la trama (*plot*), el autor, el contexto histórico, los personajes, etcétera, de esta novela. ¿Por qué cree Ud. que esta novela es tan famosa? ¿Ve paralelos entre los personajes de *Don Quijote* y los personajes del juego? Escriba un informe y entrégueselo a su profesor(a) o presente sus ideas en clase.

Sugerencia: You are now ready to play Quest 7 in **Practice Spanish: Study Abroad** (www.mhpractice.com).

EN RESUMEN En este capítulo

LEARNSMART
Visit **www.connectspanish.com** to practice the vocabulary and grammar points covered in this chapter.

AFTER STUDYING THIS CHAPTER I CAN . . .

☐ talk about sports and other pastimes (296)

☐ talk about household chores (298)

☐ use the imperfect to describe past actions (302–304)

☐ use interrogatives more effectively, especially **¿qué?** and **¿cuál(es)?** (308–309)

☐ use superlatives to describe "the most" in a category (310–311)

☐ recognize/describe at least 2–3 aspects of Puerto Rican cultures

Gramática en breve

26. The Imperfect

Regular -ar Endings
-aba, -abas, -aba, -ábamos, -abais, -aban

Regular -er/-ir Endings
-ía, -ías, -ía, -íamos, -íais, -ían

Verbs Irregular in the Imperfect
ir: iba, ibas, iba, íbamos, ibais, iban
ser: era, eras, era, éramos, erais, eran
ver: veía, veías, veía, veíamos, veíais, veían

27. Superlatives

el/la/los/las + *noun* + **más/menos** + *adjective* + **de**
el/la/los/las + **mejor(es)/peor(es)** + *noun* + **de**

28. Interrogative Words

¿qué? } = definition, explanation
= identification: + *noun* = *what/which* . . . ?

¿cuál(es)? = choice: + *verb* = *what/which (one)* . . . ?

Vocabulario

Los verbos

pelear	to fight
sonar (suena)	to ring; to sound
tocarle (qu) a uno (like **gustar**)	to be someone's turn

Repaso: deber, necesitar, tener que

Los pasatiempos, diversiones y aficiones

la afición	hobby
la diversión	fun activity

el pasatiempo	pastime
los ratos libres	spare (free) time
el tiempo libre	free time
aburrirse	to get bored
caminar	to walk
dar una caminata	to hike; to go for a hike
dar un paseo	to take a walk
hacer un *picnic*	to have a picnic
hacer planes (*m.*) **para** + *inf.*	to make plans to (*do something*)
hacer (el) yoga	to do yoga
ir...	to go . . .
a un bar / a una discoteca	to a bar / to a disco
a un museo	to a museum
al teatro / a un concierto	to the theater / to a concert
jugar (juego) (gu) al ajedrez / a las cartas / a los videojuegos	to play chess/cards/videogames
ser...	to be . . .
aburrido/a	boring
divertido/a	fun

Repaso: dar/hacer una fiesta, hacer *camping*, **ir a una fiesta / al cine / a ver una película, jugar (juego) (gu), sacar (qu) fotos, tomar el sol**

Los deportes

correr	to run
entrenar	to practice; to train
esquiar (esquío)	to ski
ganar	to win
hacer *surfing*	to surf
montar a caballo	to ride a horse
montar/pasear en bicicleta	to ride a bicycle
patinar	to skate
ser aficionado/a (a)	to be a fan (of)

Repaso: jugar (juego) (gu) al + *sport*, nadar, perder (pierdo), practicar (qu)

el ciclismo	bicycling
el deporte	sport
el equipo	team
el fútbol	soccer
el fútbol americano	football
el/la jugador(a)	player
la natación	swimming
el partido	game, match
el patinaje	skating
la pelota	ball

Cognados: el basquetbol, el béisbol, el esquí, el golf, el hockey, el tenis, el voleibol

Algunos aparatos domésticos

el aparato doméstico	home appliance
la aspiradora	vacuum cleaner
la cafetera	coffeemaker
el congelador	freezer
el horno de microondas	microwave oven
la lavadora	washing machine
el lavaplatos	dishwasher
el refrigerador	refrigerator
la secadora	clothes dryer
la tostadora	toaster

Repaso: la estufa

Los quehaceres domésticos

el quehacer doméstico	household chore
barrer el piso	to sweep the floor
hacer la cama	to make the bed
lavar	to wash
limpiar (la casa)	to clean (house)
pasar la aspiradora	to vacuum
planchar	to iron
poner la mesa	to set the table
quitar la mesa	to clear the table

sacar (qu) la basura	to take out the trash

Repaso: la cama, la casa, hacer, la mesa, los platos, poner, la ropa

Otros sustantivos

la escuela	school
el/la niñero/a	baby-sitter

Los adjetivos

deportivo/a	sporting, sports (*adj.*); sports-loving
doméstico/a	domestic, related to the home
libre	free, unoccupied
pesado/a	boring; difficult
-ito/a	small, little

Palabras adicionales

al aire libre	outdoors
de adolescente	as an adolescent
de niño/a	as a child
en la actualidad	currently, right now
mientras	while

Repaso: ¿a qué hora?, ¿adónde?, ¿cómo?, ¿cuál(es)?, ¿cuándo?, ¿cuánto/a?, ¿cuántos/as?, ¿de dónde?, ¿de quién(es)?, ¿dónde?, ¿por qué?, ¿qué?, ¿quién(es)?

Vocabulario personal

11

La salud°

La... *Health*

|SPANISH

www.connectspanish.com

En este capítulo

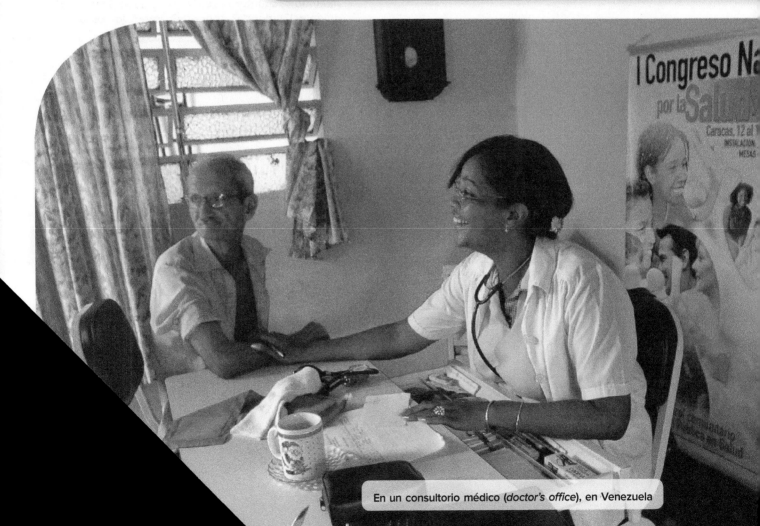

En un consultorio médico (*doctor's office*), en Venezuela

VENEZUELA
29 millones de habitantes

- Venezuela es un país muy rico en petróleo. Petróleos de Venezuela S.A.* (PDVSA) es una de las empresas (compañías) petroleras más grandes del mundo. Es una corporación del estado que controla la exploración, producción y venta[a] de todo el petróleo del país.

- La Fundación del Estado para el Sistema Nacional de las Orquestas Juveniles e Infantiles de Venezuela (FESNOJIV) es una iniciativa que fomenta la instrucción musical «como instrumento de organización social y desarrollo[b] comunitario».

[a]sale [b]development

- ¿Cómo es su salud en general? ¿Lleva Ud. una vida sana[a]?
- ¿Hace Ud. ejercicio con frecuencia? ¿Hizo Ud. ejercicio ayer?
- ¿Cuándo fue la última vez que Ud. fue al médico? ¿Fue por algo grave o fue una visita rutinaria?

[a]healthy

CECILIA FIGUEROA MARTÍN CONTESTA LAS PREGUNTAS.

- Creo que mi salud es excelente, afortunadamente. ¡Toco madera![a] La verdad es que llevo una vida sana[b] por lo general. Como bien, no bebo mucho, no fumo nada...

- Sí, trato de[c] hacer ejercicio por lo menos tres o cuatro días a la semana: voy al gimnasio o corro tres o cuatro millas. Ayer corrí.

- La última vez que fui al médico fue el mes pasado, para mi chequeo anual.

[a]¡Toco... *Knock on wood!* [b]*healthy* [c]*trato... I try to*

---

*S.A. = Sociedad Anónima (*Inc.*)

La salud y el bienestar°

La... Health and well-being

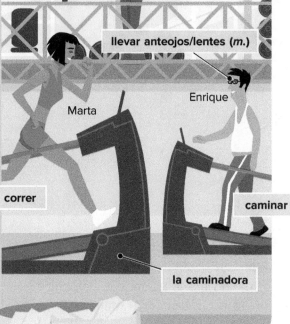

el cuerpo humano
- el ojo
- la nariz (*pl.* narices)
- el cerebro
- la oreja
- la boca
- la garganta
- los pulmones
- el corazón
- el estómago
- el brazo
- la mano
- los dedos (de la mano)
- la pierna
- el pie
- los dedos del pie

- levantar pesas — Laura
- llevar anteojos/lentes (*m.*)
- Marta
- Enrique
- correr
- caminar
- la caminadora

El cuerpo humano

la cabeza	head
el oído	inner ear

Para cuidar de la salud

comer comidas sanas	to eat healthy food
cuidarse	to take care of oneself
dejar de + *inf.*	to stop (*doing something*)
dormir (duermo) (u) lo suficiente	to get enough sleep

You can hear the pronunciation of theme vocabulary words and phrases in the Connect eBook.

hacer ejercicio	to exercise; to get exercise
hacer...	to do . . .
ejercicios aeróbicos	aerobics
(el método) Pilates	Pilates
llevar lentes (*m.*) de contacto	to wear contact lenses
llevar una vida sana/tranquila	to lead a healthy/ calm life
practicar (qu) deportes	to practice, play sports
respirar	to breathe

Así se dice

los anteojos, los lentes = las gafas (*Sp.*)

los lentes de contacto = las lentes de contacto (*Sp.*), las lentillas (*Sp.*)

la caminadora = la cinta de andar (*Sp.*), la cinta de correr, la cinta rodante, la trotadora (*P.R.*), la rueda de molino

Comunicación

A. Asociaciones

Paso 1. ¿Qué partes del cuerpo humano asocia Ud. con las siguientes palabras?
¡OJO! A veces hay más de una respuesta posible.

1. un ataque	**5.** pensar	**9.** la música
2. comer	**6.** la digestión	**10.** el perfume
3. cantar	**7.** el amor (*love*)	**11.** caminar
4. los anteojos	**8.** fumar	**12.** una flor

Paso 2. ¿Qué verbos asocia Ud. con las siguientes partes del cuerpo?

1. los ojos	**3.** la boca	**5.** el estómago
2. los dedos	**4.** el oído	**6.** los pulmones

B. Hablando de la salud. ¿Qué significan para Ud. las siguientes oraciones?

MODELOS: Se debe comer comidas sanas. →
Eso quiere decir (*means*) que es necesario comer muchas verduras, que...
También significa que no debemos comer muchos dulces o...

1. Se debe dormir lo suficiente todas las noches.
2. Hay que hacer ejercicio.
3. Es necesario llevar una vida tranquila.
4. En general, uno debe cuidarse mucho.
5. Es importante llevar una vida sana.

> **Vocabulario útil**
>
> **Eso quiere decir...**
> **Esto significa que...**
> **También...**

C. ¿Cómo vive Ud.? ¿Cómo vivía?

Paso 1. Indique las cosas que Ud. hace para mantener la salud y el bienestar.

	SÍ	NO
1. comer comidas sanas en general	☐	☐
2. no comer muchos dulces	☐	☐
3. comer muchas frutas y verduras	☐	☐
4. hacer ejercicio moderado diariamente	☐	☐
5. beber agua suficiente todos los días	☐	☐
6. dormir por lo menos ocho horas por noche	☐	☐
7. tomar bebidas alcohólicas en moderación	☐	☐
8. no beber mucho café o té	☐	☐
9. no fumar	☐	☐

Paso 2. Escriba un hábito malo que debe dejar y uno bueno que desea adquirir (*to acquire*).

Paso 3. Ahora, en parejas, entrevístense sobre los hábitos de los **Pasos 1** y **2**.
Luego díganle a la clase algo que tienen en común.

MODELO: **E1:** Yo como comidas sanas, pero como muchos dulces. ¿Y tú?
E2: Yo también. Comer muchos dulces es un hábito que quiero dejar. →
Nosotros comemos muchos dulces y es un hábito que queremos dejar.

Algo sobre...

la harina[a] de maíz blanco

La harina de maíz blanco es el ingrediente básico para hacer dos platos típicos venezolanos: las arepas y las hallacas. Las arepas son similares al pan de pita y se pueden comer como sándwiches. Las hallacas son parecidas[b] a los tamales; son una comida tradicional de la Navidad y la Nochevieja.

Una arepa

 ¿Hay algo similar a las arepas o a las hallacas en la cocina de su familia?

[a]*flour* [b]*similar*

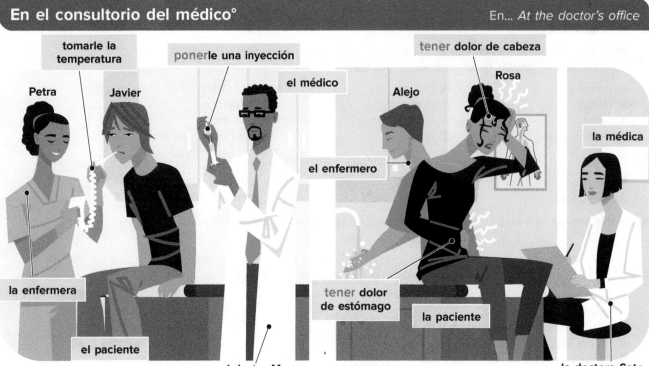

tomarle la temperatura

ponerle una inyección

el médico

tener dolor de cabeza

Rosa

Petra   Javier

Alejo

la médica

el enfermero

la enfermera

tener dolor de estómago

la paciente

el paciente

el doctor Mena

la doctora Soto

el antibiótico	antibiotic	**enfermarse**	to get sick
la cita	appointment; date	estar **sano/a**	to be healthy
el dolor	pain, ache	**guardar cama**	to stay in bed
el farmacéutico /	pharmacist	**molestar**	to bother
la farmacéutica		**resfriarse (me resfrío)**	to get/catch a cold
la fiebre	fever	**sacar (qu)**	to extract
la gripe	flu	**sacar la lengua**	to stick out one's tongue
el jarabe	(cough) syrup	**sacarle un diente /**	to extract (*someone's*)
la medicina	medicine	**una muela**	tooth/molar
la pastilla	pill	**sentirse (me siento) (i)**	to feel
la receta	prescription	tener **dolor de**	to have a
el resfriado	cold (*illness*)	**cabeza/**	headache/
la tos	cough	**estómago/muela**	stomachache/toothache
la vacuna	vaccination	tener **fiebre**	to have a fever
cansarse	to get tired	**toser**	to cough
doler (duele)	to hurt, ache		
		mareado/a	dizzy; nauseated
		resfriado/a	congested, stuffed-up

¡OJO!

Doler and **molestar** are used like **gustar**: **Me duele la cabeza. Me molestan los ojos.**

Así se dice

el resfriado = el catarro, el resfrío   la gripe = la gripa
estar resfriado/a = estar constipado/a (*Sp.*)   el consultorio = la consulta

¡OJO!

Use the term **el médico / la médica** to talk *about* doctors in general and **el/la dentista** for the dentist. However, when you use the doctor or dentist's name you should use the definite article plus the title: **el doctor Gómez, la doctora Velázquez.** To speak directly *to* him or her, just use the title **doctor(a).**

Comunicación

A. Estudio de palabras. Complete las siguientes oraciones con una palabra derivada de la palabra en rosado.

1. Si me resfrío, tengo _____.
2. La respiración ocurre cuando alguien _____.
3. Si me _____, estoy enfermo/a. Un(a) _____ me toma la temperatura.
4. Cuando alguien tose, es porque tiene _____.
5. Si me duele el estómago, tengo _____ de estómago.

B. Situaciones. Describa la situación de estas personas. Primero, indique dónde están y con quiénes están. Luego complete las oraciones que están al lado de de cada foto.

1. Rosa está muy sana. Nunca le duele(n) _____. Nunca tiene _____. Siempre _____. Más tarde hoy, ella va a _____.

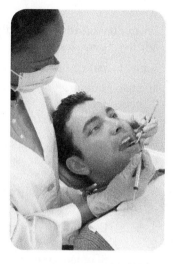

2. Anoche Martín tuvo _____. Esta mañana llamó _____ para hacer _____. El dentista va a _____. Después, Martín va a _____.

Nota cultural

El cuidado° médico en el mundo hispano   *care*

En el mundo hispano el cuidado médico puede ser muy variado. Depende principalmente del[a] nivel económico del país y después (como ocurre en este país) del nivel económico del individuo. Pero en todos los países hispanos hay excelentes médicos en todo tipo de especialidades, bien preparados[b] en las universidades de su país o en el extranjero. Aquí hay unos aspectos interesantes del cuidado médico en el mundo hispanohablante.

- **Los farmacéuticos y practicantes** Los hispanos consultan con frecuencia a estos profesionales cuando no pueden o no sienten la necesidad de acudir[c] a un médico. Por ejemplo, cuando uno tiene una enfermedad leve,[d] puede ir a la farmacia para pedir consejo sobre una medicina o conseguir un remedio, sin tener receta. Cuando se necesita un tratamiento simple, como ponerse una inyección, se puede llamar a un practicante, quien es más o menos como un enfermero.
- **Los remedios tradicionales o alternativos** Homeópatas, naturópatas, sanadores,[e] tiendas de botánica,[f]... Hay una importante tradición, de gran

A diferencia de las farmacias en este país, en las farmacias de muchos países hispanos, no se venden muchos productos para la higiene personal ni comestibles.

diversidad en el mundo hispanohablante, de consultar a personas que tienen conocimiento[g] de los remedios naturales o de curaciones basadas en la fe,[h] especialmente para las molestias y menores enfermedades más frecuentes.

¿A quién consulta Ud. cuando está enfermo/a?

[a]*on the* [b]*trained* [c]*go* [d]*minor, mild* [e]*healers* [f]*herbs*

[g]*knowledge* [h]*faith*

Nota comunicativa

C. En el consultorio del médico o del dentista. En parejas, usen los siguientes adjetivos para describir una visita al médico o dentista, según el modelo.

MODELO: malo / bueno ⟶ **Lo malo** de ir al médico es la cuenta. **Lo bueno** es...

1. malo / bueno
2. peor / mejor
3. interesante / aburrido
4. curioso (*strange*) / especial
5. insoportable (*unbearable*)

D. Refranes hispanos. Empareje una frase de la columna A con otra de la columna B para formar algunos refranes muy comunes en el mundo hispano. En algunos casos lo/la puede ayudar la rima. Luego explique lo que significan los refranes. ¿Cuál es el equivalente en inglés?

COLUMNA A	COLUMNA B
1. _____ La salud no se compra:	a. engorda (*fattens*).
2. _____ Músculos de Sansón,	b. no tiene precio.
3. _____ Si quieres vivir sano,	c. y cerebro de mosquito.
4. _____ Para enfermedad de años,	d. no hay medicina.
5. _____ Ojos que no ven,	e. acuéstate y levántate temprano.
6. _____ Lo que no mata (*doesn't kill*),	f. corazón que no siente.

¿Recuerda Ud.?

Since **Capítulo 8** you have been using first the preterite and then the imperfect in appropriate contexts. Indicate which tense you use to do each of the following.

	PRETERITE	IMPERFECT
1. to tell what you did yesterday	☐	☐
2. to tell what you used to do when you were in grade school	☐	☐
3. to describe background details, like physical or mental states	☐	☐
4. to tell about a completed action	☐	☐
5. to talk about the way things used to be	☐	☐
6. to describe an action that was in progress	☐	☐

If you understand these uses of the preterite and the imperfect, the summary of their uses in **Gramática 30** (page 330) will be very easy for you.

«Remedios para todos» Segmento 1

Antes de mirar

Cuando Ud. tiene problemas de salud, ¿a quién consulta? Indique a todas las personas de la lista que Ud. haya consultado (*may have consulted*) por razones de salud por lo menos una vez.

☐ mi madre/padre
☐ mi abuelo/a
☐ un médico / una médica
☐ un(a) homeópata
☐ un(a) naturópata
☐ ¿ ?

En esta botánica (*herb store*) se venden velas (*candles*), imágenes, collares (*necklaces*), rosarios, incienso, agua florida (*aromatic essences*) y mucho más. ¡Hasta (*Even*) imágenes de Buda para la buena suerte (*luck*)!

Este segmento

Laura presenta un reportaje sobre una botánica, una tienda tradicional típica del Caribe.

Vocabulario **del segmento**

desde luego	certainly
ahorrar	to save
el tratamiento	treatment
mezclarse	to mix up/in with
han visitado	have you visited
tuvo la amabilidad de concedernos	was kind enough to give us
sobar	to rub
la sávila	aloe vera
la quemada	burn
el catarro	**el resfriado**
broncear la piel	to tan (one's skin)
la tuna	cactus
el riñón	kidney
la limpieza	cleaning, cleansing
la hoja	leaf

Después de mirar

A. **¿Está claro?** Complete las siguientes oraciones con información del video.

   1. Las botánicas son tiendas típicas de los países _____.
   2. En una botánica se compran ingredientes naturales para hacer tés y _____ tradicionales.
   3. Los viejos y los _____ van a las botánicas.
   4. La tuna se usa para problemas del estómago y de los _____.

B. **Un poco más.** Conteste las siguientes preguntas.

   1. ¿Por qué se llaman «botánicas» las tiendas como la (*that*) de la Sra. Santiago?
   2. ¿En qué tipo de tratamientos se especializan las botánicas?
   3. ¿Qué objetos se puede comprar en una botánica? ¿Para qué sirven?

C. **Y ahora, Uds.** En grupos, hablen de las comidas y bebidas que Uds. toman cuando no se sienten bien y de las cosas que hacen cuando quieren conseguir buena suerte o necesitan calmarse. Por ejemplo, ¿soban o tocan Uds. algo, como una imagen de Buda?

GRAMÁTICA

Grammar Tutorial 30

www.connectspanish.com

30 Talking About the Past (Part 5)
Using the Preterite and the Imperfect

Gramática en acción: En el consultorio de la Dra. Méndez

DRA. MÉNDEZ: ¿Cuándo empezó a sentirse mal su hija?

MADRE: Ayer por la tarde. Estaba resfriada, tosía mucho y se quejaba de que le dolían el cuerpo y la cabeza.

DRA. MÉNDEZ: ¿Y le notó algo de fiebre?

MADRE: Sí. Por la noche le tomé la temperatura y tenía treinta y nueve grados.*

grados centígrados	36	37	38	39	40	41
grados Fahrenheit	96.8	98.6	100.4	102.2	104	105.8

DRA. MÉNDEZ: A ver... Abre la boca, por favor.

¿Y Ud.?

1. ¿Cómo se sentía Ud. ayer por la noche?
2. ¿A qué hora se acostó?

You have already learned and used the preterite (**Capítulos 8** and **9**) and imperfect tenses (**Capítulo 10**). In this chapter you will begin to use them together to talk about the past.

Keep the following points in mind.

1. The preterite and the imperfect are both past tenses.
2. They are both used to talk about the same point in the past.

They *differ* in the point of view (aspect) about the past that they each convey. This is the same as with English usage. When you decide to say *I ran, I used to run,* or *I was going to run,* you are making a decision about the aspect of the past action that you want to communicate.

Here is a summary of the main uses of the two tenses. You will learn about them on the next pages.

Pretérito	Imperfecto
• beginning/end of an action	• habitual/repeated action
• completed action	• ongoing action
• series of completed actions	• background information
• the action on the "stage"	• the setting for the action

In Dr. Méndez's office DR. MÉNDEZ: When did your daughter begin to feel ill? MOTHER: Yesterday afternoon. She was stuffed up, she was coughing a lot, and she was complaining that her body and head were hurting. DR. MÉNDEZ: And did you notice any fever? MOTHER: Yes. At night I took her temperature, and it was thirty-nine degrees. dr. méndez: Let's see . . . Open your mouth, please.

Normal body temperature is 37°C (98.6°F).

Note: |, ||, ||| = completed actions in the past, one, two, three or more
~~~ = ongoing or repeated actions in the past, background detail

Differences between the Preterite and the Imperfect / Las diferencias entre el pretérito y el imperfecto

1. Beginning/End vs. Habitual

Use the preterite to . . . |~~~||

- tell about the beginning or the end of a past action

El sábado pasado, el partido de fútbol **empezó** a la una. **Terminó** a las cuatro. El entrenador **habló** a las cinco.
Last Saturday, the soccer game began at one. It ended at four. The coach spoke (began to speak) at five.

Use the imperfect to . . . ~~~

- talk about the habitual nature of an action (something you always did)

Había un partido **todos los sábados.** Muchas personas **jugaban todas las semanas.**
There was a game every Saturday. Many people played every week.

2. Completed vs. Ongoing

Use the preterite to . . . ||

- express an action that is viewed as completed

El partido **duró** tres horas. **Ganaron** Los Lobos.
The game lasted three hours. The Lobos won.

Use the imperfect to . . .
~~~mientras~~~
Mientras~~~, ~~~

- tell about simultaneous events (with **mientras** = *while*)

Yo **estaba** en la cocina **mientras** todos **miraban** el partido.
I was in the kitchen while everyone was watching the game.

Mientras mi amigo **veía** el partido, **hablaba** con su novia.
While my friend was watching the game, he was talking with his girlfriend.

Use the imperfect and the preterite in the same sentence to . . .

|~~~ ~~~|

- tell what was happening when another action took place

Yo no vi el final del partido. **Estaba** en la cocina cuando **terminó.** (El partido **terminó** cuando **estaba** en la cocina.)
I didn't see the end of the game. I was in the kitchen when it ended. (The game ended while I was in the kitchen.)

3. Series of Completed Actions vs. Background Details

Use the preterite to . . . |||

- express a series of completed actions

Durante el partido, los jugadores **corrieron, saltaron** y **gritaron.**
During the game, the players ran, jumped, and shouted.

Use the imperfect to . . . ~~~

- give background details of many kinds: time, location, weather, mood, age, physical and mental characteristics

Todos los jugadores **eran** jóvenes; **tenían** 17 o 18 años. ¡Y todos **esperaban** ganar!
All the players were young; they were 17 or 18 years old. And all of them hoped to win!

4. Action vs. the Setting

The preterite and imperfect are also used together in the presentation of an event.

- The imperfect sets the stage, describes the conditions that caused the action, or emphasizes the continuing nature of a particular action.

~~~

- The preterite narrates the actions. ||

Era un día hermoso. **Hacía** mucho sol, pero no hacía mucho calor. Como no **tenía** que trabajar en la oficina, **salí** a comprar unas flores. Luego **me puse** camiseta y pantalones cortos y **decidí** trabajar todo el día en el jardín.
It was a beautiful day. It was very sunny, but it wasn't very hot. Since I didn't have to work at the office, I went out to buy some flowers. Then I put on a T-shirt and shorts and decided to work in the garden all day.

Remember that, when used in the preterite, **saber, conocer,** and **querer** have English equivalents different from that of the infinitives. (See page 275.) In the imperfect, the English equivalents of these verbs do not differ from the infinitive meanings.

—¿Ya sabías que se murió el abuelo de Miguel?
—Sí, lo supe el mes pasado.
*"**Did** you already **know** that Miguel's grandfather passed away?"*
*"Yes, I **found out** (**learned**) about it last month."*

—Anoche conocí a Roberto.
—¿Anoche? Yo pensaba que ya lo conocías.
"Last night I met Roberto."
"Last night? I thought you already knew him."

—¿No querías hablar con el profesor ayer?
—Sí, quise llamarlo pero no estaba en su oficina.
*"Didn't you **want** to talk to the professor yesterday?"*
*"Yes, I **tried** to call him but he wasn't in his office."*

Preterite vs. imperfect
Summary

Beginning/middle vs. habitual/repeated
Completed vs. ongoing
Actions vs. background
Action vs. setting

Práctica y comunicación

A. En la escuela secundaria

Paso 1. Autoprueba. ¿Se usa el pretérito (P) o el imperfecto (I) ?

1. para dar detalles de fondo (*background details*) y descripciones como el tiempo y la hora _____
2. para hablar de acciones habituales _____
3. para narrar acciones completadas _____
4. para hablar de hábitos personales _____
5. para hablar de una acción en progreso _____
6. para narrar una secuencia de acciones _____
7. para decir lo que pasaba cuando otra acción ocurrió _____
8. para describir condiciones y estados físicos o afectivos _____

Paso 2. ¿Cómo era su salud cuando Ud. estaba en la secundaria? ¿Sufría Ud. de alguna enfermedad física o de algún tipo de impedimento? Complete las siguientes oraciones con la forma apropiada del imperfecto o el pretérito. Use **no** cuando sea (*it's*) necesario.

Cuando estaba en la secundaria...
1. resfriarse con frecuencia
2. tener alergias
3. tener una operación
4. ir al dentista con regularidad
5. tener la gripe / mononucleosis
6. hacer mucho ejercicio
7. sufrir (*to have*) un accidente de coche
8. gustar me quedarme en casa y no ir a la escuela

Paso 3. Ahora, en parejas, túrnense para hacer y contestar preguntas basadas en las oraciones del **Paso 2.** Luego díganle a la clase algo que tienen en común.

MODELO: E1: Cuando estabas en la escuela secundaria, ¿te resfriabas con frecuencia?
E2: No, no me resfriaba con frecuencia. ¿Y tú?
E1: Yo tampoco.

Prác. A, Paso 1: Answers: 1. I 2. I 3. P 4. I 5. I 6. P 7. I 8. I

B. En el consultorio. Estos son algunos de los pacientes que el Dr. Sánchez vio ayer en el consultorio. Describa cómo se sentía cada paciente. Luego empareje cada caso con lo que hizo el Dr. Sánchez y complete esas oraciones.

LOS SÍNTOMAS DE LOS PACIENTES

1. Un paciente: tener mucho frío
2. A otro le: doler la garganta
3. Un señor: creer que estaba anémico
4. Una señora: sentirse muy mal sin saber por qué
5. Un señor mayor: querer más medicinas
6. Un niño: estar muy alto para su edad (*age*)
7. A un hombre le: doler el pecho (*chest*)

POR ESO, EL DR. SÁNCHEZ...

a. _____ hacerle muchas preguntas.
b. _____ darle una nueva receta.
c. _____ tomarle la temperatura.
d. _____ escucharle los sonidos (*sounds*) de los pulmones y del corazón.
e. _____ pedirle un análisis de sangre (*blood*).
f. _____ hacerle sacar la lengua.
g. _____ decirle que su chequeo (*check-up*) mostraba que estaba muy bien.

Nota **comunicativa**

Algunas palabras y expresiones asociadas con el pretérito y el imperfecto

Certain words and expressions are frequently associated with the preterite, others with the imperfect. Only the words that are translated are new.

Some words often associated with the preterite are:

ayer, anteayer, anoche (*last night*)   **de repente** (*suddenly*)

una vez, dos veces (*twice*)...   **en seguida**

el año pasado (*last*), **el lunes pasado**...

Some words often associated with the imperfect are:

todos los días, todos los lunes...   **mientras**

siempre, frecuentemente (*frequently*)   **de niño/a, de adolescente**

As you continue to practice using the preterite and imperfect, these expressions can help you determine which tense to use. These words do not *automatically* cue either tense, however. The most important consideration is the meaning that you want to express.

Ayer cenamos temprano.   *Yesterday we had dinner early.*

Ayer cenábamos cuando Juan llamó.   *Yesterday we were having dinner   when Juan called.*

Jugaba al fútbol **de niño.**   *He played soccer as a child.*

Empezó a jugar al fútbol **de niño.**   *He began to play soccer as a child.*

You will see these words and expressions in activities in the rest of this section and throughout the rest of *Puntos de partida.*

Algo sobre...

Simón Bolívar

Simón Bolívar fue un general y político venezolano que es conocido[a] en Latinoamérica como el Libertador. Fue la figura principal en el movimiento por la independencia de España de varios países latinoamericanos (Colombia, Panamá, el Perú, Bolivia y el Ecuador). Desde 1819 hasta 1830 fue presidente de la Gran Colombia, una unión de naciones hispanohablantes que se estableció después de ganar su independencia de España. La Gran Colombia solo duró[b] hasta 1831.

¿Quién es el gran héroe de la independencia de los Estados Unidos? ¿Qué cargos[c] tuvo?

[a]*known* [b]*lasted* [c]*positions*

Simón Bolívar (1783–1830), el Libertador

C. Pequeñas historias

Paso 1. Complete el siguiente párrafo con una de las palabras o frases de la lista. Antes de empezar, mire la foto que acompaña el párrafo para tener una idea general del tema de la historia.

VOCABULARIO: **íbamos, nos gustó, nos quedábamos, nos quedamos, nuestra familia decidió, vivíamos**

Cuando éramos niños, Jorge y yo _____¹ en la Argentina. Siempre _____² a la playa, a Mar del Plata, para pasar la Navidad. Allí casi siempre _____³ en el Hotel Fénix. Un año, _____⁴ quedarse en otro hotel, el Continental. No _____⁵ tanto como el Fénix y por eso, al año siguiente, _____⁶ en el Fénix otra vez.

Paso 2. Ahora, para completar la siguiente historia, debe escoger (*choose*) entre el pretérito y el imperfecto en cada caso. Antes de empezar, mire el dibujo que acompaña el párrafo.

Eran las once de la noche y yo (estaba / estuve¹) leyendo un libro, cuando de repente se (apagaban / apagaron^a2) todas las luces^b de la casa. (Ponía / Puse³) el libro en el suelo^c y luego (usaba / usé⁴) mi celular para tener algo de luz. La verdad es que (tenía / tuve⁵) mucho miedo. Por eso, (salía / salí⁶) a la calle.^d Entonces^e (podía / pude⁷) ver que (había / hubo⁸) un apagón por todo el barrio.^f La luz (volvía / volvió⁹) media hora después.

^aapagar = *to go out* ^b*lights* ^c*floor* ^d*street* ^e*Then* ^f*un... a power outage in the whole neighborhood*

D. La historia afectiva de Simón Bolívar

Paso 1. Complete los siguientes párrafos con la forma apropiada de los infinitivos, en el pretérito o el imperfecto.

Simón Bolívar (1783–1830) fue el gran héroe de la independencia sudamericana. Bolívar no (tener¹) una vida^a personal muy afortunada. (Ser²) hijo de una familia aristocrática española. (Tener³) tres hermanos mayores. Sus padres (morirse⁴) cuando Bolívar (ser⁵) muy pequeño y por eso (vivir⁶) varios años con otros parientes.

En 1798, cuando (tener⁷) 15 años, (irse⁸) a estudiar a Madrid. Allí (conocer⁹) a María Teresa, con quien (casarse^b10) en 1802. Bolívar (regresar¹¹) a Venezuela con su joven esposa. Pero María Teresa (morir¹²) ocho meses después, víctima de la fiebre amarilla. Bolívar (empezar¹³) su carrera^c como líder nacional viajando por Europa para soportar^d la muerte^e de María Teresa. Nunca (volver¹⁴) a casarse.

^a*life* ^b*to marry* ^c*career* ^d*deal with* ^e*death*

Paso 2. Comprensión. Conteste las siguientes preguntas.

1. En la familia de Bolívar, ¿era él hermano mayor o el menor?
2. ¿Cuántos años tenía Bolívar cuando se casó con María Teresa?
3. ¿De qué murió María Teresa?
4. ¿Por qué empezó a viajar Bolívar?

E. Rubén y Soledad

Paso 1. Complete el párrafo con la forma apropiada de los infinitivos, en el pretérito o en el imperfecto.

Una merienda típicamente española: churros (*fried dough rolled in sugar*) y chocolate

Rubén estaba estudiando cuando Soledad entró en el cuarto. Ella le (preguntar[1]) a Rubén si (querer[2]) ir al cine. Rubén le (decir[3]) que sí porque (sentirse[4]) un poco aburrido de estudiar. Los dos (salir[5]) en seguida para el cine. (Ver[6]) una película cómica y (reírse[7]) mucho. Luego, como (hacer[8]) frío, (entrar[9]) en su café favorito, El Gato Negro, y (tomar[10]) churros y chocolate. (Ser[11]) las dos de la mañana cuando por fin (regresar[12]) a casa. Soledad (acostarse[13]) en seguida porque (estar[14]) cansada, pero Rubén (empezar[15]) a estudiar otra vez.

Paso 2. Comprensión. Ahora conteste las siguientes preguntas, según el párrafo.

1. ¿Qué hacía Rubén cuando Soledad entró?
2. ¿Qué le preguntó Soledad a Rubén? (**Le preguntó si...**)
3. ¿Por qué le contestó Rubén que sí?
4. ¿Les gustó la película? ¿Cómo se sabe?
5. ¿Por qué tomaron churros y chocolate después de salir del cine?
6. ¿Qué hora era cuando regresaron a casa?
7. ¿Qué hicieron cuando llegaron a casa?

F. La fiesta de Roberto

Paso 1. Complete el párrafo con la forma apropiada de los infinitivos, en el pretérito, en el imperfecto o en el presente.

Durante mi segundo[a] año en la universidad, conocí a Roberto en una clase. Pronto nos (hacer[1]) muy buenos amigos. Roberto (ser[2]) una persona muy generosa que (dar[3]) una fiesta en su apartamento todos los viernes. Todos nuestros amigos (ir[4]). (Haber[5]) muchas bebidas y comida abundante, y todos (hablar[6]) y (bailar[7]) hasta muy tarde.

Una noche algunos de los vecinos[b] de Roberto (llamar[8]) a la policía porque les (parecer[c9]) que nosotros (hacer[10]) demasiado ruido. (Llegar[11]) dos policías al apartamento y le (decir[12]) a Roberto que la fiesta (ser[13]) demasiado ruidosa. Nosotros no (querer[14]) aguar la rumba,[d] pero ¿qué (poder[15]) hacer? Todos nos (despedir[16]) aunque[e] (ser[17]) solamente las once de la noche.

Aquella noche Roberto (aprender[18]) algo importantísimo. Ahora cuando (hacer[19]) una fiesta, siempre (invitar[20]) a sus vecinos.

[a]*second* [b]*neighbors* [c]*to seem* [d]*aguar... to spoil the party* [e]*although*

Paso 2. Comprensión. Las siguientes oraciones son falsas. Corríjalas.

1. A Roberto no le gustaban las fiestas.
2. Las fiestas de Roberto siempre terminaban temprano.
3. Los vecinos de Roberto nunca se quejaban del ruido de sus fiestas.
4. Roberto siempre invitaba a sus vecinos a sus fiestas.

G. Lo mejor de estar enfermo

Paso 1. Haga oraciones completas con la forma apropiada de los infinitivos, en el pretérito o el imperfecto.

1. Cuando yo (ser) niño, (pensar) que lo mejor de estar enfermo (ser) pasar el día en casa.
2. Lo peor (ser) que yo (resfriarse) con frecuencia durante las vacaciones.
3. Una vez (*yo:* ponerse) muy enfermo durante la Navidad.
4. Mi madre (llamar) al médico porque yo (tener) una fiebre muy alta.
5. El Dr. Matamoros (venir) a casa en seguida y (ponerme) una inyección de antibióticos porque yo (tener) una infección de la garganta.
6. Desgraciadamente (*Unfortunately*), mis padres (tener) que darme un baño de agua fría para bajarme la fiebre, y eso no (gustarme) para nada.
7. Tengo que decir que no (ser) la mejor Navidad de mi vida.
8. Mis primos (venir) a casa, pero yo (estar) demasiado enfermo para jugar.
9. ¡Pero esa Navidad mis abuelos (regalarme) mi primera Play Station!

Paso 2. Ahora vuelva a contar la historia desde el punto de vista (*point of view*) de la madre. Siga el modelo.

MODELO: Cuando **mi hijo era** niño, **él pensaba** que lo mejor...

H. Una historia famosa

Paso 1. La siguiente historia está narrada en el presente. Póngala en el pasado, usando los verbos en el pretérito.

La niña abre[1] la puerta y entra[2] en la casa. Ve[3] tres sillas. Se sienta[4] en la primera silla, luego en la segunda[a], pero no le gusta[5] ninguna. Por eso se sienta[6] en la tercera.[b] Ve[7] tres platos de comida en la mesa y decide[8] comer el más pequeño. Luego, va[9] a la alcoba para descansar un poco. Después de probar[c] las camas grandes, se acuesta[10] en la cama más pequeña y se queda[11] dormida.[d]

[a]*second* [b]*third* [c]*trying* [d]*asleep*

Paso 2. ¿Reconoce Ud. la historia? Es el cuento de Ricitos de Oro (lit. *Little Golden Curls*) y los tres osos (*bears*). Pero el cuento es un poco aburrido tal como está escrito (*as it is written*) en el **Paso 1.** Mejórelo (*Improve it*) con palabras de **Vocabulario útil** y dando detalles y descripciones (usando el imperfecto). También debe terminar el cuento: ¿Qué pasó al final?

MODELO: Había una vez una niña que **se llamaba** Ricitos de Oro. Un día la niña **fue...**

Vocabulario útil

Había una vez... + *imp.* Once upon a time there was ...
Un día... + *pret.*

el bosque forest
la casita little house

huir to flee*

---

*Present tense forms of **huir** have a **y** (rather than an **i**) in the stem-changing pattern: **huyo, huyes**... **Y** is also used in the preterite third person singular and plural forms (like **leer**): **huyó, huyeron.** The present participle is **huyendo.**

I. Intercambios

Paso 1. ¿Cuántos años tenían Uds. cuando sus padres los dejaron hacer las siguientes cosas? Hagan y contesten preguntas sobre ese tema, según el modelo.

MODELO: te dejaron cruzar la calle (*street*) solo/a →

E1: ¿Cuántos años **tenías** cuando tus padres te dejaron cruzar la calle sola?
E2: **Tenía** 7 u 8 años cuando mis padres me dejaron cruzar la calle sola.

1. te dejaron cruzar la calle (*street*) solo/a
2. te permitieron ir de compras solo/a
3. te dejaron acostarte después de las nueve
4. te dejaron estar en casa sin niñero/a
5. te permitieron usar la estufa para cocinar
6. te dejaron ver una película para mayores de 17 años («*R*»)
7. te dejaron buscar tu primer trabajo

Paso 2. Ahora haga preguntas basadas en las ideas de la siguiente lista para saber cuántos años tenía su compañero/a cuando hizo las cosas de la lista.

MODELO: aprender a pasear en bicicleta →
¿**Cuántos años tenías** cuando aprendiste a pasear en bicicleta?

¿**Cuántos años tenías** cuando...?
1. aprender a pasear en bicicleta
2. hacer su primer viaje en avión
3. tener su primera cita romántica
4. empezar a afeitarse / teñirse el pelo (*dye his/her hair*)
5. conseguir la licencia de manejar (*driver's license*)
6. abrir una cuenta (*account*) en el banco

Paso 3. Ahora, en grupos de cuatro, comparen sus respuestas. Entre todos, ¿quién tenía los padres más estrictos? ¿los menos estrictos?

J. Experiencias memorables

Paso 1. Haga preguntas sobre una de las siguientes experiencias. En el **Paso 2,** va a usar esas preguntas para entrevistar a uno de sus compañeros de clase. Haga por lo menos cinco preguntas, usando el pretérito o el imperfecto, según el contexto.

EXPERIENCIAS
el primer trabajo
la primera cita / el primer beso (*kiss*)
algo (un incidente, una situación, un caso) que lo/la hizo ponerse rojo/a
el primer día de clases en la escuela primaria o en la universidad

Paso 2. Ahora, en parejas, túrnense para hacerse preguntas sobre la experiencia del **Paso 1** que Uds. escogieron. No tiene que ser la misma experiencia.

Algo sobre...

el lago de Maracaibo

El lago de Maracaibo ocupa el puesto[a] 19 entre los lagos más grandes del mundo. En la actualidad, conecta con el golfo de Venezuela en el norte, que lo hace una bahía semicerrada salobre.[b] Pero está documentado que fue originalmente un lago cerrado, uno de los más antiguos de la Tierra. Numerosos ríos[c] vierten[d] sus aguas en el lago de Maracaibo.

¿Cuál es el lago más grande de su estado? ¿Y del país?

El lago de Maracaibo, el más grande de toda Latinoamérica

[a]*spot* [b]*bahía... semi-closed brackish bay* [c]*rivers* [d]*empty*

Que is one of the most frequently used words in the Spanish language, and it has several meanings. Review what you already know about **que** by expressing the following sentences in English.

1. ¿Qué estudias?
2. Tengo que hacer la tarea.
3. No entiendo lo que Ud. me dice.
4. Creo que la fórmula es correcta.

In **Gramática 31,** you will learn more about **que** and other related terms that you have been using for a while: **quien** and **lo que.**

Grammar Tutorial 31
connect
|SPANISH
www.connectspanish.com

31 Recognizing *que, quien(es), lo que*
Relative Pronouns

Gramática en acción: Tus médicos, tus mejores amigos

La Organización de Médicos Hispanohablantes: Siempre contigo

Tus médicos pueden ser tus mejores amigos.

- Son personas con quienes puedes hablar de TODO.
- Son personas que pueden ayudarte y explicarte TODO lo que tú necesitas saber de tu salud.
- Tienen consultorios que están CERCA de ti.
- Y además, ¡hablan ESPAÑOL!

¿Y Ud.?

Complete las oraciones con el nombre de una persona que Ud. conoce. Incluya la revlación que tiene con Ud., por ejemplo: **mi madre.**

1. Una persona que tiene mi confianza total es _____.
2. Una persona con quien hablo si necesito ayuda, no importa en qué situación, es _____.
3. Una persona que sabe todo —o casi todo— lo que pasa en mi vida es _____.

a relative pronoun / un
pronombre relativo =
a pronoun that refers
back to a noun or
phrase already
mentioned

Relative Pronouns / Los pronombres relativos

Relative pronouns (**Los pronombres relativos**) are words that connect ideas within one sentence. Most frequently they refer back to a noun or an idea that has already been mentioned. In both English and Spanish, these words make communication more efficient and fluid because they help to avoid unnecessary repetition by linking ideas. Notice how this happens in the sentences on page 339.

Your doctors, your best friends *The Organization of Spanish-speaking Doctors: Always with you. Your doctors can be your best friends.* ■ *They're people with whom you can talk about ANYTHING.* ■ *They're people that can help you and explain (to you) EVERYTHING that you need to know about your health.* ■ *They have offices that are CLOSE to you.* ■ *And besides, they speak SPANISH!*

Conozco a una **médica**. Es de Venezuela. → Conozco a una médica **que** es de Venezuela.

*I know a **doctor**. She is from Venezuela. → I know a doctor **who** is from Venezuela.*

Spanish has a rich system of relative pronouns. You will learn only three of them in this section.

1. Relative Pronouns

There are four principal *relative pronouns* in English: *that, which, who,* and *whom.* They are usually expressed in Spanish by the relative pronouns at the right, all of which you already know.

Los pronombres relativos	
que = refers to things and people	*that, which, who*
quien(es) = refers only to people	*who(m)*
lo que = refers to a situation	*what, that which*

---

2. *que* = *that, which, who*

Que is by far the most frequently used relative pronoun in Spanish. It refers to people and things.

¡OJO!

Que cannot be used after a preposition to refer to people. See Point 3.

Tuve **una cita** con el médico **que** duró una hora.
*I had an appointment with the doctor **that** lasted an hour.*

Es **un buen médico que** tiene mucha experiencia.
*He's a good doctor **who** has a lot of experience.*

---

3. *quien, quienes* = *who(m)*

Quien and **quienes** can refer only to people. They are almost always used after a preposition.

La mujer con **quien** hablaba es mi médica.
*The woman **with whom** I was speaking is my doctor. (The woman I was speaking with is my doctor.)*

Las enfermeras a **quienes** les dimos las flores cuidaron a mi padre.
*The nurses **to whom** we gave the flowers took care of my dad. (The nurses we gave the flowers to took care of my dad.)*

---

4. *lo que* = *what, that which, the thing that*

Lo que always refers to a whole situation or idea. It can refer to something that has been mentioned before or to something that will be referred to later in the sentence. It frequently starts sentences.

¡OJO!

If you can substitute *that which* for *what* in a sentence, use **lo que,** not **que.**

No entiendo **lo que dijo.**
*I don't understand **what (that which)** he said.*

Lo que necesito es **estudiar más.**
***What (The thing that)** I need is to study more.*

---

5. Relative Pronouns versus Interrogatives

Que and **quien(es)** sound like **¿qué?** and **¿quién(es)?**, but they are not the same.

- **Que** and **quien(es)** link words within a sentence.
- **¿Qué?** and **¿quién(es)?** ask questions (and they have an accent mark to distinguish them from the relative pronouns).

—¿**Qué** es eso?
—Es una cosa **que** sirve para ver mejor.
*"**What** is this?*
*"It's something **that** helps you see better."*
—¿**Quién** es ese señor?
—Es el profesor con **quien** tengo la clase de psicología.
*"**Who** is that man?"*
*"He's the professor **with whom** I have Psychology."*

Summary of Relative Pronouns

that, which, who = **que**
preposition + whom = **quien(es)**
what, that which, the thing that = **lo que**

Práctica y comunicación

A. ¿Que, quien(es) o lo que?

Paso 1. Autoprueba. Empareje los conceptos con el pronombre relativo apropiado.

1. _____ una cosa
2. _____ una idea
3. _____ a una persona
4. _____ con dos amigos

a. que
b. quien
c. quienes
d. lo que

Paso 2. Empareje los elementos de las dos columnas. **¡OJO!** Puede repetir las personas de la Columna B.

COLUMNA A

1. _____ Es lo que me dijo mi madre antes de salir para la universidad.
2. _____ Es la persona en quien yo más confío.
3. _____ Es lo que más me importa en la vida.
4. _____ Es la persona que más me apoya (*supports*).
5. _____ Es lo que necesito hacer para graduarme.
6. _____ Es la persona que me da los mejores consejos académicos.

COLUMNA B

a. «Come bien y duerme lo suficiente.»
b. mi mejor amigo/a
c. mi familia
d. mi consejero/a
e. mi madre/padre
f. sacar notas aceptables

Paso 3. Ahora, en parejas, túrnense para hacer y contestar preguntas usando las ideas de la Columna A en el **Paso 2.**

MODELO: E1: ¿Quién es la persona **que** te da los mejores consejos académicos?
E2: (Es) Mi consejero académico. ¿Quién te los da a ti?
E1: (Es) Mi consejero también.

B. El estrés, la condición humana. Lea la siguiente tira cómica y complete las oraciones.

[a]cansancio... *fatigue, restlessness, worry, nervousness, (emotional) imbalance, and anxiety*

1. Lo que quiere el padre de Libertad (= la amiga de Mafalda) es _____.
2. Lo que su padre tiene es _____.
3. Según el médico, lo que tiene su padre es _____.

C. En la preadolescencia

Paso 1. Complete las siguientes oraciones con detalles de su vida personal.

Cuando yo tenía diez años más o menos...

1. lo que más me divertía/molestaba era _____.
2. el programa de televisión que más me gustaba era _____.
3. la persona / las personas que yo más quería (*loved*) era(n) _____.

Paso 2. Ahora, en parejas, comparen sus respuestas.

_____

PrPrác. A, Paso 1: Answers: 1. a 2. d 3. b 4. c

¿Recuerda Ud.?

Before learning how to express reciprocal actions in **Gramática 32,** review the reflexive pronouns in **Gramática 14 (Cap. 5),** then provide the correct reflexive pronouns for the following sentences.

1. ___ levanté a las ocho y media.

2. Laura ___ puso el vestido.

3. Mis amigos y yo ___ sentamos en un café.

4. ¿Prefieres duchar___ o bañar___?

---

32 Expressing *each other* (Part 2)
Reciprocal Actions with Reflexive Pronouns

Grammar Tutorial 32
connect
|SPANISH
www.connectspanish.com

Gramática en acción: La amistad

Los buenos amigos...

- se conocen **bien.**
- se respetan.
- se quieren.
- se recuerdan **siempre.**

En las culturas hispanas, cuando las buenas amigas se encuentran, se besan en la mejilla.

¿Y Ud.?

Cuando Ud. y sus amigos se encuentran, ¿cómo se saludan (*do you greet each other*)? ¿Se dan la mano? ¿Se besan?

Reciprocal Actions / Las acciones recíprocas

1. Reciprocal Actions

Reciprocal actions (**Las acciones recíprocas**) are actions that involve two or more people doing something *to* or *for* each other. They are usually expressed in English with *each other* or *one another*. In Spanish, reciprocal actions are expressed with pronouns that are identical to the plural reflexive pronouns.

nos = each other (**nosotros/as**)
os = each other (**vosotros/as**)
se = each other (**Uds., ellos/as**)

Nos queremos.	*We love each other.*
¿**Os** ayudáis?	*Do you help one another?*
Se miran con ternura.	*They're looking at each other tenderly.*

2. Verbs Frequently Used to Express Reciprocal Actions

Verbs frequently used in this way include those at right, but any verb to whose meaning the phrase *each other* can be added may express a reciprocal action: **hablarse, mirarse, pelearse,** and so on.

abrazarse (c)	to embrace
besarse	to kiss each other
darse la mano	to shake hands
encontrarse	to meet (*someone*
(**se encuentran**)	*somewhere*)
quererse	to love each other; to be
	fond of each other
saludarse	to greet each other

¡OJO!

Sometimes a preposition is added in English to express the meaning of these verbs: **hablarse** = *to talk to each other,* **mirarse** = *to look at each other,* **pelearse** = *to fight with each other.* But no preposition is needed in Spanish.

Most of these verbs are new. The verbs **encontrarse** and **quererse** are new to you with their reciprocal meaning.

Friendship *Good friends . . . • know each other well. • respect each other. • are fond of each other. • always remember each other. In Hispanic cultures, when close women friends meet, they kiss each other on the cheek.*

Reciprocal Action Summary

nos, os, se + verb =
each other, one another

Práctica y comunicación

A. Los buenos amigos

Paso 1. Autoprueba. Dé el pronombre apropiado para expresar acciones recíprocas.

1. _____ miramos
2. _____ pelearon
3. _____ conocen
4. _____ llamaban
5. _____ saludamos

Paso 2. ¿Qué hace Ud. con sus buenos amigos? Conteste usando **nos** (el pronombre recíproco). Si una oración no es cierta para Ud., use **no**.

MODELO: abrazar cuando ver ⟶ **Nos abrazamos** cuando **nos vemos.**

1. ver con frecuencia
2. conocer bien
3. respetar mucho
4. ayudar cuando necesitamos ayuda
5. mandar muchos mensajes
6. hablar por teléfono con frecuencia
7. decir la verdad siempre, lo bueno y lo malo
8. ¿ ?

Paso 3. Ahora, en parejas, túrnense para hacer y contestar preguntas basadas en el **Paso 2.** Luego, díganle a la clase algo que tienen en común.

MODELO: E1: ¿Tus amigos y tú **se abrazan** cuando **se ven**?
E2: Sí, con frecuencia **nos abrazamos** cuando **nos vemos** después de un tiempo. ¿Y Uds.?
E1: Nosotros también **nos abrazamos.**

B. ¿Qué pasa entre ellos?

Describa las siguientes relaciones familiares o sociales, haciendo oraciones completas con una palabra o frase de cada columna.

MODELO: Los buenos amigos **se conocen** bien.

los buenos amigos los parientes los esposos los padres y los niños los amigos que no viven en la misma ciudad los profesores y los estudiantes los compañeros de cuarto/casa	**+** (no) **+**	visitarse con frecuencia quererse, respetarse, necesitarse, conocerse bien ayudarse mutuamente (en los quehaceres domésticos, cuando tienen problemas económicos o problemas personales) verse (todos los días, con frecuencia) llamarse por teléfono, escribirse mirarse (con cariño [*affection*]) saludarse, darse la mano quejarse sinceramente, escucharse

C. Intercambios

Paso 1. Haga por lo menos una pregunta con cada una de las siguientes frases. En el **Paso 2,** va a usar esas preguntas para entrevistar a alguien de la clase sobre sus relaciones con su pareja, sus amigos, sus padres y sus parientes. Use el tiempo presente, como en el modelo.

(Continúa.)

_____

Prác. A, Paso 1: Answers: 1. nos 2. se 3. se 4. se 5. nos

MODELOS: besarse ⟶ ¿Tu pareja y tú se besan en público?

1. verse
2. escribirse
3. mantenerse en contacto
4. llamarse por teléfono

5. abrazarse
6. besarse
7. saludarse dándose la mano
8. pelearse

Paso 2. Ahora, en parejas, túrnense para hacerse las preguntas del **Paso 1.**
Luego díganle a la clase lo que tienen en común.

Un poco de todo

A. Lengua y cultura: La leyenda del lago de Maracaibo

Paso 1. Complete the following legend with the correct form of the word in
parentheses, as suggested by context. The verbs will be in the preterite or
imperfect. When two possibilities are given in parentheses, select the correct word.

Había una vez[a] un cacique[b] indígena que se llamaba
Zapara. Este[c] tenía una hija, Maruma, que (ser[1]) muy bonita.
Al padre y a la hija (se / les[2]) (gustar[3]) pasar tiempo juntos y
caminar por el bosque.[d]

Un día Zapara (comprender[4]) que su hija ya (ser[5]) una
mujer y (se / le[6]) (decir[7]): «Debes escoger[e] esposo, pues ya
tienes edad[f] para formar una familia. Pero (su / tu[8]) esposo
debe ser guerrero,[g] como todos los hombres de nuestra
familia».

Un día, mientras su padre (estar[9]) ausente, Maruma
(salir[10]) sola a cazar[h] en el bosque. Estaba a punto de
dispararle a un ciervo[i] cuando (un / —[11]) otro cazador[j]
(matar[k12]) al animal. Maruma (ponerse[13]) muy enojada pero
el joven, (que / quienes[14]) (ser[15]) guapo y simpático, dijo: «El
ciervo es para (tú / ti[16]). Solo quiero conocerte. Me llamo
Tamaré». A partir de ese día[l] los (joven[17]) (hacerse[m18])
amigos. Pronto se enamoraron.[n]

Una niña en su barca (*boat*), en el lago de Maracaibo

Desgraciadamente, el joven no era un buen guerrero y por eso el padre de
Maruma (enojarse[19]) mucho cuando (saber[20]) que ella (querer[21]) casarse con él. Se
enfadó tanto[ñ] que la naturaleza reaccionó y (haber[22]) grandes terremotos[o] e
inundaciones:[p] las aguas cubrieron[q] las tierras del cacique Zapara y también a
Maruma y Tamaré, formando así el lago de Maracaibo. Zapara se convirtió en
una de sus pequeñas islas.

[a]Había... *Once upon a time there was* [b]*chief* [c]*He* [d]*forest* [e]*choose* [f]*ya... you're old enough* [g]*a warrior*
[h]*hunt* [i]Estaba... *She was about to shoot a deer* [j]*hunter* [k]*to kill* [l]*A... From that day on* [m]*to become* [n]*se...*
they fell in love [ñ]*Se... He was so angry* [o]*earthquakes* [p]*floods* [q]*covered*

Paso 2. Comprensión. Conteste las siguientes preguntas.

1. ¿Quién era Zapara?
2. ¿De quién se enamoró (*fell in love*) Maruma?
3. ¿Por qué se enojó Zapara?
4. ¿Cómo se formó el lago de Maracaibo?

Paso 3. Ahora, en grupos, inventen cuatro preguntas bien difíciles, pero posibles
de contestar, sobre la leyenda del lago de Maracaibo. Luego háganle sus preguntas
a la clase. ¿Qué grupo pudo inventar las preguntas más difíciles de contestar?

B. Caperucita Roja

Paso 1. Narre el cuento de Caperucita Roja, conjugando los verbos en la forma apropiada del imperfecto o del pretérito. Trate de adivinar (*Try to guess*) el significado de las palabras o expresiones subrayadas (*underlined*), usando el contexto.

Había una vez una niña que (llamarse[1]) Caperucita Roja. Todos los animales del <u>bosque</u> (ser[2]) sus amigos y Caperucita Roja (quererlos[3]) mucho. Un día su mamá (decirle[4]): —Lleva esta <u>jarrita</u> de miel[a] a casa de tu abuelita.

En el bosque, un <u>lobo</u> (salir[5]) a hablar con la niña. Le (preguntar[6]): —¿Adónde vas, Caperucita Roja? Esta[b] (contestarle[7]): —Voy a casa de mi abuelita. Le (decir[8]) el lobo: —Pues, si vas por este sendero,[c] vas a llegar antes. Él (irse[9]) por otro <u>camino</u> más corto.

El lobo (llegar[10]) primero a la casa de la abuelita y (entrar[11]). Cuando la abuela (verlo[12]), (saltar[d13]) de la cama y (correr[14]) a esconderse.[e] Caperucita Roja (llegar[15]) por fin a la casa de la abuelita. (*ella:* encontrar[16]) a su «abuelita», que (estar[17]) en la cama. Le (decir[18]): —¡Qué dientes tan largos tienes! —Son para comerte mejor! —(decirle[19]) «su abuelita». Luego...

[a]*honey* [b]*She* [c]*path* [d]*to jump* [e]*hide herself*

Paso 2. Ahora, en grupos, terminen el cuento de Caperucita Roja. Si no lo saben bien, no importa: inventen un final.

Vocabulario útil

el cazador	hunter
comérselo/la	to eat someone up
disparar	to shoot
huir	to flee
matar	to kill

En su comunidad

Entreviste a una persona hispana de su universidad o ciudad sobre el cuidado médico en su país de origen.

PREGUNTAS POSIBLES

- En su país de origen, ¿qué hace una persona cuando tiene una enfermedad que no es muy seria? ¿Va al médico? ¿Habla con el farmacéutico? ¿Va a alguna persona que cura con remedios naturales?

- ¿Qué alimentos se consideran muy sanos en su país? ¿Se usan algunos productos naturales? ¿Cuáles son? ¿Para qué sirven de remedio?

- ¿Cómo se dice *flu* en su país? ¿Y *cold*?

«Remedios para todos» Segmento 2

Antes de mirar

Cuando Ud. tiene resfriado, ¿va al médico generalmente? ¿Qué hace para curarse y sentirse mejor? ¿Tiene algún remedio casero? ¿Quién se lo enseñó?

Este segmento

En este segmento final del programa, una reportera española enseña un remedio casero contra el resfriado. Luego Ana y Víctor hablan de otros remedios caseros.

Un remedio casero (*homemade*) contra el catarro (resfriado): un empaste de mostaza (*mustard plaster*) con harina de trigo (*wheat flour*)

Fragmento del guion

Luego, lo que tenéis que poner es aceite de oliva, que lo frotáis[a] así en el pecho,[b] para que la masa[c]... lo coja[d] mejor. Entonces, podéis poner la pasta así directamente con la cuchara. Y así lo dejáis[e] unas horas. Luego así[f] ya te puedes ir a trabajar lo que queráis,[g] pero sobre todo no os lo quitéis.[h]

[a]*rub* [b]*chest* [c]*para... so that the paste* [d]*lo.. sticks to it* [e]*leave* [f]*this way* [g]*lo... whatever you want* [h]*no... don't take it off*

Vocabulario del segmento

la miel	honey	**tapar**	to cover
pon atención	pay attention	**ensuciarse**	to get dirty
la risa	laughter	**espero que**	I hope it works
constipado/a	**resfriado/a** (*Spain*)	**os funcione**	for you
probar (pruebo)	to try	**el ajo crudo**	raw garlic
el/la bisabuelo/a	great-grandparent	**fíjate**	look
el tercio	third part (*measure*)	**tuyo/a**	of yours
espeso/a	thick	**la planta**	sole (*of the foot*)

Después de mirar

A. ¿Está claro? ¿Cierto o falso? Corrija las oraciones falsas.

	CIERTO	FALSO
1. Es un remedio de su abuela.	☐	☐
2. El primer ingrediente del empaste es el aceite de oliva.	☐	☐
3. El empaste debe estar bastante (*rather*) espeso.	☐	☐
4. Se pone aceite de oliva en la mano.	☐	☐
5. La persona enferma debe llevar el empaste solo unos minutos.	☐	☐

B. Un poco más. Conteste las siguientes preguntas.

1. ¿Qué le pasa a Víctor hoy?
2. ¿Qué remedio casero le recomienda Ana a Víctor?
3. ¿Qué remedio prefiere Víctor? ¿Por qué?

C. Y ahora, Uds. En grupos, hablen de los remedios y productos que no necesitan receta médica que Uds. usan por razones de salud. ¿Qué tipo de remedios son? (¿farmacéuticos, herbales, homeopáticos,... ?) ¿Confían Uds. (*Do you trust*) en sus beneficios? ¿Les preocupan los posibles efectos secundarios?

¿Qué tipo de seguro (*insurance*) médico tiene Ud.? ¿Tiene uno para los estudiantes de la universidad o uno a través del (*through the*) trabajo de sus padres? ¿O tiene uno de su propio (*own*) trabajo?

Lectura cultural: Venezuela

El seguro[a] médico en Venezuela

En Venezuela hay un sistema de salud público y gratuito[b] que sirve, sobre todo,[c] a la gente de la clase trabajadora que no puede pagar un seguro médico privado. Hay consultorios médicos, clínicas y hospitales que proveen de todo tipo de servicios relacionados con la salud a las personas que los necesitan.

También existe la posibilidad de tener atención médica privada a través de pólizas[d] de seguro, que se contratan generalmente a través del empleador.[e] Sin embargo, los venezolanos siempre tienen acceso al sistema público, que se paga con impuestos[f] obligatorios para la seguridad social. En general, el cuidado médico de familia, privado, es mucho más barato que en los Estados Unidos y no resulta muy caro ir al consultorio del doctor y pagar la visita sin tener un seguro. En cambio,[g] los servicios de emergencia y hospitalización son muy costosos[h] y para tenerlos es indispensable[i] un seguro médico.

[a]*insurance* [b]*free* [c]*sobre... especially* [d]*a... through* policies [e]*employer* [f]*taxes* [g]*En... On the other hand* [h]*expensive* [i]*absolutely necessary*

Un venezolano, que baila el limbo durante una fiesta, en Caracas

Un símbolo venezolano: «La rumba»

Al espíritu fiestero[a] de los venezolanos se le dice[b] «la rumba». Venezuela es el principal mercado de consumo de la música popular caribeña. Al venezolano le gusta organizar y celebrar fiestas en las cuales[c] siempre se baila salsa, merengue o cualquier otro ritmo caribeño, hasta el amanecer.[d]

[a]*party-loving* [b]*se... (it) is called* [c]*las... which* [d]*dawn*

En **otros** países hispanos

- **En Latinoamérica** Es muy diversa la manera en que cada país provee de asistencia sanitaria[a] a sus habitantes: a través de[b] un sistema exclusivamente gubernamental[c] o por medio[d] de una combinación de sistemas públicos y privados. El acceso al cuidado médico también varía mucho de país a país. Hay países como la Argentina, Cuba y Costa Rica que proporcionan[e] acceso a todas las personas. Desgraciadamente, en otros países hay un considerable número de personas que no tienen acceso fácil a médicos y medicinas.

- **En España** España tiene un sistema nacional de seguridad social que cubre[f] el cuidado médico de todos sus ciudadanos. Este sistema, junto con[g] otros factores, contribuye a que los españoles tengan una de las esperanzas de vida[h] más largas del mundo.

[a]*health* [b]*a... via* [c]*government-run* [d]*means* [e]*provide* [f]*covers* [g]*junto... along with* [h]*esperanzas... life expectancies*

COMPRENSIÓN

1. ¿Qué sistema de salud usa con más frecuencia la clase trabajadora venezolana?
2. ¿Cómo se paga el sistema público de salud en Venezuela?
3. ¿Los habitantes de qué país hispanohablante tienen una de las esperanzas de vida más largas del planeta?
4. ¿Qué es «la rumba» en Venezuela?
5. ¿Qué bailan los venezolanos?

Y ahora, Uds.

¿Creen Uds que las personas de los Estados Unidos tienen «espíritu de rumba»? Expliquen su opinión, dando ejemplos especificos para ilustrar su punto de vista (*point of view*).

Del mundo hispano

Antes de leer

Un epitafio es una breve inscripción que se pone en la tumba de una persona muerta (*deceased*). En su opinión, ¿cuáles de los siguientes temas son apropiados para un epitafio?

- ☐ datos biográficos
- ☐ descripción física
- ☐ aspectos de su profesión
- ☐ un símbolo de la persona
- ☐ sus gustos y preferencias

- ☐ aspectos de su personalidad
- ☐ la descripción de algunos de sus parientes
- ☐ su filosofía de la vida
- ☐ algo memorable que dijo una vez
- ☐ cómo murió

Lectura: «Epitafio», de Nicanor Parra

De estatura mediana,[a]
con una voz[b] ni delgada ni gruesa,[c]
hijo mayor de un profesor primario[d]
y de una modista de trastienda;[e]
5   flaco de nacimiento[f]
aunque[g] devoto de la buena mesa;[h]
de mejillas escuálidas[i]
Y de más bien[j] abundantes orejas;
con un rostro cuadrado[k]
10 en que los ojos se abren apenas[l]
y una nariz de boxeador mulato
baja a la boca de ídolo azteca
—todo esto bañado[m]
por una luz entre irónica y pérfida[n]—,
15 ni muy listo ni tonto de remate[ñ]
fui lo que fui: una mezcla[o]
de vinagre y de aceite de comer
¡un embutido[p] de ángel y bestia[q]!

[a]*average* [b]*voice* [c]*hearty* [d]de escuela primaria [e]*modista... backroom seamstress* [f]*flaco... thin since birth* [g]*although* [h]*de... to good food* [i]*mejillas... thin cheeks* [j]*más... rather* [k]*rostro... square face* [l]*hardly* [m]*bathed* [n]*treacherous* [ñ]*de... hopelessly* [o]*mixture* [p]*sausage* [q]*beast*

Comprensión

A. En este epitafio. ¿Cuáles de los posibles temas para un epitafio que se mencionaron en **Antes de leer** aparecen en este poema?

B. Preguntas

Paso 1. ¿Cierto o falso? Indiquen las palabras específicas del poema que justifiquen su respuesta.

	CIERTO	FALSO
1. Esta persona era alta.	☐	☐
2. Sus padres eran médicos importantes.	☐	☐
3. Esta persona era delgada.	☐	☐
4. Tenía orejas grandes.	☐	☐
5. Era inteligentísimo.	☐	☐
6. Su personalidad era contradictoria.	☐	☐

Paso 2. Este poema es autobiográfico; es decir (*that is*), que el poeta lo escribió acerca de sí mismo (*about himself*). ¿Qué palabras del poema revelan esto?

Antes de escuchar

¿Qué precauciones toma Ud. para no enfermarse? ¿Tuvo Ud. algún resfriado el año pasado? ¿alguna gripe? ¿Fue al médico con frecuencia durante el último año?

Vocabulario para escuchar

vacunarse	to get a shot	**la vacuna**	vaccination
la muerte	death	**de alto riesgo**	high-risk
contraer (*like*	to get; to contract	**embarazadas**	pregnant
traer)	(*an illness*)	**peligroso/a**	dangerous

Después de escuchar

A. **La gripe.** Conteste las siguientes preguntas sobre esta enfermedad, según la información en el anuncio.

1. ¿Aproximadamente cuántas personas van al hospital cada año en los Estados Unidos a causa de la gripe?
2. ¿Cuántas personas mueren anualmente en los Estados Unidos a causa de la gripe, aproximadamente?
3. ¿Hay solo un tipo de virus de gripe?

B. **La vacuna.** Conteste las siguientes preguntas sobre la campaña de vacunación.

1. ¿Quiénes deben vacunarse contra la gripe?
2. ¿Quiénes se consideran personas de alto riesgo?
3. ¿Quiénes no pueden recibir la vacuna?

PRODUCCIÓN PERSONAL

¡Ahora, yo!

A. Use de modelo las preguntas y respuestas de la página 323 de este capítulo para hablar del tipo de vida que Ud. lleva y de su salud en general.

B. Filme a una persona que habla de un remedio casero (*homemade*) que se usa en su familia. Puede ser algo serio o cómico.

A ESCRIBIR

La historia de una enfermedad

Ud. ya ha hablado (*You've already talked*) en este capítulo de sus enfermedades. Ahora va a escribir un ensayo sobre una enfermedad que sufrió un compañero / una compañera de clase.

Preparar

Paso 1. En parejas, entrevístense sobre una enfermedad que sufrieron. Piensen en la información que van a necesitar para escribir la narración de un episodio de una enfermedad. Aquí hay algunos ejemplos. Uds. deben añadir por lo menos 3 o 4 preguntas. ¡OJO! Usen el pretérito y el imperfecto con cuidado.

1. ¿Fue una enfermedad grave o leve (*minor*)? ¿O era crónica?
2. ¿Cuándo ocurrió? ¿Cuántos años tenías?
3. ¿Cuáles eran los síntomas?
4. ¿ ?

Paso 2. Ahora escriba la narración, usando la información que consiguió en el **Paso 1**. O, si Ud. prefiere, puede escribir sobre la enfermedad de un amigo o un pariente. Hay más ayuda en Connect.

Más ideas para su portafolio

- Incluya 5 consejos que Ud. considera fundamentales para estar bien físicamente.

- Dé un resumenwve de su historia favorita (de un libro o una película) cuando Ud. era pequeño/a.

- Si ha estado jugando (*have been playing*) Practice Spanish: Study Abroad, en Quest 8 Ud. aprendió sobre la leyenda de los dos cadejos, una leyenda que trata del equilibrio (*balance*) entre lo bueno y lo malo. ¿Conoce Ud. otras historias sobre la armonía entre el bien y el mal? Escriba un informe que resuma la leyenda de los dos cadejos y compárela con leyendas, cuentos o creencias (*beliefs*) de su propia cultura o de otras culturas que Ud. conoce sobre el bien y el mal.

Sugerencia: You are now ready to play Quest 8 in **Practice Spanish: Study Abroad** (www.mhpractice.com).

LEARNSMART

Visit **www.connectspanish.com** to practice the vocabulary and grammar points covered in this chapter.

AFTER STUDYING THIS CHAPTER I CAN. . .

☐ name many parts of the body and activities related to a healthy life (324)

☐ talk about illnesses and medical exams (326)

☐ use the preterite and imperfect together to talk about the past and tell stories (330–332)

☐ use **que, quien,** and **lo que** to avoid repetition (338–339)

☐ express the concept of "each other" with pronouns (341)

☐ recognize/describe at least 2–3 aspects of Venezuelan cultures

Gramática en breve

30. Using the Preterite and the Imperfect

Uses of the Preterite	Uses of the Imperfect
beginning/end of an action	habitual/repeated action
completed action	ongoing action
series of completed actions	background information
the action on the "stage"	the setting for the action

31. Relative Pronouns

que = refers to things and people

quien(es) = refers only to people

lo que = refers to a situation

32. Reciprocal Actions with Reflexive Pronouns

each other = **nos, os, se**

Vocabulario

Los verbos

abrazarse (c)	to embrace
besarse	to kiss each other
darse la mano	to shake hands
encontrarse	to meet (*someone*
(me encuentro) (con)	*somewhere*)
quererse	to love each other; to be fond of each other
saludarse	to greet each other

La salud y el bienestar

el bienestar	well-being
la caminadora	treadmill
la salud	health

Repaso: la comida, el deporte

cansarse	to get tired
cuidarse	to take care of oneself
dejar de + *inf.*	to stop (*doing something*)
doler (duele) (*like* **gustar**)	to hurt; to ache
enfermarse	to get sick
guardar cama	to stay in bed
hacer	to do
ejercicios aeróbicos	aerobics
(el método) Pilates	Pilates
levantar pesas	to lift weights
llevar una vida sana/tranquila	to lead a healthy/calm life
molestar (*like* **gustar**)	to bother
ponerle una inyección / una vacuna	to give (*someone*) a shot, injection / a vaccination
resfriarse (me resfrío)	to get/catch a cold
respirar	to breathe
sacar (qu)	to extract
sacar la lengua	to stick out one's tongue
sacarle un diente / una muela	to extract (*someone's*) tooth/molar
tener dolor de	to have a pain/ache in
tomarle la temperatura	to take someone's temperature
toser	to cough

Repaso: caminar, comer, correr, dormir (duermo) (u), hacer ejercicio, hacer (el) yoga, llevar (to wear), practicar (qu), sentirse (me siento) (i)

El cuerpo humano

la boca	mouth
el brazo	arm
la cabeza	head
el cerebro	brain
el corazón	heart
el cuerpo humano	human body
el dedo (de la mano)	finger
el dedo del pie	toe
el estómago	stomach
la garganta	throat
la lengua	tongue
la mano	hand
la muela	molar, back tooth
la nariz (*pl.* **narices**)	nose
el oído	inner ear

el ojo	eye
la oreja	(outer) ear
el pie	foot
la pierna	leg
los pulmones	lungs
la sangre	blood

Repaso: el diente

Las enfermedades y los tratamientos

los anteojos	glasses
el chequeo	check-up
el consultorio	(medical) office
el dolor (de)	pain, ache (in)
la enfermedad	illness, sickness
la fiebre	fever
la gripe	flu
el jarabe	(cough) syrup
los lentes	glasses
los lentes de contacto	contact lenses
la pastilla	pill
la receta	prescription
el resfriado	cold (*illness*)
el síntoma	symptom
la tos	cough
el tratamiento	treatment

Cognados: el antibiótico, la medicina, la temperatura

El personal médico

| el/la enfermero/a | nurse |
| el/la farmacéutico/a | pharmacist |

Cognado: el/la dentista, el/la paciente

Repaso: el/la médico/a

Otro sustantivo

| la cita | date; appointment |
| la vida | life |

Los adjetivos

mareado/a	dizzy; nauseated
pasado/a	past, last
resfriado/a	congested, stuffed up
sano/a	healthy
suficiente	enough

Repaso: tranquilo/a

Palabras adicionales

anoche	last night
de repente	suddenly
desgraciadamente	unfortunately
dos veces	twice
eso quiere decir...	that means . . .
frecuentemente	frequently
lo bueno	the good thing/news
lo malo	the bad thing/news
lo suficiente	enough

Repaso: anteayer, ayer, de adolescente, de niño/a, en seguida, lo que, mientras, que, quien(es), siempre, una vez

Vocabulario personal

ÍNDICE

CAPÍTULO
7

Communicative Goals for Chapter 7

By the end of the chapter, you should be able to:

- discuss what you eat and drink ❏
- describe your favorite restaurant ❏
- order and pay for food ❏
- talk about what and who you know ❏
- answer questions negatively ❏
- tell someone to do something ❏

Grammatical Structures

You should know:

- **saber** and **conocer** ❏
- personal **a** ❏
- direct object pronouns ❏
- **acabar de** ❏
- indefinite and negative words ❏
- formal commands ❏

PRONUNCIACIÓN: LAS VOCALES

Remember that in Spanish there are only five vowel sounds. Listen carefully as your instructor pronounces the following words, then repeat.

A: agua – el agua – el agua mineral – camarones – gambas – naranja – banana – una naranja y una banana – papas – patatas – Las papas son patatas y las patatas son papas. – la carne – hambre – pan – salsa – sal – una papa sin sal

E: té – café – leche – café con leche – refresco – cerveza – arvejas – queso – helado – galletas – beber – comer – Pepe bebe leche y come galletas. – tenedor – mesa – El tenedor está en la mesa. – cena

I: vino – tinto – vino tinto – líquido – El vino tinto es un líquido. – rico – muy rico – bistec – El bistec está rico. – frijoles – sirve – aquí – Aquí sirven frijoles con chile. – piña – almíbar – piña en almíbar – oliva – mariscos

O: pollo – arroz – el arroz con pollo – El arroz con pollo está bueno. – sopa – jamón – postre – torta – limón – De postre hay torta de limón. – salmón – no – No me gusta el salmón. – melón

U: lechuga – desayuno – nunca – ¡Nunca desayuno lechuga! – verduras – gustan – ¿Te gustan las verduras? – menú – atún – No hay atún en el menú. – fruta – jugo – El jugo se hace de fruta. – zumo – legumbres – chuleta – cuchara – cuchillo – Se usa un cuchillo para cortar la chuleta.

LISTENING COMPREHENSION:
UNA NOCHE EN EL RESTAURANTE MÁLAGA

Your instructor will read a passage to you based on the drawing. The first time you hear the passage, identify the people/groups of people your instructor is describing. The second time you hear the passage, listen for details and indicate if the sentences that follow are true or false.

Vocabulario útil

el cumpleaños birthday
la propina tip

1. ☐ C ☐ F José and Beatriz will probably sit down next to the Gómez family.
2. ☐ C ☐ F Jean-Paul, when visiting the U.S., likes to eat in Arby's and Taco Bell.
3. ☐ C ☐ F The Gómez family is celebrating Mr. Gómez's birthday.
4. ☐ C ☐ F Mr. López eats in the Málaga very frequently.
5. ☐ C ☐ F Mr. Peñas is ordering for himself and his wife.
6. ☐ C ☐ F The cashier is smiling because she's in love with Mr. López.
7. ☐ C ☐ F José has good manners.
8. ☐ C ☐ F Mr. and Mrs. Peñas are returning to Argentina in two days.

HOSTERÍA DEL LAUREL
Plaza de los Venerables, 5
Teléfono 954 / 22 02 05
41004 - SEVILLA

ENTRANTES

Ensalada Mixta	5 €
Ensalada Lechuga y Tomate	4 €
Ensalada Salsa Roquefort	7,50 €
Espárragos Tres Salsas	9,50 €
Entremeses Variados	10 €
Jamón Serrano	12,30 €
Aguacate Vinagrete	9 €
Champiñones al Ajillo	8,60 €
Melón con Jamón	9 €
Consomé Jerez	3,50 €
Sopa de Ajos	3 €
Sopa de Picadillo	3,50 €
Gazpacho Andaluz	4 €

HUEVOS / PASTAS / ARROCES

Tortilla Española	6,50 €
Tortilla de Jamón	7,70 €
Paella Mixta (Min. 2 P.), 1 ración	16 €
Spaguetti Napolitana	6 €
Huevos Flamenca	6,50 €
Pan	1 €
Mantequilla	1 €
Oliva	2 €

PESCADOS

Brocheta de Mero	19 €
Fritura Sevillana	18 €
Urta Roteña	16 €
Pez Espada	18 €

CARNES

Chuleta de Cerdo	11 €
Pollo Sevillana	10 €
Menudo a la Andaluza	10 €
Riñones Jerez	9,50 €
Chuleta de Cordero	12 €
Cordero Asado	16 €
Salteado Ternera	12 €
Tournedos Hostería	16 €
Entrecote Parrilla	19 €
Solomillo Casera	26 €

POSTRES

Limón Helado	3,50 €
Helados Variados	4 €
Postre Hostería	4,50 €
Torta al Whisky	4,50 €
Flan al Caramelo	4 €
Fruta del Tiempo	3,50 €
Piña en Almíbar	3,50 €
Café Irlandés	4,50 €

¿SABER O CONOCER? WORKSHEET

I. Would you use **saber** or **conocer** in each of these sentences? Why?

1. She never (□ S □ C) <u>knows</u> the answer.

2. Do you (□ S □ C) <u>know</u> where Raul is? —No, but I (□ S □ C) <u>know</u> he's coming back later.

3. I don't (□ S □ C) <u>know</u> that girl, but I (□ S □ C) <u>know</u> she's from Chile.

4. My friend doesn't (□ S □ C) <u>know</u> how to play the guitar.

5. Do you (□ S □ C) <u>know</u> Paris well? —No, I (□ S □ C) <u>know</u> Madrid much better.

6. My friend wants to (□ S □ C) <u>meet</u> my unmarried cousin.

7. I don't (□ S □ C) <u>know</u> why she wants a dog!

8. I (□ S □ C) <u>know</u> San Francisco pretty well, but I still don't (□ S □ C) <u>know</u> all the good restaurants.

9. Do you (□ S □ C) <u>know</u> what we have to do tonight?

10. Hey, I (□ S □ C) <u>know</u> that guy!

II. Complete the following sentences with the correct form of **saber** or **conocer**.

1. (Yo) _____ a Beatriz, pero no _____ de dónde es.

2. ¡Esos chicos _____ jugar al básquetbol muy bien!

3. ¿(Tú) _____ cuánto dinero necesito para el cine?

4. Diego cocina muy bien: (él) _____ preparar muchos platos venezolanos.

5. ¿Por qué no (Uds.) _____ la respuesta?

6. —¿(Tú) _____ algo? Mi amigo Rafael quiere salir contigo.

7. —¿¿Rafael?? ¿Quién es? Yo no _____ a ningún Rafael.

8. ¿(Tú) _____ a la familia de tu novio?

9. En el futuro, quiero _____ a una mujer guapa, inteligente, simpática y rica... ¡pero (yo) _____ que eso va a ser difícil!

10. Marcos, ¿(tú) _____ si hay un examen mañana?

11. Pablo no _____ jugar al tenis pero sí _____ esquiar muy bien.

12. No (yo) _____ qué voy a hacer esta noche.

13. Ellos no _____ Centroamérica, pero _____ mucho de la política de esa región.

14. Queremos comer algo, pero no _____ dónde está el mercado.

PRÁCTICA: ¿SABER O CONOCER?

Alfredo and Raquel are looking for a place to eat. Complete their conversation with the correct form of **saber** or **conocer**, according to the context.

Raquel: Oye, Alfredo. Tengo hambre. ¿Comemos?

Alfredo: Sí, de acuerdo. ¿Por qué no comemos en este restaurante aquí? Es excelente.

Raquel: Bien, pero ... ¿cómo (1. tú) _____ que este restaurante es tan bueno?
Yo no (2.) _____ bien este barrio, y nunca vengo a comer por aquí. .

Alfredo: Pues, yo lo (3.) _____ muy bien. Como aquí casi todas las semanas.

Raquel: ¿De veras? (*Really?*)

Alfredo: Sí. Creo que (4. tú) _____ que mi tía Elenita tiene un restaurante,
¿no? Pues, es este restaurante aquí.

Raquel: ¡No me digas! (*You're kidding!*)

Alfredo: Sí, y vas a ver. Elenita (5.) _____ cocinar de maravilla. Te va a gustar
mucho.

Raquel: Ya lo creo. Me gustaría (6.) _____ a tu tía. (*Entran al restaurante.*)

(*Unos minutos más tarde.*)

Raquel: ¿Y (7. tú) _____ a nuestro camarero también?

Alfredo: No, no lo (8.) _____. Debe ser nuevo. ¿Ya
(9.) _____ qué vas a pedir?

Raquel: No, todavía no lo (10.) _____. ¿Qué me recomiendas?

Alfredo: Pues, como (11. yo) _____ que te gustan mucho las sopas, te
recomiendo la sopa de pollo. Es la especialidad de la casa, y es deliciosa.

Raquel: De acuerdo. Y después de pedir, vamos a la cocina. Quiero
(12.) _____ a Elenita.

DIRECT OBJECT PRONOUNS WORKSHEET

Answer the following questions by substituting the correct direct object pronoun in your answer. Where appropriate, use the correct indefinite or negative words.

| me | te | lo | la | nos | os | los | las |

Modelo: ¿Pierdes <u>tus llaves</u> con frecuencia? → No, no las pierdo nunca.

<u>La clase</u>

1. ¿Conoces bien <u>a todos los estudiantes</u> de la clase de español?   _____

2. ¿Hacen Uds. <u>los ejercicios</u> en el libro de texto cada día?   _____

3. ¿Cuándo haces <u>la tarea</u> para tu clase de español?   _____

4. ¿Vas a ver <u>al profesor</u> de español en la oficina hoy?   _____

5. ¿Cuándo vas a aprender <u>la gramática</u> nueva?   _____

6. ¿Empiezas a entender <u>los objetos directos</u>?   _____

7. ¿Siempre ayudas <u>a los compañeros</u> de clase?   _____

8. ¿Traes <u>tu diccionario</u> a clase siempre?   _____

<u>La comida</u>

9. Cuando comes en restaurantes elegantes ¿siempre pagas <u>la cuenta</u>?   _____

10. A veces, ¿comes <u>el postre</u> antes del plato principal?   _____

11. ¿Tomas <u>el café</u> con azúcar o sin azúcar?   _____

12. ¿Te gusta preparar <u>la cena</u>?   _____

13. ¿Traes <u>el almuerzo</u> a la universidad?   _____

<u>En casa</u>

14. ¿Siempre lavas <u>los platos</u> después de comer?   _____

15. ¿Haces <u>la cama</u> todos los días?   _____

16. ¿En qué cuarto prefieres poner <u>el teléfono</u>?   _____

17. ¿Miras <u>las noticias</u> en la televisión por la noche?   _____

18. ¿Puedes escuchar <u>la radio</u> y estudiar al mismo tiempo?   _____

PRÁCTICA: ¿QUÉ ACABAN DE HACER? ¿QUÉ VAN A HACER?

Explain what the people in the drawings have just done and what they are going to do now.

	¿Qué acaba(n) de hacer?	Ahora, ¿qué va(n) a hacer?

Paco

_____ _____

_____ _____

Lupe y Jaime

_____ _____

_____ _____

Ernesto

_____ _____

_____ _____

Ana, Raúl y Rafa

_____ _____

_____ _____

PRÁCTICA: INDEFINITE AND NEGATIVE WORDS

Ana and Estela are roommates, but are complete opposites. Explain how they differ from each other using the drawing below and rewriting the sentences to describe the other roommate.

Modelo: Ana siempre vuelve tarde a la residencia.   Estela nunca vuelve tarde
(Estela no vuelve tarde nunca.)
(Estela jamás vuelve tarde.)

Ana	**Estela**
Hay algo debajo de la cama de Ana.	1. _____
También hay una pizza en su cama.	2. _____
3. _____	Estela jamás lleva ropa vieja y sucia.
Ana tiene algunos problemas con organizarse.	4. _____
5. _____	Algunos creen que Estela es una compulsiva.
Ana conoce a muchas personas interesantes.	6. _____
A veces, alguien llama a Ana por teléfono a la una de la mañana.	7. _____
8. _____	Estela siempre se levanta temprano.
9. _____	Se acuesta temprano también.
10. _____	Nunca llega tarde a clase.

PRÁCTICA: MANDATOS FORMALES

¡El pobre Sr. Camacho tiene muchos problemas! Below is a list of some of Mr. Camacho's problems/desires. Tell him how you think he should solve his problems by giving him formal commands. Try to give both negative and affirmative commands where possible, and to suggest two solutions to each problem.

-ar → e(n)	tomar → tome
-er/ir → a(n)	beber → beba

Modelo:　　　Estoy cansado.
Soluciones:　　Tome una siesta. No trabaje ahora. ¡Descanse más!

1. Tengo hambre pero estoy a dieta.

_____

2. Estoy aburrido.

_____

3. Estoy enfermo.

_____

4. No me gusta mi trabajo (*job*).

_____

5. Tengo miedo de los perros.

_____

6. Me gustaría (*would like*) ser rico.

_____

7. Tengo dolor de cabeza (*headache*).

_____

8. Mi coche no funciona.

_____

9. Gano (*I earn*) muy poco dinero.

_____

10. Necesito perder 10 libras (*pounds*).

_____

PRÁCTICA: MANDATOS

Complete the charts as in the example. Substitute the correct pronouns for the underlined words. Put the affirmative commands in the first column and the negative commands in the second column.

comer <u>el helado</u>

Ud.	¡Cómalo!	¡No lo coma!
Uds.	¡Cómanlo!	¡No lo coman!

dar <u>la fiesta</u>

traer <u>el agua</u>

Ud.		
Uds.		

poner <u>la mesa</u>

preparar <u>los tacos</u>

Ud.		
Uds.		

hacer <u>el postre</u>

pedir <u>la paella</u>

Ud.		
Uds.		

llegar temprano

ayudar <u>a mamá</u>

Ud.

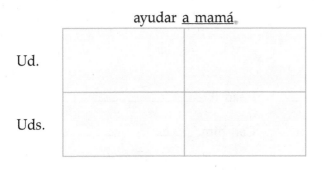

Uds.

comprar <u>la comida</u>

Ud.

Uds.

invitar <u>al profesor</u>

Ud.

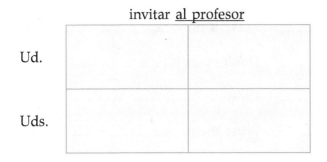

Uds.

usar <u>la tarjeta de crédito</u>

Ud.

Uds.

buscar <u>los garbanzos</u>

Ud.

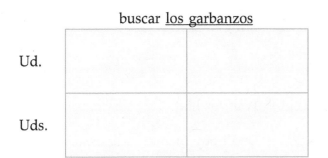

Uds.

servir <u>las verduras</u>

Ud.

Uds.

ir al café

Ud.

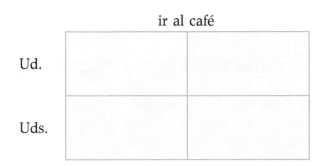

Uds.

pagar <u>la cuenta</u>

Ud.

Uds.

TRADUCCIONES: MANDATOS FORMALES

A. <u>Singular</u> (**Ud.**)

1. Read the menu. _____   Read it. _____

2. Call the professor. _____   Call him. _____

3. Don't serve that wine. _____   Don't serve it. _____

4. Don't write the letter. _____   Don't write it. _____

5. Make dinner now. _____   Make it now. _____

6. Don't open the door. _____   Don't open it. _____

7. Close the door. _____   Close it. _____

8. Bring the sandwiches. _____   Bring them. _____

9. Order the shrimp. _____   Order them. _____

10. Ask for the bill. _____   Ask for it. _____

11. Bring the ice cream. _____   Bring it. _____

B. <u>Plural</u> (**Uds.**)

1. Wait for Roberto. _____   Wait for him. _____

2. Don't buy those cookies. _____   Don't buy them. _____

3. Study Chapter 6. _____   Study it. _____

4. Invite Sofía and Sara. _____   Invite them. _____

5. Make the dessert. _____   Make it. _____

6. Don't eat that tortilla. _____   Don't eat it. _____

I. Vocabulario

1. ¿Cuáles son tres cosas que nunca comes?

   _____, _____, _____

2. ¿Cuál es tu comida favorita? _____

3. ¿Qué te gusta comer por la mañana? ¿Y por la noche? _____

II. Gramática

A. Indefinite and Negative Words. Change to the opposite.

1. Siempre estudio en la biblioteca porque me gusta mucho.

   _____

2. Algunos compañeros estudian allí también.

   _____

3. Nunca comemos en la biblioteca.

   _____

4. Nos gusta comer algo después de estudiar.

   _____

5. Tengo unos exámenes esta semana, y mis amigos también.

   _____

B. **Saber** or **conocer**. Fill in the correct form of the missing verb. If the "personal **a**" is required, include it in your answer.

1. ¿(Tú)_____ bailar el tango?

2. Yo _____ Jorge, pero no _____ dónde vive.

3. Ellas no _____ mi primo.

4. Necesitan _____ a qué hora vas a venir.

5. Acabo de _____ la madre de mi novio.

6. Quiero ir a Guatemala porque no _____ ese país.

Expresa en español.

1. I know the answer. _____

2. We'll meet Juan tomorrow. _____

3. Do you know Caracas? _____

4. I don't know when the final is. _____

5. He knows a lot of interesting people. _____

C. <u>Direct Object Pronouns</u>. Answer the questions using direct object pronouns.

1. ¿Cuándo ves tus programas de televisión favoritos?

   _____

2. ¿Con quién practicas el español?

   _____

3. ¿Cuándo vas a ver a tus amigos?

   _____

4. ¿Cuándo quieres conocer a mis amigos?

   _____

D. <u>Los mandatos</u>. Give one affirmative and one negative command to the people in El Mesón Fuentes tonight. Use the infinitive phrases given to form your commands.

1. **Ernestito y**	• comer toda la comida	_____
su hermana	• no jugar en el restaurante	_____
2. **el dueño**	• tener paciencia con los clientes	_____
	• no hacer tantas reservaciones	_____
3. **Miguel**	• pagar la cuenta	_____
	• no salir con Carmen otra vez	_____
4. **Lucía**	• ir en taxi	_____
	• no llegar tarde	_____
5. **el camarero**	• traer más vino	_____
	• no ser perezoso	_____

III. ¿Qué dices? What would you say in the following situations?

1. The waiter forgets to bring you the menu.

_____

2. You want some more water.

_____

3. Your soup is cold.

_____

4. You want to order another dish.

_____

5. You need the bill.

_____

IV. Diálogo

Write an eight-line dialogue between any two people depicted in the drawing below. The dialogue should include a description of what one of the people just ate, what they are going to do after leaving the cafeteria, and two commands.

_____

_____

_____

_____

_____

_____

_____

ENTREVISTA: ¿QUÉ TE GUSTA COMER?

First, complete the chart with your opinions of the following items using the scale below. Then find out a classmate's likes and dislikes and answer his/her questions about your own opinions. Remember to phrase your questions with the expression **¿Te gusta...?**

Escala de valores:
    1 = ¡Sí, me gusta muchísimo!
    2 = Sí, me gusta bastante.
    3 = ¡No, no me gusta para nada!

Yo		*Mi compañero/a*
	el pescado	
	la comida picante	
	la barbacoa	
	cenar en restaurantes elegantes	
	preparar comida en casa	
	la pizza con anchoas (*anchovies*)	
	la comida vegetariana	
	el café	
	el pastel de chocolate	
	la comida china	

BINGO: LA COMIDA

_____ almuerza en casa a veces.	_____ sabe cocinar muy bien.	A _____ no le gusta el pescado.	_____ toma muchísimo café.	A _____ no le gusta la comida mexicana.
_____ es vegetariano/a.	_____ está a dieta.	_____ toma vitaminas todos los días.	El restaurante favorito de _____ es «McDonalds».	_____ come postre todos los días.
A _____ le gusta beber Red Bull.	_____ no desayuna nunca.	La comida favorita de _____ es la pizza.	_____ come algo antes de acostarse.	_____ trabaja como camarero/a.
_____ no toma cerveza.	_____ es alérgico/a al chocolate.	_____ come en la biblioteca a veces.	_____ no cocina nunca.	_____ cena mientras (_while_) ve la televisión.
_____ va a cenar fuera (_dine out_) esta noche.	_____ come en una cafetería universitaria.	_____ siempre tiene hambre en la clase de español.	_____ no lava los platos después de comer.	_____ nunca tiene tiempo de almorzar

GUIDED WRITING AND SPEAKING: EN LA CAFETERÍA

A. Study the drawing and then work with a partner to form six questions about the students in the cafeteria. Use different question words for each student. Use your imagination and the vocabulary from this chapter and previous chapters.

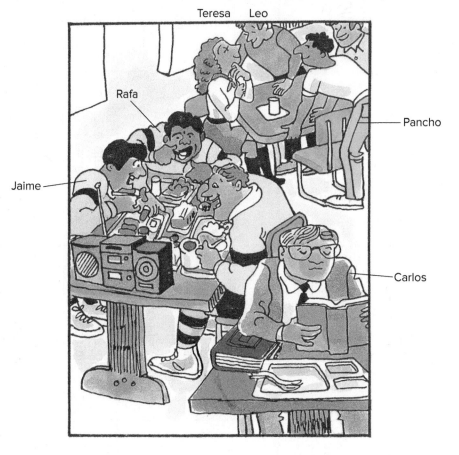

1. _____

2. _____

3. _____

4. _____

5. _____

6. _____

B. Imagine you are a new student from Panamá. Write an e-mail to your family about what kind of food you eat at the university cafeteria and what you never eat there. Then talk about some of your new classmates. Tell them who you want to know better and why.

C. With a partner, role-play a dialogue between any two characters in the drawing.

COMMUNICATIVE GOALS PRACTICE #4

Try to talk about this restaurant scene for sixty seconds. "Show off" all you have learned up to this point in the semester. Check the **Communicative Goals** boxes at the beginning of each chapter of your Supplement to see all that you should be able to do. For this fourth oral proficiency practice, the following topics are suggested. Try to use connectors (**porque, pero, y, también, por eso**) to make your description sound more fluent and natural.

1. Time
2. Description (age, personality, physical appearance, clothing)
3. Family relationships
4. Food likes and dislikes
5. Actions taking place right now
6. Future plans
7. Comparisons

After you've finished your description, imagine you are talking to the characters in the drawing. Ask at least two questions of one or more characters.

CAPÍTULO 8

Communicative Goals for Chapter 8

By the end of the chapter, you should be able to:

- talk about trips and traveling ❏
- express to whom and for whom you do ❏
  something ❏
- talk about likes and dislikes more fully ❏
- talk about things that happened in the past ❏

Grammatical Structures

You should know:

- indirect object pronouns ❏
- **dar** and **decir** ❏
- **gustar** ❏
- preterite forms ❏
- uses of the preterite ❏

PRONUNCIACIÓN: LOS SONIDOS *G, GU* Y *J*

Listen and repeat as your instructor pronounces the following sentences. Then practice with a partner.

1. No hay ningún asiento en el autobús que va al aeropuerto.

2. En el Hotel Majestad el maletero nos ayuda con un montón de maletas.

3. El piloto le pregunta al pasajero puertorriqueño si va a Pamplona o Pontevedra.

4. Recibimos tarjetas postales de Jalapa, Oaxaca, Guanajuato e Isla Mujeres.

5. Guárdame un asiento en el siguiente vuelo a Uruguay. Es urgente.

Listen as your instructor says these Spanish idiomatic expressions, then repeat. Match the Spanish expression with its English equivalent.

_____ 1. Ni decir jota.

_____ 2. Echar un jarro de agua fría.

_____ 3. De ninguna manera.

_____ 4. ¡Qué aguafiestas!

_____ 5. Me da igual.

_____ 6. No saber ni jota.

_____ 7. Se me hizo un nudo en la garganta.

_____ 8. Muy lejos, en el quinto pino.

a. *What a party-pooper!*

b. *No way.*

c. *To know absolutely nothing.*

d. *Not to say a word.*

e. *Miles from anywhere.*

f. *I got a lump in my throat.*

g. *To put a damper on it.*

h. *It's all the same to me.*

LISTENING COMPREHENSION: JAIME Y MARTA HACEN UN VIAJE

A. You will hear a short conversation between Jaime and Marta, who are getting ready for a trip. As you listen, indicate what they have already done to get ready and what they still need to do in the chart below. Place an X in the correct column, based on what you hear. Look over the list of actions before you begin.

Acción	Ya lo hicieron	Todavía necesitan hacerlo
buscar las maletas		
comprar los boletos		
ir al banco		
hacer las maletas		
llamar a la línea aérea y confirmar el vuelo		
hacer las reservaciones		
encontrar los pasaportes		
hacer una lista		
comprar pilas (*batteries*) para la cámara		
hablar con la agente de viajes		

B. Now listen as your instructor reads sentences about what Jaime and Marta like and don't like when they travel. Circle the item referred to in each statement.

1. las revistas turísticas   El Hotel Four Seasons

2. viajar en tren   los viajes en autobús

3. las hamburguesas de McDonald's   comer en restaurantes típicos

4. los museos de arte   visitar los monumentos

5. las montañas   la playa

PRÁCTICA: INDIRECT OBJECT PRONOUNS

I. Fill in the blanks with the correct indirect object pronoun, according to the context or the cues in parentheses.

me = to/for me	**nos** = to/for us
te = to/for you	**os** = to/for you (*familiar, plural*)
le = to/for you (*formal*), him, her, it	**les** = to/for you (*formal, plural*), them

En un restaurante:

1. _____ sirven el almuerzo a la una. (a nosotros)

2. _____ compro refrescos a todos mis amigos.

3. ¿Cuándo _____ va a traer el menú? (a nosotros)

4. _____ puedo recomendar el arroz con pollo y el flan. (a ti)

5. ¿_____ pasas el pan, por favor? (a mí)

De viaje:

6. La azafata _____ pide los boletos a los pasajeros.

7. Mientras hace cola, Tomás _____ guarda un puesto a María.

8. Siempre _____ mando tarjetas postales a mis amigos.

9. El agente de viaje _____ explica el precio de los boletos. (a nosotros)

10. Tengo que comprar _____ unos recuerdos (*souvenirs*) a mis padres.

11. No _____ sirven nada de comer en ese vuelo. (a ti)

II. Complete each sentence with the missing indirect object pronoun and a logical verb.
Verbos útiles: comprar / dar / decir / explicar / hacer / mandar / pagar / pedir / prestar / traer

Modelo: La profesora <u>les</u> <u>explica</u> la gramática a los estudiantes.

1. Este semestre, mis profesores _____ _____ muchísima tarea.

2. Yo _____ _____ invitaciones a mi fiesta a todos mis amigos.

3. Mis amigos _____ _____ muchos regalos bonitos para mi cumpleaños.

4. Los clientes _____ _____ el menú al camarero, y él _____ _____ la cuenta.

5. Los estudiantes _____ _____ muchas preguntas a la profesora.

6. Los pacientes _____ _____ consejos a los sicólogos.

7. Los padres _____ _____ dinero a sus hijos en la universidad.

8. Los estudiantes _____ _____:«Buenos días» al profesor.

9. A veces, mi compañero de cuarto _____ _____ su coche.

DIRECT VS. INDIRECT OBJECT PRONOUNS

Fill in the blank with the correct indirect or direct object pronoun.

Direct Object Pronouns		Indirect Object Pronouns	
me	nos	me	nos
te	os	te	os
lo, la	los, las	le	les

Las fiestas y los regalos:

1. Mañana es el cumpleaños de Ana. Beatriz y yo _____ compramos unos discos.

2. Raúl es el amigo de Laura. Él _____ llama para invitar_____ a la fiesta.

3. A José _____ gusta mucho leer. Yo pienso regalar_____ unos libros.

4. Hoy es el aniversario de mis padres. Mi hermano y yo vamos a preparar_____ una cena especial.

5. Mis amigos _____ dicen que van a comprar_____ algo para mi cumpleaños.

De viaje:

6. En el aeropuerto Roberto hace cola y _____ guarda un puesto a Sara.

7. ¿Cuál es el número de nuestro vuelo? No _____ puedo ver.

8. A nosotros no _____ gusta Tijuana, pero a Alberto _____ gusta mucho.

9. Juana _____ dice (a mí) que _____ va a traer un regalo de su viaje.

10. ¿Dónde están Paco y Rosa? No _____ veo por aquí. —Están en la playa.

Las citas:

11. Jaime sale con Inés. Él _____ ve todos los fines de semana.

12. Felipe quiere llamar a Mercedes para invitar _____ al cine.

13. Quiero a Pilar. _____ quiero porque es muy simpática.

14. Mi hermano _____ pide dinero (a mí), pero yo no _____ puedo prestar nada.

15. —¿Van a ver la nueva película de Almodóvar? —Sí, _____ vamos a ver hoy.

16. —¿Sabes el nombre de aquel chico al lado del bar? —No, no _____ sé.

17. —¿Conoces a esa mujer que baila con Pepe? —Sí, _____ conozco muy bien.

PREGUNTAS PERSONALES

Answer the following questions using direct or indirect object pronouns.

En la universidad:

1. ¿Les escribes muchos e-mails a tus padres? _____

2. ¿Tus padres te llaman todas las semanas? _____

3. ¿Puedes guardarme un asiento en la clase? _____

4. ¿Conoces al rector de la universidad? _____

5. ¿Saben Uds. cuál es la capital de Costa Rica? _____

6. ¿A qué hora haces la tarea? _____

7. ¿Siempre entiendes la gramática? _____

8. ¿Me puedes explicar el Capítulo 8? _____

9. ¿Dónde compras tus libros de texto? _____

10. ¿Pagas tus libros con cheque o con tarjeta de crédito? _____

11. ¿Ves al profesor / a la profesora cinco días a la semana? _____

El tiempo libre:

12. ¿Qué le gusta hacer a tu mejor amigo/a? _____

13. ¿Les prestas dinero a tus amigos? _____

14. ¿Les das tu número de teléfono a los compañeros de clase? _____

15. ¿Cuándo ves a tus amigos? _____

16. ¿Quieres ver la nueva película de Woody Allen? _____

17. ¿Llamas a tus amigos por teléfono todas las noches? _____

18. ¿Tus amigos te invitan a comer con frecuencia? _____

19. ¿Preparas el desayuno todos los días? _____

20. ¿Nos invitas a tu fiesta de cumpleaños? _____

21. ¿Me recomiendas las películas de Harry Potter? _____

22. ¿Siempre le dices toda la verdad a tu mejor amigo/a? _____

PRÁCTICA: *GUSTAR*

A. *Gustar* **y los objetos indirectos.** Complete the sentences with the correct indirect object pronoun, and then circle the correct form of **gustar, encantar,** or **interesar.**

1. ¿A ti _____ gusta/gustan las vacaciones de primavera?

2. A mí _____ interesa/interesan los museos arqueológicos de México.

3. A Pedro y a Marta _____ encanta/encantan viajar por América Central.

4. A mi tía Paula _____ interesa/interesan las artesanías de la gente indígena.

5. A nosotros no _____ gusta/gustan los hoteles baratos.

6. A mis padres no _____ gusta/gustan la Playa del Carmen.

7. Pero a mí _____ encanta/encantan todas las playas de México.

8. ¿A Uds. _____ gusta/gustan tomar el sol y hacer esquí acuático en Acapulco?

9. A mis amigos _____ interesa/interesan una excursión con visitas culturales.

10. A los turistas _____ gusta/gustan las comidas que sirven en la playa.

B. Los gustos de los ricos y famosos. Create six sentences about the likes and interests of the celebrities below. At least one of your sentences should be negative.

Katy Perry Tom Brady Anderson Cooper Ricky Martin y Shakira Barack Obama Angelina Jolie y Brad Pitt	gustar + (no) + interesar encantar

1. _____

2. _____

3. _____

4. _____

5. _____

6. _____

EL PRETÉRITO

REGULAR VERBS

-AR	-ER	-IR
-é	-í	-í
-aste	-iste	-iste
-ó	-ió	-ió
-amos	-imos	-imos
-asteis	-isteis	-isteis
-aron	-ieron	-ieron

IRREGULAR VERBS

DAR	HACER	IR / SER
di	hice	fui
diste	hiciste	fuiste
dio	hizo	fue
dimos	hicimos	fuimos
disteis	hicisteis	fuisteis
dieron	hicieron	fueron

I. Change the following sentences to the preterite.

1. Fabio viaja mucho.　　　　　El año pasado _____.

2. Hago las reservaciones.　　Ayer _____.

3. No escribes muchas cartas.　La semana pasada _____.

4. Comemos bien en el Mesón.　Anoche _____.

5. Juan llega hoy de Costa Rica.　_____ ayer.

6. Hacen las maletas.　　　　　Anoche _____.

7. Toman el tren a la costa.　　El año pasado _____.

8. Soy agente de viajes.　　　El año pasado _____.

9. Uds. trabajan mucho.　　　Anoche _____.

10. La agencia abre temprano.　Ayer _____.

11. Ofrecemos precios bajos.　El año pasado _____.

12. Volvemos a las once.　　　Anoche _____.

II. Preguntas personales.

1. ¿Viajaste mucho el año pasado?

_____

2. ¿Te dieron dinero tus padres para las vacaciones de primavera?

_____

3. ¿Adónde fueron tus compañeros de cuarto para la Navidad?

_____

4. ¿Cuánto dinero pagaste la última vez que hiciste un viaje por avión?

_____

5. ¿Visitaste las playas de Baja California el verano pasado?

_____

PRÁCTICA: SPELLING CHANGES IN THE PRETERITE

Verbs that end in **-car, -gar,** and **-zar** show a spelling change in the first person only.

	-car		-gar		-zar
buscar	busqué	pagar	pagué	comenzar	comencé
	buscaste		pagaste		comenzaste
	buscó		pagó		comenzó
tocar	toqué	llegar	llegué	almorzar	almorcé
	tocaste		llegaste		almorzaste
	tocó		llegó		almorzó

-AR and **-ER** stem-changing verbs show no stem change in the preterite.

Yo vuelvo. → Yo volví.   Yo pienso. → Yo pensé.
Ellos juegan. → Ellos jugaron.   Tú almuerzas. → Tú almorzaste.
Ellos comienzan. → Ellos comenzaron.

Also, an unstressed **i** between vowels becomes **y.**

> leer → leí, leíste, leyó, leímos, leísteis, leyeron
> creer → creí, creíste, creyó, creímos, creísteis, creyeron

Change the following sentences to the preterite.

1. Saco muchas fotos.   El año pasado _____
2. Él busca el mercado.   Ayer _____
3. Leemos un libro sobre México.   La semana pasada _____
4. Juego al voleibol en la playa.   Anoche _____
5. Llego a Madrid mañana.   _____ anteayer.
6. María lee la tarjeta postal.   Ayer _____
7. Almuerzo en el café de la plaza.   El lunes _____
8. Pago los boletos con cheque.   El año pasado _____
9. Comienzan su viaje mañana.   _____ la semana pasada.
10. ¿Cuándo vuelves del viaje?   ¿ _____, ayer o anteayer?
11. Se despiertan tarde y pierden el vuelo. Ayer _____
12. Empiezo a hacer la maleta ahora.   Anoche _____

EL PRETÉRITO: UN ASESINATO (*murder*)

There's been a murder in the elevator of the apartment building at Calle de las Calzadas, 29, and the police are taking reports from several people who were at the scene of the crime. Is one of these people lying? Complete each person's statement with the correct Spanish forms of the verbs in parentheses.

Catalina Alarcón de Sastre, abuela, 72 años

(1. *I left* - salir) _____ de mi casa a las ocho y cuarto, y (2. *I went* - ir) _____ al mercado para hacer las compras. Allí (3. *I bought* - comprar) _____ fruta, carne y pan. También (4. *I spoke* - hablar) _____ un rato (*for a while*) con doña Luisa. Después... ¿qué (5. *did I do* - hacer) _____ después? Ah, sí... (6. *I passed* - pasar) _____ por la farmacia por unas aspirinas. (7. *I returned* - regresar) _____ a casa a las nueve. Cuando (8. *I entered* - entrar) _____ al ascensor (*elevator*), (9. *I saw* - ver) _____ al hombre muerto (*dead*), y (10. *I screamed* - gritar) _____ «¡Socorro! ¡Socorro! (*Help!*)» Cuando (11. *arrived* - llegar) _____ el porter (*doorman*), don Ramón, yo (12. *fainted* - desmayarse) _____ y él (13. *called* - llamar) _____ a la policía. ¡Qué susto (*scare*), por Dios!

Jaime Durante, 20 años

Bueno, (1. *I woke up* - despertarse) _____ tarde, a las nueve menos cuarto. (2. *I bathed* - bañarse) _____ y (3. *I got dressed* - vestirse) _____ rapidísimo. (4. *I drank* - tomar) _____ un café negro y después (5. *I left* - salir) _____ corriendo (*running*) para la universidad. Cuando (6. *I tried* - intentar) _____ entrar al ascensor, oí (7. *I heard* - oír) _____ la voz (*voice*) de doña Catalina, gritando (*screaming*). (8. *I thought* - pensar) _____ que necesitaba ayuda, y por eso (9. *I returned* - volver) _____ a mi apartamento y (10. *I called* - llamar) _____ al hospital. La ambulancia (11. *arrived* - llegar) _____ en diez minutos. (12. *It was* - ser) _____ entonces (*then*) cuando don Ramón me (13. *explained* - explicar) _____ qué pasó. ¡Qué horrible! Y para colmo (*to top if off*), (14. *I missed* - perder) _____ mi clase.

Ramón Torrijo, portero, 57 años

De verdad no sé nada. (1. *I went out* - salir) _____ a la calle a las ocho y media, y (2. *I sat down* - sentarse) _____ en la silla que está afuera para descansar un poco. (3. *I smoked* - fumar) _____ un cigarrillo y (4. *I read* - leer) _____ el periódico. A las nueve menos cinco, (5. *rang* - sonar) _____ el teléfono, y (6. *I had* - tener) _____ que contestarlo. Pero (7. *happened* - pasar) _____ algo raro: cuando lo (8. *I answered* – contestar) _____ no había (*there wasn't*) nadie. (9. *I asked* - Preguntar) _____ «¿Quién es? ¿Quién habla?» (10. *I listened* - escuchar) _____ and (11. *I waited* - esperar) _____ unos segundos, pero nada. (12. *It was* - ser) _____ entonces cuando (13. *returned* - regresar) _____ doña Catalina. Ella (14. *entered* - entrar) _____ al ascensor y casi inmediatamente (15. *began* - empezar) _____ a gritar. ¡Qué día! ¡Vaya por Dios!

I. Vocabulario

A. Categorías.

1. Tres cosas que haces en el aeropuerto:

_____

2. Tres cosas que necesitas hacer antes de hacer un viaje:

_____

3. Tres formas de viajar:

_____

4. Tres personas que te ayudan cuando haces un viaje:

_____

B. Preguntas personales. Conteste en una o dos oraciones completas.

1. ¿Qué te gusta hacer cuando estás de vacaciones?

_____

2. ¿Cómo te gusta viajar? ¿Por qué?

_____

3. ¿Adónde te gustaría viajar? ¿Por qué?

_____

4. ¿Qué piensas hacer durante las próximas vacaciones?

_____

5. ¿Adónde fuiste el verano pasado?

_____

II. Gramática

A. <u>Pronouns</u>. Complete with the correct direct or indirect object pronoun. Read the sentences carefully to decide which pronoun is needed.

1. Mañana es el cumpleaños de Ana. _____ voy a comprar unas flores.

2. _____ voy a escribir un e-mail a mis padres después de hacer mi tarea.

3. ¿La composición? Lo siento, pero no _____ tengo conmigo.

4. Mi hermano _____ pide dinero (a mí), pero yo no _____ puedo prestar nada.

5. Los estudiantes _____ van a regalar una maleta a la profesora.

6. ¿Dónde están Paco y Rosa? No _____ vo por aquí.

7. ¿Las maletas? Tenemos que hacer _____ ahora mismo.

B. <u>Gustar</u>. Fill in the blanks with the correct pronoun and the correct form of gustar.

Modelo: No _____ _____   comer carne (a mí).
             No   me   gusta   comer carne.

1. Profesor(a), no _____ _____ la gramática. (a nosotros)

2. ¡ _____ _____ muchísimo las vacaciones! (a mí)

3. A mis padres _____ _____ mucho la música clásica, pero a mi

   hermano no _____ _____ para nada (*at all*).

4. No _____ _____ viajar en avión. Tengo miedo.

5. ¿ _____ _____ la clase de español? (a ti)

C. <u>Expresa en español</u>.

1. I don't like waiting in line at all.

   _____

2. We would like to travel in first class.

   _____

3. Many people don't like long flights.

   _____

4. I wouldn't like to be a flight attendant.

   _____

D. El pretérito. Write a short paragraph about last weekend. Include details about where you went and what you did with your friends, using the verbs below.

Modelo: El sábado, me levanté tarde...

| **Verbos útiles:** |
| levantarse   comer   salir   comprar   ir   hablar   jugar   ver   volver   acostarse |

_____

_____

_____

_____

_____

_____

_____

_____

III. Diálogo

Imagine that you are planning a trip to Mexico for spring break. Write a dialogue between you and a travel agent in which you:

- greet the agent and explain that you need two round-trip tickets for Mexico City;
- ask about hotel reservations in Mexico City and Cancún;
- ask how much it costs to fly to Cancún from Mexico City;
- confirm the times and dates you will be traveling;
- pay for your tickets.

_____

_____

_____

_____

_____

_____

_____

_____

_____

KEY LANGUAGE FUNCTIONS: DESCRIPTION, COMPARISON, EXPRESSING LIKES AND DISLIKES AND NARRATION IN THE PAST

At this point in the course, you should be able to describe, compare, discuss likes and dislikes, and narrate past events.

DESCRIBIR D	To construct a description	→ Vocabulary →	Linguistic Tools Needed: • **ser** vs. **estar** • noun-adjective agreement	
COMPARAR C	To construct a comparison	→ Vocabulary →	Linguistic Tools Needed: • noun-adjective agreement • **más/menos... que** • **tan... como** • **tanto/as/os/as... como**	
GUSTOS G	To construct a statement expressing likes and dislikes	→ Vocabulary →	Linguistic Tools Needed: • **Gustar**-type constructions • Indirect object pronouns	
PASADO P	To construct a narration of a series of past events	→ Vocabulary →	Linguistic Tools Needed: • Preterite verb forms	

Take turns with a partner talking about the following topics. Remember to pay attention to the linguistic tools (the grammar rules) you need to speak or write accurately.

DESCRIBIR D
- Describe a five-star hotel. Include the kinds of services they offer and how people feel when they go there.
- Describe a romantic restaurant. Include what they serve and how people feel when they go there.

COMPARAR C
- Compare two restaurants that you frequent.
- Compare how you feel after a great weekend with the way you feel after summer vacation.

GUSTOS G
- Tell what you like and what bothers you about vacationing with your parents.
- Tell what you think your instructor likes to do on vacation and what things interest him/her.

PASADO P
- Tell what you did yesterday from the time you got up until the time you went to bed.
- Tell where you went on your last vacation; include five things you did while you were there.

GUIDED WRITING AND SPEAKING: EN EL AEROPUERTO DE SAN JOSÉ

A. Study the drawing and then work with a partner to form six questions about the scene in the airport. Use a different question word in each question, and find a new partner to answer your questions. Use your imagination and the vocabulary from Chapter 8 and previous chapters.

1. _____
2. _____
3. _____
4. _____
5. _____
6. _____

B. Imagine you are Pepe or Julia. Write an e-mail to a friend in which you explain everything you did and everything that happened before your flight.

C. With a partner, role-play a dialogue between any two characters in the drawing.

BINGO: LOS GUSTOS

tomar el sol	los hoteles baratos	viajar en tren	hacer *camping*	los aviones
sacar fotos	los viajes por Latinoamérica	los museos	viajar con sus padres	las tarjetas postales
las comidas exóticas	la playa	las montañas	las ciudades grandes	el mar
las maletas de Gucci	los vuelos con escalas	ir en primera clase	las vacaciones de verano	los viajes en coche
viajar solo/a	los viajes en barco	los idiomas extranjeros	hacer la maleta	las islas tropicales

ENTREVISTA: BUSCA A ALGUIEN QUE...

Find classmates who did the following things. Use the model as an example and form your questions using the list below. When you find someone who answers **sí** to your question, have him/her sign in the correct blank. Be prepared to report your answers to the class.

Modelo: Find someone who took a history class last year.

Tú:	¿Tomaste una clase de historia el año pasado?
Tu compañero/a:	¡Sí!
Tú:	¡Firma aquí, por favor!

Find someone who ...	Nombre
went to the movies last night	
ate pizza last weekend	
got up late yesterday	
watched television last night	
went to a party last weekend	
lived in an apartment last semester	
got an A on the test	
talked on the phone yesterday	
did something interesting last year	
went to bed late last night	
went out with friends last weekend	
did their homework last night	
arrived late to class last week	
read the newspaper this morning	

DIÁLOGOS

With a classmate, write a short dialogue based on one of these situations. Use the cues as a guide. Be prepared to role-play your dialogue with your partner for the class.

1. **En el aeropuerto** At the airport in Santo Domingo, you run into a classmate who also spent a week in the Dominican Republic. On the plane ride home, have a conversation in which you and your classmate

- talk about what you did and where you went in the D.R.;
- exchange opinions about what you like and don't like about the island;
- explain what gifts you are going to give to friends and family and what you will tell them about your trip.

_____

_____

_____

_____

_____

_____

2. **En la República Dominicana** You and your friend are planning a trip to the Dominican Republic. With your friend, discuss

- what kind of travel you like (**ecoturismo, agroturismo, aventura, hacer camping**, etc.) and why;
- what your parents say about your plans for the trip;
- what you did to get ready and what you need to do.

_____

_____

_____

_____

_____

_____

Expresiones útiles

¡Qué casualidad! (_What a coincidence!_)
Lo que más me gustó fue...
Para mí... (_In my opinion_)
Está bien./Vale. (_Okay._)
¿Qué te pareció...? (_What did you think of ... ?_)
¿Qué opinas
Me pareció...
¡Cuéntame! (_Tell me!_)

un hotel de lujo/de cinco estrellas
(_a luxury/five–star hotel_)
De acuerdo. (_Agreed._)
Me lo pasé de maravilla. (_I had a great time._)
Bárbaro./Estupendo./Regio. (_Great._)
¿En serio? (_Really?_)
Me da igual. (_It doesn't matter to me._)

ROUND ROBIN: GRAMMAR MONITOR ACTIVITY

In this activity you will work in groups of three. Each partner will alternate roles until all three of you have (1) described what one of the characters usually does and what he/she did differently this past Saturday; (2) asked questions to get more information; and (3) served as the grammar monitor.

Partner A: Describe three things one of the characters usually does on Saturdays and then say what three things he/she did differently this past Saturday. Example: **Generalmente, ... pero el sábado pasado...** Use your imagination. Don't forget your connectors: **primero, luego, entonces, después.**

Partner B: Listen carefully as Partner A talks about the activities of one of the characters. Then ask two questions to get more information about his/her activities.

Partner C: As the grammar monitor, your job is to listen for the correct preterite verb forms. Write down the six verbs you hear. Pay special attention to the pronunciation of the preterite verbs (**pasó, regresó**, etc). When Partners A and B are finished, give them feedback on whether or not they are forming the preterite correctly and whether they are putting the stress on the accented last syllable.

Now switch roles. Partner A takes the role of Partner B (the person asking questions), Partner B takes the role of Partner C (the grammar monitor), and Partner C takes the role of Partner A (the describer of activities in the present and past).

CAPÍTULO 9

Communicative Goals for Chapter 9

By the end of the chapter, you should be able to:

- discuss special holidays and parties ❏
- talk about how you feel in different situations ❏
- give emphatic opinions and reactions ❏
- talk more about past events ❏

Grammatical Structures

You should know:

- -ísimo/a ❏
- irregular preterites ❏
- stem-changing preterites ❏
- double object pronouns ❏

PRONUNCIACIÓN: << LOS REYES MAGOS >>

Practice these verses of a carol from Argentina about the Three Kings.

Llegaron ya los reyes
y eran tres,
Melchor, Gaspar
y el negro Baltazar.
Arrope y miel
(*Syrup and honey*)
le llevarán (*will bring*)
y un poncho blanco
de alpaca real.

Changos y chinitas
(*Boys and girls*)
duérmanse,
que ya Melchor,
Gaspar y Baltazar
todos los regalos
dejarán (*will leave*)
para jugar mañana
el Redentor.

El niño Dios
muy bien lo agradeció
(*thanked*); comió
la miel y el poncho
lo abrigó.
Y fue después
que los miró,
y a medianoche
el sol se alumbró (*lit up*).

LISTENING COMPREHENSION: LOS REGALOS DE NAVIDAD

Listen as your instructor reads a passage about Carlos and Mónica's Christmas gifts and fill in the chart below as you hear the information.

	CARLOS	MÓNICA
Juguetes		
Ropa		
Animales		
Electrónicos		

Now listen again and put a check mark (✓) next to the gifts Carlos and Mónica received from **Los Reyes** and an asterisk (*) next to the gifts received from Santa Claus.

LAS EMOCIONES Y LAS REACCIONES

Answer the following questions. Try to think of two responses for each question.

Modelo: ¿En qué situaciones sonríes? →
Sonrío cuando veo a un amigo. También sonrío cuando miro el programa
Modern Family en la televisión.

1. ¿En qué situaciones te sientes feliz?

   _____

   _____

2. ¿En qué situaciones lloras?

   _____

   _____

3. ¿En qué situaciones te enojas?

   _____

   _____

4. ¿En qué situaciones te ríes?

   _____

   _____

5. ¿En qué situaciones te pones triste?

   _____

   _____

6. ¿En qué situaciones te quejas?

   _____

   _____

7. ¿En qué situaciones te pones nervioso/a?

   _____

   _____

8. ¿En qué situaciones lo pasas bien?

   _____

   _____

PRÁCTICA: ADJECTIVES OF EMPHASIS

I. Make a comparison between the pairs of items listed using the emphatic form of the adjective given.

Modelo: los hipopótamos/los elefantes (grande) → Los hipopótamos son grandes, pero los elefantes son grandísimos.

1. los coches / los aviones (rápido)

   _____

   _____

2. mis otras clases / la clase de español (interesante)

   _____

   _____

3. los perros / los chimpancés (inteligente)

   _____

   _____

4. la ciudad de Nueva York / el Distrito Federal de México (grande)

   _____

   _____

5. las ratas / las cucarachas (feo)

   _____

   _____

6. los Mercedes / los Porsches (caro)

   _____

   _____

7. Jon Stewart / Stephen Colbert (cómico)

   _____

   _____

8. Michael Dell / Bill Gates (rico)

   _____

   _____

9. la ropa de Gucci / la ropa de Chanel (elegante)

   _____

   _____

10. las composiciones / los exámenes (difícil)

   _____

   _____

II. Now give your opinion about the following people and things using an adjective of emphasis.

Modelo: los gatos → En mi opinión (Creo que) los gatos son hermosísimos.

1. tu mejor amigo/a _____

2. el programa *Empire* _____

3. Eva Longoria _____

4. el profesor/la profesora de español _____

5. las playas de México _____

6. la universidad _____

7. los «talk shows» _____

8. las margaritas _____

9. la pizza de Pizza Hut _____

10. la música de Cold Play _____

III. Now say how you feel in the following situations, using an adjective of emphasis.

1. Cuando saco una A en un examen, estoy... _____.

2. Después de una fiesta, mi apartamento está... _____.

3. Cuando estoy de vacaciones, me siento... _____.

4. Cuando mis padres me visitan, me pongo... _____.

5. Al final del semestre, estoy... _____.

EL PRETÉRITO

Complete the passages with the preterite of the verbs in parentheses.

A. Una cena con amigos

La semana pasada, Julio (1. decidir) _____ invitar a unos amigos a cenar. El jueves, (2. ir - yo) _____ con Julio para comprar los ingredientes para un arroz con pollo. El viernes, Julio y yo (3. volver) _____ a casa después de clase para limpiar (*to clean*) la casa. Él (4. pasar) _____ la aspiradora (*vacuum cleaner*) y (5. sacudir - yo) _____ los muebles (*to dust the furniture*). Después, (6. bañarse - yo) _____ y Julio (7. afeitarse) _____. Luego, Julio preparó la cena y juntos, nosotros (poner) 8. _____ la mesa (*to set the table*).

A las ocho, nuestros amigos (9. llegar) _____. Ellos nos (10. traer) _____ unas flores que (11. poner - yo) _____ encima de la mesa. A las ocho y media, (12. ir - nosotros) _____ al comedor para cenar. ¡Qué rico (13. estar) _____ el arroz con pollo! Después, (14. preparar - yo) _____ el café y se lo (15. servir) _____ a todos.

Nuestros amigos (16. quedarse) _____ hasta las tres de la madrugada (*morning*). ¡Cuánto (17. divertirse - nosotros) _____ y (18. reírse) _____! Esa noche Julio y yo (19. dormir) _____ muy bien. Nosotros no (20. levantarse) _____ hasta las dos al día siguiente. (21. Estar - Yo) _____ cansado todo el día y no (22. poder) _____ hacer nada.

B. Un aniversario de bodas

Para su quinto (*fifth*) aniversario de bodas, Antonio y Carmen (1. hacer) _____ una fiesta. (2. Invitar) _____ a todos sus parientes y amigos. Antonio (3. preparar) _____ y (4. servir) _____ unas tapas riquísimas. No (5. faltar) _____ nadie a la fiesta, y todos les (6. traer) _____ regalos preciosos. Yo les (7. regalar) _____ un álbum de fotos, y de los padres de Carmen, (8. recibir - ellos) _____ unas copas de cristal. En la fiesta, Antonio le (9. leer) _____ un poema de amor a Carmen. Ella (10. ponerse) _____ a llorar. Después, (11. calmarse - ella) _____ , y todos nosotros (12. divertirse) _____ muchísimo.

C. Una fiesta de sorpresa

La última vez que (1. dar - yo) _____ una fiesta, (2. ser) _____ un desastre. (3. Querer - Yo) _____ hacer una fiesta de para el cumpleaños de mi compañera de casa, Lourdes, pero todo (4. salir) _____ mal. (5. Empezar - Yo) _____ por invitar a unos quince amigos. Les (6. pedir - yo) _____ ayuda con los refrescos y las tapas, y todos me (7. decir) _____ que sí. Bueno... el día de la fiesta, Lourdes (8. enfermarse) _____. (9. Volver - Ella) _____ a casa y (10. acostarse) _____. Me (11. decir) _____: «No salgo de aquí. Me siento fatal». (12. Ponerse - Yo) _____ casi histérica. ¿Cómo hacer los preparativos con Lourdes en la casa enferma?

(13. Pensar - Yo) _____ unos minutos, y por fin (14. tener) _____ una idea. (15. Preparar - Yo) _____ un té con limón para Lourdes. En el té, (16. poner - yo) _____ una pastilla (*pill*) para dormir. Se lo (17. servir - yo) _____, (18. cerrar) _____ la puerta de su alcoba y (19. comenzar) _____ a limpiar (*to clean*) la casa en silencio. Pasó una hora, y (20. llegar) _____ unos invitados. Pasó media hora más y (21. venir) _____ otros. Al final, (22. terminar - nosotros) _____ de hacer los preparativos. (23. Ir - Nosotros) _____ a la sala, (24. sentarse) _____ y (25. esperar) _____.

Bueno... Lourdes no (26. despertarse) _____ aquella noche. (27. Dormir - Ella) _____ doce horas y (28. perderse) _____ la fiesta. Los invitados (29. esperar) _____ una hora, dos horas... y después me (30. dejar - ellos) _____ sola en casa con toda la comida lista, la música, el pastel, todo. Cuando Lourdes (31. salir) _____ de su alcoba al día siguiente y (32. ver) _____ todo, me (33. preguntar) _____: «Pero, chica, ¿qué es esto? ¿No sabes que mi cumpleaños fue ayer?»

PRÁCTICA: IRREGULAR AND STEM-CHANGING PRETERITES

¡Qué cambios (*changes*) más raros! With the full moon, strange things happen. Use the correct preterite forms to indicate what happened when the moon was full.

1. Típicamente los niños **duermen** muy bien, pero anoche _____ muy mal.

2. Doña Lupe siempre me **dice** «Buenas noches», pero anoche no me _____ nada.

3. Casi nunca **tengo** problemas con la tarea, pero anoche _____ muchísimos problemas con hacerla.

4. Por lo general, **puedo** terminar la tarea en una hora, pero anoche no _____ terminarla antes de las once.

5. Mis amigos generalmente **vienen** a verme por la tarde, pero ayer no _____.

6. La tía Susana casi siempre **se pone** ropa elegantísima, pero ayer _____ unos jeans viejos y una camiseta sucia.

7. Pablo casi nunca **está** enfermo, pero _____ mal todo el día ayer.

8. Mi novio me **trae** una flor todos los días, pero ayer no me _____ nada.

9. Generalmente no **hay** muchas fiestas en mi casa de apartamentos, pero anoche _____ tres o cuatro.

10. Siempre **sirven** comida riquísima en Casa Paco, pero anoche me _____ una cena horrible.

11. Mi hijo generalmente **pide** helado de postre, pero anoche _____ pastel de chocolate.

12. Mamá generalmente **se siente** feliz, pero ayer _____ muy triste.

13. Julia y Pablito **se divierten** cuando están juntos, pero ayer no _____ para nada.

14. Típicamente, el Sr. Varela **se despide** de su esposa y sale de casa a las ocho de la mañana, pero ayer no _____ hasta las nueve y media.

15. Dieguito siempre **se ríe** cuando ve *Garfield y sus amigos* en la tele, pero ayer no _____.

16. El bebé **sonríe** cuando ve a su mamá, pero ayer no _____ ni una vez.

17. Los niños típicamente **se visten** muy lento (*slowly*), pero ayer _____ muy rápido.

18. Generalmente mi amigo Raúl **puede** ayudarme con la clase de química, pero anoche él no _____ entender la tarea tampoco.

PRÁCTICA: DOUBLE OBJECT PRONOUNS

Explain who gave which anniversary gifts to Sr. and Sra. Trujillo, according to the drawing below. Use double object pronouns in your answers.

1. ¿Quién les regaló la foto?

   _____

2. ¿Quién les hizo el pastel?

   _____

3. ¿Quién les compró el televisor?

   _____

4. ¿Quién les regaló las entradas (*tickets*) para el concierto?

   _____

5. ¿Quién les compró el libro?

   _____

6. ¿Quién les organizó la fiesta?

   _____

Imagine that you are Marcos. Identify who gave you which presents at your birthday party, according to the drawing. Use double object pronouns in your answers.

1. ¿Quién te dio el regalo grande?

   _____

2. ¿Quién te regaló la camisa?

   _____

3. ¿Quién te compró el radio?

   _____

4. ¿Quién te hizo el pastel?

   _____

5. ¿Quién te regaló el libro?

   _____

6. ¿Quién te hizo la fiesta?

   _____

SEQUENCE OF OBJECT PRONOUNS: TRADUCCIÓN

1. I give it to them. (the gift)

   _____

2. I give it to her. (the invitation)

   _____

3. She gives it to me. (the cake)

   _____

4. We write it to you. (the letter)

   _____

5. They write them to us. (the questions)

   _____

6. They are going to write them to us. (the postcards)

   _____

7. I want to give it to her. (the suitcase)

   _____

8. Do you want to give it to her? (the flower)

   _____

9. Do you want to give it to me? (the money)

   _____

10. We are going to give them to them. (the appetizers)

    _____

11. Is she going to give it to us? (the photo)

    _____

12. Mary is going to buy it for us. (the tent)

    _____

13. Pablo buys them for her. (the cookies)

    _____

14. I buy them for them. (the gifts)

    _____

15. Does he tell it to her? (the answer)

    _____

16. Her parents send it to her. (the ticket)

    _____

EL PRETÉRITO Y LOS PRONOMBRES

Below is a series of questions given from one person/group of people to another about when something will happen. Answer the questions, saying the actions have already (**ya**) taken place, using the preterite and both object pronouns.

Modelo: (*you ask friends*):   ¿Cuándo van a darme Uds. mi regalo de cumpleaños?
                    (*your friends say*):   ¡Ya te lo dimos!

1. (*your mother asks*): ¿Cuándo vas a escribirle esa carta a tu tía Hortensia?

    (*you say*): _____

2. (*your professor asks the class*): ¿Cuándo van a entregarme Uds. la tarea?

    (*you say*): _____

3. (*your roommate asks*): ¿Cuándo vas a prestarme tu coche nuevo?

    (*you say*): _____

4. (*your nosy friend asks*): ¿Cuándo va a darte tu novio/a tu regalo de aniversario?

    (*you say*): _____

5. (*your Spanish class asks*): Profesora, ¿cuándo va a enseñarnos el pretérito?

    (*your professor says*): _____

6. (*your nosy friend asks again*): ¿Cuándo vas a mostrarme las fotos de tu novio/a?

    (*you say*): _____

7. (*your guilty conscience asks*): ¿Cuándo vas a mandarle esas flores a tu abuela?

    (*you say*): _____

8. (*your poor friend asks*): ¿Cuándo vas a darme el dinero que me debes (*owe*)?

    (*you say*): _____

9. (*your lazy roommate asks*): ¿Cuándo vas a lavarme los platos?

    (*you say*): _____

10. (*you ask your lazy roommates*): ¿Cuándo van a plancharme (*to iron*) la ropa?

    (*they say*): _____

REPASO: CAPÍTULO 9

I. Vocabulario

A. Párrafo. Complete this paragraph using the correct form words and phrases from Chapter 9.

Juan Ramón (1. *got angry*) _____ esta mañana porque hoy es su

(2. *birthday*) _____ y piensa que lo olvidé. Pero no lo olvidé; le voy a

(3. *give*) _____ una fiesta sorpresa. Juan Ramón va a (4. *have a good time*)

_____ Conchita y Ernesto van a preparar las (5. *appetizers*) _____

para comer, y Alberto y Angélica van a llevar los (6. *refreshments*) _____ para

beber. Quiero ver su cara (*face*) cuando gritemos (*we shout*) (7. *"Congratulations!"*)

«¡_____!» Va a (8. *become*) _____ feliz.

B. Las emociones. Complete the following sentences.

1. Me enojo cuando _____.

2. Me río cuando _____.

3. Me quejo cuando _____.

4. Me siento triste cuando _____.

C. Las asociaciones. Match the holidays in the first column with the items in the second, and add one more word that you associate with that holiday.

1. La Navidad: _____ y _____   a.   el pavo (*turkey*)

2. La Pascua: _____ y _____   b.   los huevos decorados

3. La Noche Vieja: _____ y _____   c.   muchos regalos

4. El Día de Gracias: _____ y _____   d.   besos (*kisses*) a medianoche

II. Gramática

A. Being emphatic. Translate to Spanish.

1. These gifts are extremely expensive.

_____

2. He always feels extremely sad at Christmas.

_____

3. The desserts are extremely good.

_____

B. Irregular Preterite Forms. Fill in the chart below.

Presente	Pretérito
1. pongo	1. _____
2. duermen	2. _____
3. _____	3. empecé
4. _____	4. supe
5. puede	5. _____
6. sirven	6. _____

C. Irregular and Stem-Changing Preterites. Complete the passage about Ángela's awful day with the correct form of the verb in parentheses.

Anoche ella (1. poner) _____ el despertador (*alarm clock*) para las seis.

(2. Dormir) _____ muy mal y por eso, (3. despertarse) _____

tarde, a las siete y media. Se bañó y (4. vestirse) _____ muy rápido, pero

llegó tarde a la oficina. Su jefe (5. ponerse) _____ muy enojado, y le (6. decir)

_____: «Ángela, vas a tener que terminar todo este trabajo hoy». A mediodía,

ella (7. almorzar) _____ en un restaurante cerca de su oficina. Comió muy rápido

y (8. volver) _____ a la oficina casi inmediatamente. Por eso, no (9. sentirse)

_____ bien toda la tarde. Y (10. estar) _____ trabajando hasta las diez

de la noche.

D. La fiesta de Steven Spielberg. Your friend Andrés crashed Steven Spielberg's party last night. Ask him about it, forming questions from the infinitive phrases.

Modelo: estar en la fiesta anoche (tú) → ¿Estuviste en la fiesta anoche?

1. servir tapas ricas (ellos)

_____

2. venir muchos actores famosos

_____

3. saber el teléfono de Katy Perry (tú)

_____

4. poder hablar con Chris Rock (tú)

_____

5. traerle un regalo a Steven (tú)

6. conseguir el autógrafo de Jessica Alba (tú)

7. divertirse todos

E. Double Object Pronouns. Fill in the charts with the two sets of object pronouns.

DIRECT		INDIRECT	

1. Which pronoun comes first, indirect or direct? What happens when both pronouns start with the letter **l**?

2. Substitute both objects with pronouns and rewrite the sentence.

   a. Voy a comprarle estas flores a mi amigo.

   b. Mis padres me mandaron las galletas ayer.

   c. Te voy a contar el secreto.

   d. Necesito darles estas invitaciones a mis amigos.

   e. Ella nos está explicando el problema ahora.

F. Traducciones. Use both object pronouns in the correct order.

1. They bought it for me. (**el regalo**)

2. I sent it to her. (**las flores**)

3. We gave it to them. (**la invitación**)

_____

4. She is serving them to him right now. (**las tapas**)

_____

III. <u>Diálogo</u>

You and your cousin are talking about your trip to Argentina during winter break. Write a dialogue in which:

- your cousin asks how you felt being away from the family during the holidays;
- you explain how it felt and what you did there (don't forget it was summer in Argentina in December);
- your cousin tells you what he/she did and then asks if you are going to travel again next winter during the holidays;
- you tell him/her what your plans are.

_____

_____

_____

_____

_____

_____

_____

_____

_____

BINGO: LA VIDA PERSONAL

A ___ no le gustan los días festivos.	___ va a la playa para las vacaciones de primavera.	___ faltó a clase esta semana.	___ da muchas fiestas.	___ cumple años este mes.
A ___ le encantan los fuegos artificiales. (*fireworks*)	___ se siente feliz hoy.	___ se olvidó de su libro de texto hoy.	___ llora cuando ve películas tristes.	___ discute mucho con su novio/a.
___ siempre se porta bien en la clase de español.	___ se enfermó la semana pasada.	___ odia el Día de los Enamorados.	___ gasta mucho dinero en su novio/a.	___ siempre mira el desfile en la tele el Día de Acción de Gracias.
___ estuvo en un desfile (*parade*) una vez.	___ siempre asiste a una fiesta para la Noche Vieja.	___ tuvo una quinceañera.	___ se reúne con amigos esta tarde.	La familia de ___ celebra el Día de los Reyes Magos.
___ se sintió mal el Día de Año Nuevo.	Este año, ___ no vuelve a casa para el Día de Acción de Gracias.	___ celebra su cumpleaños y su día del santo también.	___ se siente triste hoy.	___ se divirtió mucho el fin de semana pasado.

GUIDED WRITING AND SPEAKING: EN LA FIESTA DE LOS GARCÍA

A. Study the drawing and then work with a partner to form six questions about Manuel and Isabel's anniversary party. Use different interrogative words for each question. Use your imagination and the vocabulary from this chapter and previous chapters.

1. _____

2. _____

3. _____

4. _____

5. _____

6. _____

B. Imagine you are one of the characters depicted in the drawing. Write an e-mail to one of your cousins who was not able to attend the party. Tell what you did at the party, what your relatives served, and what gifts your grandparents received.

_____

_____

_____

_____

_____

_____

C. With a partner, role-play a dialogue between any two of the characters in the drawing.

COMMUNICATIVE GOALS PRACTICE #5

Try to talk about the party scene below for 60 seconds. "Show off" all you have learned up to this point in the semester. Check the **Communicative Goals** boxes at the beginning of each chapter of your Supplement to see all that you should be able to do. For this oral proficiency practice, the following topics are suggested. Try to use connectors (**porque, pero, y, también, por eso**) to make your description sound more fluent and natural.

1. Description (age, personality, physical appearance, clothing)
2. Likes and dislikes
3. Description of feelings
4. Actions taking place right now
5. What people did last weekend
6. Comparisons
7. Future plans

After you've finished your description, imagine you are talking to the characters in the drawing. Ask at least two questions of one or more characters.

10

Communicative Goals for Chapter 10

By the end of the chapter, you should be able to:

- talk about free time and household chores ❑
- talk about what you used to do ❑
- describe past conditions and states ❑
- express extremes ❑
- get information by asking questions ❑

Grammatical Structures

You should know:

- imperfect of regular and irregular verbs ❑
- question words ❑
- superlatives ❑

LISTENING COMPREHENSION: TRABAJANDO EN CASA

Listen as your instructor describes the household chores of the Pacheco family. The first time you hear the description, listen for what chores each person has already done and what he/she still needs to do, and write them next to the person. The second time, listen for the answers to the true-false statements below.

el Sr. Pacheco

Iván

Lydia

¿Cierto o falso?

1. ❑ C ❑ F Iván no es un chico muy organizado.
2. ❑ C ❑ F A Lydia le encanta planchar.
3. ❑ C ❑ F La Sra. Pacheco no ayuda en casa hoy porque está enferma.
4. ❑ C ❑ F A Lydia no le importa tener un cuarto ordenado.
5. ❑ C ❑ F El Sr. Pacheco no piensa lavar el coche solo.
6. ❑ C ❑ F El Sr. Pacheco ya puso la mesa.

EL IMPERFECTO: INTRODUCCIÓN

The imperfect (**A**) sets the scene by providing background information; (**B**) describes what was going on in the past before something else happened; (**C**) describes people, places, things, and emotions in the past; and (**D**) explains habitual actions in the past.

A. Set the scene by providing background information about time, weather, and age. Use the imperfect for each of the following pictures.

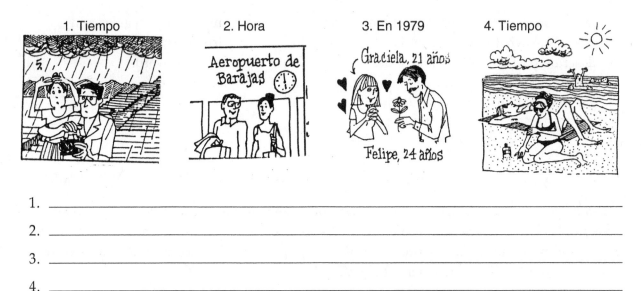

1. Tiempo   2. Hora   3. En 1979   4. Tiempo

1. _____

2. _____

3. _____

4. _____

B. Describe what was going on before something else happened. Use the imperfect to tell what each person in the house was doing before la tía Tatiana arrived.

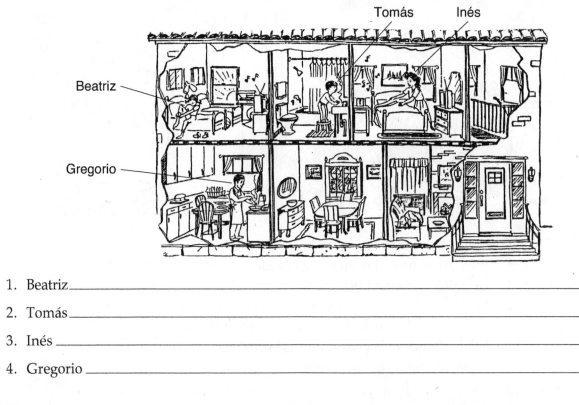

1. Beatriz _____

2. Tomás _____

3. Inés _____

4. Gregorio _____

C. Describe physical and emotional conditions in the past. Use the imperfect to describe Leo's room; how Rosa, Mari, and Diego looked at the prom; and how Rafael felt while watching the movie.

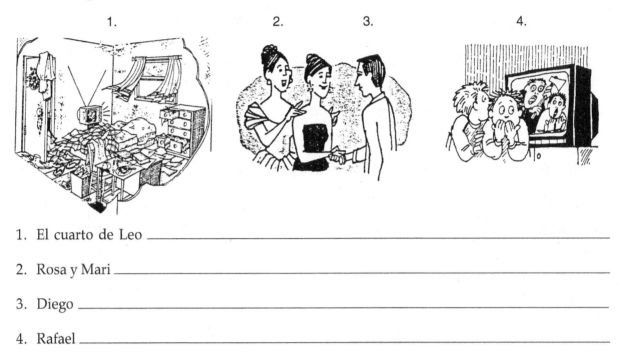

1. El cuarto de Leo _____

2. Rosa y Mari _____

3. Diego _____

4. Rafael _____

D. Talk about habitual actions in the past. Use the imperfect to describe what Pablo used to do when he was young. Mention five activities.

_____

_____

_____

_____

PRÁCTICA: EL IMPERFECTO

Complete the passages with the imperfect of the verbs in parentheses.

A. Mi niñez en México

Cuando yo (1. ser) _____ joven, (2. vivir) _____ en Jalapa, México. Todos los domingos mi familia (3. ir) _____ a la casa de mis abuelos para almorzar. Al llegar (*As soon as we arrived*), mi padre siempre (4. hablar) _____ con mis tíos sobre las noticias, y mi madre y sus hermanas (5. ayudar) _____a mi abuela en la cocina. Nosotros (6. comer) _____ a las tres de la tarde y después (7. jugar) _____ un rato en el patio. ¡Qué bonitos recuerdos! Pero cuando yo (8. tener) _____ 16 años, nos mudamos (*moved*) a la capital y solo (9. volver) _____ a Jalapa para pasar la Navidad. ¡Qué triste!

B. De vacaciones en Chile

De niña, yo (1. tener) _____ muchas oportunidades de viajar porque mi padre (2. trabajar) _____ para IBM Internacional. Todos los años mi familia (3. ir) _____ a Viña del Mar para el mes de enero. Nosotros (4. salir) _____ tres días después de la Navidad y (5. volver) _____ el primero de febrero. Mis hermanos y yo (6. pasar) _____ el invierno jugando en las playas chilenas. (7. Divertirse - Nosotros) _____ muchísimo.

C. Paco y Paquito. Paco is always complaining about his son Paquito's behavior. But Paco's mother says that Paco used to act the same way. Rewrite the paragraph about Paquito to explain what Paco used to do, according to his mother.

Cada mañana Paquito apaga el despertador (*shuts off the alarm*) y duerme media hora más. No desayuna bien y sale de la casa corriendo. Llega tarde a la escuela y no escucha a la profesora. Nunca hace su tarea y por eso tiene que quedarse en la escuela hasta las cinco cada día.

Paco, cada mañana tú también _____

_____

_____

_____

PRÁCTICA: LAS PALABRAS INTERROGATIVAS

I. <u>Los quehaceres</u>. Complete the questions about the drawing with the correct missing interrogative word. Then answer the questions, using the drawing and your imagination.

Dalila   Armando   Rogelio

Sara

1. ¿ _____ platos sucios hay en la cocina?

_____

2. ¿ _____ están enojados los padres?

_____

3. ¿ _____ hay debajo del sofá?

_____

4. ¿A _____ le toca sacar la basura?

_____

5. ¿ _____ le toca hacer a Armando?

_____

6. ¿ _____ es el quehacer que menos le gusta a Dalila?

_____

7. ¿ _____ fueron los padres?

_____

8. ¿ _____ es el problema entre Dalila y Armando?

_____

II. ¿Cuál(es)? vs. **¿Qué?** Complete the questions with the correct interrogative, then answer each based on your own experiences.

1. ¿ _____ haces en tus ratos libres?

   _____

2. En tu opinión, ¿ _____ es el pasatiempo más aburrido?

   _____

3. ¿ _____ eran tus pasatiempos favoritos cuando eras niño/a?

   _____

4. ¿ _____ programas de televisión te gustaban más?

   _____

5. ¿ _____ película quieres ver este fin de semana?

   _____

6. ¿ _____ tenías que hacer en casa cuando eras niño/a?

   _____

7. ¿ _____ te toca hacer en casa hoy?

   _____

8. En tu opinión, ¿ _____ aparato doméstico es el más necesario?

   _____

SUPERLATIVOS (I)

A. <u>En mi opinión</u>. Complete the sentences, expressing your opinions.

1. El mejor mes del año es _____, porque _____

   _____

2. La peor actriz en Hollywood es _____. Sin embargo,

   _____

3. El peor quehacer doméstico es _____. Por eso, _____

   _____

4. El mejor programa de televisión es _____, porque _____

   _____

5. El país latinoamericano más interesante es _____, porque

   _____

6. El día festivo menos divertido es _____. Sin embargo,

   _____

B. <u>Más opiniones</u>. From the items in each group, write one sentence in Spanish using the superlative construction.

Modelo:	**actores**	Ben Affleck / Matt Damon / Johnny Depp (guapo)
		Johnny Depp es el más guapo de los tres actores.

1. quehaceres   barrer el suelo / planchar la ropa / sacar la basura (difícil)

_____

2. deportes   el ciclismo / la natación / el esquí acuático (interesante)

_____

3. pasatiempos   dar un paseo / hacer un picnic / jugar a las cartas (aburrido)

_____

4. las ciudades   Acapulco / Aspen / Nueva York (divertido)

_____

5. aparatos   el horno de microondas / la estufa / el lavaplatos (necesario)

_____

SUPERLATIVOS (II)

Look at the drawings below. Who is the most or least _____? Write eight sentences about what you see in the drawings, using the superlative construction.

1. _____

2. _____

3. _____

4. _____

1. _____

2. _____

3. _____

4. _____

I. Vocabulario

A. ¿Qué puedes hacer? What activities can you do in the following situations? Choose at least two activities from Chapter 10.

1. Quieres estar afuera.

_____

2. Necesitas hacer un poco de ejercicio.

_____

3. Tienes ganas de quedarte en casa.

_____

4. Te gustaría escuchar un poco de música.

_____

5. Quieres hacer algo con un grupo de amigos.

_____

6. Hace mucho calor.

_____

B. Los quehaceres domésticos. Explain what chores you do and don't do around the house or apartment. Mention at least four chores.

_____

_____

_____

_____

C. Faltan palabras. Complete the following passage with the Spanish equivalents of the English words in parentheses.

En el mundo hispano, los (*pastimes*) _____ son tan variados y numerosos como en los Estados Unidos. Las (*activities*) _____ pueden variar, pero hay aficiones que son muy populares en todo el mundo hispano: (*going to the movies*) _____, el baile, las visitas y los (*sports*) _____. El (*cycling*) _____, el boxeo y el (*soccer*) _____ son los deportes preferidos. Y en México, el Caribe y Venezuela, el (*baseball*) _____ es muy popular.

En la Latinoamérica y España, no se televisan (*games*) _____

con la misma frecuencia que en los Estados Unidos, pero hay excepciones: las Olimpiadas,

los Juegos Panamericanos y la Copa Mundial de fútbol. Casi todos los países del mundo

hispano tienen (*teams*) _____ que participan en esta competición. Cuando

(*plays*) _____ el equipo nacional, todos los (*fans*) _____ tratan

de estar delante del televisor, y si su equipo (*wins*) _____, hay grandes fiestas y

celebraciones por todo el país.

II. Gramática

A. ¿Qué hacían cuando alguien llamó a la puerta? Write what everyone was doing when
someone knocked on the door.

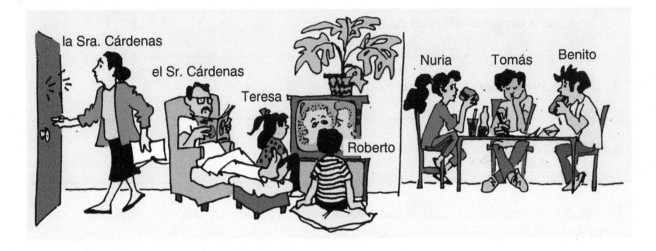

1. Tomás _____.

2. Nuria y Benito _____.

3. El Sr. Cárdenas _____.

4. Teresa y Roberto _____.

5. La Sra. Cárdenas _____.

B. En el pasado... Contesta en español.

1. ¿Cómo eras cuando tenías 15 años?

_____

2. ¿Dónde vivías antes de ir a la universidad?

_____

3. ¿Cómo era tu escuela primaria?

_____

4. ¿Qué te gustaba hacer cuando eras niño/a?

_____

5. ¿Qué hacías anoche a las siete? ¿Y a las doce?

_____

C. Los superlativos. Answer the following questions in Spanish.

1. What is the worst class you have this year?

_____

2. Where can you eat the best Mexican (Chinese, Italian) food in town?

_____

3. Who is the smartest person you know?

_____

4. What is the most difficult sport?

_____

5. What was the funniest movie you saw last year?

_____

D. Las palabras interrogativas. Leticia is telling you about her weekend plans. Create a logical question for each of her answers.

1. Tú: ¿ _____?
   Leticia: Este fin de semana, voy a un concierto.

2. Tú: ¿ _____?
   Leticia: El grupo se llama «Los Romanceros».

3. Tú: ¿ _____?
   Leticia: Ellos tocan música tejana y mexicana.

4. Tú: ¿ _____?
   Leticia: Van a tocar en el Club Paraíso.

5. Tú: ¿ _____?
   Leticia: Las entradas (tickets) cuestan 20 dólares.

6. Tú: ¿ _____?
   Leticia: El nombre de su nuevo CD es «Contigo siempre».

III. Diálogo

You're trying to set up a blind date between Alicia, a great athlete and sports fan, and Fernando, a heavy-duty partier. Write a short dialogue, in which you call up either Fernando or Alicia and:

- describe the other person to him/her;
- explain what they can do on a date;
- ask if Fernando/Alicia will call the other person.

_____

_____

_____

_____

_____

_____

_____

KEY LANGUAGE FUNCTIONS: DESCRIPTION, COMPARISON, EXPRESSING LIKES AND DISLIKES, NARRATION IN THE PAST

At this point in the course, you should be able to describe, compare, discuss likes and dislikes, and talk about the past. The chart below shows the linguistic tools needed to perform these four key language functions accurately.

DESCRIBIR D To construct a description → Vocabulary → Linguistic Tools Needed:
- **ser** vs. **estar**
- noun-adjective agreement

COMPARAR C To construct a comparison → Vocabulary → Linguistic Tools Needed:
- noun-adjective agreement
- **más/menos... que**
- **tan... como**
- **tanto/as/os/as... como**

GUSTOS G To construct a statement → expressing likes and dislikes Vocabulary → Linguistic Tools Needed:
- **Gustar**-type constructions
- Indirect object pronouns

PASADO P To construct a description → in the past Vocabulary → Linguistic Tools Needed:
- Imperfect

Take turns with a partner talking about the following topics. Remember to pay attention to the linguistic tools (the grammar rules) you need to express these key language functions accurately.

DESCRIBIR D
- Describe what your apartment or dorm room looks like the week of finals.
- Describe how you and your best friend celebrate your birthdays. Include what you give each other and how you make the day special.

COMPARAR C
- Compare Christmas in the U.S. and Christmas in Latin America.
- Compare two sports.

GUSTOS G
- Tell what your mother likes about the holidays and what bothers her about them.
- Tell what you like about Valentine's Day and what bothers you about this holiday.

PASADO P
- Tell what you were like when you were 13. Include what things you used to do at that age.
- Tell what you used to do during your favorite holiday when you were a child.

A. Using the drawing and your imagination, answer the following questions in complete Spanish sentences. Pay careful attention to the way the questions are phrased in order to use the correct structures in your answers.

1. What is Pablo doing at this moment?
2. Who bought Javi a balloon? (**el globo** = balloon)
3. What does Lola have to do later?
4. What did Marta like to do when she was little?
5. What are Juan and his friends doing?
6. Why did Luis invite Mari to the park?
7. What was Luis' old girlfriend like?
8. Who is the strangest person in the park today?
9. What plans are Lola and Marta making for the weekend?
10. What did they do last weekend?

B. Write a short paragraph describing what Marta and Lola used to do on the weekends before they had children.

C. With a partner, role-play a dialogue between any two characters in the drawing.

BINGO: ¿QUÉ HICISTE?

tomó una siesta ayer.	fue a México en marzo.	dio una fiesta el mes pasado.	miró la tele anoche.	compró algo ayer.
no asistió a clase la semana pasada.	salió con unos amigos anoche.	comió en McDonald's esta semana.	visitó a su familia el fin de semana pasado.	cenó en un restaurante la semana pasada.
escribió una carta ayer.	llegó tarde a clase ayer.	se acostó tarde el sábado.	no estudió anoche.	tomó un café esta mañana.
perdió algo la semana pasada.	leyó el periódico esta mañana.	fue de compras el fin de semana pasado.	fue a la biblioteca anoche.	hizo algo interesante el domingo.
tuvo una cita (date) el viernes.	habló por teléfono ayer.	hizo un viaje el año pasado.	vio una película buena.	tomó un examen ayer.

BINGO: ¿QUÉ HACÍAS DE NIÑO?

montaba a caballo.	nadaba con un equipo.	jugaba mucho con sus hermanos.	no limpiaba su cuarto nunca.	ayudaba mucho en casa.
odiaba los deportes.	tenía muchos quehaceres.	iba a la escuela en bicicleta.	jugaba al fútbol con un equipo.	tenía un perro.
A ____ no le gustaba viajar.	vivía en otro estado.	era travieso/a (*mischievous*).	ponía la mesa todos los días.	A ____ le gustaba la escuela.
leía mucho.	tocaba un instrumento.	tenía un gato.	quería ser astronauta.	vivía en otro país.
tenía que hacer su cama siempre.	sacaba la basura todos los días.	veía mucho la televisión.	vivía con sus abuelos.	tenía su propia computadora.

INFORMATION GAP ACTIVITY: LA FAMILIA YBARRA
(COMPAÑERO/A #1)

The chart below shows some of the things the Ybarra family used to do when they lived in Madrid a few years ago. Ask your partner questions about the activities of different family members, and fill in the missing pieces of information on your chart. Answer your partner's questions using the information you already have on your own chart. When you've finished, check with your partner to make sure you've gotten the correct answers.

Modelo:
Tu compañero/a: ¿Qué hacía Margarita los viernes por la noche?
Tú: Ella leía novelas en casa.

INFORMATION GAP ACTIVITY: LA FAMILIA YBARRA (COMPAÑERO/A #2)

The chart below shows some of the things the Ybarra family used to do when they lived in Madrid a few years ago. Ask your partner questions about the activities of different family members, and fill in the missing pieces of information on your chart. Answer your partner's questions using the information you already have on your own chart. When you've finished, check with your partner to make sure you've gotten the correct answers.

Modelo: Tu compañero/a: ¿Qué hacían Margarita y Pedro los domingos por la tarde?
              Tú: Ellos daban un paseo en el parque.

CAPÍTULO 11

Communicative Goals for Chapter 11

By the end of the chapter, you should be able to:

• talk about your health	❑
• talk about past actions and events	❑
• express reciprocal actions	❑

Grammatical Structures

You should know:

• use of the preterite and imperfect	❑
• relative pronouns	❑
• reciprocal pronouns	❑

PRONUNCIACIÓN

Listen as your instructor reads these Spanish sayings related to parts of the body, then repeat. Match the Spanish expression with its English equivalent.

_____ 1. Se escapó por los pelos.

_____ 2. No tiene pies ni cabeza.

_____ 3. Está para chuparse los dedos.

_____ 4. Más ven cuatro ojos que dos.

_____ 5. Más vale un pájaro en mano que cien volando.

_____ 6. Adonde el corazón se inclina, el pie camina.

_____ 7. En boca cerrada no entran moscas.

_____ 8. Ojos vemos, corazones no sabemos.

_____ 9. Estar hasta las narices.

a. A bird in the hand is worth two in the bush.

b. To have had it up to here.

c. Where the heart leads, the feet follow.

d. I can't make heads or tails of it.

e. You can't read a book by its cover.

f. Two heads are better than one.

g. It's finger-licking good.

h. He made it by the skin of his teeth.

i. Close your mouth; you're catching flies.

LISTENING COMPREHENSION: EL EXAMEN DE JUAN

Read the following statements. Based on the story about Juan's dilemma, decide whether they are **cierto (C)** or **falso (F)**.

1. ☐ C ☐ F A Juan le dolía la cabeza porque estudiaba mucho.

2. ☐ C ☐ F Decidió ir al hospital porque no quería tomar el examen de español.

3. ☐ C ☐ F El médico notó inmediatamente que Juan estaba muy enfermo.

4. ☐ C ☐ F Después de ver a Juan, el médico salió del cuarto y habló con otra doctora.

5. ☐ C ☐ F Cuando Juan oyó que los dos médicos hablaban de una operación, llamó a su profesora.

6. ☐ C ☐ F Juan decidió tomar el examen.

Look at the drawing below, then read the questions. Would the underlined verbs in each question be expressed with preterite (P) or imperfect (I)? Which verbs are the correct choices for the answers?

1. What <u>was</u> (□ P □ I) Sofía's dress like?
   (Fue / Era) un vestido negro y elegante.

2. Who <u>called</u> (□ P □ I) Marina?
   La (llamó / llamaba) Jorge.

3. Whom <u>did</u> Esteban <u>meet</u> (□ P □ I)
   at the party?
   (Conoció / Conocía) a Patricia.

4. What <u>did</u> Gema <u>bring</u> (□ P □ I)
   to the party?
   (Trajo / Traía) una botella de champán.

5. How <u>was</u> Jorge <u>feeling</u> (□ P □ I)?
   (Se sintió / Se sentía) bastante mal.

6. <u>Did</u> he <u>have</u> (□ P □ I) a stomachache or a headache?
   (Tuvo / Tenía) un dolor de cabeza horrible.

7. What <u>was</u> Marina <u>doing</u> (□ P □ I) when the phone <u>rang</u> (□ P □ I)?
   Ella (sirvió / servía) unas botanas cuando (sonó / sonaba) el teléfono.

8. What time <u>was</u> (□ P □ I) it when the party <u>started</u> (□ P □ I)?
   (Fueron / Eran) las ocho cuando (empezó / empezaba) la fiesta.

9. What <u>did</u> Javier's daughter <u>want</u> (□ P □ I) to do?
   (Quiso / Quería) jugar con su hermanita.

10. What <u>was</u> Javier's daughter <u>doing</u> (□ P □ I) while he <u>was talking</u> (□ P □ I) to Paco?
    Ella (lloró / lloraba) mientras su papá (habló / hablaba) con Paco.

11. How many glasses of champagne <u>did</u> Ernesto <u>have</u> (□ P □ I)?
    (Tomó / Tomaba) cinco copas de champán.

12. Why <u>was</u> (□ P □ I) Sultán, the dog, happy?
    (Estuvo / Estaba) contento porque le gustan las fiestas.

PRÁCTICA: EL EXAMEN DE REGINA

Complete the passage using the preterite and imperfect. Use the pictures to help you decide
which tense is the correct choice.

(1. Ser) _____ las nueve de la mañana cuando

Regina (2. empezar) _____ a estudiar para su

examen de historia.

Su compañera (3. levantarse) _____ a

las once, (4. llamar) _____ a su novio y

(5. poner) _____ la música muy alta. Regina

no (6. estar) _____ contenta porque (7. tener)

_____ que estudiar más.

(8. Tomar) _____ el examen a la una.

(9. Estar) _____ muy tensa porque el examen

(10. ser) _____ muy largo.

Al día siguiente cuando (11. entrar) _____ en el

salón para ver su examen, (12. estar) _____ muy

nerviosa.

Pero (13. sacar) _____ una «A». (14. Estar)

_____ contentísima.

PRÁCTICA: UNA VISITA AL MÉDICO

Juanito had to go to the doctor for a checkup yesterday. Tell what happened, using the drawings and the verbs below as a guide. Write at least two sentences for each drawing. Include one preterite or one imperfect verb in each sentence.

1. llegar / estar nervioso

_____

_____

2. hablar con la enfermera / sentirse mal

_____

_____

3. escribir / esperar

_____

_____

4. examinar / no tener miedo

_____

_____

5. dar medicina / no querer

_____

_____

6. salir / estar contento

_____

_____

PRÁCTICA: MORE PRETERITE VS. IMPERFECT

Complete with the preterite or imperfect.

1. El viernes pasado mi profesor de sociología (decir) _____ que nosotros (ir)

   _____ a tener un examen dentro de algunos días. Después de la clase, (decidir

   - yo) _____ ir a la biblioteca para leer el libro que (estar) _____

   en la lista de reserva. Se lo (pedir - yo) _____ a la señorita y ella me lo (traer)

   _____ después de unos minutos. (Haber) _____ muchos estudi-

   antes allí que (leer) _____ sus textos. Cuando (ser) _____ las

   cinco, (regresar - yo) _____ a mi casa para estudiar más.

2. Nuestro amigo Pancho tuvo mala suerte ayer. (Despertarse) _____ con un

   dolor de cabeza y (llegar) _____ tarde a la clase de español, a las ocho y

   media. ¡(Tener) _____ mucho sueño! En la clase, mientras la profesora (hablar)

   _____, Pancho (dormirse) _____ y (empezar) _____

   a roncar (*to snore*). De repente el libro de la profesora (caerse [*to fall*]) _____

   al suelo. ¡PLAS! La profesora (gritar) _____: «¡No se puede dormir en mi

   clase! ¡Fuera de aquí! (*Get out of here!*)» Pancho (levantarse) _____ y mientras

   (caminar) _____ hacia la puerta los estudiantes (reírse) _____.

3. (Hacer) _____ mucho frío y viento. (Ser) _____ una noche

   típica de invierno. Yo (leer) _____ el periódico mientras mi esposo (preparar)

   _____ la cena. De repente él (empezar) _____ a gritar. (Ir - Yo)

   _____ a la cocina y le (preguntar) _____: «¿Qué te pasa?» Él me

   (decir) _____ que un ratón (correr) _____ por la cocina. Él (tener)

   _____ miedo y yo también. ¡No me gustan los ratones!

PRÁCTICA: UNA AVENTURA EN LA SELVA

Write a story about Daniel and David's adventure in the jungle. Use the drawings, your imagination, and the suggestions in the chart to help you recount the story.

Para crear el ambiente	Para añadir emoción y descripción
Era un día caluroso...	Era...
Eran las 2:00 de la tarde...	Se sentía...
Estábamos...	Tenía/Había...
Para contar eventos	**Para resumir**
Primero..., Luego...,	Fue horrible (increíble,
De repente..., Entonces ...,	emocionante, fenomenal).
Después..., Finalmente ...	

Vocabulario útil: **la canoa** (canoe), **el chaleco salvavidas** (life jacket), **los mosquitos, la piraña** (piranha), **la selva** (jungle)

1.

2.

3.

4.

_____

_____

_____

_____

_____

_____

_____

_____

_____

¿QUE, QUIEN, QUIENES O LO QUE?

Complete each sentence with the correct relative pronoun.

Remember:
1. **que** is almost always used
2. when talking about a person, use **quien(es)** after a preposition (**de, en, con, a, acerca de**, etc.)
3. **lo que** = *the thing(s) that, what (that which)*

1. Ese es el carro _____ queremos comprar: el nuevo Honda Civic. Mi hermana, _____ tiene uno igual, dice que le gusta mucho. Y una mujer con _____ hablamos en el supermercado está muy contenta con su Honda también.

2. El programa _____ más me gusta ba de niña era *El barrio del Sr. Rogers*. _____ más me encantaba del Sr. Rogers era su sentido del humor. Creo que el Sr. Rogers fue un hombre _____ siempre entendió muy bien a los niños.

3. Los estudiantes _____ hicieron la tarea sacaron mejor nota en el examen. La profesora, con _____ hablé ayer, dijo que las notas eran bajísimas. _____ a mí me pareció muy difícil fue la sección de verbos.

4. Mamá, Papá, esta es la mujer con _____ me quiero casar (*to marry*). Se llama Laura. Queremos invitarlos a la boda (*wedding*), _____ va a ser en junio. Los padres de Laura, a _____ llamamos anoche, están muy contentos.

5. Aquellos son los chicos de _____ te hablé. El chico _____ lleva camisa anaranjada se llama Javier y el muchacho bajito con _____ está hablando ahora se llama Mauricio.

6. Este es el restaurante _____ tanto me gustó. _____ más me gusta de este lugar son las ensaladas.

7. No hay nadie a _____ yo le pueda explicar el problema. Mis amigos Roberto y Jaime, con _____ hablé anoche, no me entendieron. El problema, _____ es muy complicado, me preocupa mucho.

8. No hay nada aquí _____ podamos comer. _____ pasa es que somos todos vegetarianos. ¿Por qué no vamos a ese café macrobiótico _____ tanto te gusta?

9. ¿Sabes _____ me dijo Conchita? Me dijo que Lupe, con _____ salía Paco antes, sale ahora con Ricardo. _____ más me sorprende es que Lupe salga con un chico tan egoísta.

PRÁCTICA: RECIPROCAL PRONOUNS

Complete the passage about Romeo and Juliet with the correct form of the verbs in parentheses. You may use preterite, imperfect, or the infinitive, according to the context. Remember to use the correct reflexive pronoun to express the reciprocal action.

Al comienzo de la historia, Romeo y Julieta no (1. conocerse) _____. Ellos

(2. verse) _____ por la primera vez una noche en una fiesta en la casa de Julieta.

Esa misma noche, después de la fiesta, Romeo fue a la casa de Julieta. La vio en el balcón

de su alcoba, y los jóvenes (3. hablarse) _____ por varias horas. (4. Decirse)

_____ muchas palabras de amor y descubrieron que (5. quererse) _____

muchísimo. Cuando por fin Romeo se fue, él y Julieta (6. darse) _____ la mano en

una escena muy romántica.

Pero había un problema muy grave: las familias de Romeo y Julieta eran grandes

enemigos. Los Capulet y los Montague (7. odiarse) _____ desde hace siglos (*for*

centuries). A pesar de (*Despite*) eso, Romeo y Julieta decidieron casarse. Una tarde, ellos

(8. encontrarse) _____ en el monasterio del buen fraile (*friar*) Lorenzo, y él los casó

(*married*). Después de la ceremonia, los novios (9. besarse) _____ apasionadamente.

Por desgracia, Romeo tuvo que salir de Verona. Pero él y Julieta (10. escribirse)

_____, y en sus cartas, planearon cómo iban a (11. verse) _____

otra vez.

Todos sabemos cómo termina la trágica historia de Romeo y Julieta. Lo único bueno de

este doble suicidio fue la reconciliación de sus familias. Mientras lloraban, el padre de Romeo

y el padre de Julieta (12. abrazarse) _____. Ellos (13. decirse) _____:

«Nuestros hijos (14. quererse) _____ tanto. No seamos (*Let's not be*) enemigos más».

Así ellos (15. prometerse) _____ ser amigos en el futuro, para siempre.

REPASO: CAPÍTULO 11

I. Vocabulario

A. ¿Cuál de las medicinas usas para los siguientes síntomas?

_____ 1. una fiebre	a. Visine
_____ 2. una tos	b. Tylenol
_____ 3. el mareo (*dizziness*)	c. Dristan
_____ 4. la indigestión	d. Hall's
_____ 5. un ataque de nervios	e. Dramamine
_____ 6. un dolor de garganta	f. Preparation H
_____ 7. los ojos irritados	g. Valium
_____ 8. la nariz congestionada	h. Maalox
	i. Robitussin

II. Gramática

A. <u>Verbos</u>. Read the passage about Raquel and Paco's date, and mark each verb in parentheses with **P** or **I** depending on the context. Then write the correct preterite or imperfect form of the correct Spanish verb. After completing the passage, answer the questions.

Cuando (1. *they arrived* ☐ P ☐ I) _____ al restaurante, Raquel (2. *ordered* ☐ P ☐ I) _____ una limonada porque (3. *she had* ☐ P ☐ I) _____ muchísima sed. Después de servirle la limonada, el camarero les (4. *brought* ☐ P ☐ I) _____ el menú. Paco no (5. *[didn't] know* ☐ P ☐ I) _____ qué pedir porque no (6. *was familiar with* ☐ P ☐ I) _____ el restaurante. El camarero les (7. *recommended* ☐ P ☐ I) _____ el pollo con salsa mole, la especialidad de la casa, pero Raquel (8. *decided* ☐ P ☐ I) _____ probar (*to try*) los camarones y Paco (9. *ordered* ☐ P ☐ I) _____ las enchiladas.

Raquel y Paco (10. *waited* ☐ P ☐ I) _____ media hora para su cena porque (11. *there were* ☐ P ☐ I) _____ muchas personas en el restaurante. Paco (12. *was* ☐ P ☐ I) _____ un poco nervioso, porque los dos (13. *were going* ☐ P ☐ I) _____ al cine después y él no (14. *wanted* ☐ P ☐ I) _____ perder parte de la película. Por fin (15. *arrived* ☐ P ☐ I) _____ la cena. Todo (16. *was* ☐ P ☐ I) _____ riquísimo. Cuando (17. *they finished* ☐ P ☐ I) _____ de cenar, Paco le (18. *asked* ☐ P ☐ I) _____ a Raquel si (19. *she wanted* ☐ P ☐ I) _____ postre. Raquel (20. *said* ☐ P ☐ I) _____ que (21. *she preferred* ☐ P ☐ I) _____ tomar un helado después de la película. (22. *They paid* ☐ P ☐ I)

_____ la cuenta y (23. *they walked* ☐ P ☐ I) _____ al cine, donde (24. *they were showing* / dar ☐ P ☐ I) _____ *The Forest*.

A Raquel le (25. *liked* ☐ P ☐ I) _____ la película pero (26. *she had* ☐ P ☐ I) _____ mucho miedo. (27. *She thought* ☐ P ☐ I) _____ que los actores (28. *were* ☐ P ☐ I) _____ excelentes, pero le (29. *told* ☐ P ☐ I) _____ a Paco que no (30. *she was going* ☐ P ☐ I) _____ a pegar ojo (*was going to sleep a wink*) en toda la noche por causa del miedo. Paco (31. *said* ☐ P ☐ I) _____ que (32. *it was* ☐ P ☐ I) _____ una película muy tonta y que él no (33. *had* ☐ P ☐ I) _____ miedo. Pero eso no (34. *was* ☐ P ☐ I) _____ cierto. ¡Cuando él (35. *returned* ☐ P ☐ I) _____ a casa, (36. *he spent* ☐ P ☐ I) _____ la noche entera con las luces de su habitación encendidas (*turned on*)!

<u>Preguntas.</u>

1. ¿Qué quería tomar Raquel antes de cenar, y por qué?

   _____

2. ¿Por qué tuvieron que esperar media hora para la cena?

   _____

3. ¿Qué quería hacer Raquel después de la película?

   _____

4. ¿El cine estaba lejos o cerca del restaurante?

   _____

5. ¿Cómo le pareció la película a Raquel? ¿Y a Paco?

   _____

6. ¿Qué hizo Paco después de volver a casa?

   _____

B. Acciones recíprocas. Beatriz, Mónica and Lupe are gossiping about past and present couples. Complete their conversation with the correct form of the verb in parentheses.

Beatriz: ¿Cuándo (1. conocerse) _____ Rafael y Silvia?

Mónica: Creo que el año pasado, en una boda (*wedding*).

Lupe: Sí. Fue cuando (2. casarse [*to get married*]) _____ Margarita y Ramón, ¿se acuerdan (*remember*) Uds.?

Mónica: Sí... Rafael y Silvia (3. verse) _____ por primera vez en la recepción. Mi amigo Lourdes dice que ellos (4. mirarse) _____ toda la noche. Por fin Rafael la invitó a bailar, pero estaban tan nerviosos que casi no (5. hablarse) _____.

Beatriz: Pues, cuando los veo ahora, siempre están (6. hablarse) _____, (7. abrazarse) _____ o (8. besarse) _____.

Lupe: Sí, están muy enamorados (*in love*). (9. Quererse) _____ mucho y creo que van a (10. casarse) _____ en octubre.

C. Los pronombres relativos. Complete the passage with the correct relative pronoun.

Mi gata, 1. _____ se llama Dafne, es muy cómica. 2. _____ me parece más cómico de ella es que piensa que es una tigresa o una leona. Pero en realidad, es una gatita joven y muy chiquita. A veces, Dafne hace cosas 3. _____ después resultan un poco complicadas. Por ejemplo, le fascinan las ardillas (*squirrels*) y siempre trepa los árboles (*climbs the trees*) detrás de mi casa. Pero las ardillas, 4. _____ son muy rápidas, se le escapan. Y Dafne, 5. _____ a veces trepa árboles muy altos, no puede bajarse fácilmente. ¡Pobre gatita! Mi esposo, 6. _____ juega con la gata mucho, dice que es muy inteligente. Y dos amigos míos, a 7. _____ no les gustan los gatos por lo general, creen que Dafne es una gata realmente excepcional.

III. Diálogo

You and two classmates are talking about what happened when you went to the health center (*centro de salud*) recently. Have a conversation in which you:

- each talk about the last time you were sick or hurt;
- say what happened when you went to the health center;
- say how you felt after they treated you.

_____

_____

_____

_____

_____

_____

_____

_____

_____

_____

GUIDED WRITING AND SPEAKING: AYER EN EL CENTRO DE SALUD

A. Study the drawing and then work with a partner to form six questions about the people at the **Centro de Salud.** Use different question words for each person. Use your imagination and the vocabulary from this chapter and previous chapters.

1. _____

2. _____

3. _____

4. _____

5. _____

6. _____

B. Imagine you're an intern at the **Centro de Salud.** Write a 100-word report about what happened while you were on duty yesterday afternoon.

_____

_____

_____

_____

_____

_____

C. With a partner, role-play a dialogue between any two characters in the drawing.

BINGO: LA SALUD

lleva una vida tranquila.	quiere ser medico/a.	hace ejercicios aérobicos todos los días.	tiene un resfriado hoy.	come comidas sanas.
duerme ocho horas al día.	practica muchos deportes.	tiene dolores de cabeza frecuentemente.	necesita hacerse un chequeo pronto.	lleva gafas.
es alérgico/a a los perros.	tiene mucho miedo de las inyecciones.	camina a la universidad todos los días.	dejó de fumar el año pasado.	tiene una cita con el medico esta semana.
corre dos millas todos los días.	trabaja en una farmacia.	A le gustaría ser enfermero/a.	siempre se enferma cuando viaja en coche.	quiere ser dentista.
A le duele la garganta hoy.	A no le gusta guardar cama.	está un poco congestionado/a.	tiene miedo de los dentistas.	no descansa lo suficiente.

COMMUNICATIVE GOALS PRACTICE #6

Try to talk about the scene below for 75 seconds. "Show off" all you have learned up to this point in the semester. Check the **Communicative Goals** boxes at the beginning of each chapter of your Supplement to see all that you should be able to do. For this oral proficiency practice, some of the possible topics are listed below. Try to use connectors (**porque, pero, y, también, por eso**) to make your description sound more fluent and natural.

1. Description (age, personality, physical appearance, clothing)
2. Likes and dislikes
3. What these people usually do on weekends
4. What they did last week
5. How they felt
6. Future plans

After you've finished your description, imagine you are talking to the characters in the drawing. Ask at least two questions of one or more characters.

ADJECTIVE A word that describes a noun or pronoun.

una casa **grande**
*a **big** house*

Ana es **inteligente.**
*Ana is **smart.***

Demonstrative adjective An adjective that points out a particular noun.

este chico, **esos** libros, **aquellas** personas
***this** boy, **those** books, **those** people (over there)*

Interrogative adjective An adjective used to form questions.

¿Qué cuaderno?
***Which** notebook?*

¿Cuáles son los carteles que buscas?
Which ones are the posters (that) you're looking for?

Possessive adjective (unstressed) An adjective that indicates possession or a special relationship.

sus coches
***their** cars*

mi hermana
***my** sister*

Possessive adjective (stressed) An adjective that more emphatically describes possession.*

Es **una** amiga **mía.**
*She's **my** friend. / She's a friend **of mine.***

Es **un** coche **suyo.**
*It's **her** car. / It's a car **of hers.***

ADVERB A word that describes an adjective, a verb, or another adverb.

Roberto es **muy** alto.
*Roberto is **very** tall.*

María escribe **bien.**
*María writes **well.***

Van **demasiado** rápido.
*They are going **too** quickly.*

ARTICLE A determiner that sets off a noun.

el país
***the** country*

Definite article An article that indicates a specific noun.

la silla
***the** chair*

las mujeres
***the** women*

Indefinite article An article that indicates an unspecified noun.

un chico
***a** boy*

una ciudad
***a** city*

unas zanahorias
*(**some**) carrots*

---

*See Appendix 3 on page A–7 for more information.

CLAUSE A construction that contains a subject and a verb.

Main (Independent) clause A clause that can stand on its own because it expresses a complete thought. **Busco una muchacha.**

I'm looking for a girl.

Si yo fuera rica, **me compraría una casa.**
*If I were rich, **I would buy a house.***

Subordinate (Dependent) clause A clause that cannot stand on its own because it does not express a complete thought.

Busco a la muchacha **que juega al tenis.**
*I'm looking for the girl **who plays tennis.***

Si yo fuera rica, me compraría una casa.
***If I were rich,** I would buy a house.*

COMPARATIVE The form of adjectives and adverbs used to compare two nouns or actions.

Luis es **menos** hablador que Julián.
*Luis is **less talkative than** Julián.*

Luis corre **más** rápido que Julián.
*Luis runs **faster than** Julián.*

CONJUGATION The different forms of a verb for a particular tense or mood. A present indicative conjugation:

(yo) **hablo**	(nosotros/as) **hablamos**
(tú) **hablas**	(vosotros/as) **habláis**
(Ud.) **habla**	(Uds.) **hablan**
(él/ella) **habla**	(ellos/as) **hablan**

I speak	*we speak*
you (fam. sing.) speak	*you (fam. pl.) speak*
you (form. sing.) speak	*you (pl.) speak*
he/she speaks	*they speak*

CONJUNCTION An expression that connects words, phrases, or clauses.

Cristóbal **y** Diana
*Cristóbal **and** Diana*

Hace frío, **pero** hace buen tiempo.
*It's cold, **but** it's nice out.*

DIRECT OBJECT The noun or pronoun that receives the action of a verb.

Veo **la caja.**
*I see **the box.***

La veo.
*I see **it.***

GENDER A grammatical category of words. In Spanish, there are two genders: masculine and feminine.

	MASCULINE	FEMININE
ARTICLES AND NOUNS:	**el** disco compacto	**la** cinta
PRONOUNS:	**él**	**ella**
ADJECTIVES:	bonit**o**, list**o**	bonit**a**, list**a**
PAST PARTICIPLES:	El informe está **escrito.**	La composición está **escrita.**

IMPERATIVE *See Mood.*

IMPERFECT (*IMPERFECTO*) In Spanish, a verb tense that expresses a past action with no specific beginning or ending.

Nadábamos con frecuencia.
*We **used to swim** often.*

IMPERSONAL CONSTRUCTION One that contains a third person singular verb but no specific subject in Spanish. The subject of English impersonal constructions is generally *it*.

Es importante que...
It is important that . . .

Es necesario que...
It is necessary that . . .

INDICATIVE *See* Mood.

INDIRECT OBJECT The noun or pronoun that indicates *for who(m)* or *to who(m)* an action is performed. In Spanish, the indirect object pronoun is usually included, even when the indirect object is explicitly stated as a noun.

Marcos **le** da el suéter **a Raquel**. / Marcos **le** da el suéter.
*Marcos gives the sweater **to Raquel**. / Marcos gives **her** the sweater.*

INFINITIVE The form of a verb introduced in English by *to: to play, to sell, to come.* In Spanish dictionaries, the infinitive form of the verb appears as the main entry.

Luisa va a **comprar** un periódico.
*Luisa is going **to buy** a newspaper.*

MOOD A set of categories for verbs indicating the attitude of the speaker toward what he or she is saying.

Imperative mood A verb form expressing a command.

¡**Ten** cuidado!
***Be** careful!*

Indicative mood A verb form denoting actions or states considered facts.

Voy a la biblioteca.
***I'm going** to the library.*

Subjunctive mood A verb form, uncommon in English, used in Spanish primarily in subordinate clauses after expressions of desire, doubt, or emotion. Spanish constructions with the subjunctive have many possible English equivalents.

Quiero que **vayas** inmediatamente.
*I want you **to go** immediately.*

NOUN A word that denotes a person, place, thing, or idea. Proper nouns are capitalized names.

abogado, ciudad, periódico, libertad, Luisa
lawyer, city, newspaper, freedom, Luisa

NUMBER

Cardinal number A number that expresses an amount.

una silla, **tres** estudiantes
one chair, three students

Ordinal number A number that indicates position in a series.

la **primera** silla, el **tercer** estudiante
*the **first** chair, the **third** student*

PAST PARTICIPLE The form of a verb used in compound tenses (*see* Perfect Tenses). Used with forms of *to have* or *to be* in English and with **ser, estar,** or **haber** in Spanish.

comido, terminado, perdido
eaten, finished, lost

PERFECT TENSES Compound tenses that combine the auxiliary verb **haber** with a past participle.

Present perfect indicative This form uses a present indicative form of **haber.** The use of the Spanish present perfect generally parallels that of the English present perfect.

No **he viajado** nunca a México.
I've never ***traveled*** to Mexico.

Past perfect indicative This form uses **haber** in the imperfect tense to talk about something that had or had not been done before a given time in the past.

Antes de 2008, **no había estudiado** español.
*Before 2008, **I hadn't studied** Spanish.*

Present perfect subjunctive This form uses the present subjunctive of **haber** to express a present perfect action when the subjunctive is required.

¡Ojalá que Marisa **haya llegado** a su destino!
*I hope (that) Marisa **has arrived** at her destination!*

PERSON The form of a pronoun or verb that indicates the person involved in an action.

	SINGULAR	PLURAL
FIRST PERSON:	*I* / **yo**	*we* / **nosotros/as**
SECOND PERSON:	*you* / **tú, Ud.**	*you* / **vosotros/as, Uds.**
THIRD PERSON:	*he, she* / **él, ella**	*they* / **ellos, ellas**

PREPOSITION A word or phrase that specifies the relationship of one word (usually a noun or pronoun) to another. The relationship is usually spatial or temporal.

a la escuela
to *school*

cerca de la biblioteca
near *the library*

con él
with *him*

antes de la medianoche
before *midnight*

PRESENT PARTICIPLE The verb form that ends in *-ing* in English. Used with forms of *to be* in English and with **estar** in Spanish to form the progressive.

hablando, comiendo, pidiendo
speaking, eating, asking

PRETERITE (*PRETÉRITO*) In Spanish, a verb tense that expresses a past action with a specific beginning and ending.

Salí para Roma el jueves.
I left *for Rome on Thursday.*

PROGRESSIVE The verb that expresses continuing or developing action.

Julio **está durmiendo** ahora.
*Julio **is sleeping** now.*

Anita **estaba comiendo** cuando sonó el teléfono.
*Anita **was eating** when the phone rang.*

PRONOUN A word that refers to a person (I, you) or that is used in place of one or more nouns.

Demonstrative pronoun A pronoun that singles out a particular person, place, thing, or idea.

Aquí están dos libros. **Este** es interesante, pero **ese** es aburrido.
*Here are two books. **This one** is interesting, but **that one** is boring.*

Interrogative pronoun A pronoun used to ask a question.

¿**Quién** es él?   ¿**Qué** prefieres?
Who *is he?*   ***What*** *do you prefer?*

Object pronoun A pronoun that replaces a direct object noun or an indirect object noun. Both direct and indirect object pronouns can be used together in the same sentence.

Si **me** llamas más tarde, **te** doy el número de teléfono de David.
*If you call **me** later, I'll give **you** David's phone number.*

Veo a **Alejandro. Lo** veo.
*I see **Alejandro**. I see **him**.*

However, when the pronouns **le** or **les** appear before **lo, la, los,** or **las, le** or **les** changes to **se.**

Le doy **el libro** a Juana.
*I give the book **to Juana**.*

Se lo doy (a ella).
*I give **it** to **her**.*

Reflexive pronoun A pronoun that represents the same person as the subject of the verb.

Me miro en el espejo.
*I look at **myself** in the mirror.*

Relative pronoun A pronoun that introduces a dependent clause and denotes a noun already mentioned.

El hombre con **quien** hablaba era mi vecino.
*The man with **whom** I was talking was my neighbor.*

Aquí está el bolígrafo **que** buscas.
*Here is the pen (**that**) you're looking for.*

Subject pronoun A pronoun representing the person, place, thing, or idea performing the action of a verb.

Lucas y Julia juegan al tenis.
***Lucas and Julia** are playing tennis.*

Ellos juegan al tenis.
***They** are playing tennis.*

SUBJECT The word(s) denoting the person, place, thing, or idea performing an action or existing in a state.

Sara trabaja aquí.
***Sara** works here.*

¡**Buenos Aires** es una ciudad magnífica!
***Buenos Aires** is a great city!*

Mis **libros** y mi **computadora** están allí.
*My **books** and my **computer** are over there.*

SUBJUNCTIVE *See* Mood.

SUPERLATIVE The form of adjectives or adverbs used to compare three or more nouns or actions. In English, the superlative is marked by *most, least,* or *-est.*

Escogí el **vestido** más **caro.**
*I chose **the most expensive** dress.*

Ana es la **persona** menos **habladora** que conozco.
*Ana is **the least talkative person** I know.*

TENSE The form of a verb indicating time: present, past, or future.

Raúl **era, es** y siempre **será** mi mejor amigo.
*Raúl **was, is,** and always **will be** my best friend.*

VERB A word that reports an action or state.

Maribel **llegó.**
*Maribel **arrived**.*

La niña **estaba** cansada.
*The child **was** tired.*

Auxiliary verb A verb in conjuction with a participle to convey distinctions of tense and mood. In Spanish, one auxiliary verb is **haber.**

Han viajado por todas partes del mundo.
*They **have** traveled everywhere in the world.*

Reflexive verb A verb whose subject and object are the same.

Juan **se corta** la cara cuando **se afeita.**
*Juan **cuts himself** when he **shaves** (**himself**).*

Nominalization means using an adjective as a noun. In Spanish, adjectives can be nominalized in a number of ways, all of which involve dropping the noun that accompanies the adjective, then using the adjective in combination with an article or other word. One kind of adjective, the demonstrative, can simply be used alone. In most cases, these usages parallel those of English, although the English equivalent may be phrased differently from the Spanish.

Article + Adjective

Simply omit the noun from an *article + noun + adjective* phrase.

el **libro** azul ⟶ **el azul** (*the blue one*)
la **hermana** casada ⟶ **la casada** (*the married one*)
el **señor** mexicano ⟶ **el mexicano** (*the Mexican one*)
los **pantalones** baratos ⟶ **los baratos**
    (*the inexpensive ones*)

You can also drop the first noun in an *article + noun + **de** + noun* phrase.

la **casa** de Julio ⟶ **la de Julio** (*Julio's*)
los **coches** del Sr. Martínez ⟶ **los del Sr. Martínez**
    (*Mr. Martínez's*)

In both cases, the construction is used to refer to a noun that has already been mentioned. The English equivalent uses *one* or *ones,* or a possessive without the noun.

— ¿Necesitas el **libro** grande?
— No. Necesito **el pequeño.**
"Do you need the big book?"
"No. I need the small one."

— ¿Usamos el **coche** de Ernesto?
— No. Usemos **el de Ana.**
"Shall we use Ernesto's car?"
"No. Let's use Ana's."

Note that in the preceding examples the noun is mentioned in the first part of the exchange (**libro, coche**) but not in the response or rejoinder.
    Note also that a demonstrative can be used to nominalize an adjective: **este rojo** (*this red one*), **esos azules** (*those blue ones*).

Lo + Adjective

As seen in **Capítulo 11, lo** combines with the masculine singular form of an adjective to describe general qualities or characteristics. The English equivalent is expressed with words like *part* or *thing.*

lo mejor	*the best thing (part), what's best*
lo mismo	*the same thing*
lo cómico	*the funny thing (part), what's funny*

Article + Stressed Possessive Adjective

The stressed possessive adjectives—but not the unstressed possessives—can be used as possessive pronouns: **la maleta suya** ⟶ **la suya.** The article and the possessive form agree in gender and number with the noun to which they refer.

Este es mi **banco.** ¿Dónde está **el suyo**?
This is my bank. Where is yours?

Sus **bebidas** están preparadas; **las nuestras,** no.
Their drinks are ready; ours aren't.

No es la **maleta** de Juan; es **la mía.**
It isn't Juan's suitcase; it's mine.

Note that the definite article is frequently omitted after forms of **ser: ¿Esa maleta? Es suya.**

Demonstrative Pronouns

The demonstrative adjective can be used alone, without a noun. An accent mark can be added to the demonstrative pronoun (**éste, ése, aquél**) to distinguish it from the demonstrative adjectives if context does not make meaning clear.

Necesito este diccionario y **ese (ése).**
I need this dictionary and that one.

Estas señoras y **aquellas (aquéllas)** son las
    hermanas de Sara, ¿no?
These women and those (over there) are Sara's
    sisters, aren't they?

It is acceptable in modern Spanish, according to the **Real Academia Española,** to omit the accent on demonstrative pronouns when context makes the meaning clear and no ambiguity is possible.

APPENDIX 3   More About Stressed Possessives

When in English you would emphasize the possessive with your voice or with *of mine* (*of yours, of his*, and so on), you will use the *stressed possessives* (**las formas tónicas de los posesivos**) in Spanish. As the term implies, they are more emphatic than the *unstressed forms* (**las formas átonas de los posesivos**).

The stressed forms follow the noun, and the noun *must* be preceded by a definite or indefinite article or by a demonstrative adjective. The stressed forms agree with the noun modified in number and gender. In the following examples, boldface italic type in the English translations indicates voice stress.

Es **su** perro.	*It's her dog.*

But:

Es **un** perro **suyo.**	*It's **her** dog (i.e., not ours).* *It's a dog of hers.*
El perro **suyo** se llama King.	***Her** dog is named King.*
Ese perro **suyo** es bravo.	*That dog of hers is fierce.*

Es **su** maleta.	*It's **his** suitcase.*

But:

Es **una** maleta **suya.**	*It's **his** suitcase.*
La maleta **suya** está perdida.	***His** suitcase (i.e., not ours) is lost.*
Esa maleta **suya** está perdida.	*That suitcase of his is lost.*

The stressed possessives are often used as nouns. See **Appendix 2: Using Adjectives as Nouns.**

APPENDIX 4

Additional Perfect Forms (Indicative and Subjunctive)

As you know, some indicative verb tenses have corresponding perfect forms in the indicative and subjunctive moods. Here is the present tense system.

el presente:	yo hablo, como, pongo
el presente perfecto:	yo he hablado, comido, puesto
el presente perfecto de subjuntivo:	(que) yo haya hablado, comido, puesto

Other indicative forms that you have learned also have corresponding perfect indicative and subjunctive forms. Here are the most important ones, along with examples of their use. In each case, the tense or mood is formed with the appropriate form of **haber.**

El pluscuamperfecto de subjuntivo

yo:	hubiera hablado, comido, vivido, *and so on.*
tú:	hubieras hablado, comido, vivido, *and so on.*
Ud./él/ella:	hubiera hablado, comido, vivido, *and so on.*
nosotros:	hubiéramos hablado, comido, vivido, *and so on.*
vosotros:	hubierais hablado, comido, vivido, *and so on.*
Uds./ellos/ellas:	hubieran hablado, comido, vivido, *and so on.*

These forms correspond to **el pluscuamperfecto de indicativo (past perfect indicative) (Capítulo 15)**. The **pluscuamperfecto de subjuntivo** is most frequently used in **si** clause sentences, along with the conditional perfect. See examples in the second column.

El futuro perfecto

yo:	habré hablado, comido, vivido, *and so on.*
tú:	habrás hablado, comido, vivido, *and so on.*
Ud./él/ella:	habrá hablado, comido, vivido, *and so on.*
nosotros:	habremos hablado, comido, vivido, *and so on.*
vosotros:	habréis hablado, comido, vivido, *and so on.*
Uds./ellos/ellas:	habrán hablado, comido, vivido, *and so on.*

These forms correspond to **el futuro (Capítulo 17)** and are most frequently used to tell what *will have already happened* at some point in the future. (In contrast, the future is used to tell what *will happen*.)

Mañana **hablaré** con Miguel.
I'll speak with Miguel tomorrow.

Para las tres, ya **habré hablado** con Miguel.
By 3:00, I'll already have spoken with Miguel.

El año que viene **visitaremos** a los nietos.
We'll visit our grandchildren next year.

Para las Navidades, ya **habremos visitado** a los nietos.
We'll already have visited our grandchildren by Christmas.

El condicional perfecto

yo:	habría hablado, comido, vivido, *and so on.*
tú:	habrías hablado, comido, vivido, *and so on.*
Ud./él/ella:	habría hablado, comido, vivido, *and so on.*
nosotros:	habríamos hablado, comido, vivido, *and so on.*
vosotros:	habríais hablado, comido, vivido, *and so on.*
Uds./ellos/ellas:	habrían hablado, comido, vivido, *and so on.*

These forms correspond to **el condicional (Capítulo 18)**. These forms are frequently used to tell what *would have happened* at some point in the past. (In contrast, the conditional tells what one *would do*.)

Yo **hablaría** con Miguel.
I would speak with Miguel (if I were you, at some point in the future).

Yo **habría hablado** con Miguel.
I would have spoken with Miguel (if I had been you, at some point in the past).

Si Clause: Sentences About the Past

You have learned (**Capítulo 18**) to use the past subjunctive and conditional to speculate about the present in **si** clause sentences: what *would happen* if a particular event *were* (or *were not*) to occur.

Si **tuviera** el tiempo, **aprendería** francés.
If I had the time, I would learn French.

The perfect forms of the past subjunctive and the conditional are used to speculate about the past: what *would have happened* if a particular event *had* (or *had not*) occurred.

En la escuela superior, si **hubiera tenido** el tiempo, **habría aprendido** francés.
In high school, if I had had the time, I would have learned French.

A. Regular Verbs: Simple Tenses

Infinitive Present Participle Past Participle	INDICATIVE					SUBJUNCTIVE		IMPERATIVE
	Present	Imperfect	Preterite	Future	Conditional	Present	Imperfect	
hablar	hablo	hablaba	hablé	hablaré	hablaría	hable	hablara	
hablando	hablas	hablabas	hablaste	hablarás	hablarías	hables	hablaras	habla tú, no hables
hablado	habla	hablaba	habló	hablará	hablaría	hable	hablara	hable Ud.
	hablamos	hablábamos	hablamos	hablaremos	hablaríamos	hablemos	habláramos	hablemos
	habláis	hablabais	hablasteis	hablaréis	hablaríais	habléis	hablarais	hablad, no habléis
	hablan	hablaban	hablaron	hablarán	hablarían	hablen	hablaran	hablen
comer	como	comía	comí	comeré	comería	coma	comiera	
comiendo	comes	comías	comiste	comerás	comerías	comas	comieras	come tú, no comas
comido	come	comía	comió	comerá	comería	coma	comiera	coma Ud.
	comemos	comíamos	comimos	comeremos	comeríamos	comamos	comiéramos	comamos
	coméis	comíais	comisteis	comeréis	comeríais	comáis	comierais	comed, no comáis
	comen	comían	comieron	comerán	comerían	coman	comieran	coman
vivir	vivo	vivía	viví	viviré	viviría	viva	viviera	
viviendo	vives	vivías	viviste	vivirás	vivirías	vivas	vivieras	vive tú, no vivas
vivido	vive	vivía	vivió	vivirá	viviría	viva	viviera	viva Ud.
	vivimos	vivíamos	vivimos	viviremos	viviríamos	vivamos	viviéramos	vivamos
	vivís	vivíais	vivisteis	viviréis	viviríais	viváis	vivierais	vivid, no viváis
	viven	vivían	vivieron	vivirán	vivirían	vivan	vivieran	vivan

B. Regular Verbs: Perfect Tenses

	INDICATIVE					SUBJUNCTIVE	
	Present Perfect	Past Perfect	Preterite Perfect	Future Perfect	Conditional Perfect	Present Perfect	Past Perfect
	he	había	hube	habré	habría	haya	hubiera
	has	habías	hubiste	habrás	habrías	hayas	hubieras
	ha hablado	había hablado	hubo hablado	habrá hablado	habría hablado	haya hablado	hubiera hablado
	hemos comido	habíamos comido	hubimos comido	habremos comido	habríamos comido	hayamos comido	hubiéramos comido
	habéis vivido	habíais vivido	hubisteis vivido	habréis vivido	habríais vivido	hayáis vivido	hubierais vivido
	han	habían	hubieron	habrán	habrían	hayan	hubieran

C. Irregular Verbs

Infinitive Present Participle Past Participle	INDICATIVE					SUBJUNCTIVE		IMPERATIVE
	Present	Imperfect	Preterite	Future	Conditional	Present	Imperfect	
andar andando andado	ando	andaba	anduve	andaré	andaría	ande	anduviera	anda tú, no
	andas	andabas	anduviste	andarás	andarías	andes	anduvieras	andes
	anda	andaba	anduvo	andará	andaría	ande	anduviera	ande Ud.
	andamos	andábamos	anduvimos	andaremos	andaríamos	andemos	anduviéramos	andemos
	andáis	andabais	anduvisteis	andaréis	andaríais	andéis	anduvierais	andad, no andéis
	andan	andaban	anduvieron	andarán	andarían	anden	anduvieran	anden
caber cabiendo cabido	quepo	cabía	cupe	cabré	cabría	quepa	cupiera	cabe tú,
	cabes	cabías	cupiste	cabrás	cabrías	quepas	cupieras	no quepas
	cabe	cabía	cupo	cabrá	cabría	quepa	cupiera	quepa Ud.
	cabemos	cabíamos	cupimos	cabremos	cabríamos	quepamos	cupiéramos	quepamos
	cabéis	cabíais	cupisteis	cabréis	cabríais	quepáis	cupierais	cabed, no quepáis
	caben	cabían	cupieron	cabrán	cabrían	quepan	cupieran	quepan

C. Irregular Verbs (continued)

Infinitive Present Participle Past Participle	INDICATIVE					SUBJUNCTIVE		IMPERATIVE
	Present	Imperfect	Preterite	Future	Conditional	Present	Imperfect	
caer cayendo caído	caigo caes cae caemos caéis caen	caía caías caía caíamos caíais caían	caí caíste cayó caímos caísteis cayeron	caeré caerás caerá caeremos caeréis caerán	caería caerías caería caeríamos caeríais caerían	caiga caigas caiga caigamos caigáis caigan	cayera cayeras cayera cayéramos cayerais cayeran	cae tú, no caigas caiga Ud. caigamos caed, no caigáis caigan
creer creyendo creído	creo crees cree creemos creéis creen	creía creías creía creíamos creíais creían	creí creíste creyó creímos creísteis creyeron	creeré creerás creerá creeremos creeréis creerán	creería creerías creería creeríamos creeríais creerían	crea creas crea creamos creáis crean	creyera creyeras creyera creyéramos creyerais creyeran	cree tú, no creas crea Ud. creamos creed, no creáis crean
dar dando dado	doy das da damos dais dan	daba dabas daba dábamos dabais daban	di diste dio dimos disteis dieron.	daré darás dará daremos daréis darán	daría darías daría daríamos daríais darían	dé des dé demos deis den	diera dieras diera diéramos dierais dieran	da tú, no des dé Ud. demos dad, no deis den
decir diciendo dicho	digo dices dice decimos decís dicen	decía decías decía decíamos decíais decían	dije dijiste dijo dijimos dijisteis dijeron	diré dirás dirá diremos diréis dirán	diría dirías diría diríamos diríais dirían	diga digas diga digamos digáis digan	dijera dijeras dijera dijéramos dijerais dijeran	di tú, no digas diga Ud. digamos decid, no digáis digan

Infinitive / Present Participle / Past Participle	INDICATIVE					SUBJUNCTIVE		IMPERATIVE
	Present	Imperfect	Preterite	Future	Conditional	Present	Imperfect	
estar / estando / estado	estoy estás está estamos estáis están	estaba estabas estaba estábamos estabais estaban	estuve estuviste estuvo estuvimos estuvisteis estuvieron	estaré estarás estará estaremos estaréis estarán	estaría estarías estaría estaríamos estaríais estarían	esté estés esté estemos estéis estén	estuviera estuvieras estuviera estuviéramos estuvierais estuviera	está tú, no estés esté Ud. estemos estad, no estéis estén
haber / habiendo / habido	he has ha hemos habéis han	había habías había habíamos habíais habían	hube hubiste hubo hubimos hubisteis hubieron	habré habrás habrá habremos habréis habrán	habría habrías habría habríamos habríais habrían	haya hayas haya hayamos hayáis hayan	hubiera hubieras hubiera hubiéramos hubierais hubieran	
hacer / haciendo / hecho	hago haces hace hacemos hacéis hacen	hacía hacías hacía hacíamos hacíais hacían	hice hiciste hizo hicimos hicisteis hicieron	haré harás hará haremos haréis harán	haría harías haría haríamos haríais harían	haga hagas haga hagamos hagáis hagan	hiciera hicieras hiciera hiciéramos hicierais hicieran	haz tú, no hagas haga Ud. hagamos haced, no hagáis hagan
ir / yendo / ido	voy vas va vamos vais van	iba ibas iba íbamos ibais iban	fui fuiste fue fuimos fuisteis fueron	iré irás irá iremos iréis irán	iría irías iría iríamos iríais irían	vaya vayas vaya vayamos vayáis vayan	fuera fueras fuera fuéramos fuerais fueran	ve tú, no vayas vaya Ud. vayamos id, no vayáis vayan

Infinitive Present Participle Past Participle	INDICATIVE					SUBJUNCTIVE		IMPERATIVE
	Present	Imperfect	Preterite	Future	Conditional	Present	Imperfect	
oír oyendo oído	oigo oyes oye oímos oís oyen	oía oías oía oíamos oíais oían	oí oíste oyó oímos oísteis oyeron	oiré oirás oirá oiremos oiréis oirán	oiría oirías oiría oiríamos oiríais oirían	oiga oigas oiga oigamos oigáis oigan	oyera oyeras oyera oyéramos oyerais oyeran	oye tú, no oigas oiga Ud. oigamos oíd, no oigáis oigan
poder pudiendo podido	puedo puedes puede podemos podéis pueden	podía podías podía podíamos podíais podían	pude pudiste pudo pudimos pudisteis pudieron	podré podrás podrá podremos podréis podrán	podría podrías podría podríamos podríais podrían	pueda puedas pueda podamos podáis puedan	pudiera pudieras pudiera pudiéramos pudierais pudieran	
poner poniendo puesto	pongo pones pone ponemos ponéis ponen	ponía ponías ponía poníamos poníais ponían	puse pusiste puso pusimos pusisteis pusieron	pondré pondrás pondrá pondremos pondréis pondrán	pondría pondrías pondría pondríamos pondríais pondrían	ponga pongas ponga pongamos pongáis pongan	pusiera pusieras pusiera pusiéramos pusierais pusieran	pon tú, no pongas ponga Ud. pongamos poned, no pongáis pongan
querer queriendo querido	quiero quieres quiere queremos queréis quieren	quería querías quería queríamos queríais querían	quise quisiste quiso quisimos quisisteis quisieron	querré querrás querrá querremos querréis querrán	querría querrías querría querríamos querríais querrían	quiera quieras quiera queramos queráis quieran	quisiera quisieras quisiera quisiéramos quisierais quisieran	quiere tú, no quieras quiera Ud. queramos quered, no queráis quieran

C. Irregular Verbs (continued)

Infinitive Present Participle Past Participle	INDICATIVE					SUBJUNCTIVE		IMPERATIVE
	Present	Imperfect	Preterite	Future	Conditional	Present	Imperfect	
saber sabiendo sabido	sé sabes sabe sabemos sabéis saben	sabía sabías sabía sabíamos sabíais sabían	supe supiste supo supimos supisteis supieron	sabré sabrás sabrá sabremos sabréis sabrán	sabría sabrías sabría sabríamos sabríais sabrían	sepa sepas sepa sepamos sepáis sepan	supiera supieras supiera supiéramos supierais supieran	sabe tú, no sepas sepa Ud. sepamos sabed, no sepáis sepan
salir saliendo salido	salgo sales sale salimos salís salen	salía salías salía salíamos salíais salían	salí saliste salió salimos salisteis salieron	saldré saldrás saldrá saldremos saldréis saldrán	saldría saldrías saldría saldríamos saldríais saldrían	salga salgas salga salgamos salgáis salgan	saliera salieras saliera saliéramos salierais salieran	sal tú, no salgas salga Ud. salgamos salid, no salgáis salgan
ser siendo sido	soy eres es somos sois son	era eras era éramos erais eran	fui fuiste fue fuimos fuisteis fueron	seré serás será seremos seréis serán	sería serías sería seríamos seríais serían	sea seas sea seamos seáis sean	fuera fueras fuera fuéramos fuerais fueran	sé tú, no seas sea Ud. seamos sed, no seáis sean
tener teniendo tenido	tengo tienes tiene tenemos tenéis tienen	tenía tenías tenía teníamos teníais tenían	tuve tuviste tuvo tuvimos tuvisteis tuvieron	tendré tendrás tendrá tendremos tendréis tendrán	tendría tendrías tendría tendríamos tendríais tendrían	tenga tengas tenga tengamos tengáis tengan	tuviera tuvieras tuviera tuviéramos tuvierais tuvieran	ten tú, no tengas tenga Ud. tengamos tened, no tengáis tengan

C. Irregular Verbs (continued)

Infinitive Present Participle Past Participle	INDICATIVE					SUBJUNCTIVE		IMPERATIVE
	Present	Imperfect	Preterite	Future	Conditional	Present	Imperfect	
traer trayendo traído	traigo traes trae traemos traéis traen	traía traías traía traíamos traíais traían	traje trajiste trajo trajimos trajisteis trajeron	traeré traerás traerá traeremos traeréis traerán	traería traerías traería traeríamos traeríais traerían	traiga traigas traiga traigamos traigáis traigan	trajera trajeras trajera trajéramos trajerais trajeran	trae tú, no traigas traiga Ud. traigamos traed, no traigáis traigan
venir viniendo venido	vengo vienes viene venimos venís vienen	venía venías venía veníamos veníais venían	vine viniste vino vinimos vinisteis vinieron	vendré vendrás vendrá vendremos vendréis vendrán	vendría vendrías vendría vendríamos vendríais vendrían	venga vengas venga vengamos vengáis vengan	viniera vinieras viniera viniéramos vinierais vinieran	ven tú, no vengas venga Ud. vengamos venid, no vengáis vengan
ver viendo visto	veo ves ve vemos veis ven	veía veías veía veíamos veíais veían	vi viste vio vimos visteis vieron	veré verás verá veremos veréis verán	vería verías vería veríamos veríais verían	vea veas vea veamos veáis vean	viera vieras viera viéramos vierais vieran	ve tú, no veas vea Ud. veamos ved, no veáis vean

D. Stem-Changing and Spelling Change Verbs

Infinitive Present Participle Past Participle	INDICATIVE					SUBJUNCTIVE		IMPERATIVE
	Present	Imperfect	Preterite	Future	Conditional	Present	Imperfect	
pensar (pienso) pensando pensado	pienso piensas piensa pensamos pensáis piensan	pensaba pensabas pensaba pensábamos pensabais pensaban	pensé pensaste pensó pensamos pensasteis pensaron	pensaré pensarás pensará pensaremos pensaréis pensarán	pensaría pensarías pensaría pensaríamos pensaríais pensarían	piense pienses piense pensemos penséis piensen	pensara pensaras pensara pensáramos pensarais pensaran	piensa tú, no pienses piense Ud. pensemos pensad, no penséis piensen
volver (vuelvo) volviendo vuelto	vuelvo vuelves vuelve volvemos volvéis vuelven	volvía volvías volvía volvíamos volvíais volvían	volví volviste volvió volvimos volvisteis volvieron	volveré volverás volverá volveremos volveréis volverán	volvería volverías volvería volveríamos volveríais volverían	vuelva vuelvas vuelva volvamos volváis vuelvan	volviera volvieras volviera volviéramos volvierais volvieran	vuelve tú, no vuelvas vuelva Ud. volvamos volved, no volváis vuelvan
dormir (duermo) (u) durmiendo dormido	duermo duermes duerme dormimos dormís duermen	dormía dormías dormía dormíamos dormíais dormían	dormí dormiste durmió dormimos dormisteis durmieron	dormiré dormirás dormirá dormiremos dormiréis dormirán	dormiría dormirías dormiría dormiríamos dormiríais dormirían	duerma duermas duerma durmamos durmáis duerman	durmiera durmieras durmiera durmiéramos durmierais durmieran	duerme tú, no duermas duerma Ud. durmamos dormid, no durmáis duerman
sentir (siento) (i) sintiendo sentido	siento sientes siente sentimos sentís sienten	sentía sentías sentía sentíamos sentíais sentían	sentí sentiste sintió sentimos sentisteis sintieron	sentiré sentirás sentirá sentiremos sentiréis sentirán	sentiría sentirías sentiría sentiríamos sentiríais sentirían	sienta sientas sienta sintamos sintáis sientan	sintiera sintieras sintiera sintiéramos sintierais sintieran	siente tú, no sientas sienta Ud. sintamos sentid, no sintáis sientan
pedir (pido) (i) pidiendo pedido	pido pides pide pedimos pedís piden	pedía pedías pedía pedíamos pedíais pedían	pedí pediste pidió pedimos pedisteis pidieron	pediré pedirás pedirá pediremos pediréis pedirán	pediría pedirías pediría pediríamos pediríais pedirían	pida pidas pida pidamos pidáis pidan	pidiera pidieras pidiera pidiéramos pidierais pidieran	pide tú, no pidas pida Ud. pidamos pedid, no pidáis pidan

D. Stem-Changing and Spelling Change Verbs (continued)

Infinitive / Present Participle / Past Participle	INDICATIVE					SUBJUNCTIVE		IMPERATIVE
	Present	Imperfect	Preterite	Future	Conditional	Present	Imperfect	
reír (río) (i) riendo reído	río ríes ríe reímos reís ríen	reía reías reía reíamos reíais reían	reí reíste rio reímos reísteis rieron	reiré reirás reirá reiremos reiréis reirán	reiría reirías reiría reiríamos reiríais reirían	ría rías ría riamos riáis rían	riera rieras riera riéramos rierais rieran	ríe tú, no rías ría Ud. riamos reíd, no riáis rían
seguir (sigo) (i) siguiendo seguido	sigo sigues sigue seguimos seguís siguen	seguía seguías seguía seguíamos seguíais seguían	seguí seguiste siguió seguimos seguisteis siguieron	seguiré seguirás seguirá seguiremos seguiréis seguirán	seguiría seguirías seguiría seguiríamos seguiríais seguirían	siga sigas siga sigamos sigáis sigan	siguiera siguieras siguiera siguiéramos siguierais siguieran	sigue tú, no sigas siga Ud. sigamos seguid, no sigáis sigan
construir (construyo) construyendo construido	construyo construyes construye construimos construís construyen	construía construías construía construíamos construíais construían	construí construiste construyó construimos construisteis construyeron	construiré construirás construirá construiremos construiréis construirán	construiría construirías construiría construiríamos construiríais construirían	construya construyas construya construyamos construyáis construyan	construyera construyeras construyera construyéramos construyerais construyeran	construye tú, no construyas construya Ud. construyamos construid, no construyáis construyan
conducir (conduzco) conduciendo conducido	conduzco conduces conduce conducimos conducís conducen	conducía conducías conducía conducíamos conducíais conducían	conduje condujiste condujo condujimos condujisteis condujeron	conduciré conducirás conducirá conduciremos conduciréis conducirán	conduciría conducirías conduciría conduciríamos conduciríais conducirían	conduzca conduzcas conduzca conduzcamos conduzcáis conduzcan	condujera condujeras condujera condujéramos condujerais condujeran	conduce tú, no conduzcas conduzca Ud. conduzcamos conducid, no conduzcáis conduzcan

VOCABULARIES

This **Spanish-English Vocabulary** contains all the words that appear in the text, with the following exceptions: (1) most close or identical cognates that do not appear in the chapter vocabulary lists; (2) most conjugated verb forms; (3) diminutives ending in **-ito/a;** (4) absolute superlatives in **-ísimo/a;** (5) most adverbs ending in **-mente,** and (6) words listed or glossed in the **Vocabulario del segmento** and **Fragmento del guion** features of the **Salu2** sections. Active vocabulary is indicated by the number of the chapter in which a word or given meaning is first listed (**1** = **Capítulo 1**); vocabulary that is glossed in the text is not considered to be active vocabulary and is not numbered. Only meanings that are used in the text are given. The **English-Spanish Vocabulary** is based on the chapter lists of active vocabulary.

The gender of nouns is indicated, except for masculine nouns ending in **-o** and feminine nouns ending in **-a.** Because **ch** and **ll** are no longer considered separate letters, words beginning with **ch** and **ll** are found as they would be found in English. The letter **ñ** follows the letter **n: añadir** follows **anuncio,** for example.

Irregular verbs found in the verb charts of Appendix 5 are set all in color: andar. No changes are indicated for them in these vocabularies. Verbs with stem changes or spelling changes in the *present tense* show the **yo** form of the present tense in parentheses with the stem-vowel or spelling changes indicated in color: **sentarse (me siento); conocer (conozco); escoger (escojo); actuar (actúo).** Verbs with stem changes in the third person *preterite* and the *present participle* show the stem vowel (**i** or **u**) in parentheses after the present tense **yo** form: **preferir (prefiero) (i); morirse (me muero) (u).** Verbs with any other spelling changes in the first person *preterite* or *present subjunctive* show the change in parentheses: **buscar (qu); pagar (gu); empezar (empiezo) (c); averiguar (ü).**

The following abbreviations are used:

adj.	adjective	*inv.*	invariable form
adv.	adverb	*L.A.*	Latin America
Arg.	Argentina	*m.*	masculine
C.A.	Central America	*Mex.*	Mexico
Carib.	Caribbean	*n.*	noun
Col.	Colombia	*obj. (of prep.)*	object (of a preposition)
conj.	conjunction	*pl.*	plural
def. art.	definite article	*poss.*	possessive
d.o.	direct object	*p.p.*	past participle
f.	feminine	*prep.*	preposition
fam.	familiar	*pron.*	pronoun
form.	formal	*refl. pron.*	reflexive pronoun
gram.	grammatical term	*s.*	singular
Guat.	Guatemala	*sl.*	slang
ind. art.	indefinite article	*Sp.*	Spain
inf.	infinitive	*sub. pron.*	subject pronoun
i.o.	indirect object		
interj.	interjection		

Spanish-English Vocabulary

A

a to; at (*with time*) (1); **a base de** based on; **a causa de** because of; **a continuación** following; **a este respecto** in this regard; **a la derecha de** to the right of (6); **a la izquierda de** to the left of (6); **a la moda** in fashion, in a stylish way; **a la(s)...** at . . . (*time of day*) (1); **a menos que** unless (16); **a partir de** beyond (4); **a pesar de** in spite of; **a plazos** in installments (17); **¿a qué hora... ?** at what time . . . ? (1); **a solas** alone; **a tiempo** on time (8); **a través de** across, through; throughout; **¿a usted le gusta... ?** do you (*form. s.*) like . . . ? (1); **a veces** sometimes, at times (3); **a ver** let's see
abacería grocery store
abajo below; underneath
abandonar to abandon
abarcar (qu) to cover (*a topic*)
abarrotes *m. pl.* groceries
abecedario alphabet
abierto/a (*p.p. of* **abrir**) open (6)
abogado/a lawyer (17)
abogar (gu) to advocate
abolengo lineage
abolicionista *m., f.* abolitionist
aborto abortion
abrazar(se) (c) to embrace (11)
abrazo hug, embrace
abreviatura abbreviation
abrigo coat (4)
abril *m.* April (6)
abrir (*pp.* **abierto**) to open (3)
abrumador(a) overwhelming
absoluto/a absolute
abstenerse (*like* **tener**) to refrain
absurdo/a absurd; **es absurdo que** it's absurd that (13)
abuelo/a grandfather/grandmother (3); *m. pl.* grandparents (3)
abundante abundant
aburrido/a bored (6); **ser aburrido/a** to be boring (10)
aburrimiento boredom
aburrir (*like* **gustar**) to bore (13); **aburrirse** to get bored (10)
abuso abuse
abyecto/a wretched
acá here
acabar to finish (14); to run out of (14); **acabar de** + *inf.* to have just (*done something*) (7)
academia academy
académico/a *adj.* academic (14); **año académico** school year; **vida académica** academic life (14)

acampar to camp; **tienda de acampar** tent
acaso: por si acaso just in case (14)
acatar to obey
acceso access
accesorio accessory
accidente *m.* accident (14)
acción *f.* action; **Día** (*m.*) **de Acción de Gracias** Thanksgiving
aceite (*m.*) **(de oliva)** (olive) oil (7)
acelerado/a fast, accelerated (15)
acelerar to accelerate; to speed up
acento accent; **acento diacrítico** diacritical mark; **acento ortográfico** accent mark
acentuación *f.* accent mark
acentuado/a accentuated
aceptable acceptable
aceptar to accept
acera sidewalk (15)
acerca de *prep.* about, concerning, regarding
acercarse (qu) (a) to come near to
acertar (acierto) to guess correctly
ácido acid
acompañar to accompany
acondicionado/a: aire (*m.*) **acondicionado** air conditioning
aconsejable advisable
aconsejar to advise
acontecer to occur
acontecimiento event, happening (18)
acordarse (me acuerdo) (de) to remember (13)
acordeón *m.* accordion
acoso harassment, bullying
acostarse (me acuesto) to go to bed (5)
acostumbrarse (a) to become accustomed (to); to get used (to)
acribillar to bombard
acrílico/a acrylic
actitud *f.* attitude
actividad *f.* activity
activo/a active
acto act
actor *m.* actor (13)
actriz *f.* (*pl.* **actrices**) actress (13)
actuación *f.* performance
actual *adj.* current, present-day (12)
actualidad: de/en la actualidad currently, right now (10)
actualizar(c) to update
actuar (actúo) to act (13)
acuario aquarium; **Acuario** Aquarius
acuático/a aquatic
acudir (a) to go (to)
acueducto aqueduct

acuerdo agreement; **(no) estar de acuerdo** to (dis)agree (3)
acumular to accumulate
acusón, acusona tattler
adaptación *f.* adaptation
adaptarse (a) to adapt (to)
adecuado/a appropriate
adelante forward
adelgazar (c) to lose weight
además *adv.* moreover; **además de** *prep.* besides
adentro inside
adicción *f.* addiction
adicional additional (1)
adiós good-bye (1)
adivinar to guess (9)
adjetivo *gram.* adjective (3); **adjetivo de nacionalidad** adjective of nationality (3); **adjetivo posesivo** possessive adjective (3)
administración *f.* administration; **administración de empresas** business administration (2)
administrar to administer; to manage; to run
admiración *f.* admiration
admirar to admire
admitir to admit
adolescencia adolescence (16)
adolescente *m., f.* adolescent, teenager; **de adolescente** as an adolescent (10)
¿adónde? where (to)? (4)
adoptar to adopt
adoquinado/a cobblestoned
adorar to adore
adquirir to acquire
adquisitivo/a: poder (*m.*) **adquisitivo** purchasing power
aduana customs (*at a border*) (8); **pasar por la aduana** to go/pass through customs (8)
adulto/a adult
adverbio *gram.* adverb
adverso/a adverse
advertencia warning
adyacente adjacent
aéreo/a aerial
aeróbico/a: hacer ejercicios aeróbicos to do aerobics (11)
aerolínea airline
aeropuerto airport (8)
afán *m.* effort
afanoso/a laborious, hard
afectación *f.* affectation
afectar to affect
afectivo/a: estado afectivo emotional state (9)
afecto affection

afeitarse to shave (5)

afición *f.* hobby (10)

aficionado/a fan; **ser aficionado/a (a)** to be a fan (of) (10)

afiliación *f.* affiliation

afiliado/a (a) affiliated (with)

afín related

afinidad *f.* compatibility

afirmación *f.* statement

afirmar to affirm

afirmativo/a affirmative

afluente affluent

afortunado/a fortunate, lucky

africano/a *n., adj.* African

afroamerindo/a *n., adj.* Afro-Amerindian

afroantillano/a Afro-Antillian

afroperuano/a Afro-Peruvian

afuera *adv.* outdoors (6)

afueras *f. pl.* outskirts (12); suburbs (12)

agencia agency; **agencia de compra-venta (de coches)** used car dealership; **agencia de viajes** travel agency

agenda agenda; date book

agente *m., f.* agent (8); **agente de viajes** travel agent

ágil agile

agitar to agitate

agnóstico/a agnostic

agobiado/a overwhelmed

agosto August (6)

agotar to empty; to drain

agradable agreeable, pleasant

agradar (*like* **gustar**) to please

agradecimiento *n.* thanks

agregar (gu) to add

agresivo/a aggressive

agrícola *adj. m., f.* agricultural

agricultor(a) farmer (15)

agricultura farming, agriculture (15)

agrio/a bitter

agroturismo agritourism

agroturista *m., f.* agritourist

agroturístico/a *adj.* of rural tourism

agrupar to group

agua *f.* (*but* **el agua**) **(mineral)** (mineral) water (7)

aguacate *m.* avocado (7)

aguar (ü) to dilute; water down

agudo/a sharp

águila *f.* (*but* **el águila**) eagle

agujero hole

ahí there

ahijado/a godson/goddaughter

ahora now (2); **ahora mismo** right now (6)

ahorrar to save (*money*) (17)

ahorro savings

ahorros: cuenta de ahorros savings account

aimara *n.* Aymara

airado/a angry; annoyed

aire *m.* air (15); **aire acondicionado** air conditioning; **al aire libre** outdoors (10)

ajedrez *m.* chess; **jugar (juego) (gu) al ajedrez** to play chess (10)

ajo garlic

al (*contraction of* **a** + **el**) to the (4); **al** + *inf.* while (*doing something*); **al aire** (*m.*) **libre** outdoors (10); **al alcance** within reach; **al instante** right away; **al lado de** alongside of (6); **al menos** at least; **al principio de** at the beginning of (17)

alameda tree-lined avenue

alberca swimming pool (*Mex.*)

álbum *m.* album

alcance: al alcance within reach

alcanzar (c) to reach; to achieve

alce *m.* elk; moose

alcoba bedroom (5)

alcohol *m.* alcohol

alcohólico/a alcoholic; **bebida alcohólica** alcoholic beverage

alegrarse (de) to be happy (about) (12)

alegre happy (6)

alemán *m.* German (*language*) (2)

alemán, alemana *n., adj.* German (3)

Alemania Germany

alergia allergy

alérgico/a allergic

alerta: ojo alerta eagle eye

alfabeto alphabet

alfombra rug (5)

algo something; anything (7)

algodón *m.* cotton (4); **de algodón** *adj.* (*made of*) cotton (4)

alguien someone, anyone (7)

algún (alguna/os/as) some, any (7); **alguna vez** once; ever

alimentación *f.* diet

alimenticio/a of eating

alimento food

aliviar to alleviate

allá (way) over there (4)

allí there (4)

alma *m.* soul

almacén *m.* department store (4)

almacenamiento: espacio de almacenamiento storage space (12)

almacenar to store; to save (12)

almohada pillow

almorzar (almuerzo) (c) to have lunch (5)

almuerzo lunch (7)

¿aló? hello? (*telephone greeting*)

alojarse to lodge

alpinismo mountain climbing; **practicar (qu) el alpinismo** to mountain climb

alquilar *v.* to rent (12)

alquiler *m.* rent (12)

alrededor (de) around

alternar to take turns

alternativa *n.* alternative

alternativo/a *adj.* alternative

altiplanicie *f.* high plateau

altiplano high plateau

altitud *f.* height; altitude

alto/a tall (3); **de alta costura** high fashion; **de alto riesgo** high risk

altura altitude

alucinante incredible

alumno/a student

aluvial alluvial

amabilidad *f.* kindness

amable kind; nice (3)

amanecer *m.* dawn

amar to love (16)

amarillo/a yellow (4)

amasijo dough; mixture

Amazonas *m. s.* Amazon (River)

amazónico/a *adj.* Amazonian; **Selva Amazónica** Amazon Jungle

ambiental environmental

ambiente *m.* atmosphere; environment; **medio ambiente** environment (15)

ambigüedad *f.* ambiguity

ámbito area

ambos/as both

ambulante *adj.* traveling

América: América Latina Latin America; **Estados** (*m. pl.*) **Unidos de América** United States of America

americano/a American; **fútbol** (*m.*) **americano** football

amerindo/a *n., adj.* Amerindian

amigo/a friend (2)

amistad *f.* friendship (16)

amistoso/a friendly (16)

amo/a (*but* **el ama**) **de casa** housekeeper (17)

amoníaco ammonia

amor *m.* love (16)

amoroso/a loving

ampliar (amplío) to widen

amplio/a wide; large; spacious

amueblado/a furnished

amueblar to furnish

amuleto charm; amulet

amurallado/a walled

analfabetismo *n.* illiteracy

analfabeto/a illiterate

análisis *m. inv.* analysis

analista *m., f.* analyst; **analista de sistemas** systems analyst (17)

analizar (c) to analyze

ananá *m.* pineapple

anaranjado/a orange (4)

ancho/a wide

anciano/a *n.* old person; *adj.* old; ancient; **residencia de ancianos** nursing home (12)

Andalucía Andalusia

andaluz(a) *n., adj.* Andalusian

andante: caballero andante knight-errant

andar to walk; **andar en bicicleta** to ride a bicycle; **cinta de andar** treadmill

andino/a Andean

anécdota anecdote

anémico/a anemic

anfibio amphibian

anfitrión, anfitriona host (*of an event*) (9)

ángel *m.* angel

angelino/a *adj.* from Los Angeles; *n.* person from Los Angeles

angloparlante *adj.* English-speaking

anglosajón, anglosajona Anglo Saxon

angosto/a narrow

ángulo angle

angustia anguish

anillo ring

ánima *f.* (*but* **el ánima**) soul

animado/a lively; animated; **dibujos** (*m. pl.*) **animados** cartoons

animal *m.* animal (15); **animal de peluche** (*m.*) stuffed animal; **animal doméstico** pet

animar(se) to cheer up; **animarse a** to get up the courage to (*do something*)

ánimo: estado de ánimo state of mind

aniversario anniversary

anoche *adv.* last night (11)

anónimo/a anonymous

ansiedad *f.* anxiety (14)

ansioso/a anxious

antártico/a *adj.* Antarctic

Antártida Antarctica

ante *prep.* before; in front of

anteayer *adv.* the day before yesterday (5)

antecedente *m. gram.* antecedent

anteojos *m. pl.* glasses (11)

antepenúltimo/a third from the end

anterior previous, preceding

antes *adv.* before; **antes de** *prep.* before (5); **antes de Cristo (a.C.)** before Christ (B.C.); **antes (de) que** *conj.* before (16)

antibiótico antibiotic (11)

anticipar to anticipate

anticipo advance

anticuado/a antiquated

antídoto antidote

antiguo/a old; ancient; former

antillano/a *adj.* of/from the Antilles

Antillas (*f. pl.*) **Mayores** Greater Antilles

antipático/a unpleasant (3)

antojo appetizer

antónimo antonym

antropología anthropology

antropólogo/a anthropologist

anual annual

anualmente annually

anunciar to announce (8)

anuncio announcement; advertisement

añadir to add

año year (6); **año académico** school year; **año bisiesto** leap year; **el año entrante** next year; **Año Nuevo** New Year; **año pasado** last year; **el año que viene** next year; **cumplir años** to have a birthday (9); **este año** this year; **fin** (*m.*) **de año** end of the year (9); **tener... años** to be . . . years old (3)

apagar (gu) to turn off (12)

apagón *m.* blackout

aparato appliance; **aparato doméstico** home appliance (10)

aparcamiento parking place; parking lot

aparcar (qu) to park

aparecer (aparezco) to appear

apariencia appearance

apartamento apartment (2)

aparte also

apellido surname

apenas barely

aperitivo appetizer

apetecer (apetezco) (*like* **gustar**) to appeal to

apetito appetite

apio celery

aplicación *f.* application

aplicar (qu) to apply

aportar to contribute

apóstol *m., f.* apostle

apoyar to support

apoyo support; help

app *f.* app(lication) (12)

apreciar to appreciate

aprender to learn (3); **aprender a** + *inf.* to learn how to (*do something*) (3)

aprendizaje *m.* learning

apropiado/a appropriate

aproximadamente approximately

aproximado/a approximate

aptitud *f.* aptitude

apuntar to write down; **apuntarse** to enroll; to add one's name to the list

apuntes *m. pl.* notes (*academic*) (14)

aquel, aquella *adj.* that ([way] over there) (4); *pron.* that one ([way] over there)

aquello (*neuter pron.*) that ([way] over there) (4)

aquellos/as *adj.* those ([way] over there) (4) *pron.* those ones ([way] over there)

aquí here (2)

árabe *m.* Arabic (*language*); *n., adj. m., f.* Arab

Arabia Saudita Saudi Arabia

arábico/a *adj.* Arabic

arado *n.* plow

araña spider

árbol *m.* tree (9); **árbol genealógico** family tree

arcángel *m.* archangel

archipiélago archipelago

archivo (*computer*) file (12)

arco arch

ardilla squirrel

área *f.* (*but* **el área**) area, region

arena sand

arepa *patty made of cornmeal and flour and stuffed with different foods*

aretes *m. pl.* earrings (4)

argentino/a *n., adj.* Argentine

argumento argument; plot

árido/a arid, dry

aristocrático/a aristocratic

arma weapon

armado/a: fuerzas armadas armed forces

armar un bochinche to throw a (loud) party

armario armoire, free-standing closet (5)

armonía harmony

arpa *f.* (*but* **el arpa**) harp

arqueológico/a archaeological

arquitecto/a architect (13)

arquitectónico/a architectural

arquitectura architecture (13)

arraigado/a deeply rooted

arrancar (qu) to start up (*a car*) (15)

arreglar to fix; to repair (15)

arrepentido/a sorry; repentant

arriba (de) *prep.* above

arroba @ (12)

arrodillarse to kneel

arrogancia arrogance

arrogante arrogant

arroz *m.* (*pl.* **arroces**) rice (7)

arruinar to ruin

arte *m.* art (2); **artes** *f. pl.* the arts (13); **bellas artes** fine arts; **obra de arte** work of art (13)

arteria artery

arterial: presión (*f.*) **arterial** blood pressure

artesanía arts and crafts (13)

artesano/a artisan

Ártico *adj.* Arctic

artículo article; **artículo (in)definido** *gram.* (in)definite article

artista *m., f.* artist (13)

artístico/a artistic (13); **expresión** *(f.)* **artística** artistic expression (13)

arvejas *f. pl.* green peas (7)

asado/a roast(ed) (7); **lechón** *(m.)* **asado** roast suckling pig; **pollo asado** roast chicken (7)

asaltar to rob

asamblea assembly

ascendencia ancestry, descent

ascensor *m.* elevator (12)

asco: ¡qué asco! yuck!

asegurar to assure; **asegurarse (de que)** to make certain (that)

asentamiento settlement

asentarse (me asiento) to settle

asesinar to assassinate (18)

asesinato assassination; murder (18)

asesino *m., f.* murderer

así thus; so; **así como** as well as; **así que** therefore, consequently, so

asiático/a *adj.* Asian

asiento seat (8)

asignar to assign

asimismo additionally

asistencia sanitaria health care

asistente *(m., f.)* **de vuelo** flight attendant (8)

asistir (a) to attend; to go to (*a class, function*) (3)

asma *m.* asthma

asociación *f.* association

asociado/a associated; **estado libre asociado** commonwealth

asociar to associate

aspecto aspect

aspiradora vacuum cleaner (10); **pasar la aspiradora** to vacuum (10)

aspirante *m., f.* candidate; applicant (17)

aspirar to vacuum

aspirina aspirin

astronauta *m., f.* astronaut (17)

asumir to assume

asunto matter

asustar to scare

atacar (qu) to attack

ataque *(m.)* **(terrorista)** (terrorist) attack (18)

atar to tie

Atenas Athens

atención *f.* attention; **poner atención** to pay attention

atender (atiendo) to look after

atenerse (*like* **tener**) to accept

ateo/a atheist

ático attic

Atlántico Atlantic

atleta *m., f.* athlete

atmosférico/a atmospheric

átomo atom

atracción *f.* attraction

atractivo/a attractive

atraer (*like* **traer**) (*like* **gustar**) to draw; to attract (13)

atrás *adv.* back, backward; behind; **de atrás** backwards

atrasado/a (*with* **estar**) late (8)

atravesar (atravieso) to go through

atributo attribute

atún *m.* tuna (7)

audaz (*pl.* **audaces**) bold, daring

audiencia audience

auditivo/a aural

aula *f.* (*but* **el aula**) classroom

aumentar to increase

aumento raise

aun *adv.* even

aún *adv.* still, yet

aunque although

auriculares *m. pl.* headphones

auscultar to listen (*with a stethoscope*)

ausencia absence

ausente absent

austeridad *f.* austerity

australiano/a *n., adj.* Australian

auténtico/a authentic

auto auto (15)

autobiográfico/a autobiographical

autobús *m.* bus (8); **estación** *(f.)* **de autobuses** bus station (8); **ir en autobús** to go/travel by bus (8); **parada del autobús** bus stop (12)

autóctono/a indigenous

autoestima self-esteem

automático/a automatic; **cajero automático** automatic teller machine (ATM) (17)

automóvil *m.* automobile

automovilístico/a *adj.* automobile (15)

automutilación *f.* self-mutilation

autonomía autonomy; region

autónomo/a autonomous

autopista freeway; interstate (15)

autoprueba self-test

autor(a) author (13)

autoridad *f.* authority

autorizado/a authorized

autorretrato self-portrait

autostop: hacer autostop to hitchhike

autosuficiencia self-sufficiency

autosuficiente self-sufficient

auxiliar to help; to assist

avance *m.* preview

avanzado/a advanced

ave *f.* (*but* **el ave**) bird

avenida avenue (12)

aventura adventure

aventurero/a adventurous

aventurismo adventure tourism

aventurista *m., f.* adventure tourist

avergonzado/a embarrassed (9)

avión *m.* airplane (8); **ir en avión** to go/travel by plane (8); **volar (vuelo) en avión** to fly; to go by plane (8)

avisar to warn

aviso warning

¡ay! *interj.* ah!; ouch!

ayer yesterday; **ayer fue (miércoles...)** yesterday was (Wednesday . . .) (5)

ayuda help (7)

ayudante *m., f.* assistant

ayudar to help (7); **ayudar a** + *inf.* to help to (*do something*) (7)

ayuntamiento local government

azteca *n., adj. m., f.* Aztec

azúcar *m.* sugar (7)

azul blue (4)

azulejo tile

B

baba saliva; **se le cae la baba por** he/ she is drooling over

bacán: ¡qué bacán! fantastic!

bahía bay

bailable danceable

bailaor(a) flamenco dancer

bailar to dance (2)

bailarín, bailarina dancer (13)

baile *m.* dance (13)

bajada ebb; dip

bajar to lower; to download (12); **bajarse (de)** to get down (from) (8); to get off (of) (*a vehicle*) (8)

bajareque *n.* mud wall

bajo *prep.* under; **estar bajo muchas presiones** to be under a lot of pressure (14)

bajo/a short (*in height*) (3); low

balcón *m.* balcony

ballena whale (15)

ballet *m.* ballet (13)

baloncesto basketball

banana banana (7)

banano banana tree

bancario/a: tarjeta bancaria debit card (17)

banco bank (17)

banda band

bandeja tray

bandera flag

bandoneón *m.* large concertina

bañarse to take a bath (5)

bañera bathtub (5)

baño bathroom (5); **traje** *(m.)* **de baño** swimsuit (4)

bar *m.* bar; **ir a un bar** to go to a bar (10)

barato/a inexpensive (4)

barba beard

barbacoa barbecue (7)

barcelonés, barcelonesa of Barcelona (*Sp.*)

barco boat, ship (8); **ir en barco** to go/ travel by boat, ship (8)

barra bar

barrer (el piso) to sweep (the floor) (10)

barriga belly

barrio neighborhood (12)

barro mud

basarse en to base one's ideas/ opinions on

base *f.* base; **a base de** based on; **base de datos** data base; **con base en** based on

básico/a basic

basquetbol *m.* basketball (10)

bastante rather, sufficiently; enough (16)

bastar to be enough

basura trash (10); **sacar (qu) la basura** to take out the trash (10)

bata robe

batalla battle

batería drum set (15)

bautizo baptism

bebé *m., f.* baby

beber to drink (3)

bebida drink (5); **bebida alcohólica** alcoholic beverage

beca scholarship

béisbol *m.* baseball (10)

beisbolista *m., f.* baseball player

Bélgica Belgium

belleza beauty

bello/a beautiful (15); **bellas artes** (*f. pl.*) fine arts

bendecir (*like* **decir**) to bless; **que Dios te bendiga** God bless you

bendito/a blessed

beneficio benefit

besar to kiss; **besarse** to kiss each other (11)

beso kiss

bestia beast

Biblia Bible

biblioteca library (2)

bibliotecario/a librarian (2)

bicentenario bicentennial

bicho insect

bici *f.* bike

bicicleta bicycle; **andar en bicicleta** to ride a bicycle; **pasear en bicicleta** to ride a bicycle (10)

bien *adv.* well (1); **caerle bien a alguien** to make a good impression on someone; **empleo bien pagado** well-paid job/position (17); **está bien** it's fine, OK (6); **estar bien** to be well; to be comfortable (*temperature*) (6); **llevarse bien (con)** to get along well (with) (16); **muy bien** fine, very well (1);

pasarlo bien to have a good time (9); **portarse bien** to behave (9); **salir bien** to come/turn out well (5); to do well (5)

bienes raíces *m. pl.* real estate

bienestar *m.* well-being (11)

bienvenida *n.* welcome

bienvenido/a *adj.* welcome

bife *m.* beef

bilingüe bilingual

billete *m.* bill (*money*) (17); ticket (*Sp.*) (8); **billete de ida** one-way ticket (8); **billete de ida y vuelta** round-trip ticket (8); **billete electrónico** e-ticket (8)

binacional binational

biodiversidad *f.* biodiversity

biografía biography

biología biology

bioluminiscencia bioluminescence

bioquímica biochemistry

bisabuelo/a great-grandfather/ great-grandmother

bisiesto/a: año bisiesto leap year

bisonte *m.* bison

bistec *m.* steak (7)

blanco/a white (4); **pizarrón** (*m.*) **blanco** whiteboard (2); **vino blanco** white wine (7)

blando/a soft

blog *m.* blog (12)

bloqueador (*m.*) **solar** sunscreen (8)

bloqueo de llamadas call blocker

bluejeans *m. pl.* jeans

blusa blouse (4)

boca mouth (11)

bocadillo sandwich (*Sp.*)

bochinche: armar un bochinche to throw a (loud) party

bocina horn (*car*) (15)

boda wedding (*ceremony*) (16)

bodega grocery store (*Carib.*)

bogotano/a *adj.* from Bogotá, Colombia

bola ball

bolero love song

boleto ticket (*L.A.*) (8); **boleto de ida** one-way ticket (8); **boleto de ida y vuelta** round-trip ticket; **boleto electrónico** e-ticket (8)

bolígrafo pen (2)

bolívar *m. Venezuelan currency unit*

boliviano/a *n., adj.* Bolivian

bolso purse (4)

bomba bomb (18)

bombardeo bombing

bombero/a firefighter

bombilla light bulb

bombo legüero Argentine drum

bonanza boom (*economic*)

bongó bongo

bonito/a pretty (3)

boricua *n., adj.* Puerto Rican

Borinquen *indigenous name of Puerto Rico*

borinqueño/a *adj.* Puerto Rican

borrador *m.* draft

borrasca storm

bosque *m.* forest (15); **bosque tropical lluvioso** tropical rain forest

bostezo yawn

botanas *f. pl.* (*Mex.*) appetizers (9)

botanía botany

botánico/a botanical

botar to throw out

botas *f. pl.* boots (4)

botella bottle

botón *m.* button

boxeador(a) boxer

brasileño/a *n., adj.* Brazilian

brazo arm (11)

brecha gap; **brecha digital** digital gap; **brecha salarial** wage gap

Bretaña: Gran Bretaña Great Britain

breve brief

británico/a British

bronce *m.* bronze

broncear to tan

bruja witch

brujo wizard; warlock

bruto/a: producto nacional bruto gross national product

bucear to scuba dive; to snorkel

budismo Buddhism

budista *n., adj. m., f.* Buddhist

buen, bueno/a good (3); **¡buen provecho!** enjoy your meal! **buenas noches** good night (1); **buenas tardes** good afternoon (1); **buenos días** good morning (1); **lo bueno** the good news/thing (11); **muy buenas** good afternoon/evening (1); **tener buena suerte** to have good luck; to be lucky (14)

buey *sl.* dude (*Mex.*)

bufanda scarf

burlarse de to make fun of

buscar (qu) to look for (2); **buscar en internet** to look for on the internet (12)

búsqueda search

buzón (*m.*) **de voz** voice mailbox (12)

C

caballero knight; **caballero andante** knight-errant

caballo horse (10); **montar a caballo** to ride a horse (10)

caber to fit (*into an area*)

cabeza head (11); **dolor** (*m.*) **de cabeza** headache

cabina cabin (*on a ship*) (8)

cacerola casserole dish

cacique, cacica chief

cada *inv.* each, every (5); **cada vez más** increasingly; **cada vez mayor** greater and greater

cadena chain

caer to fall; to drop (14); **caer en** to fall on (*day of the week*); **caerle bien/ mal a alguien** to make a good/bad impression on someone; **caerse** to fall down (14); **se le cae la baba por** he/she is drooling over

café *m.* coffee (2)

cafeína caffeine

cafetal *m.* coffee plantation

cafetera coffeemaker (10)

cafetería cafeteria (2)

cafetero coffee plantation worker

caída fall (*from a height*)

caimán *m.* alligator

caja box

cajero/a cashier; teller (17); **cajero automático** automatic teller machine (ATM) (17)

cajón *m.* drawer

calabaza pumpkin; squash

calabozo prison cell

calamar *m.* squid

calcetines *m. pl.* socks (4)

calculadora calculator (2)

calcular to calculate

cálculo calculus

calefacción *f.* heating (12)

calendario calendar (14)

calentador(a) *adj.* warming

calentar (caliento) to warm

calidad *f.* quality (*excellence*)

cálido/a hot

caliente hot (*temperature*) (7)

calificación *f.* grade

caligrafía calligraphy; handwriting

callar to silence

calle *f.* street (12)

callejero/a *adj.* (of the) street

calma calm

calmarse to calm down

calor *m.* heat; **hacer (mucho) calor** to be very hot (6); **tener (mucho) calor** to be (very) warm, hot (6)

caloría calorie

caluroso/a hot

cama bed (5); **guardar cama** to stay in bed (11); **hacer la cama** to make the bed (10); **tender (tiendo) la cama** to make the bed

cámara camera (12)

camarero/a waiter/waitress (7)

camarones *m. pl.* shrimp (7)

cambiar (de) to change (12)

cambio change; **cambio climático** climate change

camélidos *m. pl.* (*zool.*) Camelidae

camello camel

caminadora treadmill (11)

caminar to walk (10)

caminata: dar una caminata to hike; to go for a hike (10)

caminero/a: furia caminera road rage

camino road; path

camión *m.* truck

camioneta station wagon (8); van (8)

camisa shirt (4)

camiseta T-shirt (4)

campamento campsite

campaña campaign; **tienda de campaña** tent (8)

campeón, campeona champion

campeonato championship

campesino/a peasant (15)

camping *m.* campground (8); **hacer camping** to go camping (8)

campo field; countryside (15)

Canadá Canada; **Día** (*m.*) **del Canadá** Canada Day

canadiense *n., adj. m., f.* Canadian

canal *m.* channel (12); canal (7)

canario canary

cancelar to cancel

cáncer *m.* cancer

cancha field; court (*tennis*)

canción *f.* song (7)

candidato/a candidate (18); **postularse (para un cargo) como candidato/a** to run (for a position) as a candidate (18)

cansado/a tired (6)

cansancio fatigue

cansarse to get tired (11)

cantante *m., f.* singer (13)

cantaor(a) flamenco singer

cantar to sing (2)

cantautor(a) singer, songwriter

cantidad *f.* quantity

cantinero/a bartender

caña sugar cane

cañonazo cannon shot

capa layer (15); **capa de ozono** ozone layer (15)

capacidad *f.* capacity

capaz (*pl.* **capaces**) able

Caperucita Roja Little Red Ridinghood

capilla chapel

capital *f.* capital city (6)

capitán, capitana captain

capítulo chapter

Capricornio Capricorn

cara face

caracola large shell

característica *n.* characteristic

característico/a *adj.* characteristic

caracterizar (c) to characterize

caramañola *torpedo-shaped meat pie of Colombia and Panama*

cárcel *f.* jail

cardinal: punto cardinal cardinal point (6)

cardiólogo cardiologist

carga load; **carga de trabajo** workload

cargar (gu) a una cuenta to charge to an account (17)

cargo (political) office (18); **postularse para un cargo (como candidato/a)** to run for a position (as a candidate) (18)

Caribe *m.* Caribbean; **mar** (*m.*) **Caribe** Caribbean Sea

caribeño/a Caribbean

caricatura caricature

cariño affection (16)

cariñoso/a affectionate (6)

carnaval *m.* carnival

carne *f.* meat (7)

carnet (*m.*) **de identificación / de identidad** identification card

carnicería butcher's shop

caro/a expensive (4)

carpa tent

carpeta folder (12)

carpintero/a carpenter

carrera career

carreta cart, wagon

carretera highway (15)

carretilla wheelbarrow

carril *m.* lane

carro (descapotable) (convertible) car (15)

carta letter (3); card; **jugar (juego) (gu) a las cartas** to play cards (10)

cartera wallet; handbag (4)

cartón *m.* cardboard

casa house, home (3); **amo/a** (*but el ama*) **de casa** housekeeper (17) **casa natal** house where someone was born; **en casa** at home (2); **limpiar la casa** to clean (the) house (10); **regresar a casa** to go home (2)

casabe *m. tortilla-type bread made of cassava*

casado/a married; **estar casado/a (con)** to be married (to) (16); **recién casado/a (con)** newlywed (to) (16); **ser casado/a** to be a married person (16)

casarse (con) to marry (16)

cascanueces *m. inv.* nutcracker

caserío hamlet; farmhouse

casero/a home-made

casi *adv.* almost (3); **casi nunca** almost never (3)

caso case; **en caso de (que)** in case (16)

castaño/a brown (chestnut-colored)

castañuelas *f. pl.* castinets

castellano Spanish (language)

castigar (gu) to punish

cata (de vino) (wine) tasting

catalán *m.* Catalan (*language*); **catalán, catalana** *adj.* Catalan

catálogo catalogue

Cataluña Catalonia

catarata waterfall

catarro cold (*health condition*)

catedral *f.* cathedral

categoría category

catolicismo Catholicism

católico/a *n., adj.* Catholic

catorce fourteen (1)

caucásico/a Caucasian

causa cause; **a causa de** because of

causar to cause

cava cellar

cazador(a) hunter

cazar (c) to hunt

CD *m.* CD (compact disc) (12)

CD-ROM *m.* CD-ROM (12)

cebolla onion (7)

cédula identity card

celda cell (*prison*)

celebración *f.* celebration

celebrar to celebrate (6)

celíaco/a gluten intolerant

celos *m. pl.* jealousy

celta *n., adj. m., f.* Celtic

celular: (teléfono) celular *m.* cell phone (2)

cementerio cemetery

cena dinner, supper (7)

cenar to have (eat) dinner, supper (7)

Cenicienta Cinderella

centavo cent

centígrado Celsius

céntrico/a central

centro center (*political*) (18); downtown (4); **centro comercial** shopping mall (4)

Centroamérica Central America

centroamericano/a Central American

cepillarse los dientes to brush one's teeth (5)

cerámica pottery; ceramics (13)

cerca *adv.* near, nearby, close; **cerca de** close to (6)

cercano/a *adj.* close, near

cerdo pork; **chuleta de cerdo** pork chop (7)

cereal *m.* cereal (7)

cerebro brain (11)

ceremonia ceremony

cero zero (1)

cerrado/a closed (6)

cerrar (cierro) to close (5); **cerrarse** to close; to finish

cerro hill

certeza certainty

cerveza beer (7)

cesárea C-section

césped *m.* lawn; grass

cesto basket

ceviche *m. raw fish dish*

champán *m.* champagne (9)

champiñones *m. pl.* mushrooms (7)

chanclas *f. pl.* flip-flops (4)

chaqueta jacket (4)

charango *stringed instrument*

charco puddle

charlar to chat

chatear to chat

chateo *n.* chat (12)

chauchas *f. pl.* green beans (*Arg.*)

cheque *m.* check (17); **con cheque** by check (17)

chequeo check-up (11)

chévere *sl.* cool

chibcha *n., adj. m., f. indigenous people of the Colombian Andes*

chicha *natural fruit soft drink*

chicle *m.* gum

chico/a guy/girl (4)

chileno/a *n., adj.* Chilean

chino Chinese (*language*)

chino/a *n., adj.* Chinese

chisme *m.* gossip

chiste *m.* joke (8)

chocante shocking

chocar (qu) con/contra to run into, bump against (14)

chocolate *m.* chocolate

chofer *m., f.* driver

choque *m.* collision, crash (18)

chuleta (de cerdo) (pork) chop (7)

churro *strip of fried dough*

cibernauto/a of the internet

ciclismo bicycling (10)

ciclo cycle

ciclón *m.* cyclone

ciego/a blind

cien one hundred (3)

ciencia science (2); **ciencia ficción** science fiction; **ciencias (***f. pl.***) naturales** natural sciences (2); **ciencias (***f. pl.***) políticas** political science (2); **ciencias (***f. pl.***) sociales** social sciences (2)

científico/a scientist

ciento one hundred (4); **ciento dos** one hundred two (4); **ciento noventa y nueve** one hundred ninety-nine (4); **ciento uno** one hundred one (4)

cierto/a true **es cierto que** it's certain that (13)

ciervo deer; stag

cifra figure, number

cigarrillo cigarette

cinco five (1)

cincuenta fifty (3)

cine *m. s.* movies (5); movie theater (5)

cineasta *m., f.* filmmaker

cinematográfico/a *adj.* movie, film

cinta: cinta de andar/correr treadmill; **cinta rodante** treadmill

cinturón *m.* belt (4)

circulación *f.* traffic (15)

circular to circulate

círculo circle

circunstancia circumstance

cirugía surgery

cisne *m.* swan

cita date; appointment (11)

citar to cite, quote

ciudad *f.* city (3)

ciudadano/a citizen (18)

cívico/a civic; **responsabilidad** (*f.*) **cívica** civic duty (18)

civil civil; **guerra civil** civil war

civilización *f.* civilization

clarificar (qu) to clarify

claro/a clear

clase *f.* class (*of students*) (2); class, course (*academic*) (2); **compañero/a (de clase)** classmate (2); **dar clases** to teach class; **salón** (*m.*) **de clase** classroom (2)

clásico/a classic(al) (13)

clasificar (qu) to classify

cláusula *gram.* clause

clave *f. n., adj.* key

clic: hacer clic to click (12)

clicar (qu) to click

cliente/a client (2)

clima *m.* climate (6)

climático/a *adj.* climate; **cambio climático** climate change

clínica clinic

cliquear to click

clóset *m.* closet

coalición *f.* coalition

cobrar to cash (*a check*) (17); to charge (*someone for an item or service*) (17)

cobre *m.* copper

coche *m.* car (3); **agencia de compra-venta (de coches)** used car dealership

cochera garage; carport

cochinilla cochineal

cocido/a *adj.* cooked

cocina kitchen (5); cuisine (7)

cocinar to cook (7)

cocinero/a cook; chef (17)
coco coconut
cocodrilo crocodile
cóctel *m.* cocktail party
codiciado/a coveted
código code
codirector(a) codirector
codo elbow
coexistir to coexist
coger (cojo) to take (*things*) (*Sp.*)
cognado *gram.* cognate
coherente coherent
cohesión *f.* cohesion
coincidencia coincidence
coincidir to coincide
cola line (*of people*) (8); **hacer cola** to stand in line (8)
colaborar to collaborate
colección *f.* collection
coleccionar to collect
colectivo bus
colega *m., f.* colleague
colegio school
colérico/a furious
colesterol *m.* cholesterol
coletilla tag (*as in tag question*)
colgar (cuelgo) (gu) to post (*on the internet*)
colina hill
collar *m.* necklace
colmado small grocery store (*Carib.*)
colocar (qu) to place
colombiano/a Colombian
colonia colony
colonización *f.* colonization
colonizador(a) colonist
colonizar (c) to colonize
colono/a settler
coloquial colloquial
color *m.* color (4)
colorado/a red-colored
colorido/a colorful
columna column
comadre *f.* godmother
combatir to combat
combinación *f.* combination
combinar to combine
comedia comedy (13)
comediante *m., f.* comedian
comedor *m.* dining room (5)
comentar to talk about
comentario comment
comentarista *m., f.* commentator
comenzar (comienzo) (c) to begin; **comenzar a** + *inf.* to begin to + *inf.*
comer to eat (3); **comerse** to eat up
comercial: centro comercial shopping mall (4)
comercio business, commerce; **libre comercio** free trade

comestibles *m. pl.* groceries, foodstuff (7)
cometa *m.* comet
cometer to commit
cómico/a funny; **tira cómica** comic strip
comida food (7); meal (7); **comida rápida** fast food
comienzo beginning
comillas *f. pl.* quotation marks
como like; as; **así como** as well as; **tan... como** as . . . as (6); **tanto como** as much as (6)
¿cómo? how?; what? (1); **¿cómo es usted?** what are you (*form. s.*) like? (1); **¿cómo está?** how are you (*form. s.*)? (1); **¿cómo estás?** how are you (*fam. s.*)? (1); **¿cómo se llama usted?** what is your (*form. s.*) name? (1); **¿cómo se llega a... ?** how do you get to . . . ? (15); **¿cómo te llamas?** what is your (*fam. s.*) name? (1)
cómoda bureau; dresser (5)
comodidad *f.* convenience
cómodo/a comfortable (4)
compacto/a: disco compacto (**CD** *m.*) compact disc (CD) (12)
compadre *m.* godfather
compañero/a companion; friend; **compañero/a (de clase)** classmate (2); **compañero/a de cuarto** roommate (2)
compañía company
comparación *f.* comparison (6)
comparar to compare
comparativo/a comparative
compartir to share
compasión *f.* compassion
compensar to make up for
competencia competition
competente competent
competición *f.* competition
competitivo/a competitive
complejo/a complex
complemento (in)directo *gram.* (in)direct object
completar to complete
completo/a complete; **trabajo de tiempo completo** full-time job (14)
complicación *f.* complication
componer (*like* **poner**) to compose (13)
comportamiento behavior
composición *f.* composition
compositor(a) composer (13)
compostero composter
comprador(a) buyer
comprar to buy (2)
compras: de compras shopping (4); **ir de compras** to go shopping (4)
compra-venta: agencia de compra-venta (de coches) used car dealership

comprender to understand (3)
comprensible understandable
comprensión *f.* understanding; comprehension
comprensivo/a *adj.* understanding
comprobar (compruebo) to prove
comprometido/a committed
compuesto/a composed; compound (*gram.*)
compulsivo/a compulsive
computación *f.* computer science (2)
computadora computer (2); **computadora portátil** laptop (computer) (2)
común common
comunicación *f.* communication; *pl.* communication (*subject*) (2); **medio de comunicación** medium of communication (18)
comunicarse (qu) to communicate
comunicativo/a communicative
comunidad *f.* community
comunión *f.* communion
comunitario/a *adj.* community
con with (2); **chocar (qu) con** to run into, bump against (14); **comunicarse (qu) (con)** to communicate (with) (18); **con base en** based on; **con cheque** by check (17); **con cuidado** carefully; **con frecuencia** frequently (2); **con permiso** excuse me (1); **¿con qué frecuencia... ?** how often . . . ? (3); **con respecto a** regarding; **con tal de** *prep.* provided (16); **con tal (de) que** *conj.* provided (that) (16); **darse con** to run into; **pegarse (gu) con** to run/bump into (14)
conceder to concede
concentración *f.* concentration
concentrar to concentrate
concepto concept
conciencia conscience
concienciación *f. n.* conscious-raising
concierto concert (10); **ir a un concierto** to go to a concert (10)
conciso/a concise
conclusión *f.* conclusion
concordancia *gram.* agreement
concreto: en concreto in particular
concursante *m., f.* contestant
concurso contest
condenado/a condemned
condición *f.* condition
condicional *gram.* conditional
cóndor *m.* condor
conducción *f.* driving
conducir (conduzco) to drive (15); **licencia de conducir** driver's license (15)
conductor(a) driver (15)

conectar to connect; **conectarse** to connect (12)

conector *m.* connector

conejo/a rabbit

conexión *f.* connection

conferencia lecture

confesional confessional

confianza confidence

confiar (confío) to trust

configurar to configure

confirmar to confirm

conflicto conflict

confluencia *n.* coming-together

confundido/a confused

congelado/a frozen; very cold (6)

congelador *m.* freezer (10)

congestión *f.* congestion

congresista *m., f.* member of congress

congreso congress; **representante** (*m., f.*) **al congreso** Congressional representative (18)

conjugación *f. gram.* conjugation

conjugar (gu) *gram.* to conjugate

conjunción *f. gram.* conjunction (16); **conjunción de tiempo** conjunction of time (17)

conjunto group

conllevar to involve

conmemorar to commemorate

conmigo with me (6)

Cono Sur Southern Cone

conocer (conozco) to know, be acquainted, familiar with (7); to meet (7); **conocerse** to meet (16)

conocimiento knowledge

conquista conquest

conquistador(a) conqueror

consciente conscious, aware

consecuencia consequence

consecutivo/a consecutive

conseguir (*like* **seguir**) to get; to obtain (9); **conseguir** + *inf.* to succeed in (*doing something*) (9)

consejero/a advisor (2)

consejo (piece of) advice (7)

conservación *f.* conservation

conservacionista conservationist

conservador(a) conservative

conservar to save; to conserve (15)

consideración *f.* consideration

considerar to consider

consigo with himself, herself, themselves

consiguiente: por consiguiente as a result

consistencia consistency

consistir (en) to consist (of)

constante constant

constar (de) to consist of

constatar to confirm

constipado/a: estar constipado/a to have a cold

constitución *f.* constitution

constituir (*like* **construir**) to constitute

construcción *f.* construction

construir (construyo) to build (15)

consuelo consolation

consulta consultation

consultar to consult

consultorio (medical) office (11); consultation

consumidor(a) consumer

consumir to consume

consumo consumption

contabilidad *f.* accounting

contable *m., f.* accountant (*Sp.*)

contacto contact; **lentes** (*m. pl.*) **de contacto** contact lenses (11); **mantenerse** (*like* **tener**) **en contacto** to stay in touch

contador(a) accountant (17)

contaminación *f.* pollution (6)

contaminado/a contaminated, polluted (15)

contaminar to pollute (15)

contar (cuento) to tell; to narrate (8)

contemplación *f.* contemplation

contemplar to contemplate

contemporáneo/a contemporary

contenedor *m.* container

contener (*like* **tener**) to contain

contenido contents

contento/a content, happy (6)

contestar to answer (7)

contexto context

contigo with you (*fam.*) (6)

continente *m.* continent

contingencia contingency

continuación: a continuación following

continuar (continúo) to continue (6)

contra against; **chocar (qu)/pegarse (gu) contra** to run into; to bump against (14); **darse contra** to run into

contrabajo double bass (*musical instrument*)

contradecir (*like* **decir**) to contradict

contraer (*like* **traer**) to contract

contrario contrary

contrarrestar to resist

contraseña password (12)

contrastar to contrast

contraste *m.* contrast

contrastivo/a contrasting

contribución *f.* contribution

contribuir (*like* **construir**) to contribute

control *m.* control; **control de seguridad** security (check) (8); **control remoto** remote control (12); **pasar por el control de seguridad** to go/pass through security (check) (8)

controlador(a) controller

controlar to control

convencer (convenzo) to convince

convención *f.* convention; system

conversación *f.* conversation

conversar to converse

convertir (convierto) (i) to convert

convivencia cohabitation; living together

convivir to live together

coordinar to coordinate

copa (wine) glass; **Copa del Mundo** World Cup (*soccer*); **Copa Mundial** World Cup (*soccer*)

copia copy; **hacer copia** to copy

copiar to copy (12)

copioso/a copious

coquí *m. small frog of Puerto Rico*

corazón *m.* heart (11)

corbata tie (4)

cordillera mountain range

coreano/a *n., adj.* Korean

cormorán cormorant (*aquatic bird*)

coro chorus

corona crown

corporación *f.* corporation

correcto/a correct

corregir (corrijo) (i) to correct

correo mail

correo electrónico e-mail (12)

correr to run (10); **cinta de correr** treadmill

correspondencia correspondence

corresponder (a) to correspond (to)

correspondiente *m., f.* correspondent; *adj.* corresponding

corrido *Mexican folk song*

corriente: cuenta corriente checking account; **estar al corriente** to be up to date

cortar to cut

cortejo courting

cortés *m., f.* polite

cortesía courtesy; **expresión** (*f.*) **de cortesía** courteous expression (1)

cortijo country house

cortina curtain

corto *n.* short segment

corto/a short (*in length*) (3); **pantalones** (*m. pl.*) **cortos** shorts (4)

cosa thing (5)

cosecha harvest; crop

cosechar to harvest

cosmético/a cosmetic

cosmopolita *m., f.* cosmopolitan

cosmovisión *f.* world view

costa coast

costar (cuesto) to cost

costarricense *n., adj. m., f.* Costa Rican

costero/a coastal

costo cost

costoso/a expensive

costumbre *f.* custom

costura: de alta costura high fashion

cotidiano/a daily

country *m.* country music

creación *f.* creation

crear to create (13)
creatividad *f.* creativity
creativo/a creative
crecer (crezco) to grow (16)
crecimiento *n.* rise, growth
credencial *f.* identity card
crédito credit; **tarjeta de crédito** credit card (7)
creencia belief
creer (en) to think; to believe (in) (3); **no creer** to not think/believe (13)
creíble believable
crema cream
cremoso/a creamy
creyente *m., f.* believer
criado/a servant
criatura child
crimen *m.* (*pl.* **crímenes**) crime
criollo/a *n., adj.* creole
cristal *m.* glass
cristianismo Christianity
cristiano/a *n., adj.* Christian
Cristo Christ; **antes de Cristo (a.C.)** before Christ (B.C.); **después de Cristo (a.D.)** Anno Domini (A.D.)
crítica criticism
criticar (qu) to criticize
crítico/a critic
crónica chronicle
crónico/a chronic
cronológico/a chronological
croqueta croquette
crucero cruise (ship) (8)
crudo/a raw
cruz *f.* (*pl.* **cruces**) cross; **Día** (*m.*) **de la Cruz** Day of the Cross
cruzar (c) to cross; **cruzarse con** to cross paths with
cuaderno notebook (2)
cuadrado *n.* square
cuadrado/a *adj.* square
cuadro painting (*specific piece*) (13); **de cuadros** plaid (4)
cuajar to fit in
cual: el/la cual, lo cual, los/las cuales which
¿cuál(es)? what? (2); which? (2); **¿cuál es la fecha de hoy?** what's today's date? (6); **¿cuál es tu onda?** what's your style?
cualidad *f.* quality (*characteristic*)
cualquier *adj.* any
cuando when
¿cuándo? when? (2)
cuanto: en cuanto as soon as (17); **en cuanto a** regarding
¿cuánto? how much? (2); **¿cuánto cuesta(n)?** how much does it (do they) cost? (4); **¿cuánto tiempo hace que... ?** how long ago (*did something happen*)? / for how long (*has something been happening*)?

¿cuántos/as? how many? (2)
cuáquero/a *n.* Quaker
cuarenta forty (3)
Cuaresma Lent
cuartel *m.* barracks
cuarto room (2); one-fourth; quarter (of an hour); **compañero/a de cuarto** roommate (2); **menos cuarto** a quarter to (*hour*) (1); **y cuarto** a quarter (fifteen minutes) after (*the hour*) (1)
cuarto/a *adj.* fourth (13)
cuate *sl. m., f.* buddy, pal
cuatro four (1)
cuatrocientos/as four hundred (4)
cubano/a *n., adj.* Cuban
cubanoamericano/a *n., adj.* Cuban American
cubierto/a (*p.p. of* **cubrir**) covered
cubiertos *m. pl.* cutlery
cubrir (*p.p.* **cubierto**) to cover (15)
cucaracha cockroach
cuchara spoon
cucharada spoonful
cuchillo knife
cuello neck
cuenta check, bill (7); **cargar (gu) a una cuenta** to charge to an account (17); **cuenta corriente** checking account
cuento story
cuerda string
cuero leather (4); **de cuero** leather (4)
cuerpo (humano) (human) body (11)
cuervo crow
cuestión *f.* question (*issue*); matter (17)
cuestionable questionable
cuestionario questionnaire
cuidado care; *interj.* careful!; **con cuidado** carefully; **tener cuidado** to be careful
cuidar a to care for; **cuidarse** to take care of oneself (11)
culebra snake
culinario/a culinary
culminar to culminate
culpa fault; **tener la culpa** to be at fault
cultivar to cultivate
cultivo cultivation
culto cult; **rendir (rindo) (i) culto** to worship
cultrún *m.* ceremonial Mapuche drum
cultura culture
cultural cultural; **tradición** (*f.*) **cultural** cultural tradition (13)
cumbia *Colombian folk dance now popular throughout Latin America*
cumbre *f.* summit
cumpleaños *m. inv.* birthday (6); **pastel** (*m.*) **de cumpleaños** birthday cake (9)
cumplir to fulfill; **cumplir años** to have a birthday (9)

cuñado/a brother-in-law, sister-in-law
cupo quota; capacity (*space*)
cupón *m.* coupon
cura cure
curación *f.* cure
curar to cure
curativo/a curing, curative
curioso/a curious
currículum *m.* résumé (17)
cursi in poor taste; trite
curso course; **programa** (*m.*) **del curso** course syllabus (14)
cuyo/a whose

D

dama lady
danza dance (13)
daño: hacerse daño to hurt oneself (14); **hacerse daño en** to hurt one's (*body part*) (14)
dar to give (8); **dar clases** to teach class; **dar un paseo** to take a walk (10); **dar una caminata** to hike; to go for a hike (10); **dar una fiesta** to throw a party (9); **darse con/contra** to run into; **darse la mano** to shake hands (11)
darwinista *m., f.* Darwinian
datar to date back to
datos *m. pl.* data; **base** (*f.*) **de datos** data base
de of (1); from (1); **de adolescente** *adj.* adolescent (10) **de algodón** *m.* (*made of*) cotton (4); **de alta costura** high fashion; **de alto riesgo** high risk; **de atrás** backwards; **de compras** shopping (4); **de cuadros** plaid (4); **de cuero** leather (4); **¿de dónde eres (tú)?** where are you (*fam. s.*) from? (1); **¿de dónde es usted?** where are you (*form. s.*) from? (1); **de estatura mediana** of medium height; **de exposición** expository; **de forma presencial** in person; **de la actualidad** currently, right now (10); **de la mañana** in the morning, A.M. (1); **de la noche** in the evening, P.M. (1); **de la tarde** in the afternoon, P.M. (1); **de lana** wool (4); **de lunares** polka-dot (4); **de manera que** so that, in such a way that; **de modo que** in such a way that; **de nada** you're welcome (1); **de niño/a** as a child (10); **de oro** gold (4); **de plata** silver (4); **¿de quién?** whose? (3); **de rayas** striped (4); **de remate** hopeless(ly); **de repente** suddenly (11); **de seda** silk (4); **de todo** everything (4); **de todo tipo** of all kinds; **de vacaciones** on vacation (8); **¿de veras?** really?; **de viaje** on a trip, traveling (8); **es de...** it is made of . . . (4)

debajo de below (6)

debate *m.* debate

debatir to debate

deber *n. m.* responsibility (18); obligation (18)

deber *v. + inf.* should, must, ought to (*do something*) (3)

debido/a a due to; because of

débito debit

década decade

decadencia decadence

decente decent

decidir to decide

décimo/a tenth (13)

decimotercer(o/a) thirteenth

decir to say; to tell (8); **eso quiere decir...** that means . . . (11)

decisión *f.* decision

declaración *f.* statement

declarar to state

decoración *f.* decoration

decorar to decorate

decorativo/a decorative

dedicarse (qu) (a) to dedicate oneself (to)

dedo (de la mano) finger (11); **dedo del pie** toe (11)

deducir (deduzco) (*like* **conducir**) to deduce

defender (defiendo) to defend

defensa defense

defensor(a) defender

deficiencia deficiency

deficiente deficient

definición *f.* definition

definido: artículo definido *gram.* definite article

definir to define

degustar to taste

dejar to leave; to let, allow; to quit (17); **dejar de** + *inf.* to stop (*doing something*) (11)

del (*contraction of* **de** + **el**) of the; from the (3)

delante de in front of (6)

delegación *f.* delegation

delfín *m.* dolphin

delgado/a thin, slender (3)

deliberado/a deliberate

delicia delicacy

delicioso/a delicious

delito crime (15)

demanda demand

demás: los/las demás the rest, others (12)

demasiado *adv.* too (9)

demasiado/a *adj.* too much (9); too many (9)

democracia democracy

demócrata *m., f.* democrat

democrático/a democratic

demonio demon, devil

demora delay (8)

demostración *f.* demonstration

demostrar (demuestro) to demonstrate

demostrativo/a *gram.* demonstrative (4)

denominación *f.* denomination

densidad *f.* density

denso/a dense (15)

dentista *m., f.* dentist (11)

dentro inside; **dentro de** inside; within; in (*time*)

departamento department

dependencia dependence

depender (de) to depend (on)

dependiente/a clerk (2)

deporte *m.* sport (10); **practicar (qu)** to play (*a sport*)

deportista *m., f.* athlete

deportivo/a *adj.* sporting, sports; sports-loving (10)

depositar to deposit (17)

depósito deposit

depresión *f.* depression

deprimido/a depressed

derecha *n.* right side; **a la derecha de** to the right of (6)

derecho right (18); **(todo) derecho** straight ahead (15)

derivación *f.* branch, offshoot

derivarse (de) to derive (from)

derramar to spill

desacuerdo disagreement

desafío challenge

desagradable disagreeable

desahogarse (gu) to let off steam; to vent

desamor *m.* lack of affection

desaparecer (desaparezco) to disappear

desarrollar to develop (15)

desarrollo development (15)

desastre *m.* disaster (14)

desastroso/a disastrous

desayunar to have (eat) breakfast (7)

desayuno breakfast (7)

descansar to rest (5)

descanso rest

descapotable: carro descapotable convertible (car) (15)

descargar (gu) to download (12)

descendiente *m., f.* descendent

descentralizado/a decentralized

descifrar to decipher; to figure out

desconectar to unplug; to disconnect

desconocido/a unknown

descontento/a unhappy

descortés *m., f.* rude, impolite

describir (*p.p.* **descrito**) to describe

descripción *f.* description

descriptivo/a descriptive

descrito/a (*p.p. of* **describir**) described

descubierto/a (*p.p. of* **descubrir**) discovered

descubrimiento discovery

descubrir (*p.p.* **descubierto**) to discover (15)

desde *prep.* from; since

desear to want (2)

desempleo unemployment

deseo wish

desequilibrio imbalance

desértico/a *adj.* desert

desesperanza desperation

desfile *m.* parade

desgracia misfortune; disgrace

desgraciadamente unfortunately (11)

deshumanización *f.* dehumanization

desierto desert

designación *f.* designation

designar to appoint; to designate

desigualdad *f.* inequality (18)

desilusión *f.* disillusion

desinflado/a: llanta desinflada flat tire (15)

desocupado/a empty; available

desordenado/a messy (6)

desorganizado/a unorganized

despacio *adv.* slowly

despedida farewell

despedir (*like* **pedir**) to let (someone) go (17); to fire (someone) (from a job) (17); **despedirse (de)** to say good-bye (to) (9)

despejado/a clear (sky)

desperdiciar to waste

desperdicio waste

despertador *m.* alarm clock (14)

despertarse (me despierto) to wake up (5)

despierto/a (*p.p. of* **despertar**) awake

despistado/a absent-minded; forgetful

después *adv.* afterwards (5); **después de** *prep.* after (5); **después de Cristo (a.D.)** Anno Domini (A.D.); **después (de) que** *conj.* after (17)

destacar (qu) to emphasize; **destacarse** to stand out

destino destination (8); destiny

destrucción *f.* destruction

destruir (*like* **construir**) to destroy (15)

desventaja disadvantage

detalle *m.* detail (9)

detective *m., f.* detective

detenerse (*like* **tener**) to stop

determinación *f.* determination

determinado/a specific

determinante decisive

determinar to determine

detestar to detest

detrás de behind (6)

deuda debt

devolver (*like* **volver**) to return (something to someone) (14)

devoto/a devout

día *m.* day (2); **buenos días** good morning (1); **Día de Acción de**

Gracias Thanksgiving; **Día de la Cruz** Day of the Cross; **Día de la Madre** Mother's Day; **Día de los Difuntos** Day of the Dead; **Día de los Muertos** Day of the Dead; **Día de San Patricio** St. Patrick's Day; **Día de San Valentín** St. Valentine's Day; **Día del Padre** Father's Day; **día festivo** holiday (9); **Día Internacional de la No Violencia Contra la Mujer** International No Violence Against Women Day; **días de la semana** days of the week (5); **estar al día** to be up to date (18); **¿qué día es hoy?** what day is today? (5); **todos los días** every day (2)

diabetes *f. inv.* **(juvenil)** (childhood) diabetes

diabético/a diabetic

diablo devil

diacrítico/a: acento diacrítico diacritical mark

diagnosticar (qu) to diagnose

diágrafo group of letters that represent a single sound

dialecto dialect

diálogo dialogue

diamante *m.* diamond

diariamente daily

diario/a daily (5)

dibujante *m., f.* comic strip artist (13)

dibujar to draw (13)

dibujo drawing (13); **dibujos** (*m. pl.*) **animados** cartoons

diccionario dictionary (2)

dicho saying

diciembre *m.* December (6)

dictador(a) dictator (18)

dictadura dictatorship (18)

dictar to dictate

diecinueve nineteen (1)

dieciocho eighteen (1)

dieciséis sixteen (1)

diecisiete seventeen (1)

diente *m.* tooth (5); **cepillarse los dientes** to brush one's teeth (5)

dieta dieta (7); **estar a dieta** to be on a diet (7)

dietético/a *adj.* diet

diez ten (1)

diferencia difference; **a diferencia de** unlike

diferenciado/a differentiated

diferente different

difícil hard, difficult (6)

dificultad *f.* difficulty

difundir to disseminate

difunto/a dead; **Día** (*m.*) **de los Difuntos** Day of the Dead

digestión *f.* digestion

digital digital; **brecha digital** digital gap

dígito digit

dignidad *f.* dignity

dilema *m.* dilemma

diligente diligent

dimensión *f.* dimension

diminutivo *gram. n.* diminutive

Dinamarca Denmark

dinero money (2); **sacar (qu) dinero** to withdraw money

dinoflagelado *type of marine plankton*

dios *m. s.* god; **Dios** God; **por Dios** for heaven's sake (14)

diosa goddess

diptongo *gram.* diphthong

dirección *f.* address (7)

directo direct; **complemento directo** *gram.* direct object

director(a) director; conductor (13)

directorio directory

dirigir (dirijo) to direct (13) (pido) (i)

discapacidad *f.* disability

discapacitado/a disabled

disco disc; **disco duro** hard drive (12)

discoteca discotheque; **ir a una discoteca** to go to a disco (10)

discriminación *f.* discrimination (18)

disculpa apology, excuse; **pedir (pido) (i) disculpas** to apologize (14)

disculpar to excuse, pardon; **disculpa, discúlpame** pardon me (*fam. s.*) (14); I'm sorry (*fam. s.*) (14); **disculpe, discúlpeme** pardon me (*form. s.*) (14); I'm sorry (*form. s.*) (14)

discurso speech

discusión *f.* argument; discussion

discutir (con/sobre) to argue (with/about) (9)

diseñador(a) designer

diseñar to design (13)

diseño design

disfraz *m.* (*pl.* **disfraces**) costume, disguise

disfrutar (de) to enjoy

disminuir (*like* **construir**) to diminish

disparar to shoot

dispensario clinic

disponible available

disposición *f.* disposition

dispositivo device

dispuesto/a ready; prepared (*to do something*)

disputarse to compete for

distancia distance

distante distant

distinción *f.* distinction

distintivo/a distinctive

distinto/a different

distracción *f.* distraction

distraer (*like* **traer**) to distract

distraído/a absentminded; distracted (14); **ir distraído/a** to be distracted (14)

distribuido/a distributed

distrito district

disuadir to dissuade

diversidad *f.* diversity

diversión *f.* fun activity (10)

diverso/a diverse

divertido/a fun; **ser divertido/a** to be fun (10)

divertirse (me divierto) (i) to have a good time; to enjoy oneself (5)

dividirse to be divided

divorciado/a (de) divorced (from) (16)

divorciarse (de) to get divorced (from) (16)

divorcio divorce (16)

divulgar (gu) to divulge

doblar to turn (15)

doble *m.* double

doce twelve (1)

dócil docile

doctor(a) doctor

doctorado doctorate

documento document

dólar *m.* dollar

doler (duele) (*like* **gustar**) to hurt; to ache (11)

dolor (*m.*) **(de)** pain, ache (in) (11); **dolor de cabeza** headache; **tener dolor de** to have a pain/ache in (11)

doméstico/a domestic, related to the home (10); domesticated, tame (15); **animal** (*m.*) **doméstico** pet; **aparato doméstico** home appliance (10); **tarea doméstica** household chore

domicilio home

dominación *f.* domination

dominar to control; to dominate

domingo Sunday (5)

dominicano/a *n., adj.* Dominican

dominio control

don *m. title of respect used with a man's first name*

donar to donate

donde where

¿dónde? where? (1); **¿de dónde eres (tú)?** where are you (*fam. s.*) from? (1); **¿de dónde es usted?** where are you (*form. s.*) from? (1)

doña *title of respect used with a woman's first name*

dormir (duermo) (u) to sleep (5); **dormir la siesta** to take a nap (5); **dormirse** to fall asleep (5)

dormitorio bedroom

dos two (1); **dos veces** twice (11)

doscientos/as two hundred (4)

drama *m.* drama (13)

dramático/a dramatic

dramatizar(c) to dramatize

dramaturgo/a playwright (13)

droga drug

dromedario dromedary

ducha *n.* shower
ducharse to take a shower (5)
duda *n.* doubt
dudar to doubt (12)
dudoso/a doubtful
duelo duel
dueño/a landlord, landlady (12); owner (7)
dulce *adj.* sweet
dulces *m. pl.* sweets; candy (7)
duración *f.* duration
duradero/a lasting
durante during (5)
durar to last (18)
duro/a hard; **disco duro** hard drive (12)
DVD *m.* DVD (12)

E

e and (*used instead of* **y** *before words beginning with stressed* **i** *or* **hi,** *except* **hie-**)
echar to throw out
ecocasa ecological house
ecología ecology
ecológico/a ecological
ecologista *m., f.* ecologist
economía economy; *s.* economics (2)
económico/a economical
economista *m., f.* economist
economizar (c) to economize (17)
ecoturismo ecotourism
ecoturista *m., f.* ecotourist
ecoturístico/a *adj.* ecotourist
ecuador *m.* equator
ecuatoguineano/a of or from Equatorial Guinea
ecuatoriano/a Ecuadoran
edad *f.* age
edificio building (2); **edificio de apartamentos** apartment building (12)
editar to edit
editorial *f.* publishing house
educación *f.* education
educador(a) educator
educarse (qu) to be educated
educativo/a educational
efectivo cash (17); **en efectivo** in cash (17)
efectivo/a effective
efecto effect
efectuar (efectúo) to carry out, execute
eficiencia efficiency
eficiente efficient
Egipto Egypt
egoísmo selfishness
egoísta *m., f.* selfish
ejecutivo/a *n., adj.* executive
ejemplar exemplary
ejemplificar (qu) to exemplify

ejemplo example; **por ejemplo** for example (14)
ejercer (ejerzo) to apply, exercise
ejercicio exercise (5); **hacer ejercicio** to exercise (5); **hacer ejercicios aeróbicos** to do aerobics (11)
ejército army (18)
el *def. art. m. s.* the; **el cual** which; **el lunes (martes...)** on Monday (Tuesday . . .) (5); **el primero de** the first of (*month*) (6); **el próximo (martes...)** next (Tuesday . . .) (5)
él *sub. pron.* he (2)
elaboración *f.* elaboration
elección *f.* choice; *pl.* election
electricidad *f.* electricity (12); electric bill (12)
electricista *m., f.* electrician (17)
eléctrico/a electrical; **energía eléctrica** electrical energy (15)
electrónica electronic equipment
electrónico/a electronic; **billete** (*m.*) (*Sp.*) / **boleto** (*L.A.*) **electrónico** e-ticket (8); **equipo electrónico** electronic equipment (12)
elefante *m.* elephant (15)
elegante elegant
elegir (elijo) (i) to select; to elect
elemento element
elevado/a high
elevador *m.* elevator
elevarse to rise
eliminar to eliminate
ella *sub. pron.* she (2)
ello: por ello therefore
ellos/as *sub. pron.* they (2); *obj. (of prep.)* them (2)
e-mail *m.* e-mail (12)
embarazada pregnant
embargo: sin embargo nevertheless
embarque: puerta de embarque boarding gate (8); **tarjeta de embarque** boarding pass (8)
emberá Embera person
emblema *m.* emblem
emblemático/a emblematic
embotellamiento traffic jam
embutido sausage
emergencia emergency
emigración *f.* emigration
emigrante *m., f.* emigrant
emigrar to emigrate
emisario/a emissary
emitir to emit
emoción *f.* emotion (9)
emocionado/a excited
emocional emotional
emocionante exciting
emocionarse to get excited
emoticono emoticon
empacar (qu) to pack

empanada *turnover pie or pastry*
emparedado sandwich
emparejar to match
empezar (empiezo) (c) to begin, start (5); **empezar a** + *inf.* to begin to (*do something*) (5) 1
empleado/a employee
empleador(a) employer
emplear to use to employ
empleo job, position (17); **empleo bien/mal pagado** well-/poorly paid job/position (17); **empleo de tiempo completo/parcial** full-/part-time job/position (17)
empresa corporation (17); business (17); **administración** (*f.*) **de empresas** business administration (2)
empresario/a businessman/woman
en in (1); on (1); at (*a place*) (1); **en casa** at home (2); **en caso de** *prep.* in case (16); **en caso de que** *conj.* in case (16); **en cuanto** as soon as (17); **en efectivo** in cash (17); **en negrilla** boldface; **en onda** in style; **en punto** on the dot (*time*) (1); **en rebaja** on sale; **en resumen** in summary; **en seguida** immediately (5); **en vez de** instead of
enamorado/a (de) in love (with) (16)
enamorarse (de) to fall in love (with) (16)
enano/a dwarf
encantado/a pleased to meet you (1); enchanted
encantar (*like* **gustar**) to like very much; to love (8)
encanto charm
encapuchado/a hooded
encarcelado/a incarcerated
encargado/a in charge
encender (enciendo) to turn on (*appliance, machine*) (12); to light
encerado blackboard
encima de on top of (6)
encomendarse (me encomiendo) a to commend yourself to
encontrar (encuentro) to find (9); **encontrarse (con)** to meet (*someone somewhere*) (11)
encuentro encounter
encuesta survey
encuestar to survey
endeble unstable
endémico/a endemic
enemigo enemy
energía energy (15); **energía eléctrica** electrical energy (15); **energía eólica** wind energy (15); **energía nuclear** nuclear energy (15); **energía renovable** renewable energy (15); **energía solar** solar energy (15)
enérgico/a energetic

enero January (6)

enfado anger

énfasis *m. inv.* emphasis

enfático/a emphatic

enfatizar (c) to emphasize

enfermarse to get sick (11)

enfermedad *f.* illness, sickness (11)

enfermero/a nurse (11)

enfermo/a sick (6)

enfilado/a in a line

enfocar (qu) to focus

enfoque *m.* focus

enfrentar(se) (a) to face

enfrente de *prep.* in front of (*across from, facing*)

englobar to encompass

engordar to gain weight; to fatten

enhorabuena congratulations

enojado/a angry (9)

enojarse (con) to get angry (with) (9)

enorme enormous

enriquecer (enriquezco) to enrich

ensalada salad (7)

ensayista *m., f.* essayist

ensayar to test

ensayo essay

enseñanza teaching

enseñar to teach (2); **enseñar a** + *inf.* to teach to (*do something*)

ensuciarse to get dirty

entender (entiendo) to understand (5)

enterarse (de) to find out; to learn (about) (18)

entero/a entire

enterrado/a buried

entidad *f.* entity

entonces then (*in that case*)

entrada entrance; ticket (*for a show*)

entrante: año entrante next year

entrañable moving, touching

entrar to enter; **entrar en internet** to go on the internet (12); **entrar en Facebook** to go onto Facebook (12)

entre *prep.* between; among (6)

entregar (gu) to hand in (8)

entrenador(a) trainer, coach

entrenamiento training

entrenar to practice, train (10)

entresemana during the week

entrevista interview (17)

entrevistado/a interviewee (17)

entrevistador(a) interviewer (17)

entrevistar to interview

entusiasmar to enthuse

envase *m.* container

envenenar to poison

enviar (envío) to send

envidia envy

envuelto/a covered

eólico/a: energía eólica wind energy (15)

episodio chapter

epitafio epitaph

época era, time (*period*)

equilibrar to balance

equilibrio balance

equipaje *m.* baggage, luggage (8); **facturar el equipaje** to check baggage (8)

equipar to equip

equipo team (10); equipment (12); **equipo electrónico** electronic equipment (12)

equivalente *m.* equivalent

equivaler (*like* **salir**) to equal

equivocarse (qu) (de) to make a mistake (about) (14)

eructar to burp, belch

erupción *f.* eruption (18)

escala stop (8); **hacer escalas** to make stops (8)

escalador(a) climber

escalar to climb

escalera staircase; *pl.* stairs (14)

escándalo scandal

escanear to scan

escáner *m.* scanner (12)

escapar(se) (de) to escape (from)

escaparate *m.* store (display) window

escaso/a scarce

escena scene (13)

escenario stage (13); scenery (13)

esclavitud *f.* slavery

esclavo/a slave

esclusa lock (*of canal*)

escoba broom

escoger (escojo) to choose; to select

escolar *adj.* school

Escorpión *m.* Scorpio

escribir (*p.p.* **escrito**) to write (3)

escrito/a (*p.p. of* **escribir**) written (14); **informe** (*m.*) **escrito** written report (14)

escritor(a) writer (13)

escritorio desk (2)

escuálido/a scrawny

escuchar to listen (to) (2)

escuela school (10); **escuela primaria** elementary school; **escuela secundaria** high school; **maestro/a de escuela** schoolteacher (17)

esculpir to sculpt

escultor(a) sculptor (13)

escultura sculpture (13)

ese/a *adj.* that (4)

esencia essence

esencial essential

esfuerzo effort

eso (*neuter pron.*) that (4); **eso quiere decir...** that means . . . (11); **por eso** for that reason; that's why (3)

esos/as *adj.* those (4)

espacial *adj.* space; **nave** (*f.*) **espacial** spaceship; **transbordador** (*m.*) **espacial** space shuttle

espacio space; **espacio de almacenamiento** storage space (12)

espacioso/a spacious

espalda back

espantapájaros *m. inv.* scarecrow

espantar to scare

español *m.* Spanish (*language*) (2)

español(a) *n.* Spaniard; *adj.* Spanish (3)

espárragos *m. pl.* asparagus (7)

especial special

especialidad *f.* specialty

especialización *f.* major (*academic*); specialization

especializarse (c) (en) to major (in)

especie *f.* species (15); **especie en peligro de extinción** endangered species (15)

especificar (qu) to specify

específico/a specific

espectacular spectacular

espectáculo show (13)

espectador(a) spectator (13); *pl.* audience (13)

especulación *f.* speculation

espejo mirror

espera wait; **llamada de espera** call-waiting; **sala de espera** waiting room (8)

esperanza hope, wish (18)

esperar to wait (for) (7); to expect (7); to hope (12)

espeso/a thick

espinaca spinach

espíritu *m.* spirit

espiritual spiritual

esplendor *m.* splendor

esposado/a handcuffed

esposo/a husband/wife (3)

esqueleto skeleton

esquema *m.* outline

esquí *m.* skiing (10)

esquiador(a) skier

esquiar (esquío) to ski (10)

esquina (street) corner (15)

esta noche tonight (6)

estabilidad *f.* stability

estable stable

establecer (establezco) to establish

estación *f.* station (8); season (6); **estación de autobuses** bus station (8); **estación de radio** radio station (18); **estación de servicio** gas station (15); **estación de trenes** train station/(8)

estacionamiento parking place/lot (15)

estacionar to park (14)

estadio stadium

estadísticas *f. pl.* statistics

estadístico/a statistical

estado state (3); **estado afectivo** emotional state (9); **estado de ánimo** state of mind; **estado libre asociado** commonwealth; **Estados** (*m. pl.*) **Unidos de América** United States of America

estadounidense *n., adj.* of the United States of America (3)

estancia stay (*in a hotel*)

estante *m.* bookshelf (5)

estar to be (2); **¿cómo está?** how are you (*form. s.*)? (1); **¿cómo estás?** how are you (*fam. s.*)? (1); **está bien** it's fine, OK (6); **está de moda** it's trendy (hot) (4); **está (muy) nublado** it's (very) cloudy, overcast (6); **estar a dieta** to be on a diet (7); **estar al corriente** to be up to date; **estar al día** to be up to date (18); **estar bajo muchas presiones** to be under a lot of pressure (14); **estar bien** to be comfortable (*temperature*) (6); **estar casado/a (con)** to be married (to) (16); **(no) estar de acuerdo** to (dis)agree (3); **estar de vacaciones** to be on vacation (8); **(no) estar seguro/a de** to (not) be sure of (13)

estatal *adj.* state, of the government

estatua statue

estatura height; **de estatura mediana** of medium height

este *m.* east (6)

este/a *adj.* this (3)

estéreo stereo

estereotípico/a stereotypical

estereotipo stereotype

estético/a aesthetic

estilizado/a slender

estilo style

estimar to estimate

estipendio stipend

estipular to stipulate

estirar to stretch

esto (*neuter pron.*) this (3)

estómago stomach (11)

estornudo sneeze

estos/as *adj.* these (3)

estrategia strategy

estrecho *n.* straight; **Estrecho de Magallanes** Strait of Magellan

estrella star

estrépito crashing

estrés *m. inv.* stress (14)

estresado/a stressed out, under stress (14)

estresante stressful

estresar to cause stress

estricto/a strict

estrofa verse (*poem*)

estructura structure

estructurar to structure

estuario estuary

estudiantado student body

estudiante *m., f.* student (2)

estudiantil *adj.* (of) student(s)

estudiar to study (2)

estudio office (*in a home*) (5); studio (*television*) pl. studies (*education*)

estudioso/a studious

estufa stove (5)

estupendo/a stupendous

etapa stage, phase (16)

etcétera etcetera

eterno/a eternal

ético/a ethical

etnia ethnicity

étnico/a ethnic

etnolingüístico/a ethnolinguistic

Europa Europe

europeo/a *n., adj.* European

euskera *m.* Basque (*language*)

evaluación *f.* evaluation

evangélico/a *n., adj.* evangelical

evangelismo evangelism

evento event

evidencia evidence

evidente evident

evitar to avoid (15)

evolución *f.* evolution

exacto/a exact

exagerado/a exaggerated

examen *m.* exam, test (4)

examinar to examine

exceder to exceed

excelencia excellence

excelente excellent

excepción *f.* exception

excepcional exceptional

excepto except

excesivo/a excessive

exceso excess

exclamar to exclaim

excluir (*like* **construir**) to exclude

exclusivo/a exclusive

excursión *f.* excursion

excusa excuse

exigente demanding

exigir (exijo) to demand

exiliarse to go into exile

existencia existence

existir to exist

éxito success; **tener éxito** to be successful

exitoso/a successful

exótico/a exotic

expandir to expand

expectativa expectation

expedición *f.* expedition

experiencia experience

experto/a expert

expiatorio/a expiatory

explicación *f.* explanation

explicar (qu) to explain (8)

exploración *f.* exploration

explorador(a) explorer

explotación *f.* exploitation

explotar to exploit

exponer (*like* **poner**) (*p.p.* **expuesto**) to display; to propose

exportador(a) exporter

exportar to export

exposición *f.* exposition; **de exposición** expository

expresar to express

expresión *f.* expression; **expresión artística** artistic expression (13); **expresión de cortesía** courteous expression (1)

expresionista expressionist

expresivo/a expressive

expulsar to expel

expulsión *f.* expulsion

exquisito/a exquisite

extender (extiendo) to extend

extensión *f.* extension

externo/a external

extinción *f.* extinction; **especie** (*f.*) **en peligro de extinción** endangered species (15)

extinguirse (me extingo) to become extinct

extracto extract

extranjero/a *n.* foreigner (2); *adj.* foreign; **ir al extranjero** to go abroad (8); **lengua extranjera** foreign language (2)

extrañar to miss

extraño/a strange; **es extraño que** it's strange that (13); **¡qué extraño que...!** how strange that . . . ! (13)

extraordinario/a extraordinary

extravagante extravagant

extremo/a extreme

extrovertido/a extrovert(ed)

F

fábrica factory (15)

fabricar (qu) to manufacture (15)

fábula fable

fabuloso/a fabulous

Facebook *m.* Facebook (12); **entrar en Facebook** to go into Facebook (12)

fácil easy (6)

facilidad *f.* ease

facilitar to facilitate

factor *m.* factor

factura bill (17)

facturar el equipaje to check baggage (8)

facultad *f.* (*university*) department

falda skirt (4)

fallar to crash (*computer*) (12)

falso/a false

falta lack (15); absence (15)

faltar (a) to be absent (from); to not attend (9)

fama fame
familia family (3)
familiar *adj.* (of the) family
famoso/a famous
fantasía fantasy
fantasma *m.* ghost
fantástico/a fantastic
farmacéutico/a pharmacist (11)
farmacia pharmacy
faro lighthouse
fascinante fascinating
fascinar (*like* **gustar**) to fascinate (13)
fastidioso/a tedious
fatal *sl.* bad, awful
fatalista *m., f.* fatalist
fauna animal species
fauno faun
favor *m.* favor; **a favor de** in favor of; **por favor** please (1)
favorito/a favorite
fax *m.* FAX (12)
fe *f.* faith
febrero February (6)
fecha date (*calendar*) (6); **¿cuál es la fecha de hoy?** what's today's date? (6); **fecha límite** deadline; **¿qué fecha es hoy?** what's today's date? (6)
federación *f.* federation
federativo/a federative
felicidades *f. pl.* congratulations
felicitaciones *f. pl.* congratulations
felicitar to congratulate
feliz (*pl.* **felices**) happy (9)
femenino/a feminine
fenicio/a Phoenician
fénix *m.* phoenix
fenomenal phenomenal
fenómeno phenomenon
feo/a ugly (3)
feria fair
feriado/a: día (*m.*) **feriado** holiday
fertilidad *f.* fertility
festejar to celebrate
festividad *f.* festival
festivo/a festive, celebratory (9); **día** (*m.*) **festivo** holiday (9)
ficción *f.* fiction; **ciencia ficción** science fiction
ficticio/a fictitious
fiebre *f.* fever (11); **tener fiebre** to have a fever
fiel faithful (3)
fiesta party (2); **dar/hacer una fiesta** to have/give/throw a party (9); **fiesta patronal** party dedicated to a patron saint
fiestero/a happy; fond of parties
figura figure
fijarse (en) to notice
fijo/a set, fixed; **precio fijo** fixed, set price (4); **teléfono fijo** landline (12)

fila line
Filadelfia Philadelphia
filantrópico/a philanthropic
Filipinas *f. pl.* Philippines
filipino/a *n., adj.* Philippine
filmar to film; to record
filosofía philosophy (2)
filosófico/a philosophical
fin *m.* end; **a fines de** at the end of; **fin de año** end of the year (9); **fin de semana** weekend (2); **por fin** finally (5); **sin fines de lucro** non-profit
final *m.* end
finalmente finally (5)
financiar to finance
financiero/a financial
finanzas *f. pl.* finances
finca farm (15)
Finlandia Finland
fino/a fine
firmar to sign
física physics (2)
físico/a physical
flaco/a skinny
flamenco *music and dance form of southern Spain*
flan *m.* (baked) custard (7)
flauta flute
flexibilidad *f.* flexibility
flor *f.* flower (8)
flora plant species
flota fleet
folclore folklore
folclórico/a traditional (13)
folclorista *m., f.* folklorist
folklórico/a traditional
fomentar to encourage; to promote
fondo background; fund; bottom
fontanero/a plumber (*Sp.*)
forma form, shape (4); way; **de forma presencial** in person
formación *f.* formation; education, training
formar to form
formato format
formidable tremendous
fórmula formula
formulario form (17)
fortalecer (fortalezco) to strengthen
fortaleza fort
fosforescente phosphorescent
foto(grafía) photo(graph) (8); **sacar (qu) fotos** to take photos (8)
fotocopia photocopy (12); **hacer fotocopia** to copy (12)
fotocopiadora copy machine (12)
fotocopiar to photocopy
fotografía photography (13)
fotógrafo/a photographer (17)
fotomontaje *m.* photo montage
fragmentado/a fragmented
fragmento fragment; excerpt
francés *m.* French (*language*) (2)

francés, francesa *n.* French person; *adj.* French
Francia France
franja stripe, band; border, fringe
frase *f.* phrase; sentence
fraternidad *f.* fraternity
frecuencia frequency; **con frecuencia** frequently (2); **¿con qué frecuencia... ?** how often . . . ? (3)
frecuente frequent
frecuentemente frequently (11)
frenos *m. pl.* brakes (15)
frente a facing; **hacer frente a** to face up to
fresa strawberry
fresco: hace fresco it's cool (weather) (6)
fresco/a fresh (7)
frigorífico refrigerator
frijoles *m. pl.* beans (7)
frío cold(ness); *adj.* cold; **hace (mucho) frío** it's (very) cold (*weather*); **tener (mucho) frío** to be (very) cold (6)
frito/a fried (7); **papa/patata frita** French fried potato (7)
frituras *f. pl.* fried food
frontera border
frotar to rub
frustración *f.* frustration
frustrado/a frustrated
fruta fruit (7); **jugo de fruta** fruit juice (7)
frutería fruit store, stand
frutilla strawberry
fruto fruit
fuego fire
fuente *f.* source; fountain; serving dish
fuera *adv.* outside
fuerza force; **fuerzas** (*f. pl.*) **armadas** armed forces
fumador(a) smoker; **sala de fumadores** smoking area (8)
fumar to smoke (8); **sala de fumar** smoking area (8)
funcionamiento *n.* functioning, working
funcionar to work; to function (12); to run (*machines*) (12)
fundación *f.* foundation
fundador(a) founder
fundar to found
furia rage; **furia al volante** road rage; **furia caminera** road rage
furioso/a furious, angry (6)
fútbol *m.* soccer (10); **fútbol americano** football (10)
futbolista *m., f.* soccer player
futuro *n.* future
futuro/a *adj.* future

G

gabinete *m.* cabinet
gafas *f. pl.* glasses (4); **gafas de sol** sunglasses (4)

gaita *Colombian indigenous flute*
galán *m.* handsome man
gallego Galician (*language*)
galleta cookie (7)
gallo/a rooster, hen; **Misa del Gallo** Midnight Mass
galope *m. traditional dance of Paraguay*
galopera *traditional dance of Paraguay*
gambas *f. pl.* shrimp (*Sp.*)
ganador(a) winner
ganancia earning
ganar to win (10); to earn (*income*) (13)
ganas: tener ganas de + *inf.* to feel like (*doing something*) (4)
gandules *m. pl.* pigeon peas
ganga bargain (4)
garaje *m.* garage (5)
garantizar (c) to guarantee
garbanzos *m. pl.* chickpeas (7)
garganta throat (11)
garifunas *m. pl.* Black Caribs (*descendents of Carib indigenous people and African slaves in Honduras*)
gas *m.* gas (*not for cars*) (12)
gaseosa soft drink
gasolina gasoline (15)
gasolinera gas station (15)
gastar to spend (*money*) (9); to use (*gas*) (15)
gasto expense (12)
gastronómico/a gastronomic
gato cat (3)
gaucho *Argentine cowboy*
gazpacho *cold tomato soup of southern Spain*
gemelo/a twin
genealógico/a: árbol (*m.*) **genealógico** family tree
generación *f.* generation
general general; **en general** in general; **por lo general** generally (5)
generar to generate; to create
genérico/a generic
género genre; gender
generosidad *f.* generosity
generoso/a generous
gente *f. s.* people (8)
genuinamente genuinely
geografía geography
geográfico/a geographic
geología geology
geométrico/a geometric
gerente *m., f.* manager (17)
gerundio *gram.* gerund
gigante *adj.* giant
gimnasio gym(nasium)
ginecólogo/a gynecologist
gira tour
gitano/a *n., adj.* gypsy
globalización *f.* globalization
gobernador(a) governor

gobierno government (15)
gol *m.* goal (*soccer*)
golf *m.* golf (10)
golfo gulf
golpe *m.* blow; **golpe de estado** coup d'état
gordo/a fat (3)
gorila *m.* gorilla (15)
gorra baseball cap (4)
gótico/a Gothic
GPS *m.* GPS (12)
grabadora (tape) recorder/player
grabar to record (12); to tape (12)
gracia grace
gracias thank you (1); **Día** (*m.*) **de Acción de Gracias** Thanksgiving; **gracias por** + *noun/inf.* thanks for (9); **muchas gracias** thank you very much (1)
grado grade, year (*in school*); degree (*temperature*)
graduarse (me gradúo) (en) to graduate (from) (17)
gráfico/a graphic
grafiti *m.* graffiti
gramática grammar
gramo gram
gran, grande large, big; great (3); **Gran Bretaña** Great Britain; **pantalla grande** big screen (monitor) (12)
granero barn
granizo hail
granja farm
grano grain
grasa fat
gratis *inv.* free (of charge)
gratuito/a free (of charge)
grave serious
Grecia Greece
griego/a *n., adj.* Greek
grifo faucet
gripa flu (*Mex.*)
gripe *f.* flu (11)
gris gray (4)
gritar to shout
grito shout; cry
grueso/a thick
grupo group; band
guagua bus (*Carib.*)
guaguanco *subgenre of rumba*
guampa *cup made from a hollowed bull's horn used to drink mate; cup used to drink* **tereré**
guanábana soursop (*tropical fruit*)
guancasco *traditional dance of the Lenca of Honduras*
guante *m.* glove
guapo/a handsome; good-looking (3)
guaraní *m. indigenous language of South America*
guardacostas *m. inv.* Coast Guard

guardar to keep (12); to save (*documents*) (12); **guardar cama** to stay in bed (11); **guardar un puesto** to save a place (*in line*) (8)
guatemalteco/a *n., adj.* Guatemalan
gubernamental governmental
guerra war (18); **guerra civil** civil war
guerrero/a warrior
guía *m., f.* guide (13)
guiado/a guided
guion *m.* script (13)
güiro *Latin American musical instrument*
guitarra guitar
guitarrista *m., f.* guitarist
gustar to be pleasing (8); **¿a usted le gusta... ?** do you (*form. s.*) like . . . ? (1); **me gustaría (mucho)...** I would (really) like . . . (8); **(no,) no me gusta** (no,) I don't like . . . (1); **(sí,) me gusta...** (yes), I like . . . (1); **¿te gusta... ?** do you (*fam. s.*) like . . . ? (1)
gusto like preference; *pl.* likes (1); **mucho gusto** nice to meet you (1)

H

haber (*inf. of* **hay**) there is, there are; to have (*aux. verb*) (12)
habichuelas *f. pl.* beans
habilidad *f.* ability
habitación *f.* bedroom
habitante *m., f.* inhabitant
habitar to inhabit
hábito habit
hablante *m., f.* speaker
hablar to speak; to talk (2); **hablar con soltura** to speak fluently; **hablar por teléfono** to talk on the phone (2)
hacer to do; to make (5); **hace** + *time* + **que** + *present* to have been (*doing something*) for (*time*) (14); **hace** + *time* + **que** + *preterite* ago (14); *present* + **desde hace** + *time* to have been (*doing something*) for (*time*) (14); *preterite* + **hace** + *time* ago (14); **hace (muy) buen/mal tiempo** it's very good/bad weather (6); **hace (mucho) calor** it's (very) hot (weather) (6).; **hace fresco** it's cool (weather) (6).; **hace (mucho) frío** it's (very) cold (*weather*); **hacer autostop** to hitchhike; **hacer camping** to go camping (8); **hacer clic** to click (12) **hacer cola** to stand in line (8); **hacer (foto)copia** to copy (12); **hacer (el método) Pilates** to do Pilates (11); **hacer (el) yoga** to do yoga (10); **hacer ejercicio** to exercise (5); **hacer ejercicios aeróbicos** to do aerobics (11); **hacer escalas** to make stops (8); **hacer frente a** to face up to; **hacer la cama** to make the bed (10); **hacer la(s) maleta(s)** to pack

one's suitcase(s) (8); **hacer paradas** to make stops (8); **hacer planes** (*m.*) **para** + *inf.* to make plans to (*do something*) (10); **hacer reserva** to make a reservation; **hacer** *surfing* to surf (10); **hacer un** *picnic* to have a picnic (10); **hacer un viaje** to take a trip (5); **hacer una fiesta** to have/throw a party (9); **hacer una juerga** to throw a party; **hacer una pregunta** to ask a question (5); **hacerse daño** to hurt oneself (14); **hacerse daño en** to hurt one's (*body part*) (14); **¿qué tiempo hace?** what's the weather like? (6)

hacia *prep.* towards

hada (*but* **el hada**) fairy

hallaca *Venezuelan meat pastry*

hamaca hammock

hambre *f.* hunger; **pasar hambre** to go hungry; **tener (mucha) hambre** to be (very) hungry (7)

hamburguesa hamburger (7)

harina flour

hasta *adv.* until; even; *prep.* until; **hasta luego** see you later (1); **hasta mañana** see you tomorrow (1); **hasta pronto** see you soon; **hasta que** until (17)

hay there is/are (1); **hay que** + *inf.* it is necessary to (*do something*) (13); **no hay** there is/are not (1); **no hay de qué** you're welcome (1)

hebreo Hebrew (*language*)

hecho *n.* fact; event (9)

hecho/a (*p.p. of* **hacer**) made

hectárea *land measure equal to 2.5 acres*

helado ice cream (7)

heliconia *flowering tropical plant*

hemisferio hemisphere

herbolario/a herbalist

heredar to inherit

herencia inheritance

hermanastro/a stepbrother, stepsister

hermano/a brother/sister (3); *m. pl.* siblings (3)

hermoso/a beautiful

héroe *m.* hero

heroína heroine

hervir (hiervo) (i) to boil

híbrido/a hybrid (15)

hidalgo nobleman

hidroeléctrico/a hydroelectric

hielo ice

hierba grass

hígado liver

hijastro/a stepson, stepdaughter

hijo/a son/daughter (3); *m. pl.* children (3)

himno hymn; **himno nacional** national anthem

hipopótamo hippopotamus

hispánico/a Hispanic

hispano/a Hispanic (3)

Hispanoamérica Hispanic America

hispanoamericano/a *adj.* Hispanic American

hispanohablante *adj. m., f.* Spanish-speaking

historia history (2); story (8)

historiador (a) historian

histórico/a historical

hockey *m.* hockey (10)

hogar *m.* home

hoja leaf

¡hola! hi!; hello! (1)

Holanda Holland

hombre *m.* man (2); **hombre de negocios** businessman (17)

homeópata *m., f.* homeopath

homeopático/a homeopathic

homogeneidad *f.* homogeneity

homogéneo/a homogenous

hondureño/a *n., adj.* Honduran

honesto/a honest

hongo mushroom; toadstool; fungus; **sombrero hongo** bowler hat, derby

honor *m.* honor

honrado/a honest; honorable

hora hour; time; **¿a qué hora... ?** at what time . . . ? (1); **es hora de...** it's time to . . . ; **hora punta** peak hour **¿qué hora es?** what time is it? (1)

horario schedule (14)

horchata *Mexican drink made from rice*

hormona hormone

horno oven; **horno de microondas** microwave oven (10)

horóscopo horoscope

horror *m.* horror

hospital *m.* hospital

hospitalario/a hospitable

hospitalidad *f.* hospitality

hospitalización *f.* hospitalization

hotel *m.* hotel

hoy today (1); **¿cuál es la fecha de hoy?** what's today's date? (6); **¿qué día es hoy?** what day is today? (5); **¿qué fecha es hoy?** what's today's date? (6)

huelga strike (*labor*) (18)

huella mark; (finger)print

huerto orchard

hueso bone

huésped *m., f.* guest

huevo egg (7)

huipil *m. traditional Mayan blouse*

huir (*like* **construir**) to flee

humanidad *f.* humanity; *pl.* humanities (2)

humanista *n., adj.* humanist

humanitario/a humanitarian

humanizar (c) to make more human

humano/a human (11); **cuerpo humano** human body (11); **ser** (*m.*) **humano** human being

humedad *f.* humidity

húmedo/a humid

humilde humble

humorístico/a humorous

huracán *m.* hurricane

I

ibérico/a *adj.* Iberian

íbero/a *n.* Iberian

icónico/a iconic

ícono icon

ida: billete (*m.*) (*Sp.*) / **boleto** (*L.A.*) **de ida** one-way ticket (8); **billete** (*m.*) (*Sp.*) / **boleto** (*L.A.*) **de ida y vuelta** round-trip ticket (8)

idealista *m., f.* idealistic

idear to think up: to conceive (*idea*)

idéntico/a identical

identidad *f.* identity; **carnet** (*m.*) **de identidad** identification card

identificación *f.* identification; **carnet** (*m.*) **de identificación** identification card; **tarjeta de identificación** identification card (14)

identificar (se) (qu) to identify (oneself)

idioma *m.* language

idiomático/a idiomatic

ídolo idol

iglesia church (16)

ignorante ignorant

ignorar to ignore

igual same; equal

igualdad *f.* equality (18)

igualitario/a egalitarian

igualmente likewise; same here (1)

ilimitado/a unlimited

ilógico/a illogical

ilusorio/a false

iluminar to light up

ilustrar to illustrate

ilustrativo/a illustrative

imagen *f.* image (13)

imaginación *f.* imagination

imaginar(se) to imagine

imaginativo/a imaginative

imitar to imitate

impaciente impatient

impacto impact

impedimento impediment

impedir (*like* **pedir**) to impede

imperfecto *gram.* imperfect

imperio empire

impermeable *m.* raincoat (4); *adj.* impermeable

impertinente impertinent
implementar to implement
implicar (qu) to imply
imponer (*like* **poner**) to impose
importancia importance
importante important
importar (*like* **gustar**) to matter; to be important
imposible impossible (13); **es imposible que** it's impossible that (13); **no es imposible que** it's not impossible (13)
impresión *f.* impression
impresionante impressive
impresionar to impress
impreso/a printed
impresora printer (12)
imprimir to print (12)
improbable unlikely (13); **es improbable que** it's unlikely, improbable that (13); **no es improbable que** it's not improbable (13)
improvisar to improvise
impuesto tax
impulsivo/a impulsive
inalámbrico/a wireless
inauguración *f.* inauguration
inca *n. m., f.* Inca; *adj. m., f.* Incan
incaico/a *adj.* Inca
incapacidad *f.* inability
incendio fire
incidente *m.* incident
incienso incense
inclinación *f.* inclination
inclinarse to lean
incluir (*like* **construir**) to include
incómodo/a uncomfortable
incompleto/a incomplete
inconcebible inconceivable
inconveniencia inconvenience
inconveniente *n. m; adj.* inconvenient
incorporar to incorporate; to include
incorrecto/a incorrect
incrédulo/a incredulous
increíble incredible (13); **es increíble que** it's incredible that (13)
incrementar to increase
incremento increment
indefinido/a indefinite; **artículo indefinido** *gram.* indefinite article; **palabra indefinida y negativa** *gram.* indefinite and negative word (7)
indeleble indelible
independencia independence
independiente independent
independizarse (c) to become independent
indescriptible indescribable
indicación *f.* instruction; direction
indicar (qu) to indicate
indicativo *gram.* indicative

índice *m.* index
Índico Indian (Ocean)
indiferente indifferent
indígena *n. m., f.* indigenous person; *adj. m., f.* indigenous
indigenista *m., f. pertaining to indigenous topics and themes*
indio/a *n., adj.* Indian
indirecto/a indirect; **complemento indirecto** *gram.* indirect object
indiscreto/a indiscreet
indispensable indispensible, essential
indistinto/a indistinct
individualidad *f.* individuality
individuo *n.* individual
individuo/a *adj.* individual
industria industry
inesperado/a unexpected
inexistente nonexistent
infancia infancy; childhood (16)
infantil *adj.* child, children's
infatigable tireless
infección *f.* infection
inferir (infiero) (i) to infer
infiltrarse to infiltrate
infinitivo *gram.* infinitive
inflexibilidad *f.* inflexibility
influencia influence
influir (*like* **construir**) to influence
influyente influential
infografía computer graphic
información *f.* information
informar to inform (18)
informática computer science
informativo/a informative
informe *m.* **(oral/escrito)** (oral/written) report (14)
infraestructura infrastructure
infrecuente infrequent
infusión *f.* infusion
ingeniería engineering
ingeniero/a engineer (17)
ingenioso/a ingenious
Inglaterra England
inglés *m.* English (*language*) (2)
inglés, inglesa *n., adj.* English (3)
ingrediente *m.* ingredient
ingresar to deposit (*in an account*)
ingreso income
inicial *f.* initial (*letter*)
iniciar to start
iniciativa initiative
inicio beginning
injusticia injustice
injusto/a unfair
inmediato/a immediate
inmenso/a immense
inmerso/a immersed
inmigración *f.* immigration
inmigrante *n., m., f.* immigrant
inmobiliario/a *adj.* real estate; property

inmóvil unmoving
innecesario/a unnecessary
innumerable countless
inocente innocent
inolvidable unforgettable
inquilino/a tenant (12); renter (12)
inscribir(se) (*p.p.* **inscrito**) **(en)** to sign up; to register (for)
inscripción *f.* inscription
inscrito/a (*p.p. of* **inscribir**) registered
insecto insect
insistir (en) to insist (on) (12)
insoportable unbearable
inspiración *f.* inspiration
instalación *f.* facility
instalar to install (12)
instantáneo/a instantaneous
instante: al instante right away
institución *f.* institution
instituto institute
instrucciones *f, pl.* instructions
instructor(a) instructor
instrumento instrument
insulina insulin
insulto insult
integración *f.* integration
integrarse to integrate oneself
intelectivo/a cognitive
intelectual intellectual
inteligencia intelligence
inteligente intelligent (3)
intención *f.* intention
intencionadamente intentionally
intensidad *f.* intensity
intensificar (qu) to intensify
intenso/a intense
intentar to attempt to
interacción *f.* interaction
interactivo/a interactive
intercambiar to exchange
intercambio exchange
interés *m.* interest (17)
interesante interesting
interesar (*like* **gustar**) to interest (*someone*) (8)
intergaláctico/a intergalactic
interior interior; inner; **ropa interior** underwear (4)
intermedio/a intermediate
interminable endless
internacional international; **Día** (*m.*) **Internacional de la No Violencia Contra la Mujer** International No Violence Against Women Day
internauta *m., f.* internet user
internet *m.* internet (12); **buscar (qu) en internet** to look for on the internet (12); **entrar en internet** to go on the internet (12)
interno/a internal
interplanetario/a interplanetary

interpretación *f.* interpretation
interpretar to interpret
interrogación: signo de interrogación question mark
interrogativo/a *gram.* interrogative (1)
interrumpir to interrupt
interrupción *f.* interruption
intervención *f.* intervention
intimidad *f.* intimacy
íntimo/a intimate; close
intolerancia intolerance
intranquilidad *f.* restlessness
introducción *f.* introduction
introducir (*like* **conducir**) to introduce
inundación *f.* flood
inútil useless
invadido/a invaded
inválido/a disabled
invasión *f.* invasion
invasor(a) *adj.* invading
inventar to invent
inversión *f.* investment
invertir (invierto) (i) to invest
investigación *f.* investigation; research
investigador(a) researcher
investigar (gu) to investigate; to research
invierno winter (6)
invitación *f.* invitation
invitado/a guest (9)
invitar to invite (7)
invocar (qu) to invoke
inyección *f.* injection (11); **ponerle una inyección** to give (*someone*) a shot (11)
iPhone *m.* iPhone (12)
iPod *m.* iPod (12)
ir to go (4); **ir a** + *inf.* to be going to (*do something*) (4); **ir a un bar** to go to a bar (10); **ir a un concierto** to go to a concert (10); **ir a una discoteca** to go to a disco (10); **ir al extranjero** to go abroad (8); **ir de compras** to go shopping (4); **ir de safari** to go on a safari; **ir de vacaciones a...** to go on vacation in/to . . . (8); **ir distraído/a** to be distracted (14); **ir en...** to go/travel by . . . (8); **ir en autobús** to go/travel by bus (8); **ir en avión** to go/travel by plane (8); **ir en barco** to go/travel by boat, ship (8); **ir en tren** to go/travel by train (8); **irse** to leave; **vamos** let's go (4)
ira al manejar road rage
iraní (*pl.* **iraníes**) *n., adj.* Iranian
iraquí (*pl.* **iraquíes**) *n., adj.* Iraqi
iridiscencia iridescence
Irlanda Ireland
irlandés, irlandesa *n., adj.* Irish
ironía irony
irónico/a ironic
irresponsable irresponsible
isla island (6)

Islandia Iceland
islote *m.* islet
israelí (*pl.* **israelíes**) *n., adj.* Israeli
Italia Italy
italiano Italian (*language*) (2)
italiano/a *n., adj.* Italian
itinerario itinerary
-ito/a *diminuitive suffix* (10)
izquierda *n.* left-hand side; **a la izquierda de** to the left of (6)
izquierdo/a *adj.* left; **levantarse con el pie izquierdo** to get up on the wrong side of the bed (14)

J

jaguar *m.* jaguar
jamaica hibiscus
jamás never (7)
jamón *m.* ham (7)
Japón *m.* Japan
japonés *m.* Japanese (*language*)
japonés, japonesa *n., adj.* Japanese
jarabe *m.* (cough) syrup (11)
jardín *m.* garden (5)
jarra jar
jazz *m.* jazz
jeans *m. pl.* blue jeans (4)
jefe/a boss
jerarquía hierarchy
jersey *m.* sweater; pullover
jirafa giraffe
jornada de tiempo parcial part-time job
joropo *folkloric music of Venezuela*
joven *n. m., f.* (*pl.* **jóvenes**) youth; *adj.* young (3); **de joven** as a youth (10)
joyería jewelry
jubilarse to retire (17)
judaísmo Judaism
juego game; **Juegos Olímpicos** Olympic Games
juerga party; **hacer una juerga** to have/throw a party
jueves *m. inv.* Thursday (5)
jugador(a) player (10)
jugar (juego) (gu) (a, al) to play (*a game, sport*) (5); **jugar a las cartas / al ajedrez / a los videojuegos** to play cards/chess/videogames (10)
jugo (de fruta) (fruit) juice (7)
juguete *m.* toy
julio July (6)
junio June (6)
junto a *prep.* near
juntos/as together (8)
jurar to swear (*oath*)
justicia justice
justificación *f.* justification
justificar (qu) to justify
justo/a fair
juvenil *adj.* youth; youthful; **diabetes** (*f.*) **juvenil** childhood diabetes
juventud *f.* youth (16)

juzgar (gu) to judge

K

kaki: color (*m.*) **kaki** khaki
kilo(gramo) kilo(gram)
kilómetro kilometer

L

la *def. art. f. s.* the; *d.o. f. s.* you (*form.*); her, it; **a la(s)...** at . . . (*time of day*) (1); **la cual** which
labor *f.* work, job
laboral *adj.* work, work-related (17)
laboratorio laboratory
lácteo/a *adj.* dairy
lado side; **al lado de** alongside of (6); **por el otro lado** on the other hand; **por un lado** on one hand
ladrar to bark
ladrón, ladrona thief
lagarto lizard
lago lake (15)
lágrima tear
lamentar to regret; to feel sorry (13)
laminado/a laminated
lámpara lamp (5)
lana wool (4); **de lana** wool (4)
langosta lobster (7)
lapicero pen
lápiz *m.* (*pl.* **lápices**) pencil (2)
largo/a long (3)
las *def. art. s. pl.* the; *d.o. f. pl.* you (*form. pl.*); **a la(s)...** at . . . (*time of day*) (1); **las cuales** which
lasaña lasagne
lástima shame; **es una lástima que** it's a shame that (13); **¡qué lástima que... !** what a shame that . . . ! (13)
lastimarse to hurt (*a body part*) (14)
lata can
latín *m.* Latin (*language*)
latino/a *adj.* Latin; **América Latina** Latin America
Latinoamérica Latin America
latinoamericano/a *n., adj.* Latin American
lavabo (bathroom) sink (5)
lavadora washing machine (10)
lavandería laundry
lavaplatos *m. inv.* dishwasher (10)
lavar to wash (10); **lavarse** to wash (oneself)
lealtad *f.* loyalty
lección *f.* lesson
leche *f.* milk (7)
lechón *m.* suckling pig; **lechón asado** roast suckling pig
lechuga lettuce (7)
lector(a) reader
lectura reading
leer (*like* **creer**) to read (3)
legislación *f.* legislation
legumbre *f.* legume

lejos *adv.* far; **lejos de** *prep.* far from (6)
lema *m.* motto
lempira *currency of Honduras*
lengua language (2); tongue (11); **lenguas extranjeras** foreign languages (2); **sacar (qu) la lengua** to stick out one's tongue (11)
lentes *m. pl.* glasses (11); **lentes de contacto** contact lenses (11)
lentillas *f. pl.* contact lenses (*Sp.*)
lento/a slow
león *m.* lion; **león marino** sea lion
leopardo leopard
letra letter (*of the alphabet*); lyrics (*song*) (7)
levantar to raise; to lift; **levantar pesas** to lift weights (11); **levantarse** to get up (out of bed) (5); to stand up (5); **levantarse con el pie izquierdo** to get up on the wrong side of the bed (14)
leve *adj.* light
ley *f.* law (18)
leyenda legend
libanés, libanesa lebanese
liberar(se) to free (oneself)
libertad *f.* freedom, liberty
libertador(a) liberator
libra pound (*measurement*)
libre free, unoccupied (10); **al aire** (*m.*) **libre** outdoors (10); **estado libre asociado** commonwealth; **libre comercio** free trade; **ratos** (*m. pl.*) **libres** spare (free) time (10); **tiempo libre** free time (10)
librería bookstore (2)
libro book (2); **libro de texto** textbook (2)
licencia license (15); **licencia de manejar/conducir** driver's license (15)
licor *m.* liqueur
licuar (licúo) to liquefy
líder *m., f.* leader
liga league
ligero/a light, not heavy (7)
lima lime
limeño/a *adj.* from Lima, Peru
limitación *f.* limitation
limitar to limit
límite *m.* limit; **fecha límite** deadline; **límite de velocidad** speed limit (15)
limón *m.* lemon
limonada lemonade
limonero lemon tree
limosina limousine
limpiar (la casa) to clean (the) house (10)
limpieza cleanliness
limpio/a clean (6)
lindo/a pretty

línea line
lingüístico/a linguistic
linterna flashlight
lío problem; trouble; **meterse en líos** to get into trouble
liquidación *f.* liquidation
líquido liquid
Lisboa Lisbon
lista list
listo/a smart; clever (3); **estar listo/a** to be ready
literario/a literary
literatura literature (2)
litoral *m.* coast
llamada call; **bloqueo de llamadas** call blocker
llamar to call (7); **¿cómo se llama usted?** what is your (*form. s.*) name? (1); **¿cómo te llamas?** what is your (*fam. s.*) name? (1); **llamarse** to be called (5); **me llamo...** my name is . . . (1) **llamarse** to be called (5)
llanero Venezuelan cowboy
llanero/a of or pertaining to the plains
llano *n.* plain
llanta (desinflada) (flat) tire (15)
llanura *n.* plain
llave *f.* key (5)
llegada arrival (8)
llegar (gu) to arrive (3); **¿cómo se llega a... ?** how do you get to . . . ? (15); **llegar a ser** to become
llenar to fill (up) (15); to fill out (*a form*) (17)
lleno/a full
llevar to wear (4); to carry (4); to take (4); **llevar una vida sana/tranquila** to lead a healthy/calm life (11); **llevarse bien/mal (con)** to get along well/ poorly (with) (16)
llorar to cry (9)
llover (llueve) to rain (6); **llueve** (it's raining) (6)
lluvia rain
lluvioso/a *adj.* rainy; of rain; **bosque** (*m.*) **tropical lluvioso** tropical rain forest
lo *d.o. m. s.* you (*form.*); him; it; **lo bueno** the good news/thing (11); **lo cual** which; **lo malo** the bad news/thing (11); **lo que** what, that which (5); **lo siento (mucho)** I'm (very) sorry (14); **lo suficiente** enough (11); **por lo general** generally (5); **por lo menos** at least (9); **por lo regular** in general
lobo/a wolf
localidad *f.* ticket (*to movie, play*)
localización *f.* location
loco/a crazy (6)
locutor(a) commentator
lógico/a logical
logotipo logo

lograr to achieve
logro achievement
Londres London
longitud *f.* longitude
los *def. art. m. pl.* the; *d.o. m. pl.* you (*form. pl.*) them; **los cuales** which; **los lunes (los martes...)** on Mondays (Tuesdays . . .) (5)
lotería lottery
lubricar (qu) to lubricate
lucha fight, struggle (18)
luchar to fight (18)
lucro: sin fines de lucro non-profit
luego then, afterward, next (5); **hasta luego** see you later (1)
lugar *m.* place (2)
lujo luxury
lujoso/a luxurious
luminiscente luminescent
luminoso/a lit up
luna moon; **luna de miel** honeymoon (16)
lunares: de lunares polka-dot (4)
lunes *m. inv.* Monday (5); **el lunes** on Monday (5); **los lunes** on Mondays (5); **el lunes que viene** next Monday (5)
Luxemburgo Luxembourg
luz *f.* (*pl.* **luces**) light (14)

M

madera wood
madrastra stepmother
madre *f.* mother (3); **Día** (*m.*) **de la Madre** Mother's Day
madrileño/a of or pertaining to Madrid
madrina godmother
madrugada dawn
madurez *f.* middle age (16)
maduro/a mature
maestría master's degree
maestro/a (de escuela) schoolteacher (17); *adj.* master; **obra maestra** masterpiece (13)
Magallanes: Estrecho de Magallanes Strait of Magellan
mágico/a *adj.* magic
magnífico/a magnificent
mago wizard
mahones *m. pl.* jeans
maíz *m.* (*pl.* **maíces**) corn
mal *adv.* poorly (2); **caerle mal a alguien** to make a bad impression on someone; **empleo mal pagado** poorly paid job/position (17); **llevarse mal (con)** to get along poorly (with) (16); **pasarlo mal** to have a bad time (9); **portarse mal** to misbehave (9); **salir mal** to come/turn out badly; to do poorly (5)
mal, malo/a *adj.* bad (3); **lo malo** the bad news/thing (11); **tener mala**

suerte to have bad luck; to be unlucky (14)

maleducado/a spoiled

malestar *m.* discomfort

maleta suitcase (8); **hacer la(s) maleta(s)** to pack one's suitcase(s) (8)

maletero porter (8)

malvado/a evil

mamá mother, mom (3)

mami mom, mommy

mamífero mammal

mancha stain

mandar to send (2); to order (*someone to do something*) (12); **mandar un mensaje** to (send a) text (2)

mandarín *m.* Mandarin (*language*)

mandato command (7)

manejar to drive (12); to operate (a *machine*) (12); **ira al manejar** road rage; **licencia de manejar** driver's license (15)

manera way, manner; **de manera que** so that, in such a way that

manga sleeve

manifestación *f.* demonstration, march (18)

maniquí *m.* mannequin

mano *f.* hand (11); **darse la mano** to shake hands (11)

mansión *f.* mansion

mantener (*like* **tener**) to maintain; to keep (18); **mantenerse en contacto** to stay in touch

mantequilla butter (7)

manzana apple (7); (city) block

mañana tomorrow (1); **de la mañana** in the morning, A.M. (1); **hasta mañana** see you tomorrow (1); **pasado mañana** the day after tomorrow (5); **por la mañana** in the morning (2)

mapa *m.* map

mapudungun *m. language of the Mapuche people*

máquina machine

mar *m.* sea (8); **mar Caribe** Caribbean Sea

maracuyá *m.* passion fruit

maratón *m.* marathon

maravilla wonder, marvel

maravillar to delight

maravilloso/a marvelous

marca brand; label

marcar (qu) to mark

marcial martial

mareado/a dizzy (11); nauseated (11)

marido husband (3)

marihuana marijuana

marinera *folkloric dance of coastal Peru*

marino/a marine; **león** (*m.*) **marino** sea lion

mariscos *m. pl.* shellfish (7)

marítimo/a maritime; sea, marine

marketing *m.* marketing

marrón *adj., m., f.* brown

martes *m. inv.* Tuesday (5); **los martes** on Tuesdays (5)

Maruecos Morocco

marzo March (6)

más more (2); **cada vez más** increasingly; **más de** + *number* more than + *number* (6); **más... que** more (-er) . . . than (6)

masa mass; dough

máscara mask

mascota pet (3)

masculino/a masculine

masivo/a massive

masticar (qu) to chew

matar to kill (18)

mate *m. traditional drink of Argentina*

matemáticas *f. pl.* math (2)

materia subject area (2); material (4)

materialidad *f.* material aspect; outward appearance

materialista *m., f.* materialistic

maternidad *f.* maternity

materno/a maternal

matinal *adj.* morning

matriarcado matriarchy

matriarcal matriarchal

matrícula tuition (2)

matricularse to enroll; to register

matrimonio marriage; married couple (16)

máximo/a maximum

maya *n., adj. m., f.* Mayan

mayo May (6)

mayor older (6); oldest; greater; greatest; **Antillas** (*f. pl.*) **Mayores** Greater Antilles; **cada vez mayor** greater and greater

mayoría majority

mayoritariamente primarily

mayoritario/a *adj.* majority

mayúscula capital (letter), uppercase

me *d.o.* me; *i.o.* to/for me; *refl. pron.* myself; **me gustaría (mucho)...** I would (really) like . . . (8); **me llamo...** my name is . . . (1); **(no,) no me gusta** (no,) I don't like . . . (1); **(sí,) me gusta...** (yes), I like . . . (1)

mecánico/a mechanic (15)

mecanización *f.* mechanization

mecanografía typing

medalla medal

mediano/a: de estatura mediana of medium height

medianoche *f.* midnight (6)

mediante *prep.* by, with

medias *f. pl.* stockings (4)

medicamento medicine

medicina medicine (11)

médico/a (medical) doctor (3)

medio *n.* medium; means; *pl.* mass media (18); **medio ambiente** environment (15); **medio de comunicación** medium of communication (18); **medio de transporte** means of transportation (8)

medio/a *adj.* half; middle; average; **media naranja** better half; **y media** half past (*the hour*) (1)

medioambiental environmental

medioambiente *m.* environment

mediodía *m.* noon (6)

medir (mido) (i) to measure

meditar to meditate

megadiverso/a megadiverse

megalópolis *f.* super-city

mejor better; best (6)

mejora improvement

mejorar(se) to improve; to get better

mellizo/a fraternal twin

melódico/a melodious

memoria memory (12)

mencionar to mention

menonito/a *adj.* Mennonite

menor younger (6); youngest; less; least

menorá menorah

menos less; least; minus; **a menos que** *conj.* unless (16); **al menos** at least; **menos cuarto** a quarter to (*hour*) (1); **menos de** + *number* fewer than + *number* (6); **menos quince** fifteen minutes till (*hour*) (1); **por lo menos** at least (9)

mensaje *m.* message; **mandar un mensaje** to (send a) text (2)

mensual monthly

mente *f.* mind

mentir (miento) (i) to lie

mentira lie (12)

menú *m.* menu (7)

menudo: a menudo *adv.* often

mercadeo marketing

mercader *m., f.* merchant

mercado market(place) (4)

mercadotecnia marketing

merecer (merezco) to deserve

merendar (meriendo) to have a snack (7)

merengue *m. dance from the Dominican Republic*

merienda snack (7)

mes *m.* month (6)

mesa table (2); **poner la mesa** to set the table (10); **quitar la mesa** to clear the table (10)

meseta plateau

mesita end table (5)

mesoamericano/a *n.,* *adj.* Meso-American

mestizaje *m.* mixing of races

meta goal

metáfora metaphor

metal *m.* metal

metálico/a metallic

metalúrgico/a metallurgical

meteorológico/a meteorological

meter to put (*into*); to place; **meterse en líos** to get into trouble

método method; **hacer (el método) Pilates** to do Pilates (11)

metro subway; **parada del metro** subway stop (12)

metrópoli *f.* metropolis

metropolitano/a urban

mexicano/a Mexican (3)

mexicoamericano/a Mexican American

mezcla mix

mezclar to mix

mezclilla denim

mezquita mosque

mí *obj. of prep.* me (6)

mi(s) *poss. adj.* my (3)

microbio microbe

microcuento very short story

microondas: horno de microondas microwave oven (10)

microorganismo microorganism

miedo fear; **tener miedo (de)** to be afraid (of) (4)

miel *f.* honey; **luna de miel** honeymoon (16)

miembro/a member

mientras while (10)

miércoles *m. inv.* Wednesday (5); **ayer fue miércoles...** yesterday was Wednesday . . . (5)

mierda shit

mil (one) thousand (4)

milagro miracle

milenario/a thousand-year

mililitro milliliter

militar *n. m., f.* soldier; (17) *adj.* military; **servicio militar** military service (18)

milla mile

millón: un millón (de) one million (4)

millonario/a millionaire

mimar to spoil; to pamper

mineral: agua *f.* (*but* **el agua**) **(mineral)** (mineral) water (7)

minidiálogo minidialogue

mínimo minimum

ministerio ministry

ministro/a minister

minoría minority

minuto minute

mío/a(s) *poss. adj.* my; *poss. pron.* (of) mine (17)

mirada look

mirar to look at; to watch (3); **mirar la tele(visión)** to watch television (3)

misa mass; **misa del gallo** midnight mass

miseria misery

misil *n.* missile

misión *f.* mission

mismo/a same (6); **ahora mismo** right now (6)

misterio mystery

misterioso/a mysterious

mitad *f.* half

mixto/a mixed

moái *m. statue on Easter Island, Chile*

mochila backpack (2)

moda fashion; style; **a la moda** in fashion, in a stylish way; **es de última moda** it's trendy (hot) (4); **está de moda** it's trendy (hot) (4)

modales *m. pl.* manners

modelar to model

modelo model, example

módem *m.* modem (12)

moderación *f.* moderation

modernidad *f.* modernity

modernismo modernism

modernista *m., f.* modernist

moderno/a modern (13)

modificar (qu) to modify

modismo idiom

modista dressmaker

modo way, matter; mode; *gram.* mood; **de modo que** in such a way that

mole *m. Mexican sauce*

molestar (*like* **gustar**) to bother (11)

molestia *n.* bother

molesto/a annoyed (6)

molino: rueda de molino treadmill

momento moment

momia mummy

monarquía monarchy

monasterio monastery

moneda coin (17); currency

monedero coin purse

monitor *m.* monitor

monitoreo monitoring

monitorizar (c) to monitor

mono monkey

monolingüe *adj.* monolingual

monoparental *adj.* single-parent

monopatín *m.* skateboard

monotonía monotony

monótono/a monotonous

monovolumen *m.* minivan

monstruo monster

montaje *m.* montage

montaña mountain (8)

montañoso/a mountainous

montar to ride; **montar a caballo** to ride a horse (10); **montar en bicicleta** to ride a bicycle (10)

montón: un montón a lot

montuno *traditional hat of Panama*

monumento monument

morado/a purple (4)

morales *f. pl.* morals

morderse (me muerdo) to bite

moreno/a brunet(te) (3)

morir(se) ([me] muero) (u) (*p.p.* **muerto**) to die (9)

moro/a *n.* Moor; *adj.* Moorish

mosaico mosaic

mosca fly

mostrador *m.* counter (8)

mostrar (muestro) to show (8)

motivación *f.* motivation

motivo motive

moto(cicleta) motorcycle (15)

motor *m.* motor

mover (muevo) to move

móvil mobile

movimiento movement

muchacho/a young boy/girl

mucho *adv.* much (2); a lot (2); **lo siento mucho** I'm very sorry (14); **me gustaría mucho...** I would really like . . . (8); **muchísimo** an awful lot (8)

mucho/a a lot (of) (3); *pl.* many (3); **estar bajo muchas presiones** to be under a lot of pressure (14); **muchas gracias** thank you very much (1); **mucho gusto** nice to meet you (1); **tener (mucha) hambre** to be (very) hungry (7); **tener (mucha) sed** to be (very) thirsty (7); **tener muchas presiones** to be under a lot of stress (14); **tener (mucho) calor** to be (very) warm, hot (6); **tener (mucho) frío** to be (very) cold (6)

mudanza *n.* move

mudarse to move (*residence*) (12)

mueble *m.* piece of furniture (5)

muela molar, back tooth (11); **sacarle (qu) una muela** to extract (*someone's*) molar (11)

muerte *f.* death (16)

muerto/a (*p.p. of* **morir**) dead; **Día** (*m.*) **de los Muertos** Day of the Dead

mujer *f.* woman (2); wife (3); **Día** (*m.*) **Internacional de la No Violencia Contra la Mujer** International No Violence Against Women Day; **mujer de negocios** businesswoman (17); **mujer soldado** female soldier (17)

mula mule

mulato/a mulatto

multa fine

multilingüe multilingual

multinacional multinational

múltiple multiple

multiplicarse (qu) to multiply; to grow in number

multirracial multiracial

mundial *adj.* world; **Copa Mundial** World Cup

mundo world (3); **Copa del Mundo** World Cup (soccer)

municipio municipality

muñeca doll

mural *m.* mural (13)

muralismo muralism

muralista *m., f.* muralist

muralla city wall

murciélago bat

muro wall

músculo muscle

museo museum; **visitar un museo** to visit a museum (10)

música music (13)

musical musical (13)

músico *m., f.* musician (13)

musulmán, musulmana Muslim

mutuo/a mutual

muy very (1); **muy bien** fine, very well (1); **muy buenas** good morning/afternoon/evening (1)

N

nacer (nazco) to be born (16)

nacimiento birth

nación *f.* nation; **Organización** *(f.)* **de Naciones Unidas (ONU)** United Nations (U.N.)

nacional national; **himno nacional** national anthem; **producto nacional bruto** gross national product

nacionalidad *f.* nationality; **adjetivo de nacionalidad** adjective of nationality (3)

nada nothing, not anything (7); **de nada** you're welcome (1); **para nada** at all (8)

nadar to swim (8)

nadie no one, nobody, not anybody (7)

náhuatl *m.* Nahuatl (*language of the Aztecs*)

nana *fam.* grandma

naranja orange (7); **media naranja** better half

nariz *f.* (*pl.* **narices**) nose (11)

narración *f.* narration

narrador(a) narrator

narrar to narrate

natación *f.* swimming (10)

natal: casa natal house where someone was born

nativo/a native

natural natural; **ciencias** (*f. pl.*) **naturales** natural sciences (2); **recurso natural** natural resource (15)

naturaleza nature (15)

naturópata *m., f.* naturopath

náufrago shipwreck

nave *(f.)* **espacial** spaceship

navegable navigable

navegación *f.* navigation

navegar (gu) to navigate (12); **navegar la Red** to surf the internet

Navidad *f.* Christmas (9)

navideño/a *adj.* Christmas

neblina mist; fog

necesario/a necessary (3)

necesidad *f.* need, necessity

necesitar to need (2)

negación *f.* negation

negar (niego) (gu) to deny (13)

negativo/a negative; **palabra indefinida y negativa** *gram.* indefinite and negative word (7)

negociar to negotiate

negocio business; **hombre** (*m.*) **de negocios** businessman (17); **mujer** (*f.*) **de negocios** businesswoman (17)

negrilla: en negrilla boldface

negro/a black (4)

neoyorquino/a *adj.* pertaining to New York

nerviosismo nervousness

nervioso/a nervous (6)

neumático tire (*automobile*)

neutralizar (c) to neutralize

neutro/a neutral

nevar (nieva) to snow (6); **nieva** it's snowing (6)

nevera refrigerator

ni neither; nor; **ni... ni** neither . . . nor

nicaragüense *n., adj. m., f.* Nicaraguan

niebla fog

nieto/a grandson/granddaughter (3)

ningún (ninguna) no, not any (7)

niñero/a baby-sitter (10)

niñez *f.* (*pl.* **niñeces**) childhood (16)

niño/a small child; boy/girl (3); **de niño/a** as a child (10)

nivel *m.* level

no no (1); **no creer** to not think/believe (13); **no es seguro/(im)posible, (im)probable** it's not sure/(im)possible, (im)probable (13); **no estar de acuerdo** to disagree (3); **no estar seguro/a de** to not be sure of (13); **no hay** there is/are not (1); **no hay de qué** you're welcome (1); **no obstante** however; **no tener razón** to be wrong (4); **ya no** no longer

¿no? right, don't they (you...)? (4)

noche *f.* night; **buenas noches** goodnight (1); **de la noche** in the evening, P.M. (1); **esta noche** tonight (6); **por la noche** at night, in the evening (2)

Nochebuena Christmas Eve (9)

Nochevieja New Year's Eve (9)

nombrar to name

nombre *m.* name (7)

nopal *m.* cactus

noreste *m.* northeast

norma rule; norm

normal normal; **es normal que** it's normal that (13)

normalidad *f.* normality

noroeste *m.* northwest

norte *m.* north (6)

Norteamérica North America

norteamericano/a North American

nos *d. o. pron.* us; *i. o. pron.* to/for us; *refl. pron.* ourselves; **nos vemos** see you around (1)

nosotros/as *subj. pron.* we (2); *obj.* (*of prep.*) us (2)

nota grade (*academic*) (5); note

notar to note, to notice

noticias *f. pl.* news (5)

noticiero newscast (18)

notificación *f.* notification

novecientos/as nine hundred (4)

novela novel (13)

novelista *m., f.* novelist (13)

noveno/a ninth (13)

noventa ninety (3)

noviazgo engagement (16)

noviembre *m.* November (6)

novio/a boyfriend/girlfriend (6); fiancé(e) (16); groom/bride (16)

nube *f.* cloud

nublado/a cloudy; **está (muy) nublado** it's (very) cloudy, overcast (6)

nuclear: energía nuclear nuclear energy (15)

nuestro/a(s) *poss. adj.* our (3); *poss. pron.* ours, of ours (17)

nueve nine (1)

nuevo/a new (3); **Año Nuevo** New Year; **Nueva York** New York

numérico/a numerical

número number (1); **número ordinal** ordinal number (13)

numeroso/a numerous

nunca never (3); **casi nunca** almost never (3)

nupcial nuptial; **votos** (*m. pl.*) **nupciales** wedding vows

nutritivo/a nutritious

O

o or (1)

obedecer (obedezco) to obey (15)

obispo bishop

objetivo *n.* objective
objeto object (2)
obligación *f.* obligation
obligado/a customary
obligatorio/a obligatory
obra work; **obra de arte** work of art (13); **obra de teatro** play (13); **obra maestra** masterpiece (13); **obra teatral** play
obrero/a worker, laborer (17)
observación *f.* observation
observar to observe
obstáculo obstacle
obstante: no obstante however
obtener (*like* **tener**) to get; to obtain (12)
obvio/a obvious
ocasión *f.* occasion
ocasionar to cause
océano ocean (8); **océano Pacífico** Pacific Ocean
ochenta eighty (3)
ocho eight (1)
ochocientos/as eight hundred (4)
octavo/a eighth (13)
octillizo/a octuplet
octubre *m.* October (6)
oculista *m., f.* ophthalmologist
oculto/a hidden
ocupación *f.* occupation
ocupado/a busy (6)
ocupar to hold; to occupy
ocurrir to occur (14)
odiar to hate (8)
oeste *m.* west (6)
ofensivo/a offensive
off: voz en off voice over
oficial official
oficina office (2)
oficio trade (*profession*) (17)
ofrecer (ofrezco) to offer (8)
ofrenda *n.* offering
oído inner ear (11)
oír to hear (5); to listen to (*music, the radio*) (5)
ojalá (que) I hope (that) (13)
ojo eye (11); **ojo alerta** eagle eye; **¡ojo!** *interj.* watch out!
olímpico/a: Juegos (*m. pl.*) **Olímpicos** Olympic Games
oliva: aceite (*m.*) (**de oliva**) (olive) oil (7)
olor *m.* odor
olvidar to forget (9)
omnipresente omnipresent
once eleven (1)
onda wave; **¿cuál es tu onda?** what's your style?; **en onda** in style; **¿qué onda?** what's new/happening?
onomatopeya onomatopoeia
onomatopéyico/a onomatopoeic
ONU *f.* **(Organización** [*f.*] **de Naciones Unidas)** U.N. (United Nations)

opción *f.* option
opcional optional
ópera opera (13)
operación *f.* operation
opinar to think; to have/express an opinion
opinión *f.* opinion
oponerse (a) (*like* **poner**) to oppose
oportunidad *f.* opportunity
optar (por) to opt (for)
optimista *m., f.* optimist; *adj.* optimistic
opuesto/a opposite
oración *f.* sentence
oral oral (14); **informe** (*m.*) **oral** oral report (14)
órale *interj. sl.* wow!
orangután *m.* orangutan
órbita orbit
orden *m.* order
ordenado/a neat (6)
ordenador *m. Sp.* computer
ordenar to put in order
ordinal: número ordinal ordinal number (13)
ordinario/a ordinary
oreja (outer) ear (11)
orgánico/a organic
organismo organism
organización *f.* organization
organizar (c) to organize
órgano organ
orgullo pride
orgulloso/a proud
orientación *f.* orientation
oriental eastern
origen *m.* origin
originario/a native
originarse to come from
oriundo/a native
oro gold (4); **de oro** gold (4)
orquesta orchestra (13)
orquídea orchid
ortogar (gu) to give
ortografía spelling
ortográfico/a: acento ortográfico accent mark
oscuridad *f.* darkness
oso/a bear
ostra oyster
otavaleno/a resident of Otavalo (*Ecuador*)
otoño fall, autumn (6)
otorgar (gu) to grant
otro/a other, another (3); **otra vez** again; **por el otro lado** on the other hand
oveja sheep
ozono: capa de ozono ozone layer (15)

P

paciencia patience
paciente *n. m., f.* patient (11); *adj.* patient

pacífico/a Pacific; **océano Pacífico** Pacific Ocean
padrastro stepfather
padre *m.* father (3); *m. pl.* parents (3); **Día** (*m.*) **del Padre** Father's Day
padrino godfather
paella *Spanish dish made with rice, shellfish, and often chicken, and flavored with saffron*
pagado/a: empleo bien/mal pagado well-/poorly paid job/position (17)
pagar (gu) to pay (for) (2)
página page; **página web** webpage (12)
país *m.* country (3)
pájaro bird (3)
Pakistán Pakistan
pakistaní *m., f.* Pakistani
palabra word (1); **palabra indefinida y negativa** *gram.* indefinite and negative word (7)
palacio palace
palestino/a Palestinian
palma palm tree
palmera palm tree
palo stick
palomitas *f. pl.* popcorn
pampa plain (*geography, Arg.*)
pan *m.* bread (7); **pan tostado** toast (7)
panadería bakery
panameño/a *n., adj.* Panamanian
páncreas *m. inv.* pancreas
pandemia pandemic
pandilla gang
pánel (*m.*) **solar** solar panel
panhispano/a Pan-Hispanic
pánico panic
panorama *m.* panorama
pantalla (grande/plana) (big/flat) screen (monitor) (12)
pantalones *m. pl.* pants (4); **pantalones cortos** shorts (4)
pañuelo handkerchief
papa (frita) (French fried) potato (7)
papá *m.* father, dad (3); *m. pl.* parents
papel *m.* paper (2); role (13)
papi *m.* dad, daddy
par *m.* pair
para (intended) for; in order to (3); **para +** *inf.* (*do something*) (10); **para nada...** at all (8); **para que** so that (16)
parabrisas *m. inv.* windshield (15)
paracaídas *m. inv.* parachute
paracaidismo skydiving
parada stop (8); **hacer paradas** to make stops (8); **parada del autobús** bus stop (12); **parada del metro** subway stop (12)
paraguayo/a *n., adj.* Paraguayan
parar to stop (15)

parcial partial; **empleo de tiempo parcial** part-time job/position (17); **trabajo de tiempo parcial** part-time job (14)

pardo/a brown

parecer (parezco) (*like* **gustar**) to seem; **parecerse (a)** to resemble

pared *f.* wall (5)

pareja (married) couple; partner (16)

paréntesis *m. inv.* parentheses

pariente *m.* relative (3)

parlamentario/a parliamentary

parque *m.* park

parqueadero parking lot

parquear to park

párrafo paragraph

parranda Christmas party *(Cuba)*

parrilla grill

parte *f.* part (5); **por todas partes** everywhere (14)

participación *f.* participation

participante *m., f.* participant

participar to participate

particular particular; unique; **en particular** particularly

partida: punto de partida starting point

partido game, match (10); political party (18)

partir: a partir de beyond (4)

pasado/a past, last (11); **el año pasado** last year; **pasado mañana** the day after tomorrow (5)

pasaje *m.* fare, price (*of a transportation ticket*) (8)

pasajero/a passenger (8)

pasaporte *m.* passport (8)

pasar to spend (*time*) (6); to happen (6); **pasar hambre** to go hungry; **pasar la aspiradora** to vacuum (10); **pasar las vacaciones en...** to spend one's vacation in . . . (8); **pasar por el control de seguridad** to go/pass through security (check) (8); **pasar por la aduana** to go/pass through customs (8); **pasarlo bien/mal** to have a good/bad time (9)

pasatiempo pastime (10)

Pascua Easter (9)

pasear to take a walk, stroll; to go for a ride; **pasear en bicicleta** to ride a bicycle (10)

paseo walk, stroll; **dar un paseo** to take a walk (10)

pasillo aisle (8)

pasión *f.* passion

paso step

pastel *m.* cake (7); pie (7); **pastel de cumpleaños** birthday cake (9)

pastilla pill (11)

pastor(a) minister

pata leg (*of an animal*)

patata (frita) (French fried) potato (7)

paternidad *f.* paternity

paterno/a paternal

patinaje *m.* skating (10)

patinar to skate (10)

patio patio (5); yard (5)

patojo/a *sl.* young man/woman (*Guat.*)

patriarcal patriarchal

Patricio: Día (*m.*) **de San Patricio** St. Patrick's Day

patrimonio patrimony

patriota *m., f.* patriot

patriótico/a patriotic

patronal: fiesta patronal *party dedicated to patron saint*

pavo turkey (7)

paz *f.* (*pl.* **paces**) peace (18)

peca freckle

pecho chest

pedazo piece

pedir (pido) (i) to ask for (5); to order (5); **pedir disculpas** to apologize (14); **pedir prestado/a** to borrow (17)

pegar (gu) to hit (14); **pegarse con/contra** to run, bump into/against (14)

peinarse to comb/brush one's hair (5)

Pekín Peking

pelado/a *sl.* young man/woman (*Col.*)

pelear to fight (10)

pelícano pelican

película movie (5)

peligro danger; **especie** (*f.*) **en peligro de extinción** endangered species (15)

peligroso/a dangerous

pelo hair; **teñirse (me tiño) (i) el pelo** to dye one's hair; **tomarle el pelo** to pull someone's leg

pelota ball (10)

pelotero/a baseball player

peluche: animal (*m.*) **de peluche** stuffed animal

peluquero/a hairstylist (17)

pen drive *m.* memory stick (12)

pena pity

pendiente *m.* earring (*Sp.*)

península peninsula

pensar (pienso) (de/en) to think (about) (5); **pensar** + *inf.* to intend, plan to (*do something*) (5); **pensar que** to think that (5)

penúltimo/a next to last

peor worse (6)

pepino cucumber (7)

pequeño/a small (3)

percatarse to realize

percepción *f.* perception

percibir to perceive

percusión *f.* percussion

perder (pierdo) to lose; to miss (*an event*) (5)

perdón excuse me (1)

perdonar to forgive

perdurable lasting

peregrinación *f.* pilgrimage

perezoso/a lazy (3)

perfección *f.* perfection

perfecto/a perfect

pérfido/a treacherous

perfil *m.* profile

perforación *f.* drilling (*well*)

perfume *m.* perfume

periódico newspaper (3)

periodismo journalism

periodista *m., f.* journalist (17)

período period (*of time*)

permanecer (permanezco) to remain, stay

permanente permanent

permiso permission; permit; **(con) permiso** excuse me (1); **permiso de manejar** driving permit

permitir to permit, allow (12)

pero but (1)

perro dog (3)

persecución *f.* persecution

perseguir (*like* **seguir**) to chase; to pursue

persona person (2)

personaje *m.* character (*book, movie*)

personal (*m.*) **médico** medical personnel (11)

personal *adj.* personal; **pronombre** (*m.*) **personal** *gram.* personal pronoun (2)

personalidad *f.* personality

perspectiva perspective

persuasivo/a persuasive

pertenecer (pertenezco) a to belong to

perturbar to perturb, bother

peruano/a *n., adj.* Peruvian

pesado/a boring; difficult (10); heavy

pesar to weigh; **a pesar de** in spite of

pesas: levantar pesas to lift weights (11)

pescadería fish market

pescado fish (7)

pescar (qu) to fish

pesimista *m., f.* pessimistic

peso weight

pestaña eyelash

petición *f.* request

petróleo petroleum, oil (15)

petrolero/a *adj.* oil; petroleum

pez *m.* (*pl.* **peces**) fish (15)

picante hot, spicy (7)

picar (qu) to bite; to sting

picnic: hacer un *picnic* to have a picnic (10)

pico peak

pie *m.* foot (11); **dedo del pie** toe; **levantarse con el pie izquierdo** to get up on the wrong side of the bed (14)

piedra stone

piel *f.* skin

pierna leg (11)

pieza piece

pila battery; **ponerse las pilas** to get one's act together; to energize oneself

pilar *m.* pillar

Pilates: hacer (el método) Pilates to do Pilates (11)

píldora pill

piloto *m., f.* pilot (8)

pimienta pepper (*condiment*) (7)

pingüino penguin

pino pine (tree)

pinola *m. typical Nicaragua drink*

pintar to paint (13)

pintor(a) painter (13)

pintura painting (*general*) (13)

piña pineapple

pirámide *f.* pyramid

piraña piranha

Pirineos *m. pl.* Pyrenees

piscina swimming pool (5)

Piscis *m.* Pisces

pisco *alcoholic beverage of Peru and Chile*

piso floor (*of a building*) (12); **barrer (el piso)** to sweep (the floor) (10); **primer piso** first floor (second story) (12); **segundo piso** second floor (third story) (12)

pizarra chalkboard

pizarrón *m.* (chalk)board (2); **pizarrón blanco** whiteboard (2)

placa license plate

placer *m.* pleasure

plan *m.* plan (10); **hacer planes para** + *inf.* to make plans to (*do something*) (10)

planchar to iron (10)

planeación *f.* planning

planear to plan

planeta *m.* planet (15)

planetario/a planetary

plano map (*of a city*); blueprint

plano/a flat; **pantalla plana** flat screen (monitor) (12)

planta plant

planta baja ground floor (12)

plantación *f.* plantation

plasma: televisión plasma *f.* plasma television (12)

plástico plastic

plata *n.* silver (4); **de plata** *adj.* silver (4)

plátano plantain

platino platinum

plato dish; course (7); plate (5); **plato principal** main course (7)

playa beach (6)

plaza plaza, square (4)

plazo deadline (14); **a plazos** in installments (17)

pleno/a complete; full

plomero/a plumber (17)

pluma pen

plurinacional multinational

población *f.* population (15)

pobre poor (3)

pobreza poverty

poco (a) little (2); few (4); **un poco (de)** a little bit (of) (2)

poder *v.* to be able, can (4)

poder *n. m.* power; **poder adquisitivo** purchasing power

poderoso/a powerful

poema *m.* poem (13)

poesía poetry

poeta *m., f.* poeta (13)

poético/a poetic

polaco/a Polish

policía *m., f.* police officer (15); *f.* police (*force*); **mujer (*f.*) policía** policewoman

polinésico/a Polynesian

política politics; policy (18)

político/a *n.* politician (18); *adj.* political; **ciencias (*f. pl.*) políticas** political science (2)

pollera *indigenous skirt of the Andes*

pollo chicken (7); **pollo asado** roast chicken (7); **pollo frito** fried chicken

polvo dust

poner to put (5); to place (5); to turn on (*an appliance*) (12); **poner atención** to pay attention; **poner la mesa** to set the table (10); **ponerle una inyección** to give (*someone*) a shot (11); **ponerse** to put on (*an article of clothing*) (5); **ponerse** + *adj.* to become, get + *adj.* (9); **ponerse las pilas** to get one's act together; to energize oneself; **ponerse rojo/a** to blush (9)

popularidad *f.* popularity

por about (6); because of (6); through (8); for (8); by (14); **gracias por** + *noun/ inf.* thanks for (9); **por consiguiente** as a result; **por Dios** for heaven's sake (14); **por ejemplo** for example (14); **por el otro lado** on the other hand; **por ello** therefore; **por eso** for that reason (3); **por favor** please (1); **por fin** finally (5); **por la mañana** in the morning (2); **por la noche** at night, in the evening (2); **por la tarde** in the afternoon (2); **por lo general** generally (5); **por lo menos** at least (9); **por lo regular** in general; **por primera/última vez** for the first/ last time (14); **por si acaso** just in case (14); **por todas partes** everywhere (14); **por un lado** on one hand

porcentaje *m.* percentage

porción *f.* portion, part

pormenorizado/a detailed

poro pore

porotos *m. pl.* beans

porque because (3)

portafolio portfolio

portarse bien/mal to (mis)behave (9)

portátil portable; **computadora portátil** laptop (computer) (2); **ordenador** (*m.*) **portátil** (*Sp.*) laptop computer (12)

portero/a building manager; doorman (12)

portón *m.* front door; gate

portugués *m.* Portuguese (*language*)

portugués, portuguesa *n., adj.* Portuguese

posar to pose

posesión *f.* possession

posesivo/a possessive (17); **adjetivo posesivo** *gram.* possessive adjective (3)

posibilidad *f.* possibility

posible possible (3); **es posible que** it's possible that (13) **no es posible** it's not possible (13)

posición *f.* position

positivo/a positive

posponer (*like* **poner**) to postpone

postal: tarjeta postal postcard (8)

posterior later, subsequent

postre *m.* dessert (7)

postularse to run (18); **postularse como candidato/a** to run as a candidate (18); **postularse para un cargo como candidato/a** to run for a position as a candidate (18)

postura posture

potencia power

potencial *m.* potential; *adj.* potential

práctica practice

practicar (qu) to practice (2); **practicar el alpinismo** to mountain climb; **practicar un deporte** to play a sport

práctico/a practical

pradera meadow

preadolescencia preadolescence

precedente *m.* precedent

preceder to precede

precio (fijo) (fixed, set) price (4)

precioso/a precious

precipicio precipice

precipitado/a hasty

precisamente precisely

precolombino/a pre-Columbian

predicción *f.* prediction

predominante predominant

predominar to predominate

preescolar *adj.* preschool

preferencia preference (1)

preferir (prefiero) (i) to prefer (4)

¿por qué? why? (3)

pregunta question (5); **hacer una pregunta** to ask a question (5)

preguntar to ask (*a question*) (8)

prehistórico/a prehistoric

premio prize

prenda article of clothing
prender to fasten
prensa (print) press (18); news media (18); **quiosco de prensa** newsstand (18)
prensado/a pressed
preocupación f. worry
preocupado/a worried (6)
preocupar(se) to worry
preparación f. preparation
preparar to prepare (7); **prepararse** to prepare oneself; to get ready
preparatoria (**prepa**) pre-university study
preposición f. gram. preposition (5)
prescribir to prescribe
preseleccionado/a pre-selected
presencia presence
presencial: de forma presencial in person
presentación f. presentation
presentador(a) presenter; (television) anchor
presentar to introduce; to present
presente m. present (time); gram. present tense; adj. present
preservar to preserve
presidencia presidency
presidencial presidential
presidente/a president
presión f. pressure (14); **estar bajo muchas presiones** to be under a lot of pressure (14); **tener muchas presiones** to be under a lot of stress (14)
preso/a prisoner
prestado/a: pedir prestado/a to borrow (17)
préstamo loan (17)
prestar to lend (8)
prestigioso/a prestigious
presupuestario/a budgetary
presupuesto budget (17)
pretérito gram. preterite
preuniversitario/a pre-university
prevenir (like **venir**) to warn
primario/a primary; first; elementary; **escuela primaria** elementary school
primavera spring (6)
primer(o/a) first (5); **el primero de** the first of (month) (6); **primer piso** first floor (second story) (12); **por primera vez** for the first time (14)
primo/a cousin (3); m. pl. cousins (3)
princesa princess
principal main; **plato principal** main course (7)
príncipe m. prince
principiante m., f. beginner; novice
principio beginning; **al principio de** at the beginning of (17)

priorizar (c) to prioritize
prisa: tener prisa to be in a hurry (4)
privacidad f. privacy
privado/a private
privilegio privilege
probabilidad f. probability
probable probable (13); **es probable que** it's likely, probable that (13); **no es probable que** it's not probable (13)
probar (pruebo) to try, taste
problema m. problem
problemático/a problematic
procedimiento procedure
procesión f. procession
proceso process
proclamar to proclaim
procurar to procure
producción f. production
producir (like **conducir**) to produce
productivo/a productive
producto product; **producto nacional bruto** gross national product
productor(a) producer
profesión f. profession (17)
profesional n. m., f. professional, person with a profession; adj. professional
profesionista n. m., f. professional, person with a profession
profesor(a) professor (1)
profesorado faculty
profundidad f. depth
profundo/a deep
programa m. program; **programa (del curso)** (course) syllabus (14)
programación f. programming
programador(a) programmer (17)
progresivo/a progressive
progreso progress
prohibir (prohíbo) to prohibit, forbid (12)
proliferación f. proliferation
promedio average
promesa promise
prometer to promise (8)
prominente prominent
promover (promuevo) to promote
pronombre m. gram. pronoun; **pronombre personal** gram. personal pronoun (2); **pronombre relativo** gram. relative pronoun
pronosticar (qu) to forecast
pronóstico forecast
pronto soon; **hasta pronto** see you soon; **tan pronto como** as soon as (17)
prontuario guide
pronunciación f. pronunciation
pronunciar to pronounce
propiedad f. property; characteristic
propio/a own, one's own (17)
proponer (like **poner**) to propose
proporción f. proportion

proporcionar to provide
propósito purpose
prórroga extension
protagonista m., f. protagonist
protección f. protection
protector(a) protective
proteger (protejo) to protect (15)
proteína protein
protestante n., adj. m., f. Protestant
protestantismo Protestantism
protestar to protest
provecho: ¡buen provecho! enjoy your meal!
proveedor(a) provider
proveer (like **creer**) to provide
proverbio proverb
providencia providence
provincia province
provocar (qu) to cause
próximo/a next; **el próximo (martes...)** next (Tuesday . . .) (5); **la próxima semana** next week (5)
proyección f. projection
proyecto project
prudente prudent
prueba quiz; test (14); proof
psicología psychology
psicólogo/a psychologist
publicación f. publication
publicar (qu) to publish (12)
publicidad f. publicity
publicitario/a adj. advertising
público n. audience (13)
público/a adj. public (15); **transporte (m.) público** public transportation
pueblo town
puente m. bridge
puerco pig
puerta door (2); **puerta de embarque** boarding gate (8)
puerto port (8)
puertorriqueño/a n., adj. Puerto Rican
pues conj. well
puesto job; position; place (in line) (8)
pulgada inch
pulido/a polished
pulmones m. pl. lungs (11)
pulpería grocery store (C.A.)
pulpo octopus
punto point; **a punto de** + inf. about to + inf.; **en punto** on the dot (time) (1); **hora punta** peak hour; **punto cardinal** cardinal point (6); **punto de partida** starting point; **punto de vista** point of view
puntuación f. punctuation
pupusa thick stuffed corn tortilla
puro cigar
puro/a pure (15)
púrpura n. purple
purpúreo/a adj. purple

Q

que that, which (3); who (3); **así que** therefore, consequently, so; **hasta que** *conj.* until; **que Dios te bendiga** God bless you; **ya que** since

¿qué? what? which?; **¿a qué hora... ?** at what time . . . ? (1); **¿con qué frecuencia... ?** how often . . . ? (3); **¿por qué?** why? (3)

¡qué... ! what . . . !; **¡qué bacán!** fantastic! **¡qué yuca!** how difficult!

quebrarse (me quiebro) to break

quedar to remain; to be left (14); to stay; to remain (*in a place*) (6)

quehacer (*m.*) **doméstico** household chore (10)

quejarse (de) to complain (about) (8)

quemada *n.* burn

quemar to burn

querer to want (4); to love (16); **eso quiere decir...** that means . . . (11); **fue sin querer** I didn't mean to do it (14); **quererse** to love each other; to be fond of each other (11); **querido/a** dear (6)

querido/a dear (6)

queso cheese (7)

quetzal *currency of Guatemala*

quien who; whom

¿quién(es)? who? whom?; **¿de quién?** whose? (3)

química chemistry (2)

quince fifteen (1); **menos quince** fifteen minutes till (*hour*) (1); **y quince** fifteen minutes after (*the hour*) (1)

quinceañera *young woman's fifteenth birthday party; young woman who is turning fifteen* (9)

quinientos/as five hundred (4)

quintillizo/a quintuplet

quinto/a fifth (13)

quiosco de prensa newsstand (18)

quiropráctico/a chiropractor

quitar to remove; **quitar la mesa** to clear the table (10); **quitarse** to take off (*an article of clothing*) (5)

quizás *adv.* perhaps

R

rabia rutera road rage

ración *f.* portion

radiante bright, shining, radiant

radical *m. gram.* root

radio *m.* radio (*apparatus*) (12); *f.* radio (*medium*); **estación** (*f.*) **de radio** radio station (18)

radioyente *m., f.* radio listener; *m. pl.* radio audience

raíz *f.* (*pl.* **raíces**) root

rama branch

rana frog

ranchera *traditional music of Mexico sung by mariachis*

rancho ranch

rap *m.* rap music

rapanui *n. m., f. indigenous person of Easter Island*

rápido *adv.* quickly

rápido/a fast; **comida rápida** fast food

rápidos *m. pl.* rapids

raqueta racket

raro/a rare; strange

rascacielos *m. inv.* skyscraper (15)

rata rat

rato while, short time; **ratos libres** spare (free) time (10)

ratón *m.* mouse (12)

raya: de rayas striped (4)

rayar to scratch

raza race (*ethnic*)

razón *f.* reason; **no tener razón** to be wrong (4); **tener razón** to be right (4)

reacción *f.* reaction

reaccionar to react

real royal; real

realidad *f.* reality

realismo realism

realista *m., f.* realistic

realizar (c) to achieve; to attain

rebaja sale, reduction; *pl.* sales, reductions (4); **en rebaja** on sale

rebanada slice

rebasar to pass (*vehicle*)

rebelde *n. m., f.* rebel; *adj.* rebellious

rebelión *f.* rebellion

recado message

recámara bedroom

recepción *f.* reception

recepcionista *m., f.* receptionist

receptor *m.* receiver; recipient

receta recipe (7); prescription (11)

recetar to prescribe

recibir to receive (3)

recibo receipt (17)

reciclaje *m.* recycling (15)

reciclar to recycle (15)

recién recently; **recién casado/a (con)** newlywed (to) (16)

reciente recent

recipiente *m.* container

recíproco/a reciprocal

recitar to recite

recoger (recojo) to collect (14); to pick up (14)

recomendable recommendable

recomendación *f.* recommendation

recomendar (recomiendo) to recommend (8)

reconocer (like **conocer**) to recognize

reconocimiento recognition

reconquista reconquest

reconstituido/a remarried; hybrid (*of a family*)

reconstituir (*like* **construir**) to reconstitute; to reconstruct

recordar (recuerdo) to remember (9)

recrear to recreate

recreo recess

recto/a straight; **(todo) recto** straight ahead (15)

rector(a) university president

recuerdo memory

recuperación *f.* recuperation

recuperador(a) recuperative

recuperar to recuperate

recurso resource; **recurso natural** natural resource (15)

red *f.* network; internet; **navegar (gu) la Red** to surf the internet; **red social** social network (12)

redacción *f.* editing

redactar to write; to edit

reducción *f.* reduction

reducir (*like* **conducir**) to reduce

reemplazar (c) to replace

referencia reference

referirse (me refiero) (i) (a) to refer (to)

refinado/a refined

reflejar to reflect

reflexivo/a reflexive; **verbo reflexivo** *gram.* reflexive verb (5)

reforma change

refrán *m.* saying, proverb

refresco soft drink (7)

refrigerador *m.* refrigerator (10)

refrigeradora refrigerator

refugio refuge

regalar to give (*as a gift*) (8)

regalo present, gift (3)

regatear to haggle; to bargain (4)

regateo bartering

reggae *m.* reggae

régimen *m.* regime

región *f.* region

regir (rijo) (i) to govern

registración *f.* registration

registrar to register

registro register; record

regla rule

regresar to return (*to a place*) (2); **regresar a casa** to go home (2)

regulador(a) regulator

regular *adj.* so-so (1); **por lo regular** in general; *v.* to regulate

regularidad *f.* regularity

reina queen (18)

reinar to reign

reino kingdom

reírse (río) (i) (de) to laugh (about) (9)

reiterar to reiterate

reivindicación *f.* vindication

reivindicar (qu) to reclaim

reja bar (*of prison*)

relación *f.* relation; relationship; **relación sentimental** emotional relationship (16)

relacionar to relate

relajado/a relaxed

relajante relaxing

relajarse to relax

relámpago lightning

relativo/a: pronombre (*m.*) **relativo** *gram.* relative pronoun

relevante relevant

religión *f.* religion

religioso/a religious

relleno/a filled

reloj *m.* watch (4)

remarcar (qu) to remark

remate: de remate hopeless(ly)

remedio remedy

remodelado/a remodeled

remoto/a: control (*m.*) **remoto** remote control (12)

remuneración *f.* remuneration

renovable renewable (15); **energía renovable** renewable energy (15)

renovar (renuevo) to renew

rentar to rent (*Mex.*)

renunciar (a) to resign (from) (17)

reparar to repair (15)

repasar to review

repaso review

repeler to repel

repente: de repente suddenly (11)

repetición *f.* repetition

repetir (repito) (i) to repeat

repetitivo/a repetitive

reportaje *m.* report (*on a news show*)

reportar to report

reportero/a reporter (18)

represa dam

representación *f.* representation

representante *n. m., f.* representative ; **representante al congreso** Congressional representative (18)

representar to represent

representativo/a *adj.* representative

reprobar (repruebo) to fail

república republic

republicano/a republican

requerir (requiero) (i) to require

requisito requirement

rescatar to rescue

reseña review (*book, movie*)

reserva reserve; reservation (*Sp.*); **hacer reserva** to make a reservation

resfriado *n.* cold (11)

resfriado/a *adj.* congested, stuffed up (11)

resfriarse (me resfrío) to catch/get a cold (11)

residencia dormitory (2); **residencia de ancianos** nursing home (12)

residencial *m.* building (*housing*)

residente *m., f.* resident

residuos *m. pl.* waste

resistente resistant; strong

resistir to resist

resolver (resuelvo) (*p.p.* **resuelto**) to solve; to resolve (15)

respectivo/a respective

respecto: a este respecto in this regard; **(con) respecto a** regarding

respetar to respect

respeto respect

respiración *f.* breathing

respirar to breathe (11)

responder to respond

responsabilidad *f.* responsibility (18); **responsabilidad cívica** civic duty (18)

responsable responsible

respuesta answer (6)

restablecimiento re-establishment; restoration

restaurante *m.* restaurant (7)

resto rest, remainder

restricción *f.* restriction

resuelto/a (*p.p. of* **resolver**) resolved

resultado result

resumen *m.* summary; **en resumen** in summary

resumir to summarize

resurrección *f.* resurrection

retribuir (*like* **contribuir**) to reward

retrospectivo/a retrospective

retumbar to resound

reunión *f.* meeting

reunirse (me reúno) (con) to get together (with) (9)

revelar to reveal

revés: al revés backwards

revisar to check (15)

revista magazine (3)

revolucionario/a revolutionary

revolver (*like* **volver**) to stir

rey *m.* king (18)

rezar (c) to pray

Ricitos de Oro Goldilocks

rico/a rich (3); tasty, savory; rich (7)

ridículo/a ridiculous

riesgo risk; **de alto riesgo** high risk

rígido/a rigid

rima rhyme

rimar to rhyme

rincón *m.* corner

rinoceronte *m.* rhinoceros

riñón *m.* kidney

río river (15)

rioplatense *adj., m., f.* from the **Río de la Plata** area

riqueza richness

risa laughter

ritmo rhythm; **ritmo de la vida** pace of life (15)

rito rite; ritual

robar to rob; to steal

robo theft; robbery

rodante: cinta rodante treadmill

rodeado/a (de) surrounded (by)

rodear to go around

rojo/a red (4)

Roma Rome

romano/a Roman

romántico/a romantic

romper(se) (*p.p.* **roto**) to break (14); **romper (con)** to break up (with) (16)

ron *m.* rum

ropa clothing (4); **ropa interior** underwear (4)

ropero wardrobe

rosa rose; **rosa té** tea rose

rosado/a pink (4)

rosario rosary

rostro face

roto/a (*p.p. of* **romper**) broken

rotulador *m.* felt-tipped pen

rubio/a blond(e) (3)

rueda wheel, tire; **rueda de molino** treadmill

ruido noise (5)

ruidoso/a noisy

ruina ruin (13)

ruso Russian (*language*)

ruso/a *n., adj.* Russian

ruta route

rutero/a: rabia rutera road rage

rutina routine (5)

rutinario/a *adj.* routine

S

sábado Saturday (5)

saber to know (7); **saber** + *inf.* to know how to (*do something*) (7)

sabiduría wisdom

sabio/a wise

sabor *m.* flavor

sabroso/a tasty

sacar (qu) to extract (11); get (*grades*) (14); to withdraw, take out (17); **sacar dinero** to withdraw money; **sacar fotos** to take photos (8); **sacar la basura** to take out the trash (10); **sacar la lengua** to stick out one's tongue (11); **sacarle un diente / una muela** to extract (*someone's*) tooth/molar (11)

sacerdote *m.* priest

safari: ir de safari to go on a safari

Sagitario Sagittarius
sagrado/a sacred
sal *f.* salt (7)
sala living room (5); **sala de espera** waiting room (8); **sala de fumadores/ de fumar** smoking area (8); **sala de urgencias** emergency room
salarial: brecha salarial wage gap
salario pay, wages (*often per hour*) (17)
salchicha sausage; hot dog (7)
salida departure (8)
salir (de) to leave (*a place*) (5); **salir bien/mal** to come/turn out well/ badly; to do poorly/well (5); **salir (con)** to go out (with) (5); **salir de vacaciones** to leave on vacation (8); **salir (para)** to leave (for) (*a place*) (5)
salmón *m.* salmon (7)
salón (*m.*) **de clase** classroom (2)
salsa sauce (7); salsa (*music*)
salsero/a *adj.* salsa (*music*)
saltar to jump
salud *f.* health (11)
saludable healthy
saludarse to greet each other (11)
saludo greeting (1)
salvadoreño/a *n., adj.* Salvadoran
salvaje wild (15)
salvar to save
san, santo/a *n.* saint; **Día** (*m.*) **de San Patricio** St. Patrick's Day; **Día** (*m.*) **de San Valentín** St. Valentine's Day
sanador(a) healer
sancocho *stew made with meat, cassava, and plantains*
sandalias *f. pl.* sandals (4)
sandía watermelon
sándwich *m.* sandwich (7)
sangre *f.* blood (11)
sangriento/a bloody
sanitario/a health; **asistencia sanitaria** health care
sano/a healthy (11); **llevar una vida sana** to lead a healthy life (11)
santo saint
santo/a holy
santuario sanctuary
sarcástico/a sarcastic
sartén *f.* skillet
satélite *m.* satellite
satírico/a satirical
satisfacción *f.* satisfaction
satisfactorio/a satisfactory
satisfecho/a satisfied
Saudito/a: Arabia Saudita Saudi Arabia
sazonar to season
secadora clothes dryer (10)
secar(se) (qu) to dry (oneself)
sección *f.* section
seco/a dry
secretario/a secretary (2)
secreto *n.* secret

secreto/a *adj.* secret
secuencia sequence
secundario/a secondary; **escuela secundaria** high school
sed *f.* thirst; **tener (mucha) sed** to be (very) thirsty (7)
seda silk (4); **de seda** *adj.* silk (4)
sedentario/a sedentary
seducir (*like* **conducir**) to seduce
segmento segment
seguida: en seguida immediately (5)
seguidor(a) follower
seguimiento following
seguir (sigo) (i) to follow (6); to keep on going (15)
según according to (3)
segundo/a second (13); **segundo piso** second floor (third story) (12)
seguridad *f.* security; safety; **control** (*m.*) **de seguridad** security (check) (8); **pasar por el control de seguridad** to go/pass through security (check) (8)
seguro *n.* insurance
seguro/a *adj.* sure, certain (6); **es seguro que** it's a sure thing that (13) **no es seguro** it's not sure (13); **no estar seguro/a de** to not be sure of (13)
seis six (1)
seiscientos/as six hundred (4)
selección *f.* selection; choice
seleccionador(a) *adj.* selection
seleccionar to select; to choose
selva jungle; **Selva Amazónica** Amazon Jungle
selvático/a *adj.* jungle
semáforo traffic signal (15)
semana week; **días** (*m. pl.*) **de la semana** days of the week (5); **fin** (*m.*) **de semana** weekend (2); **la próxima semana** next week (5); **la semana que viene** next week (5); **una vez a la semana** once a week (3)
semanal *m., f.* weekly
sembrar (siembro) to sow, plant
semejante similar
semejanza similarity
semestre *m.* semester
semi-cerrado/a semiclosed
semilla seed
senado senate
senador(a) senator (18)
sencillo/a simple
senda path
senderismo *n.* hiking
sendero path
sensación *f.* sensation
sensibilidad *f.* sensitivity
sensible sensitive
sentarse (me siento) to sit down (5)
sentido sense
sentimental: relación (*f.*) **sentimental** emotional relationship (16)

sentimiento feeling, emotion
sentir (siento) (i) to regret; to feel sorry (13); **lo siento (mucho)** I'm (very) sorry (14); **sentirse** to feel (*an emotion*) (9)
señalar to note; to point out
señor (Sr.) *m.* man; Mr.; sir (1)
señora (Sra.) woman; Mrs.; ma'am (1)
señorita (Srta.) young woman; Miss; Ms. (1)
separación *f.* separation (16)
separar(se) (de) to separate (from) (16)
septiembre *m.* September (6)
séptimo/a seventh (13)
ser to be (1); **ayer fue (miércoles...)** yesterday was (Wednesday . . .) (5); **¿cómo es usted?** what are you (*form. s.*) like? (1); **¿de dónde eres (tú)?** where are you (*fam. s.*) from? (1); **¿de dónde es usted?** where are you (*form. s.*) from? (1); **de última moda** it's trendy (hot) (4); **eres** you are (1); **es** he/she is, you (*form. s.*) are (1); **es absurdo que** it's absurd that (13); **es cierto que** it's certain that (13); **es de...** it is made of . . . (4); **es extraño que** it's strange that (13); **es (im)posible que** it's (im)possible that (13); **es (im)probable que** it's (un) likely, (im)-probable that (13); **es increíble que** it's incredible that (13); **es la una** it's one o'clock (1); **es normal que** it's normal that (13); **es seguro que** it's a sure thing that (13); **es terrible que** it's terrible that (13); **es una lástima que** it's a shame that (13); **es urgente que** + *subj.* it's urgent that (12); **fue sin querer** I didn't mean to do it (14); **llegar (gu) a ser** to become; **no es seguro/(im)posible, (im)probable que** + *subj.* it is not sure/(im)possible, (im)probable that (13); **pasar de ser** to go from being; **¿qué hora es?** what time is it? (1); **ser aburrido/a** to be boring (10); **ser aficionado/a (a)** to be a fan (of) (10); **ser casado/a** to be a married person (16); **ser divertido/a** to be fun (10); **ser en** + *place* to take place in/at (*a place*) (9); **son las...** it's . . . o'clock (1); **(yo) soy de...** I am from . . . (1)
ser (*m.*) **humano** human being
serie *f.* series
serio/a serious
serpiente *f.* snake
servicio service (15); **estación** (*f.*) **de servicio** gas station (15); **servicio militar** military service (18)
servilleta napkin
servir (sirvo) (i) to serve (5); **servir para** to be used for (5)

sesenta sixty (3)

sesión *f.* session

setecientos/as seven hundred (4)

setenta seventy (3)

sevillano/a of or pertaining to Seville

sexismo sexism

sexo sex

sextillo/a sextuplet

sexto/a sixth (13)

si if (4); **por si acaso** just in case (14)

sí yes (1); **sí, me gusta...** yes, I like . . . (1)

sicología psychology (2)

sicólogo/a psychologist (17)

siempre always (3)

sierra mountain

siesta nap; **dormir la siesta** to take a nap

siete seven (1)

siglo century

significado meaning

significar (qu) to mean

significativo/a significant

signo sign

siguiente following (5)

sílaba syllable

silencio silence

silla chair (2)

sillón *m.* armchair (5)

simbólico/a symbolic

simbolizar (c) to symbolize

símbolo symbol

similaridad *f.* similarity

similitud *f.* similarity

simpático/a nice, likeable (3)

sin without (5); **fue sin querer** I didn't mean to do it (14); **sin duda** without a doubt; **sin embargo** nevertheless (6); **sin que** *conj.* without; unless (16)

sinagoga synagogue

sinceridad *f.* sincerity

sincero/a sincere

sino but (rather); **sino que** *conj.* but (rather)

sinónimo synonym

sintético/a synthetic

síntoma *m.* symptom (11)

siquiatra *m., f.* psychiatrist (17)

sísmico/a seismic

sismorresistente earthquake resistant

sistema *m.* system; **analista** (*m., f.*) **de sistemas** systems analyst (17)

sistemático/a systematic

sitio place, location; **sitio web** website (12)

situación *f.* situation

situado/a situated

situarse (me sitúo) to situate oneself; to be placed (*in time*)

snowboard *m.* snowboarding

soberano/a sovereign

sobre *prep.* about (4); on; on top of; over

sobremesa after-dinner conversation

sobrenatural *adj.* supernatural

sobresaliente outstanding

sobresalir (*like* salir) to stand out

sobreviviente *adj., m., f.* surviving

sobrevivir to survive

sobrino/a nephew/niece (3)

social social; **ciencias** (*f. pl.*) **sociales** social sciences (2); **red** (*f.*) **social** social network (12); **trabajador(a) social** social worker (17)

socialismo socialism

socialista *n., adj. m., f.* socialist

socializar (c) to socialize

sociedad *f.* society

socioeconómico/a socioeconomic

sociología sociology (2)

sodio sodium

sofá *m.* couch (5)

soja soybean

sol *m.* sun; **gafas** (*f. pl.*) **de sol** sunglasses (4) **hace (mucho) sol** it's (very) sunny (6.); **tomar el sol** to sunbathe (8)

solar solar; **bloqueador** (*m.*) **solar** sunscreen (8); **energía solar** solar energy (15); **pánel** (*m.*) **solar** solar panel

solas: a solas alone

soldado soldier (17); **mujer** (*f.*) **soldado** female soldier (17)

soleado/a sunny

soledad *f.* solitud

soler (suelo) to tend to

solicitante *m., f.* applicant

solicitar to apply for (*a job*) (17)

solicitud *f.* application (*form*) (17)

sólido/a solid

solitario/a solitary, lonely

solo *adv.* only (2)

solo/a *adj.* alone (5)

soltero/a single (*not married*) (16)

soltura: hablar con soltura to speak fluently

solución *f.* solution

sombra shadow; shade

sombrero hat (4); **sombrero hongo** bowler hat, derby

sonar (sueno) to ring; to sound (10)

sonido sound

sonreír (*like* reír) to smile (9)

sopa soup (7)

soportar to bear

sor *f.* sister (*religious*)

sorber to absorb

sorprendente surprising

sorprender (*like* gustar) to surprise (13)

sorpresa surprise

sospechoso/a suspicious

sostenible sustainable

sostenido/a held

su(s) *poss. adj.* his, her, its, your (*form. s.*); their, your (*form. pl.*) (3)

suave pleasant

subir (a) to go up; to get on (*a vehicle*) (8)

subjuntivo *gram.* subjunctive

subordinado/a: cláusula subordinada *gram.* subordinate clause

subregión *f.* subregion

substituir (*like* construir) to substitute

subtítulo subtitle

suburbio suburb

suceder to occur; to happen

suceso happening

sucesor(a) successor

sucio/a dirty (6)

sudadera sweatshirt (4)

Sudamérica South America

sudamericano/a South American

Suecia Sweden

sueco/a Swedish

suegro/a father-in-law, mother-in-law

sueldo salary (17)

suelo floor

sueño dream; **tener sueño** to be sleepy (4)

suerte *f.* luck (14); **tener buena/mala suerte** to have good/bad luck; to be (un)lucky (14)

suéter *m.* sweater (4)

suficiente enough (11); **lo suficiente** enough (11)

sufijo *gram.* suffix

sufrimiento suffering

sufrir (de) to suffer (from, with) (14)

sugerencia suggestion

sugerir (sugiero) (i) to suggest (9)

suicidio suicide

suizo/a Swiss

sujeto *gram.* subject

sumo/a supreme

superar to overtake

superhombre *m.* superman

superlativo *gram.* superlative

supermercado supermarket (12)

superstición *f.* superstition

supersticioso/a superstitious

supervisor(a) supervisor

suplemento supplement

suponer (*like* poner) to suppose

supremo/a supreme

supuesto: ¡por supuesto! of course! (14)

sur *m.* south (6)

sureste *m.* southeast

surfear to surf

surfing: hacer surfing to surf (10)

suroeste *m.* southwest

surrealismo Surrealism

surrealista *adj. m., f.* surrealist

suscripción *f.* subscription

suspender to suspend

suspenso suspense

sustantivo *gram.* noun (2)
sustrato essence
sutil subtle
SUV *m.* SUV (15)
suyo/a(s) *poss. adj.* your (*form. s., pl.*); his, her, its, their; *poss. pron.* (of) your, yours (*form. s., pl.*); (of) his, her, its, their; (of) theirs (17)

T

tabaco tobacco
tabla table; chart
tableta tablet
tabú *f.* taboo
tacón *m.* heel
taconeo heel tap
tailandés, tailandesa Thai
Tailandia Thailand
taíno/a *pre-Columbian culture of the Caribbean*
tal such, such a; **con tal de** provided (16); **con tal (de) que** *conj.* provided (that) (16); **¿qué tal?** how are you? (1); **tal como** just as; **tal vez** perhaps
taladro drill
talento talent
talla size
taller *m.* (repair) shop (15)
tamal *m.* tamale
tamalada *get-together to make and eat tamales*
tamaño size
también also (1)
tambor *m.* drum
tambora African drum
tampoco neither, not either (7)
tan *adv.* so; as; **tan... como** as . . . as (6); **tan pronto como** as soon as (17)
tanque *m.* tank (15)
tanto/a *adj.* as much, so much; such (a); *pl.* so many; as many; **tanto como** as much as (6); **tanto/a(s)... como** as much/many . . . as (6)
tapa lid
tapar to cover
tapas *f. pl.* appetizers (9)
tapir *m.* tapir
taquigrafía shorthand
tardar to be long / take (a long) time
tarde *adv.* late (2)
tarde *f.* afternoon; **buenas tardes** good afternoon (1); **de la tarde** in the afternoon, P.M. (1); **por la tarde** in the afternoon (2)
tarea homework (5); **tarea doméstica** household chore
tarjeta card (8); **tarjeta bancaria** debit card (17); **tarjeta de crédito** credit card (7); **tarjeta de embarque** boarding pass (8); **tarjeta de identidad** identification card; **tarjeta de identificación**

identification card (14); **tarjeta postal** postcard (8)
tarta cake
tartamudo/a stutterer
tata *fam.* grandpa
tatuaje *m.* tattoo
taza cup (14)
té *m.* tea (7); **rosa té** tea rose
teatral theatrical; **obra teatral** play
teatro theater; **ir al teatro** to go to the theater (10); **obra de teatro** play (13)
techo roof
teclado keyboard
técnico/a technician (17)
tecnología technology
tecnológico/a technological
teja tile
tejedor(a) weaver
tejer to weave (13)
tejido weaving; *pl.* woven goods (13); textiles
tela cloth
tele *f.* T.V.
telediario news program
telefonear to phone
telefonía telephone systems
telefónico/a *adj.* telephone
teléfono phone (2); **hablar por teléfono** to talk on the phone (2); **teléfono celular** cell phone (2); **teléfono fijo** landline (12)
telegrama *m.* telegram
telenovela soap opera
telespectador(a) television viewer
televidente *m., f.* television viewer
televisión (*f.*) (**plasma**) (plasma) television (12); **mirar la tele(visión)** to watch television (3)
televisor *m.* television set
tema *m.* theme, topic
temblar (tiemblo) to tremble
temblor *m.* trembling
temer to fear; to be afraid (13)
temperatura temperature (11); **tomarle la temperatura** to take (*someone's*) temperature (11)
templo temple
temporada season (*hunting, fashion, etc.*)
temporal temporary
temprano *adv.* early (2)
tendencia tendency
tender (tiendo): tender la cama to make the bed
tenedor *m.* fork
tener to have (4); **no tener razón** to be wrong (4); **tener... años** to be . . . years old (3); **tener buena/mala suerte** to have good/bad luck; to be (un)lucky (14); **tener cuidado** to be careful; **tener dolor de** to have a pain/ache in (11); **tener éxito** to be successful; **tener fiebre** to have a

fever; **tener ganas de** + *inf.* to feel like (*doing something*) (4); **tener la culpa** to be at fault; **tener miedo (de)** to be afraid (of) (4); **tener (mucha) hambre** to be (very) hungry (7); **tener (mucha) sed** to be (very) thirsty (7); **tener muchas presiones** to be under a lot of stress (14); **tener (mucho) calor** to be (very) warm, hot (6); **tener (mucho) frío** to be (very) cold (6); **tener prisa** to be in a hurry (4); **tener que** + *inf.* to have to (*do something*) (4); **tener razón** to be right (4); **tener sueño** to be sleepy (4)
tenis *m. inv.* tennis (10); *pl.* tennis shoes (4)
tensión *f.* tension; **tensión arterial** blood pressure
tentación *f.* temptation
tentempié *m.* snack
teñirse (me tiño) (i) el pelo to dye one's hair
teoría theory
terapeuta *m., f.* therapist
terapia therapy
tercer(o/a) third (13)
tereré *m. traditional Paraguayan drink*
terminación *f. gram.* ending
terminal *m.* station, terminal
terminar to finish
término term
termómetro thermometer
ternura tenderness
terraza terrace
terremoto earthquake
terreno piece of land
terrestre *adj.* earth
terrible terrible (13); **es terrible que** it's terrible that (13)
territorio territory
terrorismo terrorism (18)
terrorista *m., f.* terrorist (18); **ataque** (*m.*) **terrorista** (terrorist) attack (18)
tertulia get-together
tesis *f. inv.* thesis
testigo *m., f.* witness (18)
testimonio testimony
texteo text (message)
textil *adj.* textile
texto text; **libro de texto** textbook (2)
ti (*obj. of prep.*) you (*fam.*) (6)
tibetano/a Tibetan
tiempo weather; time (6); *gram.* tense; **a tiempo** on time (8); **conjunción** (*f.*) **de tiempo** conjunction of time (17); **empleo de tiempo completo/parcial** full-/part-time job/position (17); **hace (muy) buen/mal tiempo** it's (very) good/bad weather (6); **jornada de tiempo parcial** part-time job; **¿qué tiempo hace?** what's the weather like? (6); **tiempo libre** free time (10); **trabajo**

de tiempo completo/parcial full/part-time job (14)

tienda shop, store (4); **tienda de acampar** tent; **tienda (de campaña)** tent (8)

tierra land

Tierra Earth (15)

tigre *m.* tiger

tihuanaco/a Tiwanakan (*of or pertaining to the pre-Columbian Tiwanaku civilization of Bolivia*)

tilma poncho; shawl

timbre *m.* doorbell

tímido/a shy

tina bathtub

tinieblas *f. pl.* darkness

tinto/a: vino tinto red wine (7)

tío/a uncle/aunt (3); *m. pl.* aunts and uncles (3)

típico/a typical

tipo type, kind; **de todo tipo** of all kinds

tira cómica comic strip

tirar to throw

tiritar to shiver

títere *m.* puppet

título title

toalla towel (5)

toallero towel rack

tocar (qu) to touch; to play (*a musical instrument*) (2); to honk (15); **tocarle a uno** to be someone's turn (10)

tocineta bacon

todavía still (6)

todo *n.* everything; **de todo** everything (4); **de todo tipo** of all kinds

todo/a *adj.* all (3); every (3); **por todas partes** everywhere (14); **todo derecho/recto** straight ahead (15); **todos los días** every day (2)

todoterreno *inv.* all-terrain (15)

tolerante tolerant

tomar to take (2); to drink (2); **tomar el sol** to sunbathe (8); **tomar unas vacaciones** to take a vacation (8); **tomarle la temperatura** to take (*someone's*) temperature (11); **tomarle el pelo** to pull (*someone's*) leg

tomate *m.* tomato (7)

tono tone

toque *f.* touch

tonto/a silly, foolish (3)

torno: en torno a around

toro bull (15)

torpe clumsy (14)

torre *f.* tower

torta sandwich (*Mex.*)

tortilla potato omelet (*Sp.*); *thin unleavened cornmeal or flour pancake* (*Mex.*)

tortuga turtle

tos *f.* cough (11)

tosco/a rustic; crude

toser to cough (11)

tostado/a toasted (7); **pan** (*m.*) **tostado** toast (7)

tostadora toaster (10)

tostones *m. pl.* crispy fried plantain slices

totalidad *f.* totality

trabajador(a) *adj.* hardworking (3)

trabajador(a) *n.* worker; **trabajador(a) social** social worker (17)

trabajar to work (2)

trabajo work; job (12); report, (piece of) work (14); **carga de trabajo** workload; **trabajo de tiempo completo/parcial** full-/part-time job (14)

trabajólico/a workaholic

trabalenguas *m. inv.* tongue twister

tractor *m.* tractor

tradición *f.* tradition; **tradición cultural** cultural tradition (13)

tradicional traditional

traducción *f.* translation

traducir (*like* **conducir**) to translate

traductor(a) translator (17)

traer to bring (5)

tráfico traffic (15)

tragedia tragedy

trágico/a tragic

traje *m.* suit (4); **traje de baño** swimsuit (4)

trámite *m.* step; procedure

tranquilo/a calm (9); **llevar una vida tranquila** to lead a calm life (11)

transatlántico *n.* ocean liner

transbordador (*m.*) **espacial** space shuttle

transformar to transform

transición *f.* transition

tránsito traffic (15)

transmitir to pass on; to transmit

transnacional international

transporte *m.* transportation; **medio de transporte** means of transportation (8); **transporte público** public transportation

tras *prep.* after

trasero/a back, rear

trasladarse to move

trastienda back room (*of a store*)

tratable treatable

tratado treaty

tratamiento treatment (11)

tratar de + *inf.* to try to (*do something*) (13); **tratar de** + *noun* to deal with + *noun*

través: a través de across; through; throughout

travieso/a mischievous

trayectoria trajectory; path

trébol *m.* clover

trece thirteen (1)

treinta thirty (1); **y treinta** thirty minutes past (*the hour*) (1)

tren *m.* train (8); **estación** (*f.*) **de trenes** train station (8); **ir en tren** to go/travel by train (8)

tres three (1)

trescientos/as three hundred (4)

triángulo triangle

tribu *f.* tribe

tributo tribute

trigo wheat

trillizo/a triplet

trilogía trilogy

trimestre *m.* trimester

triste sad (6)

tristeza sadness

triunfar to triumph

trofeo trophy

trompeta trumpet

tropical tropical; **bosque** (*m.*) **tropical lluvioso** tropical rain forest

trópico *n.* tropics

tropiezo mistake

trotadora treadmill

trozo piece

trucha trout

trueno thunder

tú *subj. pron.* you (*fam. s.*) (2); **¿de dónde eres (tú)?** where are you (*fam. s.*) from? (1); **¿y tú?** and you (*fam. s.*)? (1)

tu(s) your (*fam. s.*) (3)

tuit *m.* tweet (12)

tuitear to tweet

tumba tomb

tuna cactus fruit

turismo tourism

turista *n. m., f.* tourist

turístico/a *adj.* tourist

turnarse to take turns

turno shift (*on a job*)

turrón *m.* type of candy traditionally eaten at Christmas

tutor(a) tutor

tuyo/a(s) *poss. adj.* your (*fam. s.*); *poss. pron.* yours; of yours (*fam. s.*) (17)

Twitter *m.* Twitter (12)

U

u or (*used instead of* **o** *before words beginning with* **o** *or* **ho**)

ubicación *f.* placement, location

ubicar (qu) to locate

ucraniano/a Ukranian

¡uf! *interj.* oof!; whew!

último/a last, final (14); **es de última moda** it's trendy (hot) (4); **por última vez** for the last time (14)

ultramoderno/a ultramodern

un, uno/a one (1); *ind. art.* a, an; **un millón (de)** one million (4); **un poco (de)** a little bit (of) (2); **una vez a la semana** once a week (3)

unánime unanimous

único/a *adj.* only; unique

unidad *f.* unity

unido/a united; **Estados** (*m. pl.*) **Unidos de América** United States of America; **Naciones** (*f. pl.*) **Unidas** United Nations; **Organización** (*f.*) **de Naciones Unidas (ONU)** United Nations (U.N.)

unificar (qu) to unify

unión *f.* union

unir to join (together); to unite; **unirse a** to join (*a cause, organization*)

universidad *f.* university (2)

universitario/a *adj.* (of the) university (14)

universo universe

urbanístico/a *adj.* of urban development

urbano/a urban

urgencias: sala de urgencias emergency room

urgente urgent (12); **es urgente (que)** + *subj.* it's urgent (that) (12)

uruguayo/a *n., adj.* Uruguayan

usar to wear; to use (4)

uso use

usted (Ud., Vd.) *sub. pron.* you (*form. s.*) (2); *obj.* (*of prep.*) you (*form. s.*) (2); **¿a usted le gusta... ?** do you (*form. s.*) like . . . ? (1); **¿cómo es usted?** what are you (*form. s.*) like? (1); **¿cómo se llama usted?** what is your (*form. s.*) name? (1); **¿de dónde es usted?** where are you (*form. s.*) from? (1); **¿y usted?** and you (*form. s.*)? (1)

ustedes (Uds., Vds.) *sub. pron.* you (*form. pl.*); *obj.* (*of prep.*) you (*form pl.*) (2)

usuario/a user (12)

útil useful

utilidad *f.* utility

utilizar (c) to use; to utilize

uva grape

¡uy! *interj.* oh!; ah!

V

vaca cow (15)

vacaciones *f. pl.* vacation; **de vacaciones** on vacation (8); **estar de vacaciones** to be on vacation (8); **ir de vacaciones a...** to go on vacation in/to . . . (8); **pasar las vacaciones en...** to spend one's vacation in . . . (8); **salir de vacaciones** to leave on vacation (8); **tomar unas vacaciones** to take a vacation (8)

vacuna vaccine (11)

vacunación *f.* vaccination

vacunarse to get a shot

vainilla vanilla

valenciano/a Valencian

Valentín: Día (*m.*) **de San Valentín** St. Valentine's Day

valiente courageous

valioso/a valuable

valle *m.* valley

vallenato *Colombian folk music*

valor *m.* value

valorar to value

valorización *f.* appreciation

vals *m. inv.* waltz

vampiro vampire

vanagloriarse to brag

vandalismo vandalism

vapor *m.* mist

vaquero/a cowboy/cowgirl

variación *f.* variation

variante variant

variar (varío) to vary

variedad *f.* variety

varios/as several

vasco/a *n., adj.* Basque

vasija earthenware pot; vessel

vaso (drinking) glass

vasto/a vast

vecindario neighborhood

vecino/a neighbor (12)

vegano/a *n., adj.* vegan

vegetariano/a *n., adj.* vegetarian

vehículo vehicle (15)

veinte twenty (1)

veinticinco twenty-five

veinticuatro twenty-four

veintidós twenty-two

veintinueve twenty-nine

veintiocho twenty-eight

veintiséis twenty-six

veintisiete twenty-seven

veintitrés twenty-three

veintiún, veintiuno/a twenty-one

vejez *f.* (*pl.* **vejeces**) old age (16)

vela candle (9)

velocidad *f.* speed; **límite** (*m.*) **de velocidad** speed limit (15)

vena vein

vendedor(a) salesperson (17)

vender to sell (3)

Venecia Venice

venerar to revere; to venerate

venezolano/a *n., adj.* Venezuelan

venir to come (4); **el año que viene** next year; **el lunes** (*m.*) **que viene** next Monday (5); **la semana que viene** next week (5)

venta sale

ventaja advantage

ventana window (2)

ventanilla small window (*on a plane*) (8)

ver (*p.p.* **visto**) to see (5); **a ver** let's see; **nos vemos** see you around (1)

verano summer (6)

veras: ¿de veras? really

verbo *gram.* verb (2); **verbo reflexivo** *gram.* reflexive verb (5)

verdad *f.* truth; **es verdad que** it's true that (13)

¿verdad? right, don't they (you...)? (4)

verdadero/a true; real

verde green (4)

verdura vegetable (7)

vergonzoso/a shameful

vergüenza embarrassment

verificar (qu) to verify

versión *f.* version

verso verse; line of a poem

verter (vierto) (i) to spill; to shed (*a tear*)

vestido dress (4)

vestir (visto) (i) to dress; **vestirse** to get dressed (5)

veterano/a *n.* veteran

veterinario/a veterinarian (17)

vez *f.* (*pl.* **veces**) time; **a veces** sometimes, at times (3); **alguna vez** once; ever; **cada vez más** increasingly; **cada vez mayor** greater and greater; **dos veces** twice; **en vez de** instead of; **otra vez** again; **por primera/última vez** for the first/last time (14); **tal vez** perhaps; **una vez** once; **una vez a la semana** once a week (3)

viajar to travel (8)

viaje *m.* trip (5); **agencia de viajes** travel agency; **agente de viajes** travel agent; **de viaje** on a trip, traveling (8); **hacer un viaje** to take a trip (5)

viajero/a traveler

vial *adj.* road

vicepresidente/a vice president

víctima victim (18)

victoria victory

vicuña vicuna (llama)

vida life (11); **vida académica** academic life (14); **llevar una vida sana/ tranquila** to lead a healthy/calm life (11); **ritmo de la vida** pace of life (15)

video video (12)

videocasetera video cassette recorder

videojuego videogame; **jugar (juego) (gu) a los videojuegos** to play videogames (10)

videollamada video call

videoturismo videotourism

vidrio glass

viejo/a old (3)

viento wind (6); **hace (mucho) viento** it's (very) windy (6)

viernes *m. inv.* Friday (5)

vietnamita *n., adj. m., f.* Vietnamese

vikingo/a Viking

vinagre *m.* vinegar

vino (blanco, tinto) (white, red) wine (7)

violación *f.* violation

violencia violence; **Día** (*m.*) **Internacional de la No Violencia Contra la Mujer** International No Violence Against Women Day

violento/a violent

violín *m.* violin

Virgen *f.* Virgin (Mary)

virreinato viceroyalty

virus *m. inv.* virus

visión *f.* vision

visita visit

visitante *m., f.* visitor

visitar to visit (10); **visitar un museo** to visit a museum (10)

víspera eve

vista view (12); **punto de vista** point of view

viudo/a widower/widow (16)

vivienda housing (12)

vivir to live (3)

vivo/a lively; bright (*of colors*)

vocabulario vocabulary

vocal *f.* vowel

voga: en voga in vogue

volante *m.* steering wheel; **furia al volante** road rage

volar (vuelo) to fly; **volar en avión** to fly; to go by plane (8)

volcán *m.* volcano

volcánico/a volcanic

voleibol *m.* volleyball (10)

voltear to turn (over)

volumen *m.* volume

voluntario/a volunteer

volver (vuelvo) (*p.p.* **vuelto**) to return (*to a place*) (5); **volver a** + *inf.* to (*do something*) again (5)

vos *subj. pron.* you (*fam. s. C.A., S.A.*)

vosotros/as *sub. pron.* you (*fam. pl. Sp.*); *obj.* (*of prep.*) you (*fam. pl. Sp.*) (2)

votación *f.* vote; voting

votante *m., f.* voter

votar to vote (18)

votos (*m. pl.*) **nupciales** wedding vows

voz *f.* (*pl.* **voces**) voice; **voz en off** voice over

vudú *m.* voodoo

vuelo flight (8); **asistente** (*m., f.*) **de vuelo** flight attendant (8)

vuelta: billete *m.* (*Sp.*) / **boleto** (*L.A.*) **de ida y vuelta** round-trip ticket (8)

vuelto/a (*p.p. of* **volver**) returned

vuestro/a(s) your (*fam. pl. Sp.*) (3); *poss. pron.* your (*fam. pl. Sp.*) (17)

vulnerar to violate; to hurt

W

web: página web webpage (12); **sitio web** website (12)

Y

y and (1); **y cuarto** a quarter (fifteen minutes) after (*the hour*) (1); **y media** half past (*the hour*) (1); **y quince** fifteen minutes after (*the hour*) (1); **y treinta** thirty minutes past (*the hour*) (1)

ya already (9); **ya no** no longer; **ya que** since

yacimiento deposit (*mineral*)

yerba herb

yerno son-in-law

yo *sub. pron.* I (2); **yo soy de...** I am from . . . (1)

yoga *m.* yoga; **hacer (el) yoga** to do yoga (10)

yogur *m.* yogurt (7)

yuca cassava, manioc; **¡qué yuca!** how difficult!

Z

zalamería flattery

zampoña *South American panpipe*

zanahoria carrot (7)

zancudo mosquito

zapatería shoe store

zapato shoe; *pl.* shoes (4)

zarzuela *traditional Spanish operetta*

zócalo central plaza (*Mex.*)

Zodíaco Zodiac

zona zone, area (12)

zoología zoology

zumo juice (*Sp.*)

VOCABULARIES

English-Spanish Vocabulary

A

@ **arroba** (12)

A.M. **de la mañana** (1)

able: to be able **poder** (4)

about **por** (6); **sobre** (4)

abroad: to go abroad **ir al extranjero** (8)

absence **falta** (15)

absent: to be absent (from) **faltar (a)** (9)

absentminded **distraído/a** (14)

absurd: it's absurd that **es absurdo que** (13)

academic **académico/a** (14); academic life **vida académica** (14)

accelerated **acelerado/a** (15)

accident **accidente** m. (14)

according to **según** (3)

account **cuenta** (17); to charge to an account **cargar (gu) a una cuenta** (17)

accountant **contador(a)** (17)

ache n. (in) **dolor (de)** (11); v. **doler (duele)** (like **gustar**) (11); to have an ache in **tener dolor de** (11)

acquainted: to be acquainted with **conocer (conozco)** (7)

act v. **actuar (actúo)** (13)

activity: fun activity **diversión** f. (10)

actor **actor** m. (13)

actress **actriz** f. (pl. **actrices**) (13)

additional **adicional** (1)

address **dirección** f. (7)

adjective gram. **adjetivo** (3); adjective of nationality **adjetivo de nacionalidad** (3); possessive adjective **adjetivo posesivo** (3)

administration: business administration **administración** (f.) **de empresas** (2)

adolescence **adolescencia** (16)

adolescent: as an adolescent **de adolescente** (10)

advice (piece of) **consejo** (7)

advisor **consejero/a** (2)

aerobics: to do aerobics **hacer ejercicios aeróbicos** (11)

affection **cariño** (16)

affectionate **cariñoso/a** (6)

afraid: to be afraid (of) **tener miedo (de)** (4), **temer** (13)

after prep. **después de** (5), conj. **después (de) que** (17)

afternoon: good afternoon **buenas tardes** (1); **muy buenas** (1); in the afternoon **de la tarde** (1), **por la tarde** (2)

afterward **luego** (5); afterwards **después** (5)

agent **agente** m., f. (8)

ago **hace** + time + **que** + preterite (14); preterite + **hace** + time (14)

agree **estar de acuerdo** (3)

agriculture **agricultura** (15)

ahead: straight ahead **(todo) derecho** (15), **todo recto** (15)

air **aire** m. (15)

airplane **avión** m. (8)

airport **aeropuerto** (8)

aisle **pasillo** (8)

alarm clock **despertador** m. (14)

all **todo/a** (3)

all-terrain **todoterreno** inv. (15)

allow **permitir** (12)

almost **casi** inv. (3); almost never **casi nunca** (3)

alone **solo/a** (5)

alongside of **al lado de** (6)

already **ya** (9)

also **también** (1)

always **siempre** (3)

am: I am **soy** (1); I am from **soy de** (1)

America: of the United States of America n., adj. **estadounidense** (3)

among prep. **entre** (6)

analyst: systems analyst **analista** (m., f.) **de sistemas** (17)

and **y** (1); and you? **¿y tú?** fam. s. (1), **¿y usted?** form. s. (1)

android **android** m. (12)

angry **enojado/a** (9); **furioso/a** (6); to get angry (with) **enojarse (con)** (9)

animal **animal** m. (15)

announce **anunciar** (8)

annoyed **molesto/a** (6)

another **otro/a** (3)

answer n. **respuesta** (6); v. to answer **contestar** (7)

antibiotic **antibiótico** (11)

anxiety **ansiedad** f. (14)

any **algún (alguna/os/as)** (7)

anybody: not anybody **nadie** (7)

anyone **alguien** (7)

anything **algo** (7); not anything **nada** (7)

apartment **apartamento** (2); apartment building **edificio de apartamentos** (12)

apologize **pedir disculpas** (14)

app(lication) **app** f. (12)

appetizers **botanas** f. pl. (Mex.) (9); **tapas** f. pl. (9)

apple **manzana** (7)

appliance: home appliance **aparato doméstico** (10)

applicant **aspirante** m., f. (17)

application (form) **solicitud** f. (17)

apply for (a job) **solicitar** (17)

appointment **cita** (11)

April **abril** m. (6)

architect **arquitecto/a** (13)

architecture **arquitectura** (13)

am: you (fam. s.) are **eres** (1); you (form. s.) are **es** (1)

area **zona** (12); smoking area **sala de fumadores/de fumar** (8)

argue (with/about) **discutir (con/por/sobre)** (9)

arm **brazo** (11)

armchair **sillón** m. (5)

armoire **armario** (5)

army **ejército** (18)

arrival **llegada** (8)

arrive **llegar (gu)** (3)

art **arte** m. (2); arts and crafts **artesanía** (13); the arts **artes** f. pl. (13); work of art **obra de arte** (13)

artist **artista** m., f. (13)

artistic **artístico/a** (13); artistic expression **expresión** (f.) **artística** (13)

as: as . . . as **tan... como** (6); as a child **de niño/a** (10); as a youth **de adolescente** (10); as much as **tanto como** (6); as much/many . . . as **tanto/a(s)... como** (6); as soon as **en cuanto** (17), **tan pronto como** (17)

ask (a question) **hacer una pregunta** (5), **preguntar** (8); to ask for **pedir** (5)

asleep: to fall asleep **dormirse** (5)

asparagus **espárragos** m. pl. (7)

assassinate **asesinar** (18)

assassination **asesinato** (18)

astronaut **astronauta** m., f. (17)

at **en** (1); at . . . (time of day) **a la(s)...** (1); at all **(para) nada** (8); at home **en casa** (2); at least **por lo menos** (9); at the beginning of **al principio de** (17);

at times **a veces** (3); at what time . . . ? **¿a qué hora... ?** (1)

attack: terrorist attack **ataque** (*m.*) **terrorista** (18)

attend (*class, function*) **asistir (a)** (3); to not attend **faltar (a)** (9)

attendant: flight attendant **asistente** (*m., f.*) **de vuelo** (8)

attract **atraer** (*like* **traer**) (*like* **gustar**) (13)

audience **espectadores** *m. pl.* (13); **público** (13)

August **agosto** (6)

aunt **tía** (3); aunts and uncles **tíos** *m. pl.* (3)

author **autor(a)** (13)

auto **auto** (15)

automatic teller machine (ATM) **cajero automático** (17)

automobile **auto(móvil)** *m.* (15)

autumn **otoño** (6)

avenue **avenida** (12)

avocado **aguacate** *m.* (7)

avoid **evitar** (15)

awful: an awful lot **muchísimo** (8)

B

baby-sitter **niñero/a** (10)

back tooth **muela** (11)

backpack **mochila** (2)

bad **mal, malo/a** (3); (very) bad (weather) out **(muy) mal tiempo** (6); the bad news/thing **lo malo** (11); to have a bad time **pasarlo mal** (9); to have bad luck **tener mala suerte** (14)

badly: to come/turn out badly **salir mal** (5)

baggage **equipaje** *m.* (8); to check baggage **facturar el equipaje** (8)

baked custard **flan** *m.* (7)

ball **pelota** (10)

ballet **ballet** *m.* (13)

banana **banana** (7)

bank **banco** (17)

bar: to go to a bar **ir a un bar** (10)

barbecue **barbacoa** (7)

bargain *n.* **ganga** (4); *v.* **regatear** (4)

baseball **béisbol** *m.* (10); baseball cap **gorra** (4)

basketball **basquetbol** *m.* (10)

bath: to take a bath **bañarse** (5)

bathroom **baño** (5); bathroom sink **lavabo** (5)

bathtub **bañera** (5)

battery **batería** (15)

be **estar** (2); **ser** (1), (3); to be . . . years old **tener... años** (3); to be a fan (of) **ser aficionado/a (a)** (10); to be a married person **ser casado/a** (16); to be able **poder** (4); to be absent (from) **faltar (a)** (9); to be afraid **temer** (13); to be afraid (of) **tener miedo (de)** (4); to be born **nacer (nazco)** (16); to be (very) cold **tener (mucho) frío** (6); to

be comfortable (*temperature*) **estar bien** (6); to be distracted **ir distraído/a** (14); to be fond of each other **quererse** (11); to be fun **ser divertido/a** (10); to be happy (about) **alegrarse (de)** (12); to be (very) hungry **tener (mucha) hambre** (7); to be in a hurry **tener prisa** (4); to be left **quedar** (14); to be lucky **tener buena suerte** (14); to be married (to) **estar casado/a (con)** (16); to be on a diet **estar a dieta** (7); to be on vacation **estar de vacaciones** (8); to be right **tener razón** (4); to be sleepy **tener sueño** (4); to be (very) thirsty **tener (mucha) sed** (7); to be under a lot of pressure **estar bajo muchas presiones** (14); to be unlucky **tener mala suerte** (14); to be up to date **estar al día** (18); to be used for **servir (sirvo) (i) para** (5); to be (very) warm, hot **tener (mucho) calor** (6); to be wrong **no tener razón** (4)

beach **playa** (6)

beans **frijoles** *m. pl.* (7)

beautiful **bello/a** (15)

because **porque** (3); because of **por** (6)

become + *adj.* **ponerse** + *adj.* (9)

bed **cama** (5); to get out of bed **levantarse** (5); to get up on the wrong side of the bed **levantarse con el pie izquierdo** (14); to go to bed **acostarse (me acuesto)** (5); to make the bed **hacer la cama** (10); to stay in bed **guardar cama** (11)

bedroom **alcoba** (5)

beer **cerveza** (7)

before *prep.* **antes de** (16); *conj.* **antes (de) que** (16)

begin **empezar (empiezo) (c)** (5); to begin to (*do something*) **empezar a + *inf.*** (5)

beginning: at the beginning of **al principio de** (17)

behave **portarse bien** (9)

behind *prep.* **detrás de** (6)

believe (in) **creer (en)** (3); to not believe **no creer** (13)

below *prep.* **debajo de** (6)

belt **cinturón** *m.* (4)

beside **al lado de** (6)

best **mejor** (6)

better **mejor** (6)

between *prep.* **entre** (6)

beyond **a partir de** (4)

bicycle **bicicleta** (10); to ride a bicycle **montar en bicicleta** (10); **pasear en bicicleta** (10)

bicycling **ciclismo** (10)

big **gran, grande** (3); big screen (monitor) **pantalla grande** (12)

bill **cuenta** (7); **factura** (17); electric bill **electricidad** *f.* (12); (*money*) **billete** *m.* (17)

bird **pájaro** (3)

birthday **cumpleaños** *m. inv.* (6); birthday cake **pastel** (*m.*) **de cumpleaños** (9); to have a birthday **cumplir años** (9)

black **negro/a** (4)

blog **blog** *m.* (12)

blond(e) **rubio/a** (3)

blood **sangre** *f.* (11)

blouse **blusa** (4)

blue **azul** (4)

blue jeans **jeans** *m. pl.* (4)

blush *v.* **ponerse rojo/a** (9)

board **pizarrón** *m.* (2)

boarding: boarding gate **puerta de embarque** (8); boarding pass **tarjeta de embarque** (8)

boat **barco** (8); to go/travel by boat **ir en barco** (8)

body: human body **cuerpo humano** (11)

bomb **bomba** (18)

book **libro** (2); textbook **libro de texto** (2)

bookshelf **estante** *m.* (5)

bookstore **librería** (2)

boots **botas** *f. pl.* (4)

bore **aburrir** (*like* **gustar**) (13)

bored **aburrido/a** (6); to get bored **aburrirse** (10)

boring **pesado/a** (10); to be boring **ser aburrido/a** (10)

born: to be born **nacer (nazco)** (16)

borrow **pedir prestado/a** (17)

bother **molestar** (*like* **gustar**) (11)

boy **niño** (3); **chico** (4)

boyfriend **novio** (6)

brain **cerebro** (11)

brakes **frenos** *m. pl.* (15)

bread **pan** *m.* (7)

break **romper(se)** (14); to break up (with) **romper (con)** (16)

breakfast **desayuno** (7); to have (eat) breakfast **desayunar** (7)

breathe **respirar** (11)

bride **novia** (16)

bring **traer** (5)

brother **hermano** (3)

brown **(de) color café** (4)

brunet(te) **moreno/a** (3)

brush one's hair **peinarse** (5); to brush one's teeth **cepillarse los dientes** (5)

budget **presupuesto** (17)

build **construir** (15)

building **edificio** (2); apartment building **edificio de apartamentos** (12); building manager **portero/a** (12)

bull **toro** (15)

bump against/into **chocar (qu) con/contra** (14); **pegarse (gu) con/contra** (14) bureau **cómoda** (5)

bus **autobús** *m.* (8); bus station **estación** (*f.*) **de autobuses** (8); bus stop **parada del autobús** (12); to go; to travel by bus **ir en autobús** (8)

business **empresa** (17); business administration **administración** (*f.*) **de empresas** (2)

businessman **hombre** (*m.*) **de negocios** (17)

businesswoman **mujer** (*f.*) **de negocios** (17)

busy **ocupado/a** (6)

but **pero** (1)

butter **mantequilla** (7)

buy **comprar** (2)

by **por** (14); by check **con cheque** (17)

C

cabin (*on a ship*) **cabina** (8)

cafeteria **cafetería** (2)

cake **pastel** *m.* (7); birthday cake **pastel de cumpleaños** (9)

calculator **calculadora** (2)

calendar **calendario** (14)

call **llamar** (7); to be called **llamarse** (5)

calm **tranquilo/a** (9); to lead a calm life **llevar una vida tranquila** (11)

camera **cámara** (12)

campground **camping** *m.* (8)

camping: to go camping **hacer camping** (8)

candidate (*for a job*) **aspirante** *m., f.* (17); (*political*) **candidato/a** (18); to run as a candidate **postularse como candidato/a** (18); to run for a position as a candidate **postularse para un cargo como candidato/a** (18)

candle **vela** (9)

candy **dulces** *m. pl.* (7)

cap (baseball) **gorra** (4)

capital city **capital** *f.* (6)

car **coche** *m.* (3); **carro** (15); convertible car **carro descapotable** (15)

card: (post)card **tarjeta (postal)** (8); credit card **tarjeta de crédito** (7); debit card **tarjeta bancaria** (17); identification card **tarjeta de identificación** (14); to play cards **jugar (juego) (gu) a las cartas** (10)

cardinal point **punto cardinal** (6)

care: to take care of oneself **cuidarse** (11)

carrot **zanahoria** (7)

carry **llevar** (4)

case: in case *prep.* **en caso de** (16); conj. **en caso de que** (6); just in case **por si acaso** (14)

cash (*a check*) **cobrar** (17); *n.* **efectivo** (17); in cash **en efectivo** (17)

cashier **cajero/a** (17)

cat **gato** (3)

catch a cold **resfriarse (me resfrío)** (11)

CD **CD** *m.* (12)

CD-ROM **CD-ROM** *m.* (12)

celebrate **celebrar** (6)

celebratory **festivo/a** (9)

cell phone **teléfono celular** (2)

center (*political*) **centro** (18)

ceramics **cerámica** *s.* (13)

cereal **cereal** *m.* (7)

certain **seguro/a** (6); it's certain that **es cierto que** (13)

chair **silla** (2)

champagne **champán** *m.* (9)

change **cambiar (de)** (12)

channel **canal** *m.* (12)

charge (*someone for an item or service*) **cobrar** (17); to charge to an account **cargar (gu) a una cuenta** (17)

chat *n.* **chateo** (12)

check (*bank*) **cheque** *m.* (17); (*restaurant*) **cuenta** (7); by check **con cheque** (17); *v.* **revisar** (15); to check baggage **facturar el equipaje** (8)

check-up **chequeo** (11)

cheese **queso** (7)

chef **cocinero/a** (17)

chemistry **química** (2)

chess: to play chess **jugar (juego) (gu) al ajedrez** (10)

chicken **pollo** (7); roast chicken **pollo asado** (7)

chickpeas **garbanzos** *m. pl.* (7)

child: as a child **de niño/a** (10)

childhood **infancia** (16); **niñez** *f.* (16)

children **hijos** *m. pl.* (3)

chop: (pork) chop **chuleta (de cerdo)** (7)

chore: household chore **quehacer** (*m.*) **doméstico** (10)

Christmas **Navidad** *f.* (9)

Christmas Eve **Nochebuena** *f.* (9)

church **iglesia** (16)

citizen **ciudadano/a** (18)

city **ciudad** *f.* (3)

civic duty **responsabilidad** (*f.*) **cívica** (18)

class (*of students*) **clase** *f.* (2); (*academic*) **clase** *f.* (2)

classic(al) **clásico/a** (13)

classmate **compañero/a (de clase)** (2)

classroom **salón** (*m.*) **de clase** (2)

clean *adj.* **limpio/a** (6); to clean (the) house **limpiar (la casa)** (10)

clear the table **quitar la mesa** (10)

clerk **dependiente/a** (2)

clever **listo/a** (3)

click *v.* **hacer clic** (*m.*) (12)

client **cliente/a** (2)

climate **clima** *m.* (6)

clock: alarm clock **despertador** *m.* (14)

close **cerrar (cierro)** (5)

close to *prep.* **cerca de** (6)

closed **cerrado/a** (6)

closet (*free-standing*) **armario** (5)

clothes dryer **secadora** (10)

clothing **ropa** (4)

cloudy: it's (very) cloudy **está (muy) nublado** (6)

clumsy **torpe** (14)

coat **abrigo** (4)

coffee **café** *m.* (2)

coffeemaker **cafetera** (10)

cognate **cognado** (2)

coin **moneda** (17)

cold (*illness*) **resfriado** *n.* (11); it's (very) cold (*weather*) **hace (mucho) frío** (6); to be (very) cold **tener (mucho) frío** (6); to catch/get a cold **resfriarse (me resfrío)** (11)

collect **recoger (recojo)** (14)

collision **choque** *m.* (18)

color **color** *m.* (4)

comb one's hair **peinarse** (5)

come **venir** (4); to come out badly **salir mal** (5); to come out well **salir bien** (5)

comedy **comedia** (13)

comfortable **cómodo/a** (4); to be comfortable (*temperature*) **estar bien** (6)

coming (*time*) **que viene** (5)

command **mandato** (7)

communicate (with) **comunicarse (qu) (con)** (18)

communication (*subject*) **comunicaciones** *f. pl.* (2); medium of communication **medio de comunicación** (18)

comparison **comparación** *f.* (6)

complain (about) **quejarse (de)** (8)

compose **componer** (*like* **poner**) (13)

composer **compositor(a)** (13)

computer **computadora** (2); computer file **archivo** (12); computer science **computación** *f.* (2); laptop (computer) **computadora portátil** (2)

concert **concierto** (10); to go to a concert **ir a un concierto** (10)

conductor **director(a)** (13)

congested (*with a cold*) *adj.* **resfriado/a** (11)

congratulations! **¡felicitaciones!** (9)

Congressional representative **representante** (*m., f.*) **al congreso** (18)

conjunction *gram.* **conjunción** *f.* (17); conjunction of time **conjunción** (*f.*) **de tiempo** (17)

connect **conectarse** (12)

conserve **conservar** (15)

contact lenses **lentes** (*m. pl.*) **de contacto** (11)

contaminated **contaminado/a** (15)

content *adj.* **contento/a** (6)

continue **continuar (continúo)** (6); **seguir (sigo) (i)** (6) control: remote control **control** (*m.*) **remoto** (12)

convertible car **carro descapotable** (12)

cook *v.* **cocinar** (7); *n.* **cocinero/a** (17)

cookie **galleta** (7)

cool: it's cool (weather) **hace fresco** (6)

copy *n.*: copy machine **fotocopiadora** (12); *v.* **copiar** (12); **hacer (foto)copia** (12)

corner (*street*) **esquina** (15)

corporation **empresa** (17)

cost: how much does it (do they) cost? **¿cuánto cuesta(n)?** (4)

cotton **de algodón** *adj.* (4)

couch **sofá** *m.* (5)

cough *n.* **tos** *f.* (11); cough syrup **jarabe** *m.* (11); *v.* **toser** (11)

counter **mostrador** *m.* (8)

country **país** *m.* (3)

countryside **campo** (15)

couple (*married*) **pareja** (16); **matrimonio** (16)

course (*academic*) **clase** *f.* (2); (*of a meal*) **plato** (7); course syllabus **programa** (*m.*) **del curso** (14); main course **plato principal** (7); of course! **¡por supuesto!** (14)

courteous expression **expresión** (*f.*) **de cortesía** (1)

courtesy **cortesía** (1)

cousin **primo/a** (3); *pl.* **primos** (3)

cover **cubrir** (*p.p.* **cubierto**) (15)

cow **vaca** (15)

craft: arts and crafts **artesanía** (13)

crash *n.* **choque** *m.* (18); *v.* (*computer*) **fallar** (12)

crazy **loco/a** (6)

create **crear** (13)

credit card **tarjeta de crédito** (7)

crime **delito** (15)

cruise (ship) **crucero** (8)

cry **llorar** (9)

cucumber **pepino** (7)

cuisine **cocina** (7)

cultural **cultural** (13); cultural tradition **tradición** (*f.*) **cultural** (13)

cup **taza** (14)

current *adj.* **actual** (12)

currently **en la actualidad** (10)

custard: baked custard **flan** *m.* (7)

customs (*at a border*) **aduana** (8); to go/pass through customs **pasar por la aduana** (8)

D

dad **papá** *m.* (3)

daily **diario/a** (5)

dance *n.* **baile** *m.* (13); **danza** (13); *v.* **bailar** (2)

dancer **bailarín, bailarina** (13)

date **cita** (11); (*calendar*) **fecha** (6); to be up to date **estar al día** (18); what's today's date? **¿cuál es la fecha de hoy?** (6), **¿qué fecha es hoy?** (6)

daughter **hija** (3)

day **día** *m.* (2); day after tomorrow **pasado mañana** (5); days of the week **días** (*m. pl.*) **de la semana** (5); every day **todos los días** (2); the day before yesterday **anteayer** (5); what day is today? **¿qué día es hoy?** (5)

deadline **plazo** (14)

dear **querido/a** (6)

death **muerte** *f.* (16)

debit card **tarjeta bancaria** (17)

December **diciembre** *m.* (6)

delay **demora** (8)

demonstration **manifestación** *f.* (18)

demonstrative *gram.* **demostrativo/a** (4)

dense **denso/a** (15)

dentist **dentista** *m., f.* (11)

deny **negar (niego) (gu)** (13)

department store **almacén** *m.* (4)

departure **salida** (8)

deposit **depositar** (17)

design **diseñar** (13)

designer: graphic designer **diseñador(a) gráfico/a** (17)

desk **escritorio** (2)

dessert **postre** *m.* (7)

destination **destino** (8)

destroy **destruir** (*like* **construir**) (15)

detail **detalle** *m.* (9)

develop **desarrollar** (15)

development **desarrollo** (15)

dictator **dictador(a)** (18)

dictatorship **dictadura** (18)

dictionary **diccionario** (2)

die **morir(se) ([me] muero) (u)** (9)

diet: to be on a diet **estar a dieta** (7)

difficult **difícil** (6); **pesado/a** (10)

dining room **comedor** *m.* (5)

dinner **cena** (7); to have (eat) dinner **cenar** (7)

direct **dirigir (dirijo)** (13)

director **director(a)** (13)

dirty **sucio/a** (6)

disagree **no estar de acuerdo** (3)

disaster **desastre** *m.* (14)

disc: compact disc (CD) **disco compacto (CD** *m.*) (12)

disco: to go to a disco **ir a una discoteca** (10)

discover **descubrir** (*p.p.* **descubierto**) (15)

discrimination **discriminación** *f.* (18)

dish **plato** (7)

dishwasher **lavaplatos** *m. inv.* (10)

distracted **distraído/a** (14); to be distracted **ir distraído/a** (14)

divorce *n.* **divorcio** (16); *v.* **divorciarse (de)** (16)

divorced (from) **divorciado/a (de)** (16)

dizzy **mareado/a** (11)

do **hacer** (5); do you like . . . ? **¿a usted le gusta... ?** *form. s.* (1); to (*do something*) again **volver a** + *inf.* (5); to do aerobics **hacer ejercicios** (*m. pl.*) **aeróbicos** (11); to do Pilates **hacer (el método) Pilates** (11); to do poorly **salir mal** (5); to do well **salir bien** (5); to do yoga **hacer (el) yoga** (10)

doctor (*medical*) **médico/a** (3)

dog **perro** (3)

domestic (*related to the home*) **doméstico/a** (10)

domesticated **doméstico/a** (15)

don't they (you...)? **¿no?** (4), **¿verdad?** (4)

door **puerta** (2)

doorman **portero/a** (12)

dormitory **residencia** (2)

dot: on the dot (*time*) **en punto** (1)

doubt **dudar** (12)

download **bajar** (12); **descargar (gu)** (12)

downtown **centro** (4)

drama **drama** *m.* (13)

draw **dibujar** (13); (*attract*) **atraer** (*like* **traer**) (*like* **gustar**) (13)

drawer **dibujante** *m., f.* (13)

drawing **dibujo** (13)

dress **vestido** (4)

dressed: to get dressed **vestirse (me visto) (i)** (5)

dresser **cómoda** (5)

drink *n.* **bebida** (5); soft drink **refresco** (7); *v.* **beber** (3); **tomar** (2)

drive *n.*: hard drive **discoduro** (12); *v.* **manejar** (12); **conducir (conduzco)** (15)

driver **conductor(a)** (15); driver's license **licencia de conducir/manejar** (15)

drop **caer** (14)

drum set **batería** (15)

dryer: clothes dryer **secadora** (10)

during **durante** (5)

duty: civic duty **responsabilidad** (*f.*) **cívica** (18)

DVD **DVD** *m.* (12)

E

e-mail **e-mail** *m.* (12); **correo electrónico** (12)

e-ticket **billete** (*m.*) (*Sp.*) / **boleto** (*L.A.*) **electrónico** (8)

each **cada** *inv.* (5)

ear **oreja** (11); inner ear **oído** (11)

early *adv.* **temprano** (2)

earn (*income*) **ganar** (13)

earrings **aretes** *m. pl.* (4)

Earth **Tierra** (15)

east **este** *m.* (6)

Easter **Pascua** (9)

easy **fácil** (6)

eat **comer** (3); to eat breakfast **desayunar** (7); to eat dinner, supper cenar (7); to eat lunch **almorzar (ue) (c)** (5)

economics **economía** (2)

economize **economizar (c)** (17)

economy **economía** (2)

egg **huevo** (7)

eight **ocho** (1)

eight hundred **ochocientos/as** (4)

eighteen **dieciocho** (1)

eighth **octavo/a** (13)

eighty **ochenta** (3)

either: not either **tampoco** (7)

electric bill **electricidad** *f.* (12)

electrical **eléctrico/a** (15); electrical energy **energía eléctrica** (15)

electrician **electricista** *m., f.* (17)

electricity **electricidad** *f.* (12)

elephant **elefante** *m.* (15)

elevator **ascensor** *m.* (12)

eleven **once** (1)

embarrassed **avergonzado/a** (9)

embrace **abrazarse (c)** (11)

emotion **emoción** *f.* (9)

emotional **afectivo/a** (9); emotional relationship **relación** (*f.*) **sentimental** (16); emotional state **estado afectivo** (9)

end of the year **fin** (*m.*) **de año** (9)

end table **mesita** (5)

endangered species **especie** (*f.*) **en peligro de extinción** (15)

energy **energía** (15); electrical energy **energía eléctrica** (15); nuclear energy **energía nuclear** (15); renewable energy **energía renovable** (15); solar energy **energía solar** (15); wind energy **energía eólica** (15)

engagement **noviazgo** (16)

engineer **ingeniero/a** (17)

English (*language*) **inglés** *n. m.* (2); *n., adj.* **inglés, inglesa** (3)

enjoy oneself **divertirse (me divierto) (i)** (5)

enough **bastante** (16), **suficiente** (11); **lo suficiente** (11)

environment **medio ambiente** (15)

equality **igualdad** *f.* (18)

equipment **equipo** (12); electronic equipment **equipo electrónico** (12)

eruption **erupción** *f.* (18)

evening: good evening **buenas noches** (1); **muy buenas** (1); in the evening **de la noche** (1); **por la noche** (2)

event **acontecimiento** (18); **hecho** (9)

every **cada** *inv.* (5); **todo/a** (3); every day **todos los días** (2)

everything **de todo** (4)

everywhere **por todas partes** (14)

exam **examen** *m.* (4)

example: for example **por ejemplo** (14)

excuse me **(con) permiso** (1), **perdón** (1)

exercise *n.* **ejercicio** (5); *v.* **hacer ejercicio** (5)

expect **esperar** (7)

expense **gasto** (12)

expensive **caro/a** (4)

explain **explicar (qu)** (8)

expression (phrase) **expresión** *f.* (1); artistic expression **expresión artística** (13)

extinction **extinción** *f.* (15)

extract **sacar (qu)** (11); to extract (*someone's*) tooth/molar **sacarle (qu) un diente / una muela** (11)

eye **ojo** (11)

F

Facebook **Facebook** *m.* (12); to go into Facebook **entrar en Facebook** (12)

fact **hecho** (9)

factory **fábrica** (15)

faithful **fiel** (3)

fall (*season*) *n.* **otoño** (6); *v.* **caer** (14); to fall asleep **dormirse** (5); to fall down **caerse** (14); to fall in love (with) **enamorarse (de)** (16)

familiar: to be familiar with **conocer (conozco)** (7)

family **familia** (3)

fan: to be a fan (of) **ser aficionado/a (a)** (10)

far from **lejos de** (6)

fare **pasaje** *m.* (8)

farm **finca** (15)

farmer **agricultor(a)** (15)

farming **agricultura** (15)

fascinate **fascinar** (like **gustar**) (13)

fast **acelerado/a** (15)

fat **gordo/a** (3)

father **padre** *m.* (3), **papá** *m.* (3)

FAX **fax** *m.* (12)

fear *n.* **miedo** (4); *v.* **temer** (13)

February **febrero** (6)

feel **sentir** (13); (*an emotion*) **sentirse** (9); to feel like (*doing something*) **tener ganas de** + *inf.* (4); to feel sorry **lamentar** (13)

female housekeeper **ama** (*f.*) (*but* **el ama**) **de casa** (17)

female soldier **mujer** (*f.*) **soldado** (17)

festive **festivo/a** (9)

fever **fiebre** *f.* (11)

few **poco/a** (4)

fiancé **novio** (16)

fiancée **novia** (16)

field **campo** (15)

fifteen **quince** (1); fifteen minutes till (*hour*) **menos cuarto/quince** (1); young woman's fifteenth birthday party **quinceañera** (9)

fifth **quinto/a** (13)

fifty **cincuenta** (3)

fight *n.* **lucha** (18); *v.* **luchar** (18), **pelear** (10)

file (*computer*) **archivo** (12)

fill (up) **llenar** (15); to fill out (*a form*) **llenar** (17)

final **último/a** (14)

finally **por fin** (5), **finalmente** (5)

find **encontrar (encuentro)** (9); to find out (about) **enterarse (de)** (18)

fine **muy bien** (1); it's fine **está bien** (6)

finger **dedo (de la mano)** (11)

finish **acabar** (14)

fire (*someone*) (*from a job*) **despedir** (*like* **pedir**) (17)

first *adv.* **primero** (5); *adj.* **primer(o/a)** (13); first floor (second story) **primer piso** (12); for the first time **por primera vez** (14); the first of (*month*) **el primero de** (6)

fish (*cooked*) **pescado** (7); (*live*) **pez** *m.* (*pl.* **peces**) (15)

five **cinco** (1)

five hundred **quinientos/as** (4)

fix **arreglar** (15)

fixed price **precio fijo** (4)

flat: flat screen (*monitor*) **pantalla plana** (12); flat tire **llanta desinflada** (15)

flexible **flexible** (14)

flight **vuelo** (8); flight attendant **asistente** (*m., f.*) **de vuelo** (8)

flip-flops **chanclas** *f. pl.* (4)

floor (*of a building*) **piso** (12); first/second floor (second/third story) **primer/segundo piso** (12); ground floor **planta baja** (12); to sweep the floor **barrer el piso** (10)

flower **flor** *f.* (8)

flu **gripe** *f.* (11)

fly by plane **volar (vuelo) en avión** (8)

folder (*computer*) **carpeta** (12)

follow **seguir (sigo) (i)** (6)

following *adj.* **siguiente** (5)

fond: to be fond of each other **quererse** (11)

food **comida** (7)

foodstuff **comestibles** *m. pl.* (7)

foolish **tonto/a** (3)

foot **pie** *m.* (11)

football **fútbol** (*m.*) **americano** (10)

for **para** (3); **por** (8); for example **por ejemplo** (14); for heaven's sake **por Dios** (14); for that reason **por eso** (3); for what purpose? **¿para qué... ?** (16); what for? **¿para qué... ?** (16)

forbid **prohibir (prohíbo)** (12)

foreign **extranjero/a** (2); foreign language **lengua extranjera** (2)

foreigner **extranjero/a** (2)

forest **bosque** *m.* (15)

forget **olvidar** (9)

form **forma** (4); (*to fill out*) **formulario** (17)

forty **cuarenta** (3)

four **cuatro** (1)

four hundred **cuatrocientos/as** (4)

fourteen **catorce** (1)

fourth *adj.* **cuarto/a** (13)

free (*unoccupied*) **libre** (10); free time **ratos** (*m. pl.*) **libres** (10), **tiempo libre** (10)

freeway **autopista** (15)

freezer **congelador** *m.* (10)

French (*language*) **francés** *m.* (2); French fried potato **papa/patata frita** (7)

frequently **con frecuencia** (2), **frecuentemente** (11)

fresh **fresco/a** (7)

Friday **viernes** *m. inv.* (5)

fried **frito/a** (7); French fried potato **papa/patata frita** (7)

friend **amigo/a** (2)

friendly **amistoso/a** (16)

friendship **amistad** *f.* (16)

from **de** (1); from the **del** (3); I am from . . . (yo) **soy de...** (1); where are you from? **¿de dónde eres (tú)?** *fam. s.* (1); **¿de dónde es usted?** *form. s.* (1)

front: in front of **delante de** (6)

frozen **congelado/a** (6)

fruit **fruta** (7); fruit juice **jugo de fruta** (7)

full-time job **empleo de tiempo completo** (17)

fun activity **diversión** *f.* (10); to be fun **ser divertido/a** (10)

function **funcionar** (12)

furious **furioso/a** (6)

furniture (*piece*) **mueble** *m.* (5)

G

game **partido** (10)

garage **garaje** *m.* (5)

garden **jardín** *m.* (5)

gas (*not for cars*) **gas** *m.* (12)

gas station **estación** (*f.*) **de servicio** (15), **gasolinera** (15)

gasoline **gasolina** (15)

gate: boarding gate **puerta de embarque** (8)

generally **por lo general** (5)

German (*language*) **alemán** *m.* (2); *n., adj.* **alemán, alemana** (3)

get **obtener** (*like* **tener**) (12); how do you get to . . . ? **¿cómo se llega a... ?** (15); to get **conseguir** (*like* **seguir**) (9); to get (*grades*) **sacar (qu)** (14); to get a cold **resfriarse (me resfrío)** (11); to get along poorly (with) **llevarse mal (con)** (16); to get along well (with) **llevarse bien (con)** (16); to get angry (with) **enojarse (con)** (9); to get down (from) **bajarse (de)** (8); to get dressed **vestirse (me visto) (i)** (5); to get off (of) (*a vehicle*) **bajarse (de)** (8); to get on (*a vehicle*) **subir (a)** (8); to get sick

enfermarse (11); to get tired **cansarse** (11); to get together (with) **reunirse (me reúno) (con)** (9); to get up (out of bed) **levantarse** (5); to get up on the wrong side of the bed **levantarse con el pie izquierdo** (14)

gift **regalo** (3)

girl **chica** (4), **niña** (3)

girlfriend **novia** (6)

give **dar** (8); to give (*as a gift*) **regalar** (8); to give someone a party **darle/ hacerle una fiesta a alguien** (9); to give (*someone*) a shot/vaccination **ponerle una inyección/una vacuna** (11)

glasses **anteojos** *m. pl.* (11), **lentes** *m. pl.* (11)

go **ir** (4); let's go **vamos** (4); to be going to (*do something*) **ir a** + *inf.* (4); to go abroad **ir al extranjero** (8); to go by boat/ship **ir en barco** (8); to go by bus **ir en autobús** (8); to go by plane **ir/ volar (vuelo) en avión** (8); to go by train **ir en tren** (8); to go camping **hacer** *camping* (8); to go for a hike **dar una caminata** (10); to go home **regresar a casa** (2); to go onto Facebook **entrar en Facebook** (12); to go on the internet **entrar en internet** (12); to go on vacation in/to . . . **ir de vacaciones a...** (8); to go out (with) **salir (con)** (5); to go shopping **ir de compras** (4); to go through customs **pasar por la aduana** (8); to go through security (check) **pasar por el control de seguridad** (8); to go to (*a class, function*) **asistir (a)** (3); to go to a bar **ir a un bar** (10); to go to a concert **ir a un concierto** (10); to go to a disco **ir a una discoteca** (10); to go to bed **acostarse (me acuesto)** (5); to go to the theater **ir al teatro** (10); to go to a museum **ir a un museo** (10); to go up **subir (a)** (8); to go/travel by train **ir en tren** (8)

gold **oro** (4); **de oro** (4)

golf **golf** *m.* (10)

good **buen, bueno/a** (3); good afternoon **buenas tardes** (1); good afternoon/evening **muy buenas** (1); good morning **buenos días** (1); good night **buenas noches** (1); the good news/thing **lo bueno** (11); it's (very) good weather out **hace (muy) buen tiempo** (6); to have a good time **pasarlo bien** (9), **divertirse (me divierto) (i)** (5); to have good luck **tener buena suerte** (14)

good-bye **adiós** (1); to say good-bye (to) **despedir(se)** (*like* **pedir**) **(de)** (9)

good-looking **guapo/a** (3)

goods: woven goods **tejidos** *m. pl.* (13)

gorilla **gorila** *m.* (15)

government **gobierno** (15)

GPS **GPS** *m. inv.* (12)

grade (*academic*) **nota** (5)

graduate (*from*) **graduarse (me gradúo) (en)**

granddaughter **nieta** (3)

grandfather **abuelo** (3)

grandmother **abuela** (3)

grandparents **abuelos** *m. pl.* (3)

grandson **nieto** (3)

graphic designer **diseñador(a) gráfico/a** (17)

gray **gris** (4)

great **gran, grande** (3)

green **verde** (4)

green peas **arvejas** *f. pl.* (7)

greet each other **saludarse** (11)

greeting **saludo** (1)

groceries **comestibles** *m. pl.* (7)

groom **novio** (16)

ground floor **planta baja** (12)

grow **crecer (crezco)** (16)

guess **adivinar** (9)

guest **invitado/a** (9)

guide **guía** *m., f.* (13)

H

haggle **regatear** (4)

hairstylist **peluquero/a** (17)

half past (*the hour*) **y media** (1)

ham **jamón** *m.* (7)

hamburger **hamburguesa** (7)

hand **mano** *f.* (11); to shake hands **darse la mano** (11)

hand in **entregar (gu)** (8)

handbag **cartera** (4)

handsome **guapo/a** (3)

happen **pasar** (6); **ocurrir** (14)

happening **acontecimiento** (18)

happy **alegre** (6), **contento/a** (6); **feliz** (*pl.* **felices**) (9); to be happy (about) **alegrarse (de)** (12)

hard **difícil** (6)

hard drive **disco duro** (12)

hardworking **trabajador(a)** (3)

hat **sombrero** (4)

hate **odiar** (8)

have **tener** (4); (*auxilliary verb*) **haber** (12); to have a bad time **pasarlo mal** (9); to have a birthday **cumplir años** (9); to have a good time **divertirse (me divierto) (i)** (5), **pasarlo bien** (9); to have (a lot of) stress **tener muchas presiones** (14); to have a pain/ache in **tener dolor de** (11); to have a picnic **hacer un** *picnic* (10); to have a snack **merendar (meriendo)** (7); to have bad luck **tener mala suerte** (14); to have been (*doing something*) for (*time*) **hace** + *time* + **que** + *present* (14); *present* + **desde hace** + *time* (14);

to have breakfast **desayunar** (7); to have dinner, supper **cenar** (7); to have good luck **tener buena suerte** (14); to have just (*done something*) **acabar de** + *inf.* (7); to have lunch **almorzar (almuerzo) (c)** (5); to have to (*do something*) **tener que** + *inf.* (4)

he *sub. pron.* **él** (2); he is **es** (1)

head **cabeza** (11)

health **salud** *f.* (11)

healthy **sano/a** (11); to lead a healthy life **llevar una vida sana** (11)

hear **oír** (5)

heart **corazón** *m.* (11)

heating **calefacción** *f.* (12)

heaven: for heaven's sake **por Dios** (14)

hello! **¡hola!** (1)

help *n.* **ayuda** (7); *v.* **ayudar** (7); to help to (*do something*) *v.* **ayudar a** + *inf.* (7)

her *poss. adj.* **su(s)** (3); her, (of) hers *poss. adj., poss. pron.* **suyo/a(s)** (17)

here **aquí** (2)

hi! **¡hola!** (1)

highway **carretera** (15)

hike: to go for a hike **dar una caminata** (10)

his *poss. adj.* **su(s)** (3); his, of his *poss. adj., poss. pron.* **suyo/a(s)** (17)

Hispanic **hispano/a** (3)

history **historia** (2)

hit **pegar (gu)** (14)

hobby **afición** *f.* (10)

hockey **hockey** *m.* (10)

holiday **día** (*m.*) **festivo** (9)

home *n.* **casa** (3); at home **en casa** (2); nursing home **residencia de ancianos** (12); to go home **regresar a casa** (2); *adj.* (*related to the home*) **doméstico/a** (10)

home appliance **aparato doméstico** (10)

homework **tarea** (5)

honeymoon **luna de miel** (16)

honk **tocar (qu)** (15)

hope **esperanza** (18); I hope (that) **ojalá (que)** (13); to hope **esperar** (12)

horn (*car*) **bocina** (15)

horse: to ride a horse **montar a caballo** (10)

host (*of an event*) **anfitrión, anfitriona** (9)

hot (*spicy*) **picante** (7); (*temperature*) **caliente** (7); it's (very) hot (*weather*) **hace (mucho) calor** (6); it's hot (*trendy*) **está de moda** (4); **es de última moda** (4); to be (very) hot **tener (mucho) calor** (6)

hot dog **salchicha** (7)

house **casa** (3)

household chore **quehacer** (*m.*) **doméstico** (10)

housekeeper: female housekeeper **ama** (*f.*) (*but* **el ama**) **de casa** (17); male housekeeper **amo de casa** (17)

housing **vivienda** (12)

how + *adj.*! **¡qué** + *adj.*!** (14); how strange that . . . ! **¡qué extraño que... !** (13)

how? **¿cómo?** (1); how are you? **¿cómo está(s)?** (1); **¿qué tal?** (1); how do you get to . . . ? **¿cómo se llega a... ?** (15); how many? **¿cuántos/as?** (2); how much? **¿cuánto?** (2); how much does it (do they) cost? **¿cuánto cuesta(n)?** (4); how often . . . ? **¿con qué frecuencia... ?** (3)

human **humano/a** (11); human body **cuerpo humano** (11)

humanities **humanidades** *f. pl.* (2)

hungry: to be (very) hungry **tener (mucha) hambre** (7)

hurry: to be in a hurry **tener prisa** (4)

hurt **doler (duele)** (*like* **gustar**) (11); to hurt oneself **hacerse daño** (14); to hurt (*a body part*) **lastimarse** (14); to hurt one's (*body part*) **hacerse daño en** (14)

husband **esposo** (3), **marido** (3)

hybrid **híbrido/a** (15)

I

I *sub. pron.* **yo** (2); I am **soy** (1); I am from . . . **(yo) soy de...** (1); I didn't mean to do it **fue sin querer** (14); I hope (that) **ojalá (que)** (13); I would (really) like . . . **me gustaría (mucho)...** (8); I'm sorry/ pardon me **disculpa, discúlpame** *fam. s.* (14); **disculpe, discúlpeme** *form. s.* (14); I'm (very) sorry **lo siento (mucho)** (14)

ice cream **helado** (7)

identification card **tarjeta de identificación** (14)

if **si** (4)

illness **enfermedad** *f.* (11)

image **imagen** *f.* (13)

immediately **en seguida** (5)

impossible **imposible** (13); it's impossible that **es imposible que** (13) it's not impossible **no es imposible** (13)

improbable **improbable** (13); it's improbable that **es improbable que** (13); it's not improbable **no es improbable** (13)

in **en** (1); in case **en caso de (que)** (16); in cash **en efectivo** (17); in front of **delante de** (6); in love (with) **enamorado/a (de)** (16); in order to (*do something*) **para** + *inf.* (10); in the afternoon **de la tarde** (1); in the evening **de la noche** (1); in the morning **de la mañana** (1); in the morning/afternoon/evening **por la mañana/tarde/noche** (2)

incredible **increíble** (13); it's incredible that **es increíble que** (13)

indefinite and negative word *gram.* **palabra indefinida y negativa** (7)

inequality **desigualdad** *f.* (18)

inexpensive **barato/a** (4)

infancy **infancia** (16), **niñez** *f.* (16)

inflexible **inflexible** (14)

inform **informar** (18)

injection **inyección** *f.* (11)

inner ear **oído** (11)

insist (on) **insistir (en)** (12)

install **instalar** (12)

installments: in installments **a plazos** (17)

intelligent **inteligente** (3)

intended for **para** (3)

interest *n.* **interés** *m.* (17); *v.* to interest (*someone*) **interesar** (*like* **gustar**) (8)

internet **internet** *m.* (12); to go on the internet **entrar en internet** (12); to look for on the internet **buscar (qu) en internet** (12)

interrogative *gram.* **interrogativo/a** (2); interrogative word **palabra interrogativa** (2)

interstate **autopista** (15)

interview **entrevista** (17)

interviewee **entrevistado/a** (17)

interviewer **entrevistador(a)** (17)

invite **invitar** (7)

iPhone **iPhone** *m.* (12)

iPod **iPod** *m.* (12)

iron *v.* **planchar** (10)

island **isla** (6)

issue **cuestión** *f.* (17)

it is... (*time*) **es la...** (1), **son las...** (1)

Italian (*language*) **italiano** (2)

its *poss. adj.* **su(s)** (3); (of) its *poss. adj., poss. pron.* **suyo/a(s)** (17)

J

jacket **chaqueta** (4)

January **enero** (6)

jeans **jeans** *m. pl.* (4)

job **empleo** (17), **trabajo** (12); full-time job **empleo de tiempo completo** (17), **trabajo de tiempo completo** (14); part-time job **empleo de tiempo parcial** (17), **trabajo de tiempo parcial** (14); poorly paid job **empleo mal pagado** (17); well-paid job **empleo bien pagado** (17)

joke **chiste** *m.* (8)

journalist **periodista** *m., f.* (17)

juice **jugo** (7); fruit juice **jugo de fruta** (7)

July **julio** (6)

June **junio** (6)

just in case **por si acaso** (14)

K

keep **guardar** (12); **mantener** (*like* **tener**) (18); to keep on going **seguir** (**sigo**) (**i**) (15)
key **llave** *f.* (5)
kill **matar** (18)
kind **amable** (3)
king **rey** *m.* (18)
kiss: to kiss each other **besarse** (11)
kitchen **cocina** (5)
know **conocer** (**conozco**) (7); **saber** (7); to know how to (*do something*) **saber** + *inf.* (7)

L

laborer **obrero/a** (17)
lack **falta** (15)
lake **lago** (15)
lamp **lámpara** (5)
landlady **dueña** (12)
landline **teléfono fijo** (12)
landlord **dueño** (12)
language **lengua** (2); foreign language **lengua extranjera** (2)
laptop (computer) **computadora portátil** (2)
large **gran, grande** (3)
last **pasado/a** (11); **último/a** (14); for the last time **por última vez** (14); last night *adv.* **anoche** (11); to last **durar** (18)
late *adj.* **atrasado/a** (8); *adv.* **tarde** (2)
later: see you later **hasta luego** (1)
laugh **reírse** (**de**) (9)
law **ley** *f.* (18)
lawyer **abogado/a** (17)
layer: ozone layer **capa de ozono** (15)
lazy **perezoso/a** (3)
lead a calm/healthy life **llevar una vida tranquila/sana** (11)
learn **aprender** (3); to learn (about) **enterarse** (**de**) (18); to learn how to (*do something*) **aprender a** + *inf.* (3)
least: at least **por lo menos** (9)
leather *adj.* **de cuero** (4)
leave (*a place*) **salir** (**de**) (5); to leave for (*a place*) **salir para** (5); to leave on vacation **salir de vacaciones** (8)
left: to the left of **a la izquierda de** (6); to be left **quedar** (*like* **gustar**) (14)
leg **pierna** (11)
lend **prestar** (8)
lenses: contact lenses **lentes** (*m. pl.*) **de contacto** (11)
less than **menos que** (6); less. . . than **menos... que** (6); less than + *number* **menos de** + *number* (6)
let (*someone*) go **despedir** (*like* **pedir**) (17)
let's go **vamos** (4)
letter **carta** (3)
lettuce **lechuga** (7)

librarian **bibliotecario/a** (2)
library **biblioteca** (2)
license: driver's license **licencia de conducir/manejar** (15)
lie **mentira** (12)
life **vida** (11); academic life **vida académica** (14); pace of life **ritmo de la vida** (15)
lift weights **levantar pesas** (11)
light *n.* **luz** *f.* (*pl.* **luces**) (14); *adj.* light (*not heavy*) **ligero/a** (7)
like *n.* **gusto** (1); do you like . . . ? **¿te gusta... ?** *fam. s.* (1); **¿a usted le gusta... ?** *form. s.* (1); I would (really) like . . . **me gustaría (mucho)...** (8); (no,) I don't like . . . **(no,) no me gusta** (1); to like **gustar** (8); to like very much **encantar** (*like* **gustar**) (8); what are you like? **¿cómo es usted?** *form. s.* (1); yes, I like . . . **sí, me gusta...** (1)
likeable **simpático/a** (3)
likely: it's likely that **es probable que** (13)
likewise **igualmente** (1)
limit: speed limit **límite** (*m.*) **de velocidad** (15)
line (*of people*) **cola** (8); to stand in line **hacer cola** (8)
listen to (*music, the radio*) **oír** (5); to listen (to) **escuchar** (2)
literature **literatura** (2)
little *adv.* (a) little **poco** (2); (adjective suffix) **-ito/a** (10); a little bit (of) **un poco (de)** (2); *adj.* **poco/a** (4)
live **vivir** (3)
living room **sala** (5)
loan **préstamo** (17)
lobster **langosta** (7)
long **largo/a** (3)
look at **mirar** (3); to look for **buscar** (**qu**) (2); to look for on the internet **buscar** (**qu**) **en internet** (12)
lose **perder** (**pierdo**) (5)
lot: a lot *adv.* **mucho** (2); a lot (of) **mucho/a** (3); an awful lot **muchísimo** (8); there's lots of **hay mucho/a** (6)
love *n.* **amor** *m.* (16); *adj.* in love (with) **enamorado/a** (**de**) (16); *v.* **amar** (16); **querer** (16); **encantar** (*like* **gustar**) (8); to fall in love (with) **enamorarse** (**de**) (16); to love each other **quererse** (11)
luck: to have bad/good luck **tener mala/buena suerte** (14)
lucky: to be lucky **tener buena suerte** (14)
luggage **equipaje** *m.* (8)
lunch *n.* **almuerzo** (7); to have lunch **almorzar** (**almuerzo**) (**c**) (5)
lungs **pulmones** *m. pl.* (11)
-ly (*adverbial suffix*) **-mente** (14)
lyrics **letra** (7)

M

ma'am **señora (Sra.)** (1)
machine: automatic teller machine (ATM) **cajero automático** (17)
made: it is made of . . . **es de...** (4)
magazine **revista** (3)
mailbox: voice mailbox **buzón** (*m.*) **de voz** (12)
main course **plato principal** (7)
maintain **mantener** (*like* **tener**) (18)
make **hacer** (5); to make a mistake (about) **equivocarse** (**qu**) (**de**) (14); to make plans to (*do something*) **hacer planes** (*m.*) **para** + *inf.* (10); to make stops **hacer escalas/paradas** (8); to make the bed **hacer la cama** (10)
male housekeeper **amo de casa** (17)
mall: shopping mall **centro comercial** (4)
man **hombre** *m.* (2); business man **hombre de negocios** (17)
manager **gerente** *m., f.* (17); building manager **portero/a** (12)
manufacture **fabricar** (**qu**) (15)
many **muchos/as** (3); as many . . . as **tanto/a(s) ... como** (6); how many? **¿cuántos/as?** (2)
march **manifestación** *f.* (18)
March **marzo** (6)
market(place) **mercado** (4)
marriage **matrimonio** (16)
married: to be a married person **ser casado/a** (16); to be married (to) **estar casado/a (con)** (16)
marry **casarse (con)** (16)
mass media **medios** *m. pl.* (18)
masterpiece **obra maestra** (13)
match (*game*) **partido** (10)
material **materia** (4)
math **matemáticas** *f. pl.* (2)
matter **cuestión** *f.* (17)
May **mayo** (6)
me *obj. of prep.* **mí** (6); with me **conmigo** (6)
meal **comida** (7)
mean: I didn't mean to do it **fue sin querer** (14); that means . . . **eso quiere decir...** (11)
means of transportation **medio de transporte** (8)
meat **carne** *f.* (7)
mechanic **mecánico/a** (15)
medical **médico/a** (11); medical office **consultorio** (11); medical personnel **personal** (*m.*) **médico** (11)
medicine **medicina** (11)
medium of communication **medio de comunicación** (18)
meet **conocerse** (**conozco**) (16); nice to meet you **mucho gusto** (1); to meet (*someone somewhere*) **encontrarse** (**me encuentro**) (**con**) (11)

memory **memoria** (12)

memory stick **pen drive** *m.* (12)

menu **menú** *m.* (7)

messy **desordenado/a** (6)

Mexican **mexicano/a** (3)

microwave oven **horno de microondas** (10)

middle age **madurez** *f.* (16)

midnight **medianoche** *f.* (6)

military *adj.* **militar** (18); military service **servicio militar** (18)

milk **leche** *f.* (7)

million: one million **un millón (de)** (4)

mine, (of) mine *poss. adj., poss. pron.* **mío/a(s)** (17)

mineral water **agua** (*f.; but* **el agua**) **mineral** (7)

minute: fifteen minutes till (*hour*) **menos quince** (1); thirty minutes past (*the hour*) **y treinta** (1)

misbehave **portarse mal** (9)

miss (*an event*) **perder (pierdo)** (5)

Miss **señorita (Srta.)** (1)

mistake: to make a mistake (about) **equivocarse (qu) (de)** (14)

modem **módem** *m.* (12)

modern **moderno/a** (13)

molar **muela** (11)

mom **mamá** (3)

Monday **lunes** *m. inv.* (5); next Monday **el lunes que viene** (5); on Monday **el lunes** (5); on Mondays **los lunes** (5)

money **dinero** (2)

monitor **pantalla** (12); big screen monitor **pantalla grande** (12); flat screen monitor **pantalla plana** (12)

month **mes** *m.* (6)

moped **moto(cicleta)** (15)

more **más** (2); more than **más que** (6); more . . . than **más... que** (6); more than + *number* **más de** + *number* (6)

morning: good morning **buenos días** (1); in the morning **por la mañana** (2); **de la mañana** (1)

mother **madre** *f.* (3); **mamá** (3)

motorcycle **moto(cicleta)** (15)

mountain **montaña** (8)

mouse **ratón** *m.* (12)

mouth **boca** (11)

move (*residence*) **mudarse** (12)

movie **película** (5); movie theater **cine** *m. s.* (5); movies **cine** *m. s.* (5)

Mr. **señor (Sr.)** *m.* (1)

Mrs. **señora (Sra.)** (1)

Ms. **señorita (Srta.)** (1)

much **mucho** (2); as much . . . as **tanto/a(s)... como** (6); as much as **tanto como** (6); how much? **¿cuánto?** (2); how much does it (do they) cost? **¿cuánto cuesta(n)?** (4)

mural **mural** *m.* (13)

museum **museo** (10); to visit a museum **visitar un museo** (10)

mushrooms **champiñones** *m. pl.* (7)

music **música** (13)

musical *n. m.* **musical** (13)

musician **músico/a** (13)

must (*do something*) **deber** + *inf.* (3)

my *poss. adj.* **mi(s)** (3); *poss. adj., poss. pron.* **mío/a(s)** (17)

N

name **nombre** *m.* (7); my name is . . . **me llamo...** (1); what is your name? **¿cómo se llama usted?** *form. s.* (1); **¿cómo te llamas?** *fam. s.* (1)

nap: to take a nap **dormir duermo (u) la siesta** (5)

narrate **contar (cuento)** (8)

nationality **nacionalidad** *f.* (3); adjective of nationality **adjetivo de nacionalidad** (3)

natural **natural** (15); natural resource **recurso natural** (15); natural sciences **ciencias** (*f. pl.*) **naturales** (2)

nature **naturaleza** (15)

nauseated **mareado/a** (11)

navigate **navegar (gu)** (12)

neat **ordenado/a** (6)

necessary **necesario/a** (3); it is necessary to (*do something*) **hay que** + *inf.* (13)

need **necesitar** (2)

negative: indefinite and negative word *gram.* **palabra indefinida y negativa** (7)

neighbor **vecino/a** (12)

neighborhood **barrio** (12)

neither **tampoco** (7)

nephew **sobrino** (3)

nervous **nervioso/a** (6)

network: social network **red** (*f.*) **social** (12)

never **jamás** (7), **nunca** (3); almost never **casi nunca** (3)

nevertheless **sin embargo** (6)

new **nuevo/a** (3)

New Year's Eve **Nochevieja** *f.* (9)

newlywed **recién casado/a** (16)

news **noticias** *f. pl.* (5); news media **prensa** (18); the bad news **lo malo** (11); the good news **lo bueno** (11)

newscast **noticiero** (18)

newsstand **quiosco de prensa** (18)

newspaper **periódico** (3)

next *adv.* **luego** (5); *adj.* **próximo/a** (5); next (Tuesday . . .) **el próximo (martes...)** (5); next Monday **el lunes** (*m.*) **que viene** (5); next week **la próxima semana** (5), **la semana que viene** (5)

nice **amable** (3), **simpático/a** (3); nice to meet you **mucho gusto** (1); (very) nice out **(muy) buen tiempo** (6)

niece **sobrina** (3)

night: at night **de la noche** (1), **por la noche** (2); last night *adv.* **anoche** (11)

nine **nueve** (1)

nine hundred **novecientos/as** (4)

nineteen **diecinueve** (1)

ninety **noventa** (3)

ninth **noveno/a** (13)

no **no** (1); **ningún (ninguna)** (7); no, I don't like . . . **(no,) no me gusta** (1)

no one **nadie** (7)

nobody **nadie** (7)

noise **ruido** (5)

noon **mediodía** *m.* (6)

normal **normal** (13); it's normal that **es normal que** (13)

north **norte** *m.* (6)

nose **nariz** *f.* (*pl.* **narices**) (11)

not any **ningún (ninguna)** (7)

notebook **cuaderno** (2)

notes (*academic*) **apuntes** *m., pl.* (14)

nothing **nada** (7)

noun *gram.* **sustantivo** (2)

novel **novela** (13)

novelist **novelista** *m., f.* (13)

November **noviembre** *m.* (6)

now **ahora** (2); right now **ahora mismo** (6)

nuclear energy **energía nuclear** (15)

number **número** (1); ordinal number *gram.* **número ordinal** (13)

nurse **enfermero/a** (11)

nursing home **residencia de ancianos** (12)

O

o'clock: it's . . . o'clock **son las...** (1)

obey **obedecer (obedezco)** (15)

object **objeto** (2)

obligation **deber** *m.* (18)

obtain **obtener** (*like* **tener**) (12); **conseguir** (*like* **seguir**) (9)

ocean **océano** (8)

October **octubre** *m.* (6)

of **de** (1); of course! **¡por supuesto!** (14); of the **del** (3)

off: to turn off **apagar (gu)** (12)

offer **ofrecer (ofrezco)** (8)

office **oficina** (2); (*in a home*) **estudio** (5); (*medical*) **consultorio** (11); (*political*) **cargo** (18)

often: how often . . . ? **¿con qué frecuencia... ?** (3)

oil (*cooking*) **aceite** *m.* (7); (*fuel*) **petróleo** (15)

OK: it's OK **está bien** (6)

old **viejo/a** (3); old age **vejez** *f.* (16)

older (than) **mayor (que)** (6)

olive oil **aceite** (*m.*) **de oliva** (7)

on **en** (1); on a trip **de viaje** (8); on Monday **el lunes** (5); on the dot (*time*) **en punto** (1); on top of **encima de** (6);

on Tuesdays **los martes** (5); on vacation **de vacaciones** (8)

once a week **una vez a la semana** (3)

one **uno** (1); it's one o'clock **es la una** (1)

one hundred **cien** (3); (used with 101–199) **ciento** (4)

one hundred ninety-nine **ciento noventa y nueve** (4)

one hundred one **ciento uno** (4)

one hundred two **ciento dos** (4)

one million **un millón (de** + noun**)** (4)

one thousand **mil** (4)

onion **cebolla** (7)

only adv. **solo** (2)

open v. **abrir** (p.p. **abierto**) (3); adj. **abierto/a** (6)

opera **ópera** (13)

operate (a machine) **manejar** (12)

or **o** (1)

oral **oral** (14); oral report **informe** (m.) **oral** (14)

orange n. **naranja** (7); adj. **anaranjado/a** (4)

orchestra **orquesta** (13)

order **mandar** (12); (in a restaurant) **pedir (pido) (i)** (5); in order to (do something) **para** + inf. (3)

ordinal number gram. **número ordinal** (13)

other **otro/a** (3); others **los/las demás** (12)

ought to (do something) **deber** + inf. (3)

our poss. adj. **nuestro/a(s)** (3); our, of ours poss. adj., poss. pron. **nuestro/a(s)** (17)

outdoors adv. **afuera** (6); **al aire libre** (10)

outer ear **oreja** (11)

outskirts **afueras** f. pl. (12)

overcast: it's (very) overcast **está (muy) nublado** (6)

own, one's own **propio/a** (17)

owner **dueño/a** (7)

ozone layer **capa de ozono** (15)

P

P.M. **de la noche** (1); **de la tarde** (1)

pace of life **ritmo de la vida** (15)

pack one's suitcase(s) **hacer la(s) maleta(s)** (8)

page: webpage **página web** (12)

paid: well/poorly paid job/position **empleo bien/mal pagado** (17)

pain (in) **dolor** m. **(de)** (11); to have a pain in **tener dolor de** (11)

paint **pintar** (13)

painter **pintor(a)** (13)

painting (general) **pintura** (13); (specific piece) **cuadro** (13)

pants **pantalones** m. pl. (4)

paper **papel** m. (2)

pardon me **con permiso** (1), **disculpa, discúlpame** fam. s. (14); **disculpe, discúlpeme** form. s. (14)

parents **padres** m. pl. (3)

park **estacionar** (14)

parking lot/place **estacionamiento** (15)

part **parte** f. (5)

part-time job/position **empleo de tiempo parcial** (17), **trabajo de tiempo parcial** (14)

partner **pareja** (16)

party **fiesta** (2); (political) party **partido (político)** (18); to throw a party **dar/hacer una fiesta** (9)

pass: boarding pass **tarjeta de embarque** (8)

pass through customs **pasar por la aduana** (8); to pass through security (check) **pasar por el control de seguridad** (8)

passenger **pasajero/a** (8)

passport **pasaporte** m. (8)

password **contraseña** (12)

past **pasado/a** (11)

pastime **pasatiempo** (10)

patient **paciente** n. m., f. (11)

patio **patio** (5)

pay n. (often per hour) **salario** (17); v. to pay (for) **pagar (gu)** (2)

pea: green peas **arvejas** f. pl. (7)

peace **paz** f. (pl. **paces**) (18)

peasant **campesino/a** (15)

pen **bolígrafo** (2); pen drive **pen drive** m. (12)

pencil **lápiz** m. (pl. **lápices**) (2)

people **gente** f. s. (8)

pepper (condiment) **pimienta** (7)

permit **permitir** (12)

person **persona** (2)

personal pronoun gram. **pronombre** (m.) **personal** (2)

personnel: medical personnel **personal** (m.) **médico** (11)

pet **mascota** (3)

petroleum **petróleo** (15)

pharmacist **farmacéutico/a** (11)

phase **etapa** (16)

philosophy **filosofía** (2)

phone **teléfono** (2); cell phone **teléfono celular** (2); to talk on the phone **hablar por teléfono** (2)

photo(graph) **foto(grafía)** (8); to take photos **sacar (qu) fotos** (8)

photocopier **fotocopiadora** (12)

photocopy **fotocopia** (12)

photographer **fotógrafo/a** (17)

photography **fotografía** (13)

physics **física** (2)

pick up **recoger (recojo)** (14)

picnic: to have a picnic **hacer un picnic** (10)

pie **pastel** m. (7)

piece: piece of advice **consejo** (7); piece of furniture **mueble** m. (5)

Pilates: to do Pilates **hacer (el método) Pilates** (11)

pill **pastilla** (11)

pilot **piloto** m., f. (8)

pink **rosado/a** (4)

place n. **lugar** m. (2); (in line) **puesto** (8); parking place **estacionamiento** (15); v. **poner** (5)

plaid **de cuadros** (4)

plan **plan** m. (10); to make plans to **hacer planes para** (10)

plane **avión** m. (8); to fly; to go/travel by plane **volar (vuelo) en avión** (8); **ir en avión** (8)

planet **planeta** m. (15)

plasma television **televisión** (f.) **plasma** (12)

plate **plato** (5)

play (dramatic) n. **drama** m. (13), **obra de teatro** (13); (a game, sport) v. **jugar (juego) (gu) (a, al)** (5); (a musical instrument) **tocar (qu)** (2); to play cards **jugar (juego) (gu) a las cartas** (10); to play chess **jugar (juego) (gu) al ajedrez** (10); to play videogames **jugar (juego) (gu) a los videojuegos** (10)

player **jugador(a)** (10)

playwright **dramaturgo/a** (13)

plaza **plaza** (4)

pleasantry **expresión** (f.) **de cortesía** (1)

please **por favor** (1)

pleased to meet you **encantado/a** (1), **mucho gusto** (1)

pleasing: to be pleasing **gustar** (8)

plumber **plomero/a** (17)

poem **poema** m. (13)

poet **poeta** m., f. (13)

point: cardinal point **punto cardinal** (6)

police officer **policía** m., f. (15)

policy **política** (18)

political: political office **cargo** (18); political party **partido** (18); political science **ciencias** (f. pl.) **políticas** (2)

politician **político/a** (18)

politics **política** s. (18)

polka-dot **de lunares** (4)

pollute **contaminar** (15)

polluted **contaminado/a** (15)

pollution: there's (lots of) pollution **hay (mucha) contaminación** f. (6)

pool **piscina** (5)

poor **pobre** (3); poorly paid job/position **empleo mal pagado** (17); to do poorly **salir mal** (5); to get along poorly (with) **llevarse mal (con)** (16)

poorly **mal** (2)

population **población** f. (15)

pork chop **chuleta (de cerdo)** (7)

port **puerto** (8)

porter **maletero** (8)

position **empleo** (17); full-time / part-time position **empleo de tiempo completo / parcial** (17), **trabajo de tiempo parcial** (14); poorly paid position **empleo mal pagado** (17); to run for a position (as a candidate) **postularse para un cargo (como candidato/a)** (18); well-paid position **empleo bien pagado** (17)

possessive **posesivo/a** (17); possessive adjective *gram.* **adjetivo posesivo** (3)

possible **posible** (3); it's not possible **no es posible que** (13); it's possible that **es posible que** (13)

post (*as on Facebook*) **publicar (qu)** (12)

postcard **tarjeta postal** (8)

potato **papa/patata** (7); French fried potato **papa/patata frita** (7)

pottery **cerámica** (13)

practice (*play*) **practicar (qu)** (2); (*train*) **entrenar** (10)

prefer **preferir (prefiero) (i)** (4)

preference **preferencia** (1)

prepare **preparar** (7)

preposition *gram.* **preposición** *f.* (5)

prescription **receta** (11)

present **regalo** (3)

press **prensa** (18)

pressure **presión** (14); to be under a lot of pressure **estar bajo muchas presiones** (14)

pretty **bonito/a** (3)

price (*of a transportation ticket*) **pasaje** *m.* (8); fixed, set price **precio fijo** (4)

print **imprimir** (12)

printer **impresora** (12)

probable **probable** (13); it's not probable **no es probable que** (13); it's probable that **es probable que** (13)

profession **profesión** *f.* (17)

professor **profesor(a)** (1)

programmer **programador(a)** (17)

prohibit **prohibir (prohíbo)** (12)

promise **prometer** (8)

pronoun: personal pronoun *gram.* **pronombre** (*m.*) **personal** (2)

protect **proteger (protejo)** (15)

provided **con tal de** (16); provided (that) **con tal (de) que** (16)

psychiatrist **siquiatra** *m., f.* (17)

psychologist **sicólogo/a** (17)

psychology **sicología** (2)

public *n.* **público** (13); *adj.* **público/a** (15)

publish **publicar (qu)** (12)

pure **puro/a** (15)

purple **morado/a** (4)

purpose: for what purpose? **¿para qué?** (16)

purse **bolso** (4)

put **poner** (5); to put on (*an article of clothing*) **ponerse** (5)

Q

quarter: a quarter (fifteen minutes) after (*the hour*) **y cuarto/quince** (1); a quarter to (*hour*) **menos cuarto/quince** (1)

queen **reina** (18)

question **pregunta** (5); to ask a question **hacer una pregunta** (5), **preguntar** (8)

quit **dejar** (17)

quiz **prueba** (14)

R

radio (apparatus) **radio** *m.* (12); radio station **estación** (*f.*) **de radio** (18)

rain **llover (llueve)** (6); it's raining **llueve** (6)

raincoat **impermeable** *m.* (4)

rather **bastante** (16)

read **leer** (*like* **creer**) (3)

reason: for that reason **por eso** (3)

receipt **recibo** (17)

receive **recibir** (3)

recipe **receta** (7)

recommend **recomendar (recomiendo)** (8)

record **grabar** (12)

recycle **reciclar** (15)

recycling **reciclaje** *m.* (15)

red **rojo/a** (4); red wine **vino tinto** (7)

reflexive verb *gram.* **verbo reflexivo** (5)

refrigerator **refrigerador** *m.* (10)

regret **lamentar** (13), **sentir (siento) (i)** (13)

relationship: emotional relationship **relación** (*f.*) **sentimental** (16)

relative **pariente** *m.* (3)

remain (*in a place*) **quedarse** (6); to remain; to be left **quedar** (14)

remember **acordarse (me acuerdo) (de)** (13); **recordar (recuerdo)** (9)

remote control **control** (*m.*) **remoto** (12)

renewable **renovable** (15); renewable energy **energía renovable** (15)

rent *n.* **alquiler** *m.* (12); *v.* to rent **alquilar** (12)

renter **inquilino/a** (12)

repair **arreglar** (15), **reparar** (15); repair shop **taller** *m.* (15)

report **informe** (14), **trabajo** (14); oral report **informe** (*m.*) **oral** (14); written report **informe** (*m.*) **escrito** (14)

reporter **reportero/a** (18)

representative: Congressional representative **representante** (*m., f.*) **al congreso** (18)

resign (from) **renunciar (a)** (17)

resolve **resolver (resuelvo)** (15)

resource: natural resource **recurso natural** (15)

responsibility **deber** *m.* (18), **responsabilidad** *f.* (18)

rest **descansar** (5)

restaurant **restaurante** *m.* (7)

résumé **currículum** *m.* (17)

retire (*from a job*) **jubilarse** (17)

return (*something to someone*) **devolver** (*like* **volver**) (14);

(*to a place*) **regresar** (2), **volver (vuelvo)** (5); to return home **regresar a casa** (2)

review **repaso** (2)

rice **arroz** *m.* (7)

rich (*wealthy*) **rico/a** (3); (*tasty*) **rico/a** (7)

ride: to ride a bicycle **montar en bicicleta** (10); **pasear en bicicleta** (10); to ride a horse **montar a caballo** (10)

right (*legal*) **derecho** (18); **¿no?** (4), **¿verdad?** (4); right now **ahora mismo** (6); right now (*currently*) **en la actualidad** (10); to be right **tener razón** (4); to the right of **a la derecha de** (6)

ring **sonar (suena)** (10)

river **río** (15)

roast(ed) **asado/a** (7); roast chicken **pollo asado** (7)

role (*in a play, an event*) **papel** *m.* (13)

room **cuarto** (2); waiting room **sala de espera** (8)

roommate **compañero/a de cuarto** (2)

round-trip ticket **billete** *m.* (*Sp.*) / **boleto** (*L.A.*) **de ida y vuelta** (8)

routine **rutina** (5)

rug **alfombra** (5)

ruin **ruina** (13)

run **correr** (10); to run against/into **chocar (qu) contra/con** (14); **pegarse (gu) con/contra** (14); to run as a candidate **postularse como candidato/a** (18); to run for a position **postularse para un cargo** (18); (*machines*) **funcionar** (12); to run out of **acabar** (14)

S

sad **triste** (6)

sake: for heaven's sake **por Dios** (14)

salad **ensalada** (7)

salary **sueldo** (17)

sales **rebajas** *f. pl.* (4)

salesperson **vendedor(a)** (17)

salmon **salmón** *m.* (7)

salt **sal** *f.* (7)

same **mismo/a** (6); same here (likewise) **igualmente** (1)

sandals **sandalias** *f. pl.* (4)

sandwich **sándwich** *m.* (7)

Saturday **sábado** (5)

sauce **salsa** (7)

sausage **salchicha** (7)

save **conservar** (15); (*a place in line*) **guardar un puesto** (8); (*documents*) **almacenar** (12), **guardar** (12); (*money*) **ahorrar** (17)

savory **rico/a** (7)

say **decir** (8); to say good-bye (to) **despedirse** (*like* **pedir**) **(de)** (9) scanner **escáner** *m.* (12)

scene **escena** (13)

scenery **escenario** (13)

schedule **horario** (14)

school **escuela** (10)

schoolteacher **maestro/a de escuela** (17)

science **ciencia** (2); computer science **computación** *f.* (2); natural sciences **ciencias** (*f. pl.*) **naturales** (2); political science **ciencias** (*f. pl.*) **políticas** (2); social sciences **ciencias** (*f. pl.*) **sociales** (2)

screen **pantalla** (12); big screen (monitor) **pantalla grande** (12); flat screen (monitor) **pantalla plana** (12)

script **guion** *m.* (13)

sculpt **esculpir** (13)

sculptor **escultor(a)** (13)

sculpture **escultura** (13)

sea **mar** *m.* (8)

season (of the year) **estación** *f.* (6)

seat **asiento** (8)

second **segundo/a** (13); second floor (third story) **segundo piso** (12)

secretary **secretario/a** (2)

security (check) **control** (*m.*) **de seguridad** (8); to go/pass through security (check) **pasar por el control de seguridad** (8)

see **ver** (5); see you around **nos vemos** (1); see you later **hasta luego** (1); see you tomorrow **hasta mañana** (1)

sell **vender** (3)

senator **senador(a)** (18)

send a text **mandar un mensaje** (2)

separate (from) **separarse (de)** (16)

separated from **separado/a (de)** (16)

separation **separación** *f.* (16)

September **septiembre** *m.* (6)

serve **servir (sirvo) (i)** (5)

service **servicio** (15); military service **servicio militar** (18)

set price **precio fijo** (4)

set the table **poner la mesa** (10)

seven **siete** (1)

seven hundred **setecientos/as** (4)

seventeen **diecisiete** (1)

seventh **séptimo/a** (13)

seventy **setenta** (3)

shake hands **darse la mano** (11)

shame **lástima** (13); it's a shame that **es una lástima que** (13); what a shame that . . . ! **¡qué lástima que... !** (13)

shape **forma** (4)

share **compartir** (17)

shave **afeitarse** (5)

she *sub. pron.* **ella** (2); she is **es** (1)

shellfish **mariscos** *m. pl.* (7)

ship **barco** (8); cruise ship **crucero** (8); to go/travel by ship **ir en barco** (8)

shirt **camisa** (4)

shoes **zapatos** *m. pl.* (4)

shop **tienda** (4); repair shop **taller** *m.* (15)

shopping **de compras** (4); shopping mall **centro comercial** (4); to go shopping **ir de compras** (4)

short (*in height*) **bajo/a** (3); (*in length*) **corto/a** (3)

shorts **pantalones** (*m. pl.*) **cortos** (4)

shot: to give (*someone*) a shot **ponerle una inyección** (11)

should (*do something*) **deber** + *inf.* (3)

show *n.* **espectáculo** (13); *v.* **mostrar (muestro)** (8)

shower: to take a shower **ducharse** (5)

shrimp **camarones** *m., pl.* (7)

siblings **hermanos** *m. pl.* (3)

sick **enfermo/a** (6); to get/become sick **enfermarse** (11)

sickness **enfermedad** *f.* (11)

sidewalk **acera** (15)

silk *adj.* **de seda** (4)

silly **tonto/a** (3)

silver *adj.* **de plata** (4)

sing **cantar** (2)

singer **cantante** *m., f.* (13)

single (*not married*) **soltero/a** (16)

sink: bathroom sink **lavabo** (5)

sir **señor (Sr.)** *m.* (1)

sister **hermana** (3)

sit down **sentarse (me siento)** (5)

six **seis** (1)

six hundred **seiscientos/as** (4)

sixteen **dieciséis** (1)

sixth **sexto/a** (13)

sixty **sesenta** (3)

skate *v.* **patinar** (10)

skating **patinaje** *m.* (10)

ski **esquiar (esquío)** (10)

skiing **esquí** *m.* (10)

skirt **falda** (4)

skyscraper **rascacielos** *m. inv.* (15)

sleep **dormir (duermo) (u) (u)** (5)

sleepy: to be sleepy **tener sueño** (4)

slender **delgado/a** (3)

small **pequeño/a** (3); (*adjective suffix*) **-ito/a** (10); small child **niño/a** (3)

smart **listo/a** (3)

smile **sonreír** (*like* **reír**) (9)

smoke **fumar** (8)

smoking area **sala de fumadores/ de fumar** (8)

snack **merienda** (7); to have a snack **merendar (meriendo)** (7)

snow **nevar (nieva)** (6); it's snowing **nieva** (6)

so that **para que** (16)

so-so **regular** (1)

soccer **fútbol** *m.* (10)

social: social network **red** (*f.*) **social** (12); social sciences **ciencias** (*f. pl.*) **sociales** (2); social worker **trabajador(a) social** (17)

sociology **sociología** (2)

socks **calcetines** *m. pl.* (4)

soft drink **refresco** (7)

solar energy **energía solar** (15)

soldier **militar** *m., f.* (17); **soldado** (17); female soldier **mujer** (*f.*) **soldado** (17)

solve **resolver (resuelvo)** (15)

some **algún (alguna/os/as)** (7)

someone **alguien** (7)

something **algo** (7)

sometimes **a veces** (3)

son **hijo** (3)

song **canción** *f.* (7)

soon: as soon as **en cuanto** (17), **tan pronto como** (17)

sorry: to feel sorry **lamentar** (13), **sentir (siento) (i)** (13); I'm (very) sorry **lo siento (mucho)** (14)

sound **sonar (suena)** (10)

soup **sopa** (7)

south **sur** *m.* (6)

space: storage space **espacio de almacenamiento** (12)

Spanish (*language*) **español** *m.* (2); *n., adj.* **español, española** (3)

spare (free) time **ratos** (*m. pl.*) **libres** (10)

speak **hablar** (2)

species **especie** *f.* (15); endangered species **especie en peligro de extinción** (15)

spectator **espectador(a)** (13)

speed **velocidad** *f.* (15); speed limit **límite** (*m.*) **de velocidad** (15)

spend (*money*) **gastar** (9); (*time*) **pasar** (6); to spend one's vacation in . . . **pasar las vacaciones en...** (8)

spicy **picante** (7)

sport **deporte** *m.* (10)

sporting **deportivo/a** (10)

sports, sports-loving *adj.* **deportivo/a** (10)

spring (*season*) **primavera** (6)

square **plaza** (4)

stage **escenario** (13); (*phase*) **etapa** (16)

stairs **escaleras** *f. pl.* (14)

stand up **levantarse** (5); to stand in line **hacer cola** (8)

start **empezar (empiezo) (c)** (5); to start up (*a car*) **arrancar (qu)** (15)

state **estado** (3); emotional state **estado afectivo** (9)

station **estación** *f.* (8); bus station **estación de autobuses** (8); gas station **estación de servicio** (15); radio station **estación de radio** (18); station wagon **camioneta** (8); train station **estación de trenes** (8)

stay **quedarse** (6); to stay in bed **guardar cama** (11)

steak **bistec** *m.* (7)

stick out one's tongue **sacar (qu) la lengua** (11)

still **todavía** (6)

stockings **medias** *f. pl.* (4)

stomach **estómago** (11)

stop *n.* **escala** (*in a trip*) (8), **parada** (*to board transportation*) (8); bus stop **parada del autobús** (12); subway stop **parada del metro** (12); to make stops **hacer escalas** (8), **hacer paradas** (8); to stop **parar** (15); to stop (*doing something*) **dejar de + inf.** (11)

storage (space) **(espacio de) almacenamiento** (12)

store *n.* **tienda** (4); *v.* (*computer*) **almacenar** (12)

story **historia** (8)

stove **estufa** (5)

straight ahead **(todo) derecho** (15), **todo recto** (15)

strange: how strange that . . .! **¡qué extraño que... !** (13); it's strange that **es extraño que** (13)

street **calle** *f.* (12)

street corner **esquina** (15)

stress **estrés** *m.* (14); to have a lot of stress **tener muchas presiones** (14); under stress, stressed out **estresado/a** (14)

strike (*labor*) **huelga** (18)

striped **de rayas** (4)

struggle **lucha** (18)

student **estudiante** *m., f.* (2)

study **estudiar** (2)

stuffed up (*with a cold*) **resfriado/a** *adj.* (11)

subject area **materia** (2)

suburbs **afueras** *f. pl.* (12)

subway stop **parada del metro** (12)

succeed in (*doing something*) **conseguir** (*like* seguir) **+ inf.** (9)

suddenly **de repente** (11)

suffer **sufrir (de)** (14)

sufficiently **bastante** (16)

sugar **azúcar** *m.* (7)

suggest **sugerir (sugiero) (i)** (9)

suit **traje** *m.* (4)

suitcase **maleta** (8); to pack one's suitcase(s) **hacer la(s) maleta(s)** (8)

summer **verano** (6)

sunbathe **tomar el sol** (8)

Sunday **domingo** (5)

sunglasses **gafas (f. pl.) de sol** (4)

sunny: it's (very) sunny **hace (mucho) sol** (6)

sunscreen **bloqueador (m.) solar** (8)

supermarket **supermercado** (12)

supper **cena** (7); to have (eat) supper **cenar** (7)

sure **seguro/a** (6); it's a sure thing that **es seguro que** (13); it's not sure **no es seguro que** (13); to not be sure of **no estar seguro/a de** (13)

surf **hacer surfing** (10)

surprise **sorprender** (*like* gustar) (13)

SUV **SUV** *m.* (15)

sweater **suéter** *m.* (4)

sweatshirt **sudadera** (4)

sweep (the floor) **barrer (el piso)** (10)

sweets **dulces** *m. pl.* (7)

swim **nadar** (8)

swimming **natación** *f.* (10); swimming pool **piscina** (5)

swimsuit **traje (m.) de baño** (4)

syllabus **programa (m.) del curso** (14)

symptom **síntoma** *m.* (11)

systems analyst **analista (m., f.) de sistemas** (17)

T

T-shirt **camiseta** (4)

table **mesa** (2); to clear the table **quitar la mesa** (10); to set the table **poner la mesa** (10)

take **tomar** (2); **llevar** (4); to take a bath **bañarse** (5); to take a nap **dormir (duermo) (u) la siesta** (5); to take a shower **ducharse** (5); to take a trip **hacer un viaje** (5); to take a vacation **tomar unas vacaciones** (8); to take a walk **dar un paseo** (10); to take care of oneself **cuidarse** (11); to take off (*an article of clothing*) **quitarse** (5); to take out **sacar (qu)** (17); to take out the trash **sacar (qu) la basura** (10); to take photos **sacar (qu) fotos** (8); to take place at/in (*a place*) **ser en + place** (9); to take someone's temperature **tomarle la temperatura** (11)

talk **hablar** (2); to talk on the phone **hablar por teléfono** (2)

tall **alto/a** (3)

tame **domesticado/a** (15)

tank **tanque** *m.* (15)

tape **grabar** (12)

tasty **rico/a** (7)

tea **té** *m.* (7)

teach **enseñar** (2)

teacher: school teacher **maestro/a de escuela** (17)

team **equipo** (10)

technician **técnico/a** (17)

teeth: to brush one's teeth **cepillarse los dientes** (5)

television: (plasma) television **televisión (f.) (plasma)** (12); to watch television **mirar la tele(visión)** (3)

tell **contar (cuento)** (8); **decir** (8)

teller **cajero/a** (17); automatic teller machine (ATM) **cajero automático** (17)

temperature **temperatura** (11); to take someone's temperature **tomarle la temperatura** (11)

ten **diez** (1)

tenant **inquilino/a** (12)

tennis **tenis** *m.* (10)

tennis shoes **tenis** *m. pl.* (4)

tent **tienda (de campaña)** (8)

tenth **décimo/a** (13)

terrible **terrible** (13); it's terrible that **es terrible que** (13)

terrorism **terrorismo** (18)

terrorist **terrorista** *m., f.* (18); terrorist attack **ataque (m.) terrorista** (18)

test **examen** *m.* (4); **prueba** (14)

text (*electronic*) **mensaje** *m.* (2); to (send a) text **mandar un mensaje** (2)

textbook **libro de texto** (2)

than: less . . . than **menos... que** (6); less than + *number* **menos de + number** (6); more . . . than **más... que** (6); more than + *number* **más de + number** (6); older than **mayor que** (6); younger than **menos que** (6)

thank you (very much) **(muchas) gracias** (1); thanks for **gracias por + inf./ noun** (9)

that *conj.* **que** (3); that *adj., pron.* **ese/a** (4); *neuter pron.* **eso** (4); that ([way] over there) *adj., pron.* **aquel, aquella** (4); that ([way] over there) *neuter pron.* **aquello** (4); that means . . . **eso quiere decir...** (11); that which **lo que** (5)

theater **teatro** (10); to go to the theater **ir al teatro** (10)

their *poss. adj.* **su(s)** (3); (of) theirs *poss. adj., poss pron.* **suyo/a(s)** (17)

them *obj.* (*of prep.*) **ellos/as** (2)

then **luego** (5)

there **allí** (4)

there: (way) over there **allá** (4)

there is/are **hay** (1); is there / are there? **¿hay?** (1); there is/are not **no hay** (1); there's (lots of) **hay (mucho/a[s])** (6); infinitive form of **hay haber** (12)

these *adj., pron.* **estos/as** (3)

they *sub. pron.* **ellos/as** (2)

thin **delgado/a** (3)

thing **cosa** (5); the bad thing **lo malo** (11); the good thing **lo bueno** (11)

think **creer (en)** (3); to not think **no creer** (13); to think (about) **pensar (pienso) (de/en)** (5); **pensar que** to think that (5)

third **tercer(o/a)** (13)

thirsty: to be (very) thirsty **tener (mucha) sed** (7)

thirteen **trece** (1)

thirty **treinta** (1); thirty minutes past (*the hour*) **y treinta** (1)

this *adj., pron.* **este/a** (3); *neuter pron.* **esto** (3) those *adj., pron.* **esos/as** (4); those ([way] over there) *adj., pron.* **aquellos/as** (4)

three **tres** (1)

three hundred **trescientos/as** (4)

throat **garganta** (11)

through **por** (8)

throw: to throw a party **dar/hacer una fiesta** (9)

Thursday **jueves** *m. inv.* (5)

ticket **billete** *m.* (*Sp.*) / **boleto** (*L.A.*) (8); one-way ticket **billete/bolleto de ida** (8); round-trip ticket **billete/boleto de ida y vuelta** (8)

tie **corbata** (4)

time **tiempo** (6); at what time . . . ? **¿a qué hora... ?** (1); at times **a veces** (3); conjunction of time **conjunción** (*f.*) **de tiempo** (17); for the first/last time **por primera/última vez** (14); free time **tiempo libre** (10); on time **a tiempo** (8); free time **ratos** (*m. pl.*) **libres** (10); to have a bad time **pasarlo mal** (9); to have a good time **divertirse (me divierto) (i)** (5); **pasarlo bien** (9); what time is it? **¿qué hora es?** (1)

tire **llanta** (15); flat tire **llanta desinflada** (15)

tired **cansado/a** (6); to get tired **cansarse** (11)

to **a** (1); to the **al** (4); to the left of **a la izquiera de** (6); to the right of **a la derecha de** (6)

toast **pan tostado** (7)

toasted **tostado/a** (7)

toaster **tostadora** (10)

today **hoy** (1); what day is today? **¿qué día es hoy?** (5); what's today's date? **¿cuál es la fecha de hoy?** (6), **¿qué fecha es hoy?** (6)

toe **dedo del pie** (11)

together **juntos/as** (8)

tomato **tomate** *m.* (7)

tomorrow **mañana** (1); see you tomorrow **hasta mañana** (1); the day after tomorrow **pasado mañana** (5)

tongue **lengua** (11); to stick out one's tongue **sacar (qu) la lengua** (11)

tonight **esta noche** (6)

too much **demasiado** *adv.* (9)

tooth **diente** *m.* (5); back tooth **muela** (11); to brush one's teeth **cepillarse los dientes** (5)

top: on top of **encima de** (6)

towel **toalla** (5)

trade (*profession*) **oficio** (17)

tradition: cultural tradition **tradición** (*f.*) **cultural** (13)

traditional **folclórico/a** (13)

traffic **circulación** *f.* (15), **tráfico** (15), **tránsito** (15); traffic signal **semáforo** (15)

train **tren** *m.* (8); to go/travel by train **ir en tren** (8); to train **entrenar** (10); train station **estación** (*f.*) **de trenes** (8)

translator **traductor(a)** (17)

transportation: means of transportation **medio de transporte** (8)

trash **basura** (10); to take out the trash **sacar (qu) la basura** (10)

travel **viajar** (8); to travel by bus **ir en autobús** (8); to travel by boat/ship **ir en barco** (8); to travel by plane **ir en avión** (8)

traveling **de viaje** (8)

treadmill **caminadora** (11)

treatment **tratamiento** (11)

tree **árbol** *m.* (9)

trendy: it's trendy **está de moda** (4), **es de última moda** (4)

trip **viaje** *m.* (5); on a trip **de viaje** (8); to take a trip **hacer un viaje** (5)

true: it's true that **es verdad que** (13)

try to (*do something*) **tratar de** + *inf.* (13)

Tuesday **martes** *m. inv.* (5); on Tuesdays **los martes** (5)

tuition **matrícula** (2)

tuna **atún** *m.* (7)

turkey **pavo** (7)

turn **doblar** (15); to be someone's turn **tocarle (qu) a uno** (10); to turn on (*appliance, machine*) **encender (enciendo)** (12); to turn on (*appliance, machine*) **poner** (12); to turn off (*appliance, machine*) **apagar (gu)** (14); to turn out badly **salir mal** (5); to turn out well **salir bien** (5)

tweet *n.* **tuit** *m.* (12); *v.* **Twitear** (12)

twelve **doce** (1)

twenty **veinte** (1)

twice **dos veces** (11)

Twitter **Twitter** *m.* (12)

two **dos** (1)

two hundred **doscientos/as** (4)

U

ugly **feo/a** (3)

uncle **tío** (3); aunts and uncles **tíos** *m. pl.* (3)

under stress **estresado/a** (14); to be under a lot of stress **tener muchas presiones** (14)

understand **comprender** (3); **entender (entiendo)** (5)

underwear **ropa interior** (4)

unfortunately **desgraciadamente** (11)

United States: of the United States of America *n., adj.* **estadounidense** (3)

university *n.* **universidad** *f.* (2); *adj.* **universitario/a** (14)

unless **a menos que** (16); **sin que** (16)

unlikely: it's unlikely that **es improbable que** (13)

unlucky: to be unlucky **tener mala suerte** (14)

unoccupied **libre** (10)

unpleasant **antipático/a** (3)

until *prep.* **hasta** (1); *conj.* **hasta que** (17)

up: to be up to date **estar al día** (18)

urgent **urgente** (12); it's urgent (that) **es urgente que** (12)

us *obj.* (*of prep.*) **nosotros/as** (2)

use **usar** (4); (*gas*) **gastar** (15); to be used for **servir (sirvo) (i) para** (5)

user **usuario/a** (12)

V

vacation: on vacation **de vacaciones** (8); to be on vacation **estar de vacaciones** (8); to go on vacation in/to . . . **ir de vacaciones a...** (8); to leave on vacation **salir de vacaciones** (8); to spend one's vacation at/on/in . . . **pasar las vacaciones en...** (8); to take a vacation **tomar unas vacaciones** (8)

vaccination **vacuna** (11)

vacuum cleaner **aspiradora** (10); to vacuum **pasar la aspiradora** (10)

van **camioneta** (8)

vegetables **verduras** *f. pl.* (7)

vehicle **vehículo** (15)

verb *gram.* **verbo** (2); reflexive verb *gram.* **verbo reflexivo** (5)

very *adv.* **muy** (1); very much **muchísimo** (8); very very **-ísimo** (9); very well **muy bien** (1)

veterinarian **veterinario/a** (17)

victim **víctima** (18)

video **video** (12); videogame **videojuego** (10); to play videogames **jugar (juego) (gu) a los videojuegos** (10)

view **vista** (12)

visit a museum **visitar un museo** (10)

voice mailbox **buzón** (*m.*) **de voz** (12)

volleyball **voleibol** *m.* (10)

vote **votar** (18)

W

wages (*often per hour*) **salario** (17)

wait (for) **esperar** (7)

waiter/waitress **camarero/a** (7)

waiting room **sala de espera** (8)

wake up **despertarse (me despierto)** (5)

walk **caminar** (10); to take a walk **dar un paseo** (10)

wall ***pared*** *f.* (5)

wallet **cartera** (4)

want **desear** (2); **querer** (4)

war **guerra** (18)

was **fue** (5)

wash **lavar** (10)

washing machine **lavadora** (10)

watch *n.* **reloj** *m.* (4); *v.* **mirar** (3); to watch television **mirar la tele(visión)** (3) water **agua** *f.* (*but* **el agua**) (7); mineral water **agua mineral** (7)

way over there **allá** (4)

we *sub. pron.* **nosotros/as** (2)

wear **llevar** (4), **usar** (4)

weather **tiempo** (6); what's the weather like? **¿qué tiempo hace?** (6); it's (very) good/bad weather **hace (muy) buen/ mal tiempo** (6)

weave **tejer** (13)

webpage **página web** (12)

website **sitio web** (12)

wed: newly wed **recién casado/a** (16)

wedding (*ceremony*) **boda** (16)

Wednesday **miércoles** *m. inv.* (5)

week **semana** (5); days of the week **días** (*m. pl.*) **de la semana** (5); next week **la próxima semana** (5), **la semana que viene** (5); once a week **una vez a la semana** (3)

weekend **fin** (*m.*) **de semana** (2)

weight: to lift weights **levantar pesas** (11)

welcome: you're welcome **de nada** (1), **no hay de qué** (1)

well **bien** (1); very well **muy bien** (1); to come/turn out well **salir bien** (5); to do well **salir bien** (5)

well-being **bienestar** *m.* (11)

well-paid job/position **empleo bien pagado** (17)

west **oeste** *m.* (6)

whale **ballena** (15)

what (that which) **lo que** (5)

what? **¿cómo?** (1); **¿cuál?** (2); **¿qué?** (1); at what time? **¿a qué hora... ?** (1); for what purpose? **¿para qué... ?** (16); what (a) + *noun*! **¡qué** + *noun*! (14); what a shame that . . . ! **¡qué lástima que... !** (13); what are you like? **¿cómo es usted?** *form. s.* (1); what day is today? **¿qué día es hoy?** (5); what for? **¿para qué... ?** (16); what is your name? **¿cómo se llama usted?** *form. s.* (1); **¿cómo te llamas?** *fam. s.* (1); what time is it? **¿qué hora es?** (1); what's the weather like? **¿qué tiempo hace?** (6); what's today's date? **¿cuál es la fecha de hoy?** (6), **¿qué fecha es hoy?** (6)

when? **¿cuándo?** (2)

where? **¿dónde?** (1); where (to)? **¿adónde?** (4); where are you from? **¿de dónde eres (tú)?** *fam. s.* (1); **¿de dónde es usted?** *form. s.* (1)

which *conj.* **que** (3)

which? **¿cuál?** (2)

while **mientras** (10)

white **blanco/a** (4); white wine **vino blanco** (7)

whiteboard **pizarrón** (*m.*) **blanco** (2)

who *rel. pron.* **que** (3)

who? **¿quién?** (1)

whose? **¿de quién?** (3)

why? **¿por qué?** (3)

widow **viuda** (16)

widower **viudo** (16)

wife **esposa** (3), **mujer** *f.* (3)

wifi **wifi** *m.* (12)

wild **salvaje** (15)

win **ganar** (10)

wind **viento** (6); wind energy **energía eólica** (15)

window **ventana** (2); small window (*on a plane*) **ventanilla** (8)

windshield **parabrisas** *m. inv.* (15)

windy: it's (very) windy **hace (mucho) viento** (6)

wine (white, red) **vino (blanco, tinto)** (7)

winter **invierno** (6)

wish **esperanza** (18)

with **con** (2); with me **conmigo** (6); with you *fam. s.* **contigo** (6)

withdraw (*from an account*) **sacar (qu)** (17)

without **sin** (5); **sin que** (16)

witness **testigo** *m., f.* (18)

woman **mujer** *f.* (2); business woman **mujer de negocios** (17)

wool **de lana** (4)

word **palabra** (1); indefinite and negative word *gram.* **palabra indefinida y negativa** (7); interrogative word **palabra interrogativa** (2)

work (labor) **trabajo** (12); (piece of) **trabajo** (14); to work (function) **funcionar** (12); to work (at a job) **trabajar** (2); work of art **obra de arte** (13); *adj.* **laboral** (17)

worker **obrero/a** (17); social worker **trabajador(a) social** (17)

world **mundo** (3)

worried **preocupado/a** (6)

worse **peor** (6)

woven goods **tejidos** *m. pl.* (13)

write **escribir** (*p.p.* **escrito**) (3)

writer **escritor(a)** (13)

written **escrito/a** (*p.p. of* **escribir**) (14); written report **informe** (*m.*) **escrito** (14)

wrong: to be wrong **no tener razón** (4); to get up on the wrong side of the bed **levantarse con el pie izquierdo** (14)

Y

yard **patio** (5)

year **año** (6); (*in school*) **grado** (10); end of the year **fin** (*m.*) **de año** (9); to be . . . years old **tener... años** (3)

yellow **amarillo/a** (4)

yes **sí** (1)

yesterday **ayer** (5); yesterday was . . . **ayer fue...** (5); the day before yesterday *adv.* **anteayer** (5)

yoga: to do yoga **hacer (el) yoga** (10)

yogurt **yogur** *m.* (7)

you *sub. pron.* **tú** *fam. s.* (2); **usted (Ud.)** *form. s.* (2); **vosotros/as** *fam. pl.* (*Sp.*) (2); **ustedes (Uds.)** *form. pl.* (2); *obj. of prep.* **ti** *fam. s.* (6); **usted** *form. s.;* **ustedes (Uds.)** *form. pl.* (6); and you? **¿y tú?** *fam. s.* (1); **¿y usted?** *form. s.* (1); how are you? **¿cómo está(s)?** (1), **¿qué tal?** (1); with you *fam. s.* **contigo** (6); you are *fam. s.* **eres** (1), *form. s.* **es** (1)

young **joven** (3); young woman **señorita (Srta.)** (1)

younger (than) **menor (que)** (6)

your *poss. adj.* **tu(s)** *fam. s.* (3); **su(s)** *form. s., pl.* (3); **vuestro/a(s)** *fam. pl.* (*Sp.*) (3); your, (of) yours *poss. adj., poss. pron.* **tuyo/a(s)** *fam. s.* (17); **suyo/a(s)** *form. s., pl.* (17); **vuestro/a(s)** *fam. pl.* (*Sp.*) (17)

you're welcome **de nada** (1), **no hay de qué** (1)

youth **juventud** *f.* (16); as a youth **de adolescente** (10)

Z

zero **cero** (1)

zone **zona** (12)

CREDITS

Photo Credits

Front Matter

Page iii: © Hero/Corbis/Glow Images

Chapter 1

Opener: (road) © Rodrigo Torres/Glow Images RF; p. 2 (Barcelona): © John Kellerman/Alamy; p. 2 (Mexico City): © Mark Lewis/Getty Images RF; p. 3: © Onoky Photography/SuperStock RF; p. 4 (teacher and student): © Tom Fowlks/Getty Images; p. 4 (greeting): © GoGo Images Corporation/Alamy RF; p. 5: © Hola Images/age fotostock RF; p. 8: © dynamicgraphics/Jupiterimages RF; p. 9 (woman): © Kevin Peterson/Getty Images RF; p. 9 (man): © Andersen Ross/Getty Images RF; p. 11: © America/Alamy RF; p. 13 (class): © KidStock/Blend Images LLC RF; p. 13 (signs): © Julio López Saguar/Getty Images RF; p. 15: © Bob Thomas/Popperfoto/Getty Images; p. 20-21 (all): © McGraw-Hill Education/Klic Video Productions; p. 22 (mountain): © Guy Edwardes/Getty Images; p. 22 (beach): © Pixtal/age fotostock RF; p. 22 (forest): © Adalberto Rios Szalay/Sexto Sol/Getty Images RF; p. 22 (desert): © ESO, CC BY 3.0 RF; p. 23 (glacier): © Image Source RF; p. 23 (Madrid): © Pixtal/age fotostock RF; p. 25: © Rodrigo Torres/Glow Images RF.

Chapter 2

Opener: © Simon Jarratt/Corbis/Photolibrary RF; p. 27: © Onoky Photography/SuperStock RF; p. 30: © David R. Frazier Photolibrary, Inc./Alamy; p. 32: © Lifesize/Getty Images RF; p. 33: © McGraw-Hill Education/Klic Video Productions; p. 45: © BananaStock/PunchStock RF; p. 47 (woman): © Tetra images RF/Getty Images RF; p. 47 (students): © Digital Vision/Getty Images RF; p. 48: © Digital Vision RF; p. 51: © David A. Tietz/Editorial Image, LLC; p. 53: © McGraw-Hill Education/Klic Video Productions; p. 54: © David Peevers/Lonely Planet Images/Getty Images; p. 56: © Onoky Photography/SuperStock RF; p. 57: © McGraw-Hill Education.

Chapter 3

Opener: © UpperCut Images/Alamy RF; p. 61: © Onoky Photography/SuperStock RF; p. 62 (abuelo): © Jack Hollingsworth/Getty Images RF; p. 62 (abuela): © Jose Luis Pelaez Inc/Blend Images/Getty Images RF; p. 62 (padre): © Seth Joel/Getty Images; p. 62 (madre): © Jose Luis Pelaez Inc/Blend Images/Getty Images RF; p. 62 (tio): © Jose Luis Pelaez Inc/Blend Images/Getty Images RF; p. 62 (tia): © John Henley/Blend Images/Getty Images RF; p. 62 (Patricia): © Glow Images/SuperStock RF; p. 62 (hermana): © Getty Images/Digital Vision RF; p. 62 (hermano): © Blend Images/PunchStock RF; p. 62 (dog): © G.K. & Vikki Hart/Getty Images RF; p. 62 (primo): © Ryan McVay/Getty Images RF; p. 62 (prima): © Michael Matisse/Getty Images RF; p. 64 (abuela): © Jose Luis Pelaez Inc/Blend Images/Getty Images RF; p. 64 (padre): © Seth Joel/Getty Images; p. 64 (madre): © Jose Luis Pelaez Inc/Blend Images/Getty Images RF; p. 64 (tio): © Jose Luis Pelaez Inc/Blend Images/Getty Images RF; p. 64 (tia): © John Henley/Blend Images/Getty Images RF; p. 64 (abuelo): © Jack Hollingsworth/Getty Images RF; p. 64 (Patricia): © Glow Images/SuperStock RF; p. 65: © Jose Luis Pelaez, Inc./Getty Images RF; p. 67: © McGraw-Hill Education/Klic Video Productions; p. 69: © SuperStock/Purestock RF; p. 72: © Van Vechten Collection, Library of Congress, LC-USZ62-42516; p. 73: © McGraw-Hill Education/Klic Video Productions; p. 74: © DEA/G Dagli Orti/age fotostock; p. 75 (man): © Corbis/SuperStock RF; p. 75 (woman): © Lifesize/Getty Images RF; p. 82 (1): © moodboard/SuperStock RF; p. 82 (2): © Terry Vine/Blend Images LLC RF; p. 82 (3): © Monashee Frantz/age fotostock RF; p. 82 (4): © Jose Luis Pelaez Inc/Blend RF; p. 82 (a): © McGraw-Hill Education; p. 82 (b): © Blend Images/Alamy RF; p. 82 (c): © Hero/Corbis/Glow Images RF; p. 82 (d): © Image Source RF; p. 83: © McGraw-Hill Education/Klic Video Productions; p. 85: © Sergio Salvador/Getty Images RF; p. 87: © Charlie Neuman/U-T San Diego/ZUMA Wire/Alamy; p. 88: © Pixtal/age fotostock RF; p. 89: © Ann Summa/Corbis; p. 91: © McGraw-Hill Education/Klic Video Productions; p. 92: © Anuska Sampedro/Getty Images RF; p. 93: © AP Photo/Ramon Espinosa; p. 94: © Onoky Photography/SuperStock RF; p. 95: © McGraw-Hill Education.

Chapter 4

Opener: © Danny Lehman/Corbis; p. 99: © Onoky Photography/SuperStock RF; p. 100 (young woman): © drbimages/Getty Images RF; p. 100 (woman): © Glowimages RM/Alamy; p. 100 (man): © Peopleimages/Getty Images RF; p. 101 (man): © Andresr/Getty Images RF; p. 101 (woman): © drbimages/Getty Images RF; p. 101 (couple): © 4x6/Getty Images RF; p. 103 (crayons): © Nicemonkey/Alamy RF; p. 103 (art): Artwork courtesy of La Antigua Galería de Arte Antigua Guatemala, www.artintheamericas.com; p. 104: © Barry Barker/McGraw-Hill Education; p. 105: © brianlatino/Alamy RF; p. 107: © McGraw-Hill Education/Klic Video Productions; p. 114: © Onoky Photography/SuperStock RF; p. 117: © Lissa Harrison RF; p. 119: © Diego Lezama/Lonely Planet Images/Getty Images; p. 121: © Miami In Focus, Inc.; p. 122: © Apriori, LLC/Getty Images; p. 123: © McGraw-Hill Education/Klic Video Productions; p. 124: © Dorling Kindersley/Getty Images RF; p. 126: © Onoky Photography/SuperStock RF; p. 127 (woman in library): © Fancy Collection/Fancy Collection/SuperStock RF; p. 127 (man with skateboard): © Blue Jean Images/Corbis RF; p. 127 (woman in dress): © Ed Suter/Africa Media Online/The Image Works; p. 127 (woman in coat): © pbnj productions/SuperStock RF; p. 127 (man in suit): © Kelly Redinger/Design Pics RF; p. 127: © McGraw-Hill Education.

Chapter 5

Opener: © Jon Arnold Images Ltd/Alamy; p. 131: © Purestock/Getty Images RF; p. 134: © John Mitchell/Alamy; p. 138: © McGraw-Hill Education/Klic Video Productions; p. 142: © Jan Stromme/Alamy; p. 143: © Paul Taylor/Getty Images; p. 144: © BrazilPhotos.com/Alamy; p. 152: © Nicholas Gill/Alamy; p. 155: © EPA/Roberto Escobar/Corbis; p. 157: © McGraw-Hill Education/Klic Video Productions; p. 158: © Image Source RF; p. 160: © Purestock/Getty Images RF; p. 161 (library): © Andersen Ross/Blend Images LLC RF; p. 161 (gym): © Erik Isakson/Blend Images LLC RF; p. 161 (class): © Purestock/Alamy RF; p. 161 (café): © UpperCut Images/Glow Images RF; p. 161 (steps): © Caia Image/Glow Images RF; p. 161 (video): © McGraw-Hill Education.

Chapter 6

Opener: © Paul Souders/The Image Bank/Getty Images; p. 165: © Purestock/Getty Images RF; p. 168 (all): © Bill Brooks/Alamy RF; p. 169: © DEA/S. Buonamici/Getty Images; p. 172: © McGraw-Hill Education/Klic Video Productions; p. 173: © Janis Christie/Getty Images RF; p. 175: © imagebroker/Alamy RF; p. 178 (man): © Stockbyte/Getty Images RF; p. 178 (woman): © XiXinXing/Getty Images RF; p. 180: © Rodrigo Guerrero/LatinContent/Getty Images; p. 181: © BananaStock/PictureQuest RF; p. 182: © Jenni Kirk/McGraw-Hill Education; p. 185 (Buenos Aires): © Image Source/PunchStock RF; p. 185 (San Jose): © mtcurado/Getty Images RF; p. 189 (man): © John Lund/Sam Diephuis/Blend Images LLC RF; p. 189 (woman): © Pixtal/age fotostock RF; p. 190: © Jack Hollingsworth/Getty Images RF; p. 191: © Alamy; p. 192 (boy left): © Paul Bradbury/age fotostock RF; p. 192 (boy middle): © KidStock/Blend Images LLC RF; p. 192 (girl): © JGI/Jamie Grill/Blend Images LLC RF; p. 193: © McGraw-Hill Education/Klic Video Productions; p. 194: © Jenni Kirk/McGraw-Hill Education; p. 196: © Purestock/Getty Images RF; p. 197: © McGraw-Hill Education.

Chapter 7

Opener: © Elmer Martinez/AFP/Getty Images; p. 201: © Purestock/Getty Images RF; p. 204: © Nicholas Gill/Alamy; p. 206: © John Parra/Getty Images; p. 208: © McGraw-Hill Education/Klic Video Productions; p. 213: © Image Source RF; p. 218: © Lissa Harrison RF; p. 219: © Purestock/Getty Images RF; p. 223: © JJM Stock Photography/Alamy RF; p. 225: © McGraw-Hill Education/Klic Video Productions; p. 226: © Gonzalo Azumendi/The Image Bank/Getty Images; p. 227: © Nathan King/Alamy; p. 228: © Purestock/Getty Images RF; p. 229: © McGraw-Hill Education.

Chapter 8

Opener: © Christian Kober/Robert Harding World Imagery/Alamy; p. 233: © Rafael Guerrero/Photolibrary/Getty Images; p. 237: © Michael J. Doolittle/The Image Works; p. 238 (se habla...): © Elena Rooraid/PhotoEdit; p. 238 (colmado): © Jane Sweeney/AWL Images/Getty Images; p. 240 (all): © McGraw-Hill Education/Klic Video Productions; p. 245: © Alea Image/iStock/Getty Images RF; p. 251: © Reinhard Dirscherl/WaterFrame/Getty Images; p. 255 (bill): © Studio Works/Alamy; p. 255 (woman): © Tetra Images/Getty Images RF; p. 257: © MedioImages RF; p. 259: © McGraw-Hill Education/Klic Video Productions; p. 260: © Jon McLean/Alamy; p. 261 (camel): © Ingram Publishing/SuperStock RF; p. 261 (lake): © Lissa Harrison RF; p. 261 (falls): © Exactostock/SuperStock RF; p. 262: © Rafael Guerrero/Photolibrary/Getty Images; p. 263 (hikers): © Aurora Open/SuperStock RF; p. 263 (café): © Image Source RF; p. 263 (beach): © Purestock/Superstock RF; p. 263 (library): © Fancy/Veer/Corbis/Glow Images RF; p. 263 (camping): © Brand X Pictures/age fotostock RF; p. 263 (video): © McGraw-Hill Education.

Chapter 9

Opener: © Evelyn Paley/Alamy; p. 267: © Rafael Guerrero/Photolibrary/Getty Images; p. 269: © Adalberto Roque/AFP/Getty Images; p. 270: © AP Photo/Dado Galdieri; p. 273: © McGraw-Hill Education/Klic Video Productions; p. 276: © Boston Globe/Getty Images; p. 278: © C Bockermann/CHROMOR/agefotostock; p. 280: © Carl DeAbreu/Alamy; p. 285: © Frans Schellekens/Redferns/Getty Images; p. 286: © Beren Patterson/Alamy; p. 287: © McGraw-Hill Education/Klic Video Productions; p. 288: © Purestock/Superstock RF; p. 290: © Rafael Guerrero/Photolibrary/Getty Images; p. 291 (formal): © moodboard/Alamy RF; p. 291 (wedding): © Purestock/Superstock RF; p. 291 (dinner): © Cultura Creative/Alamy RF; p. 291 (pinata): © Ariel Skelley/Blend Images LLC RF; p. 291 (video): © McGraw-Hill Education.

Chapter 10

Opener: © Sylvain Grandadam/Robert Harding Picture Library/age fotostock; p. 295: © Rafael Guerrero/Photolibrary/Getty Images; p. 296 (riding): © Comstock Images/Alamy RF; p. 296 (walking): © David Planchet RF; p. 296 (yoga): © Ingram Publishing/SuperStock RF; p. 296 (skiing): © Ben Blankenburg/Corbis RF; p. 296 (family playing): © Chris Ryan/age fotostock RF; p. 296 (running): © Mark Anderson/Getty Images RF; p. 296 (hiking): © Brand X Pictures RF; p. 296 (clubbing): © Chris Ryan/age fotostock RF; p. 297: © Beck Diefenbach/Reuters/Corbis; p. 299: © Geordie Torr/Alamy; p. 301: © McGraw-Hill Education/Klic Video Productions; p. 307: United States Coast Guard; p. 310 (Lopez): © Stephane Cardinale/Sygma/Corbis; p. 310 (del Torres): © Stefanie Keenan/WireImage/Getty Images; p. 310 (Walker): © Focus on Sport/Getty Images; p. 313: © Helen H. Richardson/Denver Post/Getty Images; p. 313: © Glyn Genin/Alamy; p. 315: © McGraw-Hill Education/Klic Video Productions; p. 316: © Medioimages/Photodisc/Getty Images RF; p. 318: © Rafael Guerrero/Photolibrary/Getty Images; p. 319 (waterfall): © Hola Images/Getty Images RF; p. 319 (video): © McGraw-Hill Education.

Chapter 11

Opener: © ZUMA Press, Inc/Alamy; p. 323: © Rafael Guerrero/Photolibrary/Getty Images; p. 325: © Nicole Braun/Retna Ltd./Corbis; p. 327 (runner): © Royalty Free/Corbis RF; p. 327 (doctor): © Mike Watson/moodboard/Corbis RF; p. 327 (farmacia): © David R. Frazier Photolibrary, Inc./Alamy; p. 329: © McGraw-Hill Education/Klic Video Productions; p. 330: © Marty Granger/McGraw-Hill Education; p. 333: © DEA/M. Seemuller/De Agostini/Getty Images; p. 334: © Imagesource/Photolibrary RF; p. 335 (food): © Boston Globe/Getty Images; p. 335 (party): © Image Source/age fotostock RF; p. 337: © Jacques Jangoux/Alamy; p. 341: © Tommy Kay/Corbis; p. 343: © Keith Dannemiller/Corbis; p. 345: © McGraw-Hill Education/Klic Video Productions; p. 346: © Paula Bronstein/Getty Images; p. 348: © Rafael Guerrero/Photolibrary/Getty Images; p. 349: © McGraw-Hill Education.

Chapter 12

Opener: © Radius/SuperStock RF; p. 353: © Daniel Ernst/iStock/Getty Images RF; p. 357: © Jose Miguel Gomez/Reuters/Corbis; p. 359: © McGraw-Hill Education/Klic Video Productions; p. 363: © Mark Dierker/McGraw-Hill Education; p. 365: © Glow Images/Superstock RF; p. 373: © Ulf Andersen/Getty Images; p. 374: © Brand X Pictures/PunchStock RF; p. 374: © Brand X Pictures/PunchStock RF; p. 375: © Dave G. Houser/Corbis; p. 377: © McGraw-Hill Education/Klic Video Productions; p. 378: © Jane Sweeney/The Image Bank/Getty Images; p. 380 (insulin): © James R Clarke/Alamy; p. 380 (man): © Daniel Ernst/iStock/Getty Images RF; p. 381: © McGraw-Hill Education.

Chapter 13

Opener: © Bernai Velarde; p. 385: © Daniel Ernst/iStock/Getty Images RF; p. 388: © mediacolor's/Alamy; p. 389: © age fotostock/Alamy; p. 391: © McGraw-Hill Education/Klic Video Productions; p. 392: © Joe Sohm/The Image Works; p. 394: Blanton Museum of Art, The University of Texas at Austin, Barbara Duncan Fund, 1975. Photo by Rick Hall; p. 397: © Melanie Stetson Freeman/The Christian Science Monitor via Getty Images; p. 399: Aryballos-shaped vessel (ceramic), Incan/Museo Regional de Cuzco, Peru/Bildarchiv Steffens Henri Stierlin/The Bridgeman Art Library; p. 400 (market): © Nigel Pavitt/AWL Images/Getty Images; p. 400 (lake): © Christophe Boisvieux/Hemis/Alamy; p. 401 (tortoise): © Cleveland Metroparks Zoo/McGraw-Hill Education; p. 401 (iquana): © FAN Travelstock/Alamy RF; p. 404: © DEA/G Dagli Orti/Getty Images; p. 405: © Iberfoto/Iberfoto/Superstock; p. 407: © McGraw-Hill Education/Klic Video Productions; p. 408: © Aizar Raldes/AFP/Getty Images; p. 410: © Daniel Ernst/iStock/Getty Images RF; p. 411 (children): © SuperStock/age fotostock; p. 411 (video): © McGraw-Hill Education.

Chapter 14

Opener: © Mariana Bazo/Reuters/Corbis; p. 415: © Daniel Ernst/iStock/Getty Images RF; p. 418 (Slim): © Gillianne Tedder/Bloomberg via Getty Images; p. 418 (Miguel): © Carlos Alvarez/Getty Images; p. 418 (Olmos): © Michael Tran/FilmMagic/Getty Images; p. 420: © tose/iStock/Getty Images RF; p. 422: © McGraw-Hill Education/Klic Video Productions; p. 423: © Yadid Levy/ Robert Harding World Imagery/Getty Images; p. 425: © Ernesto Benavides/AFP/Getty Images; p. 429: © Xinhua/Alamy; p. 434: © Jonathan Nackstrand/AFP/Getty Images; p. 435: © Photographer's Choice/Getty Images RF; p. 437: © McGraw-Hill Education/Klic Video Productions; p. 438: © Glowimages/Getty Images; p. 440: © Daniel Ernst/iStock/Getty Images RF; p. 441: © McGraw-Hill Education.

Chapter 15

Opener: © Corbis; p. 445: © Daniel Ernst/iStock/Getty Images RF; p. 453: © McGraw-Hill Education/Klic Video Productions; p. 456: © Viviane Ponti/Lonely Planet Images/Getty Images/ Getty Images; p. 461: © Daniel Garcia/AFP/Getty Images; p. 463: © Digital Vision/Getty Images RF; p. 465: © McGraw-Hill Education/Klic Video Productions; p. 466: © Cristian Lazzari/iStock/ Getty Images RF; p. 468: © Daniel Ernst/iStock/Getty Images RF; p. 469: © McGraw-Hill Education.

Chapter 16

Opener: © Jorge Adorno/Reuters/Corbis; p. 473: © Daniel Ernst/iStock/Getty Images RF; p. 475: © Frans Lemmens/SuperStock; p. 478: © McGraw-Hill Education/Klic Video Productions; p. 479: © BananaStock/PunchStock RF; p. 482: © Mike Goldwater/Alamy; p. 485: © EPA European Pressphoto Agency b.v./Alamy; p. 487: © mtcurado/iStock/Getty Images RF; p. 489: © McGraw-Hill Education/Klic Video Productions; p. 490: © Studio Works/Alamy; p. 492 (orange): © Pulp/Getty Images RF; p. 492 (woman): © Daniel Ernst/iStock/Getty Images RF; p. 493: © McGraw-Hill Education.

Chapter 17

Opener: © Paul Harris/AWL Images/Getty Images; p. 497: © Daniel Ernst/iStock/Getty Images RF; p. 499: © Marcelo Hernandez/LatinContent/Getty Images; p. 502: © Ronald Patrick/Bloomberg via Getty Images; p. 504: © McGraw-Hill Education/Klic Video Productions; p. 507: © Mago World Image/age fotostock RF; p. 509: © El Mercurio de Chile/Newscom; p. 510 (statues): © Michael Snell/Robert Harding Picture Library/SuperStock; p. 510 (wine): © Lee Foster/Alamy; p. 514: © Martin Bernetti/AFP/GettyImages; p. 515: © Jon Arnold Images Ltd/Alamy; p. 517: © McGraw-Hill Education/Klic Video Productions; p. 518: © Marcelo Hernandez/LatinContent/ Getty Images; p. 520: © Daniel Ernst/iStock/Getty Images RF; p. 521: © McGraw-Hill Education.

Chapter 18

Opener: © Pablo Blazquez Dominguez/Getty Images; p. 525: © PhotoAlto/Eric Audras/Brand X Pictures/Getty Images RF; p. 529: © People and Politics/Alamy; p. 530: © Gerard Julien/AFP/ Getty Images; p. 531: © McGraw-Hill Education/Klic Video Productions; p. 535: © Evrim Aydin/ Anadolu Agency/Getty Images; p. 537: © Patrick Forget/age fotostock; p. 538: © Pierre-Philippe Marcou/AFP/Getty Images; p. 541: © Image Source RF; p. 546: © Hermes Mereghetti Studio/ Alamy; p. 547: © McGraw-Hill Education/Klic Video Productions; p. 548: © Pixtal/age fotostock RF; p. 550 (aqueduct): © Corbis RF; p. 550 (man): © PhotoAlto/Eric Audras/Brand X Pictures/ Getty Images RF; p. 551: © McGraw-Hill Education; p. 554: © Backyard Productions/Alamy; p. 555: © Francis R. Malasig/EPA/Newscom.

Text Credits

Chapter 1
Page 7 (table): From *Fox News Latino*; p. 11 (bottom): Source: 2010 U.S. Census; p. 12 (left – table): Source: 2006 U.S. Census.

Chapter 2
Page 55 (bottom right): From Cincilingua International Language Center, Cincinnati, Ohio.

Chapter 3
Page 64 (top left): From Instituto Nacional Electoral, Mexico; p. 65 (bottom): From Mexican Government.

Chapter 4
Page 106 (top): From Quo, HF Revistas; p. 125 (middle): Gregori Dolz, "Algo mas que ropa" in *Nexos Magazine* - © Ink-Global.

Chapter 5
Page 159 (middle): From Bienes Raíces Avisos de Ocasión.

Chapter 6
Page 195 (middle): From La U El Diario de Kampussia.

Chapter 7
Page 209 (top): From www.cnpp.usda.gov; p. 224 (middle): From CONABIP.

Chapter 8
Page 239 (middle): From En Lan; p. 246 (right): www.godominicanrepublic.com; p. 258 (cartoon): From David Sebastian Ojeda, Pasaje Blanco, 1662 Moron, prov. De Buenos Aires, artepiero@hotmail.com; p. 261 (middle): © I Love Viajes - www.iloveviajes.com.

Chapter 10
Page 308 (top): From Restaurant El Boricua.

Chapter 11
Page 340 (cartoon): © Joaquín Salvador Lavado (QUINO) Toda Mafalda - Ediciones de La Flor, 1993; p. 347 (middle): Nicanor Parra, "Epitafio", POEMAS Y ANTIPOEMAS © 1954, Nicanor Parra. Used by permission.

Chapter 12
Page 358 (top): From Vodafone; p. 364 (right): From Colombia Government - Industria y turismo; p. 379 (middle): "Cuadrados y angulos" by Alfonsina Storni, 1904.

Chapter 13
Page 409 (middle): Tito Matamala, "La opportunidad de Salomón Bobadilla" in *Con pocas palabras. Muestra de microcuentos*. Used with permission.

Chapter 14
Page 433 (bottom): From Asociacion todo ellos por; p. 439 (middle): Mario Benedetti, Poem **Oh** in *Poemas de la oficina* © Fundacion Mario Benedetti, c/o Schavelzon Graham Agencia Literaria, www.schavelzongraham.com.

Chapter 15
Page 449 (top right): © UTE; 464 (cartoon - left): © Joaquín Salvador Lavado (QUINO) ¡Cuánta bondad! - Ediciones de La Flor, 1999; p. 464 (cartoon - right): Cartoon by MENA, ALI Brussels; p. 467 (middle): "Apocalipsis, I" by Marco Denevi from *Falsificaiones*.

Chapter 16
Page 491 (middle): Diego Muñoz Valenzuela, *Amor cibernauta*. Used with permission.

Chapter 17
Page 519 (middle): © Fundación Gloria Fuertes.

Chapter 18
Page 537 (cartoon): From Antonio Mingote; p. 549 (middle): Eduardo Galeano, Celebración de la voz humana/2 in *El libro de los abrazos* © Siglo XXI DE ESPAÑA EDITORES. Used by permission; p. 555 (bottom): www.hispanicfiesta.com.

INDEX

Note: The notation "n" after a page number indicates that it is a footnote.

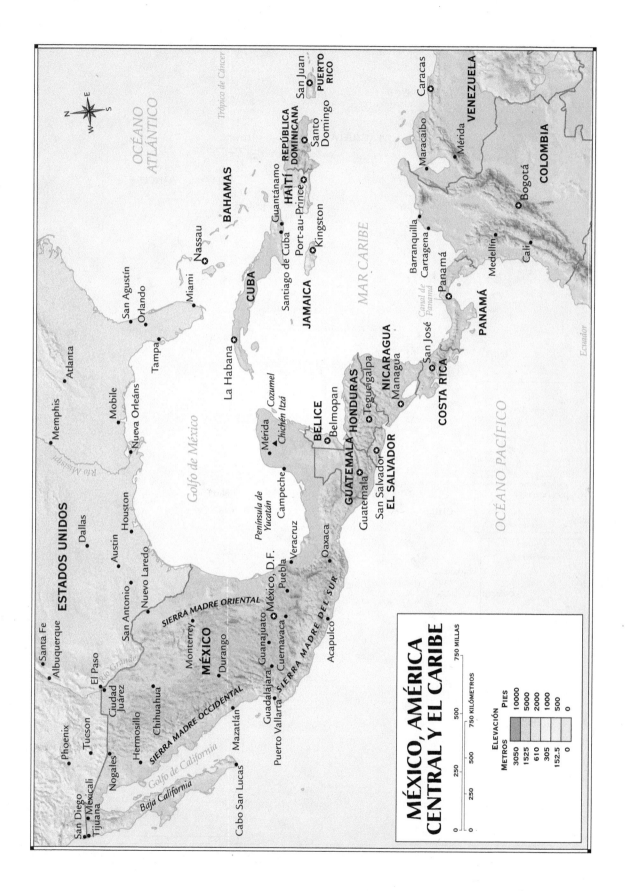

MÉXICO, AMÉRICA CENTRAL Y EL CARIBE

ELEVACIÓN

METROS	PIES
3050	10000
1525	5000
610	2000
305	1000
152.5	500
0	0

0   250   500   750 KILÓMETROS
0   250   500   750 MILLAS

ESTADOS UNIDOS

Santa Fe
Albuquerque
Phoenix
Tucson
El Paso
Ciudad Juárez
Nogales
Mexicali
San Diego
Tijuana
Hermosillo
Chihuahua
Nogales
Memphis
Atlanta
Mobile
Nueva Orleáns
San Agustín
Orlando
Tampa
Miami
Nassau

Dallas
Austin
San Antonio
Nuevo Laredo
Monterrey
Durango
Mazatlán
Cabo San Lucas

MÉXICO

SIERRA MADRE ORIENTAL
SIERRA MADRE OCCIDENTAL
SIERRA MADRE DEL SUR

Río Grande
Río Misisipi

Guadalajara
Puerto Vallarta
Guanajuato
Cuernavaca
México, D.F.
Puebla
Veracruz
Oaxaca
Acapulco

Baja California
Golfo de California

Golfo de México

Campeche
Península de Yucatán
Mérida
Cozumel
Chichén Itzá

La Habana

CUBA
BAHAMAS

Santiago de Cuba
Guantánamo

HAITÍ
Port-au-Prince
JAMAICA
Kingston

REPÚBLICA DOMINICANA
Santo Domingo
San Juan
PUERTO RICO

MAR CARIBE

OCÉANO ATLÁNTICO

Tropico de Cáncer

BELICE
Belmopan
GUATEMALA
Guatemala
HONDURAS
Tegucigalpa
EL SALVADOR
San Salvador
NICARAGUA
Managua
COSTA RICA
San José
PANAMÁ
Panamá
Canal de Panamá

OCÉANO PACÍFICO

Caracas
VENEZUELA
Maracaibo
Mérida
Barranquilla
Cartagena
Medellín
Bogotá
Cali
COLOMBIA

Ecuador

NICARAGUA
MAR CARIBE
Barranquilla
Maracaibo
COSTA
RICA
Caracas
PANAMÁ
Río Orinoco
OCÉANO
ATLÁNTICO
VENEZUELA
Medellín
Georgetown
GUYANA
Paramaribo
Bogotá
Cayenne
Cali
GUAYANA FRANCESA
COLOMBIA
SURINAM
Quito
ECUADOR
Ecuador
Guayaquil
Manaus
Belém
Río Amazonas
CORDILLERA
PERÚ
OCÉANO
PACÍFICO
BRASIL
Recife
Lima
Machu Picchu
Cuzco
OCÉANO PACÍFICO
Lago Titicaca
Isla Pinta
Isla Marchena
Arequipa
BOLIVIA
Brasília
Isla San Salvador
La Paz
Isla Santa Cruz
Sucre
Isla
Isabela
Isla San
Cristóbal
DE
Puerto
Baquerizo
Moreno
PARAGUAY
ISLAS
GALÁPAGOS
(ECUADOR)
Antofagasta
São Paulo
LOS
Asunción
Puerto Iguazú
Rio de Janeiro
100 MILLAS
CHILE
Trópico de
Capricornio
100 KILÓMETROS
Río Paraná
0   8 MILLAS
ANDES
Córdoba
0   8 KILÓMETROS
Valparaíso
OCÉANO
ATLÁNTICO
Rosario
URUGUAY
Cabo
Cummings
Santiago
Hanga Roa
Mataveri
OCÉANO
PACÍFICO
ARGENTINA
Buenos
Aires
Montevideo
Cabo Sur
Río de la Plata
ISLA DE PASCUA
(CHILE)
Concepción
Bahía Blanca

San Carlos de
Bariloche

OCÉANO
PACÍFICO

Estrecho de
Magallanes
Islas
Malvinas

Punta Arenas
Tierra del Fuego

Cabo de Hornos

AMÉRICA DEL SUR

| 0 | 250 | 500 | 750 MILLAS |
| 0 | 250 | 500 | 750 KILÓMETROS |

ELEVACIÓN

METROS	PIES
3050	10000
1525	5000
610	2000
305	1000
152.5	500
0	0

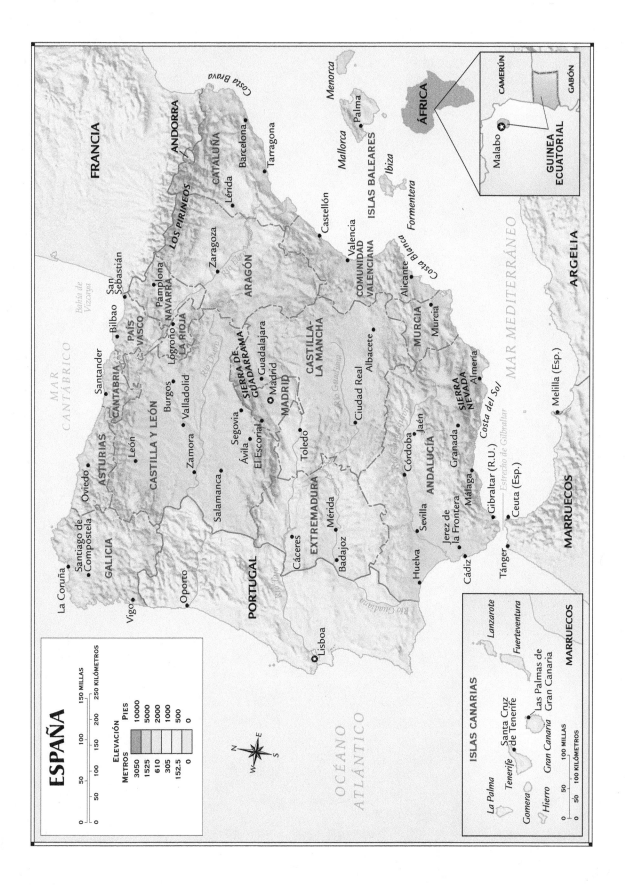

ESPAÑA

ELEVACIÓN

METROS	PIES
3050	10000
1525	5000
610	2000
305	1000
152.5	500
0	0

OCÉANO ATLÁNTICO

MAR CANTÁBRICO

Bahía de Vizcaya

FRANCIA

ANDORRA

Costa Brava

LOS PIRINEOS

CATALUÑA

Menorca

Palma

Mallorca

ISLAS BALEARES

Ibiza

Formentera

MAR MEDITERRÁNEO

ARGELIA

La Coruña
Santiago de Compostela
Vigo
Oporto
GALICIA
Oviedo
ASTURIAS
Santander
CANTABRIA
León
Zamora
CASTILLA Y LEÓN
Valladolid
Burgos
Salamanca
Bilbao
San Sebastián
PAÍS VASCO
Pamplona
NAVARRA
Logroño
LA RIOJA
Zaragoza
ARAGÓN
Lérida
Barcelona
Tarragona
Castellón
Valencia
COMUNIDAD VALENCIANA
Alicante
Costa Blanca
MURCIA
Murcia
Almería
SIERRA NEVADA
Granada
Costa del Sol
Málaga
ANDALUCÍA
Jaén
Córdoba
Ciudad Real
Albacete
CASTILLA-LA MANCHA
Guadalajara
SIERRA DE GUADARRAMA
Segovia
Ávila
El Escorial
MADRID
Madrid
Toledo
Cáceres
EXTREMADURA
Mérida
Badajoz
Sevilla
Huelva
Jerez de la Frontera
Cádiz
Tánger
Gibraltar (R.U.)
Ceuta (Esp.)
Estrecho de Gibraltar
Melilla (Esp.)
MARRUECOS

PORTUGAL
Lisboa

Río Tajo
Río Duero
Río Guadiana
Río Guadalquivir

| 0 | 50 | 100 | 150 MILLAS |
| 0 | 50 | 100 | 150 | 200 | 250 KILÓMETROS |

N
E
S
W

ISLAS CANARIAS

La Palma
Gomera
Hierro
Tenerife
Santa Cruz de Tenerife
Gran Canaria
Las Palmas de Gran Canaria
Lanzarote
Fuerteventura

MARRUECOS

| 0 | 50 | 100 MILLAS |
| 0 | 50 | 100 KILÓMETROS |

ÁFRICA

CAMERÚN

GABÓN

Malabo

GUINEA ECUATORIAL